Britons and Anglo-Saxons: Lincolnshire AD 400–650

STUDIES IN THE HISTORY OF LINCOLNSHIRE 3

BRITONS AND ANGLO-SAXONS: LINCOLNSHIRE AD 400–650

CAITLIN GREEN

Second Edition

Lincoln
HISTORY OF LINCOLNSHIRE COMMITTEE
2020

First edition published 2012 by
The History of Lincolnshire Committee, Jews' Court, Steep Hill, Lincoln
Second edition published 2020

ISBN 978 0 902668 26 3 (paperback)

Cover illustrations
Main: Looking across the Bain Valley towards the Lincolnshire Wolds north of Horncastle (Caitlin Green)
Insets: A sixth-century, gilded great square-headed brooch from the Baston inhumation cemetery (Adam Daubney, Portable Antiquities Scheme)
The sixth-century, 'Pressblech' Style I die from Garwick, used for making foil mounts (Adam Daubney, Portable Antiquities Scheme)
An early Anglo-Saxon gold-and-garnet pendant in the form of a stylized insect, discovered near Horncastle (Kevin Leahy, Portable Antiquities Scheme)

Cover design by Caitlin Green
Typeset and produced for the publisher by Kinword, Sleaford
NG34 7QE

British Cataloguing-in-Publication Data
A catalogue record for this book is obtainable from the British Library

For Frances, Evie, Tabitha and Stanley

CONTENTS

FIGURES

ABBREVIATIONS

Ant.	*Antiquity*
Antiq. J.	*Antiquaries Journal*
Archaeol. J.	*Archaeological Journal*
CBA	Council for British Archaeology
EHR	*English Historical Review*
EMC	Corpus of Early Medieval Coin Finds
HER	Lincolnshire Historic Environment Record
LHA	*Lincolnshire History and Archaeology*
LRS	Lincoln Record Society
Med. Arch.	*Medieval Archaeology*
Mid. Hist.	*Midland History*
NLSMR	North Lincolnshire Sites & Monuments Record
PAS	Portable Antiquities Scheme
SLHA	Society for Lincolnshire History & Archaeology
Trans. Royal Hist.	*Transactions of the Royal Historical Society*

A NOTE ON LINGUISTIC TERMINOLOGY

A number of historical linguistic conventions are used in what follows. Of particular note is the use of an asterisk before linguistic forms which are not attested in an extant document, but whose former existence can be inferred with reasonable certainty (for example, *Lindēs*). In contrast, where two asterisks are used, this indicates a form that is both unrecorded and believed to be philologically impossible or incorrect (for example, **Linnisfarnae*). Finally, the symbol > between two forms indicates that the former changed into the latter (for example, *Lōdēs > Loidis*), whilst the symbol < between two forms indicates that the former derived from the latter (for example, *Linnuis < *Lindēs*).

FOREWORD

I have been working on the Anglo-Saxon Kingdom of Lindsey for more than 30 years, for much of which I seemed to be ploughing a lonely furrow in the remote fastness of Scunthorpe. In 1987, Scunthorpe Museum staged an exhibition entitled 'The Lost Kingdom: the Search for Anglo-Saxon Lindsey'. This was something of a misnomer. Lindsey wasn't lost; we knew where it was, but precious little else about it. The situation had been summed up in the *Victoria History of the County of Lincoln* (1906): 'The English conquest of Lincolnshire can only be stated as a fact; it cannot be described, for all details are lacking.'

Things moved on during the twentieth century; sites were dug and finds recorded. The 'Lost Kingdom' exhibition was based on material from the Cleatham Anglo-Saxon cemetery, together with some of the metal-detector finds that we had recorded. This evidence suggested that Lindsey was perhaps not as lost as had been thought. Other people had been working on Lindsey, and in 1979 their work was drawn together by Bruce Eagles in his excellent study (B. N. Eagles, *The Anglo-Saxon Settlement of Humberside*, British Archaeological Reports British Series, 68, 2 vols, Oxford, 1979) and now we have this book by Caitlin Green.

Caitlin's book moves us on to new ground. I am just an archaeologist, good at digging holes, sticking pots together and, hopefully, getting a convincing story out of them. Here we see a multidisciplinary approach, pulling together a wide range of sources. It is obvious that the indigenous British played an important part in the Anglo-Saxon settlement of England, but Caitlin Green draws on British sources, integrating them with the archaeology to produce a stimulating narrative. Well researched and carefully argued, this is an important book and it gives me enormous pleasure to see the study of the 'Lost Kingdom' moving on.

Dr Kevin Leahy, National Adviser, Early Medieval Metalwork
The Portable Antiquities Scheme
October 2011

ACKNOWLEDGEMENTS

I should like to express my sincere and considerable thanks to the very many people who have provided invaluable assistance over the long period in which this study has been in gestation, whether in terms of detailed comments on earlier versions of the text, advice and discussion on points of detail and interpretation, additional information and images, or simply their time and encouragement. In particular, I owe debts of gratitude to Alex Bayliss, Mark Bennet, Adam Daubney, David Dumville, Bruce Eagles, Keith Kelway, Kevin Leahy, David Roffe, Katharina Ulmschneider, Ian Wood, Barbara Yorke, Jane Young and Susan Youngs. I also need to thank the two anonymous referees who read and commented on the text, as well as Wendy Atkin for her excellent editorial work, the History of Lincolnshire Committee for agreeing to publish this study, and Mick Jones for his support and assistance throughout the publication process. My considerable thanks are similarly due to Professor Helena Hamerow of the University of Oxford, whose help and support as my doctoral supervisor for the thesis version of this text was invaluable. Needless to say, all errors and interpretations do remain my own responsibility. I must, however, reserve my greatest thanks for Frances, Evie and Tabitha Green – their patience, support and usual good humour during the preparation of this book have made it possible; it is to them that this book is dedicated.

Photograph and image acknowledgements

Figs 1, 21: Society for the Promotion of Roman Studies and Cambridge University Press; Figs 2, 12: Dave Watt, English Heritage; Fig. 3: The Collection, Art and Archaeology in Lincolnshire; Fig. 4: Society for Lincolnshire History and Archaeology; Fig. 5: Naomi Field, Henry Hurst and Society for Lincolnshire History and Archaeology; Figs 7, 9, 11, 16, 18, 25, 32–4, 36, 38–41: Heritage Lincolnshire; Figs 7, 9, 11, 16, 18, 25, 33–4, 41: Katharina Ulmschneider; Figs 8, 10, 11, 20, 23, 25, 33, 41: Kevin Leahy; Fig. 9:

David Stocker and City of Lincoln Council; Fig. 13: Society for Lincolnshire History and Archaeology by David Vale; Figs 14, 26: Kevin Leahy, Portable Antiquities Scheme; Fig. 15: Susan Youngs; Figs 17, 35, 37: Adam Daubney, Portable Antiquities Scheme; Fig. 19: City of Lincoln Council; Fig. 21: Howard Williams and Nick Higham; Figs 22, 30: Society of Antiquaries of London; Fig. 24: Northern History, Maney Publishing (*www.maney.co.uk/journals/nhi*); Fig. 25: Philip Sinton, English Heritage; Fig. 28: Trustees of the British Museum; Fig. 29: Keith Kelway; Fig. 48: Akuppa (*www.flickr.com/ photos/90664717@N00/1463451575*) licensed via a Creative Commons Attribution 2.0 Generic licence. Note, map outlines used here are partially derived from OS OpenData, made available under the Open Government Licence v1.0 with the following attribution statement: Contains Ordnance Survey data © Crown copyright and database right 2011.

Acknowledgements for the second edition

As before, a significant number of people have offered invaluable assistance with the preparation and production of this new edition. In particular, I owe debts of thanks to Wendy Atkin, John Blair, Paul Cope-Faulkner, Adam Daubney, Fiona Gavin, Helena Hamerow, Catherine Hills, John Hines, Mick Jones, Kevin Leahy, Ian Simmons, Steve Willis, Hugh Willmott, Barbara Yorke and Sue Youngs. Of course, all errors and interpretations do remain my own. Finally, my greatest thanks are once again due to Frances, Evie, Tabitha and Stanley Green for their continued patience and support.

Additional photograph and image acknowledgements for the second edition

Figs A, C, H, I, J: Caitlin Green; Figs B, G, L: Portable Antiquities Scheme, used under their Creative Commons Attribution-ShareAlike 4.0 International licence; Fig. D.i: Courtesy of the Portable Antiquities Scheme and the Trustees of the British Museum; Figs D.ii, E, F: Kevin Leahy; Fig. K: Archaeological Project Services.

INTRODUCTION TO THE SECOND EDITION

Britons and Anglo-Saxons: Lincolnshire AD 400–650 first appeared in 2012 and has sold out of its first three print runs. As it is now seven years since the first edition, it was considered appropriate to provide a new preface for this reissue that offers some additional commentary and updates on various topics relating to Lincolnshire in the fifth to seventh centuries, informed by research undertaken by myself and others since this book's original drafting. It is hoped that this will be of interest to readers and add to the material treated in the main text.

Romano-British pottery in the fifth- to sixth-century Lincoln region

The question of whether Romano-British pottery continued to be produced into the fifth century AD, mentioned briefly below (pp. 111–12), is a topic of increasing interest, as most recently demonstrated by the fact that in 2016 a volume of the journal *Internet Archaeology* was entirely devoted to this question at a national level.[1] With regard to this, the Lincoln region is arguably as good a place as any to look for the continued circulation and production of Romano-British pottery into the fifth century AD. After all, the evidence discussed in the main body of this volume demonstrates that Lincoln was not only a Late Roman provincial capital that appears to have remained prosperous and remarkably vital right into the very late fourth century, but also one that subsequently lay at the heart of a significant British post-Roman territory named *Lindēs*.

As Mark Whyman and others have observed, pottery has generally been dated through its association with coins. Consequently, the fact that very few fifth-century coins appear to have found their way to Britain may well have caused archaeologists erroneously to assign a *c.* AD 400 end-date to Romano-British pottery fabrics and forms, when these actually continued in production and/or use for some time after this.[2] An awareness of such a possibility has, in recent

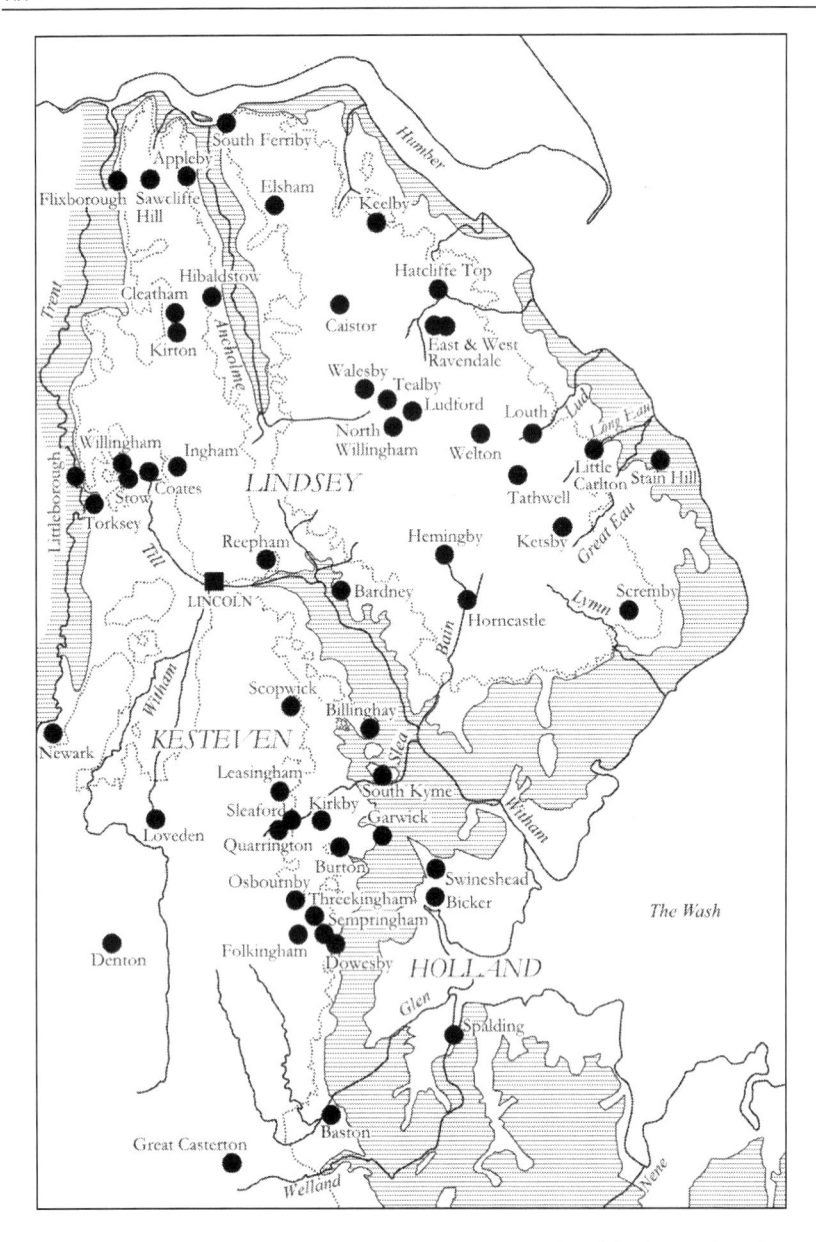

Fig. A Location map of places mentioned in this introduction.
The estimated Anglo-Saxon coastline is shown along with low-
lying land and ground above 15 metres.

years, increasingly led to the identification of very late Roman pottery wares that show some signs of having continued in production and use, albeit on a smaller scale, into the first half of the fifth century, via finds of such material in post-Roman contexts and in association with fifth-century and later items such as brooches. Notable examples here include Black Burnished ware in Dorset and Somerset, calcite-gritted wares in Yorkshire and the North, and Much Hadham and Verulamium wares in Hertfordshire.[3] In this light, Lincoln's Local Coarse Pebbly ware, with over 1,800 sherds recorded from the city, may also be of some potential interest. This relatively common wheel-thrown ware, the forms of which show a marked similarity to items produced by the Late Roman Swanpool kilns just to the south-west of Lincoln, seems to have its origins in the mid- to late fourth century. The recently published *Corpus of Roman Pottery from Lincoln* (2014) notes that this pottery is most commonly found in both assemblages of the last decades of that century – including the very late Roman pottery group that was discovered immediately outside Lincoln's Lower West Gate in 1970 and is thought likely to extend into the fifth century – and in 'post-Roman' contexts. Indeed, over fifty per cent of all Local Coarse Pebbly ware sherds come from post-Roman/sub-Roman contexts, particularly those from the Flaxengate site, in the lower Roman city, an area of Lincoln where continued urban activity into the early fifth century seems likely. In consequence, this ware is a possible candidate for a Lincoln-region analogue to the Late Roman pottery industries recently identified in other parts of Britain as continuing into the largely coin-less first half of the fifth century.[4]

If Local Coarse Pebbly ware is at the very least suggestive, it does not stand alone as the only potential evidence for a degree of continued Romano-British pottery production and/or use in the fifth-century Lincoln region. Of particular interest in this context are a number of individual pots that have been thought to be potentially of Romano-British manufacture, but which were either found in early Anglo-Saxon contexts and/or show signs of early Anglo-Saxon influence in their form or design. Perhaps the most convincing candidates here are four Roman-type pots excavated in the 1980s from the exceptionally large fifth- to sixth-century Anglo-Saxon cremation cemetery at Cleatham, Lincolnshire, located around nineteen miles to the north of Lincoln (Fig. 23). These cremation urns were all made using Romano-British wheel-throwing techniques but, as both Maggie Darling and Kevin Leahy have observed, their body-shapes and fabrics mean that they cannot be seen as re-used Roman-era pots. As was noted in Chapter 3, they are instead considered to represent products of the fifth-century 'post-Roman' British pottery industry, given their phasing in the cemetery.[5] Interestingly, another urn of the same type and manufacture was found in the fifth- to sixth-century Anglo-Saxon cremation cemetery at Millgate, Newark, sixteen miles to the south-west of Lincoln. Further fragments have been found close to Stamford at the Roman 'small town' of Great Casterton – in a destruction layer coin-dated to some point after AD 375 – and, in 2013, close to the Roman 'small town' of Littleborough (*Segelocum*), on the Trent north-west of Lincoln (Fig. B). Incidentally, with regard to these latter two finds, it is notable that the first site also possesses a well-known Late Roman to early Anglo-Saxon cemetery that is considered to offer 'a convincing case of Roman–Saxon burial continuity', whilst Littleborough appears to have still been a key site in the Lincoln region into the early seventh century and beyond.[6] Needless to say, the above evidence would consequently seem to indicate that the Late Roman wheel-thrown pottery industry in this area not only continued to function (at least to some limited degree) into the early to mid-fifth century, given the nature and contexts of these vessels, but that its products also circulated relatively widely in the region around the former provincial capital at that time, being found to both the north and the south of Lincoln.[7]

Other material may point to a connection between the remnants of the Romano-British pottery industry in this region and at least some of the locally made 'Anglo-Saxon'-style pottery found here.[8] For example, a bottle sherd from Hibaldstow – the site of a Romano-British 'small town' that was located on Ermine Street a little to the north-east of the Cleatham cemetery and which has evidence for activity into at least the late fourth/early fifth century – was found in a ditch along with Romano-British greyware and some 'normal' early–mid Saxon sherds, and is, intriguingly, in an attested local, very late fourth-century Romano-British fabric despite having the form of a 'Germanic' sixth-century bottle.[9] Similarly interesting is a fifth- or

**Fig. B A sherd from a probably mid-fifth-century greyware
vessel of the same type as the wheel-thrown, Roman-type
vessels used as urns at Cleatham; found near to Littleborough**
Source: Kevin Leahy, Portable Antiquities Scheme

sixth-century, hand-made Anglo-Saxon-style pot that is believed to show signs of Romano-British manufacture in terms of both its fabric and technique. This pot was discovered in Greetwell Villa (actually located in Lincoln's Greetwell Fields), a plausible candidate for the former Late Roman provincial governor's villa-palace at Lincoln and a notable findspot – the villa-palace here not only was maintained right into the early fifth century on the basis of the coin record, but also its estate arguably survived largely intact right through into the medieval period.[10] Also potentially intriguing is a sixth-century, Anglo-Saxon, hand-made vessel that was recovered from the flue ashes of one of the Late Roman Swanpool kilns at Rookery Lane, Lincoln. This unusual findspot has been considered significant by Ken Dark, who suggests that the pot's apparent deposition in the flue ashes may provide a date for the manufacture of the last superficially fourth-century pottery at the site.[11] Moreover, Diana Briscoe has recently pointed out that the pot itself actually features a distinctive rosette stamp motif which also occurs on some Late Roman pottery from the Swanpool kilns that was found at Flaxengate, Lincoln, a fact that she considers to be possible evidence in its own right for some sort of continuity in pottery production in the Lincoln region.[12]

We would therefore appear to have a potentially interesting situation in the post-Roman Lincoln region. Taken together, the contexts and nature of the finds of Local Coarse Pebbly ware and Cleatham-style, wheel-thrown vessels from Lincoln and its surrounding region would seem to offer a credible case for the continuance of elements of the Romano-British pottery industry here into the first half of the fifth century. Furthermore, the finds from Hibaldstow, the Lincoln villa-palace and the Rookery Lane/Swanpool kiln all hint at the possibility of a degree of continuity between the remains of this industry and at least some of the locally produced Anglo-Saxon pottery found in this region. Of course, as was noted above, we should perhaps not be too surprised. Not only is early to mid-fifth-century continuity in the Romano-British pottery industry suspected in other parts of Britain, but there is also good evidence for a significant degree of post-Roman British activity and Anglian–British interaction in Lincoln and its wider region. Finally, it is worth observing that the wheel-thrown vessels discussed above were not the only Roman-style pottery potentially present in post-Roman Lincolnshire, as small quantities of imported wares have also been identified from Lincoln. Of particular interest is a rim sherd found in Saltergate and identified on the basis of both form and fabric as being part of a fifth-century Keay's form 52 wine amphora from the central Mediterranean. In addition, a body sherd from a Biv (LRA3) eastern Mediterranean amphora found in a post-Roman deposit at Flaxengate and a possible southern Gaulish 'D ware' (DSP) bowl found in or near Lincoln in the nineteenth century are also of potential significance.[13]

Archaeology and the British 'country of *Lindēs*'

The most impressive archaeological evidence for significant post-Roman British activity in this region other than pottery continues to be the sequence of buildings excavated at St Paul in the Bail, Lincoln, and the burials that cut and post-date the second of these structures, an apsidal church. As is discussed in Chapter 2 (pp. 65–9, 82–3), although the radiocarbon results from the graves at St Paul in the Bail have often been used individually – and occasionally rather dubiously – in arguments about the dating of this apsidal church, the recent Bayesian modelling of the radiocarbon data from these burials reported below has now put things on a much sounder footing, and an Anglo-Saxon origin for this church can no longer be seen as credible. Rather, the Bayesian modelling along with a reconsideration of the other available evidence strongly indicates that the apsidal church located here was, in fact, a British church of the fifth–sixth centuries that was deliberately established in the centre of the Roman *forum* and able to hold up to 100 worshippers, and this interpretation of the radiocarbon data and Bayesian modelling of the site has recently been supported by the National Chronological Framework project led by John Hines and Alex Bayliss.[14]

It is conceivable that both this fifth- to sixth-century apsidal church and the probable earlier church that it overlay and replaced in the *forum* – possibly constructed as early as the later fourth century – are best associated with the attested Romano-British bishop of Lincoln and viewed as part of a continuing episcopal establishment in the former provincial capital. In this light, it is worth noting Steve Malone's recent suggestion that it may be possible to gain some idea of the area under the episcopal jurisdiction of the Romano-British bishop of Lincoln in the fourth century, at least, from a group of Late Roman lead tanks in Lincolnshire and Nottinghamshire that all seem to share common design elements, including the presence of cable moulding, inscriptions and/or Chi-Rho symbols on many examples.

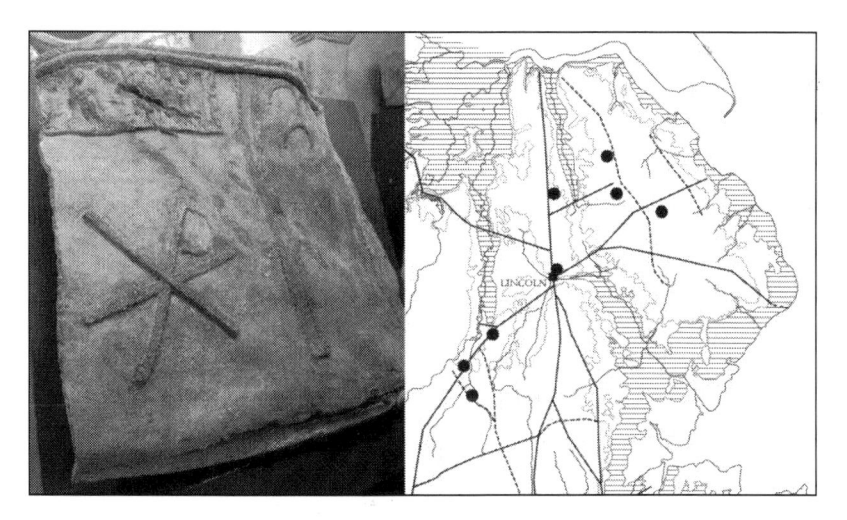

Fig. C The Walesby lead tank with a Chi-Rho symbol and the distribution of Late Roman lead tanks/fonts around Lincoln

Eight of these items are now known from the region, the most recent being reported in 2013 from only a mile to the north of Lincoln's Upper City. Malone considers that these items could well have functioned as fonts and tentatively links their distribution around the city with the 'sphere of influence of the … Episcopal see at *Lindum colonia*', given that the presence of a bishop was required at such liturgical events as baptisms, a point of considerable interest (Fig. C).[15] Mick Jones similarly considers that these artefacts probably functioned as baptismal fonts and makes the further intriguing point that the great majority of the total known from the whole of Britain (currently 28 examples) look to have been found within the potential bounds of the Late Roman province governed from Lincoln (Fig. 1).[16]

Turning to finds of fifth- to seventh-century British metalwork in the Lincoln region, six further examples of British Class 1 and Type G penannular brooches have been noted from here since 2012, bringing the total of these items now recorded from this area up to 29 or 30. This is an exceptional concentration within Britain and Ireland, and the new finds fall into and reinforce the distribution pattern observed and discussed below (pp. 69–73).[17] It should be recalled here that Class 1 brooches in particular were post-Roman British elite objects used for high-status symbolic display,[18] and Fiona Gavin has recently suggested that this was especially true of those examples decorated in the Insular Military Style like the existing brooch from East Ravendale (Fig. 14) and a new silver Class 1 brooch from Caistor (Fig. D). Such pieces are considered by her to have acted as 'important indicators of élite status' in both Britain and Ireland, and were moreover objects of 'exquisite craftsmanship and distinction'; consequently, their presence in fifth- to sixth-century Lincolnshire is clearly noteworthy.[19] Similarly, fifteen more 'Late Celtic' hanging bowls, originally high-status pieces of fifth- to seventh-century British tableware, have also been recorded since this volume was first written, raising the total number known from Lincolnshire to 49 (sixteen from Kesteven, 33 from Lindsey). Once again, the distribution of the new discoveries falls within that of the existing finds discussed in Chapter 2, below, and a similar interpretation is therefore appropriate.[20]

In addition to these brooches and hanging bowls, a rare and

**Fig. D Two objects decorated in the Insular Military Style:
(i) A British silver proto-hand-pin, found at Welton le Wold
(ii) a British post-Roman Class 1 silver penannular brooch
terminal, found at Caistor**
Source: Courtesy of the Portable Antiquities Scheme and Kevin Leahy

important British silver proto-hand-pin of the late fourth or fifth century AD has been found at Welton le Wold, near Louth (Fig. D), and this arguably also needs adding to our corpus, especially as it too is decorated in the Insular Military Style like the post-Roman Class 1 brooches mentioned above. Although given a general 'Welton village' location by the Portable Antiquities Scheme (PAS), it has subsequently been revealed that this pin was actually found on the site of what was probably a significant Late Roman villa at Welton le Wold.[21] Extensive crop- and soil-marks identified as those of a Romano-British villa have been found on the hilltop where the proto-hand-pin was discovered, and these are associated with Romano-British pottery, brooches, tile, and over 300 copper-alloy and silver coins that chiefly date from the third to the later fourth centuries (a very significant quantity of Roman coinage for this part of Lincolnshire, coin concentrations here being otherwise thin and rarely reaching into double figures).[22] Obviously, this is of considerable

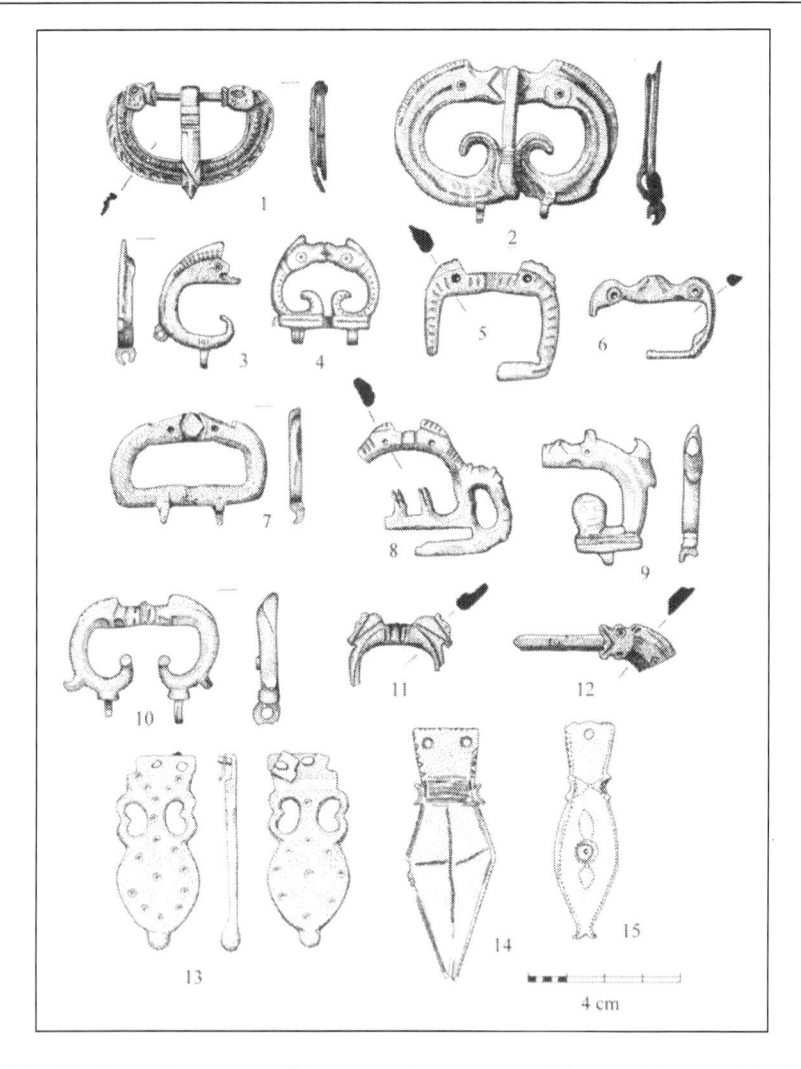

**Fig. E Late Roman military-style zoomorphic buckles and belt
fittings from Lindsey[23]**
Source: Kevin Leahy

interest, and the proto-hand-pin from here suggests that there were
still high-status Britons living at the Welton le Wold villa site at the
end of the Roman period or a little beyond. Silver proto-hand-pins
are, after all, considered by Susan Youngs to be 'prestige items' that

potentially functioned as 'a mark of official favour and status' in the late fourth century and after, with Gavin likewise arguing that they are 'highly accomplished late Roman provincial art' associated with high elites.[24] In this context, it should be noted that a very similar proto-hand-pin has been discovered in the demolition deposit of a high-status building that was standing and occupied into the fifth century AD at *Tripontium*, Warwickshire.[25]

Looking generally at the distribution and significance of such high-status British dress accessories as the Welton proto-hand-pin and the post-Roman silver Class 1 brooch from Caistor that are decorated in the Insular Military Style, Gavin has observed that British finds of this type are concentrated in both the Lincoln region and the Severn Valley/Bristol Channel area – where the origins of this style are thought to lie – with individual finds scattered between the two areas along the line of Fosse Way (the main Roman road from Exeter to Lincoln), which is intriguing.[26] Furthermore, she suggests that objects decorated in the Insular Military Style were not merely elite items, but 'served as legitimising insignia' in the very late and post-Roman periods, being used in both Britain and Ireland then to reinforce status and identity within groups facing significant change or threat, something that clearly makes sense within the context of the Lincoln region. Lastly, she argues that they are, as a class, ornamented with 'motifs and patterns drawn from the stylistic cannon of Imperial military and civilian authority'. She consequently considers that items decorated in this style may have been worn by aristocratic individuals who additionally wished to 'socially emulate military dress' and associate themselves with the trappings of Roman military organisation and militaristic power, something that is naturally of interest here.[27] In light of this last point, it may be worth considering whether there is not some link between these pieces and the apparent 'fashion' for wearing the lower-status – often poorly made – military-style zoomorphic buckles and belt fittings in Lincolnshire that Kevin Leahy has studied and associates with local Romano-British 'militias' (Fig. E). These copper-alloy items are believed to date from the end of the fourth century and the first half of the fifth, according to a recent review by Hilary Cool, and clearly reference Late Roman military belt-sets worn by soldiers and civilian officials, whilst not usually being thought to represent official military equipment. Certainly, as Fiona Gavin notes, some connection is possible, and the national distribution of such finds – with particular concentrations in Lincolnshire and the Severn Valley area – is notably reminiscent of that of the higher-status dress-accessories decorated in the Insular Military Style.[28]

With regard to the question of fifth- to sixth-century 'Anglo-Saxon' material within the Lincoln region, a number of additional clusters of finds very probably indicative of the presence of small later fifth- to sixth-century inhumation/mixed cemeteries have been recorded, with 640 individual items of this date from Lincolnshire documented by the Portable Antiquities Scheme since the research for this volume was completed.[29] These cemeteries have been mainly discovered via metal-detecting, although some of the concentrations of finds have subsequently been confirmed via a programme of archaeological work, as at Scremby near Spilsby. Here, a group of metal-detected objects – including Anglo-Saxon gilded brooches, shield-bosses and spearheads – prompted an excavation of the site by the University of Sheffield in 2017–19. This revealed it to be a late fifth- to mid-sixth-century burial ground containing more than 20 inhumations, some of which were lavishly furnished.[30] If there are thus several new 'Anglo-Saxon' small cemeteries now known, it is worth observing that these nonetheless seem to fall into the existing patterns of such cemeteries as outlined and discussed in the main chapters below. So, for example, the largest concentrations of new material indicative of an inhumation cemetery are once more found away from Lincoln – particularly at Scremby, Appleby, Leasingham and Osbournby – with only small numbers of finds being recorded from sites closer to the city.[31] Similarly, the Fenland territory of the *Spalde* (in the southern Lincolnshire district of Holland) currently continues to be, intriguingly, almost completely devoid not only of cemeteries, but also of virtually any pre-eighth-century Anglo-Saxon metalwork recorded on the PAS, with eighth- to ninth-century finds being almost as rare. This is despite both a significant quantity of material of other dates having been recorded from here by detectorists and the existence of other evidence for post-Roman activity in this area.[32]

As to the early Anglo-Saxon metalwork itself that is found in the Lincoln region, two aspects especially may deserve some further comment here. First, it should be noted that there is an increasing quantity of early Anglo-Saxon metalwork with evidence of enamelling found in the Lincoln region. Needless to say, given that enamelling in the early medieval era is generally considered to be a British decorative technique, this is of considerable interest.[33] Accordingly, mention is made in the main chapters below of the Keelby enamelled buckle, which looks to be of 'British' manufacture but is 'Anglo-Saxon' in form and is considered to carry with it implications of Anglian-British 'cultural fusion in the workshop'.[34] In addition, a number of further examples of enamelled 'Anglo-Saxon' metalwork from Lincolnshire are now recorded from the Portable Antiquities Scheme and other sources. These consist of a copper-alloy sword pommel of perhaps *c.* AD 500 from Hemingby, featuring a central, red-enamelled triangle containing one or two concentric outlined triangles; enamelled sixth-century square-headed and cruciform brooches from Sleaford, Scopwick, Baston and Tathwell; a garnet and enamel sword pyramid from Folkingham; another pyramidal mount with incised and enamelled decoration (lozenges and triangles) from South Ferriby/Barton-upon-Humber; and at least three late fifth- to sixth-century belt fittings inlaid with enamel from the excavated inhumation cemetery at Sawcliffe Hill (Sheffield's Hill) in northern Lincolnshire (Fig. F).[35]

Second, recent work on fifth- to sixth-century cruciform brooches by Toby Martin has added considerably to our understanding of such objects, which are common finds in

Fig. F Enamelled Anglo-Saxon metalwork from Lincolnshire: the Keelby buckle and two gilded and enamelled belt fittings from the Sawcliffe Hill cemetery

Source: Kevin Leahy

Lincolnshire. In particular, his new catalogue of these items rectifies the apparently sparse distribution of fifth-century cruciform brooches in northern Lincolnshire (Lindsey) as mapped in Fig. 21b, below. It is now clear that significant numbers of Martin's phase A cruciform brooches (dated by him to *c.* 420–75) are indeed found in northern Lincolnshire, as well as further south and in East Anglia.[36] As such, the distribution of the earliest cruciform brooches much more closely resembles that of the large cremation-predominant cemeteries mapped in Fig. 21a, with the vast majority of both falling within the probable boundaries of the Late Roman province administered from Lincoln (see further, pp. 93, 113).[37] Interestingly, the same distribution is maintained, and indeed concentrates and intensifies, in Martin's phase B, *c.* 475–550, something that he associates with a period of particularly intense and deliberate ethnogenesis (the construction of an ethnic identity) relating to the insular 'Anglian' immigrant identity in this region and which coincides with the spread of small inhumation cemeteries here. Martin argues that the roots of this identity lay with ambitious individuals with creditable claims to specific immigrant origins, 'or at least kin relations or political alliances with those who did', gaining local political ascendancy after or during migration and subsequently appropriating and utilising cruciform brooches as symbols of their emergent elite-group ethnic identity in order to demonstrate and legitimise their status and claimed shared descent/cultural inheritance.[38]

This coherent and focused distribution of cruciform brooches eventually breaks down in the mid-sixth century with the large and elaborate phase C brooches (*c.* 525–560/70; Fig. G), which have a more homogeneous spread across central England. These are largely evenly distributed right across into the West Midlands and what was to become the Mercian heartland, rather than heavily concentrated in Lincolnshire, Rutland and East Anglia as in phases A and B. They are also far fewer in number, being arguably restricted to a much more select elite class now and utilised in prestige gift-exchange. Martin explains these changes primarily in terms of both a shift towards more restricted elites, larger-scale political structures and formalised kingship in Anglian society at this time, and (with regard to the westwards spread) the beginnings of the Anglian Mercian dynasty in the West Midlands. Certainly, this would make sense in the context of

Fig. G A Phase C florid cruciform brooch of Martin's Type 4.7.1 from Folkingham, dated to the mid- to late sixth century; this example was gilded and silvered/tinned.
Source: Adam Daubney, Portable Antiquities Scheme

the Lincoln region, not least because – as is discussed in Chapter 3, below – the period around the mid-sixth century is thought to have indeed witnessed the emergence of a pre-eminent Anglian group in the Lincoln region and the takeover of the British 'country of *Lindēs*' to form the Anglian kingdom of *Lindissi*.[39]

Finally, with respect to the great fifth- to sixth-century 'Anglian' cremation-predominant cemeteries of our region, like Cleatham and Loveden Hill (each originally containing more than 1,500 burials), recent studies have added to our knowledge of these too. The material from the Elsham and Cleatham cemeteries in northern Lincolnshire has, for example, seen additional work by Kirsty Squires and Gareth Perry. The former has considered the skeletal material and grave furnishings found in the cremation urns from these sites, whilst the latter is concerned with the pottery itself, offering further evidence that each of these two cemeteries lay at the heart of a discrete cluster of non-funerary find sites and possessed their own territory and catchment area.[40] Looking more widely, perhaps the most significant recent contribution is that of Catherine Hills and Sam Lucy, who in the final volume on the large Spong Hill (Norfolk) cremation cemetery – published in 2013 – have argued that the earliest cremation phase both here and potentially elsewhere should be pushed back from its traditional place in the middle of the fifth century to the earlier fifth century, starting perhaps as early as *c*. AD 420. They also strongly reassert the case for large urnfields like Spong Hill showing significant cultural connections with contemporary sites on the continent and see them as reflecting the arrival of people from North-western Europe in Norfolk and Lincolnshire in the first half of the fifth century 'in sufficient numbers and force to cause a dramatic change in burial practice' – in notable contrast to regions to the west and south – resulting in cemeteries 'very like those to be found on the other side of the North Sea'.[41] Clearly, this is a point of some interest to the present work, although it does need to be emphasised once more that a significant degree of immigration from the continent and large-scale British 'survival' are not mutually exclusive propositions, and that it is likely that both were the case in at least those regions where the great cremation cemeteries are found.[42]

Place-names and history in early Anglo-Saxon Lincolnshire

Turning to the evidence of place-names, there are a handful of names that perhaps deserve some further discussion for the light they may shed on the fifth- to seventh-century Lincoln region.

The first of these is Tealby (*Tavelesbi, Teflesbi*) on the western edge of the Lincolnshire Wolds, which is now agreed to probably involve a tribal or population-group name, **Tāflas/*Tǣflas*, this being the Old English form of the continental tribal-name *Taifali*.[43] This does, of course, raise the intriguing question of how members of the *Taifali* – who are otherwise primarily attested as living in southern parts of Europe in the fourth to sixth centuries – might have ended up in early medieval Lincolnshire? One plausible answer to this involves the Late Roman *Notitia Dignitatum*, which specifies that a cavalry unit named the *Equites Taifali* was under the command of the *Comes Britanniarum* ('Count of the Britains') in the very late fourth to early fifth centuries. This unit was part of the Late Roman mobile field army, which was normally billeted in civilian areas and settlements rather than assigned to specific military forts, and was probably established between 395 and 398 from the *Taifali* who were then living in northern Italy and southern France. Naturally, this reference is most intriguing, constituting as it does the only other solid evidence for the presence of *Taifali* in Britain. In this light, it has been suggested by John Insley, Kenneth Cameron and others that the post-Roman *Taifali/*Tāflas* of Lincolnshire could have been the descendants of members (or former members) of the early fifth-century *Equites Taifali* who remained in Britain into the mid-fifth century and beyond, rather than returning to the continent.[44]

Certainly, a similar situation has recently been envisaged for northern Britain by Rob Collins, who argues that the Roman units stationed there in the early fifth century were never withdrawn and remained in place, gradually changing over time from soldiers to warriors.[45] Moreover, some potential direct support for such a scenario is available from recent work on the defence of late fourth and early fifth-century Lincolnshire. For example, Adam Daubney has argued that finds of fourth-century gold coins in Lincolnshire may be indicative of the final phase of Roman military activity in the region. The distribution of these coins appears to imply that this final phase was mainly focused on creating a defensive 'ring' around the provincial capital and episcopal see of Lincoln, with troops being stationed not in the walled forts of the region, but instead at rural strategic sites close to major routeways leading towards Lincoln and at sites close to the coastline (which accords well with the likely use of the Late Roman mobile field army, above).[46] Equally notable is the fact that finds of Roman spurs in eastern England appear to have a somewhat similar distribution around Lincoln. Such spurs are now considered to date from the end of the fourth to the early fifth century and have clear military associations, perhaps forming part of the uniform of senior officers, and Hilary Cool has suggested that their concentration in the Lincoln area likewise reflects the very late Roman defence of this region, arguably via mobile cavalry units.[47]

There would therefore seem to be a good Late Roman context for at least the presence of an element of the Late Roman mobile field army like the *Equites Taifali* in the Lincoln area at the end of the Roman period, as part of a scheme for the defence of the provincial capital at Lincoln. Indeed, it is interesting to observe that there is actually a particular concentration of such finds in the neighbouring parish to Tealby, Ludford, with a later fourth-century gold coin and *three* Late Roman spurs reported from here (one of the largest groups of these items known anywhere in Britain away from the northern frontier zone).[48] Moreover, it should be noted that this parish was both the location of a civilian 'small town' and a potential strategic site in the Late Roman period, which is likewise suggestive in light of the above, with this settlement being situated on top of the Lincolnshire Wolds on a Roman road that ran from the east coast to Lincoln, Margary 272, and also very close to the crossing point of this road with the north–south road linking the Late Roman walled forts of Caistor and Horncastle, Margary 270 (Fig. H).[49]

If the post-Roman *Taifali*/*Táflas* of Tealby (and Ludford?) did originally derive from the *Equites Taifali*, then this would arguably make sense within the fifth- to sixth-century regional context too. After all, the provincial capital of Lincoln appears to have been able to defend and maintain a significant territory all around it into the early sixth century (see Chapters 2 and 3). On the one hand, this context suggests an explanation for why members of the *Equites Taifali* might have remained in this region rather than returning to the continent, via the clear need (apparently successfully met) of those in charge at Lincoln to employ defenders for their territory as official Roman military activities in Britain drew to a close. On the other hand, the continued presence of at least some former soldiers from the Roman mobile field army – the highest-grade Roman troops –

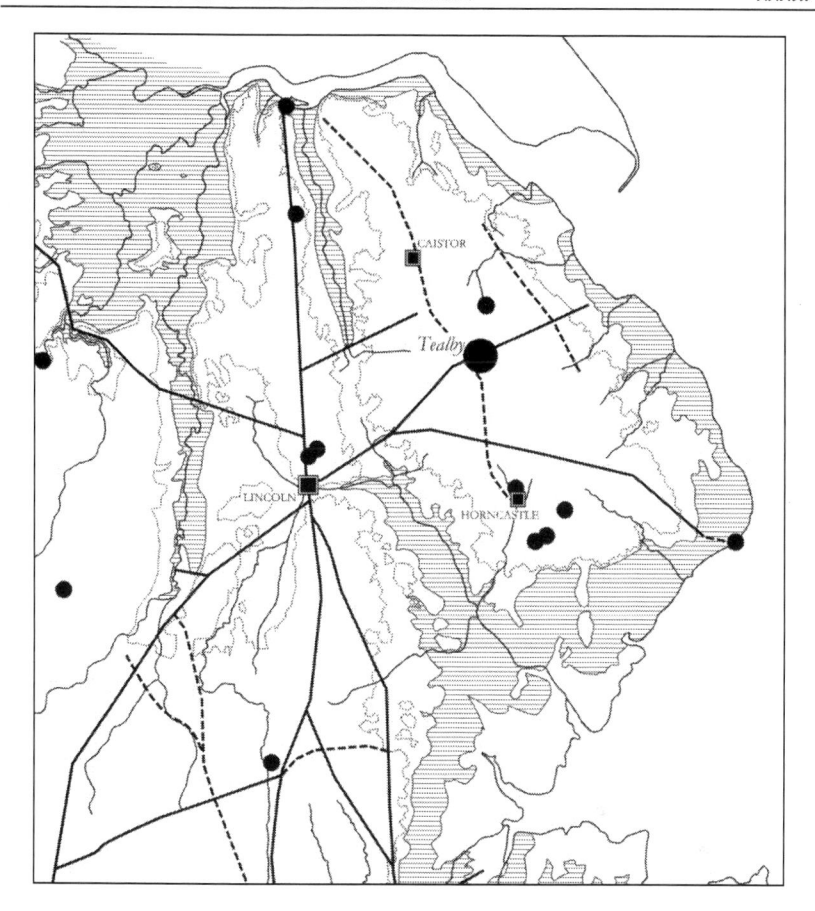

**Fig. H The distribution of Late Roman spurs around Lincoln,
with Tealby, Caistor, Horncastle and Lincoln marked**

within the British territory of *Lindēs* might help to explain why the
Britons here were seemingly so much more successful at controlling
the immigrant groups to the region during the fifth century than
many other Britons in eastern Britain seem to have been.[50] Of course,
it does need to be stressed that other explanations for the presence of
*Taifali/ *Tāflas* at Tealby in the pre-Viking era are certainly possible
(although there are potential issues with these),[51] but the above would
nonetheless seem to offer a credible solution – the context seems
sound, and such a situation as outlined above would fully explain the

evidence that we have.

The second place-name to be discussed here is Willingham. Four parishes bear this name in Lincolnshire, but they do not all share the same root. Whilst Cherry Willingham and South Willingham derive from *Willingahām, 'the estate of the *Willingas, the people/dependants of Willa', the early forms for North Willingham and Willingham by Stow point to an original *Wifelingahām, rather than *Willingahām.[52] An origin for this different first element in an unrecorded Old English personal name *Wifel formed from the insect-term wifel, 'weevil or beetle', has often been suggested, making *Wifelingahām simply 'the estate of the *Wifelingas, the people/dependants of *Wifel'. However, such a solution has been subject to a significant degree of scepticism concerning the plausibility of an early Anglo-Saxon personal name being formed from Old English wifel, and it is, moreover, not the only possible explanation of these place-names.[53]

An alternative, and highly intriguing, possibility is that these names could instead refer to Anglo-Saxon pagan priests. For example, the Old Norse name Vífill (which corresponds to Wīwila in the fifth-to sixth-century Veblungsnes runic inscription from Norway) has been argued to have originated as a term for a heathen priest, and the Old Swedish equivalent *vivil is attested in a number of place-names and is likewise believed to have been originally a designation for a cult-functionary and leader. It is, for instance, found in the place-name Vivilsta in Markims socken, Uppland, which derives from Vivils-Husar, 'portion of an administrative centre assigned to a pagan priest', and Vivelsjö in Lofta parish, Tjust, Småland, of the same meaning.[54] In light of this Scandinavian evidence, it has been suggested that the two *Wifelingahām place-names from Lincolnshire (along with one more from Cambridgeshire) are thus not, in fact, normal -ingahām names involving what is sometimes said to be an 'unattested and improbable' Old English personal name *Wifel meaning 'weevil'. Rather, it has been argued that they are better seen as containing a cognate of Old Swedish *vivil, 'pagan priest', which would take the form *wifel in Old English, and so denote Kultverbände or cultic groups under the leadership of a pagan priest.[55]

Such a possible origin for these Lincolnshire names is, of course, of considerable interest, and it is worth noting that these may not be the only place-names from eastern England that might make reference to early Anglo-Saxon *Kultverbände* and pagan priests. In particular, place-names with the form 'Ingham' – one of which is found in Lincolnshire – were re-examined as a group in 1987 by Karl Inge Sandred, who demonstrated that the old derivation of Ingham from **Ingan-hām*, 'the estate of a man named **Inga*', is unlikely to be correct. Sandred argued instead that the Ingham place-names probably all reflect Germanic **Ingwia-haimaz*, which he reads as 'the estate of the *Inguione*', a tag to mark places as the royal property of a king who claimed to be of an *Inguionic* (*i.e.* Anglian) dynasty.[56] However, as with the **Wifelingahām* place-names, this is not the only explanation of this original form that is possible. Kenneth Cameron and John Insley have more recently offered an alternative interpretation of this form that would instead see it as a cultic place-name meaning 'the estate of the devotees of the deity Ing', a Germanic god who Richard North has argued had some considerable significance in the early Anglo-Saxon period.[57]

In this context, it is noteworthy that the Lincolnshire Ingham actually lies just to the east of Willingham by Stow, separated from it only by the small former parish of Coates, which had close historical connections with Ingham parish and was probably once a part of it (Fig. I).[58] Clearly, this would seem to be a rather remarkable coincidence, although quite what its significance would be is not wholly clear. However, if the place-names Willingham and Ingham do indeed both contain references to early Anglo-Saxon *Kultverbände* – rather than one or both of them instead deriving from another of their possible meanings – then it would be worth considering whether their location next to each other could reflect a situation wherein both of these near-neighbouring parishes had once been part of a single estate belonging to an early Anglo-Saxon *Kultverband* that was led by a pagan priest, Old English **wifel*, and concerned with the worship of the deity Ing. Alternatively, if Ingham is read instead as 'the estate of the *Inguione*' and was thus an important royal centre (*villa regalis*), as is perhaps most plausible, then this would bring to mind John Blair and James Campbell's suggestion that 'the pattern by which a mid-Saxon *regio* would have two centres, a royal vill and a minster church, may perpetuate pre-Christian arrangements'. Certainly, such a situation seems to be found at Finglesham–Eastry–

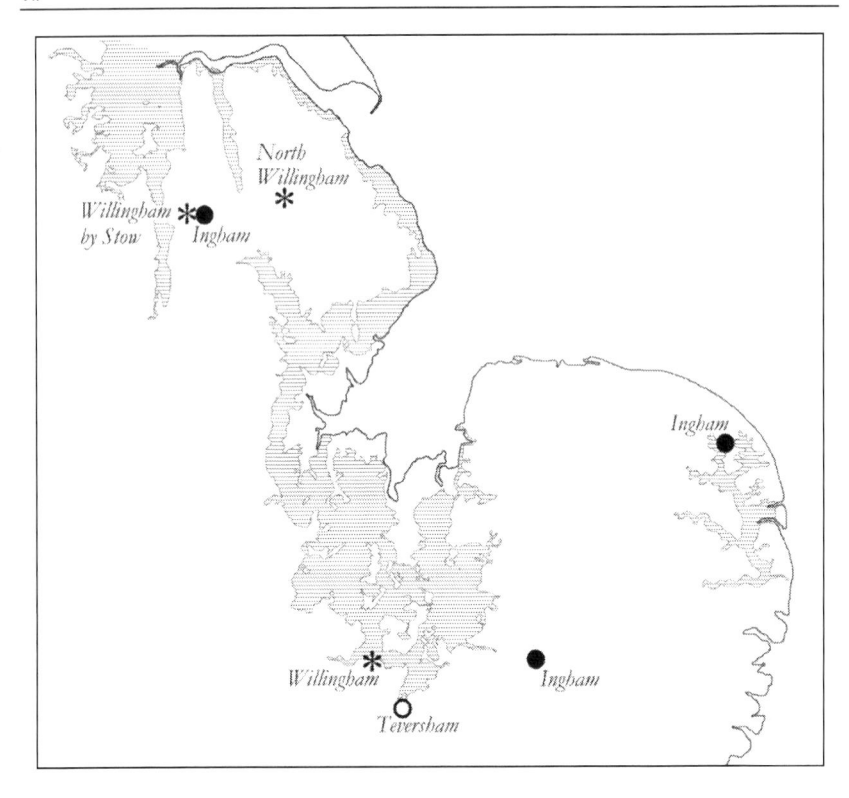

Fig. I The distribution of ***Wifelingahām*** and ***Ingwia-haimaz***
place-names in eastern England; the estimated post-Roman
coastline and extent of low-lying Fen and marshland in this area
is also shown. Note, Teversham (Cambridgeshire) is mapped
here too; this is an early name that probably means 'the
estate/homestead of the sorcerer'[59]

Woodnesborough ('Woden's mound/hill') in Kent, for example, and
it would moreover accord well with the fact that Scandinavian place-
names involving Old Swedish *vivil*, 'pagan priest', appear to have
been used as names for significant subdivisions within larger
estates/central place complexes.[60]

Finally, whatever the case may be on the above, it is intriguing to
note that a possible Middle Saxon minster (monastery) lies
immediately to the south and west of both Willingham by Stow and
Coates–Ingham. The large medieval parish of Stow that borders these

parishes is renowned as the site of the still-standing Late Saxon Stow Minster, but a case has been made for there having been a preceding pre-Viking minster church here too, based on archaeological excavations and finds.[61] This does, of course, raise the fascinating possibility that there could be a link between this potential early Christian centre and the above, neighbouring, pre-Christian estate/royal vill, perhaps even offering a direct example of the kind of Christianisation of 'pagan structure' envisaged by Campbell. As Charlotte Behr notes from a Kentish perspective, the conversion to Christianity arguably 'led to a change in religion, not to discontinuity in the religious practice where a cult site was linked to a royal villa'.[62]

Territories, central clusters and persistent places in the pre-Viking Lincolnshire landscape

With regard to the territorial and settlement landscape of Anglo-Saxon Lincolnshire, research has naturally continued over the decade since this volume was initially written. One interesting recent study is John Blair's consideration of the *regio* of the *Billingas*, a pre-Viking population-group that occupied the Kesteven Fen Edge between Billinghay and Billingborough and which was defined and discussed at length below (pp. 185–200). He makes a number of important points, including that the Car Dyke may have been used by the *Billingas* to transport goods both northwards and southwards from their important Fen Edge *wīc* (trading site) at Garwick, and confirms the existence of two 'central clusters' or core nodes within the territory of the *Billingas*, as suggested in Chapter 5, one to the north and another to the south. The northern cluster is focused on Sleaford. Blair makes the case for this having included a Middle Saxon minster church, with a dependent site at nearby Kirkby la Thorpe and perhaps another at South Kyme (given the presence of fragments of a late eighth- or early ninth-century stone chest or shrine at the latter, Fig. J), although the latter may alternatively have been an independent minster. The southern cluster is focused on the probably late seventh-century royal monastery at Threekingham/Stow Green and may also include nearby Sempringham, given finds of Middle Saxon pottery from the area of the later Priory and the reference to Sempringham in an agreement of 852 between the religious community at

Fig. J Three fragments from a late eighth- or early ninth-century stone chest or shrine from South Kyme

Medeshamstede (Peterborough) and a lay magnate called Wulfred (S 1440).[63] Blair further suggests that *Medeshamstede* had developed a significant stake in the territory of the *Billingas* by the mid-eighth century – with evidence of links to Sleaford, South Kyme and Sempringham – but that this carried with it obligations. One of these may have been the burdening of Sleaford with a Mercian royal defensive installation, indicated by the presence of a *burh* and *burh-tūn* name immediately to its east (the lost *Burg* in Kirkby la Thorpe parish and the neighbouring Burton Pedwardine).[64]

In addition to his discussion of the *regio* of the *Billingas*, John Blair has also offered some observations on Littleborough, a defended Roman 'small town' and key crossing-point on the Trent for the Roman road from Lincoln to Doncaster.[65] He notes in particular the unique concentration of 'functional *-tūn*' names around this crossing-point, which he argues are eighth- or ninth-century Mercian royal administrative names. Those found here consist of two *burh-tūnas* and two *strēt-tūnas*, along with Littleborough's own *burh* name and two significant minor names – a *stæð-ford*, 'landing-place ford', for the crossing itself, and a *þēod-þing*, 'people's meeting-place', as an alternative name for Gate Burford, with documentary evidence for this being used as a meeting-site for the whole West Riding of Lindsey. Based on this name evidence, Blair suggests that Littleborough must have been a key Mercian 'central cluster' and important node in the royal infrastructure of the eighth and ninth centuries, functioning as a strategic and defensive centre on Mercia's major communication artery, a site of assembly, and a trans-freighting point.[66]

This treatment of Littleborough is naturally of interest to the present work. As is noted in the main body of this book, the defended Roman 'small town' of Littleborough – which lay within the territory of the seventh-century kingdom of *Lindissi*, see Chapter 4 – is believed to be the site of the Roman town (*civitas*) on the Trent where Bede states Paulinus undertook the mass baptism of the *Lindisfaran*, the people of the kingdom of *Lindissi*, in AD 627–8, and to have probably been a significant element in the internal structure and administration of early Anglo-Saxon *Lindissi*. Indeed, David Stocker has observed that the mass baptism of the *Lindisfaran* in the Trent was clearly intended to be comparable with Paulinus's two other great river baptisms, in the River Glen close to the important Bernician royal centre of Yeavering and in the River Swale close to the Deiran royal centre at Catterick. He consequently argues that the *civitas* associated with the Trent baptism must be considered 'a major royal centre' of the kings of *Lindissi*, 'comparable with Yeavering and Catterick'.[67] Needless to say, the above 'central cluster' analysis by Blair adds further weight to this case for Littleborough having been an important pre-Viking royal centre. Moreover, the settlement probably continued to be a significant centre into the late ninth century, given that one of the largest assemblages of *styca* coins outside of Northumbria has been found here. These coins have an almost identical date profile to those recovered from the Viking 'Great Army' winter camp of 872–3 at Torksey (which has the largest concentration of these coins outside of Northumbria), just over a mile to the south-west of Littleborough, and their occurrence has been explained as resulting from the new, town-sized winter camp purchasing food and other resources from this site in particular, suggesting its local centrality. However, it seems unlikely that Littleborough's centrality continued much beyond this point. The establishment of a thriving Anglo-Scandinavian town and pottery industry at Torksey in the wake of the winter camp appears to have led subsequently to a decline in Littleborough's status in favour of its new neighbour (probably one of the 'seven boroughs' mentioned by the 'Anglo-Saxon Chronicle' in 1015, the others being Leicester, Lincoln, Nottingham, Stamford, Derby, and perhaps York).[68]

Another productive area for research has been the ever-increasing volume of material recorded by the Portable Antiquities Scheme (PAS) and the local Historic Environment Records (HERs). This material has recently been combined and subjected to systematic analysis by Adam Daubney, who has reached a number of interesting conclusions. Looking at the whole corpus of material from Lincolnshire from the perspective of Roman to Middle Saxon 'persistent places', he shows that nearly 88 per cent of Middle Saxon finds records on the PAS stem from sites that were previously unknown, demonstrating the value of this new resource. Furthermore, he notes that there is a clear trend in the Lincolnshire landscape whereby every identifiable 'higher status' Middle Saxon site on the PAS has also produced both early Anglo-Saxon and Romano-British finds, whereas only around 30 per cent of the 204 'lower status' Middle Saxon sites do so (although 75 per cent of these sites do include Roman material).[69] Daubney has also looked in particular detail at a number of specific sites using fine-scale mapping of the PAS and HER data. At Osbournby, for example, he notes very close spatial links between two high-status stone buildings with significant quantities of associated material indicative of activity through to the end of the Roman period, a number of finds of post-Roman 'British' metalwork, and significant scatters of early Anglo-Saxon and Middle Saxon pottery and metalwork. Exactly what this all means is, unfortunately, unclear without excavation, but it is suggested to reflect 'persistent elite activity' in this area.[70]

It is, incidentally, worth noting that a similar combination of evidence for Late Roman to Middle Saxon activity has also been noted in recent years by Steve Willis from an excavated site at Hatcliffe Top on the eastern edge of the Lincolnshire Wolds. This settlement yielded evidence for the processing of produce on a significant scale from around AD 330 through to at least the start of the fifth century, with subsequent phases of early Anglo-Saxon and Middle Saxon activity on the site indicated by finds of pottery and metalwork.[71] Likewise, attention has been recently been directed by Heinrich Härke, Helena Hamerow and John Blair to the early Anglo-Saxon to Middle Saxon settlement site at Quarrington, near Sleaford. This is thought to lie on the eastern fringes of a Romano-British settlement site (located just beyond the excavated area) and features significant evidence of both early Anglo-Saxon and Middle Saxon settlement activity, metal-working and trade. Of particular interest here is the fact that the earliest building stage consisted of three post-built roundhouses that were associated with early Anglo-Saxon pottery (Fig. K). These were subsequently replaced later in the same period by three post-built rectangular structures of the kind more normally associated with sites of this period, and the site then continued in use through until the second half of the eighth century. It goes without saying that the presence of early medieval roundhouses 'of Iron-Age and Romano-British type' on this site would seem notable; John Blair suggests that 'the complex would not look out of place in western Britain' and 'raises suspicions that Anglo-Saxon developments at a vernacular level were not wholly divorced from the post-Roman British continuum'.[72] Interestingly, another

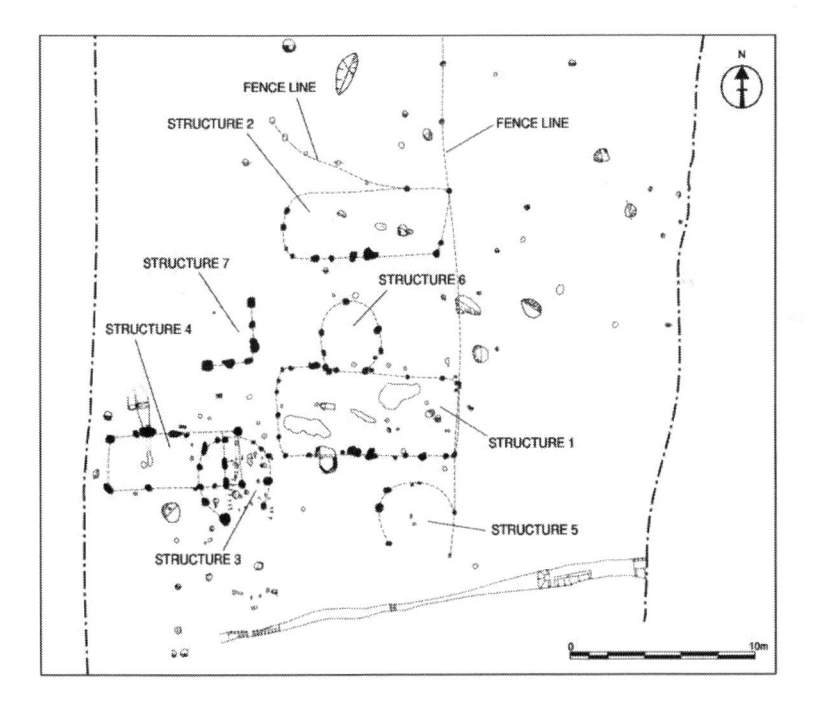

Fig. K Early Anglo-Saxon roundhouses and rectangular post-built structures excavated at Quarrington
Source: Archaeological Project Services

similar roundhouse is known from an excavated early Anglo-Saxon site at Dowsby, Lincolnshire, on the Fen Edge, around two miles south of Billingborough and Sempringham.[73]

Other 'persistent places' examined in depth by Adam Daubney include Bardney, Garwick and Little Carlton. The first of these emerges as the only site in the Witham Valley area where Roman, early Anglo-Saxon and Middle Saxon material is found together, with these finds being made just to the east of the probable site of the famous seventh-century monastery at Bardney. Curiously, the Roman material discovered from this area has been taken to tentatively suggest the presence of some sort of ritual site here, possibly a late fourth-century temple or shrine. Given both the evidence for an apparently continuous use of the River Witham for votive deposition from the pre-Roman era through to the medieval period and the relationship between this ritual activity and the establishment of Bardney and other monastic sites in the Witham Valley proposed by David Stocker and Paul Everson, this seems noteworthy.[74] Looking more widely at this site, it has been recently suggested that the seventh-century monastery at Bardney was founded on a significant local royal estate here that interlocked intriguingly with another seventh-century estate to encompass a substantial and coherent block of land north of the Witham and east of Lincoln. This second estate is argued by Everson and Stocker to have belonged to the royal reeve in charge of Lincoln (noting particularly the presence of the early name Reepham, 'the residence or estate of the reeve'), perhaps to be identified with the *praefectus ciuitatis* of *Lindocolina* – the 'Prefect of the City of Lincoln' – recorded in the early seventh century. They contend that these two estates were originally a single, albeit potentially always bipartite, unit that probably had its origins in the Roman period, arguably being ultimately associated with the suggested villa-palace of the imperial provincial governor at Lincoln, Greetwell Villa, something that is naturally of considerable interest to the present work.[75]

Garwick, in Heckington parish, is similarly important and is discussed at length in the main body of this book. This site is located right on the Fen Edge and seems to have been a pre-Viking trading site or *wīc* within the territory of the *Billingas*. Finds from the site, formerly known as the South Lincolnshire Productive Site, are prodigious; whilst Roman and early Anglo-Saxon material (including finds indicative of a small inhumation cemetery) is known, the primary interest here is the exceptionally large body of late sixth- to eighth-century coins that have been found. In Chapter 5, the total recorded coin finds from all sources as of 2009 was given, which then included around 160 very late seventh- to mid-eighth-century silver *sceattas*, a mid-seventh-century gold shilling, and thirteen high-status continental gold *tremisses* dating from the late sixth/early seventh century onwards. Since then, a number of additional finds have been made, so that the totals from Garwick now stand at just over 200 *sceattas* and seventeen *tremisses*.[76] Obviously, this constitutes an impressive corpus. Moreover, an overview of the artefact finds from Garwick indicates that there is also evidence for a 'persistent tradition of cutting down precious metals on the site', perhaps for use as forms of exchange. This apparently began in the sixth century – with a cut sixth-century silver lozenge-shaped brooch probably imported from the continent – and continued into the ninth, which is interesting, as is a potential find of a fifth- or sixth-century gold foil bracteate from here.[77] All told, Garwick is clearly a site of considerable importance for the study of the region.

Also of interest with regard to the pre-Viking trading site at Garwick is Steve Malone's recent work on the Lidar (Light Detection and Ranging) mapping of the Fenland, using airborne lasers to produce extremely accurate topographic maps that reveal the full pattern of ancient creeks/roddons in this area.[78] Of particular importance here is the fact that the resulting Lidar map shows that Garwick originally lay at the end of one arm of the former large Bicker Haven estuary and sea inlet. This arm of the estuary is Malone's feature L14, a wide 'major roddon' – an extinct, silt-filled channel that now stands higher than the surrounding land (due to differential compaction and shrinkage under drainage) – 'draining southeast towards Swineshead and Bicker Haven'. He notes that the A17 road that runs through Garwick sits atop this roddon, and suggests that this channel both dates to the early medieval period and could have offered an 'active watercourse providing a link to The Wash and North Sea' for the Fen Edge trading site.[79]

Finally, the recently discovered 'productive site' at Little Carlton is likewise fascinating. Located on a small 'island' in the marsh by the

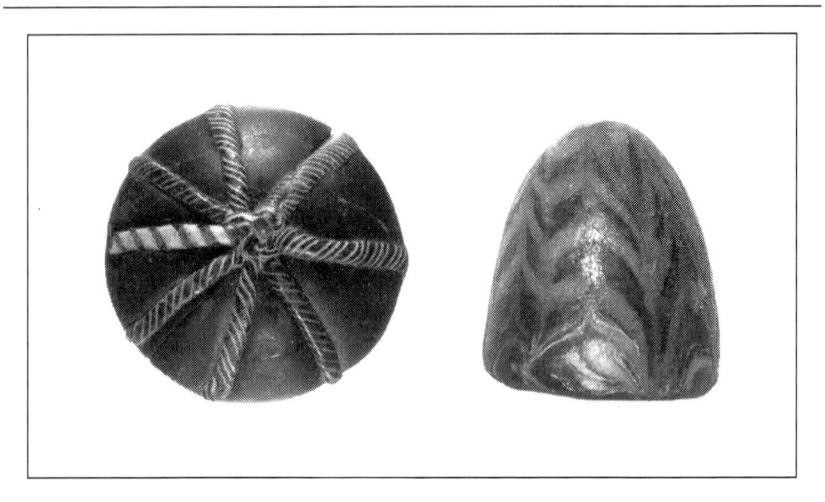

Fig. L Two Middle Saxon glass objects found at Little Carlton
Source: Adam Daubney, Portable Antiquities Scheme

Long Eau river, on the edge of the pre-Viking coastal zone, it was first discovered via metal-detecting from 2011 onwards and was subsequently excavated by the University of Sheffield. The earliest finds from here belong to the Roman and immediate post-Roman periods, including a Late Roman amphora-shaped strap end that dates from the second half of the fourth or early fifth century and a British fifth- to sixth-century Type G penannular brooch. However, the vast majority of the material – over 1,000 objects – dates from the seventh to ninth centuries.[80] It includes a large number of coins dated *c.* 680–870, styli, pins, hooked tags and strap ends, as well as handbells, glass mounts, an inscription in lead of a woman's name (*Cudburg*), and the largest collection of Middle Saxon Ipswich Ware outside of East Anglia and London, as well as some imported continental pottery (Fig. L). The excavations at Little Carlton add to this picture, revealing the presence of: industrial activity; a small wharf running out from the pre-Viking shoreline; a significant number of Middle Saxon burials; foundations that suggest the existence of a structure of considerable size; and evidence for the deliberate deposition of precious objects in a pool via an artificial platform, next to which a substantial single post was erected (indicated by a very large posthole, 1.25 metres in diameter).[81]

Taken together, the above evidence indicates that Little Carlton was a site of notable wealth and status between the seventh and ninth centuries, and bears comparison with the known sites at Flixborough (Lincolnshire) and Brandon (Suffolk). As to what the exact nature of the activity at Little Carlton was and how this changed over time, this is less clear. Hugh Willmott and Duncan Wright have commented on the presence of the strap end and penannular brooch noted above and further suggest that the deposition of precious items in the naturally accumulating central pool on the island may have its roots in a 'long-established indigenous practice', equivalent to the continuous ritual depositions in the Witham mentioned above.[82] With specific regard to the seventh- to ninth-century high-status activity, this may reflect Little Carlton being either a dependent site or part of a polyfocal 'central cluster' (of the kind observed by John Blair elsewhere in Lincolnshire) that was associated with the important Middle Saxon minster or monastery at Louth,[83] perhaps focused on trading, but also functioning as a permanent high-status, ecclesiastical settlement in its own right, given the nature of the finds from here.[84]

Of course, there is undoubtedly more that could be said regarding recent research into the fifth- to seventh-century Lincoln region,[85] but it is hoped that the above discussion at least offers a taste of some of the work most relevant to the main themes covered in this book, as well as further support for the importance and interest of this region, which lay at the heart of the core 'eastern zone' of pre-Viking England.[86]

Caitlin Green

August 2019

Notes to Introduction to the Second Edition

1   J. Gerrard (ed.), *Romano-British Pottery in the Fifth Century*, *Internet Archaeology*, 41 (2016), *intarch.ac.uk/journal/issue41/*.

2   See, for example, M. Whyman, 'Invisible people? Material culture in 'Dark Age' Yorkshire' in M. Carver (ed.), *In Search of Cult* (Woodbridge, 1992), pp. 61–8; K. R. Dark, 'Pottery and local production at the end of Roman Britain' in K. R. Dark (ed.), *External Contacts and the Economy of Late Roman and Post-Roman Britain* (Woodbridge, 1996), pp. 53–65 (p. 59); P. Rahtz, 'Anglo-Saxon Yorkshire: current research problems' in H. Geake & J.

Kenny (eds), *Early Deira: Archaeological Studies of the East Riding in the Fourth to Ninth Centuries AD* (Oxford, 2000), p. 1; J. Gerrard, 'How late is late? Pottery and the fifth century in southwest Britain' in R. Collins & J. Gerrard (eds), *Debating Late Antiquity in Britain AD 300–700* (Oxford, 2004), pp. 65–75 (p. 66); H. Cool, *Eating and Drinking in Roman Britain* (Cambridge, 2006), pp. 222–38; J. Gerrard, 'Finding the fifth century: a late fourth- and early fifth-century pottery fabric from south-east Dorset', *Britannia*, 41 (2010), 293–312; J. Gerrard, 'Roman pottery in the fifth century: a review of the evidence and its significance' in F. K. Haarer *et al* (eds), *AD 410: The History and Archaeology of Late and Post-Roman Britain* (London, 2014), pp. 87–98; K. J. Fitzpatrick-Matthews, 'Defining fifth-century ceramics in north Hertfordshire', *Internet Archaeology*, 41 (2016), *intarch.ac.uk/journal/issue41/4/*; K. J. Fitzpatrick-Matthews and R. Fleming, 'The perils of periodization: Roman ceramics in Britain after 400 CE', *Fragments*, 5 (2016), 1–33.

3   For the wares mentioned, see Gerrard, 'How late is late?', and 'Roman pottery in the fifth century'; J. Gerrard, 'The Black Burnished type 18 bowl and the fifth century', *Internet Archaeology*, 41 (2016), *intarch.ac.uk/journal/issue41/5/*; M. Whyman, 'Late Roman Britain in Transition, A.D. 300–500: A Ceramic Perspective from East Yorkshire' (University of York PhD Thesis, 2001); and Fitzpatrick-Matthews, 'Defining fifth-century ceramics'. See also, for a brief discussion, J. Gerrard, *The Ruin of Roman Britain: An Archaeological Perspective* (Cambridge, 2013), for example p. 106, where he proposes that the evidence suggests 'continued production and use, albeit on a small scale, of Romano-British pottery' in the first half of the fifth century.

4   See M. Darling and B. Precious, *A Corpus of Roman Pottery from Lincoln* (Oxford, 2014), pp. vi, 107–12, who support the possibility of this local ware continuing in production into the fifth century. With regard to the Local Coarse Pebbly ware found in the very late Roman pottery group that was discovered just outside Lincoln's Lower West Gate in 1970 (site P70), it should be noted that this group is thought 'likely to extend into the early part of the 5th century' based not only on coins found within it, but also the fact that the pottery from the latest road surfaces through the West Gate shows a 'strong resemblance' to that of this group. The *penultimate* resurfacing of this road is believed to have taken place *c.* 400, given that it contains a coin of Arcadius, and the subsequent final full road surface here moreover features further deposits that may reflect even later patching of this: M. J. Darling, *A Group of Late Roman Pottery from Lincoln* (Lincoln, 1977), p. 3; M. J. Jones, 'The Colonia era: archaeological account' in D. Stocker (ed.), *The City by the Pool: Assessing the Archaeology of the City of Lincoln* (Oxford, 2003), pp. 56–138 (p. 133); J. E. Mann, 'Roman coins' in M. Jones (ed.), *The Defences of the Lower City* (York, 1999), p. 51. With regard

to urban activity into the early fifth century at Flaxengate, see, for example, Jones, 'Colonia era', p. 133; Darling and Precious, *Corpus*, p. 215. On Lincoln's 'post-Roman' deposits and the possibility that some reflect 'sub-Roman' activity, see also A. Vince and M. Jones, 'Discussion', in K. Steane *et al*, *The Archaeology of the Lower City and Adjacent Suburbs* (Oxford, 2016), pp. 470–516 (p. 482), and Darling and Precious, *Corpus*, p. 107.

5   K. Leahy, *The Anglo-Saxon Kingdom of Lindsey* (Stroud, 2007), pp. 52–3, 86; K. Leahy, *'Interrupting the Pots': The Excavation of Cleatham Anglo-Saxon Cemetery* (York, 2007), pp. 122, 126–7. See also Gerrard, *Ruin of Roman Britain*, p. 106; Gerrard, 'Roman pottery in the fifth century', p. 93; and Fitzpatrick-Matthews, 'Defining fifth-century ceramics', section 10. On the dating of this pottery, see endnote 7 below.

6   Leahy, *Cleatham*, pp. 125, 126–7; Leahy, *Kingdom of Lindsey*, pp. 52–3; K. Leahy, 'Vessel', Portable Antiquities Scheme record FAKL-895042 (5 September 2013). For the quotation regarding the Great Casterton cemetery and Roman–Saxon burial continuity there, see S. Lucy, *The Anglo-Saxon Way of Death* (Stroud, 2000), p. 150; on Littleborough in the time of Edwin of Deira and after, see below, pp. xlii–xliii, lxv–lxvi, 136–8.

7   On the dating of this pottery, Leahy (*Cleatham*, p. 127) suggested that these urns were deposited in the late fifth century, but has more recently opted for a manufacturing date of *c.* 420–60 for this type of pottery when discussing the new find from near Littleborough: Leahy, 'Vessel', PAS FAKL-895042, 5 September 2013. This dating has also been suggested by Keith Fitzpatrick-Matthews ('Defining fifth-century ceramics', section 10), who proposes a mid-fifth-century dating for the Cleatham pottery given the recent pushing back of the start of the chronology of the great cremation cemeteries from the mid-fifth to the early fifth century at Spong Hill, see further below (pp. xxxiv).

8   See below, pp. 111–12; C. Green, 'The British kingdom of Lindsey', *Cambrian Medieval Celtic Studies*, 56 (2008), pp. 23–4; and Dark, 'Pottery and local production', pp. 58–9. See recently on such a possibility Fitzpatrick-Matthews and Fleming, 'Perils of periodization'; Fitzpatrick-Matthews, 'Defining fifth-century ceramics'; and R. Fleming, 'One British thing: a fifth-century ceramic beaker', *Journal of British Studies*, 58 (2019), 174–8.

9   C. F. Lingard and L. Bonner, *Blyborough-Brigg 300mm Gas Pipeline, 1993, Archaeological Report* (1994), pp. 21–6, 79, fig. 7.

10   J. N. L. Myres, 'Lincoln in the fifth century A.D.', *Archaeol. J.*, 103 (1946), 85–8 (pp. 87–8); J. N. L. Myres, 'The Anglo-Saxon Pottery of Lincolnshire', *Archaeol. J.*, 108 (1951), 65–99 (p. 91); J. N. L. Myres, *A Corpus of Anglo Saxon Pottery of the Pagan Period* (2 vols, Cambridge, 1977), vol. 1, p. 3; C. Green, 'An early Anglo-Saxon pot from the Greetwell villa-palace', 8 April 2015, *www.caitlingreen.org/2015/04/an-early-anglo-saxon-pot-from-greetwell.html*; Fitzpatrick-Matthews and Fleming, 'Perils of

periodization', p. 15. Myres considers it to be a 'hybrid' pot that owes 'something to a surviving tradition of Romano-British potmaking', and proposes that its presence in the villa-palace suggests 'that somebody was still living in the Greetwell villa who had a use for strongly fashioned, almost stylish, hand-made pottery at a time when it was usual to make pots of Anglo-Saxon design' (Myres, 'Lincoln', p. 88, and 'Anglo-Saxon pottery', p. 91; see also J. N. L. Myres, *The English Settlements* (Oxford, 1986), p. 182). On the survival of the villa-palace's estate into the early medieval period and beyond, see D. Stocker *et al*, 'The Greetwell villa', LARA RAZ 7.23, Heritage Connect Lincoln (2003), *www.heritageconnectlincoln.com/lara-raz/the-greetwell-villa/908*; D. Stocker and P. Everson, 'The straight and narrow way: Fenland causeways and the conversion of the landscape in the Witham valley, Lincolnshire' in M. O. H. Carver (ed.), *The Cross Goes North: Processes of Conversion in Northern Europe, A.D. 300–1300* (Woodbridge, 2002), pp. 271–88 (p. 279). For some interesting speculation regarding the wider territory of Greetwell villa-palace and its possible survival into the medieval period, see below, p. xlvi, and P. Everson and D. Stocker, *Custodians of Continuity? The Premonstratensian Abbey at Barlings and the Landscape of Ritual* (Heckington, 2011), pp. 385–91, although note that we do not have any evidence of early Anglo-Saxon burials from the villa-palace site, contrary to *Custodians*, p. 390.

11 K. R. Dark, *Britain and the End of the Roman Empire* (Stroud, 2000), p. 103, and Dark, 'Pottery and local production', pp. 58–9; see also Jones, 'Colonia era', p. 138 and G. Webster, 'A Romano-British pottery kiln at Rookery Lane, Lincoln', *Ant. Jnl.*, 40 (1960), 214–16 (who discusses the discovery of the pot and assigns it to the flue). Dark, 'Pottery', p. 59, further suggests that this pot could have been fired in the Rookery Lane kiln, but Catherine Hills (personal communication) is sceptical of this idea. See also Green, 'British kingdom', p. 23 and fn. 97, for another Romano-British kiln in the Lincoln region, at Lea, which has some curious magnetic dating results that appear to indicate that its last firing could have taken place in the mid–late fifth century – D. Tarling and N. H. Yassi note that '[i]f the kiln was not last fired at this time, then the reason for the observed deviation is not known and urgently requires further study': N. Field, 'Romano-British pottery kilns in the Trent Valley', *LHA*, 19 (1984), 100–02 (pp. 101–02).

12 D. C. Briscoe, 'Two important stamp motifs in Roman Britain and thereafter', *Internet Archaeology*, 41 (2016), *intarch.ac.uk/journal/issue41/2/*; see Darling and Precious, *Corpus*, p. 163, on the date and place of manufacture of the Late Roman vessel from Flaxengate. Also of potential interest in the present context may be the recent suggestion that twelve 'Anglo-Saxon' cremation urns from Cleatham and Millgate, Newark, which are all handmade but feature footrings, may be related to earlier Roman

wheel-made pottery and reflect local British communities making new styles of pots whilst harking back to earlier forms (Fitzpatrick-Matthews and Fleming, 'Perils of periodization', pp. 12, 18–19, 23–4, 31); however, a note of caution does need to be sounded here, as footrings are also present on some continental North-western European pottery of this era too. It is also worth noting that Colin Hayfield has argued on the basis of evidence from Barton-upon-Humber that early to middle Saxon shell-tempered pottery might in fact have a Late Roman origin: C. Hayfield, *Humberside Medieval Pottery: An Illustrated Catalogue of Saxon and Medieval Domestic Assemblages from North Lincolnshire and its Sorrounding Region* (2 vols, Oxford, 1985), vol. 1, p. 50.

13   Darling and Precious, *Corpus*, pp. 228, 241; L. A. Gilmour, *Early Medieval Pottery from Flaxengate, Lincoln* (London, 1988), p. 167; A. C. Thomas, 'Imported pottery in Dark-Age western Britain', *Medieval Archaeology*, 3 (1959), 89–111 (p. 95). Note, these finds from Lincoln are not without context in fifth-century Britain. Both Ken Dark and Maria Duggan have recently noted that finds of apparently 'post-Roman' amphorae and fineware from the Mediterranean are known not only from fifth- and sixth-century western British sites like Tintagel and Dinas Powys, but also from Roman cities and forts further east, including London, York, Wroxeter, Gloucester and Pevensey Castle (East Sussex): K. Dark, 'Western Britain in Late Antiquity' in Haarer *et al* (eds), *AD 410*, pp. 23–35 (pp. 25–6); M. Duggan, 'Ceramic imports to Britain and the Atlantic seaboard in the fifth century and beyond', *Internet Archaeology*, 41 (2016), *intarch.ac.uk/journal/issue41/3/*, section 5; PAS LON-BB27D6. Gaulish DSP is similarly now known from the east of Britain as well as the west; see the recent publication of a find from Pevensey Castle (Duggan, section 5).

14   J. Hines and A. Bayliss (eds), *Anglo-Saxon Graves and Grave Goods of the 6th and 7th Centuries AD: A Chronological Framework*, Society for Medieval Archaeology Monograph, 33 (London, 2013), pp. 549, 550. The dating and character of the St Paul in the Bail sequence argued for here has also been adopted by Nicholas Higham in N. J. Higham and M. J. Ryan, *The Anglo-Saxon World* (London, 2013), pp. 40, 106; see also B. Yorke, 'Pagan to Christian in Anglo-Saxon England' in R. Flechner and M. Ní Mhaonaigh (eds), *The Introduction of Christianity into the Early Medieval Insular World: Converting the Isles I* (Turnhout, 2016), pp. 237–57. On the probable sequence of two churches in the former Roman *forum*, see not only Chapter 2, but also Green, 'British kingdom', pp. 18–23; note, however, that the discussion below (pp. 65–9, 82–3) supersedes elements of this, especially with regard to the radiocarbon dating of the site. On the questionable use of the radiocarbon data in some prior discussions of this site – particularly P. H. Sawyer, *Anglo-Saxon Lincolnshire* (Lincoln, 1998), pp.

226–30 – see, in addition to the discussion here (especially pp. 66–7, 83), Green, 'British kingdom', 19–20, fn. 85, and A. G. Vince, 'Lincoln in the early medieval era, between the 5th and 9th centuries: the archaeological account' in Stocker (ed.), *City by the Pool*, pp. 150–1.

15   S. Malone, 'A group of Romano-British lead tanks from Lincolnshire and Nottinghamshire' in S. Malone and M. Williams (eds), *Rumours of Roman Finds: Recent Work on Roman Lincolnshire* (Heckington, 2010), pp. 138–42 (quotation at p. 142); for a sceptical view of the Christian associations of these tanks, see B. Crerar, 'Contextualising Romano-British lead tanks: a study in design, destruction and deposition', *Britannia*, 43 (2012), 135–66, although this article doesn't take into account Malone's 2010 paper, and other researchers continue to accept a Christian origin for these tanks as fonts or similar (for example, Martin Henig, commenting on a 2013 find of one of these tanks/fonts from Wiltshire – Portable Antiquities Scheme WILT-95F01A – notes that he continues to consider them to be fonts, *pace* Crerar). The 2013 find from near Lincoln is PAS LIN-9C11F6.

16   M. J. Jones, 'Recent research on the archaeology of the early Christian Church in Britain, *c.* 300–800' in S. Cresci *et al* (eds) *Acta XV Congressus Internationalis Archaeologiae Christianae (Toledo 8–12.9 2008) — Episcopus, Civitas, Territorium*, Studi Di Antichità Cristiana LXV (Vatican City, 2013), pp. 1163–78. The 28 examples known from Britain consist of 23 recorded by Crerar, 'Contextualising Romano-British lead tanks', and a further five recorded by the PAS from 2013 to 2018; almost two-thirds of these may come from Lincoln's province, depending on how it is defined.

17   There are now 21 or 22 Class 1 brooches that have been identified from the Lincoln region and eight Type G brooches. *New Class 1 brooches*: Portable Antiquities Scheme NLM-DF2FC2 (Scotter); FAKL-0F6995 (Leasingham); LIN-C445A4 (Gate Burton, see A. Booth, 'Reassessing the Long Chronology of the Penannular Brooch in Britain: Exploring Changing Styles, Use and Meaning Across a Millennium' (University of Leicester PhD Thesis, 2014), p. 263); and Gavin no. 27 (Caistor; previously listed as unprovenanced in S. Youngs, 'Britain, Wales and Ireland: holding things together' in K. Jankulak and J. M. Wooding (eds), *Ireland and Wales in the Middle Ages* (Dublin, 2007), pp. 86–7, but now identified as having come from 'Caistor, Lincolnshire or one of the surrounding parishes', see S. Youngs, 'From metalwork to manuscript: some observations on the use of Celtic art in insular manuscripts', *Anglo-Saxon Studies in Archaeology and History*, 16 (2009), 45–64 (pp. 57, 60, 62), and F. Gavin, 'Insular Ornamental Metalwork AD 300–500: 'Military Style' Inspired Art in Ireland and Britain' (2 vols, National University of Ireland, Galway, PhD Thesis, 2014), vol. 2, quotation at p. 78). *New Type G brooches*: PAS LIN-35B2BE (Little Carlton) and WILT-35008F (Glentham). There have been a number of studies of penannular brooches and related metalwork in

recent years; of particular note is Gavin, 'Insular Ornamental Metalwork', see especially vol. 1, pp. 81–6, 215–7, 229–31, 241, 266–9, 313–18, and also Booth, *Reassessing*, although the latter is mainly concerned with earlier types.

18 On Class 1 brooches in general as British elite objects, see below pp. 70–1 and, for example, Youngs, 'Holding things together', pp. 86–9; Dark, *Britain and the End of the Roman Empire*, p. 133; and Gavin, 'Insular Ornamental Metalwork', vol. 1, pp. 124–7.

19 For example, Gavin, 'Insular Ornamental Metalwork', vol. 1, pp. 81–6, 115–19, 124–7, 241, 266–9, 316–17 (quotations at pp. 126, 116); she discusses the Caistor and East Ravendale Class 1 brooches specifically in vol. 1, pp. 81–4, 217, 229–30, 295 and vol. 2, pp. 71–2, 78–9.

20 *New finds of 'Late Celtic' hanging bowls from Lindsey*: Portable Antiquities Scheme NLM-FC7404 (Blyborough); DENO-5F1F74 (Hagworthingham); LIN-CC7FA4 and LIN-CD2908/LIN-74E196 (Maltby Le Marsh); LIN-65EE1A (Waddingham); LIN-574DCD (Chapel St Leonards); NLM-C988A1 (Hatcliffe); Melton Ross (NLM-AAFD2A); NLM-07E6BC (South Ferriby/Barton-upon-Humber); NLM-A78620 (Winteringham). *New finds from Kesteven*: Portable Antiquities Scheme NLM-8EACE5 (Long Bennington); LIN-A8D424 (Osbournby); LIN-3972E3 (Aunsby and Dembleby); LIN-FA5634 (Welby); LIN-89C232 (Digby).

21 See C. Green, *The Origins of Louth: Archaeology and History in East Lincolnshire, 400,000 BC–AD 1086* (Louth, 2011), pp. 45–6, 148–9, on the actual findspot, confirmed to me by the detectorist who found the proto-hand-pin, Mark Jones. On the proto-hand-pin from Welton le Wold, see especially S. Youngs, 'After Oldcroft: a British silver pin from Welton le Wold, Lincolnshire' in N. Crummy *et al* (eds), *Image, Craft and the Classical World* (Montagnac, 2005), pp. 249–54, and Gavin, 'Insular Ornamental Metalwork', vol. 1, pp. 195, 229–31, vol. 2, pp. 10–11.

22 On the Welton villa site, see Green, *Origins*, pp. 43–6, 148–9, which established that a large body of finds recorded on the Portable Antiquities Scheme with a variety of grid references actually came from this site; see also D. Jones, 'Romano-British settlement in the Lincolnshire Wolds' in R. H. Bewley (ed.), *Lincolnshire's Archaeology from the Air* (Lincoln, 1998), pp. 69–80 (pp. 72–5); Lincolnshire HER 43544 and 41157.

23 Numbers 1 to 12 are buckles and numbers 13 to 15 are strap ends; findspots are as follows: 1 – Hibaldstow; 2, 3, 9 – Dragonby; 4 – Stickford; 5, 6, 11, – Kirmington; 7 – Osgodby; 8 – Barrow on Humber; 10 – Lincoln; 12 – Ingham; 13 – Keelby; 14 – Winterton villa; 15 – Winteringham. See futher Leahy, *Kingdom of Lindsey*, p. 29.

24 S. Youngs, 'Silver handpins from the West Country to Scotland: perplexing portable antiquities' in F. Hunter and A. Sheridan (eds.), *Ancient Lives: Object, People and Place in Early Scotland* (Leiden, 2016), pp. 303–16,

quotations at pp. 307, 312; see also Gavin, 'Insular Military Style silver pins in Late Iron Age Ireland' in F. Hunter and K. Painter (eds), *Late Roman Silver Within and Beyond the Frontier: The Traprain Treasure in Context* (Edinburgh, 2013), pp. 427–41 (quotation p. 436), and Gavin, 'Insular Ornamental Metalwork', on the aristocratic, elite character of these items. The date of manufacture of the Welton pin is open to debate: the use of niello suggests that it is unlikely to have been made later than the fifth century, but doesn't really narrow its date further than this (Gavin, 'Insular Ornamental Metalwork', vol. 1, p. 195); for what it is worth, the original report on the pin dated its manufacture to the fifth century, although a later fourth-century date has also been suggested: DCMS, *Treasure Annual Report 2001* (London, 2003), pp. 43–4; Youngs, 'After Oldcroft', p. 253.

25   Youngs, 'After Oldcroft', pp. 251 and 253, and Gavin, 'Insular Ornamental Metalwork', vol. 1, pp. 117 and 225–7, vol. 2, pp. 30–2.

26   Gavin, 'Insular Ornamental Metalwork', vol. 1, especially pp. 215–41, on the distribution of finds of metalwork decorated in the Insular Military Style, although it should be noted that this pattern is based on relatively few finds. Interestingly, the same distribution can arguably be discerned for British Class 1 and Type G brooches in Britain too, see Fig. 15 below.

27   Gavin, 'Insular Ornamental Metalwork', vol. 1, quotations at pp. 116, 126; see particularly pp. 115–27, 266–9; see further, for example, Gerrard, *Ruin of Roman Britain*, Chapter 7, especially pp. 254–5, 259–60.

28   K. Leahy, 'Soldiers and settlers in Britain, fourth to fifth century – revisited' in M. Henig and T. J. Smith (eds), *Collectanea Antiqua: Essays in memory of Sonia Chadwick Hawkes* (Oxford, 2007), pp. 133–43; Leahy, *Kingdom of Lindsey*, pp. 28–31; H. Cool, 'Objects of glass, shale, bone and metal (except nails)', in P. Booth *et al* (eds), *The Late Roman Cemetery at Lankhills, Winchester: Excavations 2000–2005* (Oxford, 2010), pp. 266–309 (p. 286); and Gerrard, *Ruin of Roman Britain*, pp. 105–06, 167–8, 255, 263–5. See also J. C. N. Coulston, 'Military equipment of the "long" 4th century on Hadrian's Wall', in R. Collins and L. Allason-Jones (eds), *Finds From the Frontier: Material Culture in the 4th–5th Centuries* (London, 2010), pp. 50–63 (pp. 52–56) on finds from the northern frontier. For Gavin's observations, see *Insular Ornamental Metalwork*, vol. 1, pp. 22–4.

29   Based on a survey of fifth- to sixth-century finds from Lincolnshire, North Lincolnshire and North East Lincolnshire recorded by the Portable Antiquities Scheme from late 2009 through to June 2019, and excluding records of British post-Roman penannular brooches. See below, p. 272, and T. F. Martin, *The Cruciform Brooch and Anglo-Saxon England* (Woodbridge, 2015), p. 165, on identifying cemeteries from metal-detected finds of early Anglo-Saxon decorative metalwork and the probable origin of most such finds in plough-disturbed graves.

30   University of Sheffield, 'Remains of Anglo-Saxon cemetery discovered', *www.sheffield.ac.uk/news/nr/remains-anglo-saxon-cemetery-discovered-1.818242*. Some of the finds from this site recorded by the Portable Antiquities Scheme include LIN-9362CB, LIN-7AC173, and LIN-7B42A2.

31   Based on a survey of the local Historic Environment Records and the Portable Antiquities Scheme; see, for example, pp. 60–4 and Fig. 33, on the existing pattern of fifth- to sixth-century Anglo-Saxon cemeteries in Lincolnshire. *Scremby*: see endnote 30. *Appleby*: a fifth- to sixth-century cemetery (PAS SWYOR-BDC012). *Leasingham*: a late fifth- to sixth-century cemetery (PAS FAKL-BD5E61); note, not the Leasingham site in the gazetteer. *Osbournby*: additional metal-detected finds, see Appendix One for the cemeteries here, e.g. PAS LIN-239908; see also A. J. Daubney, *Portable Antiquities, Palimpsests, and Persistent Places* (Leiden, 2016), pp. 120–79. Middling clusters of new finds, again all located away from Lincoln, are recorded from the Wickenby cemetery to the south of Lissingleys (see pp. 141–2, 278); the Middle Rasen cemetery (p. 279); Binbrook (p. 274); Keelby (p. 277); Miningsby in Revesby parish (not the Revesby site in the gazetteer; diffuse scatter of fifth- to sixth-century metalwork, arguably more than one site, for example PAS NCL-C7A646, DUR-8F4A7E); Riby (a different site to that listed in the gazetteer; sixth- to seventh-century cemetery: PAS NLM-FDFB3A); Melton Ross (from a site several hundred metres away from that already recorded in the gazetteer, sixth- to seventh-century cemetery: PAS NLM-8EC0B7); and South Ferriby/Barton-upon-Humber (a late fifth- to sixth-century cemetery: NLM-07F328).

32   On the *Spalde* and the primarily non-metalwork evidence for post-Roman activity in their territory, see below pp. 170–85. As of July 2019, the PAS records 1,873 finds from the territory of the *Spalde*/district of Holland, but only ten items are potentially of early medieval *and* pre-Viking date, and almost all of these belong to the eighth- or ninth-centuries, with only a single find pre-dating *c.* AD 700 (BERK-C82D3E, a seventh-century pendant from Gosberton). Other data sources, such as the EMC, add only a handful of additional finds to this total, with these again being mainly Middle Saxon in date aside from two late sixth-/seventh-century *tremisses* (EMC 2016.0319, 2014.0286). Note, there are a small number of late documentary references that have been read as indicating the survival of Britons/British-speakers in the Fenland even into the Late Saxon/Anglo-Scandinavian period: see p. 219, note 48, below, and S. Oosthuizen, 'Culture and identity in the early medieval Fenland landscape', *Landscape History*, 37 (2016), 5–24 (pp. 16–17), who considers these references to be credible; also S. Oosthuizen, *The Anglo-Saxon Fenland* (Oxford, 2017), pp. 38–9.

33   See, for example, C. Scull, 'Further evidence from East Anglia for enamelling on early Anglo-Saxon metalwork', *Anglo-Saxon Studies in*

Archaeology and History, 4 (1985), 117–24; L. Laing, 'Romano-British metalworking and the Anglo-Saxons' in N. J. Higham (ed.), *Britons in Anglo-Saxon England* (Woodbridge, 2007), pp. 42–56 (pp. 44–6); T. F. Martin, 'Identity and the Cruciform Brooch in Early Anglo-Saxon England: An Investigation of Style, Mortuary Context, and Use' (4 vols, University of Sheffield PhD Thesis, 2011), vol. 3, p. 447; Martin, *The Cruciform Brooch*, pp. 142–3.

34 Below, pp. 116, 147–8; Susan Youngs, personal communication (quotation); S. Youngs, 'Recent finds of insular enamelled buckles' in C. E. Karkov, R. T. Farrell and M. Ryan (eds), *The Insular Tradition* (Albany, 1997), pp. 192–4; S. Youngs, 'Two medieval Celtic enamelled buckles from Leicestershire', *Transactions of the Leicestershire Archaeological and Historical Society*, 68 (1993), 15–22; L. Laing, 'The Bradwell mount and the use of millefiori in post-Roman Britain', *Studia Celtica*, 33 (1999), 137–53 (p. 149); S. Youngs, 'Missing material: early Anglo-Saxon enamelling' in C. E. Karkov and H. Damico (eds), *Aedificia Nova: Studies in Honor of Rosemary Cramp* (Kalamazoo, 2008), pp. 162–75 (p. 175, n. 28). Note, the findspot was given as West Ravendale in the initial publications dealing with this piece, but it was subsequently noted to have been actually found at Keelby.

35 *Sword pommel*: British Museum accession no. 1997,0101.1 and Lincolnshire HER 43147 (Hemingby/Baumber; found close to the boundary between these two parishes and recorded under both); Youngs, 'Missing material', pp. 163, 171, 175. *Brooches*: Laing, 'Romano-British metalwork', p. 44; J. Hines, *A New Corpus of Anglo-Saxon Great Square-Headed Brooches* (Woodbridge, 1997), p. 220; British Museum 1883,0401.524; and K. Leahy, *Anglo-Saxon Crafts* (Stroud, 2003), pp. 160–1 (Sleaford & Scopwick); PAS LIN-3702B0 (Baston); PAS NLM4745 (Tathwell). *Pyramidal mounts*: PAS LIN-105D91 (Folkingham); PAS NLM-07F328 (South Ferriby/Barton). *Belt fittings*: Kevin Leahy, personal communication (Sawcliffe Hill, formerly known as Sheffield's Hill, Roxby cum Risby parish; publication forthcoming) – the items in question are objects 1 and 5 from the late fifth- or sixth-century Grave 11 (triangular copper-alloy and gilded mounts on leather, probably belt fittings, both with a circular enamel inlay) and object US005 (a probably sixth-century square gilded belt fitting with a four-petalled shape inlaid with enamel that was metal-detected from the ploughsoil of the cemtery site); two further mounts identical to the latter were also recovered by metal detecting prior to excavation (unstratified finds 1738a and 1738b), but it is unfortunately not recorded whether the central four-petalled design was inlaid on these or not.

36 Martin, *The Cruciform Brooch*, pp. 23, 25. Note, Martin, p. 175, sees his phase A, sub-group 1.1, cruciform brooches as providing potentially direct evidence for migration or continental imports; finds of these from the Lincoln region have increased markedly in recent years.

37 See J. C. Mann, 'The creation of four provinces in Britain by Diocletian', *Britannia*, 29 (1998), 340, on the Late Roman provinces of Britain. Martin, *The Cruciform Brooch*, p. 169, includes a density map of phase A cruciform brooches based on the number of finds from each site, which is more relevant in this context: almost all of the high-density area for finds of phase A brooches falls within the suggested bounds of Lincoln's province, aside from (as in Fig. 21b) an outlying concentration in eastern Kent. For an alternative, albeit arguably complementary, explanation for the overall distribution of 'Anglian' dress-accessories in eastern England, see T. Williamson, 'The environmental contexts of Anglo-Saxon settlement' in N. J. Higham and M. J. Ryan (eds), *The Landscape Archaeology of Anglo-Saxon England* (Manchester, 2010), pp. 133–56 (pp. 147–52).

38 Martin, *The Cruciform Brooch*, pp. 170 (map), 168–85, 222–38 (discussion), quotation from p. 174; Martin, 'Identity', vol. 1, pp. 171–84, vol. 2, p. 396; T. Martin, 'Women, knowledge and power: the iconography of early Anglo-Saxon cruciform brooches', *Anglo-Saxon Studies in Archaeology and History*, 18 (2013), 1–17 (p. 2). Note, the outlying concentration in eastern Kent dwindled rapidly in phase B and probably didn't outlast *c.* 500 (Martin, *The Cruciform Brooch*, p. 179). For other recent discussions of the origins of the 'Anglian' identity and the various material reflections of this, see especially J. Hines, 'The origins of East Anglia in a North Sea Zone' in D. Bates & R. Liddiard (eds), *East Anglia and its North Sea World in the Middle Ages* (Woodbridge, 2013), pp. 16–43; C. Hills, 'The Anglo-Saxon migration to Britain: an archaeological perspective' in H. Meller *et al* (eds), *Migration and Integration from Prehistory to the Middle Ages* (Saale, 2017), pp. 239–53; and C. Hills and S. Lucy, *Spong Hill IX: Chronology and Synthesis* (Cambridge, 2013), particularly pp. 305–08, 314, 327–31. On the link between the spread of furnished inhumation cemeteries in eastern England and ethnogenesis, see Martin, *The Cruciform Brooch*, pp. 222–6, 230–1, 234, and recently, for example, C. Scull, 'The *adventus saxonum* from an archaeological point of view: how many phases were there?' in G. Waxenberger and K. Kazzazi (eds), *Old English Runes: Interdisciplinary Perspectives on Approaches and Methodologies* (Berlin, forthcoming), pp. 5, 14–15, of the pre-publication version at *www.academia.edu/24427173/*; Scull suggests that the widespread adoption of a furnished inhumation burial rite (in contrast to the earlier cremation rite, see below) from the later fifth century onwards reflects ethnogenesis via a process of cultural accommodation and development between 'kindreds of continental descent' and insular groups who 'adopted elements of dress, material culture and burial rite which clearly derive from continental cultural practice' (p. 15).

39 Martin, *The Cruciform Brooch*, pp. 171 (map), 172, 185–90, 235 (discussion); Martin, 'Identity', vol. 1, pp. 184–90. On the mid-sixth-century origins of

the Anglian kingdom of *Lindissi*, see, for example, pp. 97–105, 113–5, of the present volume.

40 K. E. Squires, 'Populating the pots: the demography of the early Anglo-Saxon cemeteries at Elsham and Cleatham, North Lincolnshire', *Archaeol. J.*, 169 (2012), 312–42; K. E. Squires, 'Piecing together identity: a social investigation of early Anglo-Saxon cremation practices', *Archaeol. J.*, 170 (2013), 154–200; G. J. Perry, 'United in Death: The Pre-Burial Origins of Anglo-Saxon Cremation Urns' (University of Sheffield PhD Thesis, 2013). See also G. J. Perry, 'Beer, butter and burial: the pre-burial origins of cremation urns from the early Anglo-Saxon cemetery of Cleatham, North Lincolnshire', *Medieval Ceramics*, 32 (2011), 9–21, with regard to his interesting observations on the pre-burial origins of the urns.

41 Hills and Lucy, *Spong Hill IX*, especially pp. 229–32, 292–331; Hills, 'Anglo-Saxon migration', pp. 248–51 (quotations at p. 250). Note, Hills argues that the subsequent coherence of the late fifth- to sixth-century 'Anglian' zone – as defined by dress-accessories like those discussed above, and in notable contrast to the 'Saxon' region to the south – results and derives from the great cremation cemeteries found here and the significant immigration implied by them ('Anglo-Saxon migration', pp. 250–1). See also recently, for example, Martin, *The Cruciform Brooch*, especially pp. 174–5, 178, 184 ('large, early cremation cemeteries including Spong Hill in Norfolk and Cleatham in Lincolnshire… and their obvious parallels in northern Germany demonstrate more convincingly than anything else does that it was not just items like cruciform brooches that were brought to post-Roman Britain, but whole packages of mortuary practices, beliefs and settlement structures, for which mass migration provides the most likely vehicle.'), and Scull, 'The *adventus*', especially pp. 4–5, 10–11, 12, 14.

42 For example, below pp. 2, 108–11, 268–9; for earlier statements of this, see C. Scull, 'Approaches to the material culture and social dynamics of the migration period in eastern England' in J. Bintliff and H. Hamerow (eds), *Europe Between Late Antiquity and the Middle Ages* (Oxford, 1995), especially pp. 77–9; H. Hamerow, 'Migration theory and the Anglo-Saxon "identity crisis"' in J. Chapman and H. Hamerow (eds) *Migrations and Invasions in Archaeological Explanation* (Oxford, 1997), pp.33–44; H. Hamerow, 'The earliest Anglo-Saxon kingdoms' in P. Fouracre (ed.), *The New Cambridge Medieval History, I: c.500–c.700* (Cambridge, 2005), pp. 264–9; H. Härke, 'Population replacement or acculturation? An archaeological perspective on population and migration in post-Roman Britain' in H. L. C. Tristram (ed.), *The Celtic Englishes III* (Hiedelberg, 2003), pp. 13–28. See recently on this Nicholas Higham in Higham and Ryan, *Anglo-Saxon World*, p. 104 ('Overall… the evidence favours large-scale population continuity alongside significant migration'); Gerrard, *Ruin of Roman Britain*, pp. 181–2; and H. Härke, 'Anglo-Saxon immigration and ethnogenesis', *Med. Arch.*, 55

(2011), 1–28. For a contrary view, see S. Oosthuizen, *The Emergence of the English* (Leeds, 2019), who makes the case for a significant degree of landscape and population continuity, but also – like Richard Hodges in the 1980s – suggests that archaeological and linguistic changes in 'post-Roman' Britain can be largely explained via cultural choices/influence and without recourse to migration, although in doing this she doesn't really engage with the cremation cemetery evidence. Hills, 'Anglo-Saxon migration', forcefully restates the notion that different regions of lowland Britain are likely to have had very different experiences in the post-Roman period, and whilst significant migration may have occurred in the eastern 'Anglian zone', this was probably not the case elsewhere.

43   For a discussion, see John Insley in K. Cameron, *The Place-Names of Lincolnshire, Part Three: The Wapentake of Walshcroft* (Nottingham, 1992), pp. 135–6, and C. Green, 'Tealby, the *Taifali*, and the end of Roman Lincolnshire', *LHA*, 46 (2011), 5–10. See also K. Cameron, *Dictionary of Lincolnshire Place-Names* (Nottingham, 1998), p. 123; A. D. Mills, *A Dictionary of British Place-Names* (Oxford, 2011), p. 453; and V. Watts, *The Cambridge Dictionary of English Place-Names* (Cambridge, 2004), p. 602, all of which give this etymology. It is also supported by Carole Hough in 'Some ghost entries in Smith's *English Place-Name Elements*', *Nomina*, 17 (1994), 19–30 (p. 26). This group-name was utilised as an Old English place-name with the sense '(the settlement of) the **Tāflas/*Tǣflas*', to which the Old Danish for village (*-bȳ*) was added at some point after the Scandinavian settlements in the ninth century: Cameron, *Place-Names of Lincolnshire III*, p. 135; Green, 'Tealby', p. 5.

44   The idea that the *Taifali/*Tāflas* of Tealby had their origins in the Late Roman *Equites Taifali* was first proposed, though not discussed in any detail, by John Insley in Cameron, *Place-Names of Lincolnshire III*, pp. 135–6, and is adopted in Cameron, *Dictionary*, p. 123, and Watts, *Cambridge Dictionary*, p. 602; it is considered in depth in Green, 'Tealby', especially 5–7, which also looks at possible alternative explanations. On the billeting of the mobile field army in towns and rural sites, see, for example, P. Southern, 'The army in late Roman Britain' in M. Todd (ed.), *A Companion to Roman Britain* (Oxford, 2004), pp. 393–408 (p. 405); S. Esmonde-Cleary, *The Ending of Roman Britain* (London, 1989), p. 54; Cool, 'Objects of glass, shale, bone and metal', p. 291; and H. E. M. Cool, 'A different life' in Collins and Allason-Jones (eds), *Finds From the Frontier*, pp. 1–9 (pp. 7–9).

45   R. Collins, 'Soldiers to warriors: renegotiating the Roman frontier in the fifth century' in F. Hunter and K. Painter, *Late Roman Silver: The Traprain Treasure in Context* (Edinburgh, 2013), pp. 29–43.

46   See below, p. 117, endnote 3; A. Daubney, 'The use of gold in late Iron Age and Roman Lincolnshire' in Malone and Williams (eds), *Recent Work on Roman Lincolnshire*, pp. 64–74, especially p. 71; and Green, 'Tealby', p. 7.

47 K. Leahy, 'Three Roman rivet spurs from Lincolnshire', *Antiq. J.*, 76 (1996), 237–40; B. C. Burnham and J. Wacher, *The Small Towns of Roman Britain* (Berkeley and Los Angeles, 1990), pp. 36, 115; and especially Cool, 'A different life', pp. 4–9, fig. 1.3; Cool, 'Objects of glass, shale, bone and metal', pp. 290–1; and H. E. M. Cool, 'Which "Romans"; what "home"? The myth of the "end" of Roman Britain' in F. K. Haarer *et al* (eds), *AD 410: The History and Archaeology of Late and Post-Roman Britain* (London, 2014), pp. 13–22 (p. 17).

48 The three spurs from Ludford 'small town' are PAS NLM5355, NLM5354, and a find discussed in Leahy, 'Three Roman rivet spurs from Lincolnshire'. The Late Roman gold coin from Ludford has been reported to the local Finds Liaison Officer, Adam Daubney, but is not on the PAS database as the finder does not record with this body: A. Daubney, personal communication. For the distribution of Late Roman spurs in Britain with totals from each site, see Cool, 'A different life', fig. 1.3 (p. 6) – there are two other sites away from the northern frontier with three spurs, both on the south coast of Britain, but none with more than this.

49 Ludford 'small town' is Lincolnshire HER 40610; see also R. Bradley, R. Jackson and S. Willis, 'Ludford, Lincolnshire: small-scale investigations of a Roman roadside settlement', *LHA*, 49 (2014), 23–36. For the Roman roads, see I. D. Margary, *Roman Roads in Britain*, 3rd edn (1973).

50 See Collins, 'Soldiers to warriors', p. 39, for a similar suggestion relating to northern frontier zone.

51 See Green, 'Tealby', 6–7, 8.

52 Cameron, *Dictionary*, p. 139; Watts, *Cambridge Dictionary*, p. 681; E. Ekwall, *The Concise Oxford Dictionary of English Place-Names*, 4th edn (Oxford, 1960), p. 520; G. Fellows-Jensen, 'The Weevil's claw' in A. van Nahl *et al* (eds), *Namenwelten* (Berlin, 2004), pp. 76–89 at 82–3. Note, Willingham, Cambridgeshire, also derives from **Wifelingahām*.

53 Cameron, *Dictionary*, p. 139; Watts, *Cambridge Dictionary*, p. 681; Fellows-Jensen, 'Weevil's Claw', pp. 83–4 and 86. For significant reservations as to the existence of an Old English personal name **Wifel* formed from OE *wifel*, 'weevil or beetle', see P. Kitson, 'Quantifying qualifiers in Anglo-Saxon charter boundaries', *Folia Linguistica Historica*, 14 (1993), 29–82 at 75–7 (unlikely that anyone 'ever got lumbered with the Old English equivalent of "Cockchafer" or "Leatherjacket"'), and C. Hough, 'Wilsill in Yorkshire and related place-names', *Notes and Queries*, 50.3 (2003), 253–7 at 254 and 257 ('an unattested and improbable personal name'); it is, however, worth observing that Fellows-Jensen, 'Weevil's Claw', pp. 85–6, and John Hines, personal communication, are less sceptical with regard to its potential existence. Note, place-names involving *-ingahām* are often believed to have their origins in the late fifth to seventh centuries: K. Cameron, *English Place Names*, 2nd edn (London, 1996), p. 71.

54   J. Insley, 'Gumeningas', *Reallexikon der Germanischen Altertumskunde*, 13
       (1999), 191–3 (pp. 192–3); J. Insley, 'Kultische namen', *Reallexikon der
       Germanischen Altertumskunde*, 17 (2000), 425–37 (pp. 426–7); Fellows-
       Jensen, 'Weevil's claw', p. 85; P. Vikstrand, 'Pre-Christian sacral personal
       names in Scandinavia during the Proto-Scandinavian period' in W. Ahrens,
       S. Embleton and A. Lapierre (eds), *Names in Multi-Lingual, Multi-Cultural
       and Multi-Ethnic Contact: Proceedings of the 23rd International Congress of
       Onomastic Sciences* (Toronto, 2009), pp. 1012–18 (p. 1015); S. Brink,
       'Trading hubs or political centres of power? Maritime focal sites in early
       Sweden' in J. H. Barrett and S. J. Gibbon (eds), *Maritime Societies of the
       Viking and Medieval World* (Oxford, 2015), pp. 88–98 (pp. 89–90); S. Brink,
       'Political and social structures in early Scandinavia: a settlement-historical
       pre-study of the central place', *TOR*, 28 (1996), 235–82 (pp. 264, 266–7).
       The dating for the Veblungsnes runic inscription is taken from 'The
       Skaldic Project', *skaldic.abdn.ac.uk/db.php?table=mss&id=21858*.
55   Insley, 'Gumeningas', pp. 192–3; Insley, 'Kultische namen', pp. 426–7; J.
       Insley, 'Siedlungsnamen §2. Englische', *Reallexikon der Germanischen
       Altertumskunde*, 28 (2005), 344–53 (p. 347). See Hough, 'Wilsill', p. 257, for
       the quotation on the plausibility of a personal name **Wifel* formed from
       OE *wifel*, 'weevil or beetle', and Fellows-Jensen, 'Weevil's Claw', pp. 85–6,
       for a contrary view.
56   K. I. Sandred, 'Ingham in East Anglia: a new interpretation', *Leeds Studies in
       English*, 18 (1987), 231–40; K. I. Sandred, 'East Anglian place-names:
       sources of lost dialect' in J. Fisiak and P. Trudgill (eds), *East Anglian English*
       (Cambridge, 2001), pp. 39–61 (p. 44). Barrie Cox considered the case
       convincing in his review of the volume in which Sandred's article appeared
       (*Saga-Book of the Viking Society*, 22 (1986–89), 313–14) and references it in
       his study of early Anglo-Saxon place-names in northern Lincolnshire,
       observing that '[t]he most obvious *villa regalis* was surely in the west at
       Ingham, with its place-name derived from the pagan Germanic god Ing
       whose name in greater Germania was used as a tag to mark places as royal
       property' (B. Cox, 'The pattern of Old English *burh* in early Lindsey',
       Anglo-Saxon England, 23 (1994), 35–56 (p. 48)). The other Ingham place-
       names < **Ingwia-haimaz* are in Norfolk, Suffolk and Oxfordshire.
57   Cameron, *Dictionary*, p. 69; K. Cameron, *The Place-Names of Lincolnshire, Part
       Six: The Wapentakes of Manley and Aslacoe* (Nottingham, 2001), p. 184;
       Insley, 'Siedlungsnamen', p. 347. See also below, pp. 101–03, 162, 262, on
       Ingham. Note, Cameron and Insley's explanation of the name of Ingham,
       Lincolnshire, is largely adopted in Watts, *Cambridge Dictionary*, p. 331; John
       Hines, however, is somewhat sceptical of this interpretation (personal
       communication). On the god Ing, see R. North, *Heathen Gods in Old English
       Literature* (Cambridge, 1997); for some criticisms of the latter work, see, for
       example, Karin Olsen's review of North's book in *TijdSchrift voor*

Skandinavistiek, 19.1 (1998), 187–93. For another possible example of a *Kultverband* focused on a pagan Anglo-Saxon deity, see perhaps Tewin, Hertfordshire, which may be the '(settlement of) the worshippers of Tiw' or similar: Watts, *Cambridge Dictionary*, p. 605; T. Williamson, *The Origins of Hertfordshire* (Hatfield, 2010), p. 75.

58   P. L. Everson, C. C. Taylor and C. J. Dunn, *Change and Continuity: Rural Settlement in North-West Lincolnshire* (London, 1991), pp. 10, 11; G. Ward, 'The parish boundary of Ingham-Coates', *The Lincolnshire Magazine*, 3.2 (1936), 42–5 (pp. 42–3).

59   For Teversham, see Insley, 'Siedlungsnamen', p. 347, who considers it to be 'a name... with possible cultic implications'; Ekwall, *Oxford Dictionary*, p. 464; and Watts, *Cambridge Dictionary*, p. 605. The estimated post-Roman coastline and extent of low-lying Fen and marshland is based on Figs 7 and 25 and the sources cited there.

60   J. Blair, *Early Medieval Surrey: Landholding, Church and Settlement before 1300* (Stroud, 1991), p. 20; J. Campbell, 'Some considerations on religion in early England' in M. Henig and T. J. Smith (eds), *Collectanea Antiqua: Essays in memory of Sonia Chadwick Hawkes* (Oxford, 2007), pp. 67–73 (pp. 69–71). My thanks to Barbara Yorke for her observations on this; see also C. Behr, 'The origins of kingship in early medieval Kent', *Early Medieval Europe*, 9 (2000), 25–52 (pp. 39–45), and J. Blair, *The Church in Anglo-Saxon Society* (Oxford, 2005), p. 57. Compare also, perhaps, Yeavering, which has been seen as both a pagan cult site and a major royal centre (Blair, *Church*, pp. 56–7; D. Petts, *Pagan and Christian: Religious Change in Early Medieval Europe* (London, 2011), pp. 90–1; H. Hamerow, *Rural Settlements and Society in Anglo-Saxon England* (Oxford, 2012), pp. 106–08) and the suggested location of *Besingahearh*, '(pagan) temple of the *Besingas*' immediately next to the Cowdery's Down great hall complex (J. Blair, *Building Anglo-Saxon England* (Oxford, 2018), pp. 126, 136). On the use of place-names involving **wīvil*, see for example Brink, 'Trading hubs', pp. 89–90.

61   The medieval parish of Stow encompassed the townships of Stow, Stow Park, Normanby by Stow and the now-separate parish of Sturton by Stow. On its possible Middle Saxon origins, see K. U. Ulmschneider, *Markets, Minsters, and Metal-detectors: the Archaeology of Middle Saxon Lincolnshire and Hampshire Compared* (Oxford, 2000), pp. 30, 148; N. Field, 'Stow church', *LHA*, 19 (1984), 105–06; and Blair, *Building*, p. 278, where Stow is mapped as a Middle Saxon minster. It is worth noting that further finds of pre-Viking material have been made from Stow in recent years, including potential evidence for one or more sixth-century 'pagan' burials not far from the church itself (PAS LIN-4A4130 and LVPL-81ECA5). Additional support for a pre-Viking origin for Stow may come from the fact that the neighbouring church of Coates-by-Stow is dedicated to St Edith. This rare dedication is found seven times in Lincolnshire, and all six of the others

are found in parishes close to pre-Viking minster sites (Louth and South Kyme); see G. Jones, *Saints in the Landscape* (Stroud, 2007), p. 171, who notes that the Lincolnshire St Edith is likely to be an otherwise unknown Anglo-Saxon saint, not the tenth-century saint of the same name.

62   Behr, 'Origins of kingship', p. 45; Campbell, 'Some considerations', pp. 69–70, who further suggests that seventh-century grants of land to monasteries could have sometimes involved the granting not of the king's own estates, but rather those that formed the endowment of pagan cult centres. Certainly, from the perspective of a possible link between at least Ingham and Stow, Barrie Cox has commented that '[i]t can be no coincidence… that eventually the great Anglo-Saxon church at Stow grew up so near [to Ingham]' ('Pattern of Old English *burh*', p. 48). On the conversion of the Anglo-Saxons and possible Christianisation, see further Campbell, 'Some considerations'; Yorke, 'Pagan to Christian'; Blair, *Church*, pp. 184–6. John Blair offers a potential parallel to the proximity of these Christian and pre-Christian sites from Hampshire, where Basing minster sits directly across the River Loddon from the Cowdery's Down great hall complex and the suggested location of the pagan temple of *Besingahearh*: Blair, *Building*, pp. 126, 128, 136.

63   J. Blair, 'Beyond the *Billingas*: from lay wealth to monastic wealth on the Lincolnshire fen-edge', forthcoming (my thanks are due to John Blair for sight of this prior to publication); P. H. Sawyer, *Anglo-Saxon Charters: An Annotated List and Bibliography* (London, 1968), p. 404 (S 1440).

64   Blair, 'Beyond the *Billingas*'; see further on Mercia and *burh-tūnas* Blair, *Building*, pp. 197–221. On Sempringham, see Blair, 'Beyond the *Billingas*', and P. Cope-Faulkner, *Sempringham: Village to Priory to Mansion* (Heckington, 2011), pp. 15, 18.

65   D. N. Riley, P. C. Buckland and J. S. Wade, 'Aerial reconnaissance and excavation at Littleborough-on-Trent, Notts.', *Britannia*, 26 (1995), 253–84, which describes Littleborough/*Segelocum* as 'a substantial defended settlement' and notes that the site may well have had stone perimeter walls on the basis of Camden's description of these (pp. 253, 256).

66   Blair, *Building*, p. 206; on 'functional *-tūn*' names, see pp. 188, 193–231; according to Blair, *burh-tūnas* were elements of royal administration associated with Mercian royal defensive installations, whilst *strēt-tūnas* were strategically located holdings that controlled important long-distance roads.

67   On Littleborough's location within the kingdom of *Lindissi*, despite its situation just outside the modern district of Lindsey, see further pp. 128–36, which discuss the extent of the territory of this kingdom and its relationship with the modern district of Lindsey. For discussion of Littleborough and the mass baptism, see pp. 136–8, 202 (Fig. 41) below, for example, and B. Yorke, 'Lindsey: the lost kingdom found?' in A. Vince

(ed.), *Pre-Viking Lindsey* (Lincoln, 1993), pp. 141–2; Blair, *Church*, pp. 271–2; and D. Stocker, 'The early Church in Lincolnshire: a study of the sites and their significance' in Vince (ed.), *Pre-Viking Lindsey*, pp. 116–17 (quotations at p. 116). Note, Bede, *Historia Ecclesiastica*, II.16, describes the place where the mass baptism took place as a *civitas*, 'city', a word he used for places of importance in the Roman period that had walls/fortifications (as Littleborough seems to have had), and also gives it the name *Tiouulfingacaestir*, which contains the normal Old English word for a Roman town, *caestir/ceaster*. As such, there seems little credible doubt about the place, as only Littleborough fits the criteria whilst being both on the Trent and within *Lindissi*. The different modern name for the site need not cause any great concern either – John Blair, for example, argues that the name *Tiouulfingacaestir* was very probably replaced during the era of Mercian rule by a new, descriptive name involving *burh*, 'fortification, fortress, important node in the royal infrastructure', around the same time that the dependent *burh-tūnas* and *strēt-tūnas* names were coined. See J. Campbell, 'Bede's words for places' in J. Campbell, *Essays in Anglo-Saxon History* (London, 1986), pp. 99–119; Blair, *Churches*, pp. 247–51; Blair, *Building*, pp. 200–01, 206.

68 D. M. Hadley and J. D. Richards, 'The winter camp of the Viking Great Army, AD 872–3, Torksey, Lincolnshire', *Antiq. J.*, 96 (2016), 23–67 (p. 61); 'Anglo-Saxon Chronicle' MSS C, D, E, s.a. 1015, trans. D. Whitelock *et al* in *The Anglo-Saxon Chronicle: A Revised Translation* (London, 1961), p. 94.

69 Daubney, *Portable Antiquities*, pp. 162, 183–4, 188–91, 213. This 'persistence' also holds for some of the metal-detected sites recorded prior to the PAS, such as Stain Hill and Ketsby, both of which saw Late Roman, early Anglo-Saxon, Middle Saxon, and Anglo-Scandinavian activity. See C. Green, 'Stain Hill and the Lincolnshire Marshes in the Anglo-Saxon period', 2 November 2014, *www.caitlingreen.org/2014/11/stain-hill-anglo-saxon-marsh.html* on Stain Hill, and 'Ketsby DMV: a Roman–Early Modern settlement and pilgrimage site on the Lincolnshire Wolds', 4 February 2015, *www.caitlingreen.org/2015/02/ketsby-dmv.html* on the Ketsby finds; the latter include a late fourth- or fifth-century Romano-British buckle and a clipped silver siliqua of Arcadius (minted 395–402), as well as a late fifth-/sixth-century girdle hanger, a small-long brooch, and evidence of Middle Saxon and Anglo-Scandinavian metal-working.

70 Daubney, *Portable Antiquities*, pp. 154–68. Post-Roman material is known from a number of significant Late Roman sites in Lincolnshire, with a range of potential explanations. On the one hand, for example, a villa at Kirton-in-Lindsey has produced substantial amounts of early Anglo-Saxon pottery and metalwork along with evidence for continuity in field boundaries, with this being interpreted as potentially indicative of

continuous occupation and acculturation (J. Albone, personal communication; Green, 'British kingdom', p. 28, fn. 114). On the other hand, at Denton, near Grantham, the excavation of a Late Roman villa revealed that the villa was used for sixth-century 'Anglo-Saxon' burials which were placed in the centre of two rooms, suggesting something rather different, such as a claiming of an important point in the landscape in order to reinforce and legitimise claims to the land (J. T. Smith, 'The Roman villa at Denton', *Lincolnshire Architectural and Archaeological Society Reports and Papers*, 10 (1964), 75–104; Gerrard, *Ruin of Roman Britain*, pp. 203–05). Incidentally, it is interesting to note that the excavation at Denton found two post-*c.* 370 building stages at this villa, suggesting occupation into the fifth century, and the burials in the villa contained no roof tile, slate or similar evidence of villa destruction, only tesserae, implying that the villa still stood and had not fallen into complete disrepair even by this late date.

71 S. Willis, *The Roman Roadside Settlement and Multi-Period Ritual Complex at Nettleton and Rothwell, Lincolnshire* (London, 2013), pp. 362–3; S. Willis, 'Report on the expenditure of the grant received from The Roman Society/Roman Research Trust for specialist consultancy reporting on the pottery finds from Hatcliffe Top, North-East Lincolnshire' (March 2018), *www.romansociety.org/Portals/0/S_Willis_report.pdf*. My thanks are due to Steve Willis for discussing this site with me ahead of its publication in late 2019: S. Willis (ed.), *The Waithe Valley Through Time, I: The Archaeology of the Valley, and Excavation and Survey in the Hatcliffe Area* (London, 2019). Unfortunately, the exact nature of the early and Middle Saxon activity is unclear, due to damage of the relevant layers by ploughing.

72 Härke, 'Anglo-Saxon immigration and ethnogenesis', p. 17 (quotation); Hamerow, *Rural Settlements*, pp. 53, 91–2; Blair, *Building*, pp. 36–7 (quotation at p. 37); G. Taylor, 'An early to Middle Saxon settlement at Quarrington, Lincolnshire', *Antiq. J.*, 83 (2003), 231–80; and also F. Walker and T. Lane, *An Early to Middle Saxon Settlement at Quarrington, Lincolnshire*, Archaeological Project Services Report No. 49/96 (3 vols, Heckington, 1996). For a sceptical view, see M. Gardiner, 'An early medieval tradition of building in Britain', *Arqueología de la Arquitectura*, 9 (2012), 231–46 (pp. 238–9), and J. Hines in *The Antiquaries Journal*, 93 (2013), 431–2.

73 A. Crowson *et al*, *Anglo-Saxon Settlement on the Siltland of Eastern England* (Heckington, 2007), pp. 56–69 (pp. 64, 69); Taylor, 'Quarrington', p. 273.

74 The ritual activity and causeways in the Witham Valley are mentioned below, pp. 111, 129, 148–50, and Fig. 25. See further, for example, D. Stocker and P. Everson, 'The straight and narrow way: Fenland causeways and the conversion of the landscape in the Witham valley, Lincolnshire' in M. O. H. Carver (ed.), *The Cross Goes North: Processes of Conversion in Northern Europe, A.D. 300–1300* (Woodbridge, 2002), pp. 271– 88, and now

Everson and Stocker, *Custodians of Continuity*. On the PAS data from this area, see Daubney, *Portable Antiquities*, pp. 194–224.

75   Everson and Stocker, *Custodians of Continuity*, pp. 380–91. On the name Reepham, see Cameron, *Dictionary*, p. 101.

76   On Garwick, see below, pp. 191–4, 197–200; Daubney, *Portable Antiquities*, pp. 225–48. The totals given here represent the 2009 totals (pp. 192, 226–7), plus finds made since 2009 from the PAS and EMC (surveyed in 2014 and 2019). See Daubney, *Portable Antiquities*, pp. 235–7, on the total number of coins found here and the reporting of this based on different data sets. On Garwick's potential access to the sea via Bicker Haven, see below, p. xlvii.

77   Daubney, *Portable Antiquities*, pp. 240–3; the imported silver lozenge brooch is LIN-EDD8D2.

78   See particularly S. Malone, 'Lincolnshire Fenland Lidar', *HTL/APS Working Paper 1* (2014), *www.academia.edu/5807526*.

79   S. Malone, *Viking Link: Boygrift to North Ing Drove, Lincolnshire Onshore Cable Route – Air-Photographic and Lidar Assessment* (Nottingham, 2017), quotations at pp. 8, 17; this roddon and its significance has also been noted by Ian Simmons: I. G. Simmons, 'The emergence of the south Lindsey coast of the Wash before Domesday', *Mid. Hist.*, 42 (2017), 139–58 (p. 153), and personal communication. Note, the Old English name Swineshead for the parish immediately east of Heckington–Garwick means 'the head of the creek', whilst radiocarbon dating from the route of the A17 at Swineshead indicates that marine conditions were present here from the Late Roman/early post-Roman period: Cameron, *Dictionary*, p. 122; M. Waller, *The Fenland Project, Number 9: Flandrian Environmental Change in Fenland* (Cambridge, 1994), pp. 292–5.

80   Daubney, *Portable Antiquities*, pp. 252–4. The items mentioned are PAS LIN-0C5BF1 (see Cool, 'Objects of glass, shale, bone and metal', pp. 287–8, on the date of amphora-shaped strap ends) and LIN-35B2BE; see also on these two items H. Willmott and D. W. Wright, 'Rethinking early medieval 'productive sites': trade, wealth and worship at Little Carlton, East Lindsey' (forthcoming; my thanks to Hugh Willmott for allowing me sight of this article prior to publication). The observation that over 1,000 Middle Saxon objects are known from both metal-detecting and excavation at this site comes via H. Willmott and A. Daubney, 'Of saints, sows or smiths? Copper-brazed iron handbells in early medieval England', *Archaeol. J.*, 176 (2019), published online 31 January 2019, *doi.org/10.1080/00665983.2019.1567970*, p. 10.

81   Willmott and Wright, 'Little Carlton'; P. Townend *et al*, 'The mystery in the marsh: exploring an Anglo-Saxon island at Little Carlton', *Current Archaeology*, 313 (2016), 28–34; Daubney, *Portable Antiquities*, pp. 249–68.

82   Willmott and Wright, 'Little Carlton'.

83   On the minster at Louth, see Green, *Origins of Louth*, pp. 79–93, although note that this was written before the Little Carlton finds came to light; A. E. B. Owen, 'Herefrith of Louth, saint and bishop: a problem of identities', *LHA*, 15 (1980), 15–19, where he discusses Louth's Anglo-Saxon saint, St Herefrith (although see also his 'Louth before Domesday', *LHA*, 32 (1997), 60–4, in which he withdraws his 1980 suggestion that St Mary's at Louth had an Anglo-Saxon origin and confirms that it was never more than a chapel of ease, with most of the supposed references to St Mary's church actually relating to a chapel dedicated to St Mary in the parish church of St Herefrith–St James); and recently P. Everson and D. Stocker, '"The Cros in the Markitte Stede": the Louth Cross, its monastery and its town', *Med. Arch.*, 61 (2017), 330–71 (pp. 350–9), which includes an interesting discussion of the evidence, including the significant argument that Louth was the second, monastic, episcopal centre of Middle Saxon *Lindissi* – rather than Bardney, as previously suggested – alongside Lincoln. As to the location of the minster at Louth, I am somewhat sceptical of the suggestion in the latter article of a very large Middle Saxon monastic enclosure at Louth that reaches across both sides of the river valley. This seems out of accord with other pre-Viking minster enclosures, especially in terms of having a major river flowing through the middle of it, and appears to rely in part on Owen's withdrawn suggestion as to the status of St Mary's. More credible, perhaps, is an enclosure on the southern bank in the area of Gospelgate/Westgate, or even, as John Blair has kindly suggested, an oval enclosure between Mercer Row and the river, with St James/St Herefrith's church located just outside its west side, something that would have parallels (John Blair, personal communication).

84   See Willmott and Wright, 'Little Carlton', who suggest that Little Carlton was either a dependent site or constituted one element of a 'high-status "meshwork"', with it and the minster at Louth being 'components of an entire landscape that was exploited to meet the economic, social and political needs of elite authorities' in this part of eastern Lincolnshire; compare Blair, *Building*, pp. 174, 193–201, 254–69, on polyfocal 'central clusters'. See also Daubney, *Portable Antiquities*, pp. 258–61, and particularly Willmott and Daubney, 'Handbells in early medieval England', pp. 10–12, 17, where Little Carlton is explicitly interpreted as an important ecclesiastical site on the basis of the finds made there. Support for it as a dependent site/part of a 'central cluster' associated with the minster at Louth may perhaps be had from the presence of a St Edith dedication for the church that sits in the centre of the distribution of Middle Saxon finds. These dedications appear to be associated with pre-Viking minsters in Lincolnshire and moreover seem to have an especial distribution around Louth – see endnote 61, above; Jones, *Saints*, p. 171; and Daubney, *Portable Antiquities*, pp. 264–5.

85 Topics not covered above, for the sake of space, include the evolution and extent of the coastal zone of Lincolnshire in the Late and post-Roman periods, especially with regard to the Lincolnshire Marsh, on which see (for example) H. Fenwick, 'The Lincolnshire Marsh: Landscape Evolution, Settlement Development and the Salt Industry' (University of Hull PhD Thesis, 2007), particularly pp. 255, 264–6, 278, 290–4, 438, 480; Green, 'Stain Hill'; Green, *Origins*, pp. 47–9, 54–6, 75–6, 102–03; Simmons, 'The south Lindsey coast'; B. Simmons, 'Late Roman coastal defence around the Wash' in Malone and Williams (eds), *Recent Work on Roman Lincolnshire*, pp. 47–52; and A. Thomas, 'Rivers of Gold? The coastal zone between the Humber and the Wash in the Mid Saxon period', *Anglo-Saxon Studies in Archaeology and History*, 18 (2013), 97–118.

86 See particularly Blair, *Building*, chapter 2, on his core 'eastern zone' of pre-Viking English identity and building tradition, and compare also Catherine Hills, Toby Martin and John Hines's core zone of fifth- to sixth-century Anglian immigration, burial tradition, costume and ethnogenesis, of which Lincolnshire formed a key part: Hills, 'Anglo-Saxon migration'; Martin, *The Cruciform Brooch*; Hines, 'Origins', and J. Hines, *The Scandinavian Character of Anglian England in the pre-Viking Period* (Oxford, 1984).

INTRODUCTION

Britons and Anglo-Saxons: key questions and previous approaches

The period between the end of the fourth century and the middle of the seventh looms large in the overarching narrative of British history. From the perspective of eastern Britain, the fifth and sixth centuries were undoubtedly important. As is discussed in the first chapter, this area entered them as part of a relatively peaceful diocese of the Roman Empire, but appears to have exited as a patchwork of aggressive kingdoms and overlordships, largely ruled over by groups who claimed descent from north German and Scandinavian immigrants. Consequently, these centuries have been the subject of much discussion and research. The present study is intended as a contribution to this ongoing debate, examining the evidence from the Lincoln region with a particular focus on the question of how the former Romano-Britons interacted with the fifth- and sixth-century 'Anglo-Saxon' immigrants here.[1]

Any investigation of this sort must inevitably build upon the work of earlier researchers, and the following section offers a brief overview of previous approaches to some of the key questions concerning this period that are addressed in subsequent chapters. The first of these is the question of whether the Anglo-Saxon immigrants numerically dominated the Britons in the areas that they came to control. Certainly, such an assumption was widespread in the nineteenth century. E. A. Freeman probably describes the underlying model best in his mid-Victorian *Old English History for Children*, when he writes that:

> ...we may be sure that we have not much of their [the Britons'] blood in us, because we have so few of their words in our language... Now you will perhaps say that our forefathers were cruel and wicked men... And so doubtless it was... But anyhow it has turned out much better in the end that our forefathers did thus kill or drive out nearly all the people whom they found in the land... [since otherwise] I cannot think

that we should ever have been so great and free a people as we have been for many ages.[2]

Although such a view was never as explicitly outlined in academic work as it was in this children's history book, it would appear to underlie much of the work of Freeman and his contemporaries.[3] It is also present, at least in its historical conclusion (that the Anglo-Saxon immigrants to the east and south of Britain did not really interact with the Britons, except to drive most of them out whilst enslaving the surviving remnant as an underclass), in later work, including Geoffrey Elton's 1992 study, *The English*,[4] and recent discussions by linguists specializing in the post-Roman period.[5]

In contrast, most recent archaeological and historical research has tended to argue against the Britons forming a minority of the population and being driven out in the above manner. Instead, it is contended that the vast majority of the population of early Anglo-Saxon England is likely to have been made up of Britons.[6] Confirmation of such an alternative model has, for example, been sought in the environmental archaeology of eastern Britain, which is argued to be inconsistent with the sort of massive collapse in population density that would have resulted from Victorian ideas of Anglian–British interaction.[7] In consequence, even those archaeologists and historians who support a substantial, non-elite Anglo-Saxon migration to eastern Britain now usually assume that a significant proportion of the British population survived the 'conquest' and hence must have lived side by side with the immigrants.[8] We thus have a situation in which different disciplines seem to support different models with regard to the question of whether the Anglo-Saxon immigrants numerically dominated the Britons, and this debate extends even to new sources of evidence like genetics. So, for example, recent work on the genetic evidence from modern Britain has been interpreted as potentially reflective of either a near-total replacement of the male population by immigrants, or a post-Roman male immigration that made up only around five per cent of the total male population at the time.[9]

Another key question concerning the period relates to the British context into which the Anglo-Saxons arrived and their interaction with this. With regard to the former question, there is at present a general lack of certainty. On the one hand, a case has been made for Britain still having large-scale governance at a provincial or even a diocesan level when the Anglo-Saxon immigrants arrived. On the other hand, it has also been argued that large-scale governance could have almost entirely decayed by this point, and that the Anglo-Saxons instead encountered local territories (probably derived from the Late Roman *civitates*) ruled by local British elites, with those in the west perhaps being ruled by kings, whilst those in the east continued to be controlled by *judices*.[10] Similarly, the nature of the interaction between whatever post-Roman British territories existed and the Anglo-Saxon immigrants remains a matter of debate. In general, modern researchers have tended to place little faith in the 'historical' sources relating to this period. Most appear to contain only legends written down many centuries after the events they purport to describe,[11] and those few which seem to be contemporary or near-contemporary in date are vague in terms of their detail. Gildas's account is perhaps the most useful, being probably written sometime between the late fifth and mid-sixth centuries. He states that Anglo-Saxons were initially employed by post-Roman British rulers for defence and then subsequently rebelled. However, the lack of detail in his account means that the question of whether this model applied generally to eastern Britain or instead to a specific (and uncertain) time and place remains a matter of debate.[12] Certainly, some archaeologists have preferred a model involving largely free, rather than controlled, Anglo-Saxon settlement in parts of eastern Britain during the fifth century.[13]

With regard to the Lincoln region, previous research has tended to favour the idea of some sort of short-lived, local British territory focused on the city of Lincoln. Attention has been drawn to an apparent avoidance of Lincoln by some of the major early Anglo-Saxon cemeteries of the region in their initial stages. The archaeological evidence from the St Paul in the Bail site has also been used to suggest the survival of a British centre at Lincoln into the middle of the fifth century, although the same evidence has been interpreted as resulting from seventh- and eighth-century Anglo-Saxon activity.[14] Similarly, it has been noted that the Lincolnshire kingdom-name *Lindissi* ('Lindsey')[15] derives ultimately from British **Lindon*, which has been seen as potentially significant, although the exact import of this has not really been fully explored.[16] As to the question of how the Anglo-Saxon immigrants who settled in the Lincoln region interacted with any British polities that existed here, this has attracted little serious comment. The major cemeteries of the region are usually viewed as central burial grounds serving large surrounding territories, but whether these were established by the immigrants as part of a hostile takeover or as a consequence of a controlled settlement by British rulers is unclear.[17]

A third key question relates to the origins of the Anglo-Saxon kingdoms recorded in the seventh and eighth centuries. Once again, previous research fails to offer a consensus view on the matter. It has, for example, been argued that the Anglo-Saxon settlements and conquests of the fifth and sixth centuries resulted in an almost complete disintegration of the existing British political and administrative structures in the east of the country, with kingdoms and kings only re-emerging from the mid- to late sixth century as a result of the coalescence of many originally independent, local Anglo-Saxon territories and groups.[18] Other researchers, however, have suggested that this model is fundamentally flawed, and that a more credible one is that the Anglo-Saxons simply took over the large British territories they encountered in order to form the recorded kingdoms.[19] Which model the region around Lincoln, with its history as the seat of a Late Roman provincial capital, best fits is obviously a matter of great interest, although it is also a topic only briefly touched on in previous work. What comment there has been suggests that the second model may be the most appropriate, in light of both the apparent relationship between the Anglo-Saxon kingdom-name and British *Lindon*, and the fact that the Anglo-Saxon kingdom of *Lindissi* seems to have been partly administered from the former Roman centres of Lincoln and Littleborough.[20] However, important questions regarding the nature of any potential takeover, whether any underlying British polity was kept as a single unit, and how significant the Anglo-Saxon political debt to the British past was likely to have been, still need to be addressed in depth.

The fourth key question relates to the nature, extent and implications of Anglian–British interaction in the period after the immigrant-descended groups gained control of the region. It is now often argued, by archaeologists and historians at least, that significant numbers of Britons would have acculturated following the Anglo-Saxon takeover, adopting the material culture, language and eventually the identity of the new ascendancy.[21] Indeed, it has been suggested that most early Anglo-Saxon inhumation burials could be, in fact, those of acculturated Britons.[22] Finding evidence of this process of acculturation has proved difficult, however. A small number of cemeteries appear to include both Late Roman and culturally early Anglo-Saxon burials, implying the acculturation of a local community, but these are few and far between.[23] Cases have also been made for seeing various artefacts and burial rites – such as crouched burial, male burial without weapons, and enamelling on brooches – as indicative of acculturated Britons, although some of these have proved controversial.[24] In the Lincoln region, previous work has touched on these topics, with crouched burials observed in some cemeteries, and rites such as burial with bird bones identified as potentially 'British' in origin.[25] There has also been some linguistic analysis of the place-names of this region and the personal names in the Anglo-Saxon royal genealogy of *Lindissi*, both of which imply a degree of acculturation and interaction.[26] However, there has been little detailed discussion of acculturation in the Lincoln region, the potential nature of the Anglo-Saxon takeover here,[27] or of how the process of acculturation might have worked and what effects it might have on our understanding of questions of continuity and discontinuity of activity between the Late Roman and Middle Saxon periods here.

The fifth key question relates to the Anglo-Saxons, in particular the population groups and *regiones* they lived within during the fifth to seventh centuries. Small local or regional groups and territories have now been identified in most areas of pre-Viking England. They are often seen as originally independent or semi-independent units created by the immigrants in the fifth and sixth centuries, although some are believed to have their origins in former British territories that were taken over by the immigrants.[28] In general, there has been relatively little work done on such groups and territories within the Lincoln region, perhaps largely due to the absence of early documentary records and charters which might reveal such *regiones*. The exception here is in the south of the region, where attempts have been made to define two separate *regiones* and groups in the Fenland

and the Fen Edge using the 'Tribal Hidage' and archaeology.[29] Further north in the region it has been observed that the great cremation cemeteries all seemed to possess their own distinct territories, and two discrete 'groups' of cemeteries have been identified in North Kesteven.[30] However, there have been few attempts to define these territories and groups more closely, or to identify their origins. Equally, there has been little consideration of whether there is any evidence for Britons or acculturating Britons existing within these potential 'Anglo-Saxon' population groups, a topic of considerable significance from the perspective of the present study.

The final key question relating to Britons and Anglo-Saxons in the post-Roman period is that of the apparent expansion of the Anglo-Saxon immigrant groups beyond the primary regions of immigration into further areas controlled by British groups. That the material culture of the immigrants did indeed spread both north and west of the initial areas of settlement is in little doubt, and can be observed from a phased mapping of early Anglo-Saxon cemetery sites.[31] However, the major issue here is whether we are in fact seeing the expansion of these immigrant groups, the spread of the immigrant material culture and ethnicity, or some combination of the two.[32] Perhaps as a result, this question has often received only brief and general treatments in academic works. The chief exception has been in linguistic studies, where personal names and place-names have sometimes been used to suggest the possible movement of 'tribal' groups and powerful lineages in the early Anglo-Saxon period, most notably the suggested movement of the ancestors of the Mercian royal dynasty from East Anglia to the West Midlands.[33] With regard to the Lincoln region, discussion of the potential movement of groups from this area into either the north or the west of Britain has been largely confined to short notices in works such as Eilert Ekwall's *Concise Oxford Dictionary of English Place-Names*, although such notices have sometimes been picked up on by historical commentators.[34] However, no serious attempts have been made to assess the historical context and credibility of such suggestions, nor to try and understand the role and significance that any such groups from the Lincoln region might have played in any 'expansion', nor indeed what any such movement out of the Lincoln region might have to tell us about post-Roman Anglian–British interaction here or in the areas they moved to.

Sources of evidence and methodology

The above, then, forms the historiographical context of the present study and highlights some of the key questions addressed throughout the following chapters. However, before examining these questions in detail, we need first to confront the evidential problems of the post-Roman period. In particular, the paucity and difficulty of the available evidence is probably the major reason why even specialists in the period sometimes refer to the post-Roman centuries as a 'Dark Age'.[35] Accordingly, it is worth considering the various classes of evidence that are available to us and the potential and difficulties associated with each of these, before briefly discussing the methodology consequently adopted here.

The first type of evidence to be considered is archaeological. Much of the research into the Lincoln region in the fifth and sixth centuries has tended to focus very heavily on this material, and particularly on the Anglo-Saxon cemeteries of the region.[36] This is, perhaps, unsurprising. Not only are some of the largest Anglo-Saxon cemeteries in Britain found in the Lincoln region, with the Loveden Hill cremation cemetery probably originally containing well over 2,000 burials,[37] but there are also a considerable number of cemetery sites of all sizes and types recorded from here. Indeed, a thorough survey of the local Historic Environment Records and the Portable Antiquities Scheme datasets puts the current total at around 150 Anglo-Saxon cemeteries known or suspected in Lincolnshire.[38] In addition to the cemetery evidence, we also have a large body of material recovered from fieldwalking surveys, most notably the Fenland Survey,[39] excavation reports on a number of non-cemetery sites of this period,[40] and a substantial body of chance finds recorded by both the Portable Antiquities Scheme and the Historic Environment Records.

Given the above, the archaeological corpus from post-Roman Lincolnshire clearly has considerable potential as a source of information on the fifth and sixth centuries. Certainly, the large quantity of culturally 'Anglo-Saxon' material found in this region is of particular interest from the perspective of the current work, testifying as it does to the penetration and spread of this culture here in the post-Roman period.[41] It is also in many ways the easiest category of material to assemble and evaluate, not least because of the existence of the local Historic Environment Records and the Portable Antiquities Scheme. The former collate and index data from excavations, whilst the latter has collected a vast amount of information on metal-detected and chance finds from our region since 1997, much of which has not been used previously in analyses of this period.[42] By looking at all of this material together, we can, for example, increase the total number of finds representative of early medieval hanging bowls in Lincolnshire from the fifteen recorded by Rupert Bruce-Mitford in 1993 to at least thirty-four at present, based largely on items reported to the Portable Antiquities Scheme.[43] We can also see that the southern third of the county was not in fact entirely lacking in Anglo-Saxon cemeteries, as one recent map of Anglo-Saxon Lincolnshire suggests it to have been.[44]

On the other hand, it has to be admitted that the archaeological evidence also has a number of serious drawbacks and difficulties. At the most basic level, the quantity of the archaeological material belies its quality. Whilst some of the key sites have been properly excavated and published, notably the Cleatham and Castledyke South cemeteries, many have not.[45] Most of the Anglo-Saxon cemeteries of the region are, in fact, only known from chance or metal-detected finds; crucial sites, such as the Loveden Hill and Elsham cremation cemeteries, remain unpublished; and a significant proportion of sites were antiquarian discoveries. The latter were sometimes remarkably well excavated and reported for the period in which they were investigated, as is the case with the exceptionally large Sleaford inhumation cemetery (originally *c.* 600 or more inhumations), but in other cases they were not.[46] In consequence, barely anything is known of the apparently very extensive cremation cemetery at Quarrington, discovered in the early nineteenth century,[47] whilst the reportedly large Burton-upon-Stather cemetery was raided by treasure-hunting ironstone miners in 1928 before it could be properly recorded.[48]

More serious, from the perspective of the present work, is the fact that the archaeological material is overwhelmingly 'Anglo-Saxon' in character. The archaeological 'invisibility' of Britons in the fifth and sixth centuries (and after) is widely recognised, but it is a key issue when it comes to using the archaeological evidence as the mainstay of any analysis of these centuries, particularly given the focus here on Anglian–British interaction.[49] This is not, of course, to say that there is no archaeological evidence relating to the Britons from this region. The excavations at the site of St Paul in the Bail in Lincoln have considerable potential in this regard, and the survey of archaeological material undertaken for the present study has increased the total of known British fifth- and sixth-century penannular brooches in the Lincoln region from eleven examples in 2007 to twenty-three or twenty-four at the time of writing.[50] However, such material is very much the exception to the rule, and the vast majority of the archaeological corpus is culturally Anglo-Saxon. As such, the corpus largely represents only one side of the equation if we are interested in the questions set out above and in what actually occurred and changed during the post-Roman period. Moreover, it also needs to be remembered that the interpretation of even the Anglo-Saxon archaeology is difficult. Whilst the corpus of material can tell us about the spread and penetration of the material culture of the immigrants in this region, it can rarely tell us what this meant. In particular, were the people using this material immigrants or descendants of immigrants, or were many of them Britons who were acculturating – adopting the immigrants' culture and, ultimately, their ethnicity – and so re-emerging into archaeological 'visibility'? The second interpretation is now strongly suspected to be the correct one by many archaeologists, as is noted above, but it is potentially difficult to demonstrate from archaeological evidence alone.

A second type of evidence available to us here is linguistic. In contrast to the archaeological evidence, this has only rarely been used as a major source of evidence by archaeologists and historians studying the post-Roman Lincoln region. Nonetheless, there are a large number of place-names, district-names, river-names and personal names that are potentially relevant here. The task of assembling and assessing these names is aided considerably by the late Kenneth Cameron's detailed investigations into the place-names of Lincolnshire.[51] Although his multi-volume survey remains only partially published, the single volume *Dictionary of Lincolnshire Place-Names* (issued in 1998) details his conclusions for those names not yet covered in the main survey volumes and is a valuable companion to the various national dictionaries that have been published.[52] Recent years have also seen a significant body of work by other researchers on the names of the Lincoln region. In particular, Richard Coates has published significant and stimulating re-examinations of a large number of Lincolnshire place-names, district-names and river-names.[53] Similarly, John Insley has produced a number of important papers on the philological evidence (both place-names and personal names) relating to Lincolnshire.[54]

Needless to say, this material has considerable potential with regard to our understanding of the post-Roman period. Not only does it represent an additional large corpus of evidence that may help us to understand the situation in these centuries, but place-name evidence is also available for the whole region, unlike the Anglo-Saxon cemetery evidence, which is concentrated in certain areas.[55] So, for example, there are no early Anglo-Saxon cemeteries known from the entire Fenland district of Holland, and very few from the immediate vicinity of Lincoln. However, both areas contain several place-names that probably have their origins in the post-Roman period and are of potential significance for understanding Anglian–British interaction there.[56] Naturally, there are issues with this corpus, perhaps most notably the difficulty in identifying names that definitely or probably belong to our period of study. The mid-twentieth-century certainties regarding the relative chronology of place-name types have long since been swept away, so that we can no longer confidently state that, for instance, a name of the *x-ingas* type must reflect the presence of the first generations of Anglo-Saxon immigrants.[57] This change, and the resultant uncertainty, may explain why historians and archaeologists appear to rely less on the linguistic material than they once did. Nonetheless, there are still a significant number of names from this region that are likely to have originated in the fifth to seventh centuries, especially those involving Latin or Late British/Archaic Welsh words and names.[58] As such, the linguistic material remains of considerable interest in the current context.

Following on from this last point, the fact that the linguistic corpus includes a subset of names that derive from British or Latin words and/or reflect Anglian–British interaction is in itself significant when it comes to assessing the potential of the linguistic evidence for the present study. A good illustration of the importance of such material from this perspective can be had in the modern district-name Lindsey, which applies to the northern and eastern parts of Lincolnshire.[59] It is usually recognized in both linguistic and historical work that this district-name derives ultimately from the Anglo-Saxon kingdom-name *Lindissi/Lindesig*, and that this kingdom-name in turn derives, somehow, from a British word.[60] In addition, the analysis in Chapter 2 of the present work indicates that the underlying British root is actually a Late British tribal and territory-name involving a second element that is known to be a 'kingdom suffix', something which is naturally of considerable interest from the perspective of both the pre-Anglian political organization of this region and the origins of the Anglo-Saxon kingdom of *Lindissi*.[61] Equally noteworthy is that some Old English place-names from the Lincoln region appear to involve not only British words, but also British personal names, whilst the Anglo-Saxon royal genealogy of the kingdom of *Lindissi* includes a name that seems to be wholly British in origin.[62] Such cases obviously imply some sort of Anglian–British interaction, and potentially a degree of acculturation too. Finally, yet other names seem to reference the continued existence of Welsh speakers well into the Middle Saxon period in various parts of Lincolnshire, and some rivers within the region appear to have been known by both a British and an Old English name for a period of time.[63] As such, the linguistic material clearly has considerable potential when it comes to addressing the key questions highlighted earlier in this introduction.

Of course, there are also a number of difficulties associated with the use of such linguistic evidence. The relative uncertainty over place-name chronology when compared with previous generations has already been mentioned. Another related issue is that many names in use or originating in the fifth to seventh centuries have undoubtedly been lost, through either falling out of use or later renaming. This is a particular problem with regard to the British place-names of the period. Although we certainly have some evidence for them from this region, it is clear that the vast majority of the British place- and river-names that once existed have been lost. Similarly, it seems likely that a large number of early Anglo-Saxon place-names have also disappeared. In this context, it is worth observing that a large proportion of the place-names surviving from

Lincolnshire have their origins in the Middle Saxon or Anglo-Scandinavian periods, and in many cases it is suspected that these later names replaced earlier ones that might have had something to tell us about the post-Roman period.[64] So, for example, Maltby near Louth bears a Scandinavian name (Old Danish *Malti* + *by*, 'Malti's farmstead/village') but has produced notable finds of early Anglo-Saxon and Middle Saxon metalwork,[65] whilst the modern place-name Skegness (Old Danish *Skeggi* + Old Norse *nes*, 'Skeggi's headland') appears to have replaced an earlier-recorded name, *Tric*, which is thought to be derived from Latin *Traiectus*.[66] A final problem with the linguistic evidence is its perceived difficulty. For most historians and archaeologists, the linguistic evidence represents an unfamiliar field with its own body of scholarship, and as such it can prove difficult to engage with and use effectively. Moreover, even English place-name specialists can struggle when it comes to names that derive from British, rather than Old English, roots.[67] Nonetheless, this material and body of scholarship is worth engaging with despite these difficulties, simply because of the relevance it has for any study of this period.

The final category of evidence available to us derives from literary and historical texts. The paucity of contemporary and near-contemporary historical documentation for the fifth and sixth centuries has already been mentioned. The Anglo-Saxon immigrant groups were effectively non-literate before their conversion to Christianity and, aside from a handful of very brief (and sometimes confused) continental references to events in Britain in this era, extended contemporary and near-contemporary commentary is largely restricted to Constantius of Lyon's 'Life of St Germanus', St Patrick's *Epistola* and *Confessio*, and Gildas' *De Excidio Britanniae*.[68] Whilst these works are certainly important, none of their authors intended to provide anything approaching a detailed outline of events in lowland Britain as a whole or the Lincoln region in particular, and they do not. As such, the available corpus of historical and literary material is largely restricted to texts which postdate our period of study.

Despite this significant drawback, there remains much of potential relevance. For example, Bede (writing around 731) makes several references to the seventh-century Anglo-Saxon kingdom of

Lindissi and the Anglo-Saxon population group named the *Lindisfari* (Old English *Lindisfaran*) that inhabited it. Indeed, he makes it clear that the former Late Roman provincial capital, Lincoln, was both under the control of an Anglo-Saxon named Blæcca by the 620s and a major centre for the kingdom of *Lindissi*. Similarly, the much-debated 'Tribal Hidage' – which enumerates the large and small population groups and territories of pre-Viking England south of the Humber, and is often considered a seventh-century document – lists the *Lindisfaran* alongside at least two additional Anglo-Saxon groups (the *Spalde* and the *Gyrwe*) which can be located with confidence in this region.[69] Finally, Felix's eighth-century 'Life of St Guthlac' offers yet another illustration of the potential of such later material, as it appears to imply that there were still people speaking a form of Welsh living in the Fens of south Lincolnshire in the early eighth century.[70]

In sum, although the quantity of such historical and literary material is relatively small (especially when compared to some other areas of the country) and is focused primarily on the seventh century and after, rather than earlier periods, it is nevertheless a valuable source for understanding the Anglo-Saxons of the Lincoln region. It can also help in answering some of the key questions outlined above, providing, as it does, potential information relevant to the nature and dating of the transition from British to Anglo-Saxon rule, the character of the Anglo-Saxon kingdom of *Lindissi* and its potential British roots, the Anglo-Saxon population groups formed in this region, and the nature and duration of the process of British acculturation there.

Such Anglo-Saxon textual materials as the above are, in the main, well known and frequently discussed.[71] Less well known is the Welsh literary and historical material which may also have some bearing on our understanding of the post-Roman Lincoln region. In particular, the possible reference to men from the Lincoln region in the early Welsh poem *Y Gododdin* has not featured in discussions of this region, despite its potential importance.[72] Similarly, the significance and meaning of the reference to post-Roman battles fought in the 'country of *Linnuis*' in the ninth-century Welsh *Historia Brittonum* is rarely, if ever, seriously explored.[73] Of course, such materials can be problematic. *Y Gododdin*, for example, is only preserved in a single Welsh manuscript of the thirteenth century, although it is often argued that at least some portions of it could be as old as the seventh century.[74] In contrast, the composition of the *Historia Brittonum* is fairly securely dated to 829–30; the problem here is rather that the *Historia* appears to be in many ways unreliable when it comes to its account of supposed events in the fifth and sixth centuries.[75] However, whilst this material is undoubtedly difficult, this is not a reason to ignore it entirely. At the very least, we need to ask why the early medieval authors of these texts may have made reference to our region and what these references might signify.

The above, then, are the materials that are available to us when we seek to understand the post-Roman period and Anglian–British interaction in the Lincoln region. In light of the above discussion, the most productive approach to the fifth and sixth centuries in this region is likely to lie with an interdisciplinary methodology that brings together all of the above classes of evidence, despite the resultant burden of data collection and need to analyse material from across several disciplines which this would entail. Such a methodology has been adopted in the present study. First and foremost, using all of the available evidence gives us a greatly increased corpus of data for analysis, which is of particular importance given the generally acknowledged paucity of evidence for the post-Roman period. Moreover, it is plainly the case that all of the various classes of evidence include material that is of potential value with regard to the post-Roman Lincoln region and to addressing the key questions set out previously.

Second, using all of this material together can help to counteract some of the disadvantages and limitations observed above for the different classes of evidence. One example previously cited was the ability of the linguistic evidence to provide us with useful evidence for those areas where no Anglo-Saxon cemeteries are known. Even more important is the fact that any coherent analysis of the questions outlined above requires us to ask what was happening with the Britons in these centuries, and the archaeological evidence on its own seems insufficient to allow us to address this fully. Whilst there is certainly some archaeological material relevant to the post-Roman Britons available from the Lincoln region, the quantity of this material is relatively small, and it has often proved difficult to understand properly and evaluate the significance or context of this material when it is treated in isolation.[76] However, by considering the archaeological evidence alongside the sort of linguistic, literary and historical material described above, sufficient material can be drawn together and evaluated to allow a detailed analysis of both Anglian–British interaction and the situation in the post-Roman Lincoln region to proceed, as the following chapters seek to demonstrate.

Finally, by using all of this material together, one is able to cross-check and validate theories arising from one type of evidence against the other types. Thus, for example, the linguistic evidence seems to contradict the archaeologically derived theory of a British abandonment of the Fenland, whilst at the same time it adds weight to the archaeological evidence for significant post-Roman British activity in the area around Folkingham–Osbournby.[77]

Notes to Introduction

1   Without wishing to deny that ethnic and cultural identity in this period could be both fluid and complex (with people able to switch their primary ethnic identity and simultaneously hold several different identities), or to assert that either the Britons or the Anglo-Saxons possessed a monolithic and unvarying culture in these centuries, it is felt that the terms 'Anglo-Saxon' and 'Briton/British' continue to be useful when considering the post-Roman era. Certainly, contemporary and near-contemporary authors, such as Gildas (*Gildas: De Excidio Britanniae*, ed. and trans. M. Winterbottom, London 1978), believed that there was a genuine distinction to be drawn between 'Britons' and 'Anglo-Saxons', and this distinction is to a large degree reflected in both the archaeological evidence relating to material culture in this period and the linguistic evidence.

2   E. A. Freeman, *Old English History for Children*, 2nd edn (London, 1871), pp. 28–9.

3   See, for example, W. Stubbs, *Select Charters and Other Illustrations of English Constitutional History*, revised by H. W. C. Davis, 9th edn (Oxford, 1913), pp. 1–3, where he allows a degree of intermarriage (especially in the west of England), but little else, with the culture of the 'English' remaining untainted by the surviving 'remnant of their predecessors'.

4   G. Elton, *The English* (Oxford, 1992), p. 3, which has the Anglo-Saxons not mixing 'significantly' with the Britons but instead pushing them 'back into the western and northern uplands' over two generations of conflict.

5   See, for example, R. Coates, 'Invisible Britons: the view from linguistics' in N. J. Higham (ed.), *Britons in Anglo-Saxon England* (Woodbridge, 2007), pp. 172–91. Coates considers that the linguistic evidence can only be explained

by the sort of large-scale population replacement envisaged by Victorian historians, with the Britons largely being killed or expelled from eastern Britain. For a discussion of this position, see below, especially pp. 107–8 and the associated notes.

6   N. J. Higham, *Rome, Britain and the Anglo-Saxons* (London, 1992), makes this case at length, as do a number of other authors, including R. Hodges, *The Anglo-Saxon Achievement. Archaeology and the Beginnings of English Society* (London, 1989), and C. J. Arnold, *Roman Britain to Saxon England* (Beckenham, 1984).

7   For example, see P. Dark, 'Palaeoecological evidence for landscape continuity and change in Britain *ca* A.D. 400–800' in K. R. Dark (ed.), *External Contacts and the Economy of Late Roman and Post-Roman Britain* (Woodbridge, 1996), pp. 23–51, and P. Murphy, 'The Anglo-Saxon landscape and rural economy: some results from sites in East Anglia and Essex' in J. Rackham (ed.), *Environment and Economy in Anglo-Saxon England* (York, 1994), pp. 23–39. See further below, pp. 41–4, 108–9.

8   C. Scull, 'Approaches to the material culture and social dynamics of the migration period in eastern England' in J. Bintliff and H. Hamerow (eds), *Europe Between Late Antiquity and the Middle Ages* (Oxford, 1995), especially pp. 77–9; H. Hamerow, 'The earliest Anglo-Saxon kingdoms' in P. Fouracre (ed.), *The New Cambridge Medieval History, I: c.500–c.700* (Cambridge, 2005), pp. 264–9; H. Härke, 'Population replacement or acculturation? An archaeological perspective on population and migration in post-Roman Britain' in H. L. C. Tristram (ed.), *The Celtic Englishes III* (Hiedelberg, 2003), pp. 13–28. See also A. Woolf, 'Apartheid and economics in Anglo-Saxon England' in N. J. Higham (ed.), *Britons in Anglo-Saxon England* (Woodbridge, 2007), pp. 115–29.

9   M. E. Weale *et al*, 'Y chromosome evidence for Anglo-Saxon mass migration', *Molecular Biology and Evolution*, 19 (2002), 1008–21; M. G. Thomas *et al*, 'Evidence for an apartheid-like social structure in early Anglo-Saxon England', *Proceedings of the Royal Society*, 273 (2006), 2651–7. See below, p. 109 and the associated notes.

10 M. Welch, 'The archaeological evidence for federate settlement in Britain within the fifth century' in F. Vallet and M. Kazanski (eds), *L'Armée Romaine et les Barbares du IIIe au VIIe Siècle* (Rouen, 1993), pp. 269–77; D. N. Dumville, 'The idea of government in sub-Roman Britain' in G. Ausenda (ed.), *After Empire: Towards an Ethnology of Europe's Barbarians* (Woodbridge, 1995), pp. 180–3; B. Yorke, 'Anglo-Saxon *gentes* and *regna*' in H-W. Goetz, J. Jarnut and W. Pohl (eds), *Regna and Gentes: The Relationship Between Late Antique and Early Medieval Peoples and Kingdoms in the Transformation of the Roman World* (Leiden, 2003), pp. 395–401; R. White, *Britannia Prima: Britain's Last Roman Province* (Stroud, 2007), especially pp. 197–201; C. A. Snyder, *An Age of Tyrants: Britain and the Britons A.D. 400–600* (Stroud,

1998), pp. 225–32; K. R. Dark, *Britain and the End of the Roman Empire* (Stroud, 2000), pp. 144–9; S. Laycock, *Britannia, The Failed State* (Stroud, 2008); A. Woolf, 'The Britons: From Romans to Barbarians', in H-W. Goetz, J. Jarnut and W. Pohl (eds), *Regna and Gentes*, pp. 345–80.

11 See especially B. Yorke, 'Fact or fiction? The written evidence for the fifth and sixth centuries AD', *Anglo-Saxon Studies in Archaeology and History*, 6 (1993), 45–50, for a good overview of these sources. See also C. Green, 'The British kingdom of Lindsey', *Cambrian Medieval Celtic Studies*, 56 (2008), 38–43, for details of some of the late-recorded legends that were set in the post-Roman Lincoln region.

12 Yorke, 'Anglo-Saxon *gentes* and *regna*', pp. 381–2, and see further, D. N. Dumville and M. Lapidge (eds), *Gildas: New Approaches* (Woodbridge, 1984); N. J. Higham, *The English Conquest: Gildas and Britain in the Fifth Century* (Manchester, 1994); and P. Sims-Williams, 'Gildas and the Anglo-Saxons', *Cambridge Medieval Celtic Studies*, 6 (1983), 1–30.

13 As does Scull, 'Approaches to the material culture', pp. 75–6, for East Anglia.

14 K. Leahy, 'The Anglo-Saxon settlement of Lindsey' in A. Vince (ed.), *Pre-Viking Lindsey* (Lincoln, 1993), pp. 36–7; M. J. Jones, 'The latter days of Roman Lincoln' in A. Vince (ed.), *Pre-Viking Lindsey* (Lincoln, 1993), pp. 25–6; B. Eagles, 'Lindsey' in S. Bassett (ed.), *The Origins of Anglo-Saxon Kingdoms* (London, 1989), p. 207; P. H. Sawyer, *Anglo-Saxon Lincolnshire* (Lincoln, 1998), pp. 226–30. This is discussed at length below, pp. 65–9.

15 See S. Foot, 'The kingdom of Lindsey' in A. Vince (ed.), *Pre-Viking Lindsey* (Lincoln, 1993), pp. 128–40. The name *Lindissi* is here used for the Anglo-Saxon kingdom more commonly known as 'Lindsey' in order to distinguish this pre-Viking polity from the modern district of Lindsey (the northern half of the pre-1974 county of Lincolnshire). Although the two names are related, the district-name Lindsey is usually agreed not to derive directly from *Lindissi*, and it is moreover argued here that *Lindissi* in fact encompassed a much larger area than does the modern district of Lindsey. See, for example, K. Cameron, *The Place-Names of Lincolnshire, II* (Nottingham, 1991), pp. 2–7; M. Gelling, 'The name Lindsey', *Anglo-Saxon England*, 18 (1989), 31–2; and below, pp. 57–8, 128–36. As such, it seems best to avoid the name 'Lindsey' for the kingdom, despite its frequent usage in modern research, and instead return to the earliest recorded form of the kingdom-name.

16 B. Yorke, 'Lindsey: the lost kingdom found?' in A. Vince (ed.), *Pre-Viking Lindsey* (Lincoln, 1993), pp. 141, 143; S. Bassett, 'Lincoln and the Anglo-Saxon see of Lindsey', *Anglo-Saxon England*, 18 (1989), 7.

17 K. Leahy, *'Interrupting the Pots': The Excavation of Cleatham Anglo-Saxon Cemetery* (York, 2007), p. 6; K. Leahy, *The Anglo-Saxon Kingdom of Lindsey* (Stroud, 2007), p. 48; H. Williams, 'Cemeteries as central places – place and

identity in Migration Period eastern England' in B. Hårdh and L. Larsson (eds), *Central Places in the Migration and Merovingian Periods* (Stockholm, 2002), pp. 341–62; H. Williams, 'Assembling the dead' in A. Pantos and S. Semple (eds), *Assembly Places and Practices in Medieval Europe* (Dublin, 2004), pp. 109–34. Bassett, 'Lincoln and the Anglo-Saxon see of Lindsey', 8, fn. 40, suggests that the immigrants could have arrived in the Lincoln region as mercenaries, but says no more than this. Yorke, 'Lindsey: the lost kingdom found?', p. 142, similarly suggests that a period of controlled settlement is 'possible'.

18   S. Bassett, 'In search of the origins of Anglo-Saxon kingdoms' in S. Bassett (ed.), *The Origins of Anglo-Saxon Kingdoms* (London, 1989), pp. 3–27; C. Scull, 'Archaeology, early Anglo-Saxon society and the Anglo-Saxon kingdoms', *Anglo-Saxon Studies in Archaeology and History*, 6 (1993), 72–9; Hamerow, The earliest Anglo-Saxon kingdoms', pp. 271–88.

19   Yorke, 'Anglo-Saxon *gentes* and *regna*', especially pp. 396–401; also B. Yorke, 'Political and ethnic identity: a case study of Anglo-Saxon practice' in W. O. Frazer and A. Tyrrell (eds), *Social Identity in Early Medieval Britain* (London, 2000), pp. 82–6. See further below, pp. 163–7.

20   See especially Yorke, 'Lindsey: the lost kingdom found?', pp. 141–2, and Chapter 4, below.

21   Scull, 'Approaches to the material culture', p. 78; Thomas *et al*, 'Evidence for an apartheid-like social structure'; H. Härke, *Angelsächsische Waffengräber des 5. bis 7. Jahrhunderts* (Cologne, 1992); H. Härke, 'Changing symbols in a changing society: the Anglo-Saxon weapon burial rite in the seventh century' in M. O. H. Carver (ed.), *The Age of Sutton Hoo* (Woodbridge, 1992), pp. 149–65; C. P. Loveluck, 'The development of the Anglo-Saxon landscape, economy and society "On Driffield", East Yorkshire, 400–750 AD', *Anglo-Saxon Studies in Archaeology and History*, 9 (1996), 30–2; Hamerow, 'The earliest Anglo-Saxon kingdoms', pp. 265–6, 269–70.

22   Dark, *Britain and the End of the Roman Empire*, pp. 71–3, 75–8; Härke, *Angelsächsische Waffengräber des 5. bis 7. Jahrhunderts*; Härke, 'Changing symbols in a changing society'.

23   Hamerow, 'The earliest Anglo-Saxon kingdoms', p. 265.

24   M. Faull, 'British survival in Anglo-Saxon Northumbria' in L. Laing (ed.), *Studies in Celtic Survival* (Oxford, 1977), pp. 1–56; S. Lucy, 'Early Medieval burials in East Yorkshire: reconsidering the evidence' in H. Geake and J. Kenny (eds), *Early Deira. Archaeological Studies of the East Riding in the Fourth to Ninth Centuries AD* (Oxford, 2000), pp. 11–18; Härke, 'Changing symbols in a changing society'; E. O'Brien, *Post-Roman Britain to Anglo-Saxon England: Burial Practices Reviewed* (Oxford, 1999); C. Scull, 'Further evidence from East Anglia for enamelling on early Anglo-Saxon metalwork', *Anglo-Saxon Studies in Archaeology and History*, 4 (1985), 117–24; Loveluck, The development of the Anglo-Saxon landscape', 30–1.

25 For example, Leahy, *Anglo-Saxon Kingdom of Lindsey*, pp. 85–6; G. Drinkall, and M. Foreman, *The Anglo-Saxon Cemetery at Castledyke South, Barton-on-Humber* (Sheffield, 1998), pp. 358–9. The paucity of recently excavated and published inhumation cemeteries from the Lincoln region (see further above, p. 8) limits the availability of such evidence, unfortunately.

26 K. Cameron, *Dictionary of Lincolnshire Place-Names* (Nottingham, 1998), pp. 135, 127, 128; J. Insley and M. Eggers, 'Lindsey', *Reallexikon der Germanischen Altertumskunde*, 18 (Berlin, 2001), 477; J. Insley, 'Pre-conquest personal names', *Reallexikon der Germanischen Altertumskunde*, 23 (Berlin, 2003), 375; J. Insley, 'The study of Old English personal names and anthroponymic lexika' in D. Geuenich, W. Haubrichs and J. Jarnut (eds), *Person und Name* (Berlin, 2002), p. 164; K. H. Jackson, *Language and History in Early Britain* (Edinburgh, 1953), p. 244, n.3; P. Stafford, *The East Midlands in the Early Middle Ages* (London, 1985), p. 87.

27 The exceptions here are Eagles ('Lindsey', p. 207) and Yorke ('Lindsey: the lost kingdom found?', p. 145), who briefly discuss some possible evidence for British Christian continuity in Lincoln.

28 Bassett, 'In search of the origins of Anglo-Saxon kingdoms', offers a detailed outline of these ideas.

29 T. W. Lane and P. Hayes, 'Moving boundaries in the Fens of south Lincolnshire' in J. Gardiner (ed.), *Flatlands and Wetlands: Current Themes in East Anglian Archaeology* (Norwich, 1993), pp. 68–9; P. P. Hayes, 'Roman to Saxon in the south Lincolnshire Fens', *Ant.*, 62 (1988), 325.

30 Leahy, 'The Anglo-Saxon settlement of Lindsey', p. 36; Leahy, *Anglo-Saxon Kingdom of Lindsey*, pp. 48–9; T. M. Dickinson, 'An early Anglo-Saxon Cemetery at Quarrington, near Sleaford, Lincolnshire: report on excavations, 2000–2001', *Lincolnshire History and Archaeology*, 39 (2004), 24–5. See also Eagles, 'Lindsey', p. 211.

31 See J. Hines, 'Philology, archaeology and the *adventus Saxonum vel Anglorum*' in A. Bammesberger and A. Wollmann (eds), *Britain 400–600: Language and History* (Heidelberg, 1990), pp. 17–36, especially pp. 28, 34–6. Dark, *Britain and the End of the Roman Empire*, pp. 11, 49, offers an updated version of these maps.

32 Dark, *Britain and the End of the Roman Empire*, pp. 71–3, 75–8, for example, argues against this material being purely indicative of immigrant groups moving into new territories.

33 E. Martin, 'The *Iclingas*', *East Anglian Archaeology*, 3 (1976), 132–4; T. Williamson, *The Origins of Norfolk* (Manchester, 1993), pp. 71–2. Compare N. P. Brooks, 'The formation of the Mercian kingdom' in S. Bassett (ed.), *The Origins of Anglo-Saxon Kingdoms* (London, 1989), p. 164.

34 E. Ekwall, *The Concise Oxford Dictionary of English Place-Names*, 4th edn (Oxford, 1960), pp. 298–9; J. N. L. Myres, *The English Settlements* (Oxford,

1986), p. 199; Sawyer, *Anglo-Saxon Lincolnshire*, p. 47. See further, Chapter 6.

35 Notable instances include A. Williams *et al, A Biographical Dictionary of Dark Age Britain. England, Scotland and Wales, c. 500–c. 1050* (London, 1991); B. Crawford, (ed.) *Scotland in Dark Age Europe* (St Andrews, 1994); and J. T. Koch, *The Gododdin of Aneirin: Text and Context from Dark-Age North Britain* (Cardiff, 1997).

36 For example, Eagles, 'Lincoln'; Jones, 'The latter days of Roman Lincoln'; Leahy, 'Anglo-Saxon settlement of Lindsey'; G. Fisher, 'Kingdom and community in early Anglo-Saxon eastern England' in L. Anderson Beck (ed.), *Regional Approaches to Mortuary Analysis* (New York, 1995), pp. 147–66; Williams, 'Cemeteries as central places'; Williams, 'Assembling the dead'; Leahy, *'Interrupting the Pots'*; Leahy, *Anglo-Saxon Kingdom of Lindsey*.

37 Williams, 'Assembling the dead', p. 113; Williams, 'Cemeteries as central places', pp. 344–5.

38 See Fig. 33 and the Gazetteer on the Anglo-Saxon cemeteries of the region. By way of comparison, Leahy, 'Anglo-Saxon settlement of Lindsey', identified fifty-four cemetery sites in Lindsey and North Kesteven (not South Kesteven) in 1993, and Sawyer, *Anglo-Saxon Lincolnshire*, identified seventy-five from across the whole of Lincolnshire in 1998.

39 T. W. Lane, *The Fenland Project Number 8: Lincolnshire Survey, the Northern Fen-Edge* (Sleaford, 1992); P. P. Hayes and T. W. Lane, *The Fenland Project Number 5: Lincolnshire Survey, The South-West Fens* (Sleaford, 1992).

40 For example, G. Taylor, 'An early to middle Saxon settlement at Quarrington, Lincolnshire', *Antiq. J.*, 83 (2003), 231–80; K. Steane *et al, The Archaeology of the Upper City and Adjacent Suburbs* (Oxford, 2006).

41 For an illustration of this 'spread', see the phased maps in J. Hines, 'Britain after Rome' in P. Graves-Brown, S. Jones and C. Gamble (eds), *Cultural Identity and Archaeology: the Construction of European Communities* (London, 1996), pp. 262–3, and the discussions in Chapters 2 and 5.

42 With regard to both the PAS and HER data, the dataset on which the present analysis is based was finalized towards the end of 2009, although significant finds made after this time have also been included here. Where archaeological material is unpublished and is referred to specifically in the text or notes below, it is usually cited by either a Historic Environment Record/Sites and Monuments Record (HER) number or a Portable Antiquities Scheme (PAS) number. The HER databases are available online at *www.heritagegateway.org.uk*, and the PAS database at *finds.org.uk/database*.

43 R. Bruce-Mitford, 'Late Celtic hanging bowls in Lincolnshire and South Humberside' in A. Vince (ed.), *Pre-Viking Lindsey* (Lincoln, 1993), pp. 45–70; below, pp. 71–4 and associated notes.

44 A. G. Vince, 'Lincolnshire in the Anglo-Saxon Period, *c.* 450–1066' in S. Bennett and N. Bennett (eds), *An Historical Atlas of Lincolnshire* (Chichester, 2001), pp. 22–3. See below, Chapter 5, endnote 80, on this.

45 Leahy, *'Interrupting the Pots'*, and Drinkall and Foreman (eds), *Anglo-Saxon Cemetery at Castledyke South.*

46 G. W. Thomas, 'On excavations in an Anglo-Saxon cemetery at Sleaford in Lincolnshire', *Archaeologia*, 50 (1887), 383–406.

47 See below, pp. 187–9 and associated notes; E. Trollope, *Sleaford and the Wapentakes of Flaxwell and Aswardhurn* (London, 1887), pp. 98–100; R. Yerburgh, *Sketches Illustrative of the Topography and History of New and Old Sleaford* (Creasey, Sleaford, 1825), pp. 106–07.

48 H. Dudley, *Early Days in North-West Lincolnshire* (Scunthorpe, 1949), pp. 224–6.

49 See, for example, Härke, 'Population replacement or acculturation?', and Hamerow, 'The earliest Anglo-Saxon kingdoms', p. 265. Issues surrounding the post-Roman archaeological invisibility of the Britons are discussed in Chapters 1 and 5.

50 See further, pp. 69–71. The 2007 total for the brooches is that of Kevin Leahy, plus the two Type G brooches from the Sleaford inhumation cemetery (Leahy, *Anglo-Saxon Kingdom of Lindsey*, p. 83; T. M. Dickinson, 'Fowler's Type G Penannular brooches reconsidered', *Med. Arch.*, 26 (1982), 48, 50, 52 and figs 1–4).

51 Beginning with his *Place-Names of Lincolnshire, I*, published in 1985.

52 Cameron, *Dictionary of Lincolnshire Place-Names*. Ekwall, *Dictionary of English Place-Names* is the original national place-name dictionary and is still very useful, especially when used alongside Cameron's work and the more recent national dictionaries authored by A. D. Mills (*A Dictionary of English Place-Names*: Oxford, 1991) and V. Watts (*The Cambridge Dictionary of English Place-Names*: Cambridge, 2004).

53 R. Coates, 'Holland, the division of Lincolnshire' in R. Coates and A. Breeze, *Celtic Voices, English Places* (Stamford, 2000), pp. 162–4; R. Coates, 'Four pre-English river names in and around fenland: *Chater, Granta, Nene* and *Welland*', *Transactions of the Philological Society*, 103 (2005), 303–22; R. Coates, 'Two notes on names in *tūn* in relation to pre-English antiquities: Kirmington and Broughton, Lincolnshire', *Journal of the English Place-Name Society*, 37 (2005), 33–6; R. Coates, 'Reflections on some major Lincolnshire place-names. Part one: Algarkirk to Melton Ross', *Journal of the English Place-Name Society*, 40 (2008), 35–95; R. Coates, 'Reflections on some major Lincolnshire place-names. Part two: Ness wapentake to Yarborough', *Journal of the English Place-Name Society*, 41 (2009), 57–102.

54 J. Insley, 'Kultische namen', *Reallexikon der Germanischen Altertumskunde*, 17 (Berlin, 2000), 425–37; J. Insley, 'The study of Old English personal names and anthroponymic lexika' in D. Geuenich, W. Haubrichs and J. Jarnut

(eds), *Person und Name* (Berlin, 2002), pp. 148–76; J. Insley, 'Pre-conquest personal names', *Reallexikon der Germanischen Altertumskunde*, 23 (Berlin, 2003), 367–96; J. Insley, 'Wapentake', *Reallexikon der Germanischen Altertumskunde*, 33 (Berlin, 2006), 250–2; Insley and Eggers, 'Lindsey'.

55 See Fig. 33 (p. 177) and the Gazetteer (pp. 272–83).

56 These specific 'gaps' in the cemetery evidence are discussed at length below, pp. 62–4 and 176–85. On notable place-names in these areas, see pp. 104–5, 138, 170, 173–4, 178.

57 J. Dodgson, 'The significance of the distribution of the English place-name in *-ingas, -inga-* in south-east England', reprinted in K. Cameron (ed.), *Place-name Evidence for the Anglo-Saxon Invasion and Scandinavian Settlements* (Nottingham, 1977), pp. 27–54; B. Cox, 'The significance of the distribution of English place-names in *-hām* in the Midlands and East Anglia', *Journal of the English Place-Name Society*, 5 (1972–3), 15–73; J. Kuurman, 'An examination of the *-ingas, -inga-* place-names in the East Midlands', *Journal of the English Place-Name Society*, 7 (1974–5), 11–44; M. Gelling, 'Towards a chronology for English place-names' in D. Hooke (ed.), *Anglo-Saxon Settlements* (Oxford, 1988), pp. 59–76; M. Gelling, *Signposts to the Past. Place-names and the History of England*, 2nd edn (Chichester, 1988).

58 See Fig. 34 for the distribution of names involving British and Latin elements, based largely on the works of Cameron, Insley and Coates cited above, along with O. K. Schram, 'Fenland place-names' in B. Dickens (ed.), *The Early Cultures in North-West Europe* (Cambridge, 1950), pp. 427–41. It should be noted, for example, that four Lincolnshire place-names have their origins in Old English *wīchām*, a name which derives from Latin *vicus* and is believed to have its origins in the fifth or sixth centuries – see further below, pp. 146 and 173–4, and, for example, M. Gelling, 'English place-names derived from the compound *wīchām*' reprinted in K. Cameron (ed.), *Place-name Evidence for the Anglo-Saxon Invasion and Scandinavian Settlements* (Nottingham, 1977), p. 14, and Gelling, *Signposts to the Past*, pp. 67–74, 245–9.

59 See Fig. 24 for the modern boundaries of the three main divisions of Lincolnshire: Lindsey, Kesteven and Holland.

60 For example, Cameron, *Dictionary of Lincolnshire Place-Names*, p. 81; Sawyer, *Anglo-Saxon Lincolnshire*, p. 44; Yorke, 'Lindsey: the lost kingdom found?', p. 143.

61 Below, pp. 58–9 and associated notes. The second element in the underlying British tribal- and territory-name (**Lindēs*) became *-wys* in later Welsh; the description of *-wys* as a 'kingdom suffix' is that of John Koch, see pp. 78–9, n. 12.

62 On the place-names, see below, pp. 104–5, and, for example, Cameron, *Dictionary of Lincolnshire Place-Names*, p. 135; Insley and Eggers, 'Lindsey',

477; and Insley, 'Pre-conquest personal names', 375. On the name *Cædbæd* in the genealogy of the kings of *Lindissi*, see pp. 99–101 and Jackson, *Language and History in Early Britain*, p. 244, n.3, and J. T. Koch, (ed.) *Celtic Culture, A Historical Encyclopedia* (Oxford, 2006), p. 60.

63   See below, pp. 110, 178, 220 and 231.

64   For example, Sawyer, *Anglo-Saxon Lincolnshire*, pp. 111–13, and generally Gelling, *Signposts to the Past*, and M. Gelling, 'A brief history of English place-name studies', in M. Gelling, *Signposts to the Past*, 3rd edn (Chichester, 1997), pp. 15–18.

65   See Cameron, *Dictionary of Lincolnshire Place-Names*, p. 85, for the etymology of Maltby, and the Gazetteer (Appendix) for the small early Anglo-Saxon inhumation cemetery that was probably located here. The Middle Saxon metalwork from Maltby near Louth has been recorded by Scunthorpe Museum.

66   Cameron, *Dictionary of Lincolnshire Place-Names*, p. 110; A. E. B. Owen and R. Coates, '*Traiectus/Tric*/Skegness: a Domesday name explained', *Lincolnshire History and Archaeology*, 38 (2003), 42–4; R. Coates, *Toponymic Topics* (Brighton, 1988), pp. 35–9.

67   See below, pp. 58–9 (and n. 12) and 235–7. With regard to Celtic philology and the chronology of the mutation of British into Old Welsh, Jackson, *Language and History in Early Britain*, remains indispensable, although it needs to be paired with more recent research such as P. Sims-Williams, *The Celtic Inscriptions of Britain. Phonology and Chronology, c. 400–1200* (Oxford, 2003). See also, for example, P. Sims-Williams, 'Dating the transition to Neo-Brittonic: phonology and history, 400–600' in Alfred Bammesberger and A. Wollmann (eds), *Britain, 400–600. Language and History* (Heidelberg, 1990), pp. 217–61; P. Sims-Williams, 'The emergence of Old Welsh, Cornish and Breton orthography, 600–800: the evidence of Archaic Old Welsh', *Bulletin of the Board of Celtic Studies*, 38 (1991), 20–86; and P. Schrijver, *Studies in British Celtic Historical Phonology* (Amsterdam, 1995).

68   See, for example, Snyder, *An Age of Tyrants*, pp. 29–49.

69   Bede, *Historia Ecclesiastica*, for example at III.11, III.24, III.27, IV.3, IV.1; D. N. Dumville, 'The Tribal Hidage: an introduction to its texts and their history' in S. Bassett (ed.), *The Origins of Anglo-Saxon Kingdoms* (London, 1989), pp. 225–30. See further below, for example pp. 136–8, 167–85.

70   *Felix's Life of St Guthlac*, ed. and trans. B. Colgrave (Cambridge, 1956), pp. 108–11; see especially Graham Jones in Koch (ed.), *Celtic Culture*, p. 857.

71   See, for example, Foot, 'The kingdom of Lindsey'; Yorke, 'Lindsey: the lost kingdom found?'; Stafford, *East Midlands in the Early Middle Ages*; and Sawyer, *Anglo-Saxon Lincolnshire*.

72   J. T. Koch, 'The cynfeirdd poetry and the language of the sixth century' in B. F. Roberts (ed.), *Early Welsh Poetry: Studies in the Book of Aneirin* (Aberystwyth, 1988), p. 33; see further below, pp. 95–9.

73 For some discussion of this source and the import of this reference, see below, pp. 59–60, 89–95, and C. Green, *Concepts of Arthur* (Stroud, 2007), especially pp. 210–15.

74 *Canu Aneirin*, ed. I. Williams (Cardiff, 1938); Koch, *Gododdin of Aneirin*. See especially below, pp. 95, 119, on the dating of the poem and the stanza in question.

75 D. N. Dumville, 'The historical value of the *Historia Brittonum*', *Arthurian Literature*, 6 (1986), 1–26; N. J. Higham, *Arthur, Myth-Making and History* (London, 2002), pp. 119–69; Green, *Concepts of Arthur*, pp. 15–26, 30–8.

76 For example, finds of British Class 1 penannular brooches in Lincolnshire are discussed briefly in Leahy, *Anglo-Saxon Kingdom of Lindsey*, in a short section on 'sub-Roman/British survival' (pp. 83–4), but they are largely left to stand on their own, with little analysis of their potential context or implications.

77 Below, pp. 176–83, 212, 228 and Fig. 39.

1
THE CONTEXT OF POST-ROMAN LINCOLNSHIRE

Any account of the fifth and sixth centuries in the Lincoln region is ultimately an attempt to describe how the world of the fourth century became that of the seventh. Although both of these centuries are themselves somewhat opaque, they are nonetheless far better understood and evidenced than the period which lies between them. In consequence, an awareness of what Lincolnshire was actually like then must necessarily shape any study of the fifth and sixth centuries, as well as being a valuable source of information for it. In this context, before the detailed analysis of the historical, archaeological, literary and linguistic evidence pertaining to the post-Roman period can begin, the situation in the Lincoln region both at the end of the fourth century and during the seventh needs to be set out.

The Lincoln region in the fourth and early fifth centuries

Although fourth-century Lincolnshire was merely the northern part of the Romano-British *Civitas Corieltavorum*, which then had Leicester as its *civitas* capital, it nonetheless contained within it the important city of *Lindum Colonia* (British *Lindon*, **Lindocolōnia*), modern Lincoln. This was not only a *colonia* – a Roman colony of retired soldiers, and the highest 'rank' of Roman town – but also, in the fourth century, a Roman provincial capital and the seat of one of *Britannia*'s four bishops, Adelphius, who was present at the Council of Arles in AD 314 (Fig. 1).[1] As such, Lincoln was one of the most significant cities of fourth-century Roman Britain, and it is only right that any attempt to ascertain the nature of Late Roman Lincolnshire begins here. The new capital status that Lincoln gained at the beginning of the fourth century appears to have ensured its prosperity and remarkable vitality, when compared with non-capitals, right through to the very end of

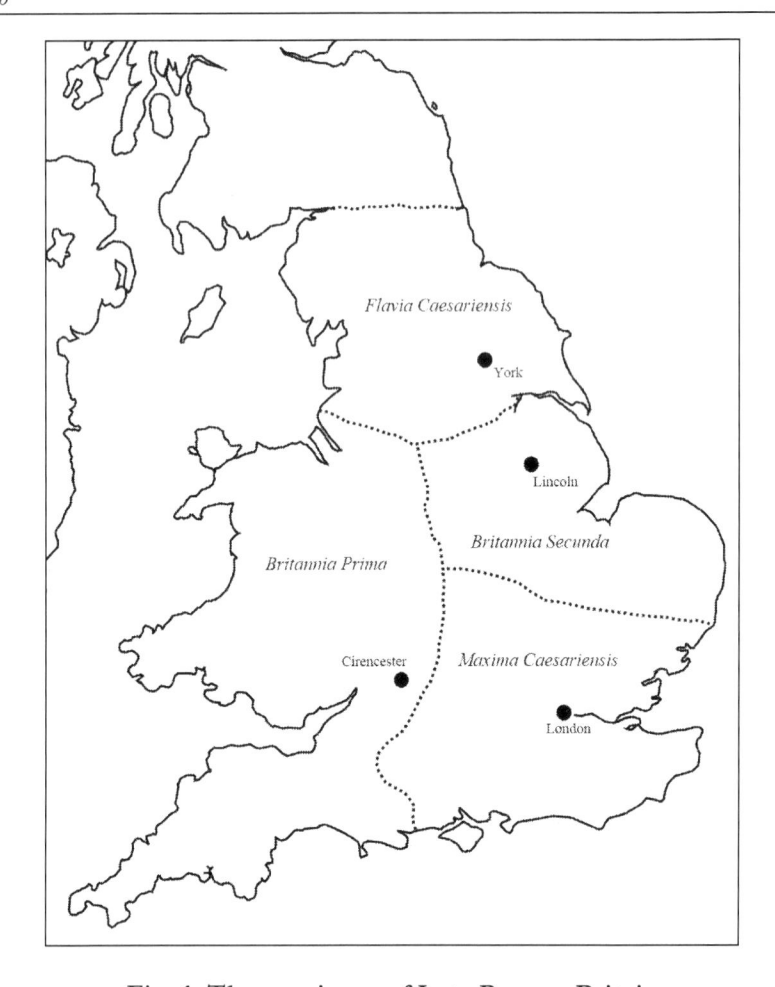

Fig. 1 The provinces of Late Roman Britain
After J. C. Mann, 'The creation of four provinces in Britain by
Diocletian', *Britannia*, 29 (1998), p. 340

the Roman period. Although Lincoln still saw the sort of general
'decline' in public buildings that can be observed in cities across the
Roman Empire at this time, the peak in activity occurs later here than
in most other Romano-British towns. For example, there is evidence
from a significant number of excavated sites for continued
occupation into the last quarter of the fourth century (Fig. 2), whilst
the peak in coin loss in Lincoln also occurs well into the second half

of the fourth century. Similarly, large-scale dumping of butchered cattle bones in the very late fourth century has been seen as indicative of specialist industry, cohesive central organization, considerable population and a thriving market at this time.[2]

There is, of course, undeniable evidence for the abandonment of some buildings in Lincoln and a reduction in scale of others, chiefly in the last quarter of the fourth century. This can hardly be dissociated from the increasing interruptions to the coinage supply to Roman Britain and the effects that this had on the market economy (with which town life seems to have been intimately linked).[3] Nonetheless, the very late fourth- to early fifth-century Roman coin finds that have so far been made are enough to indicate that organized urban life, although impoverished and reduced in scale, probably did continue across Lincoln at least some way into the fifth century. Certainly, at least one street was resurfaced after 395–402, and there is evidence for the continued official usage of the *forum*.[4] In addition, it is worth observing that the nearby Greetwell Villa (Fig. 3) similarly appears to have been occupied right up until the end of the coin sequence in the early fifth century and maintained to a high standard. This villa has been plausibly interpreted as the residence of the Roman provincial governor and, as such, its longevity may both reflect and help to explain the surprising vitality of Late Roman Lincoln.[5]

These indications of governmental and official continuity to the end of the Roman period at Lincoln are significant for any study of the post-Roman era. Whilst Lincoln's role as a truly urban centre, with a large population and a thriving market, is unlikely to have survived for long after the final end of the coin supply and the withdrawal of official support *c.* 410, this need not necessarily be true for its role as a seat of secular authority and government functions (arguably the reason why urban life was sustained so long at Lincoln).[6] However, although Lincoln was clearly important, it should not be forgotten that in Lincolnshire – as in the rest of eastern Britain – the vast bulk of the Romano-British population would appear to have lived on dispersed farmsteads and villas, not in the towns.[7] The wide distribution of Romano-British material from the region is indicative of a densely settled and worked landscape in the fourth century, with farmsteads being on average only around one kilometre apart and by no means restricted to just the best soils.[8] Indeed, field surveys have recovered significant quantities of Romano-British potsherds even from areas such as the flood-prone Lower Trent valley and the Fenland. The amount and distribution of this material suggests a fairly intensive Roman-era exploitation of these low-lying and marginal landscapes, although there does seem to be a reduction in activity in the fourth century, which has been associated with an environmental downturn.[9] In this light, what gaps there are in the distribution of settlement evidence within the region – such as on the eastern Wolds – are more plausibly explained as the result of varying intensities of fieldwork rather than an absence of Romano-Britons in these areas.

The extensive pattern of Roman-era rural settlement is partly so visible because of the general richness of fourth-century material culture compared with earlier and later periods of British history – even rural farmsteads produce fine-ware pottery, coins and stonework. This must surely reflect an increasing participation by the general Romano-British population (who spoke a mixture of Vulgar Latin and Brittonic, the ancestor of modern Welsh) in the Romanized economy of the towns and villas at this time. It is also indicative of a prosperous society that had considerable areas of land under cultivation, producing a surplus that allowed the purchase of such luxuries. Indeed, it has been observed that the archaeology of the mid- to late fourth century in Britain 'is almost overwhelming in its quantity and variety'.[10] Nevertheless, it seems reasonably clear that some areas of Lincolnshire – such as the limestone uplands in the north and south of the region – were more prosperous than others, and these were home to the majority of the 'villas' that have been so far identified here. With regard to such sites, the exact distinction between a villa and a farmstead is open to debate. Villas are usually identified by British archaeologists from their ground plans or from the presence of 'Roman' features, such as mosaics, baths, sculpted columns, marble wall-veneers, or painted plaster. Sites with such features as these are thought to represent estate centres, on the basis of a comparison with the relative wealth of other settlements present in the British landscape in this period, and they are consequently termed 'villas' to fit in with the general pattern of Roman estate organization in western Europe.[11] Of course, whilst undoubtedly

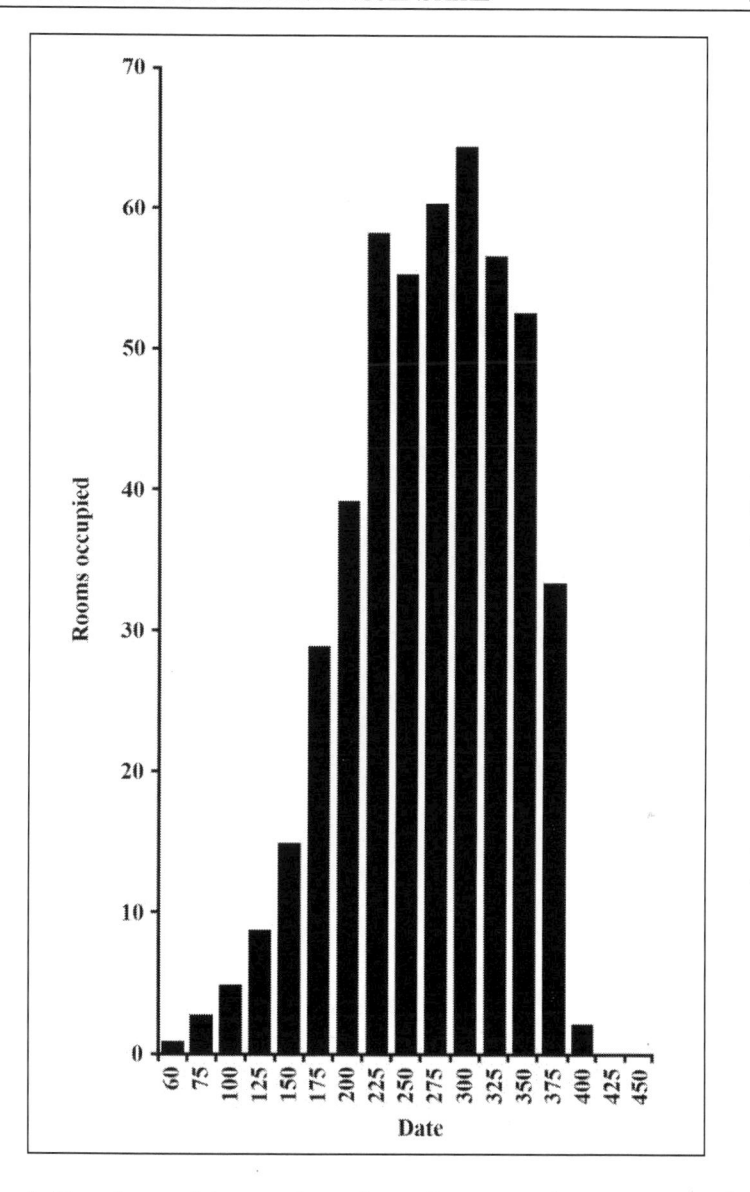

Fig. 2 Bar chart of the total number of excavated rooms occupied across Lincoln in the Roman period, showing significant activity into the last quarter of the fourth century
Copyright: English Heritage

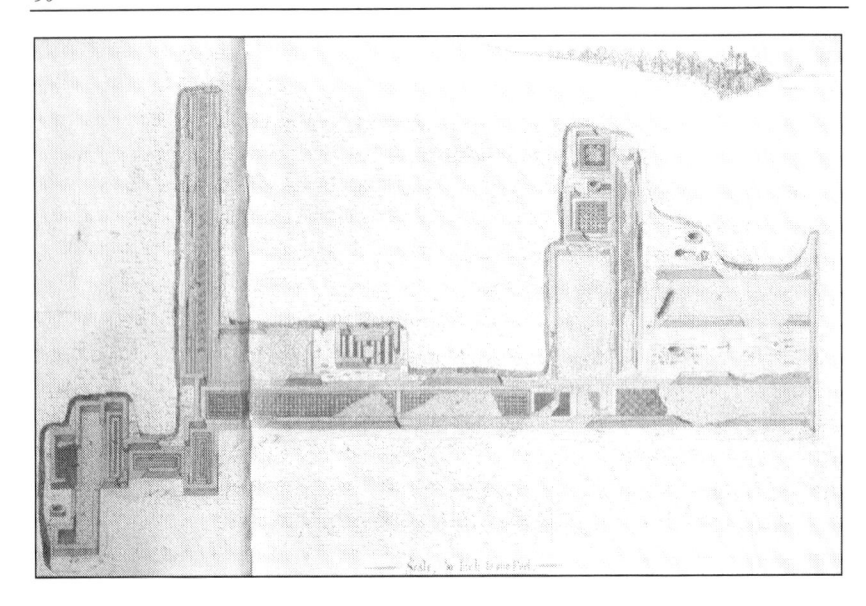

Fig. 3 Reproduction of the plan of Greetwell Villa. This appears to have been occupied through to the end of the coin sequence and is a candidate for the residence of the provincial governor
Source: The Collection: Art and Archaeology in Lincolnshire

prosperous – especially in the fourth century – the majority of British villas would be considered poor indeed if found in the Mediterranean region.[12] Nonetheless, whilst these sites are not always fully classical in form, so much as aspiring towards a Roman style, they are still potentially informative with regard to the social structure and centres of power within the Lincoln region in the fourth century. There are, for example, notably impressive villas from the region, including that found at Greetwell mentioned above. Indeed, many of the north Lincolnshire villas seem to have received new mosaic pavements in the mid- to late fourth century (for example, the Orpheus mosaic at Winterton villa), which is strongly suggestive of continued vitality and prosperity here.[13]

In terms of physical size, between the city of Lincoln and the dispersed rural farmsteads belongs a diverse class of roadside settlements and 'small towns' (Fig. 4). Included in this category are a number of unfortified but extensive sites, such as that at Kirmington. The latter seems to have covered around 20 hectares and saw very

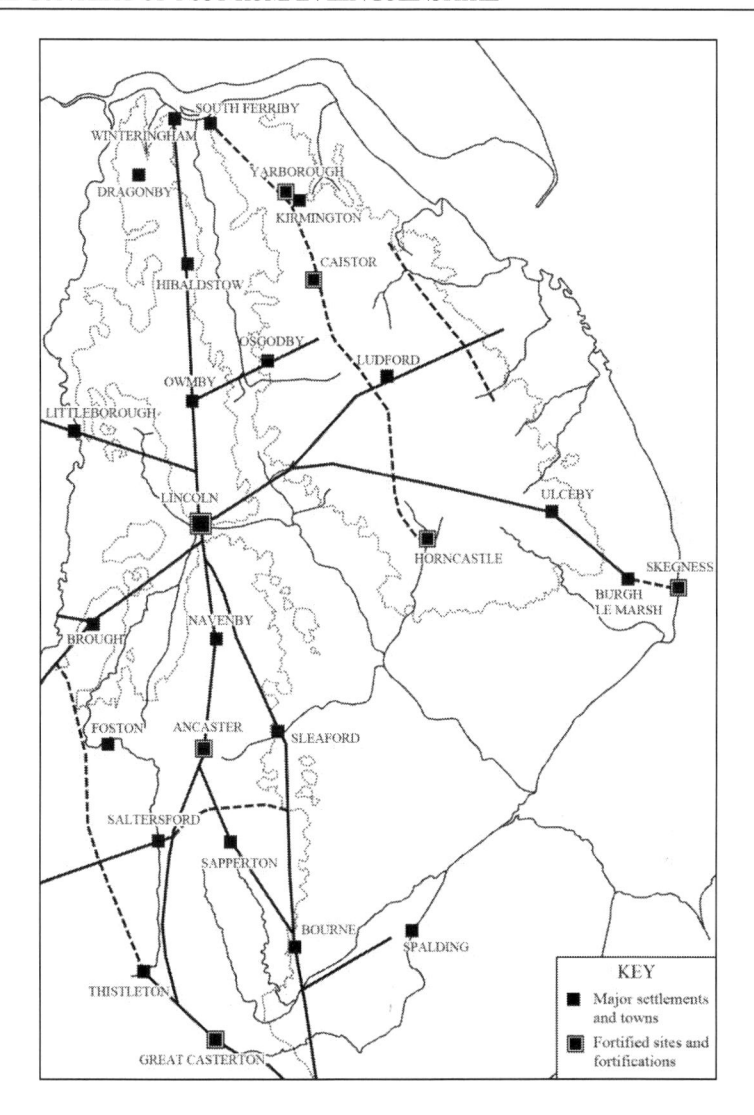

Fig. 4 Roman Lincolnshire, showing the major settlements and road-routes in the region against the modern coastline. It should be noted that, in addition to those shown here, a number of Late Roman fortifications have been suggested along the east coast, including at Yarburgh (near Louth) and Grimsby

After B. Whitwell, *Roman Lincolnshire*, 2nd edn (1992), with additions high levels of activity right up until the end of the Roman era, with 1,511 coins dated AD 364–88 and (given the context of the times) an impressive 102 examples from AD 388–402. Numerous belt fittings were also found, which may be indicative of the presence of a late fourth-century Romano-British militia.[14] Some of these sites probably acted as markets for the local area, whilst others may have been imperial posting houses, such as those on Ermine Street. Others, however – namely Ancaster, Caistor and Horncastle – were enclosed by impressive walls, which suggests that they had an additional role.[15] It has been argued that the nature of the surviving fortifications at Horncastle and Caistor places them in the same class of site as the 'Saxon Shore' forts located from north Norfolk to Portsmouth, with the thickness of their walls and the small enclosed areas being particularly noticeable (Fig. 5).[16] Why they were built and what exactly this might mean is open to debate. It should not be forgotten, for example, that Horncastle had extensive earlier occupation outside the later walls and has been described as 'one of the leading settlements in the Lincoln area'; both Horncastle and Caistor are, indeed, likely to have been important elements in the administration of the Lincoln region in the fourth century.[17] Nevertheless, it does seem plausible that in this century they took on a role both as fortified collection points for taxes paid in kind (the *annona*) and as garrisons involved in the defence of Roman Britain, with Caistor occupying a commanding position overlooking the Ancholme valley.[18] In this context, mention also ought to be made of Yarborough Camp, an important earthwork fortification that was probably refortified in the late fourth or early fifth century and would have been used in the defence of north Lincolnshire.[19] Indeed, a case has been made for several such earthwork fortifications being in use in the late fourth and early fifth centuries, including at Yarburgh (near Louth) and Grimsby, with the latter being one of the few points on the east coast where firm ground would have still reached the sea in the very Late Roman/post Roman period.[20]

We can thus extract from the available historical and archaeological evidence a picture of Lincolnshire as a fairly prosperous part of Roman Britain throughout the fourth century. It was home to the provincial capital and episcopal see of Lincoln. It also had a densely settled and exploited landscape, which included not

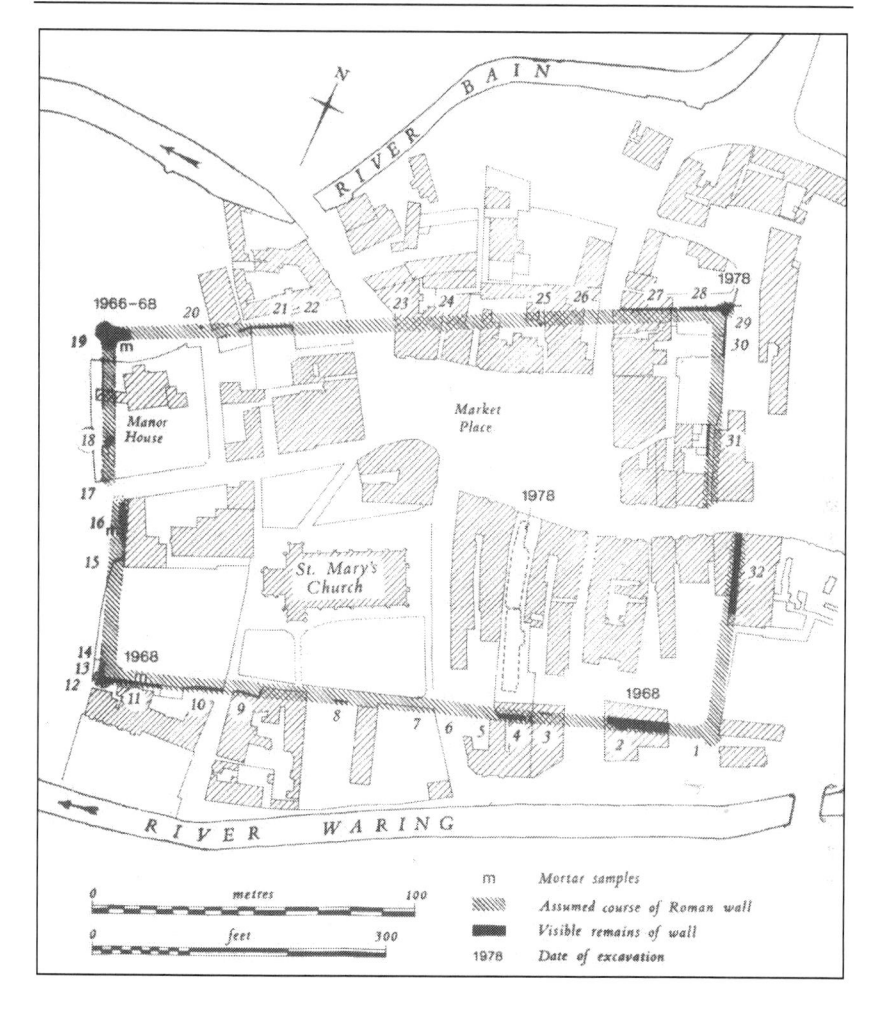

Fig. 5 Plan of the fort at Horncastle, which enclosed around two hectares within four-metre thick walls

Source: N. Field and H. Hurst, 'Roman Horncastle', *LHA*, 18 (1983)

only villas and farmsteads but also larger settlements of the type encountered at Kirmington, heavily fortified 'towns' such as Horncastle, and some earthwork fortifications as at Yarborough. The key question is, of course, how much of this continued to be occupied and to function into the period of the present study, post *c.* 400, and especially how much after *c.* 410, when Britain ceased to be part of the Roman Empire? This is a very difficult question to answer definitively. There are, as already mentioned, signs of 'decline' and abandonment in Lincoln during the last quarter of the fourth century, and to some extent this can be observed across the rest of the region too. Such a situation is, in fact, common across lowland Britain as a whole, and how these changes should be explained has been a topic that has long exercised researchers.[21] They may very well reflect, in part, an empire-wide movement of economic complexity outwards from Italy in the first century AD to Spain and Gaul in the second century, Britain and Africa in the third and fourth centuries and then to the Near East and the territories outside the borders of the Empire in succeeding centuries, with each area experiencing in turn prosperity followed by a subsequent decline.[22] On the other hand, the internal unrest in Britain recorded by Ammianus Marcellinus in the late fourth century and the increasing interruptions to the coinage supply to Britain in the last quarter of the fourth century are very likely to have played a significant role in any abandonment or 'decline' in Britain specifically. In particular, an unbroken supply of coinage to Britain was essential to the health of the urban and villa economy after the end of the London mint in the early fourth century.[23]

However, such 'decline' was by no means absolute. Whilst some rural sites, such as the large settlement at Dragonby, may not have survived to the end of the fourth century, there is evidence for continued activity of some sort at Lincoln to the very end of the Roman period, as noted previously. This is true of a number of rural sites too, including not only 'small towns', such as Kirmington and South Ferriby, but also villas and farmsteads, such as that at Deepdale (Barrow-on-Humber).[24] Furthermore, it needs to be recognized that even an absence, or near absence, of potentially early fifth-century artefacts or layers from a Late Roman site (as at Winterton Villa) cannot be considered as conclusive evidence for the last phase of this settlement certainly ending before *c.* 400, nor for any fifth-century phase necessarily representing a serious decline of the site. Whilst this could be true, the nature of the evidence for this period is such that drawing conclusions about the character and date of the final stages of Late Roman settlements is a hazardous task.

One major factor in obscuring early fifth-century phases and their nature is the simple fact that modern agricultural activity has often removed or severely damaged the latest levels of these sites, as is the case at both Winterton Villa and Hibaldstow 'small town'. This is a particular problem because of the shallow nature of very Late and post-Roman buildings, and even where the relevant levels do survive, the slightness of the traces which these buildings leave behind means that they can still escape notice.[25] In such circumstances, assumptions of abandonment before *c*. 400 – or serious decline if the site continued into the early fifth century – are obviously problematical. Moreover, this is not the only difficulty that we face when dealing with Late Roman sites where the existence or extent of any early fifth-century activity is not clear. Equally important as a factor is the declining supply of Roman coinage referred to above, with there being no new bronze coinage at all after 402 and no new gold or silver by 411.[26] This situation not only robs us of the chief source of dating evidence for the latest Romano-British levels, but it also means that no sensible chronologies can be provided for the other types of artefacts traditionally used for dating, including pottery, as these are ultimately dated from the coins too. As such, there is a legitimate concern that the final phases of some Romano-British sites, especially those not fully excavated in the modern era, may have been either missed entirely or have had their significance underestimated because of the rarity of datable artefacts for this era, as opposed to any real lack of activity. Finally, even when there is good evidence for an early fifth-century phase, the absence of later coinage can lead to an assumption that this phase was short-lived and confined to the first decade or so of the fifth century on the basis of the coin dates, despite the fact that we have no way of knowing how long these coins continued in use and thus when they were deposited on our sites. Certainly, the late fifth-century Patching hoard (found in Sussex in 1997) contained coins that were over 100 years old when they were finally deposited, which is suggestive in this regard.[27]

The end result of these evidential problems is that, from the very late fourth century onwards, British activity in the Lincoln region became at first difficult to observe and then effectively archaeologically 'invisible', with the result that we cannot easily know what was happening to them or their settlements in the landscape.

This is not, of course, to deny that 'decline' and abandonment did occur in the late fourth century, although we need to be careful not to confuse changing fashions, priorities and practices with 'decline'.[28] Nor is it to argue for anything approaching complete continuity of fourth-century Romano-British urban and villa life through the fifth century, or even beyond. Rather, it is to point out that we cannot be certain how widespread and significant the late fourth-century 'decline' was, nor how urban and villa life in Lincolnshire ultimately came to an end, nor, indeed, when. That major changes did occur seems certain, however, as the archaeological 'invisibility' of the fifth-century and later Britons is not simply a result of the lack of new coins entering the region then, but has far deeper roots. The vital economy and material culture of the fourth century was ultimately a function of the presence of the Roman Empire and its coinage through the revenue/payment cycle and its associated activities, as Simon Esmonde-Cleary has pointed out. The interruptions to the coin supply and the effects of these on the health of the Romano-British economy have already been noted as one reason for the apparent late fourth-century 'decline' observed on many sites. However, the early fifth-century withdrawal and collapse of the imperial superstructure and coinage system seems to have removed completely the main engine of the Romano-British market economy, which had sustained Romano-British towns, mass-production industry, Roman-style villa life, and Romano-British material culture in general.[29] Thus, whilst evidence for continuing activity in Lincoln in the fifth and sixth centuries is discussed in subsequent chapters, there is little to suggest that Lincoln continued to be the well-populated urban centre it had been in the late fourth century. These aspects of its role in the region had almost certainly been lost with the collapse of the Roman market economy. Similarly, whilst villa estates may well have continued to play an important role in fifth-century Lincolnshire, it is difficult to believe that the thoroughly Romanized villas themselves long survived the collapse of the Roman economy and building industry that were essential to their existence.[30] Finally, whilst a lack of fifth-century coinage means that we cannot observe the fifth-century stages of towns, villas or the pottery industry, this is not the only reason that British activity in the fifth century is hard to identify archaeologically. Quite simply, in most parts of the country the post-Roman Britons appear to have adopted – probably largely out of necessity, because of the collapse of the mass-production industries – a very different type of material culture from that which had gone before. This new culture was one which, aside from a few classes of high-status metalwork and pottery, left very little evidence for modern archaeologists to find.[31]

This, then, was the situation amongst the Britons (formerly Romano-Britons) of our region at the dawn of the period under investigation in subsequent chapters. On the one hand, theirs had been until very recently a remarkably prosperous society that enjoyed a rich material culture, although there were signs of decline – or at least change – at the very end of the period. On the other hand, the withdrawal of official Roman support for Britain would seem to have precipitated a major collapse in the economy and material culture of the Britons and rendered both them and their settlements archaeologically 'invisible'. Urban and villa life are likely to have been the chief casualties of this collapse in the Lincoln region, with there being little reason to believe that they continued into the second half of the fifth century, if they indeed survived so late. However, this is not to say that villa estates ceased to exist, nor that Lincoln and the fortified towns of the region were necessarily completely abandoned and functionless. Equally, it seems unlikely that those elements of British life and society that were less suffused with *romanitas* – and dependent upon the Roman economy – were so severely affected.

The Lincoln region in the seventh century

If a knowledge of the situation in Lincolnshire at the start of our period of study is valuable as a starting point for any investigation into the largely undocumented and obscure two centuries that follow on from the fourth, a knowledge of the situation in the seventh century is equally useful when it comes to assessing what exactly occurred in the years between 400 and 600. When we turn to look at the political landscape of the seventh century, there is a marked contrast with the situation observed in the fourth century. Fundamentally, it seems clear that the Roman diocese of *Britannia*, along with the relatively peaceful political unity that it represented, had long since dissolved by the time we reach the early seventh century. In the west of Britain, the descendants of the old Romano-British inhabitants of the island remained largely in charge of their own destiny as the rulers of the kingdoms of, amongst others, Gwynedd, Powys and Dumnonia, these being based ultimately around regional Romano-British political identities.[32] In the east of Britain there had been a similar disappearance of political unity by the seventh century. However, here the small and not-so-small kingdoms which now existed were largely ruled by lineages that believed themselves to be descended from fifth- and sixth-century 'Anglo-Saxon' immigrants to this region, who had arrived from the area of present-day north Germany, Holland, Denmark and other parts of Scandinavia (Fig. 6).[33] The degree to which these Anglo-Saxon kingdoms reflected the earlier Romano-British and post-Roman British political geography of lowland Britain is open to debate, and it is a question which the present study aims to address. Equally open to debate is how widespread this immigrant ethnic identity and language was at the start of the seventh century in the Lincoln region – was it restricted to just the elite lineages, or was it far more common? Certainly, the available evidence suggests that the vast majority of the population must have spoken Old English, rather than a descendant of Brittonic (like Archaic Welsh), by the end of the eighth century at the latest. How and why this change came about is, of course, another of the primary concerns of what follows.[34]

From a political perspective, it would seem that a very significant area of Late Roman Lincolnshire – how great a proportion is discussed in Chapter 4 – had, by the early seventh century, come to form the territory of an Anglo-Saxon kingdom named *Lindissi/Lindesig* (the latter form is the root of the modern district-name 'Lindsey'). The evidence for *Lindissi* as a real seventh-century 'Anglo-Saxon' kingdom, rather than just an administrative unit of the larger kingdom of Mercia (whose heartlands lay south-west of Lincolnshire on the Middle Trent), has been frequently rehearsed in recent years and is now beyond serious doubt.[35] Whilst we lack the detailed narratives of the deeds of its kings that we possess for the more powerful seventh-century kingdoms of Bernicia (Northumbria), Mercia and Wessex, we do have a number of items which, when taken together, are convincing. Thus there is a genealogy of the kings of *Lindissi* preserved in the eighth-century 'Anglian Collection of royal

Fig. 6 Post-Roman Britain in the seventh century, showing both the British and Anglo-Saxon kingdoms (the names of the former are in italic type)

genealogies and regnal lists', alongside those of the kings of Wessex, Kent, Mercia and Northumbria.[36] This is, naturally, of considerable importance, and its implications are supported by the 'Tribal Hidage', a list of pre-Viking Anglo-Saxon population groups and their hidations (possibly tribute assessments, reflecting some uncertain mixture of size and status). Here, *Lindissi* is assessed at the same level as the better-attested kingdoms of Essex and Sussex (7,000 hides).[37] Similarly important is the fact that Bede consistently describes *Lindissi* as a *prouincia* – his normal term for an Anglo-Saxon kingdom – in his early eighth-century *Historia Ecclesiastica*. He also portrays the people of *Lindissi* as a distinct and separate people, the *Lindisfari* (< Old English *Lindisfaran*), in this work.[38] Finally, there is the fact that Bede and other sources make it clear that the *Lindisfari/Lindisfaran* had their own bishop from the seventh until the ninth century, a point which is again indicative of *Lindissi* having been a kingdom.[39]

Although it seems apparent that *Lindissi* was indeed a seventh-century Anglo-Saxon kingdom, saying anything further about it in this period is difficult because of the aforesaid lack of narrative sources. One thing we can say is that the last king of *Lindissi* was probably named Aldfrið (an Old English name), as his is the final name in the royal genealogy that we possess for the kingdom. It used to be thought that this Aldfrið was also mentioned in a late eighth-century Mercian charter, but this belief now appears to be mistaken. Instead, a good case has been made for thinking that he was probably king up until *c.* 679, with there being no more independent rulers of *Lindissi* after him, as the kingdom was henceforth under permanent Mercian lordship.[40]

In addition to the *Lindisfaran*, there are three other population groups recorded in the 'Tribal Hidage' which can be potentially placed in the Lincoln region. One of these is the *Bilmigas*, who were assessed at 600 hides and are often associated with the *Billingas* population group that occurs in three Lincolnshire place-names: Horbling, Billingborough and Billinghay.[41] Another is the *Spalde*, who underlie the place-name Spalding. This population group, again assessed at 600 hides in the 'Tribal Hidage', has been defined through the work of the Fenland Survey and seems to have included much of the modern Fenland district of Holland in Lincolnshire.[42] Finally, there is the *Gyrwe* population group (from Old English *gyr*, 'mud'), which was assessed in two equal parts of 600 hides in the 'Tribal Hidage'. The *Gyrwe* were placed by Bede and other sources in the Fens of northern Cambridgeshire and southern Lincolnshire, with Crowland Abbey lying within their territory (Fig. 7).[43] All three of these groups are discussed in more detail in Chapter 5.

Turning away from political matters to those of material culture, rural settlement and population, the seventh century provides an equally large contrast with the situation in the fourth. Where, before, there was abundant evidence of a densely settled landscape, filled with villas and dispersed farmsteads which extended even onto marginal land, now the picture appears considerably impoverished. Certainly, nothing approaching the astonishingly rich material culture of the fourth century is apparent in early seventh-century Lincolnshire. There is, for example, no reason to think that rural settlements of any type made use of stone in their construction, nor is there any evidence for the widespread usage of fine-ware/wheel-thrown pottery or low-denomination coinage at this time. It does appear, however, that some of the handmade Anglo-Saxon pottery was traded regionally and there are some prestige imports from the continent, which suggests that the rural economy was producing a surplus.[44] Nonetheless, we really have to wait until the eighth century before we see significant evidence for inter-regional/international trade and coin usage appearing once more in the region.[45]

Potentially of equal importance is the fact that one reading of the available archaeological evidence suggests a much-reduced density of settlement – and thus overall population – across the region in the early seventh century than was the case in the fourth century. However, caution must be exercised with regard to the conclusions that can be drawn from this latter observation. Excavated early Anglo-Saxon settlements from the region are extremely rare, whilst at the same time it is difficult to be confident that fieldwalking accurately reflects the real settlement density of this period. Largely, this is a result of the aforementioned lack of the kind of rich and abundant material culture that the Lincoln area possessed in the fourth century, which is very easy to identify. In particular, attention should be drawn to the often-recognized difficulties in identifying early Anglo-Saxon pottery from fieldwalking, because of its poor quality and similarity to handmade Iron Age and Roman pottery.[46] Indeed, even when attempts have been made to rectify these issues with fieldwalking, the pattern produced is not always entirely convincing. So, recent fieldwalking and pottery collection in the north of Lindsey suggest that there was a contrast between a high early Anglo-Saxon settlement density on the Lincoln Edge and a lower one on the western part of the Chalk Wolds. This does not, however,

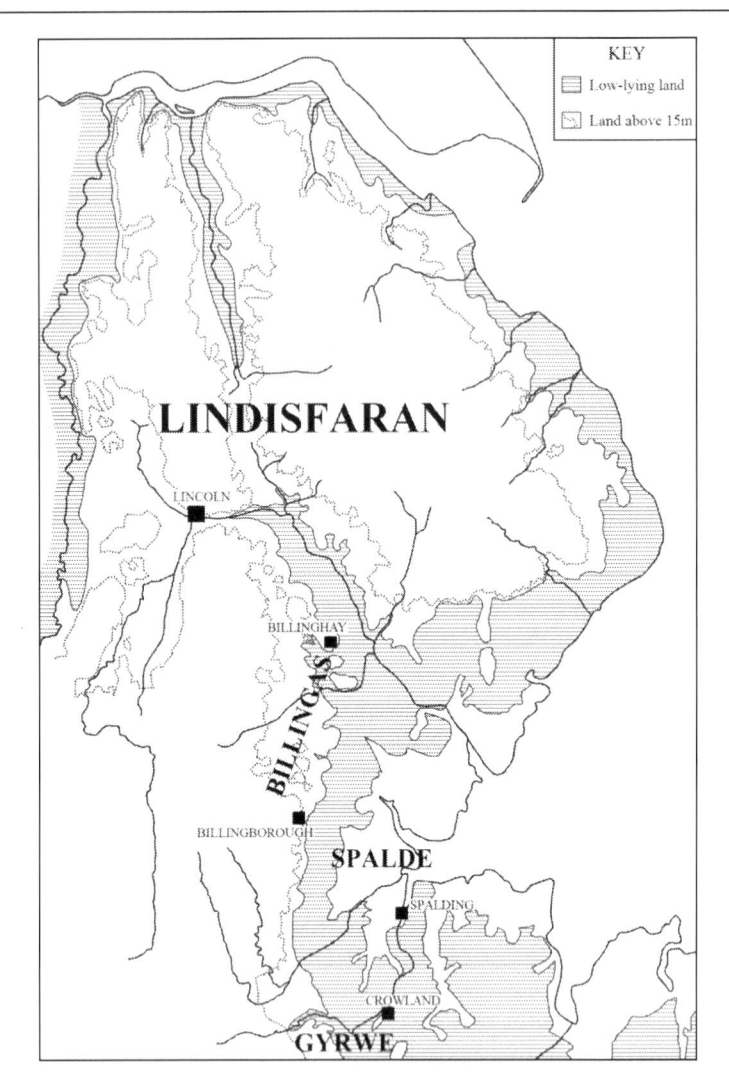

Fig. 7 Suggested locations in Lincolnshire for the Anglo-Saxon *Lindisfaran, Billingas, Spalde* and *Gyrwe* population groups. The estimated Anglo-Saxon coastline along the Fenland and marshes is shown along with low-lying land and ground above 15 metres.
Coastline and Fenland after A. Crowson *et al, Anglo-Saxon Settlement on the Siltland of Eastern England* (Heckington, 2005), and K. U. Ulmschneider, 'Settlement, economy, and the 'productive' site: Middle Anglo-Saxon Lincolnshire A.D. 650–780', *Med. Arch.*, 44 (2000)

seem to be reflected in the known distribution of early Anglo-Saxon cemeteries or in the metal-detected finds recorded by the Portable Antiquities Scheme, which indicate relatively significant populations in both areas.[47] In fact, the only pattern of early Anglo-Saxon rural settlement in Lincolnshire that seems fairly well established is one in which the low-lying marginal land (such as that on the Fens or in the Trent valley) was far less intensively exploited in the post-Roman period than it had been previously. This is likely to be at least partially due to an environmental downturn in the Late and post-Roman periods, and it is a point on which the distributions both of fieldwalked settlement evidence and of cemeteries and metal-detected finds all concur.[48] Other than this, it is hard to draw meaningful conclusions from the data currently available, especially when it comes to comparing the situation in the early Anglo-Saxon period (c. 450–650) with that in the fourth century.[49] Moreover, such difficulties are compounded by the fact that, because of the post-Roman archaeological 'invisibility' of British material culture referred to above and the normal post-Roman British rite having been burial without any grave goods, any settlements or graves of Britons living within the region who had not adopted the Anglo-Saxon material culture by c. 650 will simply not appear in the early Anglo-Saxon archaeological record, apart from in the most exceptional circumstances.[50]

The concern that there can be a significant underestimation of the density of early Anglo-Saxon rural settlement – and thus an assumption that the fifth to seventh centuries saw a sparsely populated countryside compared with the fourth century – is by no means confined to our study area. The above issues with the evidence mean that, whether we are talking about Lincolnshire or lowland Britain as a whole, we simply cannot compare rural settlement densities in the two periods using the evidence that we have available. As a result, no such assumptions of a major decline in population can be justified. This has not, of course, prevented such comparisons and assumptions inspiring theories of a catastrophic post-Roman population collapse, with this being ascribed to plague or even to the kind of land-clearing genocide that was envisaged by Victorian historians and which still finds occasional supporters.[51] That such radical explanations are unnecessary is not merely implied by the problems with evidence outlined above. The available environmental and palaeobotanical material also indicates that there was little post-Roman reforestation anywhere in lowland Britain, aside from on the most marginal land, and such reforestation ought to have occurred if there had been any significant drop in population.[52] Rather, what appears to have happened is a degree of de-intensification in land exploitation, chiefly manifested in a shift from arable to pastoral farming in some areas, which is better associated with the ending of Roman taxation and imperial demand (both of which required a significant agricultural surplus to be produced) rather than a drastic population decline.[53] As such, it seems more than credible that the landscape of early Anglo-Saxon England (including Lincolnshire), away from very marginal areas such as the Fens, was in fact almost as densely settled as it was in the Late Roman period. This position would seem to be supported by the evidence for the continued usage of Roman field systems. As Oliver Rackham and others have observed, if a field is abandoned because of a major population collapse, rather than its exploitation being shifted from arable to pastoral, then in ten years 'it will be difficult to reclaim; in thirty years it will have "tumbled down into woodland"', and it will probably be unrecoverable in terms of its boundaries.[54] In this context, not only is the lack of evidence from the pollen record for woodland regrowth (as noted above) highly significant, but so too is the fact that pre-Roman and Roman-era field systems and boundaries appear to have been still in use throughout the medieval period and in some cases right up until the modern day, with one large system having been identified around Goltho in southern Lindsey.[55]

If there seems little reason to doubt that the Lincolnshire countryside saw continuing activity at a similar level to that in the fourth century, the same cannot be said for the towns and central places of the Late Roman period. The intervening two centuries saw the disappearance of towns as densely populated centres all across Britain, and whilst some have argued that urban settlements started to re-emerge in Britain from the seventh century onwards, there is no real evidence for such a development so early in the Lincoln region.[56] However, this does not mean that the Roman-era pattern of central places, in the sense of political or administrative centres, had disappeared. With respect to Lincoln, for example, Bede makes it clear that it was one of the most important political centres for the region in the early seventh century – just as it had been at the end of the fourth – when he relates how it had a *praefectus* named Blæcca and that it was chosen as the site of the first stone church to be built in *Lindissi*.[57] Similarly, even though such early documentary evidence is lacking for the fortified 'small towns' of Ancaster, Horncastle and Caistor, archaeological and later historical evidence combines to suggest that these too may have played a significant role within early Anglo-Saxon Lincolnshire (see further, Chapter 4).

At the same time as we can observe a degree of administrative/political activity occurring on some of the same sites as it did in the fourth century, we can also recognize several new categories of 'central place' emerging by the end of the seventh century. The most significant of these, for the purposes of the present study, are those

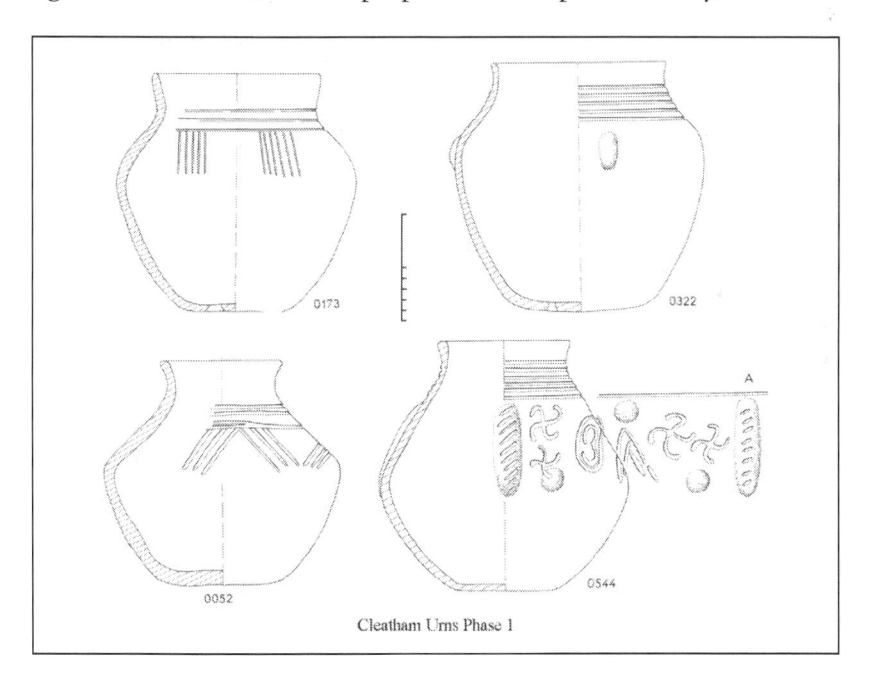

Cleatham Urns Phase 1

Fig. 8 Cremation urns from the first phase of the Anglo-Saxon cremation cemetery at Cleatham–Kirton in Lindsey
Source: Kevin Leahy

represented by the large early Anglo-Saxon cremation cemeteries or urnfields, such as are found at Cleatham (originally *c.* 1,500 burials) and Loveden Hill (*c.* 1,800 burials).[58] These cemeteries, discussed more fully in subsequent chapters, are usually considered to have been the earliest burial sites used by the Anglo-Saxon immigrants who arrived in the region in the fifth century. Furthermore, their size and widely spaced locations suggest that they each possessed a defined territory for which they acted as a central burial ground (Figs 8 and 11).[59] The monasteries which begin to appear in the Lincolnshire landscape from the middle of the seventh century, as a result of the official conversion of the kingdom to Roman-style Christianity in *c.* 627–8, represent another new type of central place. Sometimes these were founded in remote areas, as at Bardney or Crowland, but at other times they were established near to pre-existing central places (for example, Louth is the location for both a pre-Viking monastery and a major early Anglo-Saxon cremation cemetery) or significant Late Roman sites (as with Hibaldstow, which was both the site of a Roman 'small town' and the presumed location of Hygebald's monastery, mentioned by Bede).[60] As such, even though the monasteries – unlike the cremation cemeteries – were founded after the end of the period with which we are here concerned, their locations are worth investigating as a potential guide to sites that had a degree of importance in the fifth and sixth centuries (Fig. 9).

From Romano-British to Anglo-Saxon: Lincolnshire in the post-Roman period

All told, the fifth and sixth centuries in the Lincoln region seem to have represented a momentous epoch. On the one hand, the political unity of the Late Roman period appears to have been fractured, and whilst the fourth century was marked by a prosperous rural economy, vital urban centres and a widespread use of money, the seventh century in contrast appears much impoverished. Moreover, the landscape was filled with whole new classes of central places that were of no significance in the Late Roman period. At the same time, there is clear evidence for immigration into lowland Britain from continental Europe beyond the Roman frontiers. Both the material

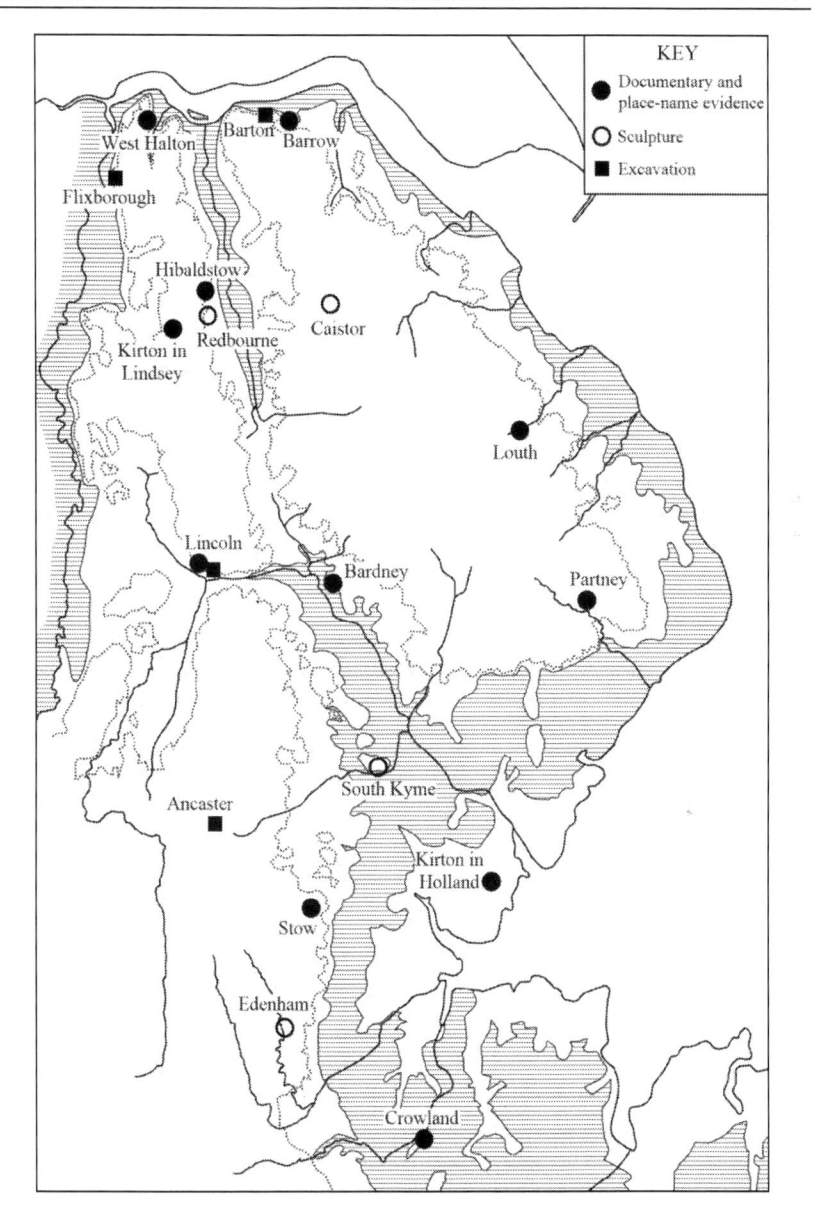

Fig. 9 The evidence for pre-Viking ecclesiastical centres in Lincolnshire
After D. Stocker, 'The early Church in Lincolnshire: a study of the sites and their significance' in A. Vince (ed.), *Pre-Viking Lindsey* (1993)

culture and language of these immigrant groups were seemingly well on their way to domination of the region by the seventh century, whilst those of the former Romano-Britons seem largely conspicuous by their absence. On the other hand, there are strong potential threads of continuity identifiable between the late fourth and the early seventh centuries. Thus, whilst seventh-century settlements are much harder to identify than Romano-British ones, there are reasons to think that the landscape of Lincolnshire probably continued to be extensively occupied into the seventh century and beyond. Similarly, Lincoln and some of the other key settlements of Late Roman Lincolnshire appear to have been important centres for the early Anglo-Saxon period too. The question is thus: how much really did change in the two centuries between *c.* 400 and *c.* 600, and is there enough evidence surviving to allow us to explain and understand the course of events which led to these changes?

Notes to Chapter 1

1   J. Wacher, *The Towns of Roman Britain*, 2nd edn (London, 1995), pp. 17–18, 87; J. C. Mann, 'The creation of four provinces in Britain', *Britannia*, 29 (1998), 339–41; M. J. Jones, 'The Colonia era: archaeological account' in D. Stocker (ed.), *The City by the Pool: Assessing the Archaeology of the City of Lincoln* (Oxford, 2003), p. 124; A. C. Thomas, *Christianity in Roman Britain to AD 500* (London, 1981), p. 197.

2   Jones, 'Colonia Era', fig. 7.69b and pp. 130–4; M. J. Jones, *Roman Lincoln: Conquest, Colony and Capital* (Stroud, 2002), pp. 124–6; K. Dobney *et al*, *Of Butchers and Breeds: Report on Vertebrate Remains from Various Sites in the City of Lincoln* (Lincoln, 1996), pp. 2–4, 57–61; K. Dobney *et al*, 'Down, but not out: biological evidence for complex economic organization in Lincoln in the late 4th century', *Ant.*, 72 (1998), 417–24. On empire-wide urban trends leading to a decline in public buildings in all areas, including Britain, see for example B. Ward-Perkins, *From Classical Antiquity to the Middle Ages* (Oxford, 1984) and S. Esmonde-Cleary, 'Britain in the fourth century' in M. Todd (ed.), *A Companion to Roman Britain* (Oxford, 2004), pp. 418–9. See N. Faulkner, 'Urban stratigraphy and Roman history' in N. Holbrook (ed.), *Cirencester: The Roman Town Defences, Public Buildings and Shops* (Cirencester, 1998), pp. 371–85 for another Late Roman provincial capital which remained prosperous late into the fourth century.

3   Jones, 'Colonia Era', pp. 133–4; Jones, *Roman Lincoln*, pp. 124, 126; S. Esmonde-Cleary, *The Ending of Roman Britain* (London, 1989), especially

chapter 4; S. Esmonde-Cleary, 'Late Roman towns in Britain and their fate' in A. Vince (ed.), *Pre-Viking Lindsey* (Lincoln, 1993), pp. 6–13.

4 Jones, 'Colonia Era', pp. 133–6; Jones, *Roman Lincoln*, pp. 125–9 – see pp. 65–9 on the usage of the *forum*.

5 Jones, 'Colonia Era', pp. 97–8, 130, 136; Jones, *Roman Lincoln*, pp. 124, 127. The evidence from Lincoln of continuing urban life in the second half of the fourth century and into the fifth obviously suggests that Reece's concept of fourth-century towns as essentially non-urban does not apply here, although Faulkner's 'post-classical urbanism' may be relevant to the last late fourth-/early fifth-century stage, as Jones has observed (R. Reece, 'The end of the city in Roman Britain' in J. Rich (ed.), *The City in Late Antiquity* (London, 1992), pp. 136–45; N. Faulkner, 'Later Roman Colchester', *Oxford Journal of Archaeology*, 13.1 (1994), 93–120; Jones, 'Colonia Era', pp. 125–7, 135).

6 See Esmonde-Cleary's *Ending of Roman Britain* (especially chapter 4) and 'Late Roman Towns' on how the collapse of the Roman market economy and withdrawal of the Roman army would have led to the rapid and final decline of towns as economic and residential *foci*.

7 See generally C. C. Taylor, *Village and Farmstead* (London, 1983); K. R. Dark and P. Dark, *The Landscape of Roman Britain* (Stroud, 1997).

8 D. Jones, 'Aerial reconnaissance and prehistoric and Romano-British archaeology in northern Lincolnshire – a sample survey', *LHA*, 23 (1988), 21; K. Leahy, *The Anglo-Saxon Kingdom of Lindsey* (Stroud, 2007), p. 21.

9 R. Van de Noort and S. Ellis, *Wetland Heritage of the Ancholme and Lower Trent Valleys: An Archaeological Survey* (Hull, 1998); T. W. Lane, *The Fenland Project Number 8: Lincolnshire Survey, the Northern Fen-Edge* (Sleaford, 1992); B. Whitwell, *Roman Lincolnshire*, 2nd edn (Lincoln, 1992), pp. xxvi–xxviii; A. E. B. Owen, 'Salt, sea banks and medieval settlement on the Lindsey coast' in N. Field and A. White (eds), *A Prospect of Lincolnshire* (Lincoln, 1984), pp. 46–9. This was also the situation in southern Lincolnshire (P. P. Hayes and T. W. Lane, *The Fenland Project Number 5: Lincolnshire Survey, the South-West Fens* (Sleaford, 1992); P. P. Hayes, 'Roman to Saxon in the south Lincolnshire Fens', *Ant.*, 62 (1988), 321–6).

10 S. Esmonde-Cleary, 'Changing constraints on the landscape' in D. Hooke and S. Burnell (eds), *Landscape and Settlement in Britain AD 400–1066* (Exeter, 1995), p. 17; Esmonde-Cleary, *Ending of Roman Britain*.

11 M. Millett, *Roman Britain* (London, 1995), pp. 67–74; Dark & Dark, *Landscape of Roman Britain*, pp. 43–51.

12 See, for example, T. W. Potter, *The Changing Landscape of South Etruria* (London, 1979).

13 Whitwell, *Roman Lincolnshire*, pp. xxix–xxxi; Leahy, *Kingdom of Lindsey*, p. 22.

14 B. Whitwell, 'Late Roman settlement on the Humber and Anglian beginnings' in J. Price and P. R. Wilson (eds), *Recent Research in Roman*

Yorkshire (Oxford, 1988), p. 59; D. Jones and B. Whitwell, 'Survey of the Roman fort and multi-period settlement complex at Kirmington on the Lincolnshire Wolds: a non-destructive approach', *LHA*, 26 (1991), 57–62; Leahy, *Kingdom of Lindsey*, pp. 30–1, 33; K. Leahy, 'Soldiers and settlers in Britain, fourth to fifth century – revisited' in M. Henig and T. J. Smith (eds), *Collectanea Antiqua: Essays in memory of Sonia Chadwick Hawkes* (Oxford, 2007), pp. 133–43.

15   Caistor and Horncastle are the only surviving examples, but it seems plausible that there was a walled fort at Skegness too. For Skegness, see John Leland, *The Itinerary of John Leland the Antiquary*, ed. T. Hearne (9 vols, Oxford, 1770), vol. 7, p. 152, and Whitwell, *Roman Lincolnshire*, pp. 51–3. The place-name *Tric* (< Latin *traiectus* 'crossing point, ferry') recorded at Domesday presumably applied to this lost settlement/fort at Skegness (Coates, *Toponymic Topics*, pp. 35–9; A. E. B. Owen and R. Coates, 'Traiectus/Tric/Skegness: a Domesday name explained', *LHA*, 38 (2003), 42–4).

16   N. Field and H. Hurst, 'Roman Horncastle', *LHA*, 18 (1983), 85–7 and tables 6–7; C. Clay, 'Roman forts in Lincolnshire' in S. Malone and M. Williams (eds), *Rumours of Roman Finds: Recent Work on Roman Lincolnshire* (Heckington, 2010), p. 41; K. Leahy, 'The Anglo-Saxon settlement of Lindsey' in Vince, *Pre-Viking Lindsey*, p. 29.

17   Field & Hurst, 'Roman Horncastle', 85.

18   As suggested by B. Whitwell, *The Coritani* (Oxford, 1982), p. 77. See particularly J. Cotterill, 'Saxon raiding and the role of the Late Roman coastal forts of Britain', *Britannia*, 24 (1993), 227–39, and M. Fulford and I. Tyers, 'The date of Pevensey and the defence of an "*Imperium Britanniarum*"', *Ant.*, 69 (1995), 1009–14, on the origins of the 'Saxon Shore' forts, which probably have more to do with Carausius (AD 286–93).

19   Leahy, *Kingdom of Lindsey*, pp. 111–14.

20   See, for example, B. Cox, 'Yarboroughs in Lindsey', *English Place-Name Society Journal*, 28 (1994–5), 50–60, and also R. Oliver, 'Possible Roman roads from Caistor and a possible fort at Cleethorpes', *LHA*, 41 (2006), 18–21.

21   For differing views as to the degree and date of 'decline' in Britain, see for example Esmonde-Cleary, *Ending of Roman Britain*; K. R. Dark, *Civitas to Kingdom: British Political Continuity 300–800* (London, 1994); G. de la Bédoyère, *The Golden Age of Roman Britain* (Stroud, 1999); N. Faulkner, *The Decline and Fall of Roman Britain* (Stroud, 2000); Esmonde-Cleary, 'Britain in the fourth century', pp. 424–5; B. Ward-Perkins, *The Fall of Rome and the End of Civilisation* (Oxford, 2005), pp. 123–4 and fig. 6.1; R. White, *Britannia Prima: Britain's Last Roman Province* (Stroud, 2007), especially pp. 177–94 and table 8.1.

22 B. Ward-Perkins, 'Specialised production and exchange' in A. Cameron *et al* (eds), *Cambridge Ancient History XIV, Late Antiquity: Empire and Successors, AD 425–600* (Cambridge, 2000), pp. 346–91.

23 E. A. Thompson, 'Ammianus Marcellinus and Britain', *Nottingham Medieval Studies*, 34 (1990), 1–15; I. N. Wood, 'Internal crisis in fourth-century Britain', *Britannia*, 22 (1991) 313–15; and Esmonde-Cleary, *Ending of Roman Britain*. The large number of later fourth-century coin hoards from Lincolnshire may offer some support for 'unrest' as a partial explanation (R. W. Higginbottom, 'Roman coin hoards from Lincolnshire', *LHA*, 15 (1980), 5–8).

24 J. May, *Dragonby: Report on Excavation at an Iron Age and Romano-British Settlement in North Lincolnshire* (2 vols, Oxford, 1996), vol. 2, pp. 637–8; Whitwell, 'Late Roman settlement'; B. Whitwell, 'Some Roman small towns in north Lincolnshire and south Humberside' in A. E. Brown (ed.), *Roman Small Towns in Eastern England and Beyond* (Oxford, 1995), pp. 95–102; Whitwell, *Roman Lincolnshire*, p. xxxi. See also below, pp. 69–71, on post-Roman British Class 1 brooches; three of these have been found on the site of Kirmington 'small town'.

25 Whitwell, 'Late Roman settlement', p. 60; Whitwell, *Roman Lincolnshire*, p. xxxv. See N. Faulkner, 'Verulamium: interpreting decline', *Archaeol. J.*, 153 (1996), 79–103, especially 87, and White, *Britannia Prima*, p. 180, with regard to the difficulty of locating Late Roman timber structures without very careful excavation of an extensive area.

26 Esmonde-Cleary, *Ending of Roman Britain*, pp. 138–9.

27 M. Whyman, 'Invisible people? Material culture in 'Dark Age' Yorkshire' in M. O. H. Carver (ed.), *In Search of Cult* (Woodbridge, 1992), pp. 61–8; K. R. Dark, 'Pottery and local production at the end of Roman Britain' in K. R. Dark (ed.), *External Contacts and the Economy of Late Roman and Post-Roman Britain* (Woodbridge, 1996), p. 58; P. Rahtz, 'Anglo-Saxon Yorkshire: current research problems' in H. Geake and J. Kenny (eds), *Early Deira: Archaeological Studies of the East Riding in the Fourth to Ninth Centuries AD* (Oxford, 2000), p. 1; K. R. Dark, *Britain and the End of the Roman Empire* (Stroud, 2000), pp. 53–7; White, *Britannia Prima*, especially pp. 20–9. Hilary Cool's demonstration that very late fourth- to fifth-century assemblages differ in composition and character from those of earlier periods may offer a partial solution to this problem (H. Cool, 'The parts left over: material culture into the fifth century' in T. Wilmott and P. Wilson (eds), *The Late Roman Transition in the North* (Oxford, 2000), pp. 47–65; H. Cool, *Eating and Drinking in Roman Britain* (Cambridge, 2006), pp. 222–38).

28 See, for example, Dark, *Britain*, pp. 56–7, who has some sensible points to make here. See Esmonde-Cleary, 'Britain in the fourth century', pp. 418–9, 424–5, on 'decline' versus 'change' in fourth-century British towns.

29   Esmonde-Cleary, *Ending of Roman Britain*, chapter 4; Esmonde-Cleary, 'Changing'; K. R. Dark, 'Proto-industrialisation and the end of the Roman economy' in Dark (ed.), *External Contacts*, pp. 1–21; Ward-Perkins, *The Fall of Rome*, especially pp. 123–4, 128 and fig. 6.1.

30   Esmonde-Cleary, *Ending of Roman Britain*, especially pp. 157–8; Dark & Dark, *Landscape of Roman Britain*, pp. 136–7; K. R. Dark, 'St Patrick's *villula* and the fifth-century occupation of Romano-British villas' in D. N. Dumville (ed.), *Saint Patrick A.D. 493–1993* (Woodbridge, 1993), pp. 19–24.

31   See, for example, P. Rahtz, 'Late Roman cemeteries and beyond' in R. Reece (ed.), *Burial in the Roman World* (London), pp. 53–64; P. Rahtz, 'Celtic society in Somerset, A.D. 400–700', *Bulletin of the Board of Celtic Studies*, 30 (1982), 176–200; M. Aston, 'Medieval settlement studies in Somerset' in M. Aston and C. Lewis (eds), *The Medieval Landscape of Wessex* (Oxford, 1994), p. 222; Ward-Perkins, *The Fall of Rome*, pp. 104, 108, 117–20. This 'invisible' material culture continues into the tenth century and even beyond in some areas.

32   Dark, *Britain*, pp. 150–202; Dark, *Civitas to Kingdom*; C. A. Snyder, *An Age of Tyrants: Britain and the Britons A.D. 400–600* (Stroud, 1998), especially pp. 225–32.

33   Attempts to deny that there was a significant migration to eastern Britain are unconvincing – see, for example, C. Scull, 'Approaches to the material culture and social dynamics of the migration period in eastern England' in J. Bintliff and H. Hamerow (eds), *Europe Between Late Antiquity and the Middle Ages* (Oxford, 1995), pp. 71–83. For the role played by immigrants from Scandinavia, see J. Hines, *The Scandinavian Character of Anglian England in the pre-Viking Period* (Oxford, 1984).

34   See M. Gelling, 'Why aren't we speaking Welsh?' *Anglo-Saxon Studies in Archaeology and History*, 6 (1993), 51–6, and below (pp. 110–11) on the place-name evidence for when British/Welsh began to die out as a spoken language in lowland Britain.

35   For example, S. Foot, 'The kingdom of Lindsey' in Vince, *Pre-Viking Lindsey*, pp. 128–40; P. H. Sawyer, *Anglo-Saxon Lincolnshire* (Lincoln, 1998), pp. 44–52; Leahy, *Kingdom of Lindsey*. For Mercia, see N. P. Brooks, 'The formation of the Mercian kingdom' in S. Bassett (ed.), *The Origins of Anglo-Saxon Kingdoms* (London, 1989), pp. 160–2.

36   D. N. Dumville, 'The Anglian Collection of royal genealogies and regnal lists', *Anglo-Saxon England*, 5 (1976), 23–50; Foot, 'Kingdom of Lindsey', pp. 129–35.

37   D. N. Dumville, 'The Tribal Hidage: an introduction to its texts and their history' in Bassett, *The Origins of Anglo-Saxon Kingdoms*, pp. 225–30. For more on the character and date of the 'Tribal Hidage', see below, pp. 163–7.

38 J. Campbell, 'Bede's *Reges* and *Principes*' in J. Campbell, *Essays in Anglo-Saxon History* (London, 1986), pp. 86, 88; Bede, *Historia Ecclesiastica*, for example at III.11, III.24, III.27, IV.3, IV.12. See below, pp. 59, 237–9 on the group-name *Lindisfaran*.

39 Foot, 'Kingdom of Lindsey', pp. 136–7.

40 F. M. Stenton, 'Lindsey and its kings' in D. M. Stenton (ed.), *Preparatory to Anglo-Saxon England* (Oxford, 1971), pp. 129–31; Foot, 'Kingdom of Lindsey', pp. 133–5, especially p. 135. For further discussion of this genealogy, see below, pp. 99–101.

41 Dumville, 'Tribal Hidage', pp. 226–7, 229; W. Davies and H. Vierck, 'The contexts of the Tribal Hidage: social aggregates and settlement patterns', *Frühmittelalterliche Studien*, 8 (1974), 233–6, 283; Hayes, 'Roman to Saxon', pp. 324–5; A. Crowson *et al*, *Anglo-Saxon Settlement on the Siltland of Eastern England* (Heckington, 2005), figs 1–2a and pp. 99, 265–6, 297, but see Sawyer, *Anglo-Saxon Lincolnshire*, pp. 47, 220–1, and below, p. 185.

42 Hayes, 'Roman to Saxon', pp. 324–25; Crowson *et al*, *Anglo-Saxon Settlement*, 1–2a and pp. 286, 298–9.

43 Dumville, 'Tribal Hidage', pp. 226–7, 229; D. N. Dumville, 'Essex, Middle Anglia and the expansion of Mercia' in Bassett, *The Origins of Anglo-Saxon Kingdoms*, pp. 130–1; D. Rollason, 'Lists of saints' resting places in Anglo-Saxon England', *Anglo-Saxon England*, 7 (1978), 89; D. Roffe, '*On middan Gyrwan fenne*: intercommoning around the island of Crowland', *Fenland Research*, 8 (1993), 80–6.

44 A. G. Vince and D. F. Williams, 'The characterization and interpretation of early to middle Saxon granitic tempered pottery in England', *Med. Arch.*, 41 (1997), 214–20; J. Huggett, 'Imported grave goods and the early Anglo-Saxon economy', *Med. Arch.*, 32 (1988), 63–96.

45 A. G. Vince, 'Lincoln in the early medieval era, between the 5th and 9th centuries: the archaeological account' in Stocker, *City by the Pool*, p. 143; M. Blackburn, 'Coin finds and coin circulation in Lindsey, *c*. 600–900' in Vince, *Pre-Viking Lindsey*, p. 83; K. U. Ulmschneider, 'Settlement, economy, and the "productive" site: Middle Anglo-Saxon Lincolnshire A.D. 650–780', *Med. Arch.*, 44 (2000), 53–79.

46 P. Everson, 'Pre-Viking settlement in Lindsey' in Vince, *Pre-Viking Lindsey*, p. 93; Taylor, *Village and Farmstead*, chapter 7. Even such a detailed and systematic field survey as the Fenland Project apparently saw some early to middle Anglo-Saxon pottery misidentified as Roman (Jane Young, personal communication).

47 Leahy, *Kingdom of Lindsey*, pp. 58, 127–8; Leahy, 'Anglo-Saxon settlement', pp. 31–2; Leahy, '*Interrupting the Pots*', p. 9.

48 Leahy, *Kingdom of Lindsey*, pp. 16–19, 58; Van de Noort & Ellis, *Wetland Heritage*; Lane, *Fenland Project Number 8*; Hayes & Lane, *Fenland Project Number 5*; Hayes, 'Roman to Saxon', pp. 321–6. However, see pp. 170–85

below on the Fenland. Whilst marine transgressions and the expansion of the freshwater fen in southern Lincolnshire would have undoubtedly led to the abandonment of some Late Roman settlements, the scale of this desertion can be vastly overestimated.

49　As also noted by, for example, Everson, 'Pre-Viking settlement', pp. 92–3.

50　There is a full discussion of this situation, and its implications, in Chapter 5, pp. 178–83; the points made there apply throughout the region. On British burial rites, see for example Rahtz, 'Late Roman cemeteries'; Rahtz, 'Celtic society'.

51　B. Ward-Perkins, 'Why did the Anglo-Saxons not become more British?', *EHR*, 115 (2000), 513–33, has some good discussion, especially his quotation from E. A. Freeman. See M. Welch, *Anglo-Saxon England* (London, 1992), p. 107, for a modern argument that the Anglo-Saxons inhabited 'a relatively empty landscape', and Wacher, *Towns of Roman Britain*, pp. 411–16, on plague. Against the notion of plague as a credible motor for fifth-century decline and population collapse, see especially M. Todd, '*Famosa pestis* and Britain in the fifth century', *Britannia*, 8 (1977), 319–25, and Esmonde-Cleary, *Ending of Roman Britain*, pp. 174–5.

52　S. P. Dark, 'Palaeoecological evidence for landscape continuity and change in Britain *ca* A.D. 400–800' in K. R. Dark (ed.), *External Contacts and the Economy of Late Roman and Post-Roman Britain* (Woodbridge, 1996), pp. 23–51; O. J. Rackham, *The History of the Countryside* (London, 1986), pp. 75–85; P. Murphy, 'The Anglo-Saxon landscape and rural economy: some results from sites in East Anglia and Essex' in J. Rackham (ed.), *Environment and Economy in Anglo-Saxon England* (York, 1994), pp. 23–39; S. Rippon, *Beyond the Medieval Village: The Diversification of Landscape Character in Southern Britain* (Oxford, 2009), for example pp. 166, 168–9.

53　See especially Murphy, 'Anglo-Saxon landscape', p. 37. It ought to be noted here that another oft-deployed argument in favour of a massive post-Roman population collapse – the supposed contrast between the estimated population in the fourth century and at Domesday – is just as methodologically flawed as that based on a comparison of supposed settlement density in the Romano-British and early Anglo-Saxon periods. One recent estimate for the population of Late Roman Britain is around 4 million (Millett, *Roman Britain*, pp. 44–6), whilst that for late eleventh-century England is perhaps 2–2.5 million (see, for example, J. S. Moore, 'Quot homines? The population of Domesday England', *Anglo-Norman Studies*, 19 (1997), 307–34), suggesting a major population fall. However, it must not be forgotten that we are not comparing like with like: Millett's figures are, on fuller examination, figures for Roman-era England, Wales, Scotland *and* Ireland. If we remove from the calculation those living outside of England then the Late Roman settled population is estimated to be around 1.5 to 2 million, which obviously removes the necessity to postulate any such massive reduction in the population between *c.* 400 and 1086.

54 Rackham, *History of the Countryside*, p. 67; Rippon, *Medieval Village*, pp. 166–7.

55 See T. Williamson, 'Settlement chronology and regional landscapes: the evidence from the claylands of East Anglia and Essex' in D. Hooke (ed.), *Anglo-Saxon Settlements* (Oxford, 1988), pp. 153–75; T. Williamson, *The Origins of Norfolk* (Manchester, 1993), pp. 24–5; S. Bassett, 'Beyond the edge of excavation: the topographical context of Goltho' in H. Mayr-Harting and R. I. Moore (eds), *Studies in Medieval History Presented to R. H. C. Davies* (London, 1985), pp. 21–39; Rippon, *Medieval Village*, pp. 156–67.

56 C. Scull, 'Urban centres in pre-Viking England?' in J. Hines (ed.), *The Anglo-Saxons from the Migration Period to the Eighth Century: An Ethnographic Perspective* (Woodbridge, 1997), pp. 269–98; Vince, 'Lincoln in the early medieval era'; K. Steane and A. Vince, 'Post-Roman Lincoln: archaeological evidence for activity in Lincoln from the 5th to the 9th centuries' in Vince, *Pre-Viking Lindsey*, pp. 71–9.

57 Bede, *Historia Ecclesiastica*, II.16. On Blæcca's status and potential links to the royal family of *Lindissi*, see below (pp. 105, 138) and, for example, S. Bassett, 'Lincoln and the Anglo-Saxon see of Lindsey', *Anglo-Saxon England*, 18 (1989), 11–12, and Leahy, *Kingdom of Lindsey*, pp. 114–15.

58 Leahy, 'Interrupting the Pots'; Leahy, 'Anglo-Saxon settlement', pp. 33, 36; Leahy, *Kingdom of Lindsey*, pp. 35–56.

59 For further discussion, see pp. 60–4, 200–09 below; Leahy, 'Anglo-Saxon settlement', p. 36; K. Leahy, 'The formation of the Anglo-Saxon kingdom of Lindsey', *Anglo-Saxon Studies in Archaeology and History*, 10 (1999), 129–30; Leahy, *Kingdom of Lindsey*, p. 49; Sawyer, *Anglo-Saxon Lincolnshire*, p. 51; H. Williams, 'Cemeteries as central places – place and identity in Migration Period eastern England' in B. Hårdh and L. Larsson (eds), *Central Places in the Migration and Merovingian Periods* (Stockholm, 2002), pp. 341–62.

60 D. Stocker, 'The early Church in Lincolnshire: a study of the sites and their significance' in Vince, *Pre-Viking Lindsey*, pp. 101–22; Bede, *Historia Ecclesiastica*, IV.3.

2
THE BRITISH COUNTRY OF *LINDĒS

Of the many questions that might be asked about the fifth and sixth centuries in this region, one of the most intriguing is how Lincoln changed from being a Roman provincial capital, controlled by a military-bureaucratic elite and populated by Romano-Britons, to a major centre of a minor Anglo-Saxon kingdom. The first part of the answer is fairly straightforward: with the withdrawal of official Roman support in AD 410, the Britons were left to fend for themselves, Britain ceased to be part of the Roman Empire, and Lincoln thus lost its official position as an imperial provincial capital.[1] For what happened next across lowland Britain as a whole, various models have been proposed. One is that a degree of central control probably persisted through at least part of the fifth century, unifying the diocese – or at least several of its provinces – under the rule of one of the former members of the Romano-British elite.[2] Alternatively, it has been suggested that the British elites took over the governance of their individual provinces, or that large-scale governance decayed completely and each local elite simply took over its local city territory.[3] In either case, there is additional uncertainty as to the fate of the resultant post-Roman British territories and whether they disappeared or were taken over by the Anglo-Saxon immigrants. It could be that, by and large, the immigrants simply overthrew the British elites in the fifth century, but then lived in relatively unstratified communities until they began organically to form new, Germanic, kingdoms in the mid–late sixth century.[4] On the other hand, it has been suggested that control of the British territories passed, peacefully or otherwise, to the Anglo-Saxons – an event often, but not always, placed in the fifth century – who then took over their rule and made use of their underlying organization.[5]

Determining which of these possible scenarios applied to eastern

Britain is generally exceedingly difficult, but we are unusually fortunate in dealing with the Lincoln area. Here a variety of linguistic, historical, literary and archaeological evidence all combines to indicate that local British elites did, at the very least, take over the territory of Lincoln itself. They were, furthermore, able to retain control of both the city and its hinterland into the sixth century. In addition, it seems clear that when the local Anglo-Saxon immigrants did gain final control of the region, they did not destroy all that they found, but instead took over the British territory within which they had settled. Naturally, the evidence for all of this is fragmentary, but its implications are clear, and the present chapter offers a detailed discussion of some of the most important material in support of this scenario. The following chapter then examines additional evidence, which not only bolsters the case, but also allows us to focus more clearly on the question of the relations between the Britons and the Anglo-Saxons in this region.[6]

Language and history in early Lincolnshire

Perhaps the best evidence for the existence of a significant British territory around Lincoln that was taken over, rather than destroyed, by the Anglo-Saxon immigrants of the fifth and sixth centuries comes from the kingdom-name *Lindissi*. Many pre-Viking, Anglo-Saxon kingdom-names from lowland Britain are of a descriptive type with solid Old English origins: for example, Wessex (the kingdom of the West Saxons), Essex (the East Saxons), Sussex (the South Saxons), East Anglia (the East Angles), and Mercia (the people of the border). *Lindissi* does, however, represent something rather different, and to understand this and its significance we have to look at the name in more detail.

The pre-Viking kingdom-name *Lindissi* (later *Lindesse*) is attested in multiple early sources, most notably throughout Bede's eighth-century *Historia Ecclesiastica* (completed AD 731). It also appears in the very early eighth-century 'Life of St Gregory', in the mid-eighth-century 'Acts of the Council of *Clofesho*' (747), and in the earliest manuscripts of the 'Anglo-Saxon Chronicle'.[7] It is not, however, the only known form of the name: *Lindesig/Lindissig* is used for this pre-Viking kingdom in both Asser's very late ninth-century 'Life of King

Alfred' (893) and a mid-eleventh-century manuscript of the 'Chronicle', and this form is ultimately the root of the medieval and modern district-name Lindsey.[8] Although there has occasionally been some debate over which of these names is the 'original' form of the pre-Viking kingdom-name (the former having an uncertain suffix, the latter Old English *-īg/-ēg*, 'island'), there seems no cogent reason for either doubting the priority and antiquity of the *Lindissi* form or treating it as being anything other than the kingdom-name that it is in all of our surviving early sources. The form *Lindesig/Lindissig* is most credibly seen as simply the result of a late misunderstanding/false explanation of the kingdom-name *Lindissi*, which involved *Lindissi*'s obscure final element being wrongly connected with Old English *-īg/ -ēg* ('island').[9]

Whatever the case may be on the kingdom-name, the key point here is that the language of the consistent first element of this kingdom-name is not, in fact, Old English at all. It is Late British, the language of the post-Roman Britons and ancestor of modern Welsh, and the element in question is actually a Late British population-group name – **Lindēs*, 'the people of *Lindon*'.[10] With regard to this name, we do need to be careful to distinguish between the ultimate provenance of a name and its actual meaning. In the case of **Lindēs*, it is almost certainly the British city-name *Lindon/*Lindocolōnia* – Lincoln – that is being referenced, not the local pool (British **lindo-*) from which the city ultimately took its name. Compare, for example, the fact that a modern-day Ludensian is someone associated with Louth (*Ludes* in Domesday), not someone associated with the 'loud river' (the Lud < Old English **hlūde*, 'the loud one') from which the town took its name. This is confirmed and taken further by an examination of similarly formed names in Welsh. Names such as **Lindēs* are never merely minor local names, nor indeed are they ever simply population-group names: they are always also district- or territory-names that refer both to a group of people *and* the territory that they inhabit.[11] Indeed, the final element in the name – Late British/Archaic Welsh *-ēs* – became *-wys* in later Welsh, and is found in major names such as that of the medieval Welsh kingdom of Powys. In this light, the notion that **Lindēs* referred only to a very small and specific group of people who lived in Lincoln, or by Brayford Pool, is untenable. The Late British tribal- and district-name

Lindēs should properly be translated as something more like 'the people of (the territory of the city of) Lincoln', with this territory being by necessity a reasonably extensive one.[12] Such a conclusion is, needless to say, important in the present context. The fact that the Anglo-Saxon kingdom-name *Lindissi/Lindesig* is derived from this Late British name does, on its own, require the pre-existence of a post-Roman British folk group and territory called *Lindēs*, which had Lincoln as its focus and which controlled a region that extended to some unknown but significant degree beyond the city. Furthermore, it indicates that the Anglo-Saxon kingdom of *Lindissi* had some sort of intimate connection with this British territory, as it took on its name.[13]

Further confirmation of the reality of this British territory, and the close links between it and the subsequent Anglo-Saxon kingdom of *Lindissi*, can be obtained from the collective group-name for the seventh-century and later Anglo-Saxon inhabitants of *Lindissi*. This, too, is found in two forms: *Lindisware* and *Lindisfaran* (Anglo-Latin *Lindisfari*). The latter is clearly the original form, being attested in multiple sources: for example, Bede's *Historia Ecclesiastica*, all manuscripts of the 'Tribal Hidage', the eighth-century 'Anglian Collection of royal genealogies and regnal lists', the pre-Viking Anglo-Saxon episcopal lists, and the subscriptions attached to the report of the Papal Legates of 786. The former is only attested once in a single, early twelfth-century manuscript of the 'Anglo-Saxon Chronicle'.[14] This group-name shares its initial element with the kingdom-name *Lindissi* – that is, Late British *Lindēs* – but that element is now paired with Old English *faran*. In light of other similar compounds of *faran* and its continental cognates in the early medieval period and the usage of this word in Old English, the meaning of this group-name is clear: the Anglo-Saxons of seventh-century *Lindissi* were, quite literally, 'the people who migrated, *faran*, to the territory of *Lindēs*'.[15] As such, the Anglo-Saxons of *Lindissi* seem not only to have borrowed the name of a pre-existing British territory for that of their kingdom, but also their own group-name actually made reference to the fact that they had arrived as immigrants to an already existing British territory called *Lindēs*.

A final confirmatory piece of linguistic evidence comes from the Cambro-Latin *Historia Brittonum*, written in 829/30 in north Wales, where we find reference to events which apparently took place *c.* 500 *in regione Linnuis* ('in the country of *Linnuis*').[16] Despite the sometimes wild guesses that have been made as to the identity of this *Linnuis*, its location is beyond reasonable doubt. Just as *Lindissi* involves the regular Old English development of Late British **Lindēs*, so too is *Linnuis* the regular ninth-century Old Welsh development of the same tribal- and territory-name: Late British **Lindēs* regularly became first Archaic Welsh **Linnēs* and then Old Welsh *Linnuis*.[17] The *Historia Brittonum*'s reference to *Linnuis* consequently suggests that some memory of a post-Roman, British population group and territory called **Lindēs* – 'the people of (the territory of the city of) Lincoln' – survived into early ninth-century Wales, something which is obviously of considerable significance in the present context. No other explanation seems plausible.[18] Furthermore, the meaning of the whole phrase *in regione Linnuis* ('in the country of *Linnuis*, **Lindēs*') supports the conclusion that this must have been an extensive territory.[19]

The archaeology of the 'country of **Lindēs*'

In Lincolnshire, the archaeological evidence for the settlement of significant numbers of Anglo-Saxons is initially concentrated in a number of large cremation cemeteries, which seem to have had their origins in the middle of the fifth century. One of the best known of these is at Cleatham, near Kirton-in-Lindsey, where 1,204 out of an original total of around 1,528 burials were recently excavated. Cemeteries such as these are suggestive of a degree of large-scale immigration.[20] Whether there were any Anglo-Saxons in the region much before the foundation of the cremation cemeteries is still very much a matter of opinion. There is a small, but fascinating, body of fourth- and early fifth-century 'Germanic' metalwork, which might be taken as indicative of a preceding stage of early and limited post-Roman 'federate' settlement (Fig. 10). However, the value of these pieces for establishing the date and nature of the settlement is questionable, given that they have usually not been found in excavated graves and thus the date of their deposition is impossible to ascertain. Indeed, finds of a similar antiquity from elsewhere in Britain have been discovered in contexts as late as the last quarter of the fifth century and beyond.[21] Given this, it is to the large cremation cemeteries that we must turn if we wish to understand early Anglo-Saxon settlement, and these have an intriguing tale to tell in the context of the above linguistic arguments for a British territory existing in the Lincoln region.

Perhaps the most striking thing about these cemeteries, from the point of view of the present work, is their distribution across the Lincolnshire landscape. Rather than being concentrated in one area, they are found at widely spaced locations around the county. This pattern is suggestive of each cemetery being at the centre of a defined territory, for which it presumably acted as both a central burial ground and a sacred and social focus and place of assembly.[22] The probable accuracy of this supposition is indicated by the subsequent history of the immediate vicinities of these cemeteries, most of which seem to have become the centres of later political and administrative territories.[23] Thus the Cleatham cemetery is actually located

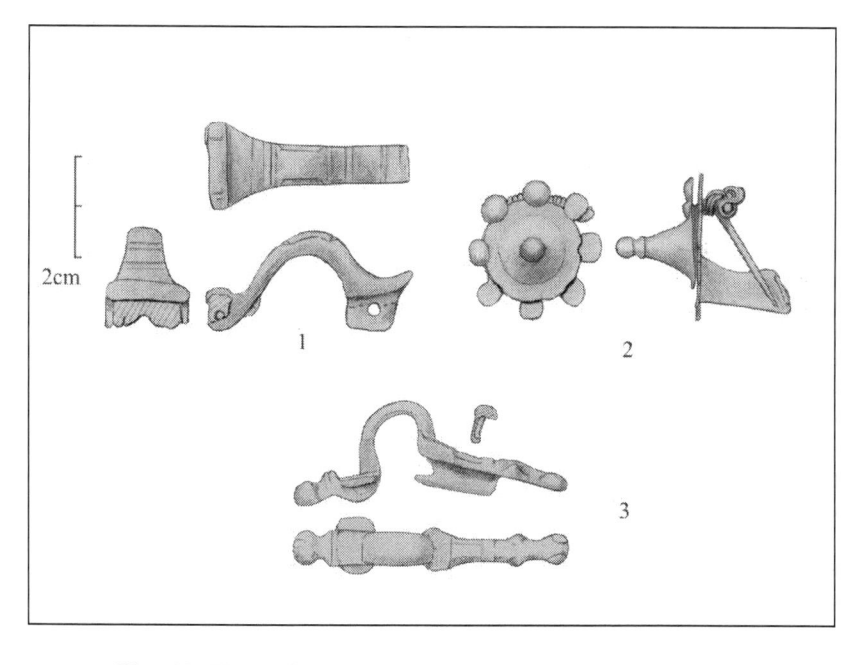

**Fig. 10 Early Germanic brooches from Lincolnshire,
1: Supporting-arm brooch, Newball. 2: Tutulus brooch,
Kirmington. 3: Group I cruciform brooch, Clixby.**
Source: Kevin Leahy

immediately to the north of Kirton-in-Lindsey (the pre-eminent Anglo-Saxon administrative centre of the West Riding of Lindsey) and is also close to the richest early Anglo-Saxon barrow-burial found in the region, at Caenby.[24] Similarly, the South Elkington cemetery (originally containing *c.* 1,200 cremation urns) is located just to the west of Louth. Louth was not only the centre of a pre-Viking monastic estate and a major Late Saxon administrative centre, but also has place-name evidence suggestive of a defined Anglo-Saxon *regio* dependent upon it: Ludborough ('the *burh*, fort, belonging to Louth'), five miles to its north, and Ludford ('the ford belonging to Louth'), eight miles to the west.[25] We find the same sort of situation elsewhere too. So the West Keal cemetery, which may have covered up to two acres and is considered to have been of a similar size to that at South Elkington,[26] is next door to Bolingbroke, a major Anglo-Saxon soke centre. Loveden Hill (the site of the second largest cremation cemetery in England, with over 1,800 burials) was the meeting place of a Late Saxon wapentake. Finally, Elsham cremation cemetery is located a couple of miles away from both the important manorial and soke centre of Barnetby-le-Wold and the meeting place of Yarborough Wapentake, the probably Late/post-Roman fort of Yarborough Camp.[27]

The key point here is, however, that these cremation cemeteries and their territories avoid Lincoln itself *entirely*, forming in effect a ring around the city. This 'ring' encloses a vast territory around Lincoln, with the closest of the large cremation cemeteries to the city being Loveden Hill (seventeen miles to the south) and Cleatham (nineteen miles to the north) (Fig. 11).[28] This avoidance is most unusual when compared with the situation found at other Roman towns in the region: York has cremation cemeteries at Heworth and The Mount; Leicester has a cremation cemetery at nearby Thurmaston and a mixed cremation and inhumation cemetery just outside of its east gate; Ancaster has a cremation cemetery to the south of its walls; and Caistor-by-Norwich has a large cemetery just outside its walls. As Kevin Leahy has argued, some explanation of this remarkable situation is demanded. The only plausible scenario is that the distribution of the early cremation cemeteries reflects some sort of British authority based at Lincoln, which continued to control the city and a significant area around it throughout the fifth century

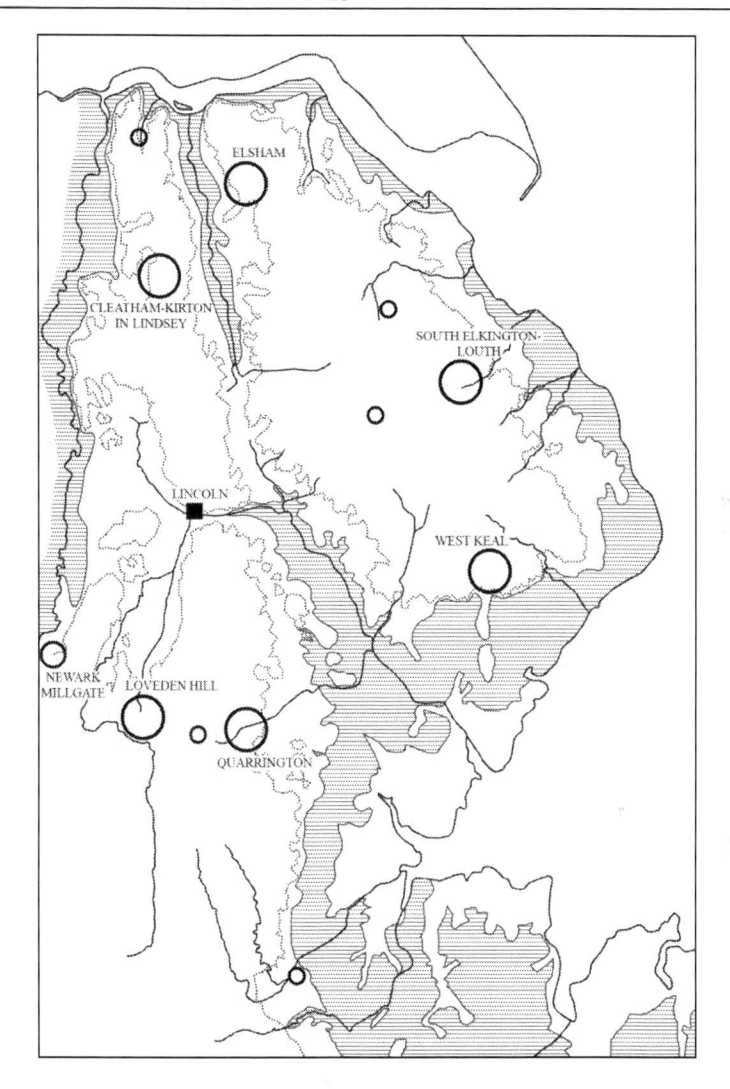

**Fig. 11 The cremation cemeteries of early Anglo-Saxon
Lincolnshire, with the larger cemeteries labelled**

and into the early sixth century, preventing the Anglo-Saxon groups
represented by the cremation cemeteries from settling in this
territory.[29]

This control only really appears to break down at some point after the early sixth century, when the small inhumation cemeteries (which first supplement and then replace the cremation cemeteries) begin to encroach upon Lincoln in a way that the earlier type of Anglo-Saxon burial grounds did not: examples are found only a few miles to both the north and south of Lincoln by the mid-sixth century. Moreover, even though this was clearly a significant development, it needs to be recognized that these inhumation cemeteries represent a very different phenomenon from the large urnfields. Whereas the latter could contain thousands of individual burials and are indicative of large-scale migration and settlement, these new inhumation cemeteries are always far smaller in scale, particularly those situated near to Lincoln. For example, the excavated sixth-century inhumation cemeteries at Welton and South Carlton have, so far, produced only eleven burials and four burials, respectively. The contrast with the huge cremation cemeteries, such as Loveden Hill and Cleatham (each containing more than 1,500 burials), is striking; but so too is that with the other local inhumation cemeteries which were located further away from Lincoln, such as Castledyke South (196 burials excavated out of *c.* 436), Sheffield's Hill I and II (129 burials), Welbeck Hill (77 burials), Ruskington (*c.* 180 burials) and Sleaford (241 graves excavated out of *c.* 600). Indeed, within Lincoln itself and its immediate hinterland there is little to no archaeological evidence for any pre-seventh-century Anglo-Saxon activity at all.[30]

Needless to say, there seems little reason to divorce the post-Roman British territory that is thus suggested by the distribution and nature of the early Anglo-Saxon burial evidence in the Lincoln region from the British 'country of **Lindēs*' that emerges from the linguistic material. As such, the burial evidence can offer considerable further support for the existence, significance and longevity of the latter territory, which appears on this basis to have been a sufficiently powerful force that it could control Anglo-Saxon settlement within its region into the early sixth century. However, the distribution of the cremation cemeteries is not the only possible source of archaeological evidence for the British 'country of **Lindēs*': even though the archaeological invisibility of the post-Roman Britons is generally a reality, we do have some positive evidence from Lincolnshire for the presence of British elites in the fifth and sixth centuries.

The first element of this comes from Lincoln itself. Whilst Lincoln may have produced little to no evidence for a pre-seventh-century Anglo-Saxon presence, this does not mean that there are no indications of activity in the city from that time. In particular, attention should be drawn to the site of St Paul in the Bail, inside the former Roman *forum*. Here there was a highly complex sequence of burials and buildings orientated east–west. One of the latter is now generally agreed to have been an apsidal timber church, and it overlays an earlier structure which belonged to the same building tradition, had the same orientation, and potentially had the same function.[31] Although there have been some attempts to identify the second of these churches as the one which Bede records Paulinus building in Lincoln *c.* 630, and which was still standing in his own day (*c.* 730), such a scenario requires an unreasonable degree of special pleading and strains both the evidence and credulity to breaking point. A far more convincing position is to see this sequence of churches as beginning in the late fourth or fifth century and then continuing in use during the early post-Roman period.[32]

Various points might be made in support of such a hypothesis. Of particular interest in this context is the position and orientation of the churches within the Roman *forum*. Both were located in the centre of the *forum* courtyard and were orientated with reasonable precision to follow the alignment of the *forum* itself. In addition, the proximity of the unexcavated west ends of both churches to the western portico of the *forum* strongly suggests that they were designed to be entered from between its columns (Fig. 12).[33] This obviously offers considerable support for the scenario outlined above, and the radiocarbon dates of a number of the burials which are found surrounding, within and cutting the walls of the second church are similarly noteworthy. One of the most important of these appears to be a foundation deposit for the second church, and this has a medial date of cal AD 441 within a likely date range from the very late fourth to the mid–late sixth century.[34] Also highly relevant are three burials which must postdate the demolition of the second church, as two of them cut the wall-line and the third comes from what had been the interior of the church, cutting a post-church layer.[35] The calibrated radiocarbon date ranges of these burials indicate that they were amongst the earliest burials from the graveyard-stage of the site,

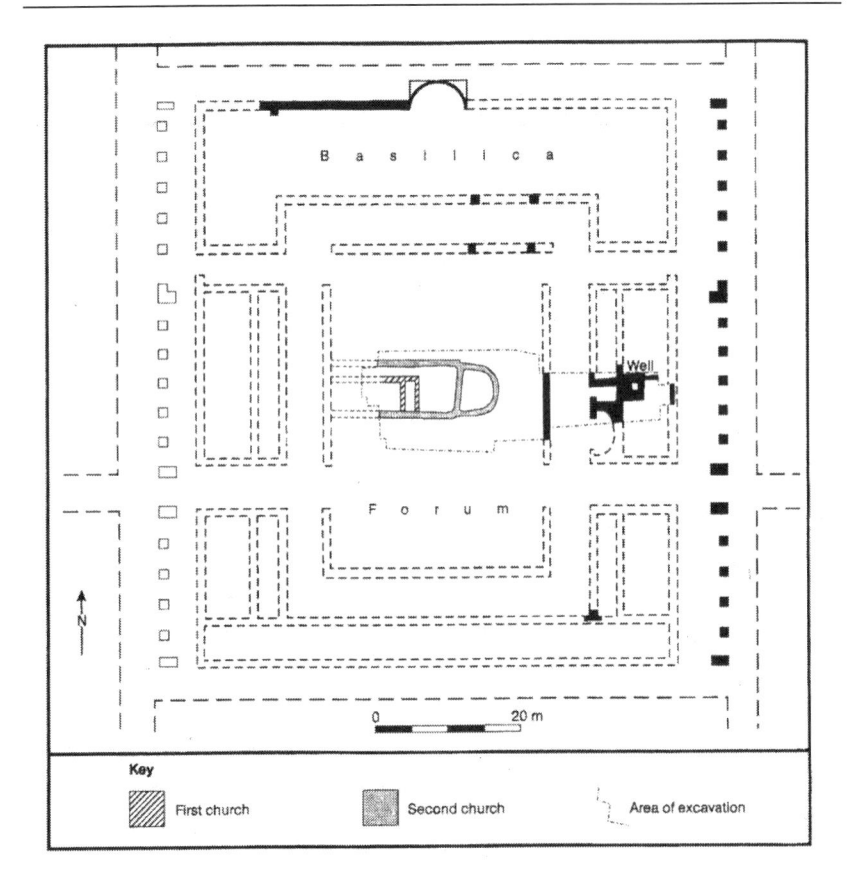

Fig. 12 The sequence of buildings at St Paul in the Bail, Lincoln, showing their relationship to the Roman *forum*
Copyright: English Heritage

which, as Brian Gilmour has demonstrated, almost certainly only began after the demolition of the second church had taken place.[36] What is especially significant here, however, is that whilst there is certainly a chance that each of these three post-church burials dates from after *c.* 600, the 'joint probability' that *all three* do so is, in fact, far lower than the probability that any single one of them does. Indeed, Bayesian modelling of the radiocarbon dates of these burials indicates that there is a high probability (>85%) that the second church was demolished before AD 600, given their relationship to this structure. Furthermore, if the graveyard stage as a whole postdates this church, as it is believed to, then an end to the church sequence before 600 becomes even more likely, although the available evidence would still just allow for a demolition as late as the early seventh century.[37]

In light of the above, it seems more than credible that we have here a late fourth- or fifth-century Romano-British church set up in a significant area of the city (the centre of the *forum*) and that this was rebuilt at some point, possibly in the mid–late fifth to early sixth centuries, into a larger apsidal structure. It then continued in use into the sixth century and perhaps a little beyond. Such a sequence of Late and post-Roman churches would certainly have a plausible context within Late and post-Roman Britain, as well as the Empire at large. After all, just about the only sin that Gildas does not accuse his fellow sixth-century Britons of is paganism, indicating that he considered them to be Christians, albeit sinful ones.[38] Any significant British polity based at Lincoln might thus be expected to have contained at least one church. Indeed, one attractive interpretation of the role and importance of the St Paul in the Bail churches stems from the fact that Lincoln seems to have had its own bishop from the early fourth century, when Adelphius, Bishop of Lincoln, was sent to the Council of Arles (314). In this context, the St Paul in the Bail sequence could be seen as part of a continuing episcopal establishment in what had been one of the capital towns of Late Roman Britain and was now the centre of a British territory.[39] Parallels for the continuing existence of such religious centres into the fifth century and beyond are to be seen in the West Midlands, where Steven Bassett has demonstrated that there were very probably British bishops in places such as Gloucester and Lichfield before there were Anglo-Saxon ones, and in other areas of Britain, such as at Exeter.[40]

Once again, then, the picture drawn from the archaeology accords very well with the linguistic evidence for a post-Roman British 'country of *Lindēs*', whilst adding yet more weight to the arguments made previously for the existence, significance and longevity of this polity. With these two successive churches in the centre of the *forum*, we have credible evidence for the existence of a British Christian community at the centre of fifth- to sixth-century Lincoln. Furthermore, this community not only appears to have

Fig. 13 Reconstruction of the apsidal church at St Paul in the Bail, Lincoln, within the Roman *forum*

Copyright: Society for Lincolnshire History & Archaeology, by David Vale

continued to use the *forum* and had a timber church there, but it also at some point decided to replace the first church with a somewhat larger structure, capable of holding around 100 worshippers, an action which was indicative of both power and confidence (Fig. 13). Finally, the likely period in which the second church was demolished and replaced by a graveyard is also telling, given that the Anglo-Saxon cemetery evidence discussed previously is indicative of a decline in the ability of Lincoln to control the settlement of Anglo-Saxons in the region during the course of the sixth century.

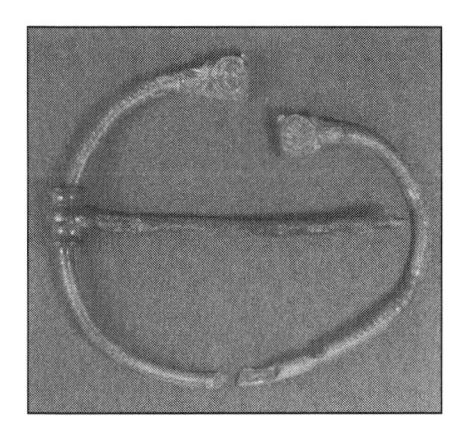

Fig. 14 An enamelled Class 1 brooch from East Ravendale
Source: Kevin Leahy, Portable Antiquities Scheme

The second major element of positive archaeological evidence for the British 'country of *Lindēs*' is represented by finds of post-Roman British metalwork from the county, especially brooches. Such brooches are rare in national terms, a consequence to some degree of the collapse in material culture suffered by the Britons in the first decades of the fifth century, and this is especially true for those areas which lie within the archaeologically described limits of fifth-century Anglo-Saxon settlement.[41] However, whilst this rule generally holds good, it fails in one specific area, namely Lincolnshire. The most important illustration of this comes from the seventeen or eighteen post-Roman, British Class 1 penannular brooches which are now known from the Lincoln region, all of which probably belong to the fifth and sixth centuries.[42] This total is comparable in size not only with the total number of these brooches known from the whole of the rest of the zone of Anglo-Saxon settlement, but also with the number recorded from the individual core areas for this class of brooch in northern and western Britain (Figs 14 and 15).[43] Such a situation naturally suggests that something quite unusual is happening

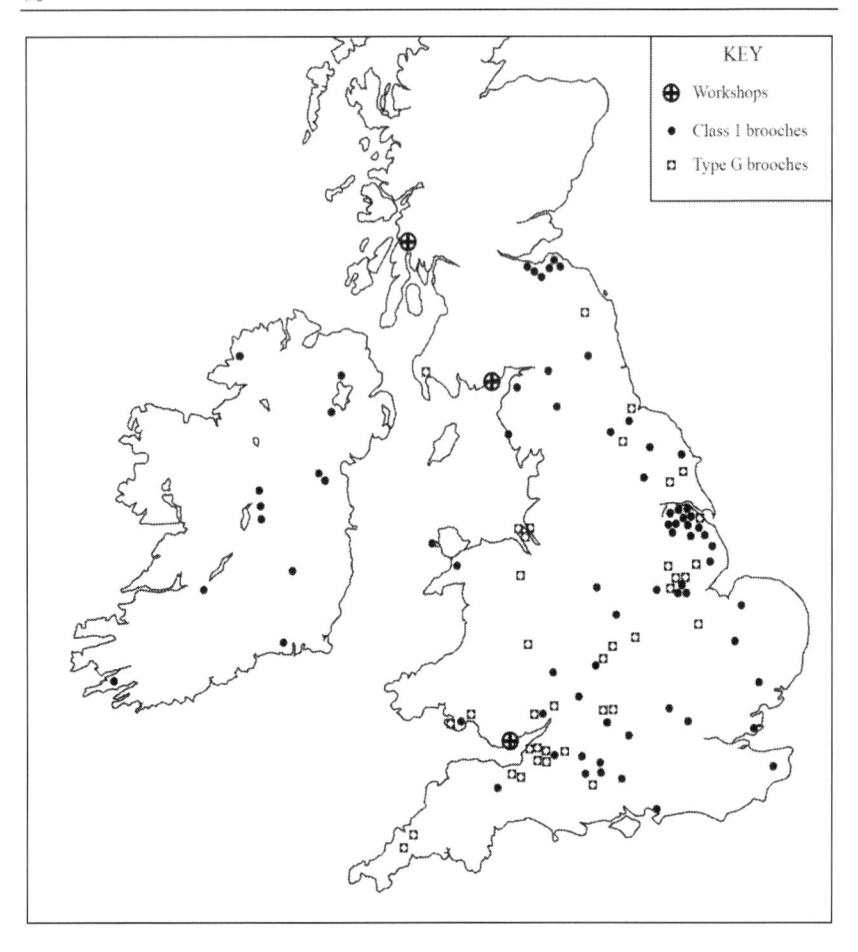

Fig. 15 The distribution of British Class 1 and Type G brooches across Britain and Ireland. Three workshops are marked with encircled crosses at (from south to north) Dinas Powys, the Mote of Mark, and Dunadd

After S. Youngs, 'Britain, Wales and Ireland: holding things together' in K. Jankulak and J. M. Wooding (eds), *Ireland and Wales in the Middle Ages* (Dublin, 2007), with additions

in Lincolnshire at this time, a sense heightened when one realizes that Class 1 brooches are considered to be British elite objects used for high-status symbolic display, and that there is evidence for the local production of at least some of the corpus in the Lincoln region itself.[44]

Consequently, we have in fifth- and sixth-century Lincolnshire a very active local tradition of not only wearing but apparently also of making these obviously non-Anglo-Saxon pieces of British elite symbolism. Given the number of Class 1 brooches involved, their rarity elsewhere in the zone of Anglo-Saxon settlement, and the evidence for their local production in the Lincoln region, it is very difficult to consider them as merely the product of trade or exchange between western/northern Britons and Lincolnshire Anglo-Saxons. A more credible alternative explanation for the significant concentration of these fifth- and sixth-century brooches in the Lincoln region is, however, available. This is that these brooches were being imported by and made for local British elites within the 'country of *Lindēs*' who wished to signal and reinforce their ethnic identity and status in response, and in opposition, to the very visible material culture of competing local Anglo-Saxon groups that had settled on the edges of this British territory in the mid–late fifth century. Certainly, in this context their quantity within Lincolnshire accords well with other early medieval evidence for the exceptional use of ethnic status symbols by elites who felt themselves threatened by neighbouring groups. This is true too of their distribution, with the brooches being found in those areas where local British elites would have directly encountered Anglo-Saxons, rather than in the apparently immigrant-free zone around the centre of the British territory, Lincoln itself (Figs 11 and 16: compare, for example, the distribution of Frankish elite display objects in the Merovingian Frankish kingdom, which follows the same pattern).[45]

If the Class 1 pennanular brooches thus offer further support for the existence and longevity of the 'country of *Lindēs*' and are indicative of fifth- and sixth-century British elites existing in its more peripheral parts, they are not the only potential positive evidence from metalwork for the existence of such elites in the Lincoln region. One might also cite, for example, the very significant concentration of British high-status fifth- to sixth-century Type G penannular brooches in the Lincoln region in support of the above, particularly as their distribution seems to both accord well with and reinforce that of the Class 1 brooches (Figs 16 and 17).[46] Similarly important is the fact that there is an astonishing number of 'Late Celtic' hanging bowls (or

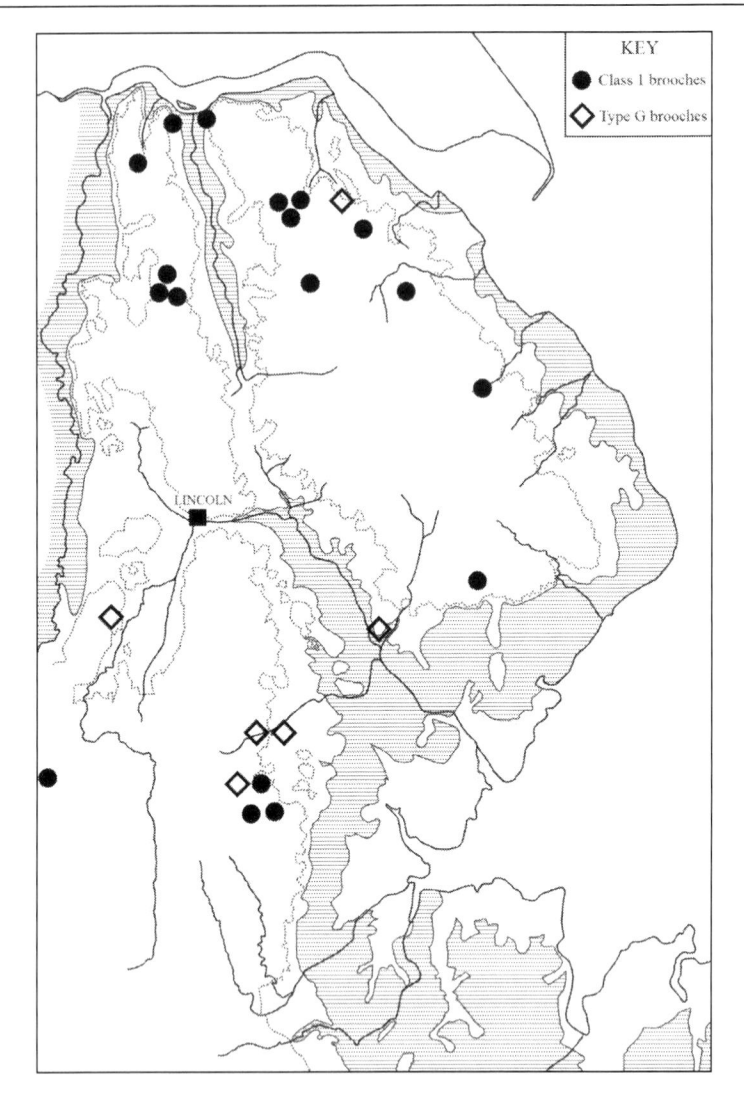

Fig. 16 The distribution of British Class 1 and Type G brooches in the Lincoln region

fragments of the same) known from the region. As with the Class 1 and Type G brooches, we again have a situation in which many more examples of these items of prestige metalwork have been found in Lincolnshire than in any other comparable area of Anglo-Saxon

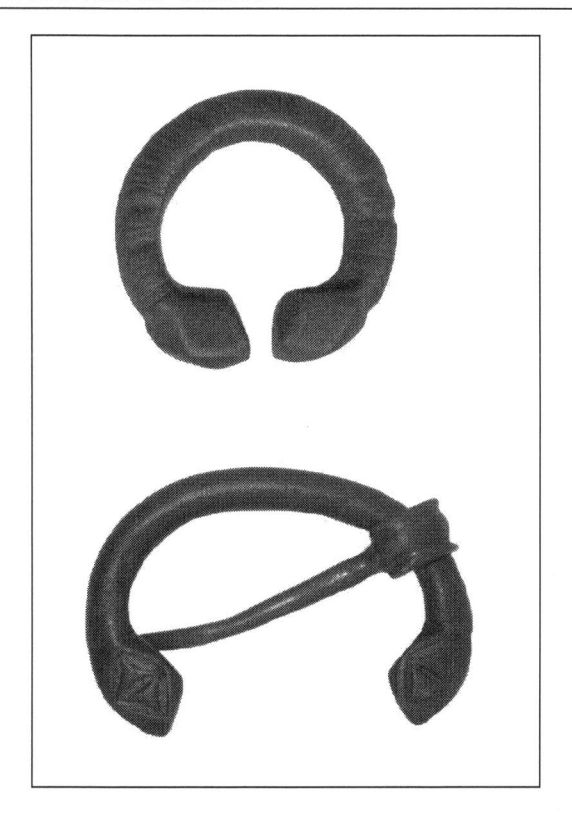

Fig. 17 British Type G brooch from Keelby in Lincolnshire (top) and an apparent hybrid Type G/Class 1 enamelled brooch from Norton Disney (bottom)
Source: Adam Daubney, Portable Antiquities Scheme

England, with twenty-three hanging bowls now known from Lindsey alone and another eleven from the south of the county (Fig. 18).[47] Although around a third of these have been found in late sixth-/seventh-century 'Anglo-Saxon' graves, it is important to recognize that this does not reflect their original function, but should be considered a secondary usage of these items. As has been reaffirmed by Rupert Bruce-Mitford and Susan Youngs, hanging bowls were probably originally high-status pieces of British tableware, made chiefly for British patrons in the fifth to seventh centuries.[48] As such, the remarkable concentration of these items all across the Lincoln region is extremely interesting and requires explanation. Seventh-century British–Anglian trading and importation is perhaps more credible as a possible mechanism for bringing some of these pieces of British prestige metalwork into Lincolnshire than is the case with the Class 1 brooches.[49] However, it still seems insufficient as an overall explanation for their presence, given the sheer number of items involved and the likely early dates of manufacture of some of the Lincolnshire bowls (notably those from Caistor and Sleaford, both probably of fifth-century date: Fig. 19).[50] Moreover, as with Class 1 brooches, such an interpretation would not address the question of why these British hanging bowls seem to have been so much more popular in this particular region than they were in other comparable parts of eastern and southern Britain. All told, it is very difficult to avoid seeking a solution to these issues in the context established above, with the number and concentration of finds in Lincolnshire thus being considered to ultimately reflect, once again, the presence here of a significant British elite in the fifth to sixth centuries. This elite would have commissioned, made use of and popularized such items of high-status British tableware, with the later Anglo-Saxon usage and demand for these pieces then stemming from this situation.[51]

The 'country of *Lindēs*': a new 'lost kingdom' found?

The evidence discussed above does not stand alone, but it is enough when taken together to require that a British 'country of *Lindēs*' must have been based at the former provincial capital, Lincoln, in the post-Roman period – no other explanation can carry conviction. Further supporting material is discussed in the following chapter, but the picture presented above is consistent and convincing. This was a polity of such significance that not only does its existence appear to have been remembered in ninth-century Wales, but the Anglo-Saxons of seventh-century *Lindissi* also used its name for their own kingdom and made explicit reference to their origins as migrants into the 'country of *Lindēs*' in their group-name, the *Lindisfaran*. Similarly, the distribution of the large Anglo-Saxon cremation cemeteries around and at some distance away from Lincoln seems indicative of an important British polity that encompassed a substantial territory to

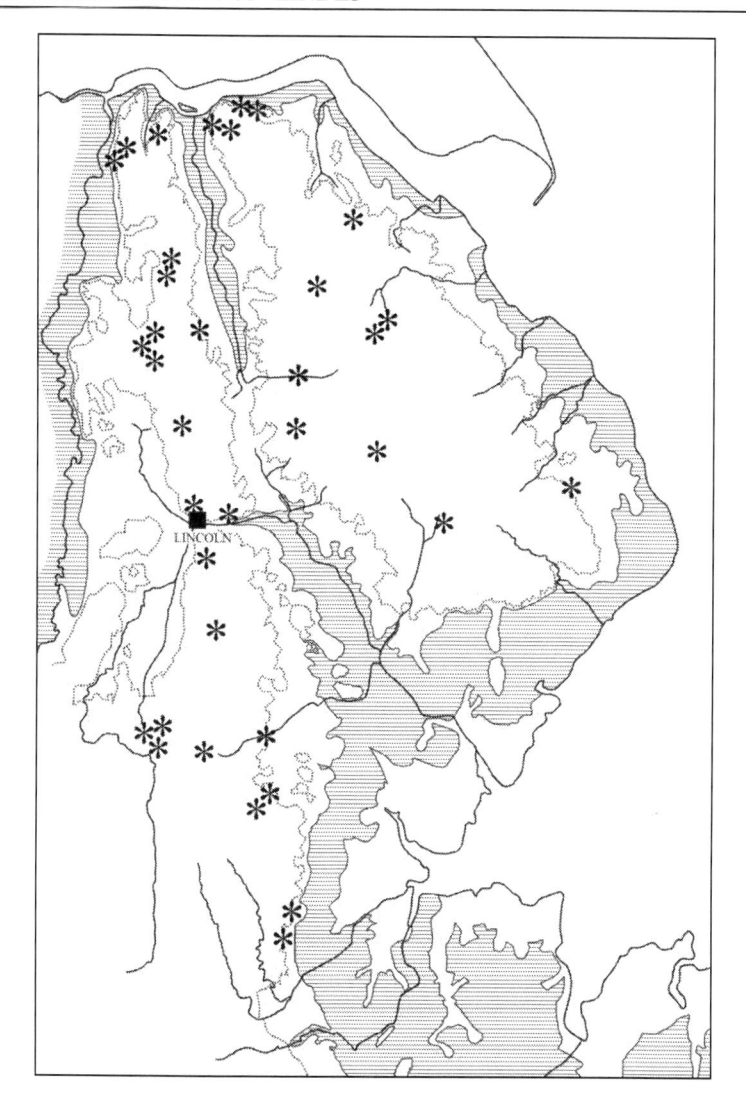

Fig. 18 The distribution of hanging bowls in Lincolnshire

both its north and south, within which significant Anglo-Saxon settlement was constrained. This situation looks to have been maintained not only throughout the fifth century, but also into the early sixth century, and this 'core' territory was only really notably encroached upon by Anglo-Saxon sites from this point onwards.

Even then, the small Anglo-Saxon inhumation cemeteries that did lie closer to Lincoln by the mid-sixth century – still not within it or its immediate hinterland – were on nothing like the scale of the earlier cremation cemeteries or even that of the contemporary inhumation cemeteries which were sited further away from Lincoln. Further confirmation of a powerful and confident British elite in post-Roman Lincolnshire is provided by the sequence of churches in the centre of Lincoln's Roman *forum* (especially the post-Roman rebuilding of the first church into a more impressive apsidal structure, which could hold around 100 worshippers), together with the astonishing concentration of British fifth- to sixth-century elite metalwork that has been found in the region.

Accepting the reality of this 'British kingdom of Lindsey', the Late Roman context established in the previous chapter provides a credible answer to the natural question of why a British polity powerful enough to survive into the sixth century might have emerged at Lincoln. Not only was Lincoln a former Roman provincial capital and the seat of one of *Britannia*'s four metropolitan bishops (a potentially very significant point in light of the evidence for Late and post-Roman Christian activity in the town), but the city also appears to have remained prosperous and centrally organized to a remarkably late date. Thus there is evidence from Lincoln for specialist industry, cohesive central organization, a considerable (though probably

Fig. 19 A probably fifth-century hanging bowl found at Caistor
Source: City of Lincoln Council, R. Bruce-Mitford, 'Late Celtic hanging bowls in Lincolnshire and South Humberside' in A. Vince (ed.), *Pre-Viking Lindsey* (Lincoln, 1993)

declining) population and a thriving market right into the very late fourth century. Furthermore, both the *forum* and the likely residence of the provincial governor – Greetwell Villa – seem to have remained in use into the fifth century. In this light, the existence and longevity of the 'country of *Lindēs*' is at least partly explicable as a function of both the high status of the city in the Late Roman period and its surprising vitality when compared with other towns at that time. The question is: if the 'country of *Lindēs*' had its origins as a polity formed out of the territory dependent upon Late Roman Lincoln (presumably by members of the local Romano-British aristocracy), how did it finally come to an end? Moreover, what was the nature of the relationship between the Britons of *Lindēs* and the Anglo-Saxons who had settled in their territory?

Notes to Chapter 2

1 S. Esmonde-Cleary, *The Ending of Roman Britain* (London, 1989), pp. 136–61; see, however, I. N. Wood, 'The final phase' in M. Todd (ed.), *A Companion to Roman Britain* (Oxford, 2004), pp. 428–42, for the suggestion that at least some Britons continued to see themselves as part of the Roman world well into the fifth century.

2 J. Morris, *The Age of Arthur* (London, 1973); M. Welch, 'The archaeological evidence for federate settlement in Britain within the fifth century' in F. Vallet and M. Kazanski (eds), *L'Armée Romaine et les Barbares du IIIe au VIIe Siècle* (Rouen, 1993), pp. 269–77; D. N. Dumville, 'The idea of government in sub-Roman Britain' in G. Ausenda (ed.), *After Empire: Towards an Ethnology of Europe's Barbarians* (Woodbridge, 1995), pp. 180–3.

3 Dumville, 'Idea of Government'; B. Yorke, 'Anglo-Saxon *gentes* and *regna*' in H-W. Goetz *et al* (eds), *Regna and Gentes: The Relationship Between Late Antique and Early Medieval Peoples and Kingdoms in the Transformation of the Roman World* (Leiden, 2003), pp. 395–401; R. White, *Britannia Prima: Britain's Last Roman Province* (Stroud, 2007), especially pp. 197–201; C. A. Snyder, *An Age of Tyrants: Britain and the Britons A.D. 400–600* (Stroud, 1998), pp. 225–32; K. R. Dark, *Civitas to Kingdom: British Political Continuity 300–800* (London, 1994), pp. 144–9.

4 See the discussion in Yorke, 'Anglo-Saxon *gentes* and *regna*', pp. 382–5; H. Hamerow, 'The earliest Anglo-Saxon kingdoms' in P. Fouracre (ed.), *The New Cambridge Medieval History, I: c.500–c.700* (Cambridge, 2005), pp. 263–88, especially pp. 281–6; S. Bassett, 'In search of the origins of Anglo-Saxon kingdoms' in S. Bassett (ed.), *The Origins of Anglo-Saxon Kingdoms* (London, 1989), pp. 3–27.

5   For example, Yorke, 'Anglo-Saxon *gentes* and *regna*', p. 396; N. P. Brooks, 'The creation and early structure of the kingdom of Kent' in Bassett, *Origins of Anglo-Saxon Kingdoms*, pp. 57–8; Bassett, 'In search', p. 24.

6   For an earlier discussion of some of this evidence, see C. Green, 'The British kingdom of Lindsey', *Cambrian Medieval Celtic Studies*, 56 (2008), 1–43.

7   B. Colgrave (ed. and trans.), *The Earliest Life of St Gregory* (Cambridge, 1968), chapter 18 (pp. 69, 102); Bede, *Historia Ecclesiastica*, Preface, II.16 etc.; Haddan and Stubbs, *Councils and Ecclesiastical Documents Relating to Great Britain and Ireland* (3 vols, Oxford, 1869–79), vol. 3, p. 362; and, for example, 'Anglo-Saxon Chronicle' MS A, s.a. 838, 873 and 874.

8   Asser, *Life of King Alfred*, ed. W. H. Stevenson (Oxford, 1904), chapters 45 and 46 (p. 34), *Lindesig/Lindissig*; 'Anglo-Saxon Chronicle' MS D, s.a. 838, *Lindesige*; note, the interest is in the use of this form for the pre-Viking kingdom, not for the post-Viking and medieval district of Lindsey. See Chapter 4, pp. 128–36, for more on the question of the relationship between *Lindissi*'s borders and the boundaries of the district of Lindsey, and also on what the form *Lindesig/Lindissig* can tell us with regard to this (especially p. 155, endnote 11). It is accepted by all recent commentators that *Lindesig/Lindissig* is a separate form from *Lindissi*, with the name 'Lindsey' deriving from *Lindesig/Lindissig* rather than from *Lindissi* – see, for example, K. Cameron, *The Place-Names of Lincolnshire*, II (Nottingham, 1991), pp. 2–7, which includes a selection of the attested forms of *Lindissi/Lindesig*; M. Gelling, 'The name Lindsey', *Anglo-Saxon England*, 18 (1989), 31–2; and V. Watts, *The Cambridge Dictionary of English Place-Names* (Cambridge, 2004), p. 374.

9   P. H. Sawyer, *Anglo-Saxon Lincolnshire* (Lincoln, 1998), pp. 9–10; Asser, *Life of King Alfred*, p. 242; B. Cox, 'The pattern of Old English *burh* in early Lindsey', *Anglo-Saxon England*, 23 (1994), 54–6; R. Coates, 'Reflections on some major Lincolnshire place-names. Part one: Algarkirk to Melton Ross', *Journal of the English Place-Name Society*, 40 (2008), 80; Watts, *Dictionary*, p. 374; and Green, 'British kingdom', 2, fn. 6, *contra* S. Bassett, 'Lincoln and the Anglo-Saxon see of Lindsey', *Anglo-Saxon England*, 18 (1989), 1–31, and Gelling, 'Lindsey'. With regard to why the name *Lindissi* was connected with *-īg*, beyond its unintelligible second element, see below, p. 155, endnote 11.

10 Green, 'British kingdom', 2–3; K. H. Jackson, *Language and History in Early Britain* (Edinburgh, 1953), pp. 332, 543; Cameron, *Lincolnshire II*, pp. 2–7.

11 See Jackson, *Language and History*, p. 543; K. H. Jackson, 'Once again Arthur's battles', *Modern Philology*, 43 (1945), 48; J. T. Koch, *The Gododdin of Aneirin: Text and Context from Dark-Age North Britain* (Cardiff, 1997), p. 133.

12 See, for example, J. T. Koch (ed.), *Celtic Culture, A Historical Encyclopedia* (Oxford, 2006), p. 1158 and p. 1498, where Koch refers to 'the *-wys*

kingdom suffix'; see Bassett, 'Lincoln', 7–8, for the rejected suggestion that *Lindēs* might refer only to the people who lived in Lincoln.

13 A comparison might usefully be made here with the Anglo-Saxon kingdom of Kent, the name of which similarly had its origins in the British past (Brooks, 'Kingdom of Kent', especially pp. 57–8). With regard to *Lindissi*, it should be noted that Richard Coates has suggested that the entire kingdom-name *Lindissi* should potentially be seen as British in origin, deriving from **Lindēssi*, 'place/territory of **Lindēs*' (Coates, 'Reflections', 80–2), rather than an uncertain Old English suffix being added to *Lindis-* (for Late British **Lindēs* > Old English *Lindis-*, compare Leeds – **Lātenses* > **Lōdēs* > *Loidis* in Bede's *Historia Ecclesiastica*, II. 14, see K. H. Jackson, 'On the name "Leeds"', *Ant.*, 20 (1946), 209–10). On the whole, the author of the present work would consider this unlikely, given the difficulty in finding appropriate parallels for such a construction and the plentiful evidence for *-ēs/-wys* names standing on their own as territory- and group-names. Indeed, having a British place-name suffix used to form (extremely infrequently) district-names added to a name which was already implicitly a district-name would not only be unparalleled but also perhaps a little odd. On the other hand, the suggestion at least has the merit of fully explaining the form *Lindissi* without relying on an uncertain Old English suffix.

14 See Green, 'British kingdom', 3–4, fn. 15, and J. Insley and M. Eggers, 'Lindsey', *Reallexikon der Germanischen Altertumskunde*, 18 (Berlin, 2001), 475. *Lindisware* is almost certainly a false creation intended to bring the *Lindissi* group-name into line with others of the type *X-ware*: for example, the *Meanware* of east Hampshire and the *Cantware* of Kent. The notion that *Lindisware* is the original form and *Lindisfaran* the false one, somehow borrowed from the name Lindisfarne (R. Coates and A. Breeze, *Celtic Voices, English Places. Studies of the Celtic Impact on Place-names in England* (Stamford, 2000), pp. 243–6), is both far-fetched and untenable, being utterly out of accord with the evidence we actually possess for this group-name. It moreover relies upon a 'Celtic' origin for the name Lindisfarne, which is itself an extremely dubious proposition. See further below, pp. 235–42, on the origin of the name 'Lindisfarne' and its relationship to the group-name *Lindisfaran*.

15 See particularly T. Charles-Edwards and P. Wormald, 'Addenda' in J. M. Wallace-Hadrill, *Bede's Ecclesiastical History of the English People: A Historical Commentary* (Oxford, 1988), pp. 234–5; Green, 'British kingdom', 3–4; and especially below, pp. 238–9. With regard to Gelling's suggested etymology for *Lindisfaran*, 'the people who resort to a place named *Lindis-*' (Gelling, 'Lindsey', p. 32), this ceases to be at all credible once we (1) reject Bassett's hypothesis that the names **Lindēs* and *Lindesig/Lindissi* were all restricted originally to Lincoln alone, rather than being the genuine territory-/

kingdom-names they clearly were (see above), and (2) give a more detailed consideration to the potential meaning of Old English *faran* in such a group-name.

16 *Historia Brittonum*, chapter 56, in J. Morris (ed. and trans.), *Nennius. British History and the Welsh Annals* (London, 1980), p. 76; J. T. Koch and J. Carey, *The Celtic Heroic Age: Literary Sources for Ancient Celtic Europe and Early Medieval Ireland and Wales* (Aberystwyth, 2003), p. 299; endnote 19, below. For date and provenance, see D. N. Dumville, 'Some aspects of the chronology of the *Historia Brittonum*', *Bulletin of the Board of Celtic Studies*, 25 (1974), 439–45, and 'The historical value of the *Historia Brittonum*', *Arthurian Literature*, 6 (1986), 1–26.

17 Green, 'British kingdom', 5; Jackson, 'Once Again', 47–8.

18 Old Welsh *Linnuis* cannot be derived from Old English *Lindissi/Lindesig*, and no **Lindēs* other than that which underlies the pre-Viking kingdom-name *Lindissi* is known from Britain for *Linnuis* to have developed from. All other suggestions, when not philologically impossible, are purely hypothetical with no evidence of their real existence outside of the *Historia Brittonum*, and most that have been made despite this fall foul of the fact that 'folk-names in *-wys* [< Old Welsh *-uis* < Archaic Welsh/Late British **-ēs*] are not formed from minor localities' (Koch, *Gododdin of Aneirin*, p. 133).

19 Jackson, 'Once Again', p. 48; Koch & Carey, *Celtic Heroic Age*, p. 299. Compare the usage of this term for various kingdoms (including Gwynedd) in the *Historia Brittonum*, for example in chapter 40.

20 See K. Leahy, 'Interrupting the Pots': The Excavation of Cleatham Anglo-Saxon Cemetery* (York, 2007); C. Scull, 'Approaches to the material culture and social dynamics of the migration period in eastern England' in J. Bintliff and H. Hamerow (eds), *Europe Between Late Antiquity and the Middle Ages* (Oxford, 1995), pp. 71–83.

21 K. Leahy 'The Formation of the Anglo-Saxon kingdom of Lindsey', *Anglo-Saxon Studies in Archaeology and History*, 10 (1999), 129; Welch, 'Federate Settlement'; J. Hines, 'Philology, archaeology and the *adventus Saxonum vel Anglorum*' in A. Bammesberger and A. Wollmann (eds), *Britain 400–600: Language and History* (Heidelberg, 1990), pp. 21–2.

22 K. Leahy, 'The Anglo-Saxon settlement of Lindsey' in A. Vince (ed.), *Pre-Viking Lindsey* (Lincoln, 1993), p. 36; K. Leahy, *The Anglo-Saxon Kingdom of Lindsey* (Stroud, 2007), p. 48. For the role of cremation cemeteries as early Anglo-Saxon 'central places', see generally H. Williams, 'Cemeteries as central places – place and identity in Migration Period eastern England' in B. Hårdh and L. Larsson (eds), *Central Places in the Migration and Merovingian Periods* (Stockholm, 2002), pp. 341–62, and H. Williams, 'Assembling the dead' in A. Pantos and S. Semple (eds), *Assembly Places and Practices in Medieval Europe* (Dublin, 2004), pp. 109–34.

23 Leahy, *Kingdom of Lindsey*, p. 49; Leahy, 'Interrupting the Pots', p. 6; Sawyer, *Anglo-Saxon Lincolnshire*, p. 51; B. Eagles, 'Lindsey' in Bassett, *Origins of Anglo-Saxon Kingdoms*, p. 211; P. Everson, 'Pre-Viking settlement in Lindsey' in Vince, *Pre-Viking Lindsey*, p. 98; Williams, 'Cemeteries as central places'. See also below, chapter 5, especially pp. 185–209. For a comparable situation in Norfolk, see T. Williamson, *The Origins of Norfolk* (Manchester, 1993), pp. 68, 102–4.

24 Everson, 'Pre-Viking settlement', pp. 96–8; Leahy, *Kingdom of Lindsey*, pp. 49, 95–6; Leahy, 'Interrupting the Pots', p. 6. Leahy suggests that Caenby may well have been a royal burial, and notes that its mound (excavated in 1849) was larger than that which covered the famous Sutton Hoo ship burial.

25 See below, pp. 203–05 and Fig. 43; Green, 'British kingdom', 16, fn. 72; Sawyer, *Anglo-Saxon Lincolnshire*, p. 51; K. Cameron, *The Place-Names of Lincolnshire, IV* (Nottingham, 1996), pp. 25–6; A. E. B. Owen, 'Roads and Romans in south-east Lindsey' in A. R. Rumble and A. D. Mills (eds), *Names, Places and People* (Stamford, 1997), p. 263; A. E. B. Owen, 'Louth before Domesday', *LHA*, 32 (1997), 60–4.

26 F. H. Thompson, 'Anglo-Saxon sites in Lincolnshire: unpublished material and recent discoveries', *Antiq. J.*, 36 (1956), 190.

27 Leahy, *Kingdom of Lindsey*, pp. 49, 114; Leahy, 'Interrupting the Pots', p. 6; Everson, 'Pre-Viking settlement', p. 98.

28 Leahy, 'Anglo-Saxon settlement', pp. 36–7; Sawyer, *Anglo-Saxon Lincolnshire*, p. 44; Leahy, *Kingdom of Lindsey*, p. 50 and fig. 8; Leahy, 'Interrupting the Pots', p. 11.

29 Leahy, 'Anglo-Saxon settlement', pp. 36–7; Leahy, *Kingdom of Lindsey*, p. 50; Sawyer, *Anglo-Saxon Lincolnshire*, p. 44; Leahy, 'Interrupting the Pots', p. 11. See also Fig. 33. This avoidance of Lincoln by the large cremation cemeteries is replicated by the distribution of all pre-*c.* 525 Anglo-Saxon cemeteries (inhumation and cremation), something which helps to confirm its reality – see J. Hines, 'Britain after Rome' in P. Graves-Brown *et al* (eds), *Cultural Identity and Archaeology: the Construction of European Communities* (London, 1996), pp. 262–3 (figs 17.1–2), and below. See also below (pp. 63–4) on the fact that cemeteries in the Lincoln region remain tiny throughout the early Anglo-Saxon period when compared with those in the areas where the cremation cemeteries were founded, which is again a significant point in this context (see Fig. 33 for a density map of all early Anglo-Saxon cemetery evidence from Lincolnshire).

30 Green, 'British kingdom', 17–18; Leahy, *Kingdom of Lindsey*, pp. 50, 59; Leahy, 'Anglo-Saxon settlement', p. 37; Sawyer, *Anglo-Saxon Lincolnshire*, p. 46; Leahy, 'Interrupting the Pots', pp. 10–11; Hines, 'Britain after Rome', pp. 262–3 (figs 17.1–2); A. G. Vince, 'Lincoln in the early medieval era, between the 5th and 9th centuries: the archaeological account' in D. Stocker (ed.), *The City by the Pool. Assessing the Archaeology of the City of Lincoln*

(Oxford, 2003), pp. 145–6, 152. In addition to the three cemeteries near Lincoln cited here, there may well have also been another very small inhumation cemetery at North Hykeham (a little to the south-west of Lincoln). The evidence for this consists of four or five metal-detected brooches, a pin and a girdle-hanger, which are indicative of perhaps two female graves (Adam Daubney, personal communication and, for example, Portable Antiquities Scheme LIN-DB6F46, LIN-DB1483). Although one of the women was buried with a mid-fifth-century brooch, all of the other associated finds are later in date, indicating that this was an heirloom piece. The assemblage as a whole suggests that the two burials had probably taken place by the middle of the sixth century.

31   M. J. Jones, 'St Paul in the Bail, Lincoln: Britain in Europe?' in K. Painter (ed.), *Churches Built in Ancient Times: Recent Studies in Early Christian Archaeology* (London, 1994), pp. 328–30 and fig. 5; M. J. Jones, 'The Colonia era: archaeological account' in Stocker, *City by the Pool*, pp. 127–9, 137; K. Steane, *The Archaeology of the Upper City and Adjacent Suburbs* (Oxford, 2006), p. 192; M. J. Jones, *Roman Lincoln: Conquest, Colony and Capital* (Stroud, 2002), p. 127; *pace* B. Gilmour, 'Sub-Roman or Saxon, pagan or Christian: who was buried in the early cemetery at St-Paul-in-the-Bail, Lincoln?' in L. Gilmour (ed.), *Pagans and Christians – from Antiquity to the Middle Ages* (Oxford, 2007), pp. 229–56.

32   See Jones, 'St Paul in the Bail'; K. Steane, 'St Paul-in-the-Bail – a dated sequence?', *Lincoln Archaeology*, 3 (1990–1), 28–31; Jones, 'Colonia era', pp. 127–9, 137; Jones, *Roman Lincoln*, pp. 127–9; Green, 'British kingdom', 19–20. Sawyer, *Anglo-Saxon Lincolnshire*, pp. 226–30 offers the theory of a seventh- to eighth-century date for the second church, with regard to which see Green, 'British kingdom', 19–20, especially fn. 85; Vince, 'Lincoln in the early medieval era', pp. 150–1. It should be noted that this theory, somewhat bizarrely, would still have the *first* church as a Late Roman or post-Roman British church, as Alan Vince has noted ('Lincoln', p. 149). Gilmour's ('Sub-Roman or Saxon') suggestion of a mid-sixth-century *de novo* start for the church-stage of the site seems less plausible than the scenario supported here, especially given both the points made below and the fact that British **Lindēs* probably came to end around this time (see below, pp. 114–15).

33   Jones, 'Colonia Era', p. 129 and fig. 7.70; Steane, 'Dated Sequence?'; M. J. Jones, 'The latter days of Roman Lincoln' in Vince, *Pre-Viking Lindsey*, p. 25; Eagles, 'Lindsey', p. 207, *pace* Gilmour, 'Sub-Roman or Saxon'. See the excellent visualization by David Vale in Jones, *Roman Lincoln*, p. 128, reproduced here as Fig. 13.

34   Sample number 34: see Gilmour, 'Sub-Roman or Saxon', pp. 247–9, 252; Steane, *Archaeology of the Upper City*, p. 157; Jones, 'Colonia Era', p. 129;

Sawyer, *Anglo-Saxon Lincolnshire*, p. 230. Note, the abbreviation 'cal' indicates a calibrated radiocarbon date.

35 Sample numbers 30, 29 and 26 – see Steane, *Archaeology of the Upper City*, especially pp. 160–1; Gilmour, 'Sub-Roman or Saxon', pp. 249, 252.

36 Gilmour, 'Sub-Roman or Saxon', pp. 248–50, 252–3.

37 The three post-church burials have date ranges, at the 95.4% confidence level, of cal AD 420–690 (sample 30), cal AD 450–770 (sample 29), and cal AD 390–680 (sample 26), according to the recently published excavation report (Steane, *Archaeology of the Upper City*, pp. 161, 210; see Gilmour, 'Sub-Roman or Saxon', p. 247, for a recalculation of these, which adjusts them slightly). It should be noted that, whilst each post-church burial on its own could conceivably date from after AD 600 on the basis of the above date ranges, all three would need to post-date 600 in order for the apsidal church to have been in use after the end of the sixth century, and this is where issues over 'joint probability' come into play. My thanks are due here to Alex Bayliss, the Head of Scientific Dating at English Heritage, for constructing a preliminary Bayesian model of the St Paul in the Bail site to look at this issue for me, and for her analysis and advice with regard to the radiocarbon dates and chronology of this site. A more detailed discussion of the probability of the second church being demolished before AD 600 must await the construction of a full Bayesian model, although the preliminary results are believed to be almost certainly in the right area.

38 Gildas, *De Excidio Britanniae*, ed. and trans. M. Winterbottom (1978).

39 Jones, 'St Paul in the Bail'; Jones, 'Colonia Era', pp. 127–9, 137; A. C. Thomas, *Christianity in Roman Britain to AD 500* (London, 1981), p. 197; Leahy, *Kingdom of Lindsey*, p. 117.

40 S. Bassett, 'Church and diocese in the West Midlands' in J. Blair and R. Sharpe (eds), *Pastoral Care Before the Parish* (London, 1992), pp. 13–40; S. Bassett, 'Medieval ecclesiastical organisation in the vicinity of Wroxeter and its British antecedents', *Journal of the British Archaeological Association*, 145 (1992), 1–28; B. Yorke, 'Lindsey: the lost kingdom found?' in Vince, *Pre-Viking Lindsey*, p. 145; Jones, 'Colonia Era', p. 137.

41 See S. Laycock, *Britannia, The Failed State* (Stroud, 2008), p.173, for a recent plot of fifth-century Anglo-Saxon sites, which updates K. R. Dark, *Britain and the End of the Roman Empire* (Stroud, 2000), p. 11, fig. 1.1; see also Hines, 'Philology', p. 34. S. Youngs, 'Britain, Wales and Ireland: holding things together' in K. Jankulak and J. M. Wooding (eds), *Ireland and Wales in the Middle Ages* (Dublin, 2007), p. 96, gives the distribution of Class 1 brooches, as does Dark, *Britain*, p. 131.

42 On the Lincolnshire examples and the dating of Class 1 penannular brooches (Fowler's type F/F1), see Leahy, 'Formation', p. 132; Leahy, *Kingdom of Lindsey*, pp. 83–4; Leahy, *Cleatham*, pp. 146–7; Green, 'British kingdom', pp. 24–5, 27, fns. 101, 109; Dark, *Britain*, p. 132; J. Graham-

Campbell, 'Dinas Powys metalwork and the dating of enamelled zoomorphic penannular brooches', *Bulletin of the Board of Celtic Studies*, 38 (1991), 220–32; R. Collins, 'Brooch use in the 4th- to 5th-century frontier' in R. Collins and L. Allason-Jones (eds), *Finds From the Frontier: Material Culture in the 4th–5th Centuries* (London, 2010), pp. 64–77. However, compare Youngs, 'Holding things together', p. 82. As a group, Class 1 brooches are usually dated to the fifth and sixth centuries, a chronology followed by Kevin Leahy for the Lindsey finds he records. Similarly, Ken Dark dates them generally from the fifth to seventh centuries and is sceptical as to whether the one example from Britain thought potentially to pre-date *c.* 400 actually does so (Dark, *Britain*, p. 132). With regard to date, see also below (pp. 103 and 122, endnote 46) on some Lincolnshire examples found in sixth-century contexts; the hybrid British Type G/Class 1 brooch from Norton Disney (Portable Antiquities Scheme, DENO-DD5FA4) may also be of some significance here. Most recently, Rob Collins has argued that an analysis of northern finds of Class 1 brooches supports the view that they are a post-Roman class, perhaps first emerging in the mid- to late fifth century (Collins, 'Brooch use', especially pp. 72–3). In addition to the fourteen Lincolnshire examples of Class 1 brooches noted by Leahy, *Kingdom of Lindsey*, and Green, 'British kingdom', we can now add an additional find from Folkingham (Portable Antiquities Scheme, LIN-1AB297; this was found at a different site from the first example), one apparently found in the Louth area (Geoff Hill, personal communication), and another located to the south of Lincoln, just outside of the county (Fig. 16; Susan Youngs, personal communication). A fragment of a probable Class 1 brooch, to judge from the decoration and implied diameter, has also been recently found near Miningsby, to the south-east of Horncastle (PAS NCL-1D90A3 and Rob Collins, personal communication).

43   Green, 'British kingdom', 25; Youngs, 'Holding things together', p. 96, and personal communication. Note, the Portable Antiquities Scheme database was checked for all British finds of Class 1 brooches, not just those from Lincolnshire.

44   Leahy, *Kingdom of Lindsey*, p. 84, and personal communication; Youngs, 'Holding things together', pp. 86–9; Dark, *Britain*, p. 133. See also M. R. Niecke, 'Penannular and related brooches: secular ornament or symbol in action?' in R. M. Spearman and J. Higgitt (eds), *The Age of Migrating Ideas: Early Medieval Art in Northern Britain and Ireland* (Edinburgh, 1993), pp. 128–34, and D. Janes, 'The golden clasp of the Late Roman state', *Early Medieval Europe*, 5.2 (1991), 127–53.

45   Green, 'British kingdom', 26–8; L. Hedeager, 'Kingdoms, ethnicity and material culture: Denmark in a European perspective' in M. O. H. Carver (ed.), *The Age of Sutton Hoo. The Seventh Century in North-western Europe*

(Woodbridge, 1992), pp. 279–300, especially figs 53–5 and pp. 299–300. See also, for example, G. Halsall, 'Social change around A.D. 600: an Austrasian perspective' in Carver, *The Age of Sutton Hoo*, pp. 265–78, especially fig. 49 and p. 275. Susan Youngs similarly sees these brooches as being made for and worn by British elites living in Lincolnshire. She also considers that the vast majority of the Lincolnshire examples are likely to have been made locally rather than imported from the west, emerging from a local British tradition of wearing penannular brooches (personal communication; Youngs, 'Holding things together').

46 There are now more of these known from Lincolnshire than from any other part of early Anglo-Saxon England: see T. M. Dickinson, 'Fowler's Type G Penannular brooches reconsidered', *Med. Arch.*, 26 (1982), 48, 52 and figures 1–4; Portable Antiquities Scheme, NLM1052, LIN-7866F3, DENO-DD5FA4 and perhaps NLM6301; and compare the national distribution of these brooches in Fig. 15 and Youngs, 'Holding things together', p. 96.

47 R. Bruce-Mitford, 'Late Celtic hanging bowls in Lincolnshire and South Humberside' in Vince, *Pre-Viking Lindsey*, pp. 45–70; S. Youngs, 'Insular metalwork from Flixborough, Lincolnshire', *Med. Arch.*, 45 (2001), 216–20; Leahy, *Kingdom of Lindsey*, pp. 84–5 and p. 106 for a distribution map of fifteen of the bowls from Lindsey, to which should be added the following: two from Flixborough (Youngs, 'Flixborough', and Kevin Leahy, personal communication) and six from the Portable Antiquities Scheme – LIN-75B9C3 (Lissington), NLM6251 (Winterton), NLM-3D8081/NLM-A6E546 (Binbrook), LIN-B86833 (Blyborough), and NLM-C057A6 (Swinhope). Note that the respective find-spots of the hanging-bowl rim and escutcheon from Willoughton are sufficiently widely separated to necessitate them being considered representative of two different bowls: see Lincolnshire Historic Environment Record 50941 and 50942. For the south of Lincolnshire, the following should be added to Bruce-Mitford's total: Lincolnshire Historic Environment Record 60962 (Bracebridge Heath) and Portable Antiquities Scheme LIN-E64595 (Walcot near Folkingham), NLM948 (Ancaster), NLM716 (Bourne), LVPL-300957 (Boothby Graffoe), LIN-836777 (Osbournby), and LIN-36AFB5 (Morton and Hanthorpe). Yet another hanging-bowl mount has been recently found just outside the south-eastern county boundary, at Whatton: Portable Antiquities Scheme, DENO-E207B6.

48 Youngs, 'Insular metalwork', 219–20; Dark, *Britain*, pp. 132–3; R. Bruce-Mitford, *A Corpus of Late Celtic Hanging Bowls* (Oxford, 2005), especially pp. 32, 34–40; Susan Youngs, personal communication. On the use of these bowls in Anglo-Saxon graves, see H. Geake, 'When were hanging bowls deposited in Anglo-Saxon graves?', *Med. Arch.*, 43 (1999), 1–18.

49 In general, Anglo-Saxon interest in these bowls is chiefly a seventh-century phenomenon (Geake, 'Hanging Bowls').
50 Bruce-Mitford, *Corpus*, p. 26.
51 See further, pp. 147–8 below.

3

ANGLIAN–BRITISH INTERACTION AND THE END OF THE 'COUNTRY OF *LINDĒS'

The origins of Anglian–British interaction: invasion or invitation?

That there must have been some interaction between the Britons and Anglo-Saxons of Lincolnshire is implicit in the evidence discussed in the previous chapter. The distribution of the great cremation cemeteries – in particular, the fact that there is no significant Anglo-Saxon encroachment into a large area around Lincoln until after the early sixth century – is strongly suggestive of the Britons of the 'country of *Lindēs' being able to physically constrain the immigrants to the region at this time. This apparent ability to control Anglo-Saxon settlement from the mid-fifth century onwards is most intriguing. It naturally raises the question of whether the textually derived 'Gildas model' of Germanic immigration to fifth-century Britain might not be an inappropriate one for understanding the situation in the 'country of *Lindēs'. According to this model, the actual settlement of the immigrants was directed and controlled by the elites of post-Roman Britain, rather than being simply a matter of invasion and the military conquest of land by the immigrants.

Two points can be made in support of this position. First, the distribution of fifth- and sixth-century British metalwork (especially Class 1 brooches) is indicative of British elites continuing to exist in those areas of fifth- and sixth-century Lincolnshire where the Anglo-Saxons were settled, these elites using such items there to signal and reinforce their identity and status as a reaction to the presence of these new immigrant groups (Figs 11 and 16). Such arguably defiant 'Britishness' close by and surrounding the immigrant centres does, of course, carry with it the strong implication that these peripheral areas remained at least nominally within the borders of the 'country of

Lindēs' through the fifth century and into the sixth, in order for the British elites there to have been able to maintain their identity and status so late.[1] This in turn argues that the British control over the Anglo-Saxon settlement was not limited simply to using military force to prevent invading immigrants from encroaching upon the core of their territory. Whilst military force may well have played a part (see below), the suggestion must be that the Anglo-Saxon immigrants were deliberately settled within the boundaries of the 'country of *Lindēs'* by the leaders of this territory, for whatever reason, and were controlled within this area into the sixth century.

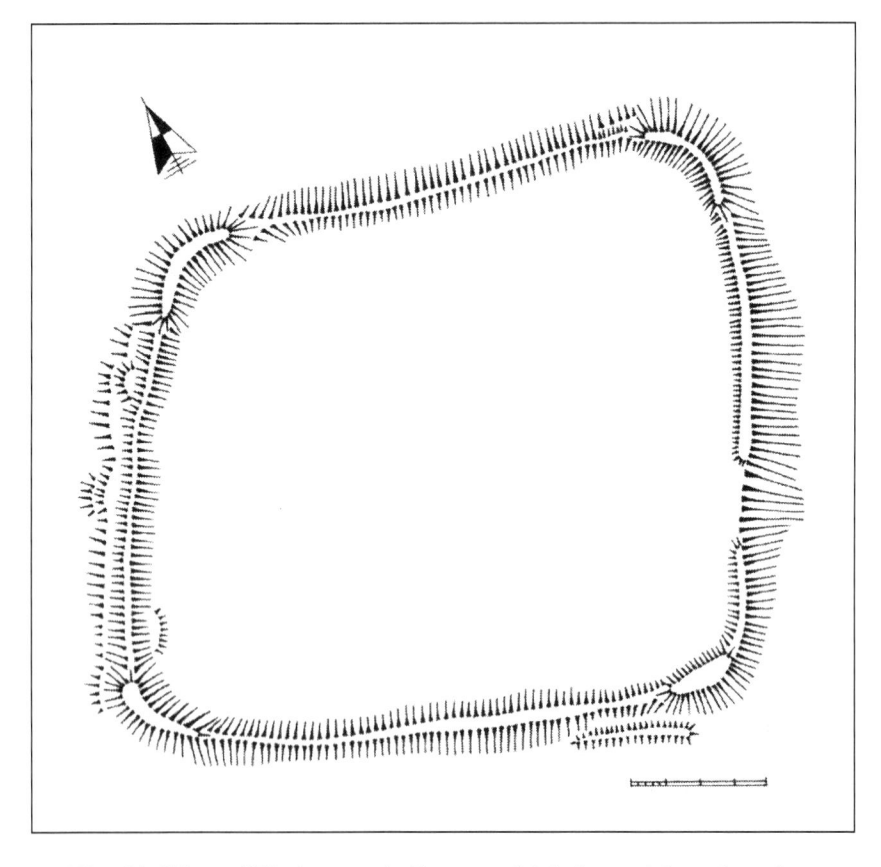

Fig. 20 Plan of Yarborough Camp, which is positioned at the important east–west Kirmington Gap
Source: Kevin Leahy

An explanation of this situation, along with further support for it, is provided by the second point, which is that the large Anglo-Saxon cremation cemeteries were not only distributed in a clear ring around Lincoln, but were also often close to likely strategic sites for the defence of British *Lindēs*. So, for example, Elsham cremation cemetery was located around two miles away from the important earthwork fortification known as Yarborough Camp (Old English *eorð-burh*, 'earthen fortification'). This site is believed to have been refortified in the late fourth or early fifth century, lay on a major east–west route and would have been crucial in the defence of post-Roman northern Lincolnshire (Fig. 20). In the same way, the South Elkington cremation cemetery was located south-west of another *eorð-burh* (Yarburgh), which may have been similarly used in the Late/post-Roman period; the West Keal cemetery was situated at a high and imposing point overlooking the Witham valley (one of the major entry points for Lincolnshire and Lincoln itself); and the Cleatham cemetery was placed just off the chief road-route from the Humber estuary to Lincoln.[2] As such, the distribution and siting of the great cremation cemeteries is – like the distribution of the Class 1 brooches – suggestive of the deliberate direction of Anglo-Saxon settlement *within* the British 'country of *Lindēs*' by its rulers in order to provide for the defence of their territory from other, hostile, groups. Such a situation would certainly offer an explanation as to why these cemeteries appear to have remained, at least into the early sixth century, within the borders of the 'country of *Lindēs*'. Taken together, these points seem to indicate that a model of invitation and directed settlement is more plausible than one simply of invasion when it comes to explaining the presence of Anglo-Saxons in the Lincoln region.[3]

In regione Linnuis: Anglian–British battles in post-Roman *Lindēs*

If the 'country of *Lindēs*' did indeed include the Anglo-Saxon cremation cemeteries within its bounds (at least into the early sixth century) and was able to control, direct and initially utilize Anglo-Saxon settlement in the region, perhaps for the purposes of defence, this does not mean that relations between the British elite and the

Germanic immigrants were always necessarily harmonious. Indeed, such was probably the case even before the balance of power in the region began to shift decisively away from the Britons (as it must have). When making this observation, we do not have to rely solely on the traditional, but non-specific, Gildasian narrative, in which the controlled settlement of Anglo-Saxons by British authorities (for the purposes of defence) was subsequently followed by a breakdown in relations and military conflict. We can instead look to the context of the early ninth-century Welsh reference to events *in regione Linnuis* (**Lindēs*). So, what did the Welsh claim had happened in the post-Roman British 'country of **Lindēs*'? The answer is quite simple: four battles between the Britons and the Anglo-Saxon immigrants, fought around the year 500, all of which were won by the Britons.

In general there have been two approaches to this supposed ninth-century remembrance of post-Roman Anglo-British warfare: the first is uncritical credulity, and the second is dismissive scepticism. Whilst there is no reason to doubt the genuineness of the name *Linnuis*, and hence the implications that it carries for the existence of a British territory of **Lindēs*, the problem is that there are numerous reasons to be sceptical of the *Historia Brittonum*'s claim to be a repository of genuine information about fifth- and sixth-century events.[4] Furthermore, it does need to be recognized that the British victor of the battles fought *c.* 500 *in regione Linnuis* was said by the author of the *Historia* to have been a *dux bellorum* ('leader of battles') named Arthur. The latter point in particular is the reason for the widely varying attitudes to the question of whether the *Historia*'s account can be used as any sort of proof that battles were indeed fought in the 'country of **Lindēs*' in the fifth or sixth century. If one is inclined to accept that the list of twelve 'Arthurian' battles that the ninth-century *Historia* provides is broadly trustworthy and reflects post-Roman realities and the deeds of a real war-leader, then there is little barrier to accepting that battles were fought *in regione Linnuis* by no less a personage than the *dux bellorum*, Arthur, himself. Such a position was not unknown in academia a generation or two ago and is still predominant amongst amateur researchers today.[5] On the other hand, present-day historians and Celticists are usually considerably more cautious with regard to questions of both Arthur's existence and the historicity of his associated battle-list. Put simply, on the basis of a study of all the surviving early references to Arthur, it seems far more credible that Arthur was originally a folkloric – or even a mythical – Hero Protector of Britain, defending the country against supernatural threats, who was historicized by the author of the *Historia*, with the battle-list being invented as part of this process.[6] Certainly, such a situation is far from unparalleled; the portrayal of fictional or mythical heroes as historical is a relatively regular occurrence in both classical and medieval literature.

Given the above, the adoption of a thoroughly sceptical approach to the reality of the *Linnuis* battles is understandable. However, it may well be a mistake simply to leave these battles in a state of limbo without further investigation; after all, even if the battle-list as a whole and its victor, the 'historical Arthur', were ninth-century inventions with no genuine historicity, it is still worth asking how the list was created and whether it included, at some level, genuine information about fifth- and sixth-century events. An investigation of this sort does, in fact, suggest that there is a solid core of history in the list, albeit well hidden. Of the twelve battles ascribed to Arthur in the *Historia Brittonum*, only one definitely did take place *c.* 500, namely the Battle of Badon Hill, but its context is telling. In Gildas's sixth-century *De Excidio Britanniae*, Ambrosius Aurelianus is given prominence as the initiator of the British counter-attack against the Anglo-Saxon immigrants, which, after the fighting of several battles, culminates in the Battle of Badon Hill. Likewise, Arthur in the *Historia Brittonum* initiates the British counter-attack against the Anglo-Saxon immigrants, which, after the fighting of several battles, culminates in the Battle of Badon Hill.[7] This is both striking and important. The most credible explanation is that the ninth-century historicization of Arthur was fundamentally based around a framework of deeds borrowed from the genuinely historical Ambrosius Aurelianus.[8] Moreover, both Oliver Padel and Michael Wood have recently argued that the earliest manuscript of Gildas has the Battle of Badon Hill – the crowning victory of Arthur in the *Historia Brittonum* – reading 'naturally as the victory that crowned the career of Ambrosius Aurelianus' himself, rather than any subsequent British leader, which places the above contention on an even sounder footing.[9]

How was this basic framework filled out? Three mechanisms

seem to be at play. Some of the battles – those with no easily identifiable real-world location – may well have been spontaneously invented for the purposes of 'bulking out' the battle-list. Others appear to have been originally mythical or folkloric Arthurian conflicts – involving demonic monsters, fighting trees, former pagan gods and werewolves – which were historicized alongside Arthur himself. Finally, some look to have been genuine historical battles of various dates that had become part of a generalized corpus of stock battles, whose original details, dates and victors had become obscured, and which were freely used and re-attributed by medieval Welsh authors in their own works.[10] In this context, the etymology of the four *Linnuis* battles means that they most plausibly belong in the last of these three categories, which in turn suggests that they are based on real battles fought at some point *in regione Linnuis*. Furthermore, given that this British territory had certainly disappeared by the early seventh century (when the Anglo-Saxon Blæcca was *praefectus* of Lincoln[11]), the implication must be that they are remembrances of at least one genuinely fifth- or sixth-century battle, a conclusion of considerable importance here. Indeed, it is difficult to avoid associating such a remembrance of post-Roman battles fought by the Britons of the 'country of **Lindēs*' with the archaeological evidence for these Britons being able to physically constrain the areas of Anglo-Saxon settlement in their region.

Can this be taken any further? Perhaps. The battles *in regione Linnuis* are the only ones from the *Historia*'s list for which an origin as a genuine remembrance of conflicts against Anglo-Saxon settlers of *c.* 500 – as opposed to later enemies – seems defensible, aside from the Battle of Badon Hill itself. Such a coincidence is intriguing, and naturally leads to the question of whether one or more battles *in regione Linnuis* might not actually have been part of the same framework of historicization that Badon was. In other words, it is possible that one or more battles in the 'country of **Lindēs*' were, in fact, similarly remembered as part of the historical campaign of Ambrosius Aurelianus.[12] With regard to this possibility, it needs to be recognized that neither Ambrosius Aurelianus's general area of operations nor the site of the Battle of Badon Hill have ever been satisfactorily established, beyond the obvious requirement that both must have been located near to where Anglo-Saxons were present in the late fifth century. In this context, it is worth noting that Baumber in Lindsey (*Badeburg* at Domesday) has as good a claim to be the site, or near to the site, of the Battle of Badon Hill as any of the other candidates which have been proffered over the years. All rest almost exclusively on etymological grounds, and *Badeburg*, located on a Roman-era road-route running north from the fortress of Horncastle, is one of several names which might potentially derive from *Badon* + Old English *burh*, 'fortress'.[13]

The above is potentially important, not least from the perspective of establishing what was happening in the Lincoln region in the fifth and sixth centuries, as it would imply that the Gildasian narrative was indeed directly applicable to the Lincoln region. Certainly, in light of the evidence discussed in the previous chapter, the former provincial capital of Lincoln – with its continuing Christian establishment in the centre of the *forum* and its apparent ability to control the Anglo-Saxon immigrants of the region – does not appear to be an inappropriate nor an implausible place for Ambrosius, 'the last of the Romans', to have been based.[14] Furthermore, there are some slight indications that Lincoln could be even more appropriate for Ambrosius' base than the evidence for a powerful 'country of **Lindēs*' alone allows. Barbara Yorke, following the lead of Alan Vince, has recently argued that Lincoln may have actually retained control of its whole province at least partway through the fifth century. In particular, she notes that the probable course of the boundary between the fourth-century provinces centred on Lincoln and London broadly corresponds with the archaeologically observable boundary between 'Anglian' and 'Saxon' cultural areas in the fifth century, with the vast majority of the Anglian material being found within the bounds of Lincoln's province and the vast majority of Saxon lying within the bounds of London's.[15] Needless to say, the implication would appear to be that the former provinces were still in existence as political units and able to exercise control over fifth-century Anglo-Saxon settlement (Fig. 21). In such circumstances, a link between Ambrosius Aurelianus and the provincial capital of Lincoln is more than credible.

Of course, both Ambrosius and Badon could well have been located in some other area of the country, and the *Linnuis* battles may not be part of the framework of historicization at all, but simply

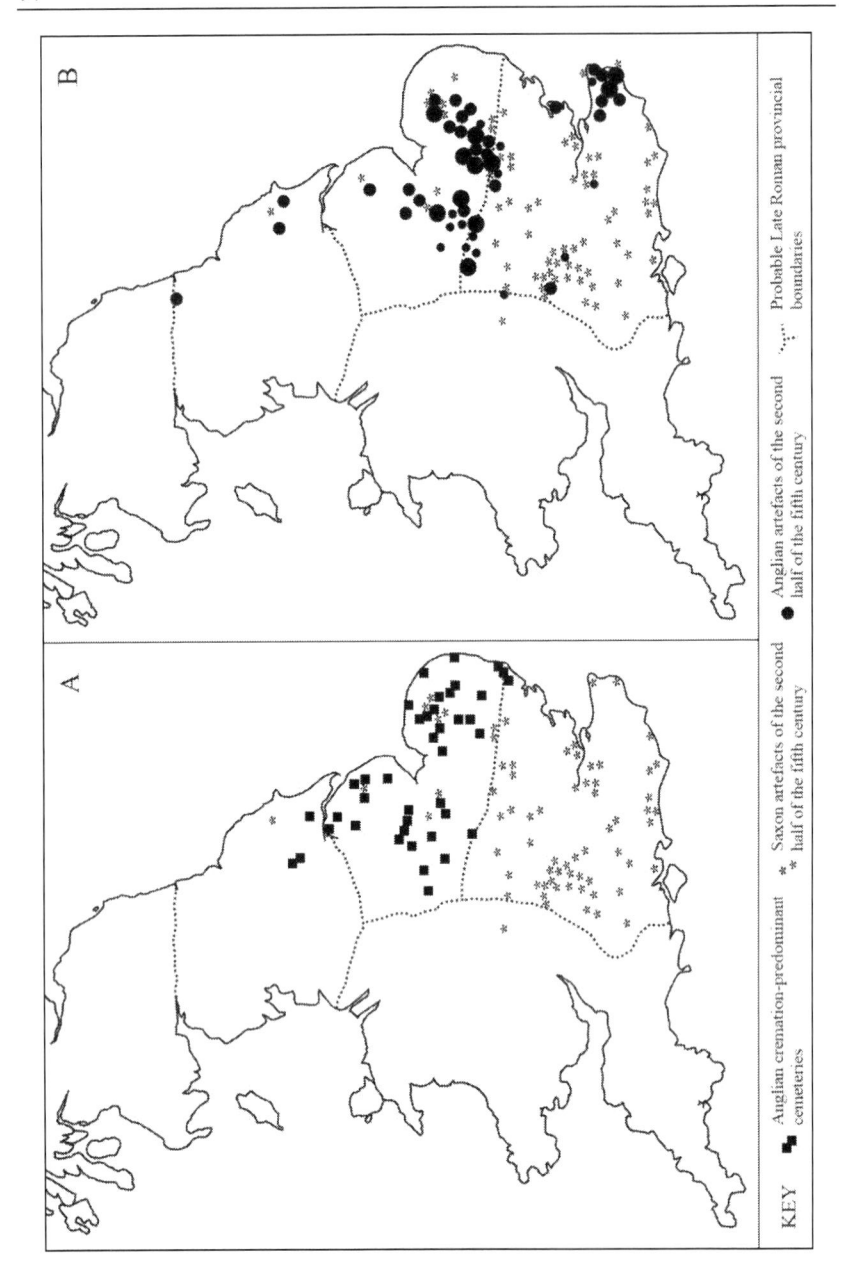

For caption, see next page

Fig. 21 The distribution of Anglian archaeology plotted against the probable Late Roman provincial boundaries. The maps plot, respectively, Anglian cremation-predominant cemeteries and Anglian artefacts of the second half of the fifth century against Saxon artefacts of the same period. Note that the apparent scarcity of early Anglian brooches in northern Lincolnshire up to the early 1990s has been corrected in recent years as a result of excavations and metal-detecting
After H. Williams, 'Cemeteries as central places – place and identity in Migration Period eastern England' in B. Hårdh and L. Larsson (eds), *Central Places in the Migration and Merovingian Periods* (Stockholm, 2002), and N. J. Higham, *Rome, Britain and the Anglo-Saxons* (London, 1992)

'stock events' that became associated with it by the author of the *Historia Brittonum*. Nevertheless, the possibility raised above deserves some serious consideration. Even leaving it to one side, the fact remains that there seems little reason to doubt that the four battles *in regione Linnuis* ultimately reflect a ninth-century Welsh remembrance of at least one fifth- or sixth-century battle fought by the Britons of the 'country of **Lindēs*' to control the Anglo-Saxon immigrants who were settled in their territory.

Y Gododdin and the 'men of *Linnuis*'

From the materials examined so far, we can begin to construct an outline narrative of events in the Lincoln region in the fifth and sixth centuries. However, we still have to address the key questions of when and how the British 'country of **Lindēs*' came to an end. In this context, there is one further Welsh reference to *Linnuis/*Lindēs* which may be of relevance, namely that contained in the Welsh poem (strictly speaking, a collection of heroic death-songs) known as *Y Gododdin*.

Although this poem is now only preserved in the thirteenth-century 'Book of Aneirin', it is traditionally ascribed to a sixth-century poet named Aneirin, and John Koch has made a good linguistic case for believing that at least some of its stanzas had their origins in the seventh and eighth centuries.[16] The poem as a whole is concerned with a disastrous mid- to late sixth-century battle fought at *Catraeth* (usually thought to be Catterick in North Yorkshire) by the war-band of the British kingdom of the Gododdin and their allies against another British kingdom and its allies.[17] It is these various allies that are of interest to us here: according to *Y Gododdin*, they included not only Anglo-Saxons (potentially on both sides), but also warriors from other British kingdoms, such as Elmet, Aeron, Strathclyde and, quite likely, *Linnuis* (**Lindēs*) too.[18] The stanza in question (A.15), which John Koch considers to date from the mid-seventh century, is given here and has been translated as follows:

> *O vreithyell gatraeth pan adrodir.*
> *maon dychiorant eu hoet bu hir.*
> *edyrn diedyrn amygyn dir.*
> *a meibyon godebawc gwerin enwir.*
> *dyforthynt lynwyssawr gelorawr hir.*[19]

> It is concerning *Catraeth*'s variegated and ruddy [land] that it is told –
> the followers fell; long were the lamentations for them, the
> immortalised men; [but] it was not as immortals that they fought for
> territory against the descendants of Godebawg, the rightful faction [*or*
> 'an evil people']: long biers bore off *lynwyssawr*.[20]

In all mainstream translations of the poem, the obscure Middle Welsh word *lynwyssawr* (which would have been **linuissaur* in Old Welsh) is rendered as something akin to 'blood-stained bodies'. However, the translation of Middle and Old Welsh is a difficult matter and several different readings are often possible, a fact that can be obscured by modern translations, which are forced to choose one single version. This is the case here. *Lynwyssawr*, **linuissaur*, could be at least equally legitimately translated as 'men of *Linnuis* (< **Lindēs*)', as the present author and a number of others have pointed out, resulting in the line 'long biers bore off men of *Linnuis*'. Given that the presence in the poem of men from British kingdoms other than the Gododdin is now widely recognized, and the fact that the 'country of *Linnuis*/**Lindēs*' now appears to have been a significant – potentially a very significant – British polity of the fifth and sixth centuries, there is no obvious reason why this reading should not be adopted. Such a reading would indeed have a good context not only in the poem as a whole but also in the stanza itself.[21]

Pursuing this further, if the suggested reading is adopted then we need to ask who these warriors were thought to be and on which side they were considered to have fought. With regard to the second question, the most natural reading of the above passage is that the author considered the British *meibyon godebawc* – 'descendants of *Godebawc*' – to have been the enemy against whom the Gododdin warriors were contending and the 'men of *Linnuis*' to have been part of the Gododdin's own war-band, with the above lines forming a lament for their loss at *Catraeth* (although *gwerin enwir* might be translated as 'the rightful faction', it is more plausibly understood as indicating that the *meibyon godebawc* were 'an evil people').[22] Certainly, such a scenario would accord well with the rest of the poem, with other stanzas similarly claiming that the Gododdin's doomed war-band contained non-Gododdin warriors.[23]

If the 'men of *Linnuis*' thus ought to be probably considered the much-lamented 'followers' of the second line and so, reputedly, fallen members of the Gododdin war-band at *Catraeth*, what then was their identity? One very credible answer here is that the men from the British 'country of *Linnuis/*Lindēs*' were simply conceived of in the same way as those from the other British kingdoms (for example, Aeron, Gwynedd and Strathclyde) that were said to have provided warriors in *Y Gododdin*: that is to say, they were all thought to be British warriors from kingdoms beyond the Gododdin's borders, who had joined the sixth-century Gododdin war-band and took part in the assault on *Catraeth*.[24] In such circumstances, a claim that 'men of *Linnuis/*Lindēs*' were present at *Catraeth* would indicate that the author of these lines must have believed that the British territory of **Lindēs* continued in existence until at least the mid-sixth century, in order that he could consider that British warriors from this territory might have been killed at *Catraeth*. Needless to say, if the suggested reading is correct, then this is a point of considerable interest.

In addition, if the claim that the Gododdin war-band included *lynwyssawr* was more than merely the contention of a later author, and British warriors from the British 'country of *Linnuis/*Lindēs*' really were fighting for the Gododdin at *Catraeth* in the sixth century, then this would naturally raise the question of why they were doing this so far from home. In this context, Craig Cessford's theory that the *lynwyssawr* of this stanza were kingdomless British warriors, who had found a place at another British court after the recent final loss of their homeland to the Anglo-Saxon immigrants, would be both attractive and plausible.[25] Not only would it fit well with the other available evidence for the end of the British 'country of *Lindēs' (such as the presence of Anglo-Saxon cemeteries within a few miles of Lincoln by the mid-sixth century and the likely demolition of the apsidal church at Lincoln before *c.* 600),[26] but it would also imply that some members of the British warrior-elite from *Lindēs* had felt it necessary to leave their homeland behind when the balance of power shifted to the immigrant groups. This would be telling from the perspective of the present chapter.

On the other hand, all of the above depends upon the *lynwyssawr* of *Y Gododdin* having been considered not only 'men of *Linnuis*', but also Britons from the British 'country of *Linnuis/*Lindēs*'. Whilst such an origin would undoubtedly have had a good context within the poem, it ought to be acknowledged that if 'men of *Linnuis/*Lindēs*' really did fight and die at *Catraeth,* then they could conceivably have been Anglo-Saxons rather than Britons. Put simply, if a group of Anglo-Saxons moved into the Gododdin region from *Lindēs* sometime before *Catraeth* in the mid-sixth century and fought alongside the Gododdin warriors in this battle, then it is not impossible that a contemporary or near-contemporary Welsh poet would have described them as 'men of *Linnuis/*Lindēs*', despite their non-British origins. This possibility would perhaps not be worth pursuing except for the curious fact that there is linguistic and archaeological material indicative of just such a mid-sixth-century movement into what is likely to have been the southern part of the Gododdin kingdom (the area around Lindisfarne and the Tweed valley) by Anglo-Saxons from the Lincoln region.[27] Of course, the arrival of these Anglo-Saxons could be entirely unrelated to the occurrence of *lynwyssawr* in *Y Gododdin,* but the coincidence is arresting. As such, if the claim that 'men of *Linnuis*' fought for the Gododdin was based in reality rather than in later poetic speculation as to the participants in this battle, then the possibility that these *lynwyssawr* were actually Anglo-Saxons from *Linnuis/*Lindēs* would deserve to be taken reasonably seriously. Indeed, such a scenario may even help to explain how and why the archaeologically and linguistically evidenced Anglo-Saxon migrants from the Lincoln region were able to establish a lasting and important foothold in an area far to the north of any other early Anglo-Saxon activity.[28]

All told, the Welsh poem *Y Gododdin* may be a source of considerable potential interest for the present study if the reading argued for here is adopted. If the *lynwyssawr* were considered Britons from *Linnuis/*Lindēs*, then it would add yet more weight to the case for British **Lindēs* having continued at least part-way into the mid-sixth century, and it may even hint at the reactions of some of the Britons of the region to the Anglo-Saxon takeover of their homeland. If they were thought to be Anglo-Saxons, then it may help us to understand better the evidence for a secondary Anglo-Saxon migration from Lincolnshire to Northumbria, discussed in subsequent chapters.

From **Lindēs* to *Lindissi*: the nature of the transition

Although there may be hints that some of the Britons of **Lindēs* decided to leave, rather than remain in the Lincoln region as power shifted from British to Anglo-Saxon hands, this need not mean that the transition was solely characterized by antipathy and hostility between the two groups. In fact, there is good reason to think that, sometimes at least, the opposite might have been the case.

Of all the available sources of evidence for such a scenario, undoubtedly the best known is the royal genealogy of the kings of *Lindissi*, which ends with the name Aldfrið. This is preserved in the late eighth-century 'Anglian Collection of royal genealogies and regnal lists', along with the genealogies and regnal lists of the Anglo-Saxon kings of Wessex, Kent, Mercia and Northumbria.[29] It used to be thought that the Aldfrið of this genealogy was also mentioned in a late eighth-century Mercian charter, wherein Sir Frank Stenton followed Birch in reading one *Ealdfrid rex* as a witness, but such a position now appears to be untenable.[30] In consequence, the question of Aldfrið's *floruit* is open to debate, although Sarah Foot has made a good case for presuming that he was king *c.* 679 and that after this date there were no more (semi-)independent rulers of *Lindissi*.[31]

The chief interest in the genealogy of the kings of *Lindissi* comes seven generations down, where we find a certain *Cædbæd* named as one of Aldfrið's ancestors who would have probably lived in the early to mid-sixth century. This name is now generally considered to be an

Anglicized form of a wholly British Celtic name, its origins lying in British *Catuboduos*, Archaic Welsh *Cadbodu*, and as such it is extremely suggestive.[32] It does, of course, have to be asked whether this genealogy can be trusted to preserve genuine information from the sixth century. Certainly, parts of it have been viewed with some suspicion in the past, most particularly because of the fact that the names alliterate in groups of two and three.[33] On the other hand, such alliteration between generations seems to have been a common practice and is also found in other Anglo-Saxon genealogies, and it might even be viewed as a positive argument in favour of the antiquity of the genealogy.[34] Similarly, whilst the presence of the name *Biscop* in the genealogy has occasionally worried some, it seems to have been a perfectly good Old English name, and the fact that it was also borne by a famous seventh-century Northumbrian noble ought not to be considered a serious cause for scepticism. Indeed, this is particularly the case given that at least some of the Northumbrian elite may have had their origins in the early Anglo-Saxon Lincoln region, with the suggestion recently being made that the Northumbrian Biscop was actually so named owing to his descent from the royal house of *Lindissi*.[35] In this light, it is worth pointing out that the fact that the genealogy is not standardized to the suspicious fourteen generations back to Woden found in all the other 'Anglian Collection' genealogies, but instead consists of only eleven generations, has been seen as a reason to consider it untampered with.[36] Another reason is the very rare and obscure nature of many of the names found within the genealogy, such as *Cueldgils*, *Cretta*, *Bubba* and *Winta*. Stenton long ago observed that there 'can be no doubt that a series like this represents a genuine tradition.'[37]

All told, it seems reasonable to treat the genealogy as representing something like the genuine lineage of a probably late seventh-century king of *Lindissi* named Aldfrið, reflecting his own concept of his own ancestry. However, even if this were not the case, the most significant consideration from our perspective is the simple fact that – whether the genealogy has been otherwise tampered with or not – it is extremely difficult to see what possible motivation there could have been for the late fabrication of a sixth-century ancestor with an anglicized British Celtic name in the *Lindissi* royal line. As a consequence of the above, the majority of modern historians have been inclined to regard 'the Celtic *Cædbæd* as the most trustworthy element in the entire genealogy, aside from Aldfrið's immediate family. It is also seen as indicative of sixth-century contact and, very likely, intermarriage between local British elites and the Anglo-Saxon group which provided the ruling lineage of *Lindissi*.[38] This is naturally of considerable import in the present circumstances. Not only would it, once again, offer support for there having been high-status Britons in the Lincoln region in the early sixth century, but it may also imply that relations between these Britons and the immigrants could be more than cordial, or at least not consistently marked by violence and antagonism.

It is worth asking, in this context, where the Anglo-Saxons involved in any such potential Anglian–British rapprochement might have been based, before they took over *Lindēs*. After all, the evidence discussed previously suggests that the Britons were still the dominant power in the region at the likely time that *Cædbæd* would have been named. Moreover, the kind of intermarriage envisaged above would in any case perhaps most credibly belong to a period in which the immigrants were gaining in influence but had not yet taken control of the British 'country of *Lindēs*'. In order to answer this, we need to direct our attention to the major fifth- and sixth-century cremation cemeteries of the region. Each of these appears to have had a large territory dependent upon it, which was probably inhabited by a distinct, early Anglo-Saxon group, and the lineage which eventually took over *Lindēs* presumably emerged from the most influential or powerful of these groups.[39] One group in particular stands out as a likely candidate here, namely that based around Cleatham–Kirton in Lindsey. Not only was this group focused upon an exceptionally large cremation cemetery, but the richest barrow burial in Lincolnshire also appears to be associated with this group (Caenby, Fig. 22), and Kirton was clearly an extremely important centre in the Anglo-Saxon period.[40] Furthermore, the place-name 'Ingham' occurs around three miles to the south of the Caenby burial. This name appears to denote a major early Anglo-Saxon royal possession and perhaps cult centre, deriving from Germanic *Ingwia-haimaz*, which can be read as either 'the estate of the *Inguione*', a tag to mark places as the royal property of a king who claimed to be of an

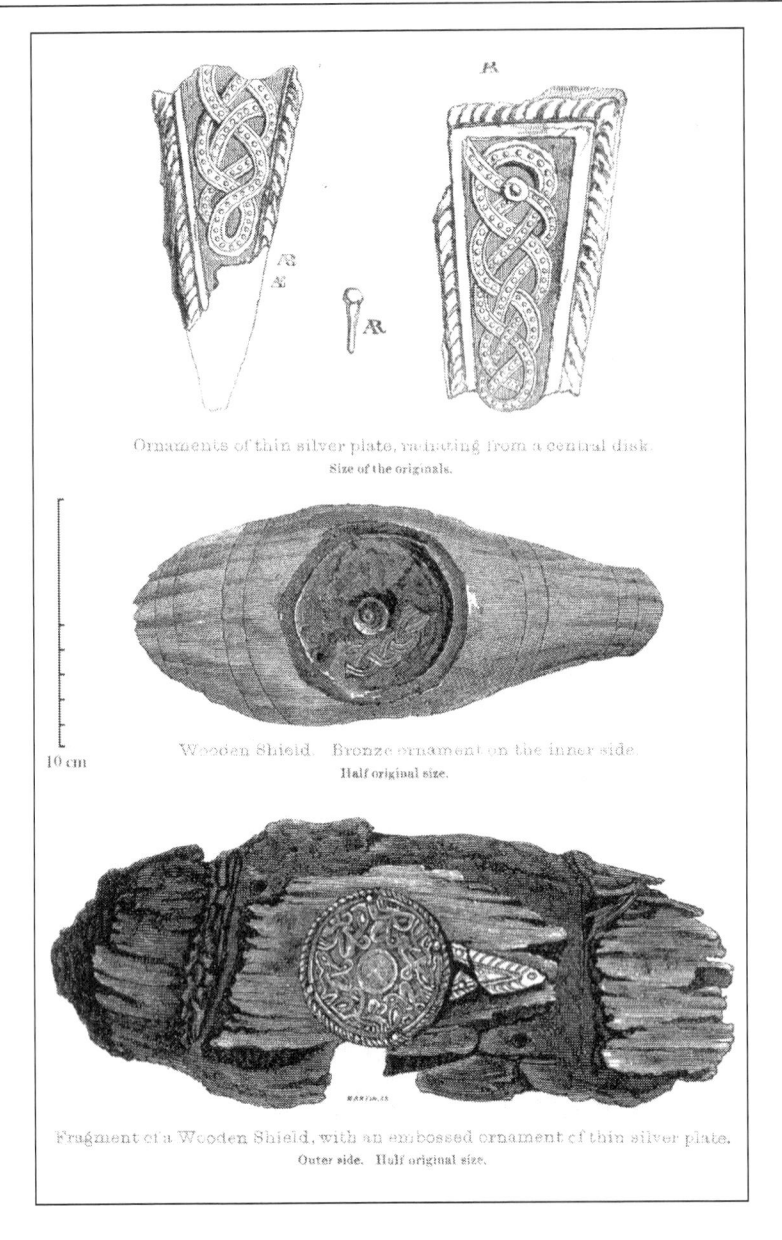

Ornaments of thin silver plate, radiating from a central disk.
Size of the originals.

10 cm

Wooden Shield. Bronze ornament on the inner side.
Half original size.

Fragment of a Wooden Shield, with an embossed ornament of thin silver plate.
Outer side. Half original size.

Fig. 22 Mounts from the great Caenby barrow
Source: Society of Antiquaries of London

Inguionic dynasty, or 'the estate of the devotees of the deity *Ing*'.[41]

In addition to such solid arguments, it can also be observed that this group was centred on the main north–south Roman road from the river Humber to Lincoln. At the point where this road meets the Humber we find two neighbouring place-names, Winterton and Winteringham. Both contain the rare name *Wintra*, which is found in the variant form *Winta* in the *Lindissi* royal genealogy, where it is the first name to appear after the mythical Woden.[42] Whilst not conclusive, this is certainly suggestive, especially as the latter place-name, at least, would be considered to have its origins in the 'pagan' period on the basis of current place-name chronologies, referring to a settlement or estate belonging to an early Anglo-Saxon population group named the *Wintringas* – 'the family, or dependants, of *Wint(r)a*'.[43] Such a group-name is, needless to say, more than plausible as the otherwise unrecorded collective name for the royal dynasty of *Lindissi*. Compare, for example, the Kentish royal *Oiscingas*, named from their early supposed ancestor Oisc, and the Mercian royal *Iclingas*, named from their early supposed ancestor Icel.[44]

If the name *Cædbæd* may provide good evidence for some degree of relatively civil interaction between the British elite of *Lindēs* and the immigrants at the start of the period in which the balance of power shifted from the Britons to the Anglo-Saxons, it does not stand alone. So, for example, whilst some of the seventeen or eighteen fifth- to sixth-century British Class 1 brooches from the region have been found at sites such as the Roman 'small town' at Kirmington,[45] three of these British elite items were recovered from local Anglo-Saxon cemeteries: one was unearthed during the excavation of Cleatham cremation cemetery, another was found in a sixth-century inhumation at Sheffield's Hill cemetery, and the last was metal-detected from the site of a large, unexcavated sixth- to seventh-century inhumation cemetery at Osbournby.[46] This situation requires explanation. As we have already seen, these brooches were probably primarily made for and worn by local high-status Britons, who lived close to the sites where the Anglo-Saxon immigrants had been settled. They felt sufficiently threatened by the incomers that they wore these brooches (and whatever associated clothing) to help reinforce and assert their ethnic identity and status.[47] However, such arguably defiant Britishness would presumably only be practical for local peripheral British elites whilst there were British leaders of influence at Lincoln who could support them. After the point at which the balance of power in the region shifted decisively away from the Britons in the sixth century, it is quite conceivable that some members of these same elites would have then felt a need to align themselves with the new ascendant power and adopt the immigrant culture in order to survive and protect their status. In this context, the presence of three of these British Class 1 brooches in local Anglo-Saxon cemeteries in Lincolnshire is perhaps explicable: they would simply be there as testimony to the ultimate acculturation and assimilation of some members of the local British elite by the immigrants' ascendancy.[48]

A consideration of the place-name Washingborough is similarly instructive. It is found close by Lincoln, on the south bank of the Witham, and derives from Old English *Wassingaburh*, 'the fortified place of the *Wassingas*', that is 'the family or dependants of **Wassa*'. However, whilst *Wassingas* is a perfectly regular Old English group-name, **Wassa* is not a Germanic personal name. Rather, it is a British Celtic name deriving from Celtic *vasso-*, equivalent to the attested Cornish name *Was(s)o* and related to the Continental Celtic names *Vasso-rix* and *Dago-vassus*.[49] This strongly suggests that the founder of the *Wassingas*, a fort-owning 'Anglo-Saxon' population group based close to Lincoln, was either a locally powerful Briton who adopted the immigrant culture and language after the Anglo-Saxon takeover in order to maintain his status and local influence, or that he was the product of the same type of intermarriage which arguably produced the name *Cædbæd* in the *Lindissi* royal genealogy. Both possibilities are, of course, of considerable interest to us here. Furthermore, Washingborough is not the only instance of a Lincolnshire-based, early Anglo-Saxon population group taking its title from a founder whose name appears to be of British derivation. Such a combination of an *-ingas* group-name plus a Brittonic personal name probably also underlies both Threekingham (**Tric-*) in the south of the county and Cammeringham (**Cadmor*) in the north.[50]

A further possible instance of this situation can be observed in the place-name Torksey, Old English *Turces ige* ('**Turc*'s Island'), which presumably originally referred to an extensive island of land alongside the river Trent. **Turc* is otherwise unrecorded as an Old

English personal name, and both Kenneth Cameron and John Insley have argued that it derives from British *torco-, Archaic Welsh *turc, 'boar' (compare, for example, the Old Breton name Turch, which also derived from this root).[51] However, this is somewhat less clear-cut as an example of either intermarriage or assimilation than Washingborough, Threekingham and Cammeringham. Whilst *Wassa founded an 'Anglo-Saxon' population group, the Wassingas, there is no evidence to suggest whether *Turc was similarly integrated in early Anglo-Saxon society or if he was merely remembered as a former British owner of the island in question. On the whole, the former situation seems the more plausible, not least because the latter sort of commemoration would be highly unusual in eastern Britain, but certainty on this matter is impossible.

Alongside the above we can also set the evidence from Lincoln. Although an Anglo-Saxon named Blæcca – whose name alliterates with some of the ancestors of Aldfrið, leading to the reasonable speculation that he may have been a member of the royal family of Lindissi[52] – was in charge of Lincoln in the 620s, various factors suggest that at least some of the high-status British Christian community based there remained in situ when control passed from British to Anglo-Saxon hands. In particular, attention should be drawn once again to the St Paul in the Bail site, with its sequence of two churches and a succeeding Christian graveyard, which continued in use into and through the Middle Saxon period.[53] Whether this cemetery was founded and the second church demolished before the end of the sixth century – the most probable scenario – or in the early seventh century, the implication of this sequence remains the same: that there were Christian Britons still in Lincoln after the Anglo-Saxon takeover around the middle of the sixth century, and that the new Anglo-Saxon rulers of Lincoln and Lindissi therefore tolerated British religious practices and perhaps even organization, at least until the Anglo-Saxons themselves were converted by the Roman church in the 620s.[54]

Certainly, such a scenario is not unparalleled within Britain. There are hints that St Augustine encountered a British Christian community in Kent which had survived under pagan Anglo-Saxon rule, venerating an otherwise unknown (probably Romano-British) St Sixtus. In addition, reference has already been made to British bishoprics which probably continued to function under similar circumstances in the West Midlands until the Anglo-Saxon rulers there converted to the Roman brand of Christianity in the mid-seventh century.[55] Moreover, it has been suggested that Bede's curiously undetailed allusion to miracles taking place in Lincoln (despite the fact that he seems very well informed about the region and was usually keen to give a detailed account of such happenings) is explicable if these were associated with the continued veneration of a (Romano-)British saint – the Lincoln equivalent of the Kentish St Sixtus – with Bede being consequently unwilling to go into details owing to his own opposition to insular 'Celtic' Christianity.[56]

That such a peaceful accommodation between pagan Anglo-Saxons and British Christians in the region could occur is further signified by recent work on dedications to St Helen, which are usually found in association with springs and watercourses. Dedications to St Helen are more common in Britain than in anywhere else in the Christian world, and the Lincoln region has been shown to lie in the core zone of British sites with such dedications, alongside Elmet and Deira (Yorkshire). It has been plausibly argued that these dedications actually have nothing to do with St Helen (the mother of Constantine the Great), but instead represent a Christianization of the well-attested Romano-British pagan veneration of springs, wells and watercourses, in this case of sites dedicated to the British goddess *Alauna*, whose name could easily deform to 'Helen'; compare, for example, the river Ellen (< *Alauna*) in Cumbria.[57] Such Christianization is likely to have been undertaken by fourth- and fifth-century British Christians, given Gildas's lack of knowledge of sixth-century British paganism. The Christian veneration of these sites must then have continued throughout the period in which the Lincoln region was ruled by pagan Anglo-Saxons in order for the dedications to have survived.

After *Lindēs*: the fate of the Britons

It thus appears that, in the course of the transition from British to Anglo-Saxon dominance, some of the Britons of *Lindēs* may have intermarried with the immigrant groups. Others may have decided to leave the region to join the war-bands of other British kingdoms (assuming that *Y Gododdin*'s reference to *lynwyssawr* reflects real British warriors from **Lindēs*). Finally, yet others may have accepted the changing circumstances, and over time adopted many aspects of the Anglo-Saxon ethnicity, even if most of them perhaps kept their own religion whilst the Anglo-Saxons remained pagan. In addition, it is not implausible that some of the Britons may have fought and died in an unsuccessful attempt to prevent the final end of the 'country of **Lindēs*', via a repetition of the kind of victories that the *Historia Brittonum* suggests that the Britons of **Lindēs* won around the year 500. There is, however, no surviving evidence for this, other than supposition, and the above indications that British religious practices were tolerated suggests that the takeover, when it came, was not primarily characterized by antagonism and violence. However, whilst these different approaches to the demise of **Lindēs* and the transition to Anglo-Saxon rule can be enumerated, this still leaves open the question of what actually happened to the vast majority of the Britons who inhabited the Lincoln region after the Anglo-Saxon takeover. Did they follow one of the paths outlined above? If so, which one did they follow, how many of them were involved, and over what period of time?

Earlier generations of historians imagined that virtually all of the Britons of eastern England must have either fled to the west or died in the course of the 'Anglo-Saxon conquest'. Their view was based largely on the belief that a lack of British words in Old English could only be explained by near-complete population replacement and the consequent racial and linguistic purity of the English.[58] Such an interpretation does not, however, accord well with the evidence discussed above with regard to at least some of the British elite managing to survive and adapt to the new ascendancy and perhaps become part of it, nor does it appear to offer any plausible context for the indications of continued Christian worship which we find in this region. Moreover, recent studies of the question of language replacement in early Anglo-Saxon England have offered more sophisticated and nuanced explanations (and analogues) for the lack of influence of Late British/Archaic Welsh on Old English, explanations which do not require either genocide or numerical dominance on the part of the Anglo-Saxons. They argue that the replacement of Late British with English could just as credibly have resulted from a situation in which Old English-speakers socially, politically and linguistically dominated the British/Archaic Welsh-speakers of lowland Britain, against a background of such factors as a pre-existing low social and political status for the Brittonic language and the fact that the Britons had just experienced, over the course of 30 years or so, the kind of economic and material-culture collapse which took several centuries to complete in southern Italy. Certainly, there is social and legal discrimination against Welsh-speakers evident in, for example, the late seventh-century 'Laws of Ine'. Furthermore, it has been suggested that the degree to which Late British/Archaic Welsh influenced English as a whole could, in any case, have been greatly underestimated by previous commentators. Indeed, it has been argued that the available evidence of this influence in fact appears to imply both Celtic-English bilingualism in the early–middle Anglo-Saxon periods and the eventual assimilation of a British majority by the Anglo-Saxon ascendancy.[59]

If we accept that linguistic arguments can therefore no longer be used as a source of support for the idea that all lowland Britons were 'killed or driven out',[60] leaving a virtually empty landscape for 'true Englishmen' to inhabit, we must look to the other available evidence for indications of what actually did occur. Perhaps the best indication that most of the Britons of lowland Britain did indeed remain where they had always been, adopting an Anglo-Saxon ethnicity over time, comes from the environmental and palaeobotanical evidence discussed in the first chapter.[61] This material indicates that models which would include a very significant population drop at some point in the post-Roman period are not credible; as such, if we were to assume that the majority of the Britons disappeared when the Anglo-Saxons took control then we would also have to assume that a large proportion of any shortfall in population was made up by immigrant Anglo-Saxons. However, whilst few would nowadays dispute that there had been a notable degree of mass-migration to eastern England in the post-Roman period (particularly to Lincolnshire, with its large cremation cemeteries), such a proposition is highly improbable. As Bryan Ward-Perkins has observed, even if we go out of our way to overestimate greatly the number of Anglo-Saxons who might have migrated to Britain (putting them at 200,000, the approximate number of Goths on the move in Late Antiquity, a very much larger grouping of people than the 'Anglo-Saxons') and to underestimate greatly the likely number of Britons who were living in lowland Britain (800,000 to 1,000,000), we still end up with a situation in which the missing Britons simply cannot have been replaced by an equal number of immigrant Anglo-Saxons.[62] Given that the real figures are more credibly in the region of 50,000 to 100,000 Anglo-Saxons and perhaps 1.5 million Britons, there seems little chance that the death or disappearance of the majority of these Britons would not have made an impact on the environmental evidence. In other words, the available evidence cannot be explained away, except by an assumption of a large-scale British survival in England.

We thus have a situation in lowland Britain whereby the most credible scenario is that there was both large-scale Anglo-Saxon immigration from the continent *and* large-scale British survival, with these Britons then adopting the Anglo-Saxon ethnic identity. In general, this scenario is in harmony with the data obtained from genetic studies of the modern populations of England and Wales. Although early attempts at using genetic material as a means of understanding events in the post-Roman period were claimed to indicate an extraordinary replacement of the male population of lowland Britain by Anglo-Saxon immigrants (fifty per cent at a minimum), these studies suffered from a host of methodological problems and dubious assumptions.[63] In contrast, more recent studies have far greater credibility, not least because they take account of the likely reproductive advantage that the immigrants would have had once they were in control and the Britons were at an economic, social, legal and political disadvantage, as they clearly were in the seventh-century 'Laws of Ine' and quite possibly in the early Kentish law-codes too. In this light, the present-day genetic evidence is readily explicable in terms of an Anglo-Saxon male immigration totalling as little as five per cent of the total male population.[64] In other words, current interpretations of the genetic evidence similarly would seem to imply that, whilst there must have been mass-migration to eastern England, it is also entirely credible that the vast majority of the native Britons remained in place there after the Anglo-Saxons took over.

With specific regard to our study area, as one of the primary areas of Anglo-Saxon settlement it is likely to have had a higher ratio of immigrants to native Britons than was found in areas further to the west. However, this is not sufficient reason to remove Lincolnshire from the general judgement on British 'survival' offered above, and we do need to be careful not to overestimate how many Anglo-Saxons would have arrived here and how many Britons would have left or died resisting the takeover. As was noted above, there is evidence from Lincolnshire for Britons living under Anglo-Saxon rule (including, potentially, a significant rural British Christian population), with a suggestion that the transition may have been relatively free of violence. Although we need to acknowledge that there were almost certainly more Anglo-Saxon immigrants here than there were in more westerly and northern parts of Britain, this does not mean that the Anglo-Saxons formed anything like the majority of the population. Indeed, as Kevin Leahy has recently observed, even if we interpret the plentiful early Anglo-Saxon (*c.* 450–650) cemetery evidence from Lindsey very generously indeed, the total number of 'Anglo-Saxons' it represents can, given the lack of evidence for woodland regeneration on non-marginal land, scarcely have made up much more than around five per cent or so of the likely total population of Lindsey in the post-Roman period. Needless to say, the 'missing thousands' who do not appear in the burial record would most credibly be seen as archaeologically 'invisible' Britons who, by the end of the early Anglo-Saxon period (*c.* 650), had not yet adopted the Anglo-Saxon material culture.[65]

The positive evidence for such a large British element in the population of Anglo-Saxon Lincolnshire (which was beginning to adopt the immigrant material culture, but was not fully acculturated by the mid-seventh century) is not merely limited to that discussed above. We might also cite, for example, those Lincolnshire place-names which seem to imply the presence of Welsh-speakers in the region, such as Walcot (three instances: near Folkingham, Billinghay and Alkborough), Walton, *Cumbre hole* (now lost, Barrow on Humber area), Cumberworth, and perhaps *Walcroft* (now lost, Fleet parish), Walesby, and the wapentake-name Walshcroft. Kenneth Cameron and Margaret Gelling have both argued that place-names involving *walh/cumbre*, 'Briton' or 'Welsh-speaker', are generally of a mid- to late eighth-century coinage and are reflective of a period at which Welsh-speakers had finally become rare enough in the landscape to inspire comment in place-names.[66] In this context it may well be significant that there are hints in Felix's 'Life of St Guthlac' that there were still people living in the Fens of south Lincolnshire in the early eighth century who spoke a form of Welsh.[67] Certainly, this should not surprise us overmuch. Current models for the 'Anglo-Saxonization' of the Britons suggest that it would have been several centuries before the process was complete, beginning probably with the elites and only later moving on to encompass the rural agricultural population.[68] This does, of course, raise the question of whether we have been right in the past to dismiss that large number of Romano-British settlements in Lincolnshire which have later sixth-, seventh- or even eighth-century Anglo-Saxon material on top of (or close by) them as potential sites where there is continuity of occupation, preferring to treat them as simply later re-occupation of a deserted farmstead.[69]

Other material which might be brought to bear includes potential evidence for Romano-British burial rites in the 'Anglo-Saxon' cemeteries of the region, especially the use of bird bones, as found in six graves at Castledyke South cemetery, Barton-upon-Humber.[70] It is also worth noting that the sequence of buildings and burials at St Paul in the Bail (Lincoln) and the wells and churches dedicated to St Helen (cited above) may not be the only indications from the region for a degree of continuity in British cult practices and sites into the Anglo-Saxon era and beyond: there now appears to be good evidence for the continued use of the river Witham for ritual deposits from the pre-Roman through to the medieval period, which is similarly strongly suggestive of such continuity.[71] Finally, we ought not to forget the very limited, but intriguing, evidence for some degree of continuity in the Romano-British pottery industry around Lincoln. So, for example, a sixth-century Anglo-Saxon stamped pot that was found in the flue ashes of a supposedly fourth-century Romano-British pottery kiln at Swanpool, near Lincoln, has been sometimes considered both to date and represent the last firing of this kiln. Moreover, some of the urns used in the Cleatham cremation cemetery now look to have been Anglo-Saxon pots made using Roman wheel-throwing techniques (Fig. 23).[72] When we put alongside this the possible evidence for a Romano-British kiln at Lea (near Gainsborough) having last been fired in the mid- to late fifth century, and some of the intriguing chance finds of pots from the county that appear Anglo-Saxon in

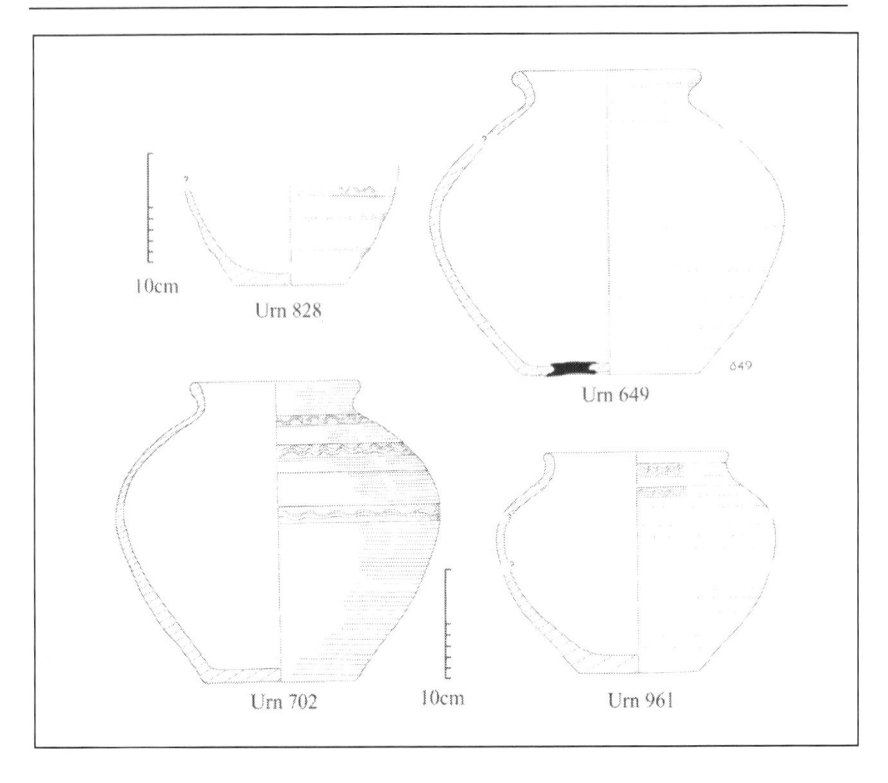

10cm

Urn 828

Urn 649

649

Urn 702

10cm

Urn 961

Fig. 23 Roman-type pots used for cremations at the Cleatham cemetery
Source: Kevin Leahy

form but Romano-British in fabric, we have a potentially very interesting situation.[73] On the whole, the best explanation may be that the absence of fifth-century and later coinage has obscured the final phase of the Romano-British pottery industry in the region, and that the British potters here not only continued to work through the fifth century for the Britons of *Lindēs*, but also subsequently started to produce pottery for the ascendant immigrant groups. Certainly, a degree of continuity for the pottery industry into the post-Roman period has been suggested elsewhere in Britain.[74] Naturally, in the present context this would once again appear to be indicative both of peaceful relations between the Britons and the Anglo-Saxons, and of the willingness of Britons to work with the new ascendancy.

Reconstructing the past: the British 'country of *Lindēs'

As was noted earlier, the chief problem with any attempt to understand the period between *c.* 400 and 600 in Lincolnshire is not that we lack material to study, but rather that what material we do have is fragmentary and often complex. Nonetheless, this does not mean that progress is impossible if a conscious attempt is made to utilize all the different strands of potential evidence. Each of the above pieces of evidence is, on its own, intriguing and suggestive. However, when put alongside each other, a clear and coherent picture of a fifth- and sixth-century British polity based around Lincoln begins to emerge. Consequently, whilst no detailed narrative of the post-Roman period in the Lincoln area survives – unless Ambrosius Aurelianus really was based in the region, as is tentatively suggested above – the following would seem to be a reasonable reconstruction of events based on all of the evidence discussed so far.

The 'country of *Lindēs'* which appears in the linguistic evidence is best seen as the post-Roman British successor to the territory associated with Lincoln, which was one of the four Late Roman provincial capitals of *Britannia* and notably prosperous in the very late fourth century. This polity would have had British leaders, drawn almost certainly from the remnants of the Late Roman aristocracy, and potentially a British bishop too, the old *forum* of the town being partly given over to a church which was entered from its western portico. Furthermore, continued commitment to both the town and its church by the Britons of the 'country of *Lindēs'* is indicated by an expansion and elaboration of this church in the post-Roman period. How long Lincoln maintained control over its entire province, rather than just an extensive area around the city, is uncertain. There are, however, hints that its wider territory did not immediately disintegrate and that Anglo-Saxon settlement in eastern Britain was – initially at least – influenced by the Late Roman provincial arrangements.

Whatever the case may be, Anglo-Saxon immigration and settlement into Lincolnshire looks to have begun at some point around the mid-fifth century, quite possibly as part of a deliberate strategy of territorial defence. Judging from the distribution of the large cremation cemeteries and their implied territories, these immigrant groups to the 'country of *Lindēs'* seem to have been controlled by the Britons and prevented – at least into the early sixth century – from significantly encroaching upon the Britons' chief settlement of Lincoln. The Welsh *Historia Brittonum* suggests that military action *c.* 500 may well have played a role in this containment. Indeed, it is not beyond the realms of possibility that such action was led by Ambrosius Aurelianus and that the Battle of Badon Hill could have been fought in *Lindēs*. In any case, it seems credible that the British leaders based at Lincoln in this period were able to exert some degree of political control over not only the immediate area around Lincoln, but also the peripheral regions settled by these Anglo-Saxons. There is, after all, evidence for the local British elites in these areas being able and willing to assert their ethnic identity in opposition to the immigrant groups through the fifth century and into the sixth, in particular via the use of Class 1 British penannular brooches. The potential survival of rural British Christian cult sites throughout the Lincoln region, indicated by dedications to St Helen, might also be explicable as a result of such a degree of continued British control over both the core of *Lindēs* and those areas settled by the immigrants.

The power and influence of this British 'country of *Lindēs*' seem to have deteriorated from the early sixth century onwards. The most obvious evidence for this is that there are no indications of a continued avoidance of the Lincoln area by those small Anglo-Saxon inhumation cemeteries which supplemented and replaced the large cremation cemeteries. Examples of these are found only a few miles to both the north and south of Lincoln by the mid-sixth century. However, it must be recognized that these sites were not on anything like the scale of the earlier cremation cemeteries or even other contemporary inhumation cemeteries from the region, and there is no evidence for such sites from Lincoln itself or its immediate hinterland. Equally, a few of the find-spots of the Class 1 penannular brooches may reflect some of these outlying elites having aligned themselves with a new ascendant power in the sixth century and adopted the immigrant culture in order to survive. This in turn implies that this period was one in which the dominant power within *Lindēs* had passed, or was beginning to pass, from British to Germanic hands. The sixth century is also very probably the period in which the apsidal church at Lincoln was demolished. Even though

Christian (and, presumably, British) burial occurred at the site subsequently, this demolition might well be taken to suggest the decline or disappearance of the leading British elites in the city.

On the whole, the best explanation of the above evidence is that the Britons of Lincoln finally lost control of the 'country of **Lindēs*' at some point during the sixth century, perhaps around its mid-point. Certainly, Bede's *Historia Ecclesiastica* indicates that there was an Anglo-Saxon (Blæcca) in control of Lincoln by the early seventh century.[75] It is also noteworthy that the bearer of the British name in the genealogy of Aldfrið, king of *Lindissi*, would have probably lived in the early–mid sixth century. The name *Cædbæd* is, after all, suggestive of intermarriage between the British elite of **Lindēs* and the pre-eminent Anglo-Saxon group in the Lincoln region. Such intermarriage would most credibly belong to a period in which the immigrants were gaining in power, but had not yet taken over the 'country of **Lindēs*'. Finally, if the *lynwyssawr* of *Y Gododdin* were Britons from *Linnuis*/**Lindēs*, placed at the battle of *Catraeth* in the mid–late sixth century, then at the very least this suggests that the Welsh author of this stanza believed that **Lindēs* still existed up to that point or had only recently been lost.

The potential evidence of high-status intermarriage mentioned above may, of course, indicate that when the takeover came it was relatively peaceful, or at least not entirely violent. This interpretation is supported by other evidence too. Most importantly, at least some of the territory of **Lindēs* was subsequently part of an Anglo-Saxon kingdom called *Lindissi*, a name which clearly derives from that of the preceding British polity. The rulers of *Lindissi* seem also to have been happy to retain both their very descriptive Anglo-Saxon folk-name *Lindisfaran* ('the people who migrated, *faran*, to the territory of **Lindēs*') and a British name in the political document that was their genealogy. This might well be taken to indicate that they were comfortable with the British past of their kingdom. It also appears likely that British Christianity was at least tolerated by the new Anglo-Saxon rulers of the Lincoln region. This is supported by the St Helen dedications apparently surviving in the countryside despite the change, and by either the British apsidal church at St Paul in the Bail being maintained into the early seventh century or, more probably, the Christian cemetery which succeeded it being in use from the sixth century through to the Middle Saxon period. Furthermore, if some of the local British elites acculturated and 'became' Anglo-Saxon in order to protect their own status, as noted above, then this too is suggestive of a takeover not entirely characterized by antipathy, and we can additionally cite here the evidence of the place-names Washingborough, Cammeringham, Threekingham and perhaps Torksey. Such acculturation and/or intermarriage may also be reflected in the British Type G brooches which have been found in Lincolnshire Anglo-Saxon cemetery contexts.[76] Finally, a relatively peaceful transition to Anglo-Saxon rule, with some members of the British elite joining the new ascendancy and a degree of toleration or sympathy towards the British past and culture, can potentially also help to explain some other aspects of early Anglo-Saxon material culture in the region. In particular, not only is there evidence to suggest that British potters turned their hand to making items for the new ascendancy, but 'Late Celtic' hanging bowls also appear to have been remarkably popular as grave goods within Anglo-Saxon Lincolnshire. These items were probably originally high-status pieces of fifth- to seventh-century British-manufactured tableware, and, as such, the above situation is highly suggestive, as is an enamelled buckle from Keelby, which looks to be of British manufacture but is Anglo-Saxon in form.[77]

Of course, whether the takeover was violent or not, it is probable that the vast majority of the Britons who lived in rural communities throughout the 'country of *Lindēs' remained in place after the transition to Anglo-Saxon rule, adopting over time the Anglo-Saxon ethnicity and material culture. This is, however, likely to have been a long process, given the great discrepancy that exists between the number of highly visible early 'Anglo-Saxon' (c. 450–650) burials and current estimates of the total population of the region at this time. Indeed, the place-name evidence and hints provided in Felix's 'Life of St Guthlac' suggest that the British language was only becoming rare enough in the Lincoln region to prompt comment by the eighth century.

In summary, it is clear that the Anglo-Saxons of the region took over a significant British territory, the 'country of *Lindēs', at some point probably around the middle of the sixth century. Thereafter they ruled over a large proportion of British-speakers, who took until perhaps the eighth century to adopt fully the immigrant ethnic identity and language. The question is, whilst there is clearly a strong British background to the Anglo-Saxon territories of the region, in particular that of *Lindissi*, just how indebted were they to the British past? Moreover, what were the Anglo-Saxons of the region doing in the period before they were converted to Christianity, besides taking control of the territory of **Lindēs* and intermarrying with British elites?

Notes to Chapter 3

1   See further, C. Green, 'The British kingdom of Lindsey', *Cambrian Medieval Celtic Studies*, 56 (2008), 27–9.

2   K. Leahy, *The Anglo-Saxon Kingdom of Lindsey* (Stroud, 2007), pp. 111–14; B. Cox, 'Yarboroughs in Lindsey', *English Place-Name Society Journal*, 28 (1994–5), 50–60; Green, 'British kingdom', 30; K. Cameron, *The Place-Names of Lincolnshire, II* (Nottingham, 1991), p. 8.

3   That the immigrant Anglo-Saxon groups were thus in some way used to fill a military and defensive role previously filled by the Romans may be further indicated by some recent work by Adam Daubney. He considers fourth-century gold coins in Lincolnshire to be indicative of the final phase of Roman military activity in the region, and in this context it is interesting to note that the distribution of these coins seems similarly to form a ring around Lincoln (A. Daubney, 'The use of gold in late Iron Age and Roman Lincolnshire' in S. Malone and M. Williams (eds), *Rumours of Roman Finds: Recent Work on Roman Lincolnshire* (Heckington, 2010), pp. 64–74, especially p. 71; A. Daubney, 'The use of precious metals in Late Roman Lincolnshire' (unpublished lecture, *End of Roman Lincolnshire* conference, 20 March 2010) and personal communication). Although this ring extends much further to the south of Lincoln than does that formed by the Anglo-Saxon cremation cemeteries (to the Spalding–Bourne area), in the north of Lincolnshire the coins often seem to be found in the same general area as the later cremation cemeteries. Indeed, Daubney has suggested that the Anglo-Saxon ring of cemeteries may in fact reflect a contraction of an earlier, late fourth-century defensive system focused on Lincoln.

4   C. Green, *Concepts of Arthur* (Stroud, 2007), pp. 15–26, 30–8; D. N. Dumville, 'The historical value of the *Historia Brittonum*', *Arthurian Literature*, 6 (1986), 1–26; N. J. Higham, *Arthur, Myth-Making and History* (London, 2002), pp. 119–69.

5   L. Alcock, *Arthur's Britain* (Harmondsworth, 1971); J. Morris, *The Age of Arthur* (London, 1973); G. Phillips and M. Keatman, *King Arthur: The True*

Story (London, 1992).

6   See especially Green, *Concepts of Arthur*, particularly pp. 8–130, 177–201; O. J. Padel, 'The nature of Arthur', *Cambrian Medieval Celtic Studies*, 27 (1994), 1–31. The change in predominant academic attitudes to Arthur from credulity to scepticism can be largely dated from 1977, when a seminal paper by David Dumville was published ('Sub-Roman Britain: history and legend', *History*, 62 (1977), 173–92).

7   Gildas, *De Excidio Britanniae*, ed. and trans. M. Winterbottom (London, 1978), chapters 25–6.

8   Green, *Concepts of Arthur*, pp. 204–16

9   Padel, 'Nature of Arthur', 16–18, quotation at 17; M. Wood, *In Search of England: Journeys into the English Past* (London, 1999), pp. 34–8; see also the discussion in Green, *Concepts of Arthur*, pp. 31–2.

10   Green, *Concepts of Arthur*, pp. 62–7, 84–5, 119–21, 207–9, 214; Padel, 'Nature of Arthur', p. 21; R. Bromwich, 'Concepts of Arthur', *Studia Celtica*, 10/11 (1975–6), 171–2.

11   See Bede, *Historia Ecclesiastica*, II.16.

12   See Green, 'British kingdom', pp. 8–10, and *Concepts of Arthur*, pp. 213–15 for some discussion of this point.

13   K. H. Jackson, 'The site of Mount Badon', *The Journal of Celtic Studies*, 2 (1953–8), 152–5; M. Gelling, 'Towards a chronology for English place-names' in D. Hooke (ed.), *Anglo-Saxon Settlements* (Oxford, 1988), pp. 60–1; Green, *Concepts of Arthur*, p. 213 and 'British kingdom', p. 9. Compare R. Coates, 'Reflections on some major Lincolnshire place-names. Part one: Algarkirk to Melton Ross', *Journal of the English Place-Name Society*, 40 (2008), 41–3, for an alternative view of this name. Although there have been no detailed archaeological investigations within the parish, an Anglo-Saxon sword pommel dated to *c.* 450–500 has been found on its edge, which may or may not be relevant here (Lincolnshire HER 43147). Note also that the second element, Old English *burh*, indicates that there was a fortification of some sort at Baumber in the Anglo-Saxon period at least.

14   Gildas, *De Excidio Britanniae*, 26.1.

15   B. Yorke, 'Anglo-Saxon *gentes* and *regna*' in H-W. Goetz *et al* (eds), *Regna and Gentes: The Relationship Between Late Antique and Early Medieval Peoples and Kingdoms in the Transformation of the Roman World* (Leiden, 2003), pp. 397–9, developing a suggestion made by Alan Vince at the 47th *Sachsen Symposium* in 1996. See also R. White, *Britannia Prima: Britain's Last Roman Province* (Stroud, 2007), pp. 197–9. Fig. 21 compares the fourth-century British provinces as reconstructed in J. C. Mann, 'The creation of four provinces in Britain by Diocletian', *Britannia*, 29 (1998), 340, with the distribution of Anglian and Saxon brooches of *c.* 450–500 (after N. J. Higham, *Rome, Britain and the Anglo-Saxons* (London, 1992), p. 163) and Anglian cremation-predominant cemeteries (after H. Williams, 'Cemeteries as central places –

place and identity in Migration Period eastern England' in B. Hårdh and L. Larsson (eds), *Central Places in the Migration and Merovingian Periods* (Stockholm, 2002), p. 344, with additions).

16   I. Williams (ed.), *Canu Aneirin* (Cardiff, 1938); J. T. Koch, 'When was Welsh literature first written down?', *Studia Celtica*, 20/21 (1985–6), 43–66; J. T. Koch, 'Gleanings from the *Gododdin* and other Early Welsh texts', *Bulletin of the Board of Celtic Studies*, 38 (1991), 111–18; J. T. Koch, *The Gododdin of Aneirin: Text and Context from Dark-Age North Britain* (Cardiff, 1997). John Koch's work on the dating and textual history of *Y Gododdin* has been the subject of much discussion amongst Celticists, but as Oliver Padel observes in his detailed review, 'linguistically we feel safe in his [Koch's] hands' (O. J. Padel, 'A new study of the *Gododdin*', *Cambrian Medieval Celtic Studies*, 35 (1998), 45). See also J. E. Caerwyn Williams, 'Review of John T. Koch, *The Gododdin of Aneirin*', *Studia Celtica*, 32 (1998), 282–91, who considers it to be, linguistically, 'scholarship of the highest standard' (291), and Green, *Concepts of Arthur*, pp. 47–8, 50–2, 251–2. Padel's main criticism with regard to Koch's *Gododdin* is that he does not separate out stanzas dated on good linguistic grounds clearly enough from those dated using other, more debatable, methods, such as textual history (see G. R. Isaac, 'Readings in the history and transmission of the *Gododdin*', *Cambrian Medieval Celtic Studies*, 37 (1999), 55–78 for another sceptical review of Koch's suggested textual history of *Y Gododdin*). In this context, it is important to note that the stanza we are concerned with below is one of those which appear to contain some Archaic Welsh features indicative of a written origin in the seventh or eighth centuries, though Koch does argue that this dating should be narrowed to the mid-seventh century on the basis of his understanding of the textual history of *Y Gododdin* (Koch, *Gododdin of Aneirin*, pp. 189–90).

17   Koch, *Gododdin of Aneirin*, pp. xxxv–xlii; C. Cessford, 'Where are the Anglo-Saxons in the Gododdin poem?', *Anglo-Saxon Studies in Archaeology and History*, 8 (1995), 95–8.

18   C. Cessford, 'Northern England and the Gododdin poem', *Northern History*, 33 (1997), 220–1; Koch, *Gododdin of Aneirin*, pp. xiii–xlii.

19   *Canu Aneirin*, ed. Williams, lines 131–5.

20   Koch, *Gododdin of Aneirin*, pp. xxv, 67. On Koch's dating, see above, endnote 16, and Koch, pp. 189–90; see Cessford, 'Northern England', p. 220, for the alternate reading of 'an evil people'.

21   See Green, 'British kingdom', 11–12; J. T. Koch, 'The cynfeirdd poetry and the language of the sixth century' in B. F. Roberts (ed.), *Early Welsh Poetry: Studies in the Book of Aneirin* (Aberystwyth, 1988), p. 33; Cessford, 'Northern England', 220–1.

22   See *Geiriadur Prifysgol Cymru (University of Wales Dictionary of the Welsh Language)*, under *Enwir*'. If the positive description of the *meibyon godebawc*

as 'the rightful faction' is still to be preferred, despite the fact that they appear to have opposed the Gododdin war-band (see further, Koch, *Gododdin of Aneirin*, p. xxv, on the *meibyon godebawc* here), this might be explained as resulting from this stanza perhaps being a summarizing interpolation composed after the text of *Y Gododdin* left the north and came into Wales, where members of the *meibyon godebawc* were probably to be found in the mid-seventh century (Koch, *Gododdin of Aneirin*, pp. xxiii-xxvi, 189-190).

23   Koch, *Gododdin of Aneirin*, pp. xxx-xxxi.

24   Green, 'British kingdom', 11–13; Cessford, 'Northern England', 220–1. Whilst it is likely that much of the defence of **Lindēs* was undertaken by the Anglo-Saxon groups settled at strategic points around the periphery of the territory, as discussed above, it does not necessarily follow that the British population of **Lindēs* was entirely civilian. Indeed, that there were at least some British warriors in **Lindēs* is, of course, implied by the *Historia Brittonum*'s reference to Anglian–British battles fought *c*. 500 *in regione Linnuis* and the fact that the Britons were actually able to control Anglo-Saxon activity in the Lincoln region into the sixth century.

25   Cessford, 'Northern England', 221; Green, 'British kingdom', 12–13.

26   See above, pp. 63–9.

27   Chapter 6 discusses the evidence for this movement in detail. See also K. R. Dark, *Britain and the End of the Roman Empire* (Stroud, 2000), pp. 206–07.

28   See further, pp. 251–2.

29   D. N. Dumville, 'The Anglian Collection of royal genealogies and regnal lists', *Anglo-Saxon England*, 5 (1976), 23–50; S. Foot, 'The kingdom of Lindsey' in A. Vince (ed.), *Pre-Viking Lindsey* (Lincoln, 1993), pp. 133–5.

30   F. M. Stenton, 'Lindsey and its Kings' in D. M. Stenton (ed.) *Preparatory to Anglo-Saxon England* (Oxford, 1971), pp. 129–31; Foot, 'Kingdom of Lindsey', p. 133; S. E. Kelly (ed.), *Charters of Selsey* (Oxford, 1998), p. 54.

31   Foot, 'Kingdom of Lindsey', pp. 133–5, especially p. 135.

32   K. H. Jackson, *Language and History in Early Britain* (Edinburgh, 1953), p. 244, n. 3; P. Stafford, *The East Midlands in the Early Middle Ages* (London, 1985), p. 87; J. Koch (ed.), *Celtic Culture, A Historical Encyclopedia* (Oxford, 2006), p. 60; D. N. Dumville, 'Kingship, genealogies and regnal lists' in P. H. Sawyer and I. N. Wood (eds), *Early Medieval Kingship* (Leeds, 1977), p. 90; and Green, 'British kingdom', 13–14, especially fn. 63, *pace* Stenton, 'Lindsey and its kings', p. 129, who thought *Cædbæd* might be an Anglian–British hybrid. Although Stenton's idea is now often dismissed as a possibility, it has recently been revived by John Insley (J. Insley and M. Eggers, 'Lindsey', *Reallexikon der Germanischen Altertumskunde*, 18 (Berlin, 2001), 477). However, his chief reason for doing so – a disbelief that a name **Catuboduos* could exist – is undermined by Koch's observation that the name **Catuboduos* is probably also the root of the attested Old Breton

name *Catuuodu* (J. T. Koch (ed.), *Celtic Culture, A Historical Encyclopedia* (Oxford, 2006), p. 60).

33 Dumville, 'Kingship, genealogies and regnal lists', p. 90; Foot, 'Kingdom of Lindsey', p. 132; P. H. Sawyer, *Anglo-Saxon Lincolnshire* (Lincoln, 1998), p. 49.

34 Dumville, 'Anglian Collection', pp. 30–7; Foot, 'Kingdom of Lindsey', p. 132. See Stenton, 'Lindsey and its kings', p. 128, for the latter viewpoint.

35 See Foot, 'Kingdom of Lindsey', pp. 132–3, who argues convincingly against the concerns of Stenton, 'Lindsey and its kings', pp. 128–9; and Leahy, *Kingdom of Lindsey*, p. 98. On the Lincolnshire connections of the Northumbrian elite, see Chapter 6 below. For the suggestion that Biscop (and Bede) was descended from the royal *Lindisfaran*, see J. Campbell, 'Bede (673/4–735)', in *The Oxford Dictionary of National Biography*, online edition (Oxford, 2004), at *www.oxforddnb.com*, and A. Thacker, 'Bede and the ordering of understanding' in S. DeGregorio (ed.), *Innovation and Tradition in the Writings of the Venerable Bede* (Morgantown, 2006), p. 40.

36 Leahy, *Kingdom of Lindsey*, p. 98. Note that the suggestion that the *Lindissi* genealogy was in fact standardized to (or originally had) the suspicious fourteen generations to Woden, and then saw three removed (owing to the addition of generations below Woden to that genealogy in the 'Anglian Collection'), seems implausible. It is further undermined by the testimony of the genealogies appended to the twelfth-century chronicle of John of Worcester (*The Chronicle of Florence of Worcester*, trans. T. Forester (London, 1854), pp. xii-xiii, 440). There we are given the Lindsey genealogy without the generations below Woden, but still with only eleven generations to him, whilst the form of the name Aldfrið (*Ealdfrith*) found there suggests an origin for this genealogy separate from that of the 'Anglian Collection' (via a West Saxon source? See Insley and Eggers, 'Lindsey', 477, 478).

37 Stenton, 'Lindsey and its kings', p. 128.

38 Stafford, *East Midlands*, p. 87; Insley and Eggers, 'Lindsey', 477; Green, 'British kingdom', 15; Dumville, 'Kingship, genealogies and regnal lists', p. 90. The exception is the unwarranted hyper-scepticism of Sawyer, *Anglo-Saxon Lincolnshire*, p. 50. An interesting comparison might be made here with the West Saxon royal genealogy, which similarly seems to include at least one 'Celtic' name in its lower reaches (R. Coates, 'On some controversy surrounding *Gewissae/Gewissei*, *Cerdic* and *Ceawlin*', *Nomina*, 13 (1990), 1–11; D. Parsons, 'British **Caraticos*, Old English *Cerdic*', *Cambrian Medieval Celtic Studies*, 33 (1997), 1–8; Koch (ed.), *Celtic Culture*, pp. 392–3).

39 K. Leahy, 'The Anglo-Saxon settlement of Lindsey' in Vince, *Pre-Viking Lindsey*, p. 36; Leahy, *Kingdom of Lindsey*, pp. 48–9; K. Leahy, *'Interrupting the Pots': The Excavation of Cleatham Anglo-Saxon Cemetery* (York, 2007), p. 6; Sawyer, *Anglo-Saxon Lincolnshire*, p. 51; P. Everson, 'Pre-Viking settlement in Lindsey' in Vince, *Pre-Viking Lindsey*, p. 98; Williams, 'Cemeteries as

central'; H. Williams, 'Assembling the dead' in A. Pantos and S. Semple (eds), *Assembly Places and Practices in Medieval Europe* (Dublin, 2004), pp. 109–34, and Chapter 5 below (especially pp. 200–09).

40 Leahy, *Kingdom of Lindsey*, pp. 93–6; Everson, 'Pre-Viking settlement', pp. 97–8; Sawyer, *Anglo-Saxon Lincolnshire*, pp. 52–3.

41 K. I. Sandred, 'Ingham in East Anglia: a new interpretation', *Leeds Studies in English*, 18 (1987), 235–6; B. Cox, 'The pattern of Old English *burh* in early Lindsey', *Anglo-Saxon England*, 23 (1994), 48; A. D. Mills, *A Dictionary of English Place-Names* (Oxford, 1991), p. 187; V. Watts, *The Cambridge Dictionary of English Place-Names* (Cambridge, 2004), p. 33; K. Cameron, *Dictionary of Lincolnshire Place-Names* (Nottingham, 1998), p. 69; K. Cameron, *The Place-Names of Lincolnshire, VI* (Nottingham, 2001), p. 184.

42 Stenton, 'Lindsey', p. 128; Insley & Eggers, 'Lindsey', p. 477; Cameron, *Dictionary*, p. 141.

43 M. Gelling, *Signposts to the Past. Place-names and the History of England*, 2nd edn (Chichester, 1988), pp. 111–12.

44 Dumville, 'Kingship, genealogies and regnal lists', p. 91.

45 On Kirmington, see pp. 30–2, 146–7.

46 Incidentally, the fact that the Sheffield's Hill and Osbournby contexts for these brooches are both sixth-century (or, in the case of the latter, just possibly seventh-century) helps to confirm that Class 1 brooches do indeed belong to the fifth and sixth centuries. See further on dating, Green, 'British kingdom', 24–5 and fn. 101. Note, neither of the two Class 1 brooches from Folkingham comes from the sixth-century metal-detected cemetery in the parish.

47 See above, p. 71.

48 See further, Green, 'British kingdom', 27–9.

49 Cameron, *Dictionary*, p. 135; Insley & Eggers, 'Lindsey', p. 477; J. Insley, 'Pre-conquest personal names', *Reallexikon der Germanischen Altertumskunde*, 23 (Berlin, 2003), 375; J. Insley, 'Old English personal names and anthroponymic lexika' in D. Geuenich *et al* (eds), *Person und Name* (Berlin, 2002), p. 164.

50 Coates, 'Reflections', 50–1; Cameron, *Dictionary*, p. 127.

51 Cameron, *Dictionary*, p. 128; Insley & Eggers, 'Lindsey', p. 477; Insley, 'Personal names', 163; Watts, *Cambridge Dictionary*, p. 622. The earliest spelling of Torksey (*æt Tureces iege, c.* 900) implies that the place-name derives from a personal name **Turoc* rather than **Turc*, but all other spellings from the later tenth century onwards point instead to **Turc* (for example, *æt Turces ige, in Turcesige*), which suggests that the earliest form is probably an error.

52 Leahy, *Kingdom of Lindsey*, p. 115; S. Bassett, 'Lincoln and the Anglo-Saxon see of Lindsey', *Anglo-Saxon England*, 18 (1989), 11–12; B. Gilmour, 'Sub-Roman or Saxon, pagan or Christian: who was buried in the early cemetery

at St-Paul-in-the-Bail, Lincoln?' in L. Gilmour (ed.), *Pagans and Christians – from Antiquity to the Middle Ages* (Oxford, 2007), pp. 252–3.

53 See K. Steane, *The Archaeology of the Upper City and Adjacent Suburbs* (Oxford, 2006); Gilmour, 'Sub-Roman or Saxon', p. 248, fig. 15. Note, David Stocker has suggested (in D. Stocker (ed.), *The City by the Pool: Assessing the Archaeology of the City of Lincoln* (Oxford, 2003), pp. 157–8) that we cannot rule out the possibility that the earliest burials at this site were all 'final phase' (seventh- to eighth-century) pagan Anglo-Saxon interments, which could account for the seemingly Christian lack of burial goods and the east–west orientation. However, this interpretation seems unlikely, particularly in light of the fact that it is generally agreed that the cemetery follows on from an apsidal church and that the site was subsequently a Christian focus in the city. In addition, it ought not to be forgotten that a re-evaluation of the radiocarbon data indicates that the cemetery very probably began before the end of the sixth century rather than during the seventh (see above, pp. 65–7).

54 See above, endnote 53 and pp. 65–7, on the dating of the graveyard. If the apsidal church did manage to survive into the early seventh century then the conversion of the Anglo-Saxon rulers of *Lindissi* to Roman-style Christianity by Paulinus might provide a plausible context for the demolition of the church and Paulinus's building of a new stone church in the city (Bede, *Historia Ecclesiastica*, II.16). Certainly, Steven Bassett has suggested that British ecclesiastical organization continued in the West Midlands until the seventh century, when the conversion of the Anglo-Saxon rulers there led to the silent replacement of British bishops with Anglo-Saxon ones (S. Bassett, 'Church and diocese in the West Midlands' in J. Blair and R. Sharpe (eds), *Pastoral Care Before the Parish* (London, 1992), pp. 13–40).

55 N. P. Brooks, *The Early History of the Church of Canterbury* (London, 1984), p. 20; above, endnote 54 and p. 67.

56 B. Yorke, 'Lindsey: the lost kingdom found?' in Vince, *Pre-Viking Lindsey*, p. 145; *Historia Ecclesiastica*, II.16.

57 G. Jones, 'Holy wells and the cult of St Helen', *Landscape History*, 8 (1986), 59–75; Yorke, 'Lindsey', p. 142. See Jackson, *Language and History*, p. 309, and E. Ekwall, *The Concise Oxford Dictionary of English Place-Names*, fourth edition (Oxford, 1960), p. 163, for *Alauna > Ellen*.

58 For example, the great Victorian medieval historian E. A. Freeman wrote of the Britons in the late nineteenth century that 'we may be sure that we have not much of their blood in us, because we have so few of their words in our language' (*Old English History for Children*, 2nd edn (London, 1871), p. 28).

59 See especially Bryan Ward-Perkins' excellent study, 'Why did the Anglo-Saxons not become more British?', *EHR*, 115 (2000), 513–33; T. Charles-

Edwards, 'Language and society amongst the insular Celts, AD 400–1000' in M. Green (ed.), *The Celtic World* (London), pp. 703–36, particularly pp. 729–33; A. Woolf, 'Apartheid and economics in Anglo-Saxon England' in N. J. Higham (ed.), *Britons in Anglo-Saxon England* (Woodbridge, 2007), pp. 115–29; M. Filppula *et al, English and Celtic in Contact* (London, 2008); and H. L. C. Tristram, 'Why don't the English speak Welsh?' in Higham, *Britons in Anglo-Saxon England*, pp. 192–214. See R. Coates, 'Invisible Britons: the view from linguistics' in Higham, *Britons in Anglo-Saxon England*, pp. 172–91, for an unconvincing attempt to reassert the Victorian position, which allows no validity to evidence other than linguistic, fails to engage properly with Ward-Perkins' points or proposed analogues, and is potentially undermined at its core by Filppula *et al* and Tristram's discussions of the evidence for Late British influence on the English language. For the pre-existing low social and political status of Brittonic/Welsh and how this helps to explain the extent of the linguistic acculturation of the Britons, see Charles-Edwards, 'Language and society', pp. 729–36. For the Italian post-Roman material-culture collapse, see B. Ward-Perkins, 'Specialised production and exchange' in A. Cameron *et al* (eds), *Cambridge Ancient History XIV, Late Antiquity: Empire and Successors, AD 425–600* (Cambridge, 2000), pp. 354–5 (also p. 325 of the same volume); N. Christie, 'Italy and the Roman to medieval transition' in J. Bintliff and H. Hamerow (eds), *Europe Between Late Antiquity and the Middle Ages* (Oxford, 1995), pp. 99–110; and B. Ward-Perkins, *The Fall of Rome and the End of Civilisation* (Oxford, 2005), especially pp. 123–4 and fig. 6.1. Needless to say, such a rapid culture collapse in eastern Britain cannot but have had a concomitant destabilising effect on all aspects of post-Roman lowland British culture and identity. For further probable factors in the linguistic acculturation of the Britons, see, for example, Ward-Perkins, 'Why did', especially pp. 527–30, and Charles-Edwards, 'Language and society', pp. 732–3.

60 Freeman, *Old English History*, p. 28. Note that he allows that the British men might have left behind a few of their womenfolk, who would have been – in his view – made into slaves or forced to marry their new masters.

61 See above, pp. 43–4. See also, for example, H. Härke, 'Population replacement or acculturation? An archaeological perspective on population and migration in post-Roman Britain' in H. L. C. Tristram (ed.), *The Celtic Englishes III* (Hiedelberg, 2003), pp. 16–17.

62 Ward-Perkins, 'Why did', 522–3. See also M. E. Jones, *The End of Roman Britain* (Ithaca, 1996), pp. 8–9, 26–8, 266–8.

63 M. E. Weale *et al*, 'Y chromosome evidence for Anglo-Saxon mass migration', *Molecular Biology and Evolution*, 19 (2002), 1008–21, is a good example of such a flawed study, which was characterized by a small and very restricted sample-set and a remarkable degree of historical naivety. The latter, in particular, led to poor models of events and a lack of

awareness of how circumstances over the intervening 1,500 years might have affected the results they took. So, for example, no awareness is shown of the fact that their two Welsh 'control' sites are in areas which medieval texts claim saw major post-Roman immigration from Ireland and southern Scotland (see, for example, Koch, *Gododdin of Aneirin*, pp. xcvii–xcix, and J. T. Koch, 'Marwnad Cunedda a diwedd y Brydain Rufeinig' in P. Russell (ed.), *Yr Hen Iaith: Studies in Early Welsh* (Aberystwyth, 2003), pp. 171–97). Similarly, they allow for a single, post-Roman migration event with Britons and Anglo-Saxons thereafter breeding at the same rate, both of which assumptions are implausible (see M. G. Thomas *et al*, 'Evidence for an apartheid-like social structure in early Anglo-Saxon England', *Proceedings of the Royal Society*, 273 (2006), 2651–7). Finally, their Central England site is at the meeting point of six eighteenth- and nineteenth-century coaching roads and is thus likely to have been subject to much population churn, of which they show no awareness, and their East of England sites are all from areas where mass migration is readily admitted anyway and, furthermore, where there was a second major immigration from the continent in the intervening period (the Vikings). See also B. McEvoy *et al*, 'The *Longue Durée* of genetic ancestry: multiple genetic marker systems and Celtic origins on the Atlantic facade of Europe', *American Journal of Human Genetics*, 75 (2004), 699, for some further points.

64 Thomas *et al*, 'Evidence for an apartheid-like social structure'. See also A. Woolf, 'Apartheid and economics', and Charles-Edwards, 'Language and society', pp. 732–3.

65 Leahy, 'Anglo-Saxon settlement', p. 38; Leahy, *Kingdom of Lindsey*, pp. 82–3. It should be noted that some, at least, of the 'Anglo-Saxons' buried in these cemeteries are likely to have been Britons who *had* already acculturated before the mid-seventh century – see further below.

66 See K. Cameron, 'The meaning and significance of Old English *walh* in English place-names', *Journal of the English Place-Name Society*, 12 (1980), 1–53; M. Gelling, 'Why aren't we speaking Welsh?', *Anglo-Saxon Studies in Archaeology and History*, 6 (1993), 54; and Gelling, *Signposts*, pp. 95–6. With regard to the dating of such names, a key point is that the second elements are indicative of these compound names being formed 'in the mid to late eighth century' (Gelling, 'Why Aren't We Speaking Welsh?', 54; see also Cameron, 'The meaning and significance,' 33–4). See for the Lincolnshire examples, C. J. Balkwill, 'Old English *wīc* and the origin of the hundred', *Landscape History*, 15 (1993), 11; Cameron, *Lincolnshire II*, p. 30; K. Cameron, *The Place-Names of Lincolnshire, III* (Nottingham, 1992), p. 172; Cameron, *Dictionary*, pp. 134, 135; Mills, *Dictionary*, p. 99; O. K. Schram, 'Fenland place-names' in B. Dickens (ed.), *The Early Cultures in North-West Europe* (Cambridge, 1950), 431; and A. Crowson *et al*, *Anglo-Saxon Settlement on the Siltland of Eastern England* (Heckington, 2005), p. 298.

67   Felix, *Life of St Guthlac*, ed. and trans. B. Colgrave (Cambridge, 1956), pp. 108–11. Such an interpretation of this passage has been most recently advocated by Graham Jones in Koch (ed.), *Celtic Culture*, p. 857. See also A. G. Vince, 'Lincoln in the early medieval era, between the 5th and 9th centuries: the archaeological account' in Stocker, *City by the Pool*, p. 143; and D. Stocker, 'The early Church in Lincolnshire: a study of the sites and their significance' in Vince, *Pre-Viking Lindsey*, pp. 101, 106.

68   C. Scull, 'Approaches to the material culture and social dynamics of the migration period in eastern England' in Bintliff and Hamerow, *Europe Between Late Antiquity and the Middle Ages*, p.78; Thomas *et al*, 'Evidence for an apartheid-like social structure'; H. Härke, *Angelsächsische Waffengräber des 5. bis 7. Jahrhunderts* (Cologne, 1992); H. Härke, 'Changing symbols in a changing society: the Anglo-Saxon weapon burial rite in the seventh century' in M. O. H. Carver (ed.), *The Age of Sutton Hoo* (Woodbridge, 1992), pp. 149–65; and H. Härke, 'Early Anglo-Saxon social structure' in J. Hines (ed.), *The Anglo-Saxons from the Migration Period to the Eighth Century: An Ethnographic Perspective* (Woodbridge, 1997), pp. 125–60.

69   Everson, 'Pre-Viking settlement', p. 91; see further below, pp. 178–83.

70   Leahy, *Kingdom of Lindsey*, pp. 85–6. See also E. O'Brien, *Post-Roman Britain to Anglo-Saxon England: Burial Practices Reviewed* (Oxford, 1999).

71   D. Stocker and P. Everson, 'The straight and narrow way: Fenland causeways and the conversion of the landscape in the Witham valley, Lincolnshire' in M. O. H. Carver (ed.), *The Cross Goes North: Processes of Conversion in Northern Europe, A.D. 300–1300* (Woodbridge, 2002), pp. 271–88. See further below, Chapter 4, pp. 148–50, and Fig. 25.

72   See K. R. Dark, 'Pottery and local production at the end of Roman Britain' in K. R. Dark (ed.), *External Contacts and the Economy of Late Roman and Post-Roman Britain* (Woodbridge, 1996), pp. 58–9, for the pot from one of the Swanpool kilns. See Leahy, *Kingdom of Lindsey*, pp. 52–3 and 86, and Leahy, 'Interrupting the Pots', pp. 126–7, on the Cleatham urns.

73   N. Field, 'Romano-British pottery kilns in the Trent valley', *LHA*, 19 (1984), 100–02, and Green, 'British kingdom', 23 and fn. 97.

74   Compare, for example, M. Whyman, 'Invisible people? Material culture in 'Dark Age' Yorkshire' in M. O. H. Carver (ed.), *In Search of Cult* (Woodbridge, 1992), pp. 61–8.

75   Bede, *Historia Ecclesiastica*, II.16.

76   T. M. Dickinson, 'Fowler's Type G Penannular brooches reconsidered', *Med. Arch.*, 26 (1982), 48, 50, 52 and figs. 1–4, for the two Sleaford brooches. The Keelby and Osbournby examples are probably also from early Anglo-Saxon cemeteries.

77   Susan Youngs, personal communication; S. Youngs, 'Recent finds of insular enamelled buckles' in C. E. Karkov, R. T. Farrell and M. Ryan (eds), *The Insular Tradition* (Albany, 1997), pp. 192–4; and S. Youngs, 'Two

medieval Celtic enamelled buckles from Leicestershire', *Transactions of the Leicestershire Archaeological and Historical Society*, 68 (1993), 15–22. See also K. U. Ulmschneider, 'The archaeology of Middle Saxon England: the evidence of Lincolnshire and Hampshire compared' (2 vols, D.Phil thesis, University of Oxford, 1998), vol. 2, p. 363, and Portable Antiquities Scheme LIN-3702B0 (an enamelled cruciform brooch from Baston) and NLM4745 (an enamelled head of a cruciform brooch from Tathwell). See further below, pp. 147–8.

4

LINDISSI *AND THE LEGACY OF* *LINDĒS

The political legacy of *Lindēs*

The previous chapter was concerned with both the end of the British 'country of *Lindēs*' and the question of the fate of its British inhabitants during the transition from British to Anglo-Saxon rule, and the points made in that chapter apply to the whole of *Lindēs*. However, whilst the British experience of, and reaction to, the change in rulers was treated at length there, the political results of this transition were not. In particular, although it seems clear that the transition to Anglo-Saxon rule may have been relatively peaceful, we do need to determine exactly what form the post-*Lindēs* Anglo-Saxon lordships took. For example, was *Lindēs* taken over as a single whole, with little change aside from an Anglicization of its name to *Lindissi*, or was it split (perhaps along pre-existing internal divisions) into a number of polities of which *Lindissi* was the major one? Furthermore, in either case, just how much did the Anglo-Saxon administration and organization of the region owe to this earlier British territory?

Perhaps the most obvious approach to answering the first of these questions is to examine the boundaries of Anglo-Saxon *Lindissi*. When we first have the means to define accurately the medieval extent of the district of Lindsey, whose name is closely related to the kingdom-name *Lindissi*, it appears, like the modern district, to cover only Lincolnshire to the north and east of both Lincoln and the river Witham.[1] In contrast, the distribution of both post-Roman British metalwork and early Anglian cremation cemeteries in the region indicates that the British 'country of *Lindēs*' probably encompassed a substantial area all around Lincoln into the sixth century, including the whole of modern Lindsey and northern Kesteven (the district to the south of Lincoln and the Witham) down to the Folkingham area.[2] The question therefore becomes, when did the southern third of the territory of *Lindēs become detached from that portion which still bears a name derivative of *Lindēs? Unfortunately, this is extremely difficult to ascertain. In particular, opinion is currently very much divided as to whether Lindsey, as defined in the twelfth-century 'Lindsey Survey', was coterminous with seventh-century *Lindissi* or not, and thus whether the areas south of the Witham were lost during the transition from British to Anglo-Saxon rule or at some point subsequent to this.

If the first scenario is correct, then one might hypothesize that a south Lincolnshire immigrant group, based around the exceptionally large cremation cemetery at Loveden Hill, perhaps took advantage of the temporary uncertainty and instability engendered by a north Lincolnshire group's (probably Cleatham–Kirton in Lindsey) final takeover of the British 'country of *Lindēs' to seize control of some of the territory to the south of Lincoln.[3] The most commonly cited arguments in favour of such a sequence of events include the fact that all of the places which Bede names as being within the kingdom of *Lindissi* are within modern Lindsey and that the Witham and its surrounding fen would be credible as a kingdom-boundary.[4] Unfortunately, these points are not as powerful as they might appear. Bede, for example, only actually identifies three sites other than Lincoln itself as being definitely within *Lindissi*, and so the significance of this point must be in doubt.[5] Similarly, whilst the Witham is certainly a very significant landscape feature for the region, it does not necessarily follow that it *must* have been the southern boundary of *Lindissi*.[6] The existence of *Lindēs demonstrates that an early medieval polity could exist on both sides of the river, and the archaeological and landscape evidence for several causeways linking the solid ground to the north and south of the Witham from the pre-Roman period until the later Middle Ages (with continuous ritual use of the river itself) suggests that too much can be made of the river as a divisive feature in the landscape – it may even have been a unifying focus.[7] In this context, it should be noted that both Steven Bassett and Barbara Yorke have considered that it is entirely plausible that *Lindissi* did include a substantial territory to the south of the Witham throughout its lifespan, and that the restriction of its territory to just the region north and east of Lincoln and the Witham postdates the end of the kingdom and was even potentially an Anglo-Scandinavian development.[8]

Some of the other arguments which have occasionally been made in support of *Lindissi* being coterminous with modern Lindsey are more credible than those noted above, but they are still in no way conclusive or convincing. Thus the fact that the Archbishopric of York does not seem to have laid claim to ecclesiastical authority in Lincolnshire south of the River Witham in the tenth and eleventh centuries is potentially suggestive, given that York had probably inherited the authority of the pre-Viking bishops of *Lindissi*.[9] However, even if accepted as evidence, this can only rule out a post-Viking separation of northern Kesteven from *Lindissi*, not one which occurred at some point before the middle of the ninth century, perhaps during the final absorption of *Lindissi* into Mercia in the late seventh century (the period in which, incidentally, the diocese of *Lindissi* was created).[10] Similarly, if Lissingleys' probable role as the rural meeting place for the whole of Late Saxon Lindsey really can be pushed back into the pre-Viking period (see below, pp. 140–2), this would necessitate Lindsey being a distinct territory at that time too. However, whilst this is interesting if it can be sustained, it would only in fact tell us that Lindsey existed as an administrative unit with a meeting place in the pre-Viking period. It would not tell us whether this unit was coterminous with the kingdom of *Lindissi* or if it was, rather, simply an important but subordinate territory within a more extensive kingdom, which had inherited the lands of **Lindēs* to both the north and the south of the Witham.[11]

All told, it is perhaps not unreasonable to treat modern Lindsey – representing around two thirds of the likely area of the 'country of **Lindēs*' – as a distinct core territory of the kingdom of *Lindissi*. Such would explain much of the available evidence discussed above, and the two names are obviously related. However, this does not mean that the kingdom of *Lindissi* did not also encompass other areas before its late seventh-century end, nor that it did not in fact include almost all of the territory of the British 'country of **Lindēs*' – both to the north and the south of the Witham – within its bounds. There is, quite simply, no credible evidence to suggest that this was not the case, and one can, moreover, make several points in favour of such a scenario.

The first point is relatively straightforward, but important nonetheless. Essentially, it might be thought likely that at least some of the territory immediately to the south of Lincoln (that is, northern Kesteven) did in fact lie within the kingdom of *Lindissi*. If not, then what would seem to have been the chief centre of *Lindissi* was located on a hill on the very borders of its territory, overlooking lands belonging to another kingdom, which is a problematical proposition.[12] Equally, the apparent continued maintenance of most of the British votive causeways on both the northern and southern banks of the Witham after the demise of the 'country of **Lindēs*' is perhaps most readily explicable if the Witham had not become a kingdom-boundary and both banks had remained within a single polity, first *Lindissi* and later Mercia.[13]

In this context, it needs to be remembered that there is a total absence of positive historical evidence to suggest that northern Kesteven was under the rule of a kingdom other than *Lindissi* from the mid-sixth to the late seventh century, other than the contention that *Lindissi's* territory *must* have been coterminous with Lindsey (on which, see both above and point two below) and therefore that someone else *must* have ruled northern Kesteven. So, whilst one can hypothesize a kingdom focused on Loveden Hill, which had taken possession of the whole of the southern part of the territory of **Lindēs* in the sixth century, preventing *Lindissi* from occupying it, there is in fact no reason to believe that such a kingdom ever existed. The only potential Kesteven-based, pre-Viking 'kingdom' which we know of is that of the *Bilmigas*, who are mentioned in the 'Tribal Hidage' and have often been associated with the *Billingas* of south Lincolnshire, an Anglo-Saxon population group recorded in the Fen Edge place-names Billinghay, Horbling and Billingborough.[14] However, there are serious problems with the equation of the *Bilmigas* and the *Billingas*, and if this cannot be sustained then there is no credible basis for thinking that the *Billingas* were ever an independent kingdom or 'people'.[15] Furthermore, even if they can be equated, there seems no justification for considering the resulting *Bilmigas/Billingas* to have been anything more than a small Fen Edge group, whose territory extended not much further inland than the Sleaford area.[16] Indeed, the idea that the small 'Tribal Hidage' groups like the *Bilmigas* must have originally been independent 'kingdoms' does, in any case, no longer appear as convincing as it once did.[17] As such, any attempt to identify the *Billingas* as the kingdom focused on Loveden Hill conjectured above, covering the whole of northern Kesteven, would be both unwarranted and highly speculative. Of course, it might alternatively be suggested that the recorded Mercian kingdom took control of northern Kesteven in the mid-sixth century. However, this suggestion would once again be purely speculative and without any evidential support. In the absence of any actual evidence for northern Kesteven having belonged to an early Anglo-Saxon polity other than *Lindissi* – and bearing in mind both Lincoln's location and the continuing causeways across both sides of the Witham Fens – any hypothesis that the area south of Lincoln had become separated from the rest of the former territory of British **Lindēs* in the mid-sixth century would seem to be both unnecessary and even problematical, if the contention that *Lindissi*'s territory *must* have been coterminous with Lindsey from the mid-sixth century onwards is unsound.

The second point relates directly to the preceding one and argues that we do in fact have some solid evidence which indicates that Lindsey was indeed just the core of the Anglo-Saxon kingdom of *Lindissi*, rather than its entirety. Although present-day Lindsey is largely bordered on the west by the Trent (another apparently 'natural boundary' like the Witham), there is a good case to be made for *Lindissi* having included within it a sizeable district beyond this river, with the attachment of the Isle of Axholme to modern Lindsey being but a small remnant of this. In the pre-Viking era, the Isle of Axholme is thought to have formed the north-eastern part of a district known as *Hæthfelth* (Hatfield), which was described in the early eighth-century 'Life of St Gregory the Great' as a *regio*, a term for an administrative district of a kingdom in Anglo-Latin texts.[18] The actual extent of the *regio* of Hatfield is uncertain, but it seems to have included not only the Isle of Axholme and Hatfield in South Yorkshire, but also the large Hatfield Division of Bassetlaw Wapentake in Nottinghamshire and at least the North Clay division of the same (Fig. 24).[19] The key point here is not simply that Axholme remains a part of Lindsey, although this is undoubtedly significant, but rather that the whole district of Hatfield was in fact

Fig. 24 The three divisions of Lincolnshire plotted alongside the suggested original extent of the *regio* of Hatfield
After M. S. Parker, 'The province of Hatfield', *Northern History*, 28 (1992). The south-eastern boundary of Hatfield is open to debate, with two possibilities shown. The dashed line bisecting Kesteven reflects the southern limit of **Lindēs*, so far as it can deduced from the distribution of cremation cemeteries and British brooches

clearly linked to the kingdom of *Lindissi* as a subordinate unit in the 'Tribal Hidage': *Lindes farona syfan þusend hyda mid hæþ feld lande*, '[the territory of] the *Lindisfaran*, seven thousand hides with Hatfield land'.[20] Consequently, it is more than credible that the main kingdom of which Hatfield was an administrative district (*regio*) was the kingdom of *Lindissi*, and thus that *Lindissi* did indeed extend beyond the borders of modern Lindsey.[21]

How long the *regio* of Hatfield had been a subdivision of the kingdom of *Lindissi* is uncertain. Some recent commentators have assumed that the fact it is mentioned specifically in the 'Tribal Hidage' implies that it was an originally independent unit which had somehow become attached as a sub-unit to *Lindissi*.[22] However, the most detailed study of the *regio* of Hatfield considers it to have been a 'lower tier of organization' within *Lindissi*, rather than anything else, with the specific reference to 'Hatfield land' as part of *Lindissi*'s assessment in the 'Tribal Hidage' being due to the status of Hatfield – 'open country of the heath, wasteland' – as marginal land west of the Trent, unlike the rest of the kingdom of *Lindissi*.[23] Indeed, the character of Hatfield in the Early Medieval period renders as somewhat implausible any attempt to see the district as an originally independent territory. Not only is the name itself indicative of its marginal quality, but also environmental evidence points to both an increase in wetness and significant woodland regeneration there during the post-Roman period, whilst at the same time no early or middle Anglo-Saxon cemeteries have been excavated in this district. Although chance-finds indicate that Hatfield was not abandoned in this era, it was clearly not an area which saw significant pre-Viking Anglo-Saxon settlement activity.[24]

Whatever the case may be on its origins, that Hatfield was indeed a subdivision of the kingdom of *Lindissi*, and fully integrated into this, finds additional support from the sequence of events surrounding Hatfield narrated in the 'Life of St Gregory the Great'. Here it is related that, at some point between 675 and 704, a Deiran priest named Trimma was told in a dream to go and retrieve the body of King Edwin from the site where he was slain 'in that district (*regio*) which is called Hatfield'. When Trimma asks how he is to locate the body without further details, he is instructed to go to a 'village in *Lindissi*' where he will find a peasant householder who can show him the exact spot, something which he eventually does.[25] This is, needless to say, significant. The natural question here is why a peasant householder from the kingdom of *Lindissi* would have been able to identify where Edwin's body lay, given that the site was almost certainly Edwinstowe – located well within the Hatfield Division of Nottinghamshire's Bassetlaw Wapentake – and that around fifty years or more had passed since Edwin had died?[26] Such knowledge might be more than remarkable if the peasant lived many miles from the site in a village in the modern district of Lindsey, but not if his 'village in *Lindissi*' was in fact close by the site in question, because the village, the battle-site and the *regio* of Hatfield were all within the normal and recognized seventh-century boundaries of the kingdom of *Lindissi*.

The third and final point is that a situation wherein Lindsey was the core of a kingdom which also included areas south of the Witham would not actually be unparalleled. As Jeffrey May has argued, modern Lindsey seems to have been the core territory of the *Corieltavi*, the British tribe which inhabited Lincolnshire and Leicestershire in the pre-Roman and Romano-British eras. Although the Romans made Leicester the nominal tribal capital, the original Iron-Age focus of *Corieltavi* power seems to have lain in modern Lindsey, with a southward spread to the Ancaster–Sleaford area and beyond occurring in the late first century BC.[27] Given the evidence for both high-status post-Roman Britons in the Lincoln region and some revival of British tribal identities in the post-Roman period, this may be of particular relevance here.[28]

This is the limit of the available evidence, but it is probably enough to reach some conclusions on the question of the political fate of the 'country of *Lindēs'. It seems clear, especially in the light of the second point set out above, that it can no longer be plausibly argued that *Lindissi*'s territory *must* have been coterminous with modern Lindsey – and thus that northern Kesteven *must* have become detached from the rest of *Lindēs during the transition from British to Anglo-Saxon rule in the region – as it clearly was not. The arguments in favour of such a position were already weak and sometimes dubious, and the evidence of Hatfield renders them largely untenable. Lindsey may very well have represented a distinct core district within *Lindissi*, as it appears to have done for the earlier kingdom of the *Corieltavi*, but there is no need to see it as being anything more than this. Furthermore, not only do we no longer have any reason to place *a priori* the complete separation of northern Kesteven from Lindsey in the sixth century rather than in, say, the late seventh or the ninth, but there is in any case no evidence for this region ever having been in the possession of a kingdom other than *Lindissi* before the late seventh century. Indeed, there are positive indications that *Lindissi* probably did include at least a part of northern Kesteven within its bounds (as noted in the first point above). All told, the most credible scenario, given our present state of knowledge, may well be that the fifth- and sixth-century British 'country of **Lindēs*' was taken over largely intact in order to form the kingdom of *Lindissi*, just as the linguistic origins of the kingdom-name *Lindissi* (< **Lindēs-*) would suggest (Fig. 25).[29]

The organization and administration of Anglo-Saxon *Lindissi*

From a political perspective, the legacy of **Lindēs* in the 'post-British' period was not simply limited to the name and territory of the kingdom of *Lindissi*; as might perhaps be expected, given the likely nature of the takeover, there are also reasons to think that some aspects of the internal organization of *Lindissi* similarly owed a debt to the British past. In particular, attention has recently been drawn to the role that Late/post-Roman 'central places' played in Paulinus' early seventh-century evangelization of *Lindissi* and its northern and western neighbours, Elmet and Deira. All three kingdoms appear to have been British territories taken over by Anglo-Saxon rulers, and in all three cases Paulinus seems to have worked primarily from former Roman forts or towns that were apparently being used for early Anglo-Saxon royal administration. As Barbara Yorke has argued, this would seem to suggest that there was a degree of British–Anglian continuity in terms of the internal organization and administration of all of these formerly British territories.[30] With specific regard to the kingdom of *Lindissi*, the case does not seem unreasonable. Bede, after all, makes it very clear that the focus of the British 'country of **Lindēs*', Lincoln, was a principal centre of the kingdom of *Lindissi* in the early seventh century too, being under the control of an Anglo-Saxon named Blæcca. This is where Paulinus began his mission to the kingdom and it was where he completed a new stone church, seemingly before even York was accorded this honour, this church being later used to consecrate the next Archbishop of Canterbury.[31] Similarly, the mass baptism of the *Lindisfaran* by Paulinus in the Trent is most credibly seen as occurring near to the Roman town of

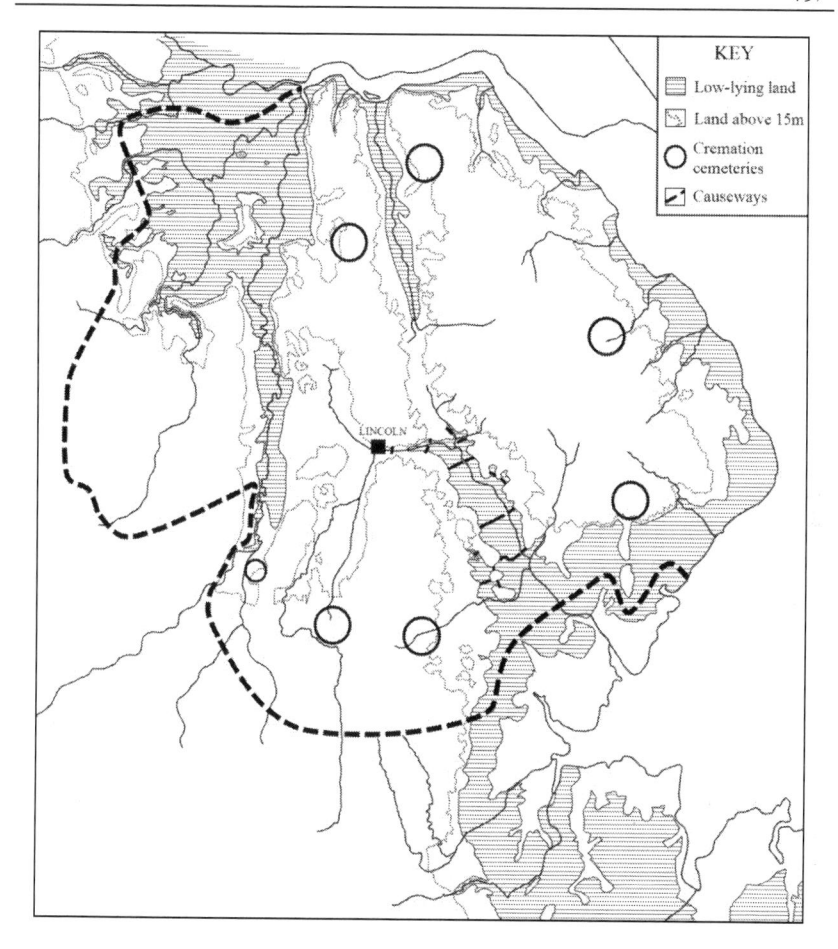

Fig. 25 The suggested boundaries of the Anglo-Saxon kingdom of *Lindissi*, on the basis of the argument offered here (pp. 128–36). Also shown are the major cremation cemeteries of Anglo-Saxon Lincolnshire (see Fig. 11) and the causeways across the Witham valley

The latter after P. Everson and D. Stocker, "'Coming from Bardney...'" – the landscape context of the causeways and finds groups of the Witham valley' in S. Catney and D. Start (eds), *Time and Tide, The Archaeology of the Witham Valley* (Sleaford, 2003). *Copyright:* English Heritage

Littleborough (*Segelocum*), which was probably within *Lindissi*'s boundaries at that time, given the evidence discussed above.

Such potential continuity in the likely internal organization of *Lindēs* and *Lindissi* is obviously of considerable interest from the perspective of the political legacy of *Lindēs*. Indeed, that Lincoln was of considerable importance to the Anglo-Saxons of *Lindissi* is not only apparent from Bede's testimony, it is also evident in the unusual history of the name 'Lincoln' itself. This name appears to derive directly from the British form of the name, so that Late British *Lindogolunia/*Lindgolun* was preserved as *Lindocolina*, *Lindcylene*, and *Lindcolun*, unaltered apart from the expected Old English vowel substitutions and mutations. The last of these forms is the root of present-day 'Lincoln'; the other two forms are attested in Anglo-Saxon England but have no Modern English descendants.[32] This contrasts greatly with the situation found at other Roman cities in eastern and southern Britain where the (Romano-)British name was often lost, either wholly or partially; indeed, Lincoln's name even lacks the usual addition of Old English *ceaster*, 'Roman walled town/fort', which suggests that the second element of Late British *Lindogolunia/*Lindgolun* (< Latin *colonia*, 'colonial town', the highest rank of Roman town[33]) was actually recognized by the Anglo-Saxons of the region as making the addition of *ceaster* unnecessary.[34] In this context, it may also be worth pointing out that the description of Blæcca – who may have been a member of the royal family of *Lindissi*, or even one of its kings – as the *praefectus ciuitatis* of *Lindocolina* (the 'Prefect of the City of Lincoln') has been seen as potentially indicative of the new Anglo-Saxon rulers not only taking on the physical rule of Lincoln and its territory, but also a post-Roman British title that went with this.[35] Certainly this does not have to be the case: *praefectus* was used in Anglo-Saxon England for people of varying status, including sub-kings, and as such it would not be unlikely that an Anglo-Saxon ruler of Lincoln and/or *Lindissi* in a period of Northumbrian domination of the kingdom would be described thus.[36] On the other hand, the notion of an inherited title is not impossible and deserves some consideration.

If Lincoln and Littleborough's roles in the administration of early seventh-century *Lindissi* were thus potentially a legacy of their status as British/Romano-British 'central places', what of the other sites which were important to the internal organization of *Lindissi*? Certainly, a case has recently been made that the Late Roman fortified

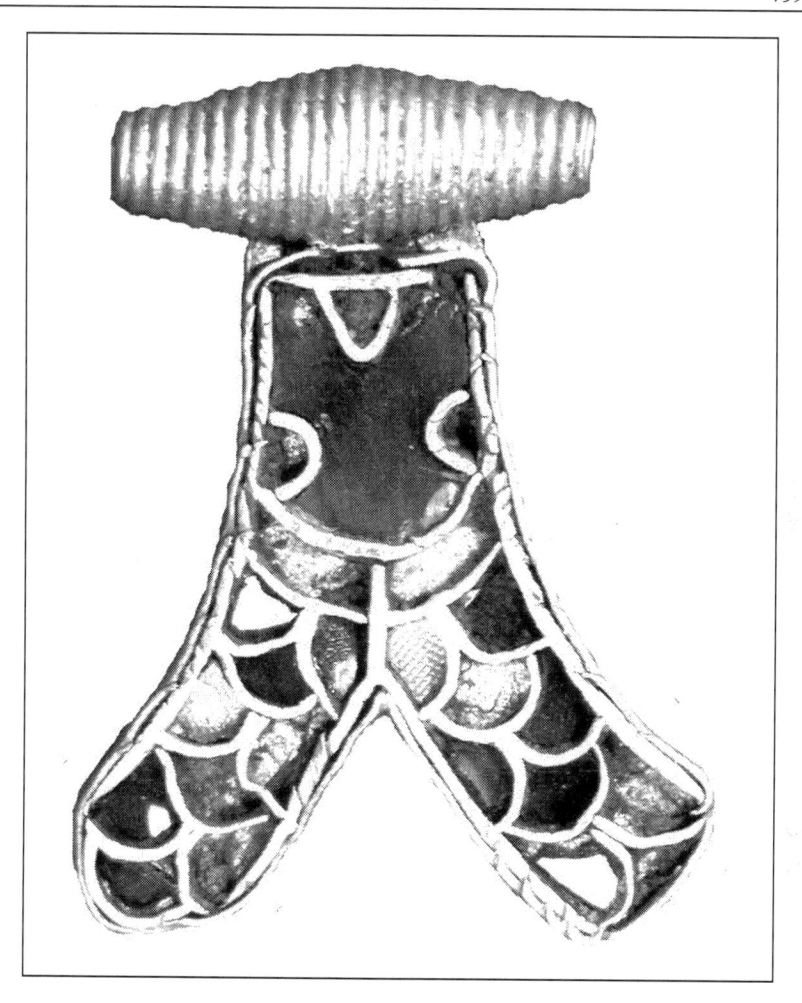

**Fig. 26 An early Anglo-Saxon gold-and-garnet pendant in the form
of a stylized insect, discovered near Horncastle**
Source: Kevin Leahy, Portable Antiquities Scheme

'small town' of Horncastle was the focus of a seventh-century Anglo-Saxon royal estate, which was centred on the Roman fort but stretched down to the Witham, with a royal residence perhaps inside Horncastle's walls where the manor house now stands.[37] In this context, it can be observed that Horncastle was the centre of an Anglo-Saxon royal soke, a type of Anglo-Saxon administrative unit

often thought to have its origins in the pre-Viking period.[38]
Moreover, recent finds of early and middle Anglo-Saxon metalwork
from the town and its hinterland – in particular, a late sixth- to
seventh-century gold-and-garnet pendant (Fig. 26) and a silver boar's-
head mount from a helmet of the same period – strongly suggest that
members of the local Anglo-Saxon elite were present in the
Horncastle area in the period after the likely mid-sixth-century Anglo-
Saxon takeover of the region.[39] It thus seems probable that
Horncastle had a significant role to play in the administration of
Lindissi in the early Anglo-Saxon period, and in such circumstances it
is not implausible that its importance – like that of Lincoln – resulted
from British–Anglian continuity in the internal organization of the
region. In fact, such a situation would help to explain the fact that the
probable Romano-British name of this fort, *Bannovallum*, appears to
have been preserved in the name Horncastle, with Old English *horn*
apparently directly translating British **banno-*, a point which is
indicative both of local bilingualism and a degree of continued
significance for the site.[40]

Another site which is likely to have been of central importance to
the administration of Anglo-Saxon *Lindissi* was Lissingleys. Up until
its enclosure in 1851, Lissingleys was the name of an area of pasture
situated approximately ten miles to the north-east of Lincoln, the
common use of which was shared between a number of surrounding
settlements which lay in different Wapentakes and Ridings of
Lindsey. However, its original import would seem to have gone far
beyond this. As David Roffe has demonstrated, this common land
was located at the exact point where the three Anglo-Scandinavian
Ridings of Lindsey met, and a consideration of the available evidence
and relevant parallels suggests that it is very likely that Lissingleys was
in fact the rural meeting place of the whole of Late Saxon Lindsey.[41]
This is, of course, a point of considerable significance, and it naturally
raises the question of whether such a Late Saxon role for Lissingleys
could have developed from a similar or related function for the site in
the pre-Viking period. In this context, the West Riding certainly has a
rather odd and artificial eastern boundary, which looks to have been
deliberately adopted in order to ensure that all three of the Ridings
converged at Lissingleys (Fig. 27). The implication is that this site
already had some considerable significance before the Ridings were

created,[42] and such a proposition finds additional support in the known early Anglo-Saxon archaeology of this area. Thus, metal-detecting over a number of years by Keith Kelway and others has uncovered evidence for as many as three separate early Anglo-Saxon cemeteries in the immediate vicinity of Lissingleys. This is, in itself, quite remarkable, and some of the Anglo-Saxon material recovered from these cemeteries is, moreover, clearly indicative of the presence of members of the Anglo-Saxon 'elite' in the Lissingleys area. Although an enamelled mount from a 'Late Celtic' hanging bowl is, of course, suggestive in this regard, the most impressive finds have been a rare mid- to late sixth-century silver sword ring and a silver sword mount, both probably from the same weapon (Fig. 28). Such 'ring-

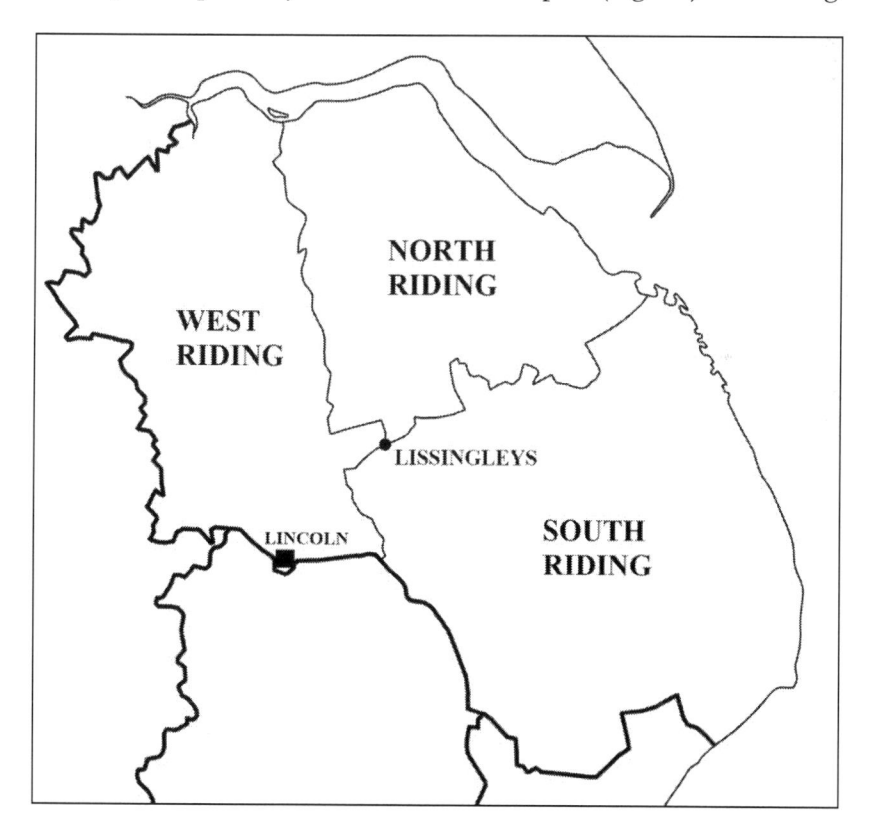

Fig. 27 Map of the Anglo-Scandinavian Ridings of Lindsey, showing the location of Lissingleys

swords' have an almost exclusively Frankish and Kentish distribution and are thought to be symbolic of exalted social status, even in those areas where they are more common. Furthermore, this particular example has a malachite setting at the apex of its pyramidal mount, the use of which is extremely rare in the post-Roman period and otherwise unknown in an early Anglo-Saxon context.[43]

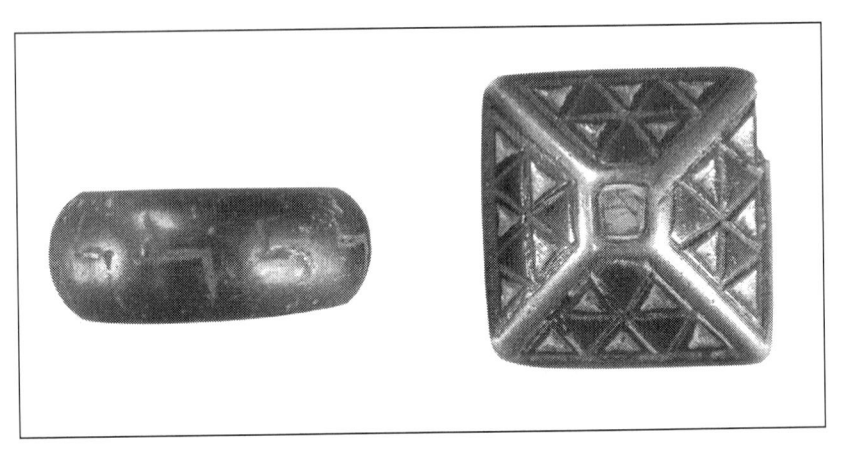

Fig. 28 A sixth-century, silver sword ring and mount, probably from the same weapon, discovered at Lissington by Keith Kelway
Source: Trustees of the British Museum

Taken together, the historical and archaeological evidence for Lissingleys implies that this was probably the location of some sort of pre-Viking 'central place' for the Anglo-Saxons of *Lindissi*, and potentially one which had a crucial role in the internal structure of the kingdom (or at least of its core district, modern Lindsey). The question is, was this apparent status as a 'central place' a new development or is it possible that this too was partly a legacy of the British and/or Romano-British background to *Lindissi*? Whilst metal-detecting has revealed Anglo-Saxon activity in the immediate area of Lissingleys, this is not all that it found. The major discovery was actually a very significant and extensive concentration of Iron Age and Romano-British material located to the south of where the Ridings meet. Finds from here include pre-Roman brooches, pottery and five gold and silver coins, along with extremely large numbers of

Roman-era brooches and coins (primarily third- to fourth-century), pointing to a site in constant use from the pre-Roman Iron Age through to the late fourth century.[44]

As to the nature of this activity, the limited excavations to date have unfortunately not encountered any structural remains and are largely inconclusive. Finds of roof tile, box-flue tile and wall plaster imply a substantial Romano-British building somewhere on the site, and there is some evidence of domestic, military and small-scale industrial activity, but what exactly this represents remains unclear.[45] Perhaps potentially more informative is a subset of the metal-detected material, which constitutes a collection of finds indicative of votive and ritual activity. In particular, a sceptre head in the form of a helmeted Mars has been found in the southern part of the site, which is strongly suggestive of there being a rural temple or shrine of some sort here. In this context it is also interesting to note that two silver rings bearing the inscription 'ToT' have also been recovered. These reference the Romano-Celtic deity Mars Toutatis, who appears to have been particularly venerated by the *Corieltavi* of Lincolnshire. In addition to such votive finds, there are some which look to be ceremonial in origin, including a fine bronze bowl and a high-quality bronze ox-head spout from a shallow bowl, perhaps used for wine-pouring on special occasions, which is again suggestive (Fig. 29).[46] In sum, the number and nature of finds from this site is intriguing, and at present the most convincing suggestion is that there was a Romano-Celtic rural temple/shrine here, in addition to any other activity at the site. Moreover, it is tempting to speculate that this shrine was particularly associated with Mars Toutatis, an important tribal deity for the region.

Could this potential pre-Roman and Romano-British significance for the Lissingleys area at least partially explain its importance under Anglo-Saxon rule from the second half of the sixth century onwards? Certainly the coincidence is noteworthy, and it is not impossible that the site might have retained a degree of local and tribal importance even after the conversion of the British to Christianity, which was probably largely complete by the sixth century on the basis of the testimony of Gildas (note here the continued local importance of rural Romano-British pagan cult sites after the conversion, suggested by dedications to St Helen and post-Roman votive deposition in the

Fig. 29 A sceptre head (in the form of a helmeted Mars) and an ox-head spout, found by Ken Toyne on the Roman site to the south of Lissingleys
Source: Keith Kelway

Witham).

In support of some sort of relationship between the Romano-British activity and the early Anglo-Saxon, two pieces of evidence can be cited. The first is the distribution of the probable sixth-century Anglo-Saxon cemeteries: these were situated immediately to the north of the Romano-British site, immediately to its south, and – still close but a little further away – to its east.[47] In other words, early Anglo-Saxon cemeteries have been found all around and close to the Romano-British site, but not on it. This might well be taken to imply that their location was dictated by this earlier centre, but that the Anglo-Saxons were avoiding burying on the site itself for some reason. Needless to say, both points suggest that the site still had a recognizable function in the sixth century. The second piece of evidence comes from the name Lissingleys and the neighbouring, and clearly related, name Lissington. Early forms of the latter – the earlier recorded of the two – include *Lessintone, Lissigtuna, Lissingtun, Lissington* and *Lissinctona*.[48] The two place-names mean, respectively, the *lēah*, probably 'clearing', and the *tūn*, 'village', associated with (medial connective *-ing-*) *Lissa.[49] Usually, *Lissa is thought to be an unrecorded, shortened (hypocoristic) form of the Old English personal name *Lēofsige*.[50] However, an origin for *Lissa in the word which produced the place-name Liss (early forms include *Lis, Lissa, Lisse, Lysse*[51]) in Hampshire seems worthy of consideration too. This word is Late British/Archaic Welsh **liss-*, the root of Welsh *llys*, for which the *Geiriadur Prifysgol Cymru* offers early-attested definitions including 'court, hall' and 'parliament, gathering of nobles', with Lissingleys/Lissington becoming on this model 'the clearing/village associated with the *Liss'.[52] Such an origin for Lissingleys/Lissington would obviously strengthen the notion that this site was an important (and multi-purpose) centre in both the Roman and post-Roman periods and perhaps offers a context for this importance. It would also provide considerable support for the view that the probable role of Lissingleys as a meeting place within pre-Viking *Lindissi* was another example of British–Anglian continuity in the internal administration of the region.

It would therefore appear that Barbara Yorke's case for at least a degree of British–Anglian continuity in the internal organization and administration of *Lindissi* is more than credible. Lincoln, Littleborough, Horncastle and Lissingleys were all arguably significant elements in the internal structure of Anglo-Saxon *Lindissi*, and in each case it seems likely that this significance can be related to the site's importance in the preceding British and Romano-British periods. Such a situation would, of course, accord well with the evidence discussed in previous chapters for a relatively non-destructive Anglo-Saxon takeover, which saw continuity not only in the kingdom-name and territory, but also potentially in other aspects of post-Roman British life, including pottery production, metalworking, landscape exploitation, and religion.

Needless to say, we need to be wary of pressing this too far – some early Anglo-Saxon administrative centres, such as Loveden Hill and Bolingbroke–West Keal, have no immediately obvious antecedents. On the other hand, there is a very credible case to be made for the early Anglo-Saxon 'central place' of Sleaford–Quarrington having inherited its territory and significance from the Roman 'small town' of Old Sleaford. Similarly, if Caistor's demonstrable Middle Saxon importance as an ecclesiastical centre resulted from an early Anglo-Saxon secular significance, then it would not be implausible that this too was a legacy of the (Romano-)British organization of the region, given the importance of this fortified 'small town' in the Late Roman period.[53] It ought to be noted here that Caistor was, like Horncastle, the centre of an Anglo-Saxon royal soke, that there were three early Anglo-Saxon cemeteries located close by, and that there is a deserted medieval village named 'Wykeham' in the neighbouring parish. This name derives from Old English *wīchām*, which in turn comes from Latin *vicus* + Old English *hām*. *Vici* were Roman settlements that were often the administrative centres for the *pagi* (subdivisions of the *civitates*) in the Romano-British period, and names which derive from *wīchām* have often been plausibly considered to be indicative of some sort of administrative continuity between the Late Roman and early Anglo-Saxon periods. This is, of course, a point of considerable interest given the proximity of Wykeham to Caistor.[54] It might equally be seen as significant that the small Roman town of Hibaldstow – occupied from probably the first century through to the fifth century, and another likely Late Roman *vicus* – lay just to the north-east of Cleatham–Kirton in Lindsey, a major Anglo-Saxon administrative centre from the very early Anglo-Saxon period onwards.[55] Likewise, the fortified 'small town' of Ancaster had a small fifth- to sixth-century cremation cemetery founded just outside its walls, which Howard Williams has recently considered indicative of Ancaster having functioned as an early Anglo-Saxon 'central place'.[56] Finally, both the Elsham and South Elkington cremation cemeteries – which were early Anglo-Saxon funerary, social and sacred *foci* – were located near to the probable Late/post-Roman forts of Yarborough Camp and Yarburgh.[57] Indeed, Elsham is also only three miles from Kirmington 'small town' (itself a mile to the south-east of Yarborough Camp), which seems to have been a significant British centre in the Late and post-Roman periods on the basis of the very strong and late coin sequence there, the three high-status Class 1 brooches found on the site, and the fact that the name Kirmington – *Chernitone* at Domesday – may well preserve the town's British name.[58]

All told then, it would not seem unreasonable to argue that the type of British–Anglian continuity in the internal administration of the region discussed in detail above was potentially more the general rule than the exception, and that *Lindissi*'s administrative debt to the preceding British 'country of *Lindēs' was thus potentially both considerable and widespread, just as might in fact be expected given the longevity of *Lindēs and the apparent nature of Anglian–British interaction in the region.

Material culture and religion

The political and administrative legacy of *Lindēs described above was not, of course, the only lasting impact that the British past had on the Anglo-Saxon kingdom of *Lindissi*. One other probable inheritance was a large British population, the management and integration of which would most likely have remained an issue well into the eighth century, to judge from the place-name evidence and hints in Felix's 'Life of St Guthlac'. Lincolnshire was not, of course, unique in this regard; such must have been the case throughout much of lowland Britain. However, there are reasons to think that the fact that these Britons had been in charge of an extensive territory around Lincoln some way into the sixth century may have meant that this population legacy had a more noticeable effect here than it did in some other parts of Anglo-Saxon England.

On the material culture front, one might, for example, point to the Keelby enamelled buckle – with its implications of Anglian–British 'cultural fusion in the workshop'[59] – and the British hanging bowls used as Anglo-Saxon grave goods. With specific regard to the hanging bowls, although they are indeed found elsewhere in eastern and southern Britain, the quantities found in Lincolnshire are remarkable. This is true both in terms of the overall corpus of bowls and of that subset which has been discovered in late sixth-/seventh-century Anglo-Saxon funerary contexts.[60] It might, of course, be argued that the reason why the Anglo-Saxons of the Lincoln region had such exceptional access to these pieces of elite British tableware is simply that they inherited them from the sixth-century 'country of

Lindēs and its elites. This is certainly very likely to be a major factor in explaining the Anglo-Saxon usage of these pieces.[61] However, it cannot represent the entire story, as some of the hanging bowls from the region post-date the sixth century and thus the likely end-date of *Lindēs*. This implies that a rich material inheritance was not the only factor dictating the popularity of such British metalwork in Lincolnshire, a conclusion supported by the Keelby buckle and other such items.[62] All told, the number and date-range of the Lincolnshire hanging bowls point to the Anglo-Saxons of the region having developed a particular interest in obtaining and possessing such pieces of British prestige metalwork, and it is difficult to dissociate this especial interest from their unusually extended contact with – and, perhaps most importantly, probable partial absorption of – the British elite of the 'country of *Lindēs*', discussed in the preceding chapters.

In addition to indicating a long-lasting fascination with 'Celtic' elite metalwork in the Lincoln region, one of the find-spots of these hanging bowls can also point us to another potential arena in which the British background to *Lindissi* left a major cultural legacy. As David Stocker and Paul Everson have recently argued, the river Witham appears to have been a major votive cult site for the people of Lincolnshire from the prehistoric era onwards. Detailed landscape research has managed to identify ten prehistoric causeways leading out into the Witham, which appear to have been used for the ritual deposition of various items into the river. Seven of these causeways and deposition sites look to have continued in existence through the Romano-British period and then into the medieval, with the famous Witham hanging bowl probably representing one Middle Saxon instance of this recurring ritual activity (Figs 25 and 30).[63] Such continuity in ritual activity from prehistory into the Anglo-Saxon period and beyond (the last votive depositions date from the fourteenth century) is, of course, most unusual. Needless to say, it seems reasonable to relate its survival to both the apparent lateness of the Anglo-Saxon takeover in the region and the other available evidence for the Anglo-Saxon rulers of *Lindissi* being tolerant of British religious practices. In particular, attention might be once again drawn to the Christian continuity evidenced at the St Paul in the Bail site and the possible continuity in rural British cult sites that appears

Fig. 30 The famous Witham hanging bowl, discovered during drainage works on the River Witham in 1816, but since mislaid
Source: Society of Antiquaries of London

to underlie the many dedications to St Helen in the region.

The importance of *Lindissi*: a symbolic inheritance?

If the British background to *Lindissi* may have left a cultural legacy as well as a political and administrative one, this is not necessarily the end of the matter. Some aspects of the seventh-century history of *Lindissi* suggest that there may also have been a symbolic legacy.

One of the most curious aspects of the seventh-century history of *Lindissi* is the apparent eagerness of the great Anglian kingdoms of Mercia and Northumbria to control and lay claim to the kingdom. The likely late seventh-century final annexation of *Lindissi* by Mercia came at the end of a number of decades in which the kings of *Lindissi* appear to have been under the constant overlordship of either Mercia or Northumbria. When Bede first mentions the kingdom of *Lindissi* it is under the overlordship of Edwin, king of Northumbria, who sponsored a mass baptism of the *Lindisfaran* in the Trent and the building of a stone church at Lincoln *c.* 627–8. It is not clear whether *Lindissi* passed under Mercian overlordship after the death of Edwin (633) at the hands of Penda, king of Mercia, or whether it regained its independence. Whatever the case may be, the people of *Lindissi* remembered Oswald, king of Northumbria 634–42, as a 'conqueror', so he must have retaken the kingdom at some point soon after its escape from Northumbrian overlordship.[64] After the death of Oswald, it is generally assumed that *Lindissi* continued to be subordinate to the two larger kingdoms, being first under Mercian overlordship until Penda's death in 655, then Northumbrian until 658, and then once more Mercian under Wulfhere until *c.* 674.[65] At this point it appears that the Mercians were defeated in battle by the Northumbrians, and Bede relates that Ecgfrith of Northumbria won the kingdom of *Lindissi* around this time, presumably as a result of this same battle. Finally, Æthelred of Mercia defeated Ecgfrith at the battle of the Trent in 679, which appears to have been the final change in fortune for the kingdom of *Lindissi* – from this point onwards it remained firmly under Mercian control.[66]

Quite why *Lindissi* was so contested in the seventh century is, of course, a matter of considerable interest here. Its changing overlordship may simply have been a by-product of the larger conflict between Mercia and Northumbria in the seventh century, with its proximity to the contested boundary where these two overlordships met and location on the Roman road network between them resulting in it being a natural, but coincidental, prize for the victor after each battle. On the other hand, it may well be that the overlordship of *Lindissi* was, in fact, specifically part of what was ultimately being fought over in these repeated battles, as has sometimes been suggested. Certainly, this is implied by Bede's account of the period and its battles: for instance, his reference to 'the kingdom of *Lindissi*, which King Ecgfrith had recently won by conquering Wulfhere and putting him to flight'.[67] In this context it ought to be remembered that a number of the key battles between Mercia and Northumbria do seem to have been fought either on the borders of the kingdom of *Lindissi* or even within the westernmost marches of it. So, given that *Lindissi* appears to have extended west of the Trent to take in the district of Hatfield in the seventh century, it is clear that at least one of the above major battles took place within the borders of the kingdom. This was the battle of Hatfield, *Hæthfelth*, at which Penda and his allies defeated and killed Edwin of Northumbria in 633, removing *Lindissi* from Northumbrian overlordship. Furthermore, it is quite likely that the site of the battle at which Æthelfrith of Northumbria, another overlord, was taken by surprise and killed *c.* 616 similarly lay within the *regio* of Hatfield. A case has also been made that the unidentified site of the battle of *Maserfelth* – at which Oswald of Northumbria was killed by Penda in 642 – ought to be looked for within *Lindissi*, and the same could well be said for that of the Battle of the Trent (679).[68]

In this light, the idea that the overlordship of *Lindissi* was one of the primary considerations in motivating these battles (as is implied by Bede) may not seem so strange, and if control of this kingdom was indeed the major bone of contention in the seventh-century wars then it does, of course, raise some intriguing questions about the status and role of Lincoln and its territory in the fifth, sixth and early seventh centuries. So, why might *Lindissi* have been so important to Mercia and Northumbria? On the one hand, it is certainly credible that *Lindissi*'s location, controlling the north–south Roman road network, both banks of the lower Trent (which was navigable into Mercia at least as far as Nottingham[69]) and the southern bank of the

Humber, made it an attractive strategic conquest for both kingdoms rather than simply a coincidental one. Moreover, *Lindissi* appears to have been both wealthy and well connected to the outside world: not only are a remarkable number of high-status 'Late Celtic' hanging bowls known from here, but there are also notable concentrations of continental gold coins and imported Baltic amber.[70] Such a situation would, of course, have made the kingdom an even more desirable prize, especially from the perspective of land-locked Mercia.[71]

On the other hand, it might well be wondered whether strategic advantage and the control of an economically significant region, whilst undoubtedly powerful motivating forces, fully explain the Mercian and Northumbrian interest in controlling *Lindissi*. Obviously, no certainty can be had on this matter, but if **Lindēs* really did have some measure of post-Roman provincial control over the initial Anglian settlement in the fifth century and continued to remain a powerful force in the region into the sixth century, then a remembrance of this might have made the control of Lincoln and *Lindissi* a symbolic prize of sufficient interest to be disputed between the two leading *imperium*-building Anglian dynasties of the seventh century. Such would certainly explain *Lindissi*'s manifest attraction to these two kingdoms. In addition, there appears to have been a direct road-route between Mercia and Deira that ran considerably west of the Trent, a point which might in any case undermine the case for *Lindissi* as simply a strategic conquest.[72]

In support of such a symbolic legacy of British **Lindēs* lying at the root of *Lindissi*'s turbulent seventh-century history, two tentative points might be made. The first is the curious fact, noted above, that Edwin of Deira – the early seventh-century overlord of *Lindissi*, whose interest in establishing an *imperium* that harked back to the Roman era is well established[73] – oversaw the completion of a stone church in Lincoln before even York. Furthermore, it was in this church that the consecration of the next Archbishop of Canterbury, Honorius, took place. This would seem to suggest that Lincoln was considered a very significant location by Edwin, and perhaps more suitable for the symbolically important consecration of Honorius as archbishop than any place within his Northumbrian kingdom proper.[74] The second is the possibility, mentioned above, that the Anglo-Saxon rulers of *Lindissi* were making use of an inherited 'sub-

Roman' title; if so, this would suggest that the British past of the kingdom was indeed acknowledged and of symbolic value in the early seventh century.

It is also conceivable that the control of *Lindissi* could have had a more personal symbolic content for the rulers of Mercia and Northumbria. As is argued at length in Chapter 6, there is a good case to be made for significant population groups within Northumbria, and quite possibly Mercia, having in fact originated in the Lincoln region. To give but one example here, the kings of Bernicia are most credibly seen as in origin *Lindisfaran*, who had migrated to the Lindisfarne–Bamburgh region in the middle of the sixth century.[75] Indeed, it is not beyond the realms of possibility that members of the Northumbrian elite up to and including the Bernician ruling house itself could even have had blood links to the kings of *Lindissi*; certainly, such a link has been recently suggested for one powerful mid-seventh-century Northumbrian noble.[76] Naturally, all of this is very suggestive from the present perspective, and in this context it is surely likely that both the Northumbrian and the Mercian kings would have felt that they had a legitimate claim on the kingdom of *Lindissi* and would have seen its possession as a personal symbolic victory.

The significance of **Lindēs*

This is probably as far as we need to go. The following chapters touch on some additional indications of the lasting impact of **Lindēs* on the internal structure of the region, the early history of Anglo-Saxon England, and the legends which surround the post-Roman period, but they do not fundamentally alter the overall picture provided by the material discussed above. Essentially, it is clear that the 'country of **Lindēs*' cannot be considered a mere historical curiosity. Instead, there seem to be good reasons to think that the Britons based at Lincoln in the fifth and sixth centuries left a political, administrative, cultural, and even potentially a symbolic, legacy for the succeeding centuries. This is, naturally, something which is of considerable interest in the overall context of Anglian–British interaction in this region: such interaction appears not to have simply consisted of Britons adapting to the new Anglo-Saxon ascendancy (acculturation) but also the new ascendancy having been influenced – to some greater or lesser degree – by the British context from which it emerged. The question is, can we know anything more about those who were thus affected by the legacies of *Lindēs*?

Notes to Chapter 4

1   F. M. Stenton, 'Lindsey and its kings' in D. M. Stenton (ed.), *Preparatory to Anglo-Saxon England* (Oxford, 1971), pp. 133–4; C. W. Foster and T. Longley (eds), *The Lincolnshire Domesday and the Lindsey Survey* (Lincoln, 1924). See above, pp. 57–8, on the relationship between the names 'Lindsey' and *Lindissi*.

2   C. Green, 'The British kingdom of Lindsey', *Cambrian Medieval Celtic Studies*, 56 (2008), 27, 35 and fn. 131. The southern limits of the British *Lindēs* are best defined by the distribution of the cremation cemeteries and the Class 1 and Type G brooches (the most southerly of which come from Folkingham), given that it was argued in previous chapters that these all belong to the peripheral regions of *Lindēs*. Indeed, all but two of the Lincolnshire hanging bowls and all of the Old English *-ingas* group-names formed from British personal names fall within this area too, and 'Kesteven' itself appears to be a Scandinavianized British district-name deriving from British *cēto-*, 'wood' (K. Cameron, *Dictionary of Lincolnshire Place-Names* (Nottingham, 1998), p. 72; Green, 'British kingdom', 35 and fn. 132).

3   For example, Green, 'British kingdom', 35 and fn. 133; B. Eagles, 'Lindsey' in S. Bassett (ed.), *The Origins of Anglo-Saxon Kingdoms* (London, 1989), p. 211. See above, pp. 101–03, on the royal family of *Lindissi* perhaps having their origins in the population group focused on the Cleatham cemetery.

4   Stenton, 'Lindsey', pp. 132–5; K. Leahy, *The Anglo-Saxon Kingdom of Lindsey* (Stroud, 2007), pp. 11–14; P. H. Sawyer, *Anglo-Saxon Lincolnshire* (Lincoln, 1998), p. 45; D. Roffe, 'Lissingleys and the meeting place of Lindsey' (2000).

5   Green, 'British kingdom', p. 36.

6   Stenton, 'Lindsey', p. 134.

7   D. Stocker and P. Everson, 'The straight and narrow way: Fenland causeways and the conversion of the landscape in the Witham valley, Lincolnshire' in M. O. H. Carver (ed.), *The Cross Goes North: Processes of Conversion in Northern Europe, A.D. 300–1300* (Woodbridge, 2002), pp. 271–88; P. Everson and D. Stocker, '"Coming from Bardney..." – the landscape context of the causeways and finds groups of the Witham valley' in S. Catney and D. Start (eds), *Time and Tide, The Archaeology of the Witham Valley* (Sleaford, 2003), pp. 6–15.

8   S. Bassett, 'Lincoln and the Anglo-Saxon see of Lindsey', *Anglo-Saxon*

England, 18 (1989), 2–3; B. Yorke, 'Lindsey: the lost kingdom found?' in A.
Vince (ed.), *Pre-Viking Lindsey* (Lincoln, 1993), pp. 142–3, 147–8.

9   Roffe, 'Lissingleys'; Sawyer, *Anglo-Saxon Lincolnshire*, pp. 149–53.

10   The final conquest of *Lindissi* by Mercia probably took place in 679: S.
Foot, 'The kingdom of Lindsey' in Vince, *Pre-Viking Lindsey*, p. 135.
Although the diocese of *Lindissi* was first created in 678, this was an act of
Northumbrian overlordship, and it is likely that the boundaries of this
diocese under Mercian rule would only have been finally established after
the division and reorganization of the Mercian see *c.* 690 (see S. Keynes,
The Councils of Clofesho (Leicester, 1994); S. Keynes, 'Diocese and cathedral
before 1056' in G. Aylmer and J. Tiller (eds), *Hereford Cathedral: A History*
(London, 2000), p. 7; S. Keynes, 'Between Bede and the *Chronicle*: London,
BL, Cotton Vespasian B. vi, fols. 104–9' in K. O. O'Keeffe and A.
Orchard (eds), *Latin Learning and English Lore: Studies in Anglo-Saxon literature
for Michael Lapidge* (Toronto, 2005), pp. 56–7).

11   Roffe, 'Lissingleys'; the available evidence suggests that Lissingleys was an
important pre-Viking 'central place'/meeting place of some sort, but not
necessarily that it was used as the meeting place of the whole of Lindsey
before the late ninth century (see below, pp. 140–2). If the Lindsey place-
names involving Old English *burh* ('fortress') really did all date from early
in the seventh century and represent a coherent defensive network for
Lindsey, then this too might support the notion that Lindsey and *Lindissi*
were coterminous (B. Cox, 'The pattern of Old English *burh* in early
Lindsey', *Anglo-Saxon England*, 23 (1994), 35–56, especially 54 and 56).
However, this hypothesis seems both unlikely and implausible, as a
number of commentators have pointed out (Sawyer, *Anglo-Saxon
Lincolnshire*, pp. 84–6; J. Blair, *The Church in Anglo-Saxon Society* (Oxford,
2005), p. 250). Furthermore, Cox omitted to mention at least one *burh*
name in Kesteven (a lost site, east of Sleaford), and in light of this his
'network', if it existed in a meaningful way, might be thought to have
extended down the Kesteven Fen Edge in any case. A more plausible
argument may be found in the fact that *Lindesig/Lindissig* looks to be an
unhistorical form of the kingdom-name *Lindissi*, created when the final
element of *Lindissi* was wrongly connected with the Old English word for
island, *-īg* (above, pp. 57–8; Sawyer, *Anglo-Saxon Lincolnshire*, pp. 9–10).
This connection between *Lindissi* and *-īg* most credibly results from the
then island-like properties of the district of Lindsey (see Stenton, 'Lindsey',
p. 134) and, as such, the new name *Lindesig/Lindissig* is most likely to have
been created only after the name *Lindissi* had become restricted to the
district of Lindsey. However, as the first instance of the name
Lindesig/Lindissig being used for *Lindissi* occurs in the late ninth century,
this can tell us little more than that the loss of northern Kesteven to
Lindissi is likely to have occurred before the late ninth century.

12 See, for example, Bede, *Historia Ecclesiastica*, II.16, on Lincoln's centrality to *Lindissi*.

13 See Stocker and Everson, 'Straight and narrow way', especially p. 275, for a summary of the evidence; Fig. 25.

14 D. N. Dumville, 'The Tribal Hidage: an introduction to its texts and their history' in S. Bassett (ed.), *The Origins of Anglo-Saxon Kingdoms* (London, 1989), pp. 226–7, 229; Cameron, *Dictionary*, pp. 14, 65–6; W. Davies and H. Vierck, 'The contexts of the Tribal Hidage: social aggregates and settlement patterns', *Frühmittelalterliche Studien*, 8 (1974), 233–6, 283. See further, Chapter 5.

15 See Sawyer, *Anglo-Saxon Lincolnshire*, pp. 49, 220–1, and further below, p. 185.

16 The low assessment of the *Bilmigas* in the 'Tribal Hidage' (600 hides compared with *Lindissi*'s 7,000) combined with the Fen Edge focus of the *Billingas* place-names suggest that it is most unlikely that the *Bilmigas*/*Billingas*, if they existed, covered the whole of northern Kesteven; see Chapter 5 on the likely extent of the *regio* of the *Billingas*, which can be defined with a reasonable degree of confidence because of an unusual coincidence of evidence.

17 Recent studies have challenged the very notion that most of the smaller population groups that occur in the 'Tribal Hidage' and other documents, such as the *Bilmigas*, were originally independent 'peoples' and polities rather than merely distinct, but always subordinate, population groups which existed within the borders of larger kingdoms like *Lindissi* (B. Yorke, 'Political and ethnic identity: a case study of Anglo-Saxon practice' in W. O. Frazer and A. Tyrrell (eds), *Social Identity in Early Medieval Britain* (London, 2000), pp. 82–6; B. Yorke, 'Anglo-Saxon *gentes* and *regna*' in H-W. Goetz *et al* (eds), *Regna and Gentes: The Relationship Between Late Antique and Early Medieval Peoples and Kingdoms in the Transformation of the Roman World* (Leiden, 2003), pp. 381–408, especially p. 401; A. Woolf, 'Community, identity and kingship in early England' in W. O. Frazer and A. Tyrrell (eds), *Social Identity in Early Medieval Britain* (London, 2000), pp. 91–109). This question is discussed further below, pp. 163–7.

18 M. S. Parker, 'The province of Hatfield', *Northern History*, 28 (1992), 42–69; B. Colgrave (ed. and trans.), *The Earliest Life of St Gregory* (Cambridge, 1968), § 18 (pp. 102–03); J. Campbell, 'Bede's *Reges* and *Principes*' in J. Campbell, *Essays in Anglo-Saxon History* (London, 1986), pp. 86–7.

19 See Parker, 'Hatfield', on the extent of the *regio* of Hatfield.

20 Dumville, 'Tribal Hidage', pp. 226–7; Parker, 'Hatfield', 46.

21 As also observed by Yorke, 'Lindsey', pp. 142–3; Sawyer, *Anglo-Saxon Lincolnshire*, pp. 72–3; Parker, 'Hatfield', 46–9; and David Roffe, personal communication. Such a situation is also implicit in Bassett, 'Lincoln', 2.

22 N. J. Higham, *The Kingdom of Northumbria, AD 350–1100* (Stroud, 1993), pp.

87–9; Davies & Vierck, 'Contexts', p. 281.

23   Parker, 'Hatfield', 46–8, 60.

24   R. Van de Noort, *The Humber Wetlands: The Archaeology of a Dynamic Landscape* (Bollington, 2004), p. 129; K. R. Dark, *Britain and the End of the Roman Empire* (Stroud, 2000), p. 11; S. Lucy, *The Anglo-Saxon Way of Death* (Stroud, 2000), pp. 141–3.

25   Colgrave, *Earliest Life of St Gregory*, § 18 (pp. 102–03, 151), written by a monk of Whitby. The event is said to have occurred 'in the days of their [the Mercian's] king Æthelred' (p. 103), who ruled from 675 to 704. Colgrave (p. 47) suggests that it must have occurred after 680, as the 'Life' also dates the event in relation to Eanflæd (Edwin's daughter), who took control of Whitby with her daughter Ælfflæd when Hild died in 680. However, the 'Life of St Gregory' specifies only that the event in question happened 'while Eanflæd was still living and in the monastic life' (p. 103), which she probably was from the death of her husband in 670 (B. Yorke, *Nunneries and the Anglo-Saxon Royal Houses* (London, 2003), p. 32), and Colgrave himself considers the reference later in the chapter to Whitby as the monastery of Ælfflæd to be the Whitby author's own comment, not part of the tale he was relating (pp. 47–8).

26   See Parker, 'Hatfield', 45–6, on the location of Edwin's body.

27   J. May, *Dragonby: Report on Excavation at an Iron Age and Romano-British Settlement in North Lincolnshire* (2 vols, Oxford, 1996), vol. 2, pp. 638–44; J. May, 'The later Iron Age' in S. Bennett and N. Bennett (eds), *An Historical Atlas of Lincolnshire* (Chichester, 2001), pp. 12–13.

28   C. A. Snyder, *An Age of Tyrants: Britain and the Britons A.D. 400–600* (Stroud, 1998), p. 232; Yorke, 'Anglo-Saxon *gentes* and *regna*', pp. 396–7; S. Laycock, 'Britannia: the threat within', *British Archaeology*, 87 (2006), 10–15; S. Laycock, *Britannia, The Failed State* (Stroud, 2008); Green, 'British kingdom', 35–6.

29   With regard to when northern Kesteven was split off from the core territory of *Lindissi*, see further below, pp. 197–200.

30   Yorke, 'Lindsey', pp. 141–2. See also Blair, *Church*, pp. 271–2. On the British origins of Deira and Elmet, see R. G. Gruffydd, 'In search of Elmet', *Studia Celtica*, 28 (1994), 63–79; Higham, *Northumbria*, p. 81; J. T. Koch, *The Gododdin of Aneirin: Text and Context from Dark-Age North Britain* (Cardiff, 1997), pp. xxxi–xxxii, xl.

31   Bede, *Historia Ecclesiastica*, II.16 and II.18 (see *HE*, II.14, for York's stone church being still unfinished at the time of Edwin's death).

32   K. H. Jackson, *Language and History in Early Britain* (Edinburgh, 1953), especially p. 309.

33   J. Wacher, *The Towns of Roman Britain*, 2nd edn (London, 1995), pp. 17–18, 87.

34   K. Cameron, *The Place-Names of Lincolnshire, I* (Nottingham, 1985), pp. 1–3.

35   Gilmour, 'Sub-Roman or Saxon, pagan or Christian: who was buried in the early cemetery at St-Paul-in-the-Bail, Lincoln?' in L. Gilmour (ed.), *Pagans and Christians – from Antiquity to the Middle Ages* (Oxford, 2007), pp. 252–3; K. Leahy, 'The Anglo-Saxon settlement of Lindsey' in Vince, *Pre-Viking Lindsey*, p. 36. On Blæcca and the possibility that he was a member of the ruling family of *Lindissi*, see above, p. 105; as Kevin Leahy (*Kingdom of Lindsey*, p. 115) rightly points out, we possess a genealogy rather than a king-list for *Lindissi*, and so the absence of Blæcca's name from this genealogy does not mean that he was not in fact the king of the *Lindisfaran* during Edwin's overlordship, only that Aldfrið was not descended from him.

36   Sawyer, *Anglo-Saxon Lincolnshire*, p. 51; Bassett, 'Lincoln, 11–12; Leahy, *Kingdom of Lindsey*, p. 115; Eagles, 'Lindsey', p. 210.

37   See further, D. A. Hinton, *A Smith in Lindsey: The Anglo-Saxon Grave at Tattershall Thorpe, Lincolnshire* (London, 2000), especially pp. 103–04, 114.

38   Sawyer, *Anglo-Saxon Lincolnshire*, pp. 51, 84, 108, 113–14; see further below, pp. 190–1.

39   Leahy, *Kingdom of Lindsey*, p. 59 and plates 13 and 16, for the early Anglo-Saxon finds (see also NLM-B895B4 from Thimbleby), and pp. 131, 144–45 and 159, for the Middle Saxon. On the status-symbolism of Anglo-Saxon 'military' items, see H. Härke, 'Changing symbols in a changing society: the Anglo-Saxon weapon burial rite in the seventh century' in M. O. H. Carver (ed.), *The Age of Sutton Hoo* (Woodbridge, 1992), pp. 149–65.

40   Cameron, *Dictionary*, p. 66.

41   Roffe, 'Lissingleys'.

42   Roffe, 'Lissingleys'. See also the map in D. Roffe, 'Medieval administration' in Bennett and Bennett, *Historical Atlas of Lincolnshire*, pp. 38–9. Roffe argues that the Ridings may be pre-Viking in origin too, but this is not necessary for Lissingleys to have had pre-Viking significance, as noted above. A pre-Viking origin for them has been, in any case, doubted (Sawyer, *Anglo-Saxon Lincolnshire*, pp. 137–9).

43   Keith Kelway, personal communication; DCMS, *Treasure Annual Report 2001*, p. 49; DCMS, *Treasure Annual Report 2002*, pp. 66–67; Portable Antiquities Scheme, LIN-75B9C3. On ring-swords, see H. Stuer, 'Helm und Ringschwert. Prunkbewaffnung und Rangabzeichen germanischer Krieger. Eine Übersicht', *Studien zur Sachsenforschung*, 6 (1987), 190–236, and V. I. Evison, 'The Dover ring-sword and other ring-swords and beads', *Archaeologia*, 101 (1967), 63–118.

44   Keith Kelway, personal communication; Adam Daubney, unpublished finds report; Wessex Archaeology, *Blackhills Farm and The Hollys, Wickenby, Lincolnshire. Archaeological Evaluation and Assessment of Results* (Salisbury, 2008).

45   Wessex Archaeology, *Wickenby*, pp. 2, 10, 17; Lincolnshire Historic

Environment Record 55173; Adam Daubney, unpublished finds report.

46   Adam Daubney, unpublished finds report; Keith Kelway, personal communication; Wessex Archaeology, *Wickenby*, pp. 2–3; Lincolnshire Historic Environment Record 55193; Portable Antiquities Scheme NLM-5FBEB7, NLM-5DF5D6 and SWYOR-6429A2; A. Daubney, 'The cult of Totatis' in S. Worrell *et al* (eds), *A Decade of Discovery: Proceedings of the Portable Antiquities Scheme Conference 2007* (Oxford, 2010), catalogue numbers 8 and 62. Note, a sceptre foot is also known from this area (LIN-A7EF01), as is a small figurine of Mercury (LIN-3A2272). On Mars Toutatis and Lincolnshire, see Daubney, 'The cult of Totatis"; A. Daubney, 'Ancient British cult of Toutatis discovered in Lincolnshire', published on the Portable Antiquities Scheme website (12 July 2007), *www.finds.org.uk/wordpress/?p=329*.

47   Keith Kelway, personal communication.

48   Cameron, *Dictionary*, p. 81.

49   That the first element is **Lissa* is apparent from the early forms (E. Ekwall, *The Concise Oxford Dictionary of English Place-Names*, fourth edition (Oxford, 1960), p. 30; R. Coates, 'Reflections on some major Lincolnshire place-names. Part one: Algarkirk to Melton Ross', *Journal of the English Place-Name Society*, 40 (2008), 82). See, however, M. Gelling and A. Cole, *The Landscape of Place-Names*, 2nd edn (Stamford, 2003), p. 237, on the second element of 'Lissingleys/Lissinglea' having the potential meaning 'pasture, meadow' rather than 'clearing, wood', which might fit well with its historical character.

50   Ekwall, *Dictionary*, p. 300; Cameron, *Dictionary*, p. 81. Coates, 'Reflections', 82, very tentatively offers **Lindis(s)ing-leas/ *Lindis(s)ing-tun*, 'the clearings/village associated with the [polity of] Lindsey', as an alternative. However, as he notes, **Lindis(s)-* would require a very drastic reduction to get to **Liss-* and is thus unlikely.

51   V. Watts, *The Cambridge Dictionary of English Place-Names* (Cambridge, 2004), p. 375.

52   Jackson, *Language and History*, p. 285; *Geiriadur Prifysgol Cymru (University of Wales Dictionary of the Welsh Language)*, s.v. *Llys*. On the potential names 'the clearing/village associated with the **Lis*', compare Toynton All Saints and Toynton St Peter, *Totintun* and *Totingtun*, arguably 'the estate/village associated with the *tōt*, the look-out hill' (A. D. Mills, *A Dictionary of English Place-Names* (Oxford, 1991), pp. xvii, 333; Green, 'British kingdom', 30, fn. 120). Kirmington (*Chernitone, Chirningtun*) may well provide a comparable example of a British place-name compounded with *tūn* – see R. Coates, 'Two notes on names in *tūn* in relation to pre-English antiquities: Kirmington and Broughton, Lincolnshire', *Journal of the English Place-Name Society*, 37 (2005), 33–4. See also, perhaps, Penistone in South Yorkshire (*Pengestone, Peningestone*), which appears to derive from Archaic Welsh *penn*

(Mills, *Dictionary*, p. 256).

53 See below, pp. 195–6, on Sleaford. On Caistor, see D. Stocker, 'The early Church in Lincolnshire: a study of the sites and their significance' in Vince, *Pre-Viking Lindsey*, p. 117; Leahy, *Kingdom of Lindsey*, pp. 125–6, 205.

54 C. J. Balkwill, 'Old English *wīc* and the origin of the hundred', *Landscape History*, 15 (1993), 5–12; Yorke, 'Anglo-Saxon *gentes* and *regna*', p. 396; M. Gelling, 'English place-names derived from the compound *wīchām*', reprinted in K. Cameron (ed.), *Place-name Evidence for the Anglo-Saxon Invasion and Scandinavian Settlements* (Nottingham, 1977), pp. 8–26; M. Gelling, *Signposts to the Past. Place-names and the History of England*, 2nd edn (Chichester, 1988), pp. 67–74, 245–7; M. Gelling, 'Latin loan-words in Old English place-names', *Anglo-Saxon England*, 6 (1977), 1–5; S. Oosthuizen, 'The origins of Cambridgeshire', *Antiq. J.*, 78 (1998), 95–6.

55 See K. Leahy, *'Interrupting the Pots': The excavation of Cleatham Anglo-Saxon cemetery* (York, 2007), and p. 206 on Cleatham–Kirton in Lindsey. See also H. Williams, 'Cemeteries as central places – place and identity in Migration Period eastern England' in B. Hårdh and L. Larsson (eds), *Central Places in the Migration and Merovingian Periods* (Stockholm, 2002), pp. 341–62; H. Williams, 'Assembling the dead' in A. Pantos and S. Semple (eds), *Assembly Places and Practices in Medieval Europe* (Dublin, 2004), pp. 109–34. On Hibaldstow, see B. Whitwell, 'Some Roman small towns in north Lincolnshire and south Humberside' in A. E. Brown (ed.), *Roman Small Towns in Eastern England and Beyond* (Oxford, 1995), pp. 98–9; Hibaldstow Roman 'town' covered over half a square mile. Note that Anglo-Saxon 'pagan' pottery has been recorded from the site of the town itself, and that there is notable evidence of British–Anglian continuity from this area (Green, 'British kingdom', 24 and 28, fn. 114).

56 Williams, 'Cemeteries as central places', pp. 347–50. See also, perhaps, the probable Roman fort at Skegness, the name of which appears to have survived into the eleventh century (A. E. B. Owen and R. Coates, 'Traiectus/Tric/Skegness: a Domesday name explained', *LHA*, 38 (2003), 42–4; R. Coates, *Toponymic Topics* (Brighton, 1988), pp. 35–9).

57 B. Cox, 'Yarboroughs in Lindsey', *English Place-Name Society Journal*, 28 (1994–5), 50–60; Leahy, *Kingdom of Lindsey*, pp. 111–14; Green, 'British kingdom', 30; above, p. 89. On cremation cemeteries as 'central places', see Williams, 'Cemeteries as central places'; Williams, 'Assembling the dead'; and further below, pp. 200–09.

58 Whitwell, 'Roman small towns', pp. 100–02; Leahy, *Kingdom of Lindsey*, p. 84; Coates, 'Kirmington and Broughton', 33–4; above, pp. 30–1.

59 Susan Youngs, personal communication; S. Youngs, 'Recent finds of insular enamelled buckles' in C. E. Karkov, R. T. Farrell and M. Ryan (eds), *The Insular Tradition* (Albany, 1997), pp. 192–4. See also S. Youngs, 'Two medieval Celtic enamelled buckles from Leicestershire', *Transactions of*

the *Leicestershire Archaeological and Historical Society*, 68 (1993), 15–22.

60   See S. Youngs, 'Insular metalwork from Flixborough, Lincolnshire', *Med. Arch.*, 45 (2001), 216–17, and H. Geake, 'When were hanging bowls deposited in Anglo-Saxon graves?', *Med. Arch.*, 43 (1999), 3 and 4, for the fifty bowls known from Anglo-Saxon graves to 1999, to which we should add the recent find from Bracebridge Heath (Lincolnshire Historic Environment Record 60962). A disproportionate twenty per cent of the total known from all funerary contexts across the whole of Anglo-Saxon England come from Lincolnshire graves.

61   See, for example, the probably fifth-century hanging bowl found in what seems to be a seventh-century grave at Sleaford (Geake, 'Hanging bowls', 13).

62   See R. Bruce-Mitford, 'Late Celtic hanging bowls in Lincolnshire and South Humberside' in Vince, *Pre-Viking Lindsey*, pp. 45–70, for some examples of probably seventh-century British hanging bowls from the region. See also the enamelled cruciform brooches mentioned above, p. 127, endnote 77.

63   See Stocker & Everson, 'Straight and narrow way'; Everson & Stocker, 'Coming from Bardney'.

64   Bede, *Historia Ecclesiastica*, II.16, III.11; Leahy, *Kingdom of Lindsey*, pp. 114–15, 117; Sawyer, *Anglo-Saxon Lincolnshire*, pp. 57, 58.

65   Foot, 'Kingdom of Lindsey', p. 135; Sawyer, *Anglo-Saxon Lincolnshire*, p. 57; Bede, *Historia Ecclesiastica*, IV.3; D. Tyler, 'An early Mercian hegemony: Penda and overkingship in the seventh century', *Mid. Hist.*, 30 (2005), 1–19.

66   Bede, *Historia Ecclesiastica*, IV.12, IV.21; Foot, 'Kingdom of Lindsey', p. 135; Sawyer, *Anglo-Saxon Lincolnshire*, p. 58.

67   Bede, *Historia Ecclesiastica*, IV.12. See, for example, C. Stancliffe, 'Oswald, "most holy and victorious king of the Northumbrians"' in C. Stancliffe and E. Cambridge (eds), *Oswald: Northumbrian King to European Saint* (Stamford, 1995), p. 55; N. J. Higham, 'Northumbria's southern frontier: a review', *Early Medieval Europe*, 14.4 (2006), 400.

68   *Historia Ecclesiastica*, II.12, IV.12; A. Thacker, '*Membra disjecta*: the division of the body and the diffusion of the cult' in C. Stancliffe and E. Cambridge (eds), *Oswald: Northumbrian King to European Saint* (Stamford, 1995), p. 99; Parker, 'Hatfield'.

69   Sawyer, *Anglo-Saxon Lincolnshire*, p. 18.

70   See J. Huggett, 'Imported grave goods and the early Anglo-Saxon economy', *Med. Arch.*, 32 (1988), 64–5; G. Drinkall and M. Foreman, *The Anglo-Saxon Cemetery at Castledyke South, Barton-on-Humber* (Sheffield, 1998), p. 262; A. G. Vince, 'Coinage and urban development: integrating the archaeological and numismatic history of Lincoln' in B. Cook and G. Williams (eds), *Coinage and History in the North Sea World, c. AD 500–1200*

(Leiden, 2006), p. 527; and chapter five, below.

71   See especially below, pp. 197–200.

72   Parker, 'Hatfield', 46–7.

73   See Bede, *Historia Ecclesiastica*, II.16.

74   Bede, *Historia Ecclesiastica*, II.16, II.18; N. J. Higham, *An English Empire.
      Bede and the Early Anglo-Saxon Kings* (Manchester, 1995), p. 59.

75   See below, pp. 244–50.

76   J. Campbell, 'Bede (673/4–735)', in *The Oxford Dictionary of National
      Biography*, online edition (Oxford, 2004), *www.oxforddnb.com*; A. Thacker,
      'Bede and the ordering of understanding' in S. DeGregorio (ed.), *Innovation
      and Tradition in the Writings of the Venerable Bede* (Morgantown, 2006), p. 40.
      It should perhaps be noted here that there is place-name evidence
      suggestive of the kings of *Lindissi* considering themselves an *Inguionic*
      dynasty, deriving from continental Anglian *Inguiones*, a claim which may
      also be embodied in the Bernician royal genealogy (see below, p. 262,
      endnote 54, and M. Miller, 'Royal pedigrees of the insular Dark Ages: a
      progress report', *History in Africa*, 7 (1980), 213; R. North, *Heathen Gods in
      Old English Literature* (Cambridge, 1997), especially pp. 42–3; and K. I.
      Sandred, 'Ingham in East Anglia: a new interpretation', *Leeds Studies in
      English*, 18 (1987), 234–5). An alternative possibility – that the Bernician
      kings considered the pagan god *Ing* to have been their divine patron and
      that the cult of *Ing* was an important one within early Anglo-Saxon *Lindissi*
      (see above, pp. 101–03) – would, of course, be equally intriguing.
      However, in either case we do need to be cautious with regard to how
      much can be read into the Bernician pedigree, given the differing versions
      of this which survive and the evidence for tampering/invention in the
      generations below Ida (see pp. 259–60, endnote 35 below).

5

THE POPULATION GROUPS OF EARLY ANGLO-SAXON LINCOLNSHIRE

The 'Tribal Hidage', population groups and kingdoms

Any attempt to understand what political identities existed within early Anglo-Saxon Lincolnshire will inevitably come up against the 'Tribal Hidage'. This document consists of a list of Anglo-Saxon population groups, which are given hidations (possibly tribute assessments, reflecting some uncertain mixture of size and status) ranging from 300 to 100,000 hides. On the whole, there is general agreement that at least parts of this list must have their origins in the pre-Viking period, perhaps in seventh-century Mercia, and as such it is a potentially very valuable resource.[1] Some of the population groups named are the same peoples and kingdoms that we know of from other early sources, such as Bede's *Historia Ecclesiastica*, including the *Lindisfaran*, the Mercians and the East Saxons. However, in addition to these, the list includes a large number of much smaller groups, nearly all of which are not only mentioned in this document alone, but also appear to be chiefly locatable in the East Midlands, including some that may belong to southern Lincolnshire (Fig. 31).[2]

These small groups are probably to be related to other small Anglo-Saxon population groups and *regiones*, such as the *Stoppingas*, who appear in charters and other documents as subgroups within the boundaries of the recognized larger kingdoms. However, what the actual significance of these smaller groups was in the early Anglo-Saxon period is at present unclear, depending to a large degree upon the model of early Anglo-Saxon kingdom formation that is adopted. The first model has the Anglo-Saxons lacking leaders with more than local authority before the middle of the sixth century, on the basis of an apparent absence of evidence for significant social stratification and kingship in the archaeological record.[3] It is argued that the

Fig. 31 One possible reconstruction of the locations of the Tribal Hidage population groups. The vast majority ought probably to be placed in the Middle Anglian area between Mercia and East Anglia
Based on C. Hart, 'The Tribal Hidage', *Transactions of the Royal Historical Society*, fifth series, 21 (1971)

immigrant Anglo-Saxons of the fifth and earlier sixth centuries generally ignored or destroyed all but the most local of British territories which they encountered. Instead, they lived in small population groups (like those found in the 'Tribal Hidage' and various charters), which may have had local leaders but not permanent dominant lineages/dynasties, at least until the second half of the sixth century. These groups are consequently considered to represent genuine 'peoples' and once-independent territories, with most of the larger kingdoms attested in the seventh century being formed through the coalescence of these smaller units via a process of conquest and absorption, which also produced the first kings. The 'Tribal Hidage' would, on this model, represent a stage in the evolution of Anglo-Saxon kingdoms wherein the majority of these small units had already coalesced into the larger historical kingdoms, with the exception of those based primarily in the East Midlands (the area termed Middle Anglia in Bede and other sources), which still retained a degree of their original independence, for some uncertain reason.[4]

Such an interpretation, although in many ways attractive, has nonetheless been seriously challenged. The original independence of the small population groups in the above model is largely an assumption. Indeed, it has been recently demonstrated that seventh- and early eighth-century sources, such as Bede's *Historia Ecclesiastica*, appear to have drawn a clear distinction between such small groupings and genuine, larger, kingdoms and peoples, with evidence for most of the small population groups we know of as truly autonomous units being chiefly conspicuous by its absence. In the light of this, it can be argued that many of the smaller Anglo-Saxon groups are better seen as simply having always been what they are in these sources: distinct, but subordinate, population groups, which inhabited settlement units/subdistricts (*regiones*) within larger kingdoms and territories and which never actually had any fully independent existence.[5] If this is the case, then the presence of large numbers of subordinate groups in the 'Tribal Hidage' can be explained in one of two ways. On the one hand, this document could have its origins in the region where most of these groups were probably located – the East Midlands (Middle Anglia) – reflecting an especial interest in the organization of this area. On the other hand, the 'Tribal Hidage' might be more credibly considered a tenth-/eleventh-century antiquarian composite of pre-Viking hidations, created primarily from a survey of the internal subdivisions of the kingdom of Middle Angles (which ought to be considered a genuine, large kingdom and people, to judge from Bede's testimony, that just so happens to be missing from the 'Tribal Hidage'). The aggregate hidages for the other large kingdoms were then added to this material, along with the details of a few additional small groups that happened to be available to the compiler, obtained from unknown pre-Viking materials.[6]

This interpretation of both the 'Tribal Hidage' and the small population groups and *regiones* of pre-Viking England would obviously imply a very different general model of kingdom formation from that outlined above, as the recorded Anglo-Saxon kingdoms cannot have emerged from the coalescence of many originally independent, smaller groups and territories if there is no reason to think that these independent groups ever existed. Indeed, in this context the notion that there was an almost complete disintegration of the Late Roman and post-Roman British administrative framework followed by a gradual rebuilding from the ground up – which is largely based on the supposed evidence for numerous small, independent population groups and territories in the early Anglo-Saxon period[7] – would also seem to be unnecessary and even unlikely. As Barbara Yorke has suggested, in such circumstances the most credible solution may well be that the recorded Anglo-Saxon kingdoms in fact had their origins in the takeover of sizeable British territories, such as those of the *civitates*, with the small population groups simply being groups which inhabited subdistricts within these. Certainly, there is nothing inherently implausible in this. Both Deira and Bernicia are, in fact, usually seen as originally British kingdoms, and a credible relationship can also be posited between, for example, the kingdoms of Kent, East Anglia, Essex and Sussex and the *civitates* of the *Cantiaci, Iceni, Trinovantes* and *Regni*.[8] Moreover, the lack of archaeological evidence for the existence of true early Anglo-Saxon kings and dynasties before the middle of the sixth century need not be a major problem here. On this model, it is envisaged that any large territories taken over before the mid-sixth century would have been initially administered along the same lines as the continental Old Saxon province – which had no kings, but was instead made up of a number of semi-autonomous subdistricts that were controlled by local leaders (*satrapes*), who might temporarily unite under one leader in times of war – with this situation then developing into true kingship during the course of the sixth century.[9]

Which of these two models is correct is perhaps too complex an issue to pursue more fully here. Nonetheless, it is worth pointing out that the relationship between British **Lindēs* and Anglo-Saxon *Lindissi* argued for in the present study would offer considerable support for the second model, and this model is more in line with the evidence that we actually possess regarding the nature of the small population groups. Furthermore, it is interesting to note that the territory of the Middle Angles does in fact coincide to a striking degree with a coherent and archaeologically identifiable late fifth- to sixth-century cultural group, which is distinct from that of the surrounding regions and seems to represent 'an economic, a social, and an ideological unit'.[10] Given that most of the small 'Tribal Hidage' groups are found in this area, this is especially suggestive. Indeed, it would once again seem to offer significant support to the second model of early Anglo-Saxon kingdom formation and political organization, wherein the smaller population groups were never truly independent, but rather always part of a larger whole. However, whether or not the small population groups in the 'Tribal Hidage' were originally independent units or merely important population groups within larger territories and kingdoms, the key point is that they were clearly of some considerable significance within lowland Britain in the early Anglo-Saxon period. The question, therefore, becomes: what small population groups do we have evidence for in the Lincoln region?

1.   The *Gyrwe* of southern Lincolnshire

The first Lincolnshire population group to be considered here is also the one about which we know the most, namely the *Gyrwe*, whose name derives from Old English *gyr*, 'mud', and should be taken to mean something akin to 'the fen dwellers'. In the 'Tribal Hidage' this group is split into two halves, the 'North' and the 'South *Gyrwe*' (600 hides each), and it has the distinction of being the only small East Midlands group named in that document which unambiguously occurs outside of it too. So Bede, for example, refers to a *princeps* of the South *Gyrwe* named *Tondberct*, who married the daughter of a king of East Anglia at some point before *c.* 660, and he also notes that *Medeshamstede* (Peterborough) was in territory of the *Gyrwe* and that the first bishop of East Anglia came from the *prouincia Gyruiorum*.[11] Exactly how much of the territory of this group lay within Lincolnshire is unclear, but some of it – probably the most northerly part – certainly did: Crowland Abbey, which was probably a cell of *Medeshamstede* and founded *c.* 700 by St Guthlac, was said to have lain in the midst of the fen belonging to the *Gyrwe* ('*on middan Gyrwan fenne*') in a text which probably has its origins in the late ninth century.[12]

Just what the nature of this north Cambridgeshire and southern Lincolnshire population group was is an important question, given how much we actually know of it compared with other small population groups. On the one hand, Bede's references to *Tondberct*'s marriage and to the territory of the *Gyrwe* as a *prouincia* have been taken to suggest that this is one of those very few cases where we actually have some reason to think that a small Anglo-Saxon population group was an independent, rather than subordinate, political unit.[13] On the other hand, the evidence we have regarding the *Gyrwe*'s possible independence is not conclusive, and a case might be equally made for them having been a subordinate, if important, unit within the kingdom of the Middle Angles.[14]

One element of this case is that the evidence in favour of autonomy is less secure than is often admitted. Thus whilst *prouincia* is certainly Bede's normal word for a kingdom, he does sometimes use it for subdivisions and subordinate population groups too: for example, his references to the *prouincia* of the *Meanware* and the *prouincia Undalum*.[15] Confirmation that he was using it in the latter sense when referring to the *Gyrwe* comes from the fact that he later describes the *Gyrwe*'s territory as a *regio*, a term which, in contrast, he uses without exception to refer to subordinate districts rather than known kingdoms.[16] Similarly, whilst the South *Gyrwe* were certainly assigned a mid-seventh-century ruler named *Tondberct* by Bede, something which has been seen as very significant, *Tondberct* is in fact described as a *princeps* of the South *Gyrwe*, not their king. This term, *princeps*, is a difficult one; Bede seems to have consistently used it for those who had authority over extensive lands, but who were also subordinate and inferior to a king, with the normal Old English equivalent of the term being *ealdorman*.[17] The strong implication is thus that *Tondberct* was not truly autonomous, but instead subordinate to some larger unit and its king. This might be speculated to be a king of all of the *Gyrwe*, North and South, but we have no reason to think that it must have been, or even that such a king or kingdom ever existed, especially given that Bede refers to the territory of the *Gyrwe* as a *regio*. Indeed, even if we could be sure that *Tondberct* was a member of a royal dynasty – something perhaps implied by his marriage to an East Anglian princess[18] – it would not necessarily follow that he was a representative of an independent Gyrwean royal house, as has often been assumed. He could instead have been, for example, a minor member of the lost Middle Anglian dynasty – which probably existed before Peada was made king of the Middle Angles by his father (Penda of Mercia) in 653 – who had simply been appointed as a *princeps* to take charge of 'the fen dwellers' (*Gyrwe*) within the kingdom, or even a member of the Mercian or Northumbrian dynasty who had been appointed to this position during their mid-seventh-century overlordships.[19]

The other element of this case consists of positive evidence in favour of *Gyrwe* lying within the borders of Middle Anglia. This evidence comes in the form of Felix's early- to mid-eighth-century 'Life of St Guthlac', which includes two important points. The first is that Crowland, located in the midst of the Fen of the *Gyrwe*, appears to have been under Middle Anglian ecclesiastical jurisdiction, as the bishop of Mercia and Middle Anglia (Headda) ordained Guthlac and consecrated his church. This is, of course, suggestive, though it is not conclusive. More interesting, however, is the fact that, as Bertram Colgrave noted, the two manuscripts of the 'Life of St Guthlac' which are most closely connected with Crowland describe the fen in which Crowland lay ('the Fen of the *Gyrwe*') as being in the land of the Middle Angles.[20] Taken together, these two points do seem to indicate that the territory of the *Gyrwe* was thought to have been located within the bounds of Middle Anglia in the first half of the eighth century. When combined with the fact that Bede refers to the territory of the *Gyrwe* as a *regio* and the issues raised with regard to assumptions about both the meaning of *prouincia* and *Tondberct*'s status and origins, there consequently appears to be a reasonable case to answer for the *Gyrwe* having been a subordinate, though important, population group within Middle Anglia, rather than a truly independent kingdom.

Whatever their status, the *Gyrwe* only just qualify as an early Anglo-Saxon population group of the Lincoln region. Their primary focus is generally thought to lie in Cambridgeshire, and Crowland (a parish on the Lincolnshire side of the border with Cambridgeshire) probably lay within their northern periphery. Certainly, the territory of the *Gyrwe* seems to have extended far to the south of Lincolnshire, at least as far as Conington in Huntingdonshire, and it has been suggested that Ely represents the territory of the South *Gyrwe*.[21] As such, it is unlikely that the *Gyrwe* were within the area directly ruled by the British 'country of **Lindēs*' in the later fifth and sixth centuries.[22] On the other hand, it is not impossible that the Anglo-Saxons of the middle and southern Fens would have been influenced by this British polity, especially if Anglian settlement as a whole was initially controlled from Lincoln; some possible evidence for such an influence is discussed in the next chapter.

2. The *Spalde/Spaldingas* of Holland

Another population group mentioned in the 'Tribal Hidage' is the *Spalde/Spaldas*, assessed at only 600 hides. The exact location of this group's territory has been an occasional cause of dispute, with some trying to place it in the vicinity of Spaldwick (Huntingdonshire) or Spalford (Nottinghamshire), largely on the basis that these names may involve the group-name *Spalde*; that the Fens around Spalding in the Holland district of Lincolnshire were uninhabitable in the early Anglo-Saxon period; and that the place-name 'Spalding' derives from the group-name *Spaldingas*, rather than *Spalde* directly.[23] Such a rejection of a south Lincolnshire location for the *Spalde* is, however, dubious on several grounds. First, both Spaldwick and Spalford are more credibly interpreted as simply local topographic names, rather than ones involving the group-name *Spalde*, meaning respectively 'the dwelling or farm by a trickling stream or ditch' and 'the ford over a trickling stream or ditch'.[24] Second, the Fenland Survey has clearly demonstrated that the Fenland around Spalding was permanently inhabited during the early Anglo-Saxon period.[25] Third, the group-name *Spalde* refers to the inhabitants of a district whose name derived from Old English **spald*, 'ditch'; as such, a Fenland location for the *Spalde* would be more than appropriate. Fourth and finally, there is little obvious reason why the name 'Spalding' cannot be used to localize this population group, especially in light of the first point above. Modern 'Spalding' derives from the group-name *Spaldingas*, which can be either read as a name which means 'the people of the *Spalde*' or – better, perhaps – as an alternative form of the group-name *Spalde*, formed from the underlying district-name (**Spald*), meaning 'the dwellers in (the district of) **Spald*'. Whatever the case may be, Spalding would consequently be a settlement belonging to the *Spalde*, and the existence of this name and its origins would thus seem reasonable grounds for localising the *Spalde* of the 'Tribal Hidage' in the Lincolnshire Fenland.[26]

Given the above, the association of the *Spalde/Spaldas* with the area around Spalding seems secure; the question is, are we able to say any more about them than this? Although we lack further explicit documentary references to the *Spalde*, the work of the Fenland Survey means that we do in fact know a reasonable amount about this group. The crucial point here is that the evidence for early and middle Anglo-Saxon settlement in the Lincolnshire Fens recovered from the Survey is not distributed evenly across the area of Fenland studied. Rather, it falls into two separate and distinct groups: one on the western Fen Edge and another on the Wash Silts. These silts – on which modern Spalding is also located, although it was outside of the area of the Fenland Survey – seem to have formed, in effect, an island in the early and middle Anglo-Saxon periods, isolated from the rest of Lincolnshire and the Fen Edge by an intervening stretch of uninhabited, freshwater peat fen (Fig. 32).[27] As such, the finds from the silts would appear to reveal the existence of a previously unevidenced and distinct, early and middle Anglo-Saxon settlement unit based on the siltland of the Spalding region, clearly separated from the rest of Anglo-Saxon Lincolnshire by a physical barrier. This is obviously of considerable importance in the present context, and the geographical impression of a separate pre-Viking Spalding area settlement unit and community is furthered by the fact that the settlements on the Wash Silts seem to have remained dispersed into the eighth century, whilst those on the Kesteven Fen Edge appear to have nucleated around the middle of the seventh. Similarly, the medieval documentary evidence suggests that the Late Saxon and earlier Lincolnshire siltland originally constituted a discrete single unit, which was neither dependent on the surrounding upland nor had any significant tenurial relationship with it. In the light of all of this, it can be very credibly maintained that the 600-hide territory of the *Spalde* is relatively easy to identify: it was the Lincolnshire siltland and its associated settlements, which later became the district of Holland.[28]

If the territory of the *Spalde* is thus reasonably easy to define, what then of its origins? Unfortunately, the Fenland Survey produced few artefacts from the siltland beyond animal bone and pottery, but those sherds of early Anglo-Saxon pottery recovered which can be dated more precisely than simply to the early Anglo-Saxon period in

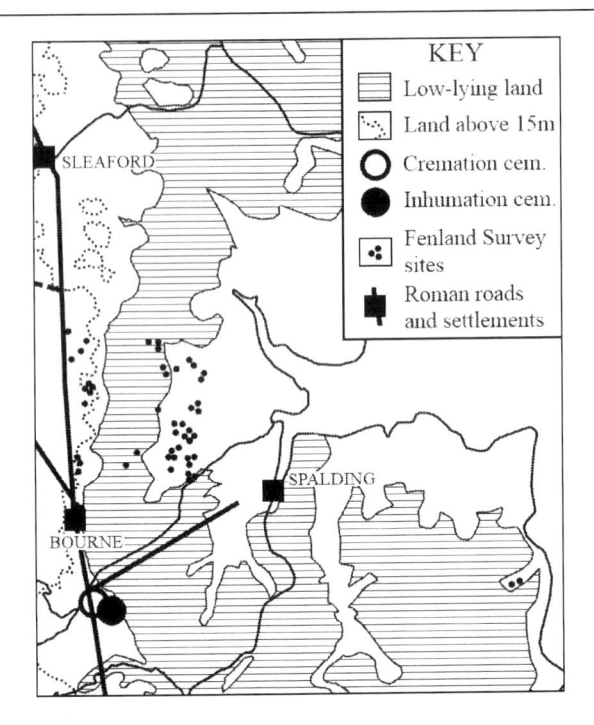

**Fig. 32 Map of the Fenland Survey results for south Lincolnshire,
showing the siltland of Holland, the Roman background and the
two large Anglo-Saxon cemeteries at Baston**
After A. Crowson *et al, Anglo-Saxon Settlement on the Siltland of Eastern
England* (Heckington, 2005)

general suggest that some of the settlements had their beginnings in
the sixth century, if not before.[29] The origins of the *Spalde* population
group and its territory presumably belong to the same period, and this
is supported by the available place-name evidence (see below), but the
exact circumstances of their emergence must remain a matter of
debate. However, given the evidence discussed earlier for a degree of
continuity in the Lincoln region between (Romano-)British
administrative centres and territories and those of the early Anglo-
Saxon period (not least *Lindēs/Lindissi*), it may be worth considering
whether the territory of the *Spalde* was the successor to some sort of
Roman administrative unit based in the Fens around Spalding. Was it,
perhaps, originally a sub-unit within the hypothesized Roman

imperial estate which covered the whole Fenland, or, if the existence of this estate is rejected, simply an administrative unit for the extensive Romano-British Lincolnshire Fen settlements?[30]

There are certainly some indications that the area immediately around Spalding (which, although outside the zone investigated by the Fenland Survey, is reasonably presumed to have been an important centre for the *Spalde* in light of its etymology)[31] had a degree of significance in the Roman period: it is strategically placed on the probable common estuary of the prehistoric courses of the rivers Glen and Welland; it appears to have been a focus for Roman-era activity in the Fenland; and there seems to have been a Roman road leading from Roman King Street to the Spalding area, known as the Baston Outgang, which is highly suggestive of something of note existing here.[32] Perhaps the most significant point from our perspective, however, is the survival of the place-name 'Wykeham' just to the north of Spalding. This derives from Old English *wīchām*, which in turn comes from Latin *vicus* and the early Old English element *hām*, and it is of particular interest here for three major reasons.[33] First, place-names with this derivation are generally agreed to date from the fifth or sixth century, an extremely important point in and of itself when it comes to considering the origins of the *Spalde*.[34] Second, these names are all considered to derive their Latin first element from their close proximity to a Romano-British settlement, which was known colloquially as a *vicus* in the Late and post-Roman periods, with *vici* in this context being probably Romano-British settlements which functioned as local administrative centres.[35] The existence of such a name next to Spalding consequently implies the presence of a Romano-British administrative centre of some sort in its immediate vicinity, a situation which would provide a context for the Roman road heading in this direction, noted above. Third and finally, it has been argued that such names not only reflect the nearby presence of a *vicus*, but are also indicative of some sort of administrative continuity between the Late Roman and early Anglo-Saxon periods, which is very significant in the present context.[36] All told, in the absence of further survey work and excavation specifically in the Spalding area, no certainty is possible, but what little evidence we do have is perhaps sufficient to suggest that an origin for the *Spalde* in a Romano-British administrative unit based in the

Lincolnshire Fens deserves at least some serious consideration.

Turning to the nature and political affiliations of the *Spalde*, any conclusions in this regard do to a large degree depend upon our attitude to the 'Tribal Hidage', as this contains the only documentary reference to the *Spalde*. If all of the small 'Tribal Hidage' population groups are considered to represent originally independent polities and tribes, then the *Spalde* ought to be seen in this light too.[37] However, if the legitimacy of assuming that a population group was originally independent based purely on its presence in the 'Tribal Hidage' is rejected, along with the model of kingdom-formation which goes with it, then the *Spalde* could well have been an important early and middle Anglo-Saxon population group inhabiting a geographically defined settlement unit and *regio* within a larger 'true' territory or kingdom, rather than a genuine 'tribal polity'.[38] On the whole, the arguments in favour of the latter approach to both the 'Tribal Hidage' and the *Spalde* seem the more convincing, but this naturally raises the question of which Anglo-Saxon kingdom the *Spalde* consequently belonged to. With regard to this, we have two credible options, namely *Lindissi* and Middle Anglia. In favour of the former is the proximity of the northern fringes of the likely territory of the *Spalde* to areas which are placed within *Lindissi*, based on the discussion in the previous chapter: that is, northern Kesteven and the south-eastern part of modern Lindsey. However, there is little beyond this proximity which can be offered in support of the case, and the lands of the *Spalde* were not only geographically and tenurially separated from Lindsey and northern Kesteven (Fig. 25), but they also extended far to the south of the probable southern periphery of both **Lindēs* and *Lindissi*.[39]

In contrast, the case in favour of the *Spalde* being a subgroup within the Middle Angles has at least some potential points in its favour. The first of these is that the 'Tribal Hidage' probably ought to be seen as a composite document, based primarily around a survey of the internal subdivisions of the kingdom of Middle Angles, to which had been added both pre-Viking aggregate hidages for the large kingdoms and information on a few other small groups that just happened to be available to the compiler.[40] The *Spalde* could, on this basis, be one of the last category of groups, but their location in the East Midlands immediately to the north of the probably Middle

Anglian *Gyrwe* suggests that they too were a subgroup within Middle Anglia, rather than a haphazard addition to the list. The second point is that the previously mentioned manuscripts of Felix's 'Life of St Guthlac' have the entire Fenland 'as far north as the sea' as part of the land of the Middle Angles. This description is suggestive for the *Spalde*, who were located on the Wash Silts between the Fen and the sea, although we do need to recognize that the siltland around and east of Wisbech also borders on the sea and it is this that could be intended here: these silts were almost certainly the lands of the *Wisse*, a population group mentioned in Felix's 'Life' and the *Spalde*'s eastern neighbour, probably to be identified with the Middle Anglian *Wille* and/or *Wixan* in the 'Tribal Hidage'.[41] In addition to these two points, if the territory of the *Spalde* was indeed related to a Late and post-Roman Fenland administrative unit, then a southerly connection may, in any case, be more plausible for this group than a northerly one. Thus the Roman road that travels into the Fens towards Spalding and Wykeham runs north-east and is connected to the main road network near to Kate's Bridge in the very far south of the county, suggesting a southern outlook for the Roman-era Lincolnshire Fenland (Fig. 32).[42] Equally, one major hypothesis with regard to the Fenland is that it was a single imperial estate, the centre of which probably lay in the south, whilst at the same time there are indications from Ptolemy that the Fenland was not actually considered part of the territory of the *Corieltavi* of Lindsey and Kesteven, instead belonging to the *Catuvellauni* tribe in the Late Iron Age and early Roman periods.[43]

On the whole then, the available evidence suggests that the *Spalde* were a significant early and middle Anglo-Saxon population group that inhabited the whole of the Lincolnshire siltland of Holland. Their territory may have had its origins in a Late and post-Roman administrative unit based in the Spalding/Wykeham area, with the earliest artefacts and place-names from the region indicating Anglo-Saxon influence and settlement from at least the sixth century. Finally, although it is possible that the *Spalde* constituted an originally independent 'tribe' controlling this territory, it seems more credible that they were in fact the inhabitants of a *regio* – an important subdistrict – of the Middle Anglian kingdom, as were their neighbours to the east (the *Wisse*) and to the south (the *Gyrwe*). This is really the limit of the available positive evidence; the only other potential source of information is that of Anglo-Saxon burial archaeology, and this is mostly notable by its absence, rather than anything else. Quite why we currently know of no early Anglo-Saxon cemeteries from the siltland associated with the *Spalde*, despite the fact that there is some evidence for Anglo-Saxon settlement here from at least the sixth century, is uncertain.[44] It may well be that we simply have not yet found the cemetery sites, perhaps because of a lack of fieldwork on the silts not immediately bordering the peat fen. It is worth noting in this context that, away from Lindsey and northern Kesteven, early Anglo-Saxon burial sites in the region do become much scarcer and far smaller in size (Fig. 33).[45] However, a simple failure to look in the right places is not fully convincing; we would still expect to find at least *some* evidence of Anglo-Saxon graves, if only from antiquarian discoveries or via modern metal-detecting.

One possibility is that the paucity of known cemeteries from within the territory of the *Spalde* may reflect a greater-than-normal British element within this 'Anglo-Saxon' population group, with some of these Britons perhaps making pragmatic use of early Anglo-Saxon everyday material culture, such as pottery, but not taking part in the distinctive and archaeologically 'visible' Anglo-Saxon burial rite. The normal post-Roman British rite appears to have been burial without any grave goods, thus making British graves of this period effectively archaeologically 'invisible' in most circumstances. Indeed, it is likely that the majority of the Britons who lived within the Anglo-Saxon kingdom of *Lindissi* do not appear in the early Anglo-Saxon burial record there, with the recorded graves of this period representing only five per cent or so of the likely total population.[46] Consequently, if the ratio of Britons to Anglo-Saxons in the territory of the *Spalde* was significantly higher than it was in *Lindissi* – a 'primary' area of Anglo-Saxon settlement, unlike Holland – then this situation might well help to account for the lack of 'Anglo-Saxon' graves here. Certainly, an absence of identifiable Anglo-Saxon burials has been associated with the significant presence of Britons elsewhere in eastern England.[47] In this context, it is worth recalling the hints in Felix's 'Life of St Guthlac' that there were still people speaking a form of Welsh in the Fens of south Lincolnshire in the early eighth

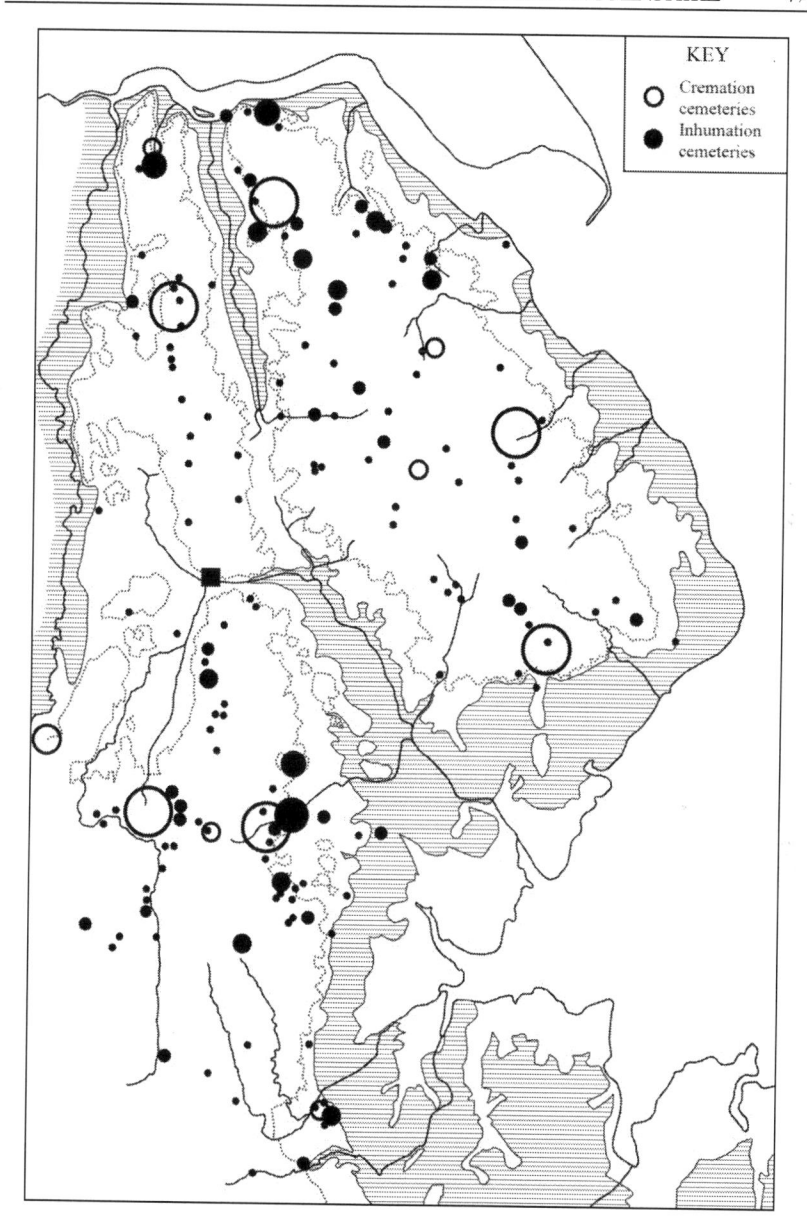

Fig. 33 The distribution of all fifth- to seventh-century Anglo-Saxon cemeteries in Lincolnshire. The diameters of the circles reflect the likely relative size of each cemetery

century. Such a situation could well underlie the names *Walcroft* and (less certainly, perhaps) *Bretlond* recorded in Fleet parish to the east of Spalding.[48] It would also accord well with the argument that the district-name Holland is of Neo-Brittonic (Archaic Welsh) origin, as may be the Fenland place-name Tydd and the first element of Lutton too (Fig. 34). Similarly, it has often been observed that the river-names of the Fenland are overwhelmingly pre-English in origin, with some having both a Celtic and an Old English name which co-existed and competed for dominance; so, the Lincolnshire Glen was known as both the Glen (< British **glanos*, 'pure, clear (water)') and the Baston Ea/Edyke (< Old English *ēa*, 'river', compare the Barlings Eau in Lindsey) in the medieval period.[49]

Of course, such a situation would seem to conflict with claims that there was a 'profound discontinuity' in terms of settlement within the Lincolnshire Fenland at the end of the Roman period.[50] Certainly many Romano-British settlements in the Fenland would have been badly affected by the spread of the freshwater fen, marine transgressions, and other environmental changes, with some being found buried under two metres of silt. It is very likely that a de-intensification of production associated with the end of the Roman state and its demands would have also had an effect.[51] However, this is a long way from saying that the post-Roman Britons virtually abandoned the whole of the Holland district, not just those areas most significantly affected by the environmental changes, with subsequent early Anglo-Saxon activity in the region being on a smaller scale and largely unrelated to that which had gone before, as sometimes seems to be suggested.[52] The evidence in favour of such a scenario as this consists almost entirely of two observations, namely that only a small number of Romano-British Fenland sites have produced early Anglo-Saxon material during fieldwalking and that early Anglo-Saxon sites discovered by the Fenland Survey are far less numerous than Romano-British ones, even in areas not directly affected by the environmental downturn. As such, the hypothesis of a post-Roman British abandonment of the Fenland does need to be viewed with considerable suspicion.

The concern here falls into two parts. Leaving to one side the important point that large areas of the Fenland, including the Spalding area, remain unsurveyed, it has to be recognized that early

Anglo-Saxon settlement patterns derived from fieldwalking can sometimes bear only a very dubious relationship to reality.[53] In particular, the notion that Romano-British and early Anglo-Saxon settlement patterns recovered from fieldwalking can be directly compared to produce conclusions about changing landscape exploitation and settlement density (and thus population levels) is open to serious doubt. After all, on this basis a dramatic decline in the post-Roman settlement density and population might be observed and hypothesized for most areas of eastern Britain, despite the fact that the environmental and palaeobotanical evidence indicates that this did not occur.[54] Part of the problem is that Late Roman artefacts are so much easier to identify and more numerous than their early Anglo-Saxon counterparts, with the poor quality of early Anglo-Saxon pottery and its similarity to handmade Iron Age and Roman wares causing significant difficulties in terms of both locating sites of this period and identifying evidence for Anglo-Saxon activity on Romano-British sites.[55] This is, needless to say, a point of considerable importance in the present context. However, it is not the whole story, as the notion that a simple comparison of Romano-British and early Anglo-Saxon find-scatters enables us to say anything useful about whether the Britons abandoned this region is vulnerable to a more fundamental methodological objection.

Essentially, the only 'early Anglo-Saxon' period sites (that is, *c.* 450–650) which will be revealed by fieldwalking – or even, in many cases, excavation – are those where the inhabitants made at least partial use of early Anglo-Saxon material culture, as post-Roman British settlements and settlement-stages are effectively archaeologically 'invisible' and aceramic in this period.[56] In such circumstances, observations based on the relative frequencies of early Anglo-Saxon 'sites' versus Romano-British ones, or (especially) the number of Romano-British sites with early Anglo-Saxon material on them, cannot credibly be used to hypothesize a near-complete disappearance of the Britons from the Lincolnshire Fenland after the fourth century or a general collapse in settlement density. The problem is quite simply that the field survey will be deficient in two key areas. First, it will miss any settlements of 'early Anglo-Saxon' unacculturated Britons present in the region – and it should be noted here that it seems likely that many Britons did not in fact acculturate

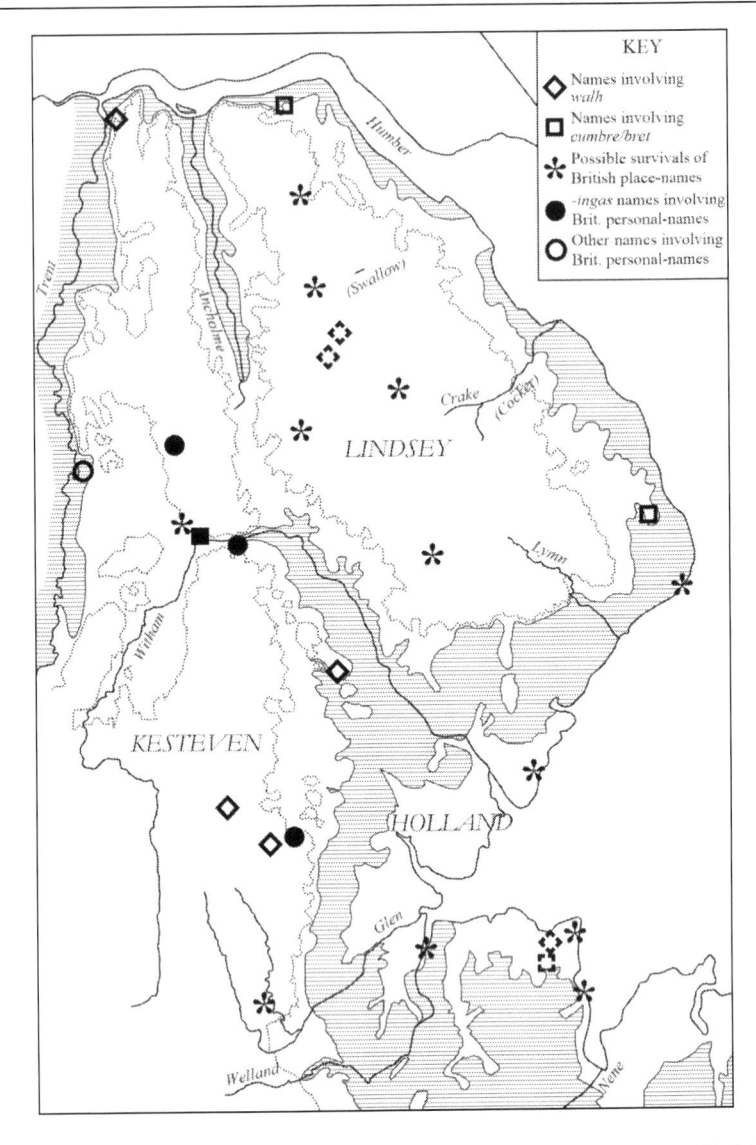

Fig. 34 The distribution of linguistic evidence for Anglian–British interaction in Lincolnshire. District- and river-names are shown where they derive from a pre-English name: where enclosed by brackets, this name survives only in a settlement-name. Note, where a place-name only possibly involves *walh, cumbre* or *bret,* the icon is given a broken line

until after the mid-seventh century (that is to say, not until the 'Middle Saxon' period), and some not even until the mid–late eighth century, or possibly a little later.[57] Second, it will miss any post-Roman British stages to the early Anglo-Saxon sites which are discovered. Thus, for example, supposedly abandoned Romano-British settlements might have indeed been abandoned *c.* 400, but even if they had in fact continued in use for several centuries, they would still be indistinguishable on the ground from those which really were abandoned then, so long as their inhabitants had not acculturated whilst they lived there (and if they had, this could easily be misread as 're-occupation'). Similarly, if the Britons of the Fenland had relocated to new settlement sites in the period before they acculturated (perhaps in the face of marine transgressions, the general environmental downturn, or as a result of other factors, such as the well-established phenomenon of early medieval settlement mobility and drift across the landscape), then these new sites would not appear in the record at all, until or unless the Britons who lived there began to adopt the Anglo-Saxon material culture. Moreover, if they did acculturate, then their settlement might be easily misinterpreted as one founded *de novo* in the early or middle Anglo-Saxon period.[58]

In this context, it is worth noting that it is usually agreed that almost all of the sites discovered by the Fenland Survey were abandoned before the end of the Middle Saxon period, with settlement relocating and nucleating onto the unsurveyed high silts at the sites of the present villages.[59] Although 'by the early ninth century' is the date most recently given for this, a number of settlements look to have been abandoned by *c.* 700 and, whilst there is a very small quantity of Ipswich-ware pottery (dating *c.* 725–850) from some of the sites, it is perfectly credible that the relocation and nucleation was generally well under way by the middle of the eighth century.[60] If so, then the general abandonment of almost all dispersed settlements within the Fenland Survey area would have been begun before any process of British acculturation was completed, given both the general chronology proposed for this acculturation by modern commentators and the hints of surviving Welsh-speakers provided in the eighth-century 'Life of St Guthlac' and Holland place-names.[61] Needless to say, any Britons who moved to the nucleated settlements on the high silts before they acculturated would be completely 'invisible' to the Fenland Survey.

None of this is, of course, to deny that there was a significant decline in settlement density in some parts of the Fenland in the post-Roman period, to be associated with environmental changes and a de-intensification of production, with some Romano-British settlement sites being buried by marine transgressions. However, any claims of a post-Roman British near-abandonment of the whole district of Holland, followed by an unrelated early Anglo-Saxon resettlement, do rest on dubious evidential and methodological grounds. Fundamentally, the Fenland Survey results could just as easily arise from a situation in which there continued to be a significant number of Britons living in the Lincolnshire Fenland, who only gradually acculturated over the course of the pre-Viking period, as they could from a wholesale British landscape-abandonment in the early fifth century. This is particularly the case given that we do have reason to think that post-Roman Britons were present in this area and there is a conspicuous absence of diagnostic early Anglo-Saxon graves from the region, despite evidence for 'early Anglo-Saxon' settlement activity. Indeed, it ought to be noted here that not only do the apparent references to Welsh-speakers in both the eighth-century 'Life of St Guthlac' and place-names suggest that unacculturated Britons still lived in the Lincolnshire Fenland until a relatively late date, but also some of the Celtic etymologies for Fenland names appear actively to require the survival of Welsh-speakers into at least the sixth century or after in order to account for the forms taken.[62] Moreover, for what it is worth, the author of chapter 56 of the ninth-century *Historia Brittonum* certainly seems to have considered there to have been British activity in the area north of Spalding in the post-Roman period. He refers to a battle fought *c.* 500 between the Britons and the immigrant Anglo-Saxons *in ostium fluminis quod dicitur Glein*, 'at the mouth of the river called *Glein*'.[63] This river-name derives from British **glanos* ('pure, clear') and would be **Glain* in Modern Welsh, but no river with this form of the name currently exists. The only two possible identifications of the *Glein* generally admitted are, in fact, the Glen in Northumberland and the Lincolnshire Glen; of the two, only the latter is credible if this is to be considered a real battle against Anglo-Saxons fought *c.* 500, given that there is no evidence for Anglo-Saxon activity in the area of the Northumberland Glen before *c.* 550. Moreover, the case for its reality is perhaps bolstered by the possibility of a Lincolnshire core for this chapter of the *Historia*, as discussed above.[64]

Of course, the idea of a very large British element in the territory of the *Spalde* can potentially be pushed too far as well. When all is said and done, the *Spalde* seem to have been at least nominally an 'Anglo-Saxon' population group, not a 'British' one, to judge purely from their name and the occurrence of probable early place-names in their territory, such as Wykeham, which indicate the presence of Old English-speakers. However, this still leaves the question of the absolute lack of burials. A large British element within the population group can certainly help to explain the severe paucity of early Anglo-Saxon burials in Holland when compared with *Lindissi*, along with the reference in the 'Life of St Guthlac', but perhaps not the total absence of graves. What, then, are we to make of this? There are only really two possibilities which seem credible, if we consider it likely that there were at least some immigrant-descended Anglo-Saxons in the region from the sixth century onwards. The first is that, once again, their graves have not yet been discovered, and if immigrant-descended Anglo-Saxons were in far more of a minority here than elsewhere then this might certainly make finding their graves even more difficult.

The second, speculative, possibility is that the graves may not actually be on the siltland itself. If one follows the Roman road running south-west from the likely Romano-British and Anglo-Saxon centre of the Fenland, Spalding/Wykeham, then shortly after it crosses the Car Dyke and exits the Fenland to join the main Roman road network, we find not one, but probably two, significant fifth- to sixth-century cemeteries just to the south of the probable junction. One of these is Baston small cremation cemetery, which is usually considered to have been fully excavated. This contained forty-four cremations and two inhumations, dating from the late fifth and sixth centuries. The other is a sizeable fifth- to sixth-century inhumation cemetery recorded via metal-detecting a little distance away from the cremation cemetery, with finds including two mid-fifth-century Aberg group I brooches.[65] These cemeteries need not, of course, have anything to do with the *Spalde*, but their location just to the south of the junction of the road leading into the *Spalde*'s territory

**Fig. 35 A sixth-century, gilded great square-headed brooch from
the Baston inhumation cemetery**
Source: Adam Daubney, Portable Antiquities Scheme

is certainly intriguing, and they do stand out in terms of size in
southern Kesteven (Figs 33 and 35).[66] In this context, it might be
speculated that the graves of those of the *Spalde* who did bury in an
Anglo-Saxon manner, and probably considered themselves descended
from fifth- and sixth-century immigrants, are invisible in the Fenland
not only because they were potentially few in number, but also
because they chose to inter their dead on the beginnings of the
uplands at the very edge of their territory, next to the route into their
regio.[67] This would, of course, require that the *Spalde*'s territory
included at least this small part of southern Kesteven, something
which might seem to conflict with the historical indications that pre-
Norman Holland was a distinct territory that was not dependent
upon the surrounding upland and Fen Edge.[68] On the whole, there
seems no good reason to challenge this judgement, but it is perhaps

worth wondering whether a relationship in the opposite direction, wherein a small part of the Fen Edge was dependent on the siltland, would be as problematical. It would certainly not seem impossible that the Roman route across the Fens to Spalding/Wykeham, along with any attendant maintenance obligations, lay wholly within the jurisdiction of the *Spalde* in the post-Roman period, with this Fen Edge dependency perhaps being lost once the road went out of use (as it is now suggested to have done, rather than survive into the twelfth century and beyond as was once thought).[69]

3.   The *Bilmigas* and the *regio* of the *Billingas*

The only other small 'Tribal Hidage' population group to be considered in detail here is the *Bilmigas*.[70] The *Bilmigas* have often been equated with a Kesteven-based group called the *Billingas* ('the people of *Billa*'), who are known from the place-names Billinghay ('the island of the *Billingas*'), Billingborough ('the fort of the *Billingas*') and Horbling ('the muddy settlement of the *Billingas*'), all of which lie within the boundaries suggested previously for **Lindēs/Lindissi*.[71] Unfortunately, this equation is, at best, debatable. Not only would it require that *Bilmigas* is in error for an original **Bilingas*, but all of the manuscripts of Recension C of the 'Tribal Hidage' give the group-name a consistent extra syllable (*Bilmiligas, Birmiligas, Biliniligas, Silimligas, Bilmiligas* and *Biliniligas*), which makes an emendation to **Bilingas* difficult to sustain.[72] As such, an equation between the *Bilmigas/Bilmiligas* and the *Billingas* is probably best left to one side as unconvincing and unsafe on present evidence, with the *Bilmigas/Bilmiligas* simply being one of the groups mentioned in the 'Tribal Hidage' whose location is unknown.[73] However, whilst such a rejection of an equation of the *Bilmigas/Bilmiligas* and the *Billingas* is important to note, it leaves unanswered the question of what the three *Billingas* place-names actually represent, and whether they have any historical significance.

In general, the meaning of *-ingas* group-names which are recorded in a single place-name is very much open to debate, and in many cases they may well only represent very local kin groups which inhabited the area in the immediate vicinity of that place-name.[74] On the other hand, where we have more than one place-name referring to a single *-ingas* group, and especially when these are spread over a sizeable area, the situation is somewhat different. We are likely then to be dealing with a more substantial grouping, and we do need to bear in mind here that *-ingas* names are in fact found as those of significant population groups and *regiones* in pre-Viking England: for example, the *Stoppingas*, the *Feppingas*, the *Hæstingas*, the *Geddingas*, the *Sunningas*, and probably the *Hroðingas*.[75] In light of this, it is worth asking whether there is any evidence which might support a contention that our three *Billingas* place-names reflect such a significant population group and *regio* within the kingdom of *Lindissi*.

Certainly, in this context, the wide separation of the *Billingas* place-names, which are found at opposite ends of a thirteen-mile stretch of the northern Kesteven Fen Edge, indicates that the *Billingas* were a population group which encompassed an area comparable in extent with the territories of the known *-ingas* population groups and *regiones*, such as those of the *Sunningas* or the *Hroðingas*.[76] This in itself is very suggestive, and a reasonable working hypothesis might consequently be that Billinghay and Billingborough represented the northern and southern limits of the *Billingas* population group and *regio* within *Lindissi* – something supported by the fact that the southern boundary of *Lindēs*/*Lindissi* is unlikely to have been located much further south than Billingborough[77] – with this *regio* then extending to some unknown degree inland from the Fen Edge between these two places.[78] Such a hypothesis finds very considerable support in the early Anglo-Saxon archaeology of Kesteven. As has often been observed, most recently by Tania Dickinson, the early Anglo-Saxon cemeteries of northern Kesteven fall into two clearly distinct geographic groups: one on and to the west of the limestone edge in the centre of northern Kesteven between Lincoln and Ancaster (the largest of these cemeteries being the Loveden Hill cremation cemetery), and another on the lower ground to the east of the uplands stretching to the Fen Edge, focused around Sleaford and Ruskington.[79] The distribution maps which reveal this pattern need updating to include the early Anglo-Saxon cemeteries discovered in recent years by metal-detecting and excavation, along with a number of other cemeteries which have sometimes been missed off the distribution maps, and this has been done in Fig. 36.[80] However, these additions only serve to confirm and strengthen the pattern of two discrete groups previously observable. The only significant changes are that the Loveden Hill region appears as more of a focus for the first group than it did previously, and the second group can now be seen to have extended south of Sleaford to the Osbournby and Folkingham area. What is particularly interesting here is that the second geographic group does in fact fall between, and inland of, Billinghay–Billingborough. In other words, these cemeteries seem to represent a coherent and discrete grouping – distinct in terms of distribution from the other early Anglo-Saxon cemetery group in Kesteven – which just so happens to cover a significant proportion of the sort of territory which might be predicted for any *regio* of the *Billingas*.

The sense, derived from their distribution and separation from the other cemeteries of northern Kesteven, that the Ruskington–Sleaford–Folkingham group of cemeteries may represent a genuine early Anglo-Saxon 'settlement unit' and territory is heightened by a closer examination of the archaeology of this part of northern Kesteven. Of particular interest here is the fact that the large cremation cemeteries of *Lindēs*/*Lindissi* not only formed, in effect, a ring around Lincoln, but they also appear to have been spaced out across the landscape and usually located at or close by the centres of documented early political and administrative territories. Indeed, in light of recent research into the nature and role of such exceptionally large cemeteries, it seems likely that each of these sites functioned as an early Anglo-Saxon social and sacred 'central place' for a sizeable territory and its inhabitants, many of whom were in fact buried in the main cemetery, whilst others were buried in surrounding subordinate small inhumation and mixed cemeteries, perhaps because they were excluded from the main burial ground.[81] As such, it is important to note that the most easterly of the three cremation cemeteries known from northern Kesteven is in fact found at the heart of our Ruskington–Sleaford–Folkingham group of cemeteries, close by Sleaford itself, which was a Late Saxon soke-centre and the focus of a documented pre-Viking estate.[82]

The cemetery in question was discovered at Quarrington, immediately to the west of Sleaford, during gravel-digging in the early nineteenth century, and looks to have been in use from the fifth through to the seventh century. Specific details are thin on the

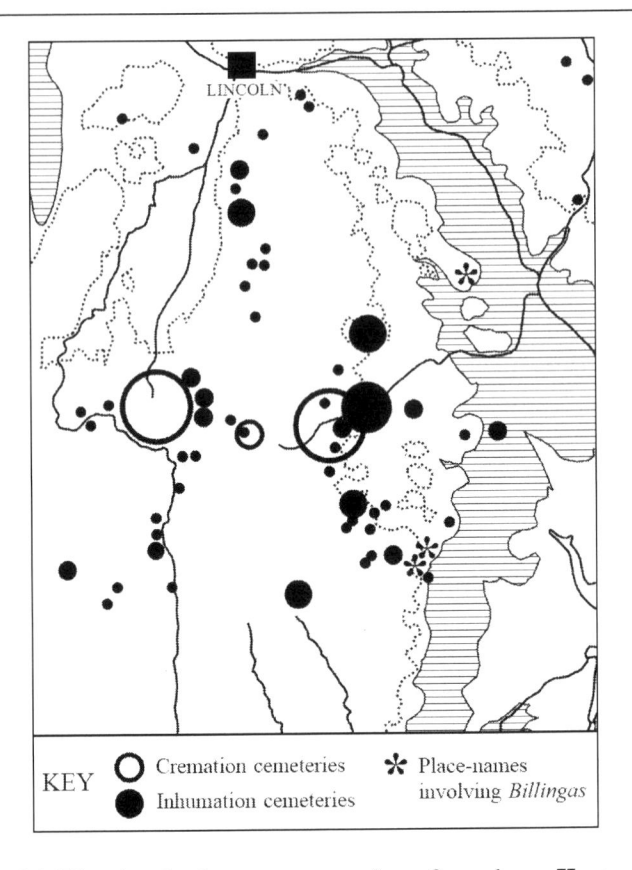

KEY

⭕ Cremation cemeteries

⬤ Inhumation cemeteries

✳ Place-names involving *Billingas*

Fig. 36 The Anglo-Saxon cemeteries of northern Kesteven, overlaid with the *Billingas* place-name evidence, marked by asterisks (north to south: Billinghay, Horbling, Billingborough)

ground because of the date and method of discovery of the site. However, it appears to have been primarily a cremation cemetery with some accompanying inhumations (as is also the case at the Cleatham, Elsham and Loveden Hill cemeteries), and the description of the site suggests that it was probably comparable in extent to the other large cremation cemeteries of the Lincoln region.[83] Furthermore, at Sleaford, only one and a half miles to the east of Quarrington, we also find one of the largest early Anglo-Saxon inhumation cemeteries in England. It dates from the late fifth to the sixth/early seventh centuries, and on its own seems to have been equivalent in size to many cremation cemeteries (*c.* 600 or more burials; Elsham cremation cemetery, for example, contained 625 cremations and five inhumations).[84] Given both the evidence from the other large cemeteries in Lincolnshire and current perspectives on the role which such large cemeteries played as social and sacred *foci* in early Anglo-Saxon England, it would appear very likely that Sleaford–Quarrington represented the 'central place' of a significant fifth- to seventh-century Anglo-Saxon population group and territory.[85] Needless to say, in the present context it is difficult to avoid relating this population group and its territory to the geographically distinct early Anglo-Saxon cemetery group/'settlement unit' focused on Ruskington–Sleaford–Folkingham discussed above. In other words, it seems probable that we can here identify archaeologically both an early Anglo-Saxon 'central place' (Sleaford–Quarrington) and also the likely extent of its territory, as observable from the separate and coherent grouping of small cemeteries that occurs to the north and south of this centre, these credibly representing the burial grounds of those who made use of the social and sacred functions of the 'central place', but not, for whatever reason, its funerary function.

This is obviously of considerable interest to the present investigation. Not only does the suggested territory of any *regio* of the *Billingas* happen to coincide reasonably well with a geographic group of fifth- to seventh-century cemeteries, but it also seems likely that the distribution of these cemeteries reflects the territory of a major early Anglo-Saxon group focused on Sleaford–Quarrington. In such circumstances, the above contention regarding the existence of a *regio* of the *Billingas* would seem to be largely confirmed. Put simply, there is good archaeological evidence for an early Anglo-Saxon territory and population group existing in the area that is hypothesized as the likely territory of the *Billingas*. As such, there seems little obvious reason not to consider the *Billingas* of our three widely spaced place-names to have been – like other multiply attested *-ingas* groups – a real early Anglo-Saxon population group and *regio*, to be identified with the Sleaford–Quarrington territory and group.

Whether the Sleaford–Quarrington group was indeed known as the *Billingas* or as something else entirely, we do still need to ask what else can be learnt about this population group and its territory/*regio*, as it was clearly a significant element within the kingdom of *Lindissi*.

One way of approaching this is to examine the evidence for Middle Saxon and later territories existing in this region, in order to see whether there are any later echoes of the early Anglo-Saxon territory. With regard to this, the area of the Ruskington–Sleaford–Folkingham early Anglo-Saxon cemetery group seems to fall wholly within the likely territories of two neighbouring Anglo-Saxon estates, which is intriguing. The first of these estates was based at Sleaford. An estate here is mentioned in a genuine, ninth-century charter, and although we certainly cannot assume that all Domesday sokes reflect much earlier estates, it has been argued that the sokes based at and around Sleaford (and possibly Ruskington) do derive ultimately from a pre-Viking estate focused on Sleaford, which probably originally straddled the wapentakes of Flaxwell and Aswardhurn.[86] The second estate is the Soke of Folkingham, which encompassed not only the settlements in the northern part of Aveland wapentake but also most of those in the southern half of Aswardhurn wapentake; once again, whilst not all sokes derive from Middle Saxon estates, it has been suggested that this one may well do so.[87] That these two estates together seem to have covered all of the area of the fifth- to seventh-century cemetery group is unlikely to be a coincidence. As such, they are probably best seen as confirming that this geographically separate cemetery group did indeed represent the early Anglo-Saxon territorial unit dependent upon Sleaford–Quarrington, with this territory having been split in two in perhaps the Middle Saxon period. In this context it is important to note that David Roffe has argued that the site of a recorded late seventh-century royal monastery, Stow Green, is found only one and a half miles to the north-east of Folkingham village. The Middle Saxon foundation of this monastery would provide a convincing explanation for the division of the territory dependent upon Sleaford–Quarrington, as one would expect that at some point an estate would have had to be created out of the lands of the *regio* in which Stow Green lay, in order to cater for the needs and maintenance of this royal ecclesiastical centre.[88] Certainly, the carving up of early *regiones* in order to provide estates and minster territories for monasteries appears to have been a common occurrence elsewhere in Middle Saxon England. We might, for example, compare here the carving of the Chertsey monastic estate in Surrey out of the *regio* of the *Woccingas*, or the Farnham estate out of the *regio* of the

Godhelmingas.[89]

If the evidence for pre-Viking estates based at Sleaford and Folkingham can thus help both to confirm and potentially further delimit the extent of the early Anglo-Saxon territory/*regio* dependent upon Sleaford–Quarrington, and also tell us something of its later history and division, what of the archaeological evidence? Although we know too little about the Quarrington cemetery to comment any further, several points can be made with regard to the neighbouring large inhumation cemetery at Sleaford. In particular, it needs to be recognized that this cemetery was not only exceptionally large, but also exceptionally well connected to the outside world. Thus, for example, many more amber beads – around 981 in total – have been found in the Sleaford cemetery than in any other Anglo-Saxon cemetery in England, these being mainly used in the sixth century and probably imported from the Baltic.[90] Similarly, there is a notable concentration of imported walrus- or elephant-ivory rings in the Sleaford cemetery, and this cemetery also has produced more than twice as many probably imported crystal beads (again, primarily a sixth-century artefact) as any other Anglo-Saxon cemetery.[91] Needless to say, this all adds yet more weight to the case for Sleaford's importance in the early Anglo-Saxon period. Fundamentally, it seems that at least some of the people who buried their dead in the Sleaford inhumation cemetery had far greater access to imported and high-status items than did those in the surrounding region, where such luxury imports are considerably rarer. Indeed, on this basis it has been credibly suggested that Sleaford may have been the burial ground used by local leaders who maintained a tight control over the regional redistribution of these prestige items.[92] Certainly, the fact that around 250 of the amber beads were found in a single grave in the Sleaford cemetery (the average was 16 beads per grave) might well support the view that access to these luxury imports was tightly controlled and preferential. Also important in this regard is the fact that those graves at Sleaford which lacked imported amber beads appear to have had restricted access to other types of artefacts too, such as disc brooches, earrings, bracelets, pendants, small-long brooches and bags.[93]

One interesting question in view of the above is where the trading point used by these leading members of the local early Anglo-Saxon community might have been. Although no absolute certainty can be obtained, one extremely good possibility is that it was at Heckington, located on the Fen Edge halfway between Billinghay and Billingborough. Heckington was part of the probably Middle Saxon estate focused on Sleaford, and Adam Daubney has recently revealed that the important 'South Lincolnshire Productive Site' was located in this parish.[94] Although in Lindsey there appear to have been numerous minor markets and trading sites located all across the region, testified to by the presence of Middle Saxon coinage and other finds, in Kesteven almost all trading activity appears to have been channelled through this single site.[95] Katharina Ulmschneider recorded over 90 coins in total from here in 2000, and this number has continued to increase. As of 2009, there were about 160 very late seventh- to mid-eighth-century *sceattas* known in addition to other types, making this, after the *Hamwic* (Southampton) finds, the largest non-hoarded group of Middle Saxon coins in England.[96] In this context, it may well be significant that the finds have been made to the east of Heckington village, at a hamlet on the very Fen Edge – just beyond the Car Dyke – called Garwick, either 'the *wic* (trading site) on a triangular piece of land' or 'belonging to *Gæra*'.[97] What is particularly relevant here, however, is the fact that the site was in use before the late seventh century. In particular, a mid-seventh-century gold shilling, thirteen high-status continental gold coins (*tremisses*), which date from the late sixth/early seventh century onwards, and a gold blank flan have all been found at Garwick. Given the rarity of these coins, this is a very significant concentration indeed and certainly a far greater quantity than is found on any other 'productive site' in the region or, in fact, across the whole of Lindsey.[98] Moreover, there is also a sixth-century 'Pressblech' Style I die from the site for making foil mounts, which is suggestive of very early trading activity here, whilst other finds are indicative of the presence of a sixth- to seventh-century Anglo-Saxon inhumation cemetery (Figs 37 and 38).[99]

All told, this is an exceedingly interesting site, not least because there is evidence for trade activity here much earlier than on most other 'productive sites', even into the sixth century on the basis of the 'Pressblech' die. Two points are of especial relevance to the present focus. First, the history of the site, its context within Kesteven, and the fact that some sort of trading activity seems to have been taking

Fig. 37 The sixth-century, 'Pressblech' Style I die from Garwick, used for making foil mounts
Source: Adam Daubney, Portable Antiquities Scheme

place here from potentially as early as the sixth century, mean that the suggestion that the luxury imports – such as amber and ivory – found in sixth-century graves at Sleaford came through here must be seen as more than credible. Second, even without reference to its probable role in the importation of the luxury goods used in the Sleaford cemetery, it seems likely that this site was linked to the local early and middle Anglo-Saxon 'central place' at Sleaford–Quarrington. So, for example, Garwick seems to have been part of the probably pre-Viking Sleaford estate and the Ruskington–Sleaford–Folkingham cemetery group, and it may be worth noting here that the only other seventh-century gold *tremissis* known from Kesteven comes from the Sleaford area, as does the only other notable concentration of Middle Saxon coins.[100] Similarly, the high status of the early finds in particular suggest that Garwick probably had considerable political significance, and a link between this site and the local leaders who seem to have been buried at Sleaford – the local 'central place' – is consequently very plausible. Of course, if the amber and ivory found in the Sleaford graves did come through this trading site, as seems likely, then it ought to be recalled that local leaders are usually considered to have controlled both the supply and redistribution of these

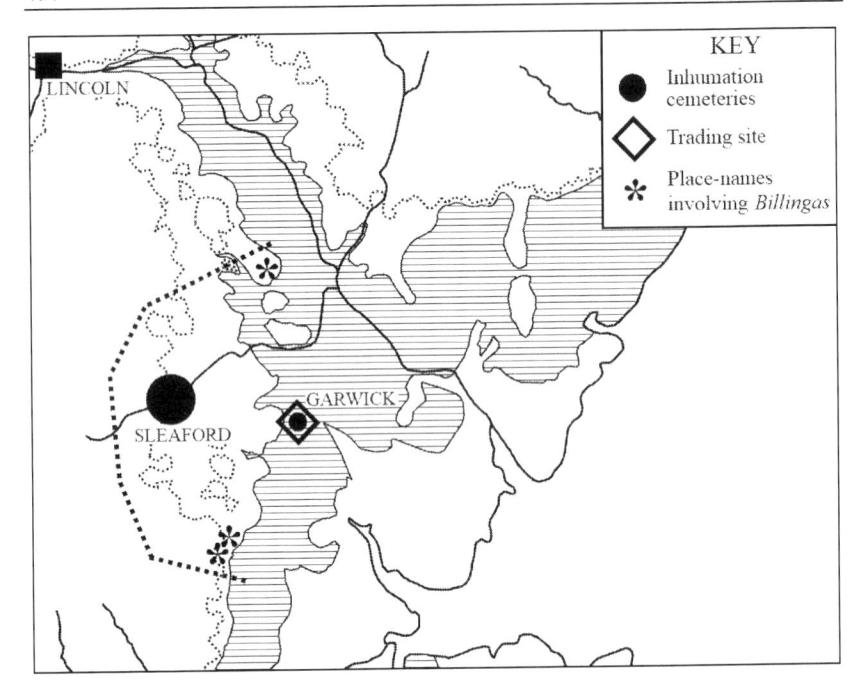

**Fig. 38 Garwick and the *Billingas*. The cemetery and trading site
at Garwick are shown, as is the Sleaford inhumation cemetery,
which contains a significant quantity of probably imported amber.
The dotted line represents the suggested minimum extent of the
Billingas, based upon the place-name and cemetery evidence**

luxury imported items in the region in the sixth century, which would
in turn presumably indicate some sort of direct control over the
trading site as well.[101]

Another important question regarding the early history of the
population group and territory/*regio* focused on Sleaford–
Quarrington is that of the relationship here between the immigrant
Anglo-Saxons and the post-Roman Britons. Given that this territory
lay within the probable bounds of both *Lindissi* and **Lindēs*, there
seems no good reason why the general model of Anglian–British
interaction within **Lindēs* proposed in the previous chapters should
not be applied here; all of the major cremation cemeteries and their
territories in the Lincoln area are most credibly seen as being the
result of a deliberate fifth-century settlement of immigrant groups on

the periphery of the 'country of *Lindēs*', with the Britons probably maintaining at least a degree of control over these territories and groups some way into the sixth century.[102] The evidence we have from the Sleaford–Quarrington region accords well with this picture, and when we turn to look at the transition to Anglo-Saxon rule, the picture is again in harmony with that established generally for *Lindēs*/*Lindissi*.[103] Thus, for example, one of the instances of an Anglo-Saxon -*ingas* group-name formed from a British personal name occurs in the south of the *regio*, at Threekingham. Similarly, high-status British brooches are known from probably sixth-century Anglo-Saxon graves here – something which may reflect acculturation and/or intermarriage – and there is place-name evidence for British/Welsh-speakers still existing within the landscape as late as the eighth century from the two Walcots, one in Billinghay parish and the other close by Threekingham (Fig. 39).[104]

This naturally raises the question of whether the territory and *regio* of Sleaford–Quarrington itself, as an element in the internal organization and administration of *Lindissi*, owed anything to the British past. After all, *Lindissi* seems to have been a British political unit taken over by an immigrant group, and it was suggested in the previous chapter that at least some elements of the internal administration of *Lindēs* were carried over with this. In this context it would be remiss not to point out that around 500 metres to the north-east of the Sleaford inhumation cemetery lay the Roman 'small town' of Old Sleaford, which was occupied from the first century BC through to at least the late fourth century AD.[105] Romano-British local administration is likely to have been based around the 'small towns', and as such it might be legitimately wondered whether the *regio* focused on Sleaford–Quarrington might not have been the Anglo-Saxon successor to the authority and territory of Old Sleaford.[106] Certainly, the likely extent of the Anglo-Saxon *regio*, as indicated by the cemetery group, bears a credible resemblance to that which might be suggested for the territory administered from Old Sleaford using Thiessen polygons (Fig. 40).[107] There is, of course, no absolute certainty possible here, but such a situation seems plausible in the general context of *Lindissi*'s apparent administrative debt to *Lindēs*. Indeed, it may well be relevant that there seems to be a similar coincidence between Hibaldstow 'small town' in the north of the

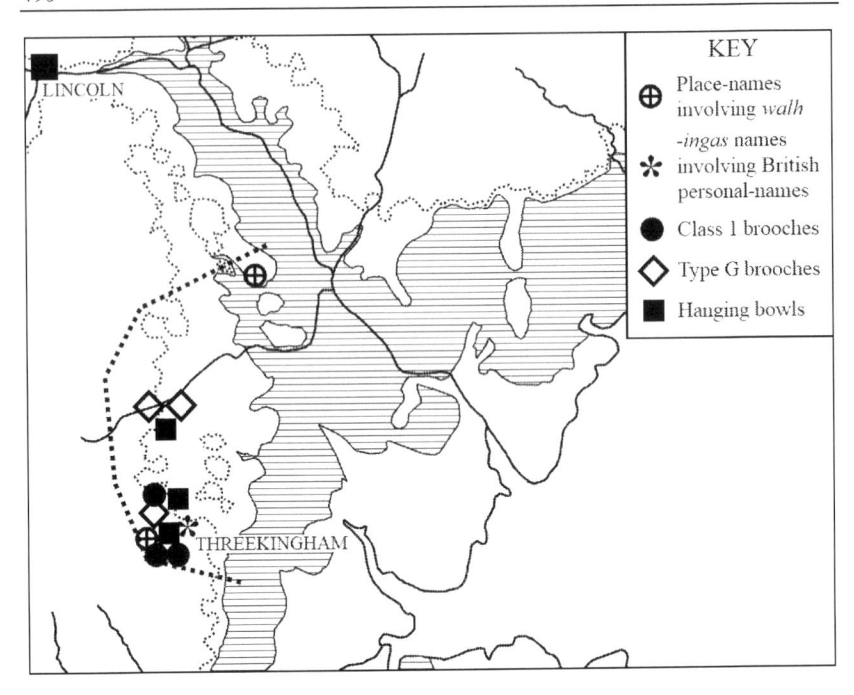

Fig. 39 The distribution of British metalwork and place-name evidence for Britons in the territory of the *Billingas*

county and both the Cleatham cremation cemetery and the Anglo-Saxon soke-centre of Kirton in Lindsey. Finally, in this light it may be worth pointing out that Sleaford's *wīc* site at Garwick also appears to have Romano-British and earlier antecedents, with finds through to the fourth century, including three British gold 'staters' and material which is indicative of the presence of some sort of votive shrine.[108]

In sum, it seems quite credible that the *Billingas* were indeed a genuine pre-Viking population group and *regio* within the kingdom of *Lindissi*, to be identified with the early Anglo-Saxon population group that was focused upon the sizeable cremation cemetery at Quarrington and the exceptionally large inhumation cemetery at Sleaford. The origins of this group ought to be sought in the Anglian–British interactions of the Lincoln region discussed in previous chapters, and the extent of their territory is probably reflected in both the spread of the discrete Ruskington–Sleaford–Folkingham cemetery group and the bounds of the probably Middle

Saxon estates of Sleaford and Folkingham. Whether this territory bears any relationship to that controlled in the Late Roman period from Old Sleaford is open to debate, but there are hints that this might be the case and such a situation would have a good regional context. In any case, there is some evidence for British elites either intermarrying or acculturating within this *regio*, in particular from the place-name Threekingham. That Sleaford–Quarrington was the 'central place' of this population group is not only indicated by its large cemeteries and later status as an estate centre, it is also implied by the wealth of some of the sixth-century graves in the Sleaford inhumation cemetery when compared with those in the surrounding area. This wealth was primarily expressed through imported luxury items, especially amber beads, the use and redistribution of which appears to have been tightly controlled by leading members of the local community. The same may also be true for the *wīc* (trading site) where this material was probably obtained, namely the 'South Lincolnshire Productive Site' located at Garwick, which appears to have functioned as a trading site from perhaps as early as the sixth century through to the mid-eighth.

If we are thus able to establish a reasonable amount about the nature and origins of this early Anglo-Saxon *regio* and population group, can anything worthwhile be said about its history after the final conquest of *Lindissi* by Mercia in 679? It should be noted here that this event actually provides a very credible context for the separation of northern Kesteven from the rest of **Lindēs/Lindissi*, something which is likely to have taken place by the mid–late ninth century at the latest and which would obviously have been of considerable significance to the northern Kesteven-based *Billingas*.[109] Indeed, not only would the kingdom of *Lindissi* probably have been particularly vulnerable to such a loss of territory in and around 679, but it may well also be that Mercia would have had an especial interest in separating and absorbing northern Kesteven at this time, rather than at any other.[110] In particular, Mercia, because of its location, appears to have had no substantial trading site (*wīc*) of its own, and from *c.* 675 until some point between *c.* 689 and 733 the Mercian kings lost their control over the originally East Saxon *wīc* at *Lundenwic* (London).[111] In such circumstances, the acquisition (through annexation) of northern Kesteven – and therefore of the

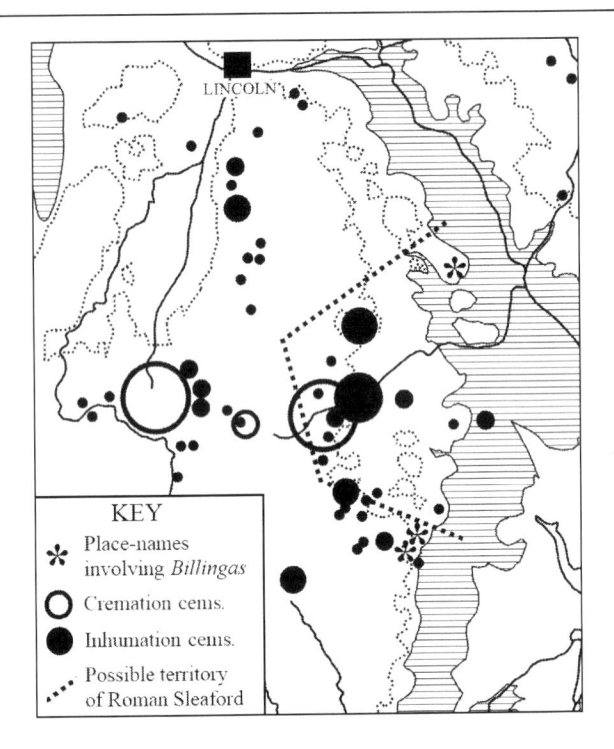

Fig. 40 The territory of Roman Sleaford as suggested by Thiessen polygons, plotted against the early Anglo-Saxon cemetery evidence and the *Billingas* place-names

important high-status trading site at Garwick – could well have seemed a particularly attractive proposition to the Mercian kings in the aftermath of their conquest of *Lindissi* in 679. The question therefore becomes, is there any evidence which might indicate that there was indeed a royal Mercian takeover and exploitation of Garwick at this time?

With regard to this, it has to be said that a royal Mercian interest of the late seventh-century onwards in the *wīc* at Garwick, perhaps prompted by their loss of control of *Lundenwic*, would certainly help to explain some of the very exceptional features of this site. Thus, whilst Garwick looks to have been an important local prestige-trading site through to *c.* 675 (based on the fifteen gold coins – including one blank – and the 'Pressblech' die found there, along with the amber and ivory found in the Sleaford cemetery), this does not really prepare us for the sheer quantity of very late seventh- to mid-eighth-century coinage which has been found. The current total of *c.* 160 *sceattas*, plus other types, is remarkable. Not only does it significantly exceed the total known from the whole of Lindsey (123 *sceattas*) – an area which is often considered to have been one of the wealthiest parts of Middle Saxon England[112] – but it is also the largest, non-hoarded group of Middle Saxon coins from England other than that from *Hamwic*, and it dwarfs the total of 51 *sceattas* known from *Lundenwic*.[113] Similarly suggestive is the fact that an examination of the Garwick coins by series indicates a very heavy Mercian and continental influence at this trading site, whilst Northumbrian issues are conspicuous by their absence, something which is not true on the 'productive sites' found across the Witham in Lindsey.[114] Indeed, around half of the Garwick *sceattas* have continental origins, which is probably further indicative of the importance of this trading site in the late seventh to mid-eighth centuries. Certainly, the fact that one fifth of the *sceattas* from *Lundenwic* (London) are continental in origin has been interpreted as a 'testimony to the range and intensity of the port's foreign contacts', and the even larger proportion of continental coins in the Garwick corpus should presumably be interpreted in the same manner.[115] Finally, it is worth observing that, whilst there are a considerable number of large, medium and small Middle Saxon 'productive sites' in Lindsey from which multiple *sceattas* have been recovered, this is not the case in southern Lincolnshire; instead, virtually all trading activity here appears to have been channelled through Garwick.[116]

In the light of Mercia's late seventh-century loss of control of *Lundenwic*, the exceptional character of the very late seventh- to mid-eighth-century finds from Garwick, and the apparent failure of other significant Middle Saxon trading/market sites to develop in southern Lincolnshire (in contrast to the situation in Lindsey), it appears more than credible that Garwick had indeed been taken over by the Mercian kings in the late seventh century, who then proceeded to exploit the site to its fullest potential. This does, of course, offer considerable support for the above position that the final conquest of *Lindissi* in 679 had led to the annexation and absorption of northern Kesteven by Mercia, with this occurring then rather than later because of the Mercian interest in directly controlling Garwick.[117] Such a scenario certainly helps to explain the available evidence, and a

Mercian takeover of the *Billingas* in the late seventh century may also provide a good context for other aspects of the history of this *regio*, such as the probable carving up of its territory into a late seventh-century Mercian royal monastic estate focused on Stow Green in the south and a 'multiple estate' focused on Sleaford in the north. The nature of the resultant Sleaford estate is particularly intriguing here, as it has been argued that the estate probably functioned as a major corn-milling centre for the region from perhaps as early as *c.* 700. Certainly, the neighbouring parish to Sleaford – Quarrington (*Corninctune* at Domesday) – bears a name which appears to derive from Old English **cweorning*, (probably 'the mill-place'), plus the common element *tūn*, giving something akin to 'the village near to the mill-place'.[118] Whether there is any direct link between the product of this possible pre-Viking corn-milling centre and the trading taking place at Garwick is uncertain, but it is tempting to see both the intensive exploitation of this *wīc* and the emergence of the Sleaford 'multiple estate' as being the result of a considerable Mercian royal interest in this area and its economy.[119]

This is just about as far as we can go with the evidence presently available, but it is enough to present a reasonably detailed and compelling picture of one of the *regiones* which made up the Anglo-Saxon kingdom of *Lindissi* and its later history. The question is, can any more such *regiones* be credibly identified?

4. Beyond the 'Tribal Hidage': possible *regiones* and population groups within *Lindissi*

The probable *regio* of the *Billingas*, as outlined above, can provide a basis for understanding the internal organization of the kingdom of *Lindissi*. We have here a fortunate coincidence of evidence which allows us to observe the coherence and character of the subdistricts and population groups which lay within early Anglo-Saxon kingdoms like *Lindissi*. Identifying other comparable early Anglo-Saxon population groups and *regiones* within *Lindissi* is not, however, an easy task. For the *Gyrwe* and the *Spalde* to the south, there is, happily, documentary evidence that attests to their existence, and with both the *Spalde* and the *Billingas* we are in the unusual position of being able to delimit the territory of the *regio*, using a combination of historical, geographical and archaeological data. By and large, we lack these advantages for the rest of *Lindissi*. Nonetheless, the quest is not without hope.

A good place to start looking for *regiones* within *Lindissi* is with the large cremation cemeteries of the Lincoln region. The wide separation of these sites has often been seen as suggestive of them acting as 'central places' for large early Anglo-Saxon territories and groups. This is a position which garners considerable support from recent research into the role that large cremation cemeteries played as funerary, social and sacred *foci* for their surrounding regions, and the fact that the vicinity of these cemeteries often coincides with the centres of historically documented Anglo-Saxon estates and administrative units.[120] Certainly, the evidence from Sleaford–Quarrington can be interpreted in this manner. In this context the simplest solution to the question of early *regiones* and population groups within *Lindissi* would perhaps be to use Thiessen polygons to reconstruct the likely territories dependent on both these cemeteries and the four centres discussed in the previous chapter (Lincoln, Littleborough, Caistor and Horncastle). The latter do not appear to have had major cremation cemeteries located near to them, but they were, arguably, British administrative centres which retained their importance into the early Anglo-Saxon period (Fig. 41). This is certainly an interesting exercise, but it has to be admitted that it is plagued by doubts. Not only is the legitimacy of using Thiessen polygons to reconstruct early medieval territories open to debate, but there also are specific questions here. For example, what should be done about the 'minor' cemeteries where cremation predominated, such as Wold Newton? Should these be given their own polygon, or treated as offshoots of the larger cemeteries and subordinate to them?[121] Similarly, it might be wondered whether one should somehow weight the polygon focused on Lincoln, given that the location of the cremation cemeteries within the region may well have been dictated by the Britons based there.[122] Finally, whilst the pattern produced appears reasonably credible in some areas, notably to the south of Lincoln, in others it fails to respect apparent natural boundaries, as is the case with the northern part of the River Ancholme.

In such circumstances, we need to look to the area around the

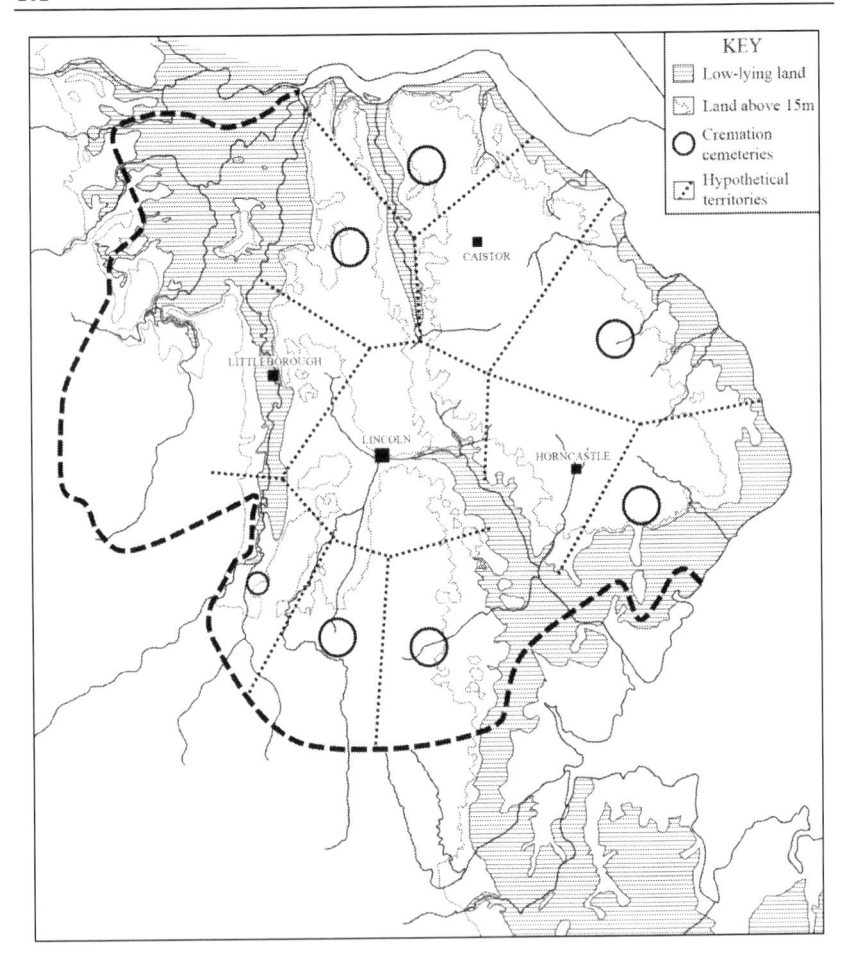

Fig. 41 Map of the kingdom of *Lindissi*, showing probable central places and their hypothetical territories, as reconstructed using Thiessen polygons. For the major cremation cemeteries, see Fig. 11

actual 'central places' themselves, to see if there is any evidence available that is less theoretical and which might help to delimit and analyse the groups and territories dependent upon these centres. Given that the sites of the Lincolnshire cremation cemeteries were probably used as meeting places and ritual sites for the regional communities which they served, it is perhaps worth considering whether the wapentakes of pre-Norman Lincolnshire might be relevant here, given that they seem to have had a similar function (Fig. 42). Wapentakes were, in origin, assemblies of free men from the surrounding region, who met at a specific site to discuss and arrange the business of the locality. Whilst the name of these institutions is Scandinavian in origin (Old English *wæpengtac* < Old Norse *vápnatak*, 'the taking of weapons', denoting the symbolic taking or brandishing of weapons at an assembly), in many cases both the units themselves and the local groups and territories which were served by them probably had their origins in the pre-Viking period, as is indicated by the Old English origins of many of the names of the Lincolnshire wapentakes and their meeting places.[123] In this context it is intriguing to note that most of the fifth- to seventh-century 'central places' and meeting places under consideration here were located either at or near to the meeting place of a later wapentake or, alternatively, on the very borders of its territory. This might well be taken to imply that the wapentakes either inherited the social role and quite possibly the territory/group associated with the cremation cemeteries, or were created via a division of this role and territory/group.[124]

The cemetery at West Keal, for example, was probably of a similar size to South Elkington cremation cemetery (*c.* 1,200 burials) and was located on Hall Hill, overlooking Old Bolingbroke village and the surrounding low-lying ground.[125] Not only was Bolingbroke the centre of a sizeable Anglo-Saxon soke, but it also gave its name to the large wapentake in which both it and the cremation cemetery lay, and it is likely that Hall Hill was actually the meeting place for this wapentake.[126] As such, it would not seem unreasonable to consider Bolingbroke wapentake to have been in some way related to the territory inhabited by the population group for which the West Keal cemetery was a focus and meeting place; certainly, the wapentake was of a credible extent for such an early Anglo-Saxon *regio*. Similarly, the South Elkington–Louth cremation cemetery was located on a hill overlooking the town of Louth, which was the centre of the large wapentake that met at Louthesk, 'the ash tree at Louth', the location of which is unknown.[127] Indeed, the existence of a pre-Viking territory focused on Louth would seem to be confirmed by the Old English place-names Ludborough and Ludford ('the fort/ford

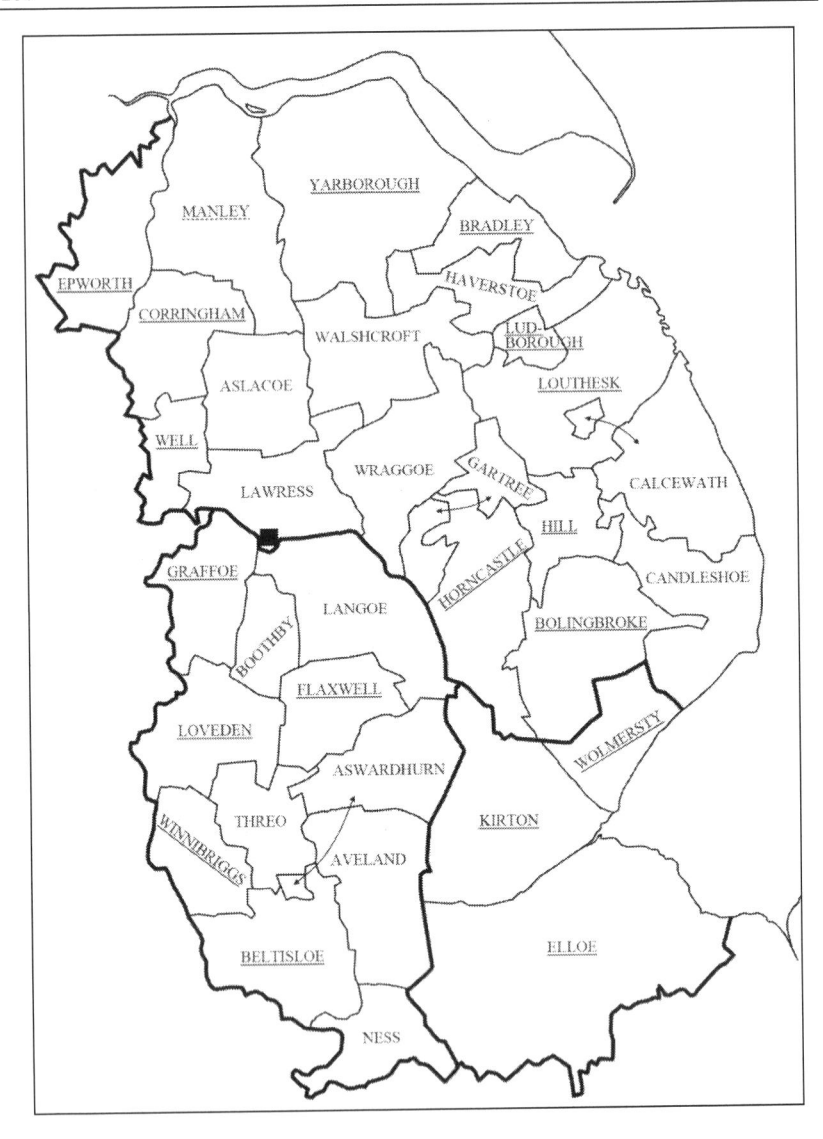

Fig. 42 The medieval Lincolnshire wapentakes. Wapentake-names of Old English derivation are underlined; those of mixed or debatable origin are underlined with a dashed line

After C. W. Foster and T. Longley (eds) *The Lincolnshire Domesday and the Lindsey Survey*, LRS, vol. 19 (Lincoln, 1924), and S. Turner, 'Aspects of the development of public assembly in the Danelaw', *Assemblage*, 5 (2000) belonging to Louth') to the north and west of Louth, and perhaps Meers Bank (< Old English *(ge)mære*, 'boundary') to the south-east. The fact that all three lie on or just outside of the recorded bounds of Louthesk wapentake is highly suggestive in the present context.[128] In consequence, it seems more than credible that the early Anglo-Saxon population group that was dependent upon South Elkington–Louth inhabited a territory which was broadly equivalent to the later territory of Louthesk wapentake (Fig. 43).[129] Finally, the cremation cemetery at Elsham was located just two miles away from the meeting place of the large wapentake of Yarborough. The notion that there may thus have been a degree of administrative continuity between the community that inhabited this territory and met here and the early Anglo-Saxon population group for whom Elsham was the primary burial centre is supported by the fact that the meeting-place of the

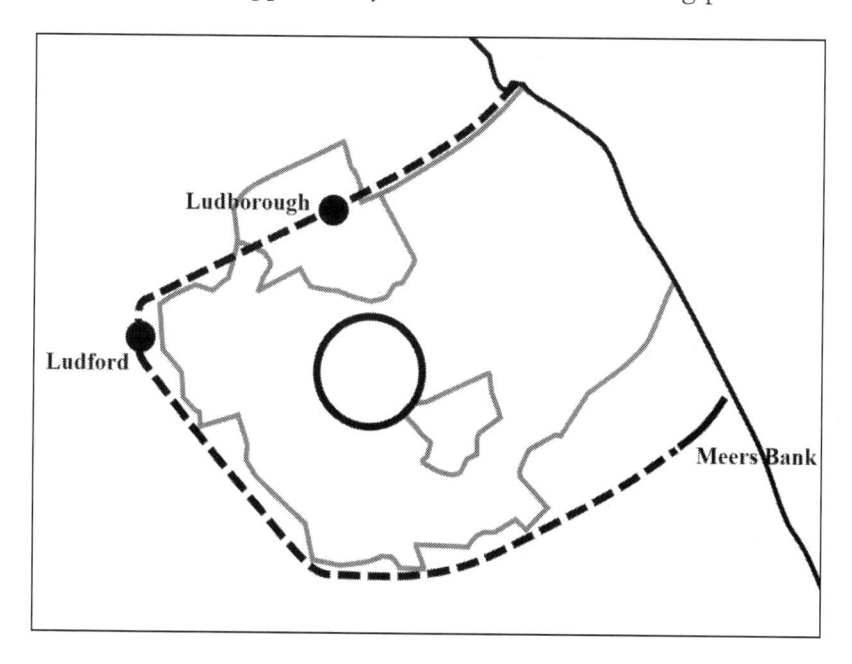

Fig. 43 The territorial context of the South Elkington–Louth cremation cemetery. Shown here are the cemetery, the later wapentake boundaries of Louthesk (in grey), and the place-name evidence for a pre-Viking territory focused on Louth, together with its suggested boundaries

wapentake was Yarborough Camp. This important earthwork fortification seems to have been refortified in the late fourth or early fifth century, and it can be argued that the Anglo-Saxons who buried their dead at Elsham had probably been initially settled in this area in order to make use of this fort in the defence of northern *Lindēs*. As such, they were intimately associated with this site from the very start.[130]

In contrast, the third largest Anglo-Saxon cemetery in Britain, located at Cleatham (*c.* 1,528 burials), is sited on the boundary between Corringham and Manley wapentakes, and just a few miles to the north of the boundary between these two wapentakes and that of Aslacoe.[131] In this light, it might be tentatively suggested that these three wapentakes had originally constituted a single territory, which looked to Cleatham as its primary social, sacred and funerary centre, in the manner suggested above. Certainly it is potentially significant that the exceptionally large soke based at Kirton in Lindsey, which may well have had its origins in the pre-Viking period and be related to Cleatham's role as a 'central place' (Cleatham cemetery lies between the villages of Kirton and Manton), covered all three wapentakes.[132] Similarly, the 'princely' barrow-burial at Caenby in Aslacoe wapentake (which originally had a mound larger than that which covered the Sutton Hoo ship burial) is probably also to be associated with the Cleatham group.[133] Moreover, an analogous situation can also be observed at Sleaford–Quarrington, with the Quarrington cremation cemetery and the Sleaford large inhumation cemetery lying very near to the boundary between Flaxwell and Aswardhurn wapentakes. Here the territory of the population group dependent upon Sleaford–Quarrington certainly seems to have originally stretched across both of these wapentakes.[134]

Another, probably comparable, instance of a cremation cemetery sited near to the borders of later wapentakes is that of the largest cremation cemetery in the Lincoln region, Loveden Hill. Over 1,800 burials have been excavated from this site, with the cemetery itself being located on top of a notable hill which would have been visible for many miles around, and its centrality in the early Anglo-Saxon period is clearly apparent in the early Anglo-Saxon archaeology of the surrounding region (Fig. 44).[135] Not only do the other cemeteries in the western half of northern Kesteven appear to have been far smaller in scale, containing at most around 80 burials, but Loveden Hill is also centrally located within the general distribution of cemeteries here. This point is underlined by the fact that a phasing of these cemeteries indicates that it is in the Loveden Hill area that the earliest of them are found, with those to the north and the south of this site appearing to be generally later in date (post *c.* 525).[136] With regard to the relationship between this 'central place' and the later wapentakes, it is important to note that Loveden Hill was actually the meeting place of Loveden wapentake, a key point in itself.[137] However, it was also located in the very far south of the wapentake, within a mile or so of the border with the wapentake of Threo and only a few miles from the boundary with Winnibriggs wapentake. This location is most intriguing, and it raises the possibility that we have here another instance of the territory served by a cremation cemetery having been divided up, although in this instance the cemetery site retained its role as the meeting place for one of the resultant divisions, unlike at Cleatham. In considerable support of this interpretation is the fact that the probable meeting place of the wapentake to the south-east of Loveden, Threo, appears to have been located in the very far north-west of *its* territory, on the high ground above – and only a mile and a half to the south-east of – Loveden Hill. This would certainly seem to be suggestive of these two wapentakes, at least, having been originally part of a single pre-Viking territory which was focused on Loveden Hill. On this basis it seems quite credible that the territory of the population group based around Loveden Hill included much of the wapentake of Loveden, whilst also extending southward into the neighbouring wapentakes of Threo and Winnibriggs.[138]

The above scenario gains additional weight from a consideration of the available archaeological evidence. So, for example, one possible way of identifying the community which made use of the Loveden Hill cemetery is to look for pyre sites, which are indicative of bodies being cremated close to the settlements they came from before they were transported to the main cremation cemetery for interment. One such site has been identified from the cremated remains of a sixth-century small-long brooch found around one and a half miles from Loveden Hill, but another possible example is represented by the foot of a cremated cruciform brooch from Great Ponton.[139] Although this

Fig. 44 Loveden Hill: the site of Loveden Hill cremation cemetery

is located some distance (around nine miles) to the south of Loveden Hill, it may similarly represent a pyre site associated with this cemetery. If so, it would suggest that the population group using Loveden Hill extended considerably to the south of Loveden wapentake. In this context it may well be relevant that there is no local cremation cemetery known in the vicinity of this find-spot, and the territory dependent upon Sleaford–Quarrington looks to have been of a similar extent to that which would be implied for Loveden Hill by this find (Fig. 45).[140]

The general distribution of early Anglo-Saxon cemeteries in the western half of Kesteven is also potentially informative, especially given that such evidence was used above to help define the Sleaford–Quarrington population group and that Loveden Hill appears to lie at the centre of this distribution, both geographically and temporally. Of course, caution must be urged here: the geographically distinct distribution of cemeteries around Sleaford–Quarrington, which can be plausibly suggested to reflect a single early Anglo-Saxon population group and its territory, is relatively unusual.[141] Certainly, it is worth noting that there seem to have been at least two distinct 'groups' within the distribution in the west, with the cemeteries from Welbourn northwards looking to be geographically distinct from those to the south (including Loveden Hill) and probably being representative of the post-*c.* 525 Anglo-Saxon encroachment northwards into the territory controlled from Lincoln, discussed in previous chapters.[142] On the other hand, the southern 'group' of cemeteries, although somewhat spread out, is actually distributed within the wapentakes of Loveden, Threo and Winnibriggs. As such, they might be tentatively seen to reflect and offer further confirmation of the territory of the Loveden Hill population group proposed above.[143]

All told, there do seem to be grounds for thinking that it is possible to gain at least a general idea of the extent of the population groups dependent upon the cremation cemeteries of the Lincoln region, through a combination of Thiessen polygons and the available historical and archaeological evidence. Of course, giving a name to any of these groups is rather more difficult – the Sleaford–Quarrington group was probably known as the *Billingas*, but beyond this it is presently impossible to go. Although most of the population groups based around the cremation cemeteries have place-names derived from *-ingas* group-names within their probable territories, these are best seen as simply representing the names of local late fifth- to late seventh-century subgroups which existed within the larger units, inhabiting the area in the immediate vicinity of that place-name.[144] For example, there was a group named the *Ælfingas* that had a settlement at Alvingham, but there is no good reason to think that this name applied to the whole of the population group dependent upon South Elkington–Louth, whilst within a five-mile radius of Cleatham–Kirton in Lindsey we find settlements belonging to the *Mæssingas*, the *Grægingas*, and the *Wadingas*, which only serves to underline this point.[145] However, even if we cannot name most of the population groups and their *regiones* which existed within the kingdom of *Lindissi*, we can identify their 'central places' with a high degree of confidence, and also their likely territories, which is an important point for the history of pre-Viking Lincolnshire.

Summary: a question of origins

As the preceding discussion demonstrates, we are able to establish a reasonable amount about the Anglo-Saxon population groups which inhabited the pre-Viking *regiones* of the Lincoln region, if we make full use of the historical, linguistic and archaeological evidence which is available. Several key points emerge from this evidence, but one in

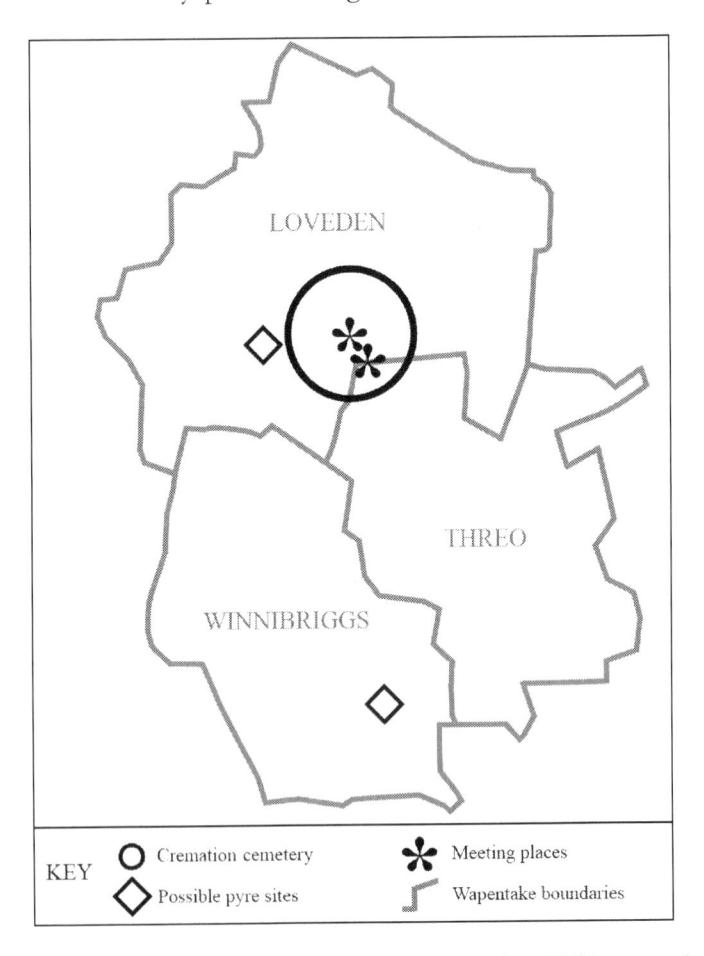

Fig. 45 The territorial context of the Loveden Hill cremation cemetery. The surrounding wapentake boundaries are shown in grey, alongside the meeting places of Loveden and Threo wapentakes and possible pyre sites

particular deserves some brief, final comment before we move on, given the overarching interests of the present study. Fundamentally, whether or not such *regiones* and their groups represented originally independent territories and 'peoples' (a proposition which seems generally dubious and specifically implausible in the case of those located within *Lindissi*, given its origins in the British 'country of **Lindēs*'), we do need to ask just how much they owed to the British past. It was argued in the previous chapter that many of the early Anglo-Saxon 'central places' in the region – including most of the cremation cemeteries – were situated at or very close by sites which were highly likely to have played a significant role in the Late Roman and British administration of this area. The consequent implication is that there may well have been a significant degree of internal administrative continuity between Anglian *Lindissi* and British **Lindēs*. This perhaps should not be too surprising, given the longevity of **Lindēs* and the apparently intimate relationship which existed between these two polities and their inhabitants, and there is other evidence, aside from the coincidence of sites, which would appear to offer support for this position.[146] The present chapter, with its detailed investigation into the extent and character of the *regio* of the *Billingas*, reinforces this. Not only was the 'central place' of this population group/*regio* probably to be found at Sleaford–Quarrington, just to the west of the Roman 'small town' of Old Sleaford, but there is also a case to be made for the extent of this *regio* being broadly equivalent to the territory administered from Old Sleaford in the Late Roman period. Indeed, such local administrative continuity would appear to be credible even outside of **Lindēs*/*Lindissi*, with the probable 'centre' of the Middle Anglian *Spalde* – Spalding – being at or close by a Roman *vicus*. How much more widely this might have applied is an interesting question. No suggestions have been made above with regard to the origins of the *Gyrwe* ('the fen dwellers'), but in the present context it may be at least worth pondering the fact that the important Gyrwean monastery of *Medeshamstede* (Peterborough) was located only around four and a half miles west of the Roman town of *Durobrivae*, a probable Late Roman administrative centre for the Fenland.[147]

Such indications of potential British–Anglian continuity are also encountered when considering the Anglo-Saxon population groups which made use of these 'central places' and inhabited the *regiones*. Even in an area of apparently significant Anglo-Saxon immigration such as northern Kesteven, we find evidence to suggest that the resultant 'Anglo-Saxon' population groups included considerable numbers of Britons, and not merely as slaves or agricultural workers. One can, for example, point to the interesting concentration of high-status, post-Roman British Class 1 and Type G brooches and hanging bowls in the south of the probable territory of the *Billingas*, which looks to be associated both with an 'Anglo-Saxon' *-ingas* group whose founder had a British name and with place-name evidence for the continued use of Archaic Welsh into the eighth century.[148] Such a scenario seems even more credible with regard to those Anglo-Saxon population groups which were based away from the major immigrant centres, in areas where early Anglo-Saxon cemeteries are considered large if they contain tens of graves, never mind hundreds or thousands. Thus, for example, the available evidence from the territory of the *Spalde* suggests that this population group is likely to have included a very substantial 'British' element, and something similar has recently been argued for north Nottinghamshire, whose *regio* of *Hæthfelth* (Hatfield) was almost certainly part of *Lindissi*.[149]

In sum, an investigation into the population groups of the Lincoln region can not only help us to establish a clearer picture of the internal structure of the Anglo-Saxon kingdoms based here, but also to flesh out some of the conclusions reached earlier in this study with regard to the nature of Anglian–British interaction in the region and the territorial and administrative relationship between British **Lindēs* and Anglo-Saxon *Lindissi*.

Notes to Chapter 5

1   Needless to say, opinions on the origins of at least some parts of the 'Tribal Hidage' vary enormously, but a seventh-century Mercian one is still clearly the majority interpretation (W. Davies and H. Vierck, 'The contexts of the Tribal Hidage: social aggregates and settlement patterns', *Frühmittelalterliche Studien*, 8 (1974), 226–7; D. N. Dumville, 'Essex, Middle Anglia and the expansion of Mercia' in S. Bassett (ed.), *The Origins of Anglo-Saxon Kingdoms* (London, 1989), pp.132–3; H. Hamerow, 'The earliest Anglo-Saxon kingdoms' in P. Fouracre (ed.), *The New Cambridge Medieval History, I: c.500–c.700* (Cambridge, 2005), p. 282). On the hidations, see P.

Featherstone, 'The Tribal Hidage and the ealdormen of Mercia' in M. P. Brown and C. A. Farr (eds), *Mercia. An Anglo-Saxon Kingdom in Europe* (London, 2001), pp. 28–9.

2   C. Hart, 'The Tribal Hidage', *Trans. Royal Hist.*, fifth series, 21 (1971), 133–57; Davies & Vierck, 'Contexts'; Featherstone, 'Tribal Hidage', p. 28.

3   See especially Hamerow, 'Anglo-Saxon Kingdoms', pp. 271–88, and C. Scull, 'Archaeology, early Anglo-Saxon society and the Anglo-Saxon kingdoms', *Anglo-Saxon Studies in Archaeology and History*, 6 (1993), 72–9.

4   S. Bassett, 'In search of the origins of Anglo-Saxon kingdoms' in S. Bassett (ed.), *Origins of Anglo-Saxon Kingdoms* (London, 1989), especially pp. 17–18, 26; Scull, 'Archaeology'; Hamerow, 'Anglo-Saxon Kingdoms', especially p. 282.

5   B. Yorke, 'Political and ethnic identity: a case study of Anglo-Saxon practice' in W. O. Frazer and A. Tyrrell (eds), *Social Identity in Early Medieval Britain* (London, 2000), pp. 82–6; B. Yorke, 'Anglo-Saxon *gentes* and *regna*' in H-W. Goetz *et al* (eds), *Regna and Gentes: The Relationship Between Late Antique and Early Medieval Peoples and Kingdoms in the Transformation of the Roman World* (Leiden, 2003), pp. 381–408; A. Woolf, 'Community, identity and kingship in early England' in W. O. Frazer and A. Tyrrell (eds), *Social Identity in Early Medieval Britain* (London, 2000), pp. 91–109.

6   See especially J. Blair, 'The Tribal Hidage' in M. Lapidge *et al* (eds), *The Blackwell Encyclopedia of Anglo-Saxon England* (Oxford, 1999), p. 456, and D. P. Kirby, *The Earliest English Kings*, 2nd edn (London, 2000), p. 9, on a composite origin; see also S. Keynes, 'England, 700–900' in R. McKitterick (ed.), *The New Cambridge Medieval History, II: c.700–c.900* (Cambridge, 1995), pp. 21–5. I would agree with James Campbell ('Bede's *Reges* and *Principes*' in J. Campbell, *Essays in Anglo-Saxon History* (London, 1986), pp. 88, 90), D. P. Kirby (*Earliest English Kings*, pp. 8–9), Barbara Yorke ('Political and ethnic identity', p. 74) and others that Middle Anglia was probably a genuine, large early Anglo-Saxon kingdom, not one 'invented' in the mid-seventh century, on the basis of Bede's references to them as a genuine early Anglo-Saxon *gens* (Bede, *Historia Ecclesiastica*, III.21). H. M. Chadwick's *The Origin of the English Nation* (Cambridge, 1924), pp. 7–10, though now rarely read, includes a very useful survey of the evidence for Middle Anglia as a real kingdom, and the 'Tribal Hidage' groups as sub-units of this.

7   As Hamerow, 'Anglo-Saxon Kingdoms', p. 284.

8   See Yorke, 'Anglo-Saxon *gentes* and *regna*', especially pp. 396–401, and also, for example, N. J. Higham, *The Kingdom of Northumbria, AD 350–1100* (Stroud, 1993), pp. 80–1, on Deira and Bernicia; Bassett, 'In search', p. 24, on Essex; N. P. Brooks, 'The creation and early structure of the kingdom of Kent' in S. Bassett (ed.), *The Origins of Anglo-Saxon Kingdoms* (London, 1989), pp. 57–8, on Kent; P. Warner, *The Origins of Suffolk* (Manchester,

1996), p. 148, and S. Oosthuizen, 'The origins of Cambridgeshire', *Antiq. J.*, 78 (1998), 89–90, on East Anglia. See also S. Laycock, *Britannia, The Failed State* (Stroud, 2008), pp. 197–236, especially p. 204 onwards.

9 Yorke, 'Anglo-Saxon *gentes* and *regna*', especially from p. 400; see Bede, *Historia Ecclesiastica*, V.10, on the Old Saxons.

10 J. Hines, 'The Anglo-Saxon archaeology of the Cambridge region and the Middle Anglian kingdom', *Anglo-Saxon Studies in Archaeology and History*, 10 (1999), quotation at p. 144.

11 Bede, *Historia Ecclesiastica*, III. 20, IV.6 and IV.19. See W. T. W. Potts, 'The pre-Danish estates of Peterborough Abbey', *Proceedings of the Cambridge Antiquarian Society*, 65 (1974), 13–27, for the argument that the seventh-century estate of *Medeshamstede* was equivalent to the territory of the North *Gyrwe*.

12 Davies & Vierck, 'Contexts', 231; Dumville, 'Expansion of Mercia', pp. 130–1; D. Rollason, 'Lists of saints' resting places in Anglo-Saxon England', *Anglo-Saxon England*, 7 (1978), 89; D. Roffe, '*On middan Gyrwan fenne*: intercommoning around the island of Crowland', *Fenland Research*, 8 (1993), 82–3.

13 Dumville, 'Expansion of Mercia', pp. 130–1. Barbara Yorke has suggested that the reason why the *Gyrwe* ('the fen dwellers') may have had some autonomy, whilst most other small population groups did not, may be because of their unusual geographical situation (Yorke, 'Political and ethnic identity', pp. 83–4).

14 Chadwick, *Origin of the English Nation*, p. 9.

15 Campbell, 'Bede's *Reges* and *Principes*', p. 86; Chadwick, *Origin of the English Nation*, p. 9; Bede, *Historia Ecclesiastica*, IV.13, and V.19.

16 Bede, *Historia Ecclesiastica*, IV.6; Yorke, 'Political and ethnic identity', pp. 74–5; Campbell, 'Bede's *Reges* and *Principes*', pp. 86–7.

17 Campbell, 'Bede's *Reges* and *Principes*', p. 89; note, *princeps* is in fact translated as *ealdorman* in the Old English translation of Bede (T. Miller (ed.), *Old English Version of Bede's Ecclesiastical History* (2 vols, London, 1890 and 1898), vol. 1, p. 316).

18 Dumville, 'Expansion of Mercia', p. 131.

19 See Kirby, *Earliest English Kings*, pp. 8–9, and Chadwick, *Origin of the English Nation*, pp. 7–10, on the kingdom of Middle Anglia. If it was a kingdom before Peada, as suggested, then we should expect there to have been a pre-Peada dynasty too. Note that, in the twelfth-century *Liber Eliensis*, *Tondberct*'s death is placed at some point between 652 (the year of his marriage) and 654–5; could his death have been linked somehow to Peada's takeover of Middle Anglia? If so, it might support the case for seeing him as a member of a lost Middle Anglian dynasty. With regard to the notion that he could have been a member of the Mercian or Northumbrian dynasties, it is interesting to note that the first element of

his name (*Tond-*) has been described as a 'characteristically Northumbrian' name-element (J. Insley, 'Gyrwe', *Reallexikon der Germanischen Altertumskunde*, 13 (Berlin, 1999), 230), though this circumstance might alternatively be explained in terms of the links between the *Gyrwe* and Northumbria discussed in Chapter 6 (below, pp. 246–7).

20   Felix, *Life of St Guthlac*, ed. and trans. B. Colgrave (Cambridge, 1956), pp. 2, 86–7, 142–5 (see especially Colgrave's comments on p. 2 with regard to the reference to Crowland being in Middle Anglia); Insley, 'Gyrwe', p. 231; Chadwick, *Origin of the English Nation*, pp. 9–10. Compare Hines, 'Middle Anglian kingdom', 144.

21   With regard to the *Gyrwe*'s southern frontier, we know that in a tenth-century charter, *Gyruwan fen* formed part of the boundary of Conington (Huntingdonshire), around twenty-one miles south-east of Peterborough, which would tend to confirm that the vast majority of the *regio* of the *Gyrwe* lay south of Crowland (Davies & Vierck, 'Contexts', 231). Although the *Liber Eliensis* suggests that the lands of the South *Gyrwe* included or were equivalent to the island of Ely, and John Hines has considered such an identification to be 'highly plausible' ('Middle Anglian kingdom', 144; see also P. Courtney, 'The early Saxon Fenland: a reconsideration', *Anglo-Saxon Studies in Archaeology and History*, 2 (1981), 95–6), this may well be a late invention and speculation by the author of the *Liber Eliensis*, rather than a reflection of seventh-century reality (see especially Hart, 'Tribal Hidage', 143, and B. Yorke, *Nunneries and the Anglo-Saxon Royal Houses* (London, 2003), pp. 32–3).

22   See above, pp. 128–9, 154, on the probable extent of the British 'country of **Lindēs*'.

23   Davies & Vierck, 'Contexts', for example 232, 234, 285.

24   A. D. Mills, *A Dictionary of English Place-Names* (Oxford, 1991), p. 304; V. Watts, *The Cambridge Dictionary of English Place-Names* (Cambridge, 2004), p. 564.

25   P. P. Hayes and T. W. Lane, *The Fenland Project Number 5: Lincolnshire Survey, The South-West Fens* (Sleaford, 1992); P. P. Hayes, 'Roman to Saxon in the south Lincolnshire Fens', *Ant.*, 62 (1988), 321–6; A. Crowson *et al*, *Anglo-Saxon Settlement on the Siltland of Eastern England* (Heckington, 2005), figs. 1–2a, pp. 18–48, 211, 214–15. Note, although it has been suggested that the early and middle Anglo-Saxon settlements discovered by the Fenland Survey in the Lincolnshire Fenland were seasonal rather than permanent in nature, recent archaeological work indicates that this position is untenable (K. U. Ulmschneider, 'Settlement, economy, and the 'productive' site: Middle Anglo-Saxon Lincolnshire A. D. 650–780', *Med. Arch.*, 44 (2000), 70–1; Crowson *et al*, pp. 217–18, 228, 261–2, 293).

26   K. Cameron, *Dictionary of Lincolnshire Place-Names* (Nottingham, 1998), p. 114; Mills, *Dictionary*, p. 303. Old English **spald* is cognate with Old High

German *spalt*, 'a ditch, trench'. See also Courtney, 'Early Saxon Fenland', 97.

27   Hayes & Lane, *The Fenland Project Number 5*, especially pp. 213–15, 257; Crowson *et al*, *Anglo-Saxon Settlement*, figs. 1–2a.

28   Hayes, 'Roman to Saxon', 324–5; T. W. Lane and P. Hayes, 'Moving boundaries in the Fens of south Lincolnshire' in J. Gardiner (ed.), *Flatlands and Wetlands: Current Themes in East Anglian Archaeology* (Norwich, 1993), pp. 66, 68; Crowson *et al*, *Anglo-Saxon Settlement*, pp. 277–80, 283, 285–6. See further below, p. 181, on the date of nucleation in Holland.

29   Hayes, 'Roman to Saxon', 323–4; Crowson *et al*, *Anglo-Saxon Settlement*, p. 215; Hayes & Lane, *The Fenland Project Number 5*, pp. 249, 252.

30   On the debate over the reality of this estate, see, for example, P. Salway, 'The Roman Fenland' in C. W. Phillips (ed.), *The Fenland in Roman Times* (London, 1970), p. 10; M. Millett, *The Romanization of Britain* (Cambridge, 1990), pp. 120–3; Lane & Hayes, 'Moving boundaries', p. 65; S. Rippon, 'Romano-British reclamation of coastal wetlands' in H. F. Cook and T. Williamson (eds), *Water Management in the English Landscape* (Edinburgh, 1999), pp. 113–17; J. Taylor, 'Stonea in its Fenland context: moving beyond an Imperial Estate', *Journal of Roman Archaeology*, 13 (2000), 647–58. See also T. W. Potter, 'The Roman Fenland: a review of recent work' in M. Todd (ed.), *Research on Roman Britain: 1960–89* (London, 1989), who suggests that the Fenland could potentially have been administered from several centres. In this context it is perhaps worth recalling that Ptolemy places a centre called *Salinae* ('saltworks') near the coast of the Wash. In the past, this has been seen as a mistake, but given the considerable evidence for Iron Age and Romano-British saltworking discovered by the Fenland Survey in the Spalding region, there now seems to be no good reason to reject Ptolemy's testimony. See further, Hayes & Lane, *The Fenland Project Number 5*, pp. 218–29; Lane & Hayes, 'Moving boundaries', pp. 64–5; B. Whitwell, *Roman Lincolnshire*, 2nd edn (Lincoln, 1992), p. xxviii; T. W. Lane, 'Invisible and irretrievable? Consideration of some non-ceramic aspects of Fenland salt production' in T. Lane and E. L. Morris (eds), *A Millennium of Saltmaking: Prehistoric and Romano-British Salt Production in the Fenland* (Heckington, 2001), p. 463. A. Strang, 'Explaining Ptolemy's Roman Britain', *Britannia*, 28 (1997), 23, identifies *Salinae* with the probable fort at Skegness, but place-name evidence suggests rather that this was called *Traiectus* (A. E. B. Owen and R. Coates, '*Traiectus*/*Tric*/Skegness: a Domesday name explained', *LHA*, 38 (2003), 42–4). Note also that Ptolemy puts *Salinae* in the territory of the *Catuvellauni*, whilst Skegness is most credibly associated with the *Corieltavi*.

31   See especially J. Campbell, 'Bede's words for places' in J. Campbell, *Essays in Anglo-Saxon History* (London, 1986), p. 113; also Yorke, 'Political and ethnic identity', pp. 84–5. See, for example, P. H. Sawyer, *Anglo-Saxon*

Lincolnshire (Lincoln, 1998), p. 49, for support for the idea that Spalding 'may well have been a centre of some local importance' in the pre-Viking period.

32 Whitwell, *Roman Lincolnshire*, p. 48; S. J. Hallam, *Settlement and Society. A Study of the Early Agrarian History of South Lincolnshire* (Cambridge, 1965), pp. 111–13; Hayes & Lane, *The Fenland Project Number 5*, pp. 171–2, 257; S. Malone, '"Rumours of Roman finds": updating Roman Lincolnshire' in S. Malone and M. Williams (eds), *Rumours of Roman Finds: Recent Work on Roman Lincolnshire* (Heckington, 2010), p. 8. See also below, pp. 183–5, 222–3 (endnote 69), for its survival into the post-Roman period, but perhaps not as late as has been claimed (the twelfth century).

33 Cameron, *Dictionary*, p. 145; M. Gelling, *Signposts to the Past. Place-names and the History of England*, 2nd edn (Chichester, 1988), p. 246.

34 On the date of *wīchām* names, see for example M. Gelling, 'English place-names derived from the compound *wīchām*' reprinted in K. Cameron (ed.), *Place-name Evidence for the Anglo-Saxon Invasion and Scandinavian Settlements* (Nottingham, 1977), p. 14. Spalding is another name from this area which seems likely to have its origins in this period, and the same may possibly be true of the name Quadring (the 'fen *Hæferingas*'), if it refers to a subgroup within the *Spaldingas/Spalde*. See K. Cameron, *English Place-Names*, 2nd edn (London, 1996), p. 71, on *-ingas* group-names necessarily pre-dating the name of the settlement to which they eventually become attached, and probably mostly belonging to the late fifth to seventh centuries.

35 Gelling, '*wīchām*'; Gelling, *Signposts to the Past*, pp. 67–74, 245–9, especially pp. 70–1; M. Gelling, 'Latin loan-words in Old English place-names', *Anglo-Saxon England*, 6 (1977), 1–5; Cameron, *English Place-Names*, p. 42; Yorke, 'Anglo-Saxon *gentes* and *regna*', p. 396; C. J. Balkwill, 'Old English *wīc* and the origin of the hundred', *Landscape History*, 15 (1993), 5–12, especially 11. See also Oosthuizen, 'Origins of Cambridgeshire', 95–6.

36 See especially Balkwill, 'Old English *wīc*'; Yorke, 'Anglo-Saxon *gentes* and *regna*', p. 396; Gelling, *Signposts to the Past*, pp. 71–4.

37 As they are in Lane & Hayes, 'Moving boundaries', p. 68, and Hayes, 'Roman to Saxon', 325.

38 Note, the different dates of settlement-nucleation on the Fen Edge and the siltland have been used as evidence for the *Spalde* being a semi-independent tribe, apparently on the basis that the Fen Edge communities were fully conquered in the seventh century and forced to nucleate, whilst the *Spalde* of the siltland retained 'a fair degree of independence', so they did not nucleate and instead became a buffer-state between East Anglia and Mercia (Lane & Hayes, 'Moving boundaries', p. 68; Hayes, 'Roman to Saxon', 325). Needless to say, there is absolutely no necessity to posit such complex political machinations lying behind the nucleation and lack of nucleation observed. That the two areas represent distinct settlement units

with their own histories and trajectories is clear, but it is impossible to say anything more than this on the basis of this evidence alone, without veering off into the realms of pure speculation. At best, the above scenario relies fully on the presumption of the *Spaldë*'s original independence before it can even begin to have any credibility; it certainly cannot be used to prove this independence.

39   See above, pp. 128–36.

40   Blair, 'Tribal Hidage', p. 456, and above, pp. 163–7.

41   See especially Roffe in Crowson *et al*, *Anglo-Saxon Settlement*, pp. 285–6, also p. 298; Hart, 'Tribal Hidage', 144; Felix, *Life of St Guthlac*, pp. 2, 86–7, 168–9. Note, the group-names used here are the nominative plural forms (for example, *Wixan*); the forms in the 'Tribal Hidage' are genitives (for example, *Wixna*). The same applies, incidentally, to the group-name *Spalde* ('Tribal Hidage' *Spalda*).

42   Hayes & Lane, *The Fenland Project Number 5*, p. 172.

43   Rippon, 'Coastal wetlands', pp. 113–17; Potter, 'Roman Fenland'; Lane & Hayes, 'Moving boundaries', p. 65; Whitwell, *Roman Lincolnshire*, p. xxviii.

44   Welch faces a similar situation with the *Hæstingas* of Sussex, who look to have been a pre-Viking population group and *regio*, but who were located in a region without any early Anglo-Saxon burials (M. Welch, 'The kingdom of the South Saxons: the origins' in S. Bassett (ed.), *The Origins of Anglo-Saxon Kingdoms* (London, 1989), p. 78). Welch's suggestion is that they emerged in the Middle Saxon period, a solution which does not seem to be available in this case, given the presence of both early Anglo-Saxon pottery and settlements on the siltland and the place-name Wykeham.

45   It might be suggested that the lack of cemeteries indicates that the siltland settlements were seasonal rather than permanent, belonging to people normally living on the uplands. However, as noted above (p. 215, endnote 25), the results of the excavation of these settlements indicate that this is not the case and that they were instead used year-round as permanent settlements. Hallam (in C. W. Phillips (ed.), *The Fenland in Roman Times* (London, 1970), p. 294), notes a possible 'Saxon' cremation cemetery at Donington (in Holland). However, if one follows up the references, this is clearly a case of mistaken identity, with a possible cemetery from 'Donington on the Bane' (Donington on Bain, in Lindsey), noted in 1834, being wrongly assigned to the Fenland in the gazetteer because of 'on the Bane' being omitted in an intermediate source used to create it.

46   On British burial rites see, for example, P. Rahtz, 'Late Roman cemeteries and beyond' in R. Reece (ed.), *Burial in the Roman World* (London, 1977), pp. 53–64; P. Rahtz, 'Celtic society in Somerset, A.D. 400–700', *Bulletin of the Board of Celtic Studies*, 30 (1982), 176–200; H. Härke, 'Population replacement or acculturation? An archaeological perspective on population and migration in post-Roman Britain' in H. L. C. Tristram (ed.), *The Celtic*

Englishes III (Hiedelberg, 2003), p. 19. See above, pp. 106–12, on Britons within *Lindissi*; also K. Leahy, *The Anglo-Saxon Kingdom of Lindsey* (Stroud, 2007), pp. 82–3. It would seem that even acculturated Britons buried within early Anglo-Saxon cemeteries were not accorded the full, normal Anglo-Saxon burial rites: see, for example, H. Härke, 'Changing symbols in a changing society: the Anglo-Saxon weapon burial rite in the seventh century' in M. O. H. Carver (ed.), *The Age of Sutton Hoo* (Woodbridge, 1992), pp. 149–65; H. Härke, *Angelsächsische Waffengräber des 5. bis 7. Jahrhunderts* (Cologne, 1992); and N. P. Brooks, 'Historical introduction' in L. Webster and J. Backhouse (eds), *The Making of England. Anglo-Saxon Art and Culture, AD 600–900* (London), p. 10, for the frequent suggestion that 'Anglo-Saxon' burials without grave goods were those of Britons living within Anglo-Saxon communities.

47   For example, K. R. Dark, *Britain and the End of the Roman Empire* (Stroud, 2000), pp. 97–103, and J. T. Baker, *Cultural Transition in the Chilterns and Essex Region, 350 AD to 650 AD* (Hatfield, 2006).

48   Felix, *Life of St Guthlac*, pp. 108–11; such an interpretation of this passage has been most recently advocated by Graham Jones in J. Koch (ed.), *Celtic Culture, A Historical Encyclopedia* (Oxford, 2006), p. 857. For the names, see O. K. Schram, 'Fenland place-names' in B. Dickens (ed.), *The Early Cultures in North-West Europe* (Cambridge, 1950), p. 431, and Crowson *et al*, *Anglo-Saxon Settlement*, p. 298; see generally K. Cameron, 'The meaning and significance of Old English *walh* in English place-names', *Journal of the English Place-Name Society*, 12 (1980), 1–53, and M. Gelling, 'Why aren't we speaking Welsh?', *Anglo-Saxon Studies in Archaeology and History*, 6 (1993), 54, on names involving *walh* and similar being suggestive of the continued presence of Welsh-speakers into perhaps the mid–late eighth century. In addition, H. C. Darby has some possible evidence for there still being Britons in the Fenland as late as the Late Saxon period ('The Fenland frontier in Anglo-Saxon England', *Ant.*, 8 (1934), 192–4).

49   R. Coates, 'Holland, the division of Lincolnshire' in R. Coates and A. Breeze, *Celtic Voices, English Places* (Stamford, 2000), pp. 162–4; R. Coates, 'Invisible Britons: the view from linguistics' in N. J. Higham (ed.), *Britons in Anglo-Saxon England* (Woodbridge, 2007), p. 181; R. Coates, 'Reflections on some major Lincolnshire place-names. Part one: Algarkirk to Melton Ross', *Journal of the English Place-Name Society*, 40 (2008), 83; R. Coates, 'Reflections on some major Lincolnshire place-names. Part two: Ness wapentake to Yarborough', *Journal of the English Place-Name Society*, 41 (2009), 85–7; Schram, 'Fenland place-names', p. 430; R. Coates, 'Four pre-English river names in and around fenland: *Chater, Granta, Nene* and *Welland*', *Transactions of the Philological Society*, 103 (2005), 303–22. For the Glen/Baston Ea (Edyke) in the medieval period and after, see Hayes & Lane, *The Fenland Project Number 5*, p. 161; Cameron, *Dictionary*, p. 50.

Something similar to the Glen/Baston Ea situation can perhaps also be seen in the fact that there seem to be two district-names for the Lincolnshire Wash Silts: Holland and *Spald*. Schram also notes a lost *ad Cricum* in Freiston on the Wash Silts, which may also be relevant here as it contains the Archaic Welsh *cruc*, 'hill, mound, barrow' (Schram, p. 430; see Coates, 'Invisible Britons', p. 181, and M. Gelling and A. Cole, *The Landscape of Place-Names*, 2nd edn (Stamford, 2003), pp. 159–63). See also the place-name Wykeham, above, pp. 173–4.

50   Hayes, 'Roman to Saxon', 324.

51   On environmental change in the Fenland and its effects, see for example Crowson *et al*, *Anglo-Saxon Settlement*, p. 10, and Hayes & Lane, *The Fenland Project Number 5*, p. 213. On the end of the Roman state, compare P. Murphy, 'The Anglo-Saxon landscape and rural economy: some results from sites in East Anglia and Essex' in J. Rackham (ed.), *Environment and Economy in Anglo-Saxon England* (York, 1994), p. 37, on East Anglia. De-intensification may have played a particular role if the Fenland remained an imperial estate to the end of the Roman period.

52   For example, Hayes, 'Roman to Saxon', 324, who refers to an abrupt and universal 'discontinuity between Roman and Saxon' (a 'profound discontinuity'), which cannot be explained as a 'simple response to environmental change'. He further contends that the frequent close proximity of Saxon and Roman sites in the Fenland is not evidence for continuity, but instead merely results from coincidence. This notion of a landscape 'mostly abandoned' by the Britons at the end of the Roman period has influenced later commentators, including M. E. Jones, *The End of Roman Britain* (Ithaca, 1996), p. 200, fn. 45, and Crowson *et al*, *Anglo-Saxon Settlement*, especially pp. 291–2.

53   See above, pp. 41–3.

54   See the discussion in Chapter 1 above, pp. 43–4. See also, for example, N. J. Higham, *Rome, Britain and the Anglo-Saxons* (London, 1992), pp. 111–13, on a similar situation in Suffolk.

55   P. Everson, 'Pre-Viking settlement in Lindsey' in Vince (ed.), *Pre-Viking Lindsey* (Lincoln, 1993), p. 93; C. C. Taylor, *Village and Farmstead* (London, 1983), chapter 7. The difficulty in identifying Anglo-Saxon material from Romano-British sites has been an issue across the East Midlands, and one which has only really been fully addressed in recent years. Thus, if we look to neighbouring Leicestershire, it is striking that in the last 20 years there have been numerous instances of Romano-British sites with 'Anglo-Saxon' material coming from them recorded in the *Transactions of the Leicestershire Archaeological and Historical Society*, but if we examine the finds recorded in the 1970s and 1980s in the same journal, hardly any are noted. Note, with regard to the problems of misidentifying early Anglo-Saxon pottery as Romano-British or Iron Age, a subsequent examination of some of the

Fenland Survey finds suggests that this project, despite its careful design, was certainly not immune from issues of misidentification (Jane Young, personal communication).

56   Indeed, Somerset appears to have remained aceramic from the end of the Roman period right through until the tenth century, whilst Devon is aceramic until the eleventh, causing significant issues in terms of identifying early medieval settlements in these areas (S. Rippon, *Beyond the Medieval Village: The Diversification of Landscape Character in Southern Britain* (Oxford, 2009); M. Aston, 'Medieval settlement studies in Somerset' in M. Aston and C. Lewis (eds), *The Medieval Landscape of Wessex* (Oxford, 1994), p. 222).

57   See above, pp. 110–11, 116–17; Härke, *Angelsächsische Waffengräber*; Härke, 'Changing symbols'; Härke, 'Population replacement', p. 23; and Gelling, 'Why Aren't We Speaking Welsh?', who, on the basis of the place-name evidence, suggests that there were still Welsh-speakers in eastern England in the mid–late eighth century. Darby ('Fenland frontier', 192–4) details hints of post-Viking Britons in the Fenland, though we should be right to be sceptical here.

58   See, for example, H. Hamerow, 'Settlement mobility and the "Middle Saxon Shuffle": rural settlements and settlement patterns in Anglo-Saxon England', *Anglo-Saxon England*, 20 (1991), 1–18, on pre-Viking settlement drift. The examples are, obviously, all Anglo-Saxon, but we have no good reason to think the same imperatives would not have led to a similar drifting of post-Roman British sites in eastern England too. Certainly many of the early–middle Anglo-Saxon sites on the Fens are close by Romano-British ones.

59   Hayes, 'Roman to Saxon', 325; Crowson *et al*, *Anglo-Saxon Settlement*, pp. 292. 293.

60   Crowson *et al*, *Anglo-Saxon Settlement*, pp. 14, 211–16; the 'by the early ninth century' dating is given on p. 293.

61   One might compare here the situation on the heavy clays of Suffolk, where it has been suggested that the Britons who lived here only really began to acculturate in the eighth and ninth centuries (Härke, 'Population replacement', p. 23).

62   For example, Coates, 'Reflections', 83; Coates, 'Holland', p. 163. Note also, to the east of Holland, the names Nene and (King's) Lynn (see Coates, 'River names', 317, on the Nene).

63   *Historia Brittonum*, chapter 56, ed. and trans. J. Morris in *Nennius. British History and the Welsh Annals* (London, 1980), p. 73.

64   K. H. Jackson, 'Once again Arthur's battles', *Modern Philology*, 43 (1945), 46; C. Green, *Concepts of Arthur* (Stroud, 2007), pp. 214–15; pp. 89–95, above. See Fig. 32 for the mouth of the Glen in the early Anglo-Saxon period. On the origins and date of Anglian settlement north of Hadrian's Wall, see

below, pp. 242–6.

65 For the cremation cemetery, see P. Mayes and M. J. Dean, *An Anglo-Saxon Cemetery at Baston, Lincolnshire* (Lincoln, 1976). On the full extent of this cemetery having been discovered, see Lincolnshire Historic Environment Record 33387, although Howard Williams ('Cemeteries as central places – place and identity in Migration Period eastern England' in B. Hårdh and L. Larsson (eds), *Central Places in the Migration and Merovingian Periods* (Stockholm, 2002), p. 351) considers it possible that the cremation cemetery was originally larger in scale, but was partially destroyed by medieval and post-medieval quarrying. For the inhumation cemetery, see Williams, 'Cemeteries as central places', pp. 350–2, and the Gazetteer (below, p. 273). The two mid-fifth-century brooches, both of which consist only of the lower portions, are Portable Antiquities Scheme, NLM960 and NLM959. See also NLM975 for a fragment of a fifth-century great square-headed brooch, which comes from another site in Baston. Note, there are indications of two additional small burial sites in the parish.

66 If the two cemeteries are not to be associated with the *Spalde* then they might be alternatively – and very tentatively – linked to either the North *Gyrwe* or the *Wideriggas* (below, p. 223, endnote 70). See, for example, Williams, 'Cemeteries as central places', pp. 350–2, who relates the cemeteries to other evidence for early Anglo-Saxon activity in the area around the junction of these Roman roads, suggesting that they belong in a south Kesteven context.

67 That neither cemetery appears to contain seventh-century burials is interesting. It is possible that the Anglo-Saxons of the *Spalde* could have ceased to use their distinctive rite by the seventh century under the influence of their British neighbours. Certainly, this seems to have occurred in other areas where Anglo-Saxons lived alongside very large numbers of Britons, such as in the West Midlands, where it is suggested that the Anglo-Saxons abandoned their burial rite at the end of the sixth century as a result of their conversion to Christianity by the Britons (P. Sims-Williams, *Religion and Literature in Western England, 600–800* (Cambridge, 1990), pp. 64–83).

68 Crowson *et al*, *Anglo-Saxon Settlement*, pp. 277–80, 283, 285–6.

69 The case for this road (the Baston Outgang) surviving into the medieval period was made in Hallam, *Settlement and Society*, pp. 111–13, but has been seriously challenged in Hayes & Lane, *The Fenland Project Number 5*, p. 172, where it is argued that the supposed references to it in the twelfth century and afterwards are illusory. However, whilst the evidence for it still existing in the twelfth century has been called into question, there is no especial reason to think that the road would not still have been used and maintained in the immediately post-Roman period, particularly given the

evidence for the continued maintenance of the Roman and pre-Roman causeway roads across the Witham Fens and the location of the important names Spalding and Wykeham at the apparent siltland endpoint of the road.

70 It is possible that Stamford and its immediate vicinity belonged to the probably Middle Anglian *Wideriggas* – assessed at 600 hides in the 'Tribal Hidage' – if this population group is correctly associated with the place-name Wittering (variously *Witheringaeige*, *Witheringham* and *Witeringa*). Wittering lies only three miles to the south of Stamford, just over the county boundary (Dumville, 'Tribal Hidage', pp. 226–7; Davies & Vierck, 'Contexts', pp. 233, 234, 292; Hart, 'Tribal Hidage', 134, 152–3; Mills, *Dictionary*, p. 366). The most detailed discussion of this group is in G. Foard, 'The administrative organisation of Northamptonshire in the Saxon period', *Anglo-Saxon Studies in Archaeology and History*, 4 (1985), 195–6 and fig. 5, where it is tentatively associated with Rutland and the adjacent parts of Northamptonshire and southern Lincolnshire.

71 For the names and forms, see Cameron, *Dictionary*, pp. 14, 65–6, and Mills, *Dictionary*, pp. 35, 178. An origin for all three of these names in a population group called the *Billingas*, 'the people of *Billa*' – with *Billa* being either a personal name or Old English *bill*, 'sword' – certainly seems far more credible than Victor Watts' (*Dictionary*, p. 56) suggestion that they were all independently generated from a place-name **Billing*, 'place at/by the ridge'. For the link between this group and the *Bilmigas* of the 'Tribal Hidage', see for example Davies & Vierck, 'Contexts', pp. 234–6. On the boundaries of **Lindēs/Lindissi*, see above, pp. 128–36 and Fig. 25.

72 Davies & Vierck, 'Contexts', p. 292; Sawyer, *Anglo-Saxon Lincolnshire*, p. 221 – note, the MS C versions are given in the nominative plural form.

73 Sawyer, *Anglo-Saxon Lincolnshire*, pp. 49, 220–1; A. R. Rumble, 'An edition and translation of the Burghal Hidage, together with Recension C of the Tribal Hidage' in D. Hill and A. R. Rumble (eds), *The Defence of Wessex: The Burghal Hidage and Anglo-Saxon Fortifications* (Manchester, 1994), p. 23.

74 Davies & Vierck, 'Contexts', p. 239; David Roffe in Crowson *et al*, *Anglo-Saxon Settlement*, p. 280.

75 Yorke, 'Political and ethnic identity', pp. 84–5; Davies & Vierck, 'Contexts', pp. 239–40; G. Fellows-Jensen, 'The light thrown by the early place-names of Southern Scandinavia and England on population movement in the Migration Period' in E. Marold and C. Zimmermann (eds), *Nordwestgermanisch* (Berlin, 1995), p. 69; Bassett, 'In search', pp. 18–19, 21–3; K. Bailey, 'The Middle Saxons' in S. Bassett (ed.), *The Origins of Anglo-Saxon Kingdoms* (London, 1989), pp. 114–19; J. Blair, 'Frithuwold's kingdom and the origins of Surrey' in S. Bassett (ed.), *The Origins of Anglo-Saxon Kingdoms* (London, 1989), pp. 97–107; Dumville, 'Expansion of Mercia', pp. 133–4; J. M. Dodgson, 'The significance of the distribution of

the English place-name in *-ingas, -inga-* in south-east England' reprinted in K. Cameron (ed.), *Place-name Evidence for the Anglo-Saxon Invasion and Scandinavian Settlements* (Nottingham, 1977), pp. 36–7.

76 See Bassett, 'In search', pp. 19 and 22, and Blair, 'Frithuwold's kingdom', pp. 99 and 104, for maps of the likely extent of some of these *regiones* bearing *-ingas* names.

77 On the basis that Loveden Hill, Ancaster and Quarrington cremation cemeteries were all probably within the peripheral zone of **Lindēs*, as were probably Folkingham and Threekingham (above, pp. 128–9, 154).

78 Note, the surviving *Hæstingas* place-names similarly seem to be located on the margins of their territory (Welch, 'Kingdom of the South Saxons', p. 78).

79 T. M. Dickinson, 'An early Anglo-Saxon Cemetery at Quarrington, near Sleaford, Lincolnshire: report on excavations, 2000–2001', *LHA*, 39 (2004), 24–5; Davies & Vierck, 'Contexts', p. 274.

80 In producing this map, I have followed the methodology set out by Kevin Leahy in creating his gazetteer of Anglo-Saxon cemeteries from Lindsey (K. Leahy, 'The Anglo-Saxon settlement of Lindsey' in A. Vince (ed.), *Pre-Viking Lindsey* (Lincoln, 1993), pp. 39–42). The non-metal-detected cemeteries to the south of Loveden Hill are missing from Leahy's gazetteer and map (pp. 31–2), but this is because he was only concerned with Lindsey and the most northerly sites in Kesteven. Unfortunately, this distribution has been carried over into other publications concerned with the whole of Lincolnshire or just with Kesteven, producing a somewhat skewed view of the archaeology of the region (A. G. Vince, 'Lincolnshire in the Anglo-Saxon Period, *c.* 450–1066' in S. Bennett and N. Bennett (eds), *An Historical Atlas of Lincolnshire* (Chichester, 2001), pp. 22–3; Dickinson, 'Quarrington', 25).

81 See above, pp. 61–2, and especially Williams, 'Cemeteries as central places', and H. Williams, 'Assembling the dead' in A. Pantos and S. Semple (eds), *Assembly Places and Practices in Medieval Europe* (Dublin, 2004), pp. 109–34. See Williams, 'Assembling the dead', pp. 114–15, on the relationship between the large and small cemeteries in these territories. Note, it might well be wondered if some, at least, of these smaller and probably subordinate cemeteries did not include the burials of acculturating Britons: see Härke, 'Changing symbols', and *Angelsächsische Waffengräber* on Britons in other parts of the country not being assigned the full, normal, Anglo-Saxon burial rites even after acculturation; and C. Scull, 'Approaches to the material culture and social dynamics of the migration period in eastern England' in J. Bintliff and H. Hamerow (eds), *Europe Between Late Antiquity and the Middle Ages* (Oxford, 1995), p. 78. Another group which might have been buried in such small cemeteries rather than the central urnfield might be any of John Hines' 'second wave' of late fifth-/early sixth-century

Scandinavian immigrants who moved into already established Anglian territories (J. Hines, *The Scandinavian Character of Anglian England in the pre-Viking Period* (Oxford, 1984)).

82   The three cremation cemeteries – that is, those where cremation predominated rather than where it was a minority rite, as it is at a number of inhumation cemeteries – are Loveden Hill, Ancaster and Quarrington (Leahy, 'Anglo-Saxon settlement', p. 31). For Sleaford as a soke-centre and the focus of a large and probably Middle Saxon estate, see D. Roffe, 'Origins', *South Lincolnshire Archaeology*, 3 (1979), 11–16, particularly 15–17 and fig. 7; Roffe, 'The lost settlement of *Burg* refound?' (2000); S. Pawley, 'Grist to the mill: a new approach to the early history of Sleaford', *LHA*, 23 (1988), 37–41. Note that an estate at Sleaford is mentioned in a genuine Middle Saxon charter (S 1140) of 852: Sawyer, *Anglo-Saxon Lincolnshire*, p. 231; A. J. Robertson, *Anglo-Saxon Charters* (Cambridge, 1939), no. 7.

83   Leahy, 'Anglo-Saxon settlement of Lindsey', p. 41; Sawyer, *Anglo-Saxon Lincolnshire*, p. 217; E. Trollope, *Sleaford and the Wapentakes of Flaxwell and Aswardhurn* (Sleaford, 1887), pp. 98–100, especially p. 99. Trollope indicates both that cremations predominated and that, although the gravel pit where the finds were initially made (see R. Yerburgh, *Sketches Illustrative of the Topography and History of New and Old Sleaford* (Creasey, Sleaford, 1825), pp. 106–07) lay to the north of the Sleaford–Grantham road, the cemetery extended 'over some portion of the field on the other [southern] side of that road' too. See also Dickinson, 'Quarrington', 42–3, who identifies two possible gravel pits north of the road that may be that referred to; whichever is the correct one, the implication is that this was a very sizeable cemetery. A second cemetery ('Quarrington II'), containing 15 inhumations, was excavated around 400 yards to the west in 2000–01. This is likely to be either a separate site or a separate inhumation-only cluster of the original cemetery (see Dickinson, 42).

84   Leahy, 'Anglo-Saxon settlement', p. 41; Sawyer, *Anglo-Saxon Lincolnshire*, p. 217; H. Geake, 'When were hanging bowls deposited in Anglo-Saxon graves?', *Med. Arch.*, 43 (1999), 13, who argues for at least one grave belonging to the early seventh century. For further on this cemetery, see G. W. Thomas, 'On excavations in an Anglo-Saxon cemetery at Sleaford in Lincolnshire', *Archaeologia*, 50 (1887), 383–406, and Mike Turland's unpublished paper 'The Anglian Cemetery at Sleaford'. On the size, Thomas excavated 242 graves and estimated that he had excavated less than one third of the cemetery, which therefore contained 'at least six hundred' (Thomas, p. 385). It should be noted here that there are various other graves from Sleaford which may suggest additional burial clusters, helping to confirm the centrality of this locality (see Gazetteer, p. 281). Quite why this exceptionally large cemetery existed just to the east of a probably similarly large and contemporary cremation cemetery is a matter

of speculation (perhaps based around the two groups mentioned in endnote 81), but its existence does offer additional strong support for the Sleaford–Quarrington area being an extremely significant social/sacred/funerary focus for the region.

85 Potentially beginning early in the fifth century too. Not only is cremation an early rite, but just to the north of Sleaford there has been found a 'heavy bronze cicada shaped mount, probably of Germanic type and of late 4th–5th century date' (Lincolnshire Historic Environment Record, 65301).

86 Roffe, 'Origins', particularly 15–17 and fig. 7; Roffe, '*Burg*'; Pawley, 'Grist to the mill'; S. Pawley, 'Medieval Old Sleaford' in S. M. Elsdon, *Old Sleaford Revealed. A Lincolnshire settlement in Iron Age, Roman, Saxon and Medieval Times: Excavations 1882–1995* (Oxford, 1997), 68–9; Sawyer, *Anglo-Saxon Lincolnshire*, p. 231; Robertson, *Anglo-Saxon Charters*, no. 7. What the exact relationship is between the sokes and the Sleaford estate mentioned in the charter is open to debate.

87 D. Roffe, 'Osbournby' (2000); D. Roffe, 'The distribution of sokeland in south Kesteven', *South Lincolnshire Archaeology*, 1 (1977), 30–3, especially 31.

88 D. Roffe, 'The seventh century monastery of Stow Green, Lincolnshire', *LHA*, 21 (1986), 31–3. Such an estate could have been created at the supposed first foundation of the site in honour of St Æthelthryth in the late seventh century, or perhaps most credibly when King Æthelred of Mercia entrusted the site to St Werburg, his niece, at some point before the end of the seventh century (she died *c.* 700 in this community): see Roffe, 'Stow Green', and further below, p. 200.

89 Blair, 'Frithuwold's kingdom', pp. 102–5; J. Blair, *The Church in Anglo-Saxon Society* (Oxford, 2005), pp. 154–5.

90 J. Huggett, 'Imported grave goods and the early Anglo-Saxon economy', *Med. Arch.*, 32 (1988), 64–5; Arnold, *Archaeology of the Early Anglo-Saxon Kingdoms*, pp. 103–5.

91 Huggett, 'Imported grave goods and the early Anglo-Saxon economy', 68–71; C. J. Arnold, *An Archaeology of the Early Anglo-Saxon Kingdoms*, 2nd edn (London, 1997), p. 105.

92 Arnold, *Archaeology*, p. 121; Huggett, 'Imported grave goods', 89, 91; Hamerow, 'Anglo-Saxon Kingdoms', p. 285.

93 Huggett, 'Imported grave goods', 64–6, 91; Hamerow, 'Anglo-Saxon Kingdoms', p. 285; Arnold, *Archaeology*, p. 123.

94 Roffe, 'Origins', particularly fig. 7; Roffe, '*Burg*'; Daubney, 'The South Lincolnshire Productive Site'. My thanks to Adam Daubney for allowing me access to the unpublished text of his 2009 lecture to the CBA; page numbers cited below are taken from the printout of this. The location of the 'South Lincolnshire' find-spot has been previously narrowed down to the 'Sleaford area' in Leahy, *Kingdom of Lindsey*, p. 130.

95   See especially Ulmschneider, 'Middle Anglo-Saxon Lincolnshire', 64;
     Leahy, *Kingdom of Lindsey*, p. 130.
96   Ulmschneider, 'Middle Anglo-Saxon Lincolnshire', 63–5 (she records 90
     coins in total, some of which are not *sceattas*); A. G. Vince, 'Coinage and
     urban development: integrating the archaeological and numismatic history
     of Lincoln' in B. Cook and G. Williams (eds), *Coinage and History in the
     North Sea World, c. AD 500–1200* (Leiden, 2006), p. 527; Daubney, 'South
     Lincolnshire Productive Site', p. 3, and personal communication. For
     examples, see Portable Antiquities Scheme LIN-DEC3F4 (Series C,
     c. 680–710); LIN-EEFB05 (Series E, variant D, *c.* 700–735); LIN-B3D8D0
     ('Saroaldo' group, *c.* 705–715); LIN-DEE7D1 (a copper alloy copy of a
     Series E *sceatta, c.* 680–710); LIN-DE6F30 (Series J, *c.* 710–750).
97   Daubney, 'South Lincolnshire Productive Site', pp. 1–2, 6. See Cameron,
     Dictionary, p. 49, for the early forms (*Gerewic, Gerewik, Gerwyk*). He sees the
     first element as a personal name (**Gæra*) rather than Old English *gāra*
     ('triangular plot of land'), and treats *wīc* as having one of its other
     meanings. The first is certainly very possible – compare the trading
     settlement at Ipswich, *Gipeswic*, 'the *wīc* belonging to **Gip*' – though Adam
     Daubney argues for a derivation from *gāra*, on the basis of the shape
     formed by the surrounding parish boundaries. On the meaning of *wīc*, the
     revelation that Garwick is the location of the 'South Lincolnshire
     Productive Site' makes it virtually certain that it has the meaning 'trading
     settlement, trading centre' here (compare *Hamwic*, Southampton, and the
     other *wīc* sites). E. Ekwall, *The Concise Oxford Dictionary of English Place-
     Names*, fourth edition (Oxford, 1960), p. 192, lists the site as 'Garrick' and
     suggests the first element is *gāra*, noting that the attested spellings of this
     element would indicate that the place-name has been 'Scandinavianized' at
     some point.
98   Daubney ('South Lincolnshire Productive Site', p. 2) notes ten *tremisses*,
     plus one additional recent find via personal communication (July 2009).
     The Corpus of Early Medieval Coin Finds (EMC), based at the Fitzwilliam
     Museum (*www.fitzmuseum.cam.ac.uk/dept/coins/emc/*), lists the gold shilling
     (2000.0537) and twelve *tremisses*, not including the most recent find, hence
     the total given here (note, one of the coins – 2000.0069 – may have been
     minted in Ipswich rather than on the continent); Sawyer, *Anglo-Saxon
     Lincolnshire*, p. 258, lists the gold blank flan. See also Vince, 'Numismatic
     History of Lincoln', p. 527, and R. Abdy and G. Williams, 'A catalogue of
     hoards and single finds from the British Isles, *c.* AD 410–675' in Cook and
     Williams, *Coinage and History*, pp. 44–5, 49, 52, 53, 55, 61. Leahy, *Kingdom of
     Lindsey*, p. 158, notes two gold shillings and eight *tremisses* from Lindsey.
     Using Sawyer's list, the EMC, the PAS, and Abdy and Williams, the total
     of *tremisses* from Lindsey can be increased to twelve, including one *tremissis*
     of the Byzantine Emperor Maurice, 582–602 (Portable Antiquities Scheme

LVPL-9C93A2).

99 Portable Antiquities Scheme LIN-4F6CE7 (Style I die); Daubney, 'South Lincolnshire Productive Site', p. 2. Other finds include a sword pommel (Portable Antiquities Scheme LIN-7B7528), which was possibly originally gold-plated.

100 Abdy & Williams, 'A catalogue', p. 54; Vince, 'Numismatic History of Lincoln', p. 527; Ulmschneider, 'Middle Anglo-Saxon Lincolnshire', 64, 70. The gold *tremissis* is Corpus of Early Medieval Coin Finds item 1998.0041; this database also lists eleven eighth-century *sceattas*, one ninth-century *styca*, and two coins of Offa from 'near Sleaford'.

101 For example, Hamerow, 'Anglo-Saxon Kingdoms', p. 285.

102 See above, Chapters 2 and 3, especially pp. 113–15.

103 With regard to the Sleaford–Quarrington district, not only do we have a probably sizeable cremation cemetery and associated territory located some considerable distance from Lincoln, but all three types of post-Roman British metalwork – Class 1 brooches (Folkingham and Osbournby), Type G brooches (Sleaford and Osbournby) and hanging bowls (Sleaford, Walcot near Folkingham, and Osbournby) – are found in this region. See further, pp. 69–74, for the implications of these items.

104 Above, pp. 103–04, 110, 126 (endnote 76). Is there some link between the two Class 1 brooches from Folkingham; the group-name which underlies Threekingham and almost certainly pre-dates *c.* 600, given the origins of its first element; the Welsh-speakers referenced in the place-name Walcot and the escutcheon from a sixth-/seventh-century hanging bowl found there; and the Class 1 brooch, Type G brooch, and hanging bowl fragment found at Osbournby, given that all four parishes abut each other? This is certainly an extremely intriguing coincidence of evidence, if nothing else. The other two British brooches from Anglo-Saxon graves in this region are from the Sleaford cemetery, as is the other hanging bowl (T. M. Dickinson, 'Fowler's Type G Penannular brooches reconsidered', *Med. Arch.*, 26 (1982), 48, 50, 52 and figs. 1–4; R. Bruce-Mitford, *A Corpus of Late Celtic Hanging Bowls* (Oxford, 2005), pp. 26, 34–5, 212–14).

105 Elsdon, *Old Sleaford Revealed*, especially pp. 39, 76.

106 J. Wacher, *The Towns of Roman Britain*, 2nd edn (London, 1995), p. 40; Yorke, 'Anglo-Saxon *gentes* and *regna*', pp. 396–7.

107 This is based on Ben Whitwell's map (in 'Roman Lincolnshire' in Bennett and Bennett, *Historical Atlas of Lincolnshire*, pp. 14–15), on the assumption that most Romano-British 'small towns' in Lincolnshire are now known, and thus an analysis of likely territories for these 'towns' using Thiessen polygons is legitimate. As Helena Hamerow observes, in such circumstances territories reconstructed using these techniques can correspond well with reality (H. Hamerow, *Early Medieval Settlements* (Oxford, 2002), pp. 101–2).

108 Daubney, 'South Lincolnshire Productive Site', p. 7. Sawyer, *Anglo-Saxon Lincolnshire*, p. 258, lists two 'staters'; the third is the recent find Portable Antiquities Scheme LIN-F4A8B4. It is tempting to compare the finds of Late Iron Age gold coins, evidence for a Romano-British votive shrine, and the presence of a sixth-century cemetery, with the Iron Age/Romano-British/Anglo-Saxon site at Lissingleys discussed above, pp. 140–5. The chief difference seems to be the use the site was put to subsequently: a '*wīc*' here and a meeting place at Lissingleys. There is also more Romano-British material currently known from the latter site, though Roman and Iron Age material continues to be found at Garwick.

109 See further above, pp. 128–36.

110 A date of separation before *c.* 690 would also be helpful with regard to explaining why York never claimed ecclesiastical authority south of the Witham, see pp. 130 and 155 (endnote 10).

111 J. R. Maddicott, 'London and Droitwich, *c.* 650–750: trade, industry and the rise of Mercia', *Anglo-Saxon England*, 34 (2005), 7–58, especially 16–21; R. Cowie, 'Mercian London' in M. P. Brown and C. A. Farr (eds), *Mercia. An Anglo-Saxon Kingdom in Europe* (London, 2001), pp. 194–210, especially p. 195. The documentary *terminus ante quem* for the re-establishment of full Mercian control over *Lundenwic* comes in 733, when Æthelbald of Mercia granted remission on tolls due on one ship '*in portu Lundoniae*' to the Bishop of Rochester.

112 Leahy, *Kingdom of Lindsey*, p. 159. Ulmschneider, 'Middle Anglo-Saxon Lincolnshire', 78; M. Blackburn, 'Coin finds and coin circulation in Lindsey, *c.* 600–900' in A. Vince (ed.), *Pre-Viking Lindsey* (Lincoln, 1993), p. 83.

113 Daubney, 'South Lincolnshire Productive Site', p. 3; Maddicott, 'London and Droitwich', 9–10. Of course, Middle Saxon coins are almost certainly easier to recover from the Garwick site than they are from *Lundenwic*.

114 Ulmschneider, 'Middle Anglo-Saxon Lincolnshire', 63–5, 66; Daubney, 'South Lincolnshire Productive Site', p. 4.

115 Maddicott, 'London and Droitwich', 9–10; Ulmschneider, 'Middle Anglo-Saxon Lincolnshire', 66.

116 Ulmschneider, 'Middle Anglo-Saxon Lincolnshire', 63–5 (especially fig. 6), 67–9; Leahy, *Kingdom of Lindsey*, pp. 129–30.

117 Whether Garwick ever made the move from being a 'trading site' to being a permanent trading settlement – as found at London, Ipswich and Southampton – is impossible to say without detailed fieldwalking and excavation. There is a significant quantity of lead melt, spindle whorls and weights from the site, but the Fen Edge location and lack of subsequent significant settlement may suggest that it did not. On the whole, Garwick appears to be an unusually tightly controlled market on a marginal site, rather than a true trading settlement.

118 Pawley, 'Grist to the mill'; Pawley, 'Medieval Old Sleaford', p. 69. See also Roffe, '*Burg*'. On the name Quarrington, see Cameron, *Dictionary*, p. 99, and Mills, *Dictionary*, p. 266.

119 As to why there is no evidence for Garwick continuing to function as a major regional trading site after the middle of the eighth century, various explanations seem possible (Daubney, 'South Lincolnshire Productive Site', pp. 4–5). One additional possibility is that, if this was a royal Mercian site, then the kings of Mercia may have simply begun to favour *Lundenwic* once they had established full control over it (by 733).

120 Leahy, 'Anglo-Saxon settlement', p. 36; Leahy, *Kingdom of Lindsey*, pp. 48–9; K. Leahy, *'Interrupting the Pots': The Excavation of Cleatham Anglo-Saxon Cemetery* (York, 2007), p. 6; Sawyer, *Anglo-Saxon Lincolnshire*, p. 51; Everson, 'Pre-Viking settlement', p. 98; Williams, 'Cemeteries as central places'; Williams. 'Assembling the dead'.

121 On Thiessen polygons, compare K. R. Dark, *Civitas to Kingdom: British Political Continuity 300–800* (London, 1994), pp. 113–15, and Hamerow, *Early Medieval Settlements*, pp. 101–2. It might also be wondered whether Skegness/*Tric* ought to have its own polygon, on account of its probable Late Roman fort and the place-name evidence discussed in Owen and Coates, *'Traiectus/Tric/Skegness'*. Note also the recent find of a late sixth- to mid-seventh-century gold *tremissis* from Skegness (EMC 2001.0741) and the significant quantity of eighth- and ninth-century metalwork from 'near Skegness' (Ulmschneider, 'Middle Anglo-Saxon Lincolnshire', 65).

122 C. Green, 'The British kingdom of Lindsey', *Cambrian Medieval Celtic Studies*, 56 (2008), 17–18, 27–30; above, pp. 60–4, 87–9.

123 Sawyer, *Anglo-Saxon Lincolnshire*, pp. 84, 125–6, 134–6, 138; Leahy, *Kingdom of Lindsey*, pp. 49, 113; D. M. Hadley, *The Vikings in England: Settlement, Society and Culture* (Manchester, 2006), pp. 90–2; J. Insley, 'Wapentake', *Reallexikon der Germanischen Altertumskunde*, 33 (Berlin, 2006), 251; and especially S. Turner, 'Aspects of the development of public assembly in the Danelaw', *Assemblage*, 5 (2000).

124 Compare, for example, Balkwill, 'Old English *wīc*'.

125 Williams, 'Cemeteries as central places', pp. 352–5; F. H. Thompson, 'Anglo-Saxon sites in Lincolnshire: unpublished material and recent discoveries', *Antiq. J.*, 36 (1956), 189–92, especially p. 190.

126 Everson, 'Pre-Viking settlement', p. 98; D. Roffe, 'Medieval administration' in Bennett and Bennett, *Historical Atlas of Lincolnshire*, pp. 38–9; Lincolnshire Historic Environment Record 43906.

127 Roffe, 'Medieval administration', p. 39; Cameron, *Dictionary*, p. 82; K. Cameron, *The Place-Names of Lincolnshire, IV* (Nottingham, 1996), p. 26.

128 Green, 'British kingdom', 16, fn. 72; Sawyer, *Anglo-Saxon Lincolnshire*, p. 51; Cameron, *Lincolnshire IV*, pp. 25–6; A. E. B. Owen, 'Roads and Romans in south-east Lindsey' in A. R. Rumble and A. D. Mills (eds), *Names, Places*

and People (Stamford, 1997), pp. 263, 267; A. E. B. Owen, 'Herefrith of Louth, saint and bishop: a problem of identities', *LHA*, 15 (1980), 15–19; A. E. B. Owen, 'Louth before Domesday', *LHA*, 32 (1997), 60–4. I would thus consider Ludborough wapentake to be a late creation, carved out of Louthesk, as its size and relationship to the northern boundary of Louthesk would suggest. Similarly, it is not implausible that the parts of the wapentake of Calcewath north of Meers Bank were an addition to this wapentake: see further, Fig. 43 and Roffe, 'Medieval Administration', p. 39, for the wapentake boundaries.

129 It is perhaps worth observing here that, although Louth takes its name from the river Lud (**hlūde*, 'the loud one'), North Cockerington (*Cocrinton* at Domesday) is located further downstream and seems to preserve the British name for the river in its etymology, 'the village, *tūn*, associated with the (river) Cocker', as Cocker is a Celtic river-name (Cameron, *Dictionary*, pp. 32, 82). Given that place-names involving *tūn* are now considered to be chiefly of a mid-eighth-century or later date (see B. Cox, 'The place-names of the earliest English records', *English Place-Name Society Journal*, 8 (1976), 12–66), this suggests that both the British and Old English names for the river were in use throughout much of the pre-Viking period. In this context it is similarly interesting to note that a spring dedicated to St Helen lies in the heart of the town, and that one of the tributaries of the Lud – the Crake, which runs along Welton le Wold parish boundary – appears to bear a Celtic river-name (E. Ekwall, *English River-Names* (Oxford, 1928), pp. 261, 101-02). See the Cleatham cemetery for another major cremation cemetery which has potential evidence for post-Roman Britons living in its immediate vicinity (Green, 'British kingdom', 24, 28 and fn. 114).

130 Leahy, *Kingdom of Lindsey*, pp. 111–14; Green, 'British kingdom', p. 30; B. Cox, 'Yarboroughs in Lindsey', *English Place-Name Society Journal*, 28 (1994–5), 50–60; above, p. 89. It is certainly conceivable that Yarborough Camp could have always been the meeting place for the Elsham group, particularly as the cemetery site is not topographically distinct, unlike those at (for example) Loveden Hill, West Keal and Louth. Although not within modern Lincolnshire, the Newark Millgate cemetery is also relevant here as it formed part of the ring of cremation cemeteries around Lincoln. The evidence from here accords well with the relationship described above between cremation cemeteries and wapentakes, with Newark being the centre of an Anglo-Scandinavian wapentake. Furthermore, there is evidence to suggest that the wapentake of Newark was in fact independent of Nottinghamshire before *c*. 950 and possibly attached to Lincolnshire (D. Roffe, *Nottinghamshire and the North: A Domesday Study* (1987/2002), chapter 8, fn. 21).

131 Leahy, *'Interrupting the Pots'*, p. 6; Leahy, *Kingdom of Lindsey*, p. 49; Roffe, 'Medieval administration', p. 39.

132 See Everson, 'Pre-Viking settlement', pp. 97–8.

133 Leahy, *Kingdom of Lindsey*, pp. 93–6; Everson, 'Pre-Viking settlement', pp. 97–8; Sawyer, *Anglo-Saxon Lincolnshire*, pp. 52–3.

134 See especially above, pp. 185–97, and also Pawley, 'Grist to the mill', 37. The northern half of Aveland wapentake also looks to have been originally dependent upon Sleaford–Quarrington, though this relationship may have been severed by the probable carving up of the *regio* of the *Billingas* in the late seventh century by the Mercian rulers (above, pp. 197–200).

135 On the location, see Williams, 'Cemeteries as central places', p. 355, and Williams, 'Assembling the dead', pp. 111, 119–20.

136 J. Hines, 'Britain after Rome' in P. Graves-Brown *et al* (eds), *Cultural Identity and Archaeology: the Construction of European Communities* (London, 1996), pp. 262–3 (figs. 17.1 and 17.2), phases the early Anglo-Saxon cemeteries known up to the mid-1990s into those which were certainly in existence by *c.* 525 and those which were certainly in existence by *c.* 560. An examination of the finds from the most recently discovered sites (listed in the Appendix) gives us no good reason to dispute this conclusion. Although there are a very small number of individual 'early' items from the north and south of the cemetery group, these may well be heirloom pieces (see above, p. 82, endnote 30, on the North Hykeham brooch), and the early cemeteries are still all in this central zone, with Loveden itself being the most obvious example. In terms of the early Anglo-Saxon centrality of Loveden Hill, it may also be relevant that there seem to have been some very high-status burials in this cemetery in the seventh century, as indicated by finds of a Coptic bowl and a sceptre (Williams, 'Assembling the dead', pp. 123–4; T. Page, 'Coptic bowl from Loveden Hill', *LHA*, 21 (1986), 76–7; Lincolnshire Historic Environment Record 30280).

137 Williams, 'Assembling the dead', pp. 123–4; Williams, 'Cemeteries as central places', p. 353.

138 For the probable meeting place of Threo wapentake, Spellar Wood (first recorded in the early twelfth century), see Lincolnshire Historic Environment Record 35331; Roffe, 'Medieval administration', p. 39, maps the medieval wapentake boundary here.

139 Portable Antiquities Scheme NLM6073 and NLM963; Williams, 'Cemeteries as central places', pp. 356–7; Williams, 'Assembling the dead', p. 121. See also Williams, 'Assembling the dead, p. 114 and fig. 5.7, on pyre sites.

140 See Leahy, *'Interrupting the Pots'*, p. 12, for the argument that we are now aware of most – if not all – significant cremation cemeteries in the region. As such, the Great Ponton pyre site seems likely to be associated with Loveden Hill to the north – although there was a mixed cremation and inhumation cemetery at Woolsthorpe, this is still a significant distance from Great Ponton and it is likely to have only served a local community.

141 See, for example, Courtney, 'Early Saxon Fenland', 94, on the general issues with assuming that all 'cemetery groups' relate to only a single population group.

142 This expansion is discussed above, pp. 63–4. See above, pp. 207 and 232 (endnote 136), on the phasing and dating of cemeteries in this region. All of these cemeteries fall to the north of Loveden wapentake, which may be significant (see Roffe, 'Medieval administration', p. 39).

143 One possible problem with treating these southern cemeteries as a single coherent 'group' focused on Loveden Hill is that the small Ancaster cremation cemetery, containing 40 or so burials, has been considered indicative of an early Anglo-Saxon 'central place' in its own right (Williams, 'Cemeteries as central places', pp. 347–50). However, this cemetery does seem to have been far smaller in scale than that at Loveden Hill, and it could perhaps therefore be treated as a subordinate cemetery within the eastern edge of Loveden Hill's territory, potentially laying claim to the Roman fort there. One might compare here the small cremation cemetery of Wold Newton (containing 20 or so burials), which probably lay on the northern edge of the territory dependent upon South Elkington–Louth, and the possible small cremation cemetery just to the north of Hibaldstow Roman 'small town', which was almost certainly within the territory of Cleatham–Kirton in Lindsey.

144 See Davies & Vierck, 'Contexts', p. 239; David Roffe in Crowson *et al*, *Anglo-Saxon Settlement*, p. 280. On the date of the *-ingas* names, see Cameron, *English Place-Names*, p. 71.

145 Cameron, *Dictionary*, pp. 2 (Alvingham), 53 (Grayingham), 88 (Messingham), and 133 (Waddingham). As already noted (pp. 185–6), we can only really be confident in seeing an *-ingas* group as having more than local import when we have several instances of it in place-names, or a documentary reference to a *regio* named after it. The three *Billingas* names are the only clearly convincing case of this from within *Lindissi*, although the two neighbouring *Wintringas* place-names (Winteringham and Winterton) are potentially interesting given the coincidence of the name *Wint(r)a* in the *Lindissi* royal genealogy (above, p. 103). Whilst we do have two settlements or estates named after groups called the *Willingas* (Cherry Willingham and South Willingham), they are around twelve miles apart, and a coincidence cannot be easily discounted. Similarly, there are two settlements or estates linked to groups called the *Wifelingas* (Willingham by Stow and North Willingham), but these are eighteen miles apart and the *Wifelingas* in both instances are perhaps better treated not as early Anglian population groups, but rather as *Kultverbände* under the leadership of pagan priests, Old English **Wifel* (J. Insley, 'Kultische namen', *Reallexikon der Germanischen Altertumskunde*, 17 (Berlin, 2000), 426, but see G. Fellows-Jensen, 'The Weevil's claw' in A. van Nahl *et al* (eds), *Namenwelten* (Berlin,

2004), pp. 76–89).

146 See Chapter 4, pp. 136–47, above. There does, for example, seem to be an unusual amount of evidence for the survival of the names of (Romano-)British 'central places' in the Lincoln region. Thus the name Lincoln derives directly from the Late British *Lindgolun*; the first element of the name Horncastle directly translates the first element of the British name of this site (Old English *horn-*, British **banno-*); Lissingleys looks to derive from Late British/Archaic Welsh **liss-* (see Welsh *llys*, 'court, hall, parliament, gathering of nobles, etc.'); the name of the probable fort at Skegness looks to have been preserved in the eleventh-century place-name *Tric* (< Latin *Traiectus*); and the name Kirmington may well derive from the British name of Kirmington 'small Roman town'. It is also worth noting here that Caistor Roman town has a *wīchām* (< Latin *vicus*) close by it, which is equally suggestive.

147 Potter, 'Roman Fenland', pp. 171–2. See, for example, Courtney, 'Early Saxon Fenland', 96, for the suggestion that Peterborough lay at the heart of at least the North *Gyrwe*.

148 Above, pp. 195, 228 (endnote 104).

149 M. W. Bishop, *An Archaeological Resource Assessment of Anglo-Saxon Nottinghamshire* (2000), pp. 1–2. On this *regio*, see above, pp. 132–5.

6

LINDISFARNE, THE LINDISFARAN AND THE ORIGINS OF ANGLO-SAXON NORTHUMBRIA

When considering the Anglo-Saxon inhabitants of the kingdom of *Lindissi* and their historical significance, it has often been wondered whether there is some sort of relationship between the place-names Lindsey/*Lindissi* and Lindisfarne and, if so, what the meaning of this might be.[1] That such a link is not inconceivable is to a large degree confirmed by an examination of both the group-name for the inhabitants of *Lindissi* (Anglo-Latin *Lindisfari*, Old English *Lindisfaran*) and the early forms of the place-name Lindisfarne (Anglo-Latin *insula Lindisfarnensis*, Old English *Lindisfarnae*, *Lindisfarena ea*).[2] In what follows, the evidence for such a relationship is examined in detail, looking first at the linguistic case for and against this, and then moving on to the historical and archaeological evidence which might have some bearing upon its plausibility, before examining the question of the significance of any such relationship.

The etymology of Lindisfarne

Broadly speaking, there have been two main approaches to the question of the etymology of the name Lindisfarne. The first of these has been to consider that any morphological similarity between Old English *Lindisfarnae*/*Lindisfarena ea* and the Lincolnshire group-name *Lindisfaran* is entirely coincidental. Such explanations independently derive the first element of the place-name *Lindisfarnae*/*Lindisfarena ea* from British **lindo-* ('pool, lake'), with reference to either the stretch of water which lies between the island of Lindisfarne and the mainland, or some pool of fresh water on the island itself. The second element of the name is then either left as an unidentified British word, for a wholly British etymology of Lindisfarne, or treated as Old English *faran*, in which case Lindisfarne would probably be the island belonging to the people who travelled across the water between the island and the mainland.[3]

Whilst such an independent British or part-British etymology for Lindisfarne has proved convincing for some commentators, there are in fact a number of very serious problems with such a hypothesis. One is quite simply that both the British and the Irish names for the island of Lindisfarne are already known, and whilst they are clearly related, in neither case do they resemble anything remotely like *Lindisfarnae/Lindisfarena ea*. Rather, the name of the island was in Old Welsh *Medcaut/Metcaud* and in Old Irish *Inis Medcoit/Insula Medgoet*, both of which derive from a Latin place-name *medicāta (insula)*, the 'island of healing', borrowed in the Late or post-Roman period. The significance of this point is, needless to say, considerable.[4]

Another major problem stems from the notion that the first element of *Lindisfarnae/Lindisfarena ea* is independently generated from British **lindo-* ('pool, lake'). On the one hand, in those theories where **lindo-* would refer to the waters between the mainland and the island, such a usage of the word would be highly unusual and unparalleled in either Welsh or Irish place-names.[5] On the other, in those theories where **lindo-* would refer to a fresh-water pool on the island itself, *faran* would not be a plausible second element, and instead we would have to leave the entire second half of the name unexplained, which is hardly a satisfactory situation.[6] Even more important, however, is the fact that it is extremely unlikely that any independent derivation of Old English *Lindisfarnae/Lindisfarena ea* from British **lindo-* would produce either of these forms rather than the non-existent forms ***Linnisfarnae/**Linnisfarena ea*, whatever **lindo-* referred to.

The issue here is that, if one wishes to derive the English place-name Lindisfarne directly from British **lindo-*, then one must place the adoption of the name Lindisfarne by the Bernician Anglo-Saxons before the mutation of *-nd-* to *-nn-* in Late British/Archaic Welsh, as otherwise the name should be recorded as ***Linnisfarnae*, not *Lindisfarnae*.[7] If this mutation was only complete by around 600, as is usually assumed in studies of the name Lindisfarne, then the form *Lindisfarnae* causes no problems, as both the written and the archaeological evidence suggests that Anglo-Saxons were in the Lindisfarne region from about 550, or a little later, and so would have adopted the name before *-nd-* became *-nn-*.[8] Unfortunately, however, such an end-date for this mutation refers to the orthographically conservative British epigraphic and written evidence, and any mid–late sixth-century Anglo-Saxon borrowing would have instead occurred orally; the significance of this is that, orally, the change from -*nd*- to -*nn*- in Late British/Archaic Welsh is likely to have been completed much earlier, by around 500 at the latest. As such, the notion that a name for the island independently derived from British *lindo*- and adopted by the Anglo-Saxons around 550 or a little later would take the Old English form *Lindisfarnae*, rather than non-existent ***Linnisfarnae, is open to very serious doubt indeed.[9] When taken together with the other concerns outlined above, especially the fact that we already know the post-Roman British name for the island, the theory of a British origin for the place-name Lindisfarne must consequently be rejected.

The second approach to the question of the etymology of Lindisfarne has been to admit that there is almost certainly a direct relationship between either *Lindissi* or *Lindisfaran* and the place-name *Lindisfarnae*/*Lindisfarena ea*. However, where we go after this is somewhat disputed. Most have argued that *Lindissi*/*Lindisfaran* are the earliest and primary names and that *Lindisfarnae*/*Lindisfarena ea* is a secondary, Old English formation based upon one of them. On the other hand, Richard Coates has recently suggested that *Lindisfaran* is the later, secondary, name and that it was actually borrowed from the island-name *Lindisfarnae*/*Lindisfarena ea*. This latter theory is based around two related hypotheses: one, that the group-name *Lindisfaran* was not the 'true' form of the name for the inhabitants of the kingdom of *Lindissi* (which was 'correctly' *Lindisware*) but was instead a false misapplication of the name of Lindisfarne to the people of *Lindissi*, with *Lindisfaran* being inherently implausible as a group-name; and, two, that whilst a British root for *Lindisfarnae*/*Lindisfarena ea* must be rejected, we have a plausible alternative to seeing *Lindisfarnae* as etymologically derivative of *Lindissi*/*Lindisfaran* in a hypothetical Archaic Irish **Lindis-feranna, 'domains at/of (a stream named) *Lindis*'.[10]

Concerning the first hypothesis, it has to be said that the suggestion that *Lindisware*, not *Lindisfaran*, is the original form of the name of the population group which inhabited *Lindissi* strains credulity beyond breaking point. Quite simply, *Lindisware* ('*Lindis*-

dwellers') is attested as the group-name for the inhabitants of *Lindissi* only a single time: in one early twelfth-century manuscript that reflects in part an early eleventh-century recension of the 'Anglo-Saxon Chronicle'.[11] In contrast, *Lindisfaran* is attested on multiple occasions – for example, in Bede's early eighth-century *Historia Ecclesiastica*, all manuscripts of the originally pre-Viking 'Tribal Hidage', the eighth-century 'Anglian Collection of royal genealogies and regnal lists', the pre-Viking Anglo-Saxon episcopal lists, and the subscriptions attached to the report of the Papal Legates of 786.[12] In other words, it is quite clear which is the correct and original pre-Viking form, and it is not *Lindisware*. Rather than adopting a frankly far-fetched and untenable hypothesis, wherein the 'true' group-name of the people of *Lindissi* – *Lindisware* – is somehow mysteriously replaced in all Anglo-Saxon documents (other than a single, twelfth-century manuscript of the 'Chronicle') by the name of the island of Lindisfarne, it is far simpler to treat *Lindisware* as a false and very late creation intended merely to bring the *Lindissi* group-name into line with others of the more familiar *X-ware* type, such as the *Meanware* of east Hampshire and the *Cantware* of Kent.[13]

As to the claim that *Lindisfaran* is inherently implausible as a group-name, it ought to be acknowledged that the name has caused problems in the past and there have consequently been some implausible translations of *Lindisfaran* (for example, '*Lindis*-goers, the people who resort to a place named *Lindis*-'), about which we would be right to be sceptical.[14] However, this is not to say that the name *Lindisfaran* itself is in any way implausible as a group-name for the inhabitants of *Lindissi*, only that some of the suggested translations of this name are implausible, and this has more to do with an insufficient consideration of the potential meanings of Old English *faran* in such a group-name rather than anything else.[15] In fact, if one does consider more carefully the range of meanings possible for *faran*, based on the Anglo-Saxon and continental evidence, then *Lindisfaran* is readily and clearly explicable as a group-name which would be more than appropriate for an Anglo-Saxon population group of the 'migration period'. The Anglo-Saxons of *Lindissi* were, on this basis, quite literally 'the people who migrated (*faran*) to the territory of *Lindēs* (> Old English *Lindis*)'.[16] Furthermore, this notion that *Lindisfaran* is in no way implausible as an early Anglo-Saxon group-name is strongly supported by the evidence for the existence of other closely related group-names in the early medieval period. One might, for example, point to the *Burgundofarones/Burgundaefarones* who appear in the seventh-century 'Chronicle of Fredegar' as the ruling group within Frankish Burgundy, and it is worth observing here that the eighth-century Franco-Burgundian *Passio sancti Sigismundi regis* states that *Burgundofarones* was actually the original group-name for the Burgundian tribe.[17] Similarly pertinent are the Lombard *farae*, the name apparently given to the Lombard groups (clans, extended kin groups and/or military 'followings') which migrated into northern Italy in the sixth century and took over territories there. Indeed, it has been argued that this organization of the migrating groups into *farae* was common not only to the Lombards but also to the Burgundians and the Ostrogoths.[18] Finally, it should be noted that in the Old English poem *Widsið* we find reference to another supposed kingdom and population group whose name involves Old English *faran*: *Hringweald wæs haten Herefarena cyning*, 'Hringweald was called the king of the *Herefaran*'.[19]

Taken together, the above two points – that *Lindisfaran*, not *Lindisware*, was clearly the original name for the population group which inhabited the kingdom of *Lindissi*, and that *Lindisfaran* is in no way implausible as a group-name – fatally undermine the case for the similarity between the place-name *Lindisfarnae* and the group-name *Lindisfaran* being due to a bizarre misapplication of the place-name *Lindisfarnae* to the people of *Lindissi*. In such circumstances, *if* the name Lindisfarne is potentially of Irish origin – as the second hypothesis which underpins this theory holds, seeing it as coined by the seventh-century Irish monks who founded the monastery at Lindisfarne – then we would need to start thinking about a rather remarkable coincidence having occurred in order to produce two rare and near-identical, but unrelated, names. The question is, does the evidence for an Irish origin for Lindisfarne justify positing such a coincidence? There are, needless to say, once again several very serious issues with such an etymology, which suggest that the answer to this must be in the negative.

One of these is the question of redundancy. As was noted above, we already know of both the Welsh name for Lindisfarne (*Medcaut/Metcaud* < Latin *medicāta (insula)*) and the Irish one (*Inis*

Medcoit/Insula Medgoet), with the latter appearing to be an Archaic Irish borrowing of the Welsh form of the name.[20] As such, it might well be legitimately wondered how credible it is that the Irish monks would have felt the need to coin a second Archaic Irish name for the island.[21] This would not, perhaps, be so much of a stumbling block if the suggested Archaic Irish etymology for Lindisfarne – *Lindis-feranna* ('domains at/of (a stream named) *Lindis*')[22] – were clear, plausible and uncontentious, but it is not. Thus, for example, the hypothetical Irish form *Lindis-feranna* would involve a first element that was a derivative of Archaic Irish *lind-* ('pool, lake') utilized as a stream-name, which is dubious, and its first and second elements would, moreover, be used in a way which is effectively unique and unparalleled in other Irish place-names.[23] Even leaving to one side such considerable linguistic concerns, there are other sound reasons for rejecting this Irish etymology for Lindisfarne. Quite simply, the name 'domains at/of (a stream named) *Lindis*' seems implausible as a name for the island chosen by its new monastic owners; the plural 'domains, territories' (*feranna*) is curious to say the least, and there were surely far more obvious defining geographical features which could have been referenced in any such name other than a stream, especially as the stream supposedly known as *Lindis* is only two feet wide.[24] All told then, not only do we already know the Archaic Irish name for the island, but the proposed etymology would also seem both to involve an exceptional degree of special pleading and to produce a name which does, in any case, seem implausible. In consequence, it is impossible to see a derivation from a hypothetical Archaic Irish *Lindis-feranna* as a credible explanation of the name Lindisfarne.[25]

We thus have a situation in which the proposed British and Irish etymologies of Lindisfarne must be rejected as far too problematical and speculative, but at the same time an explanation for both the name Lindisfarne and its similarity to the group-name *Lindisfaran* is still very much required. Fortunately, there is a more than credible solution to this dilemma available to us, in the form of a perfectly legitimate and frequently noted Old English etymology for *Lindisfarnae/Lindisfarena ea* that consists simply of Old English *Lindisfaran* plus Old English *ēg*, giving 'the island (*ēg*) of the *Lindisfaran*', with the first element taking the genitive plural form

(-*ena*). Given that this etymology would easily and fully explain the name Lindisfarne, and that, in the light of the above discussion, there is no plausible, available alternative, nor any other way of explaining the similarity of the names *Lindisfaran* and Lindisfarne, it must therefore be asked why Lindisfarne was named the 'island of the *Lindisfaran*'.[26]

One hypothesis is that the group-name *Lindisfaran* could here be an independent coining formed from the first part of the Old English kingdom-name *Lindissi* plus Old English *faran*, meaning something akin to 'the people who have been to or regularly go to *Lindissi*'.[27] This, however, seems both implausible and problematical as an explanation of the name. Not only would it require a remarkable coincidence whereby the group-name *Lindisfaran* was independently coined not just once but twice over (and with a different meaning on each occasion), but it is also very difficult to see why *Lindissi* would have been so immensely important to the people of Lindisfarne that they would have chosen to name themselves (or were named) the *Lindisfaran* after their supposed travels back and forth to this kingdom far to their south.[28] It is surely far more convincing and credible to treat the *Lindisfaran* referenced in the name *Lindisfarnae/Lindisfarena ea* ('the island of the *Lindisfaran*') as simply members of the well-attested Lincolnshire population group called the *Lindisfaran*, who had taken possession of this island at some point. The appearance of this group-name in the only acceptable etymology for Lindisfarne is, after all, both singular and striking, and the notion that there was a second, independent, coining of the same group-name for the people of Lindisfarne might well be seen to be special pleading designed to avoid the obvious implications of the etymology 'the island of the *Lindisfaran*'. As Thomas Charles-Edwards and Patrick Wormald have noted, a direct link between the *Lindisfaran* of Lincolnshire and the *Lindisfaran* of Lindisfarne is 'as certain as anything in place-name studies can be'. Consequently, there seems little credible option but to accept Eilert Ekwall's primary interpretation that the name *Lindisfarnae/Lindisfarena ea* signified that the island was settled by the *Lindisfaran* (that is to say migrants or colonists from *Lindissi*), presumably at some point before the foundation of the monastery at Lindisfarne in 635.[29] Rather than trying to think up alternative etymologies in order to avoid this conclusion, we would perhaps do better to ask what the context and implications of this transparent etymology might actually be.

The *Lindisfaran* in Northumbria: the historical and archaeological context

The above conclusion that the name Lindisfarne is almost certainly Old English in derivation and probably means 'the island ($\bar{e}g$) belonging to/settled by members of the *Lindisfaran* population group of Lincolnshire' gains a very credible context from a consideration of the history and archaeology of early Anglo-Saxon Bernicia and Deira, the two kingdoms which made up later Northumbria.

The key point is that, whilst the available archaeological evidence clearly indicates that there was a notable degree of Anglo-Saxon activity in the Lindisfarne region from the middle of the sixth century onwards (as evidenced by, for example, the settlements and cemeteries at Yeavering, Milfield, Thirlings and Bamburgh), there is no convincing evidence for significant pre-seventh-century Anglo-Saxon activity south of this region until we reach Hadrian's Wall. Even here the significance and meaning of the Anglo-Saxon material discovered is open to debate, perhaps being best explained as a result of a continued British control of the Wall that involved a partial employment of Anglo-Saxon mercenaries, rather than anything else (Fig. 46).[30] Needless to say, this is suggestive in the present context, and it might well be taken to imply that the area around Lindisfarne was indeed settled by an Anglo-Saxon group which had arrived there via the sea. Certainly, the alternative hypothesis, that the Anglo-Saxon settlements and cemeteries of the Lindisfarne region were the result of a northwards, land-based expansion of Anglo-Saxon rule from the area around Hadrian's Wall – this thus being the original 'core' of the kingdom of Bernicia – would seem implausible, given both the distribution of the sixth-century finds and the nature of the evidence from the Wall.[31] Moreover, such a scenario would also conflict with the evidence for the Lindisfarne region being itself the early 'core area' of the kingdom of Bernicia, not an outlying and later northern dependency. Bede's testimony strongly implies that, for him at least, Lindisfarne and Bamburgh (four miles to the south of the island, on the mainland coast) represented very significant royal possessions and the historical core of the kingdom of Bernicia. This is supported by the legends included in the ninth-century *Historia Brittonum*, where both Bamburgh and Lindisfarne feature as the chief strongholds of

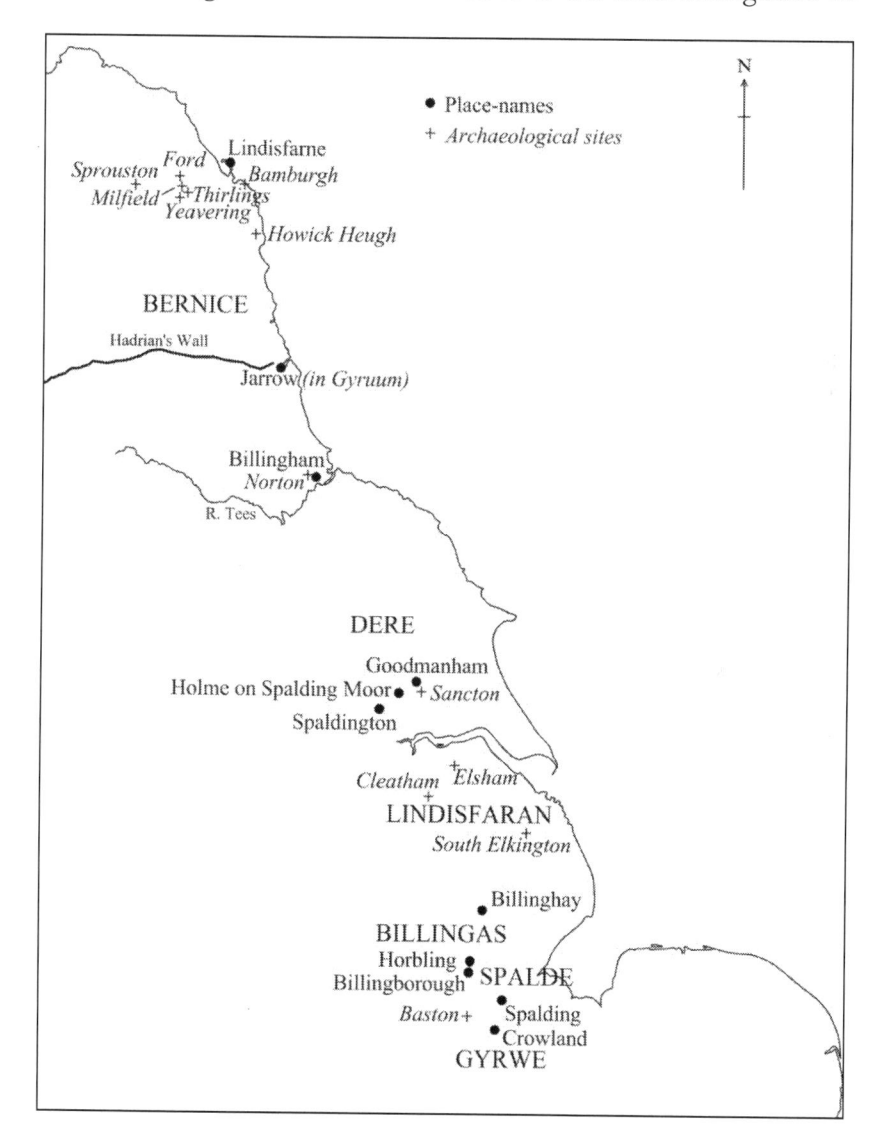

Fig. 46 Map of Lincolnshire, Lindisfarne and the North, showing key sites, groups and place-names discussed in Chapter 6

the Bernician kings from the middle of the sixth century onwards (Figs 47 and 48).[32] Indeed, even if the literary references are left to one side, it has to be recognized that the archaeological evidence is fully in accord with the idea that it was the Lindisfarne–Bamburgh region, not that around Hadrian's Wall, which was the main heartland of the kingdom of Bernicia in the sixth and earlier seventh centuries. Not only are several early 'palace' sites known from this region, including that at Yeavering, but the cemeteries at Bamburgh and Sprouston also dwarf all other known Bernician cemeteries.[33]

All told, the etymologically derived notion that Lindisfarne was settled by *Lindisfaran* – colonists from *Lindissi*, far to the south – finds some very considerable support in the archaeology of the region. The available evidence strongly suggests that Anglo-Saxon activity in the

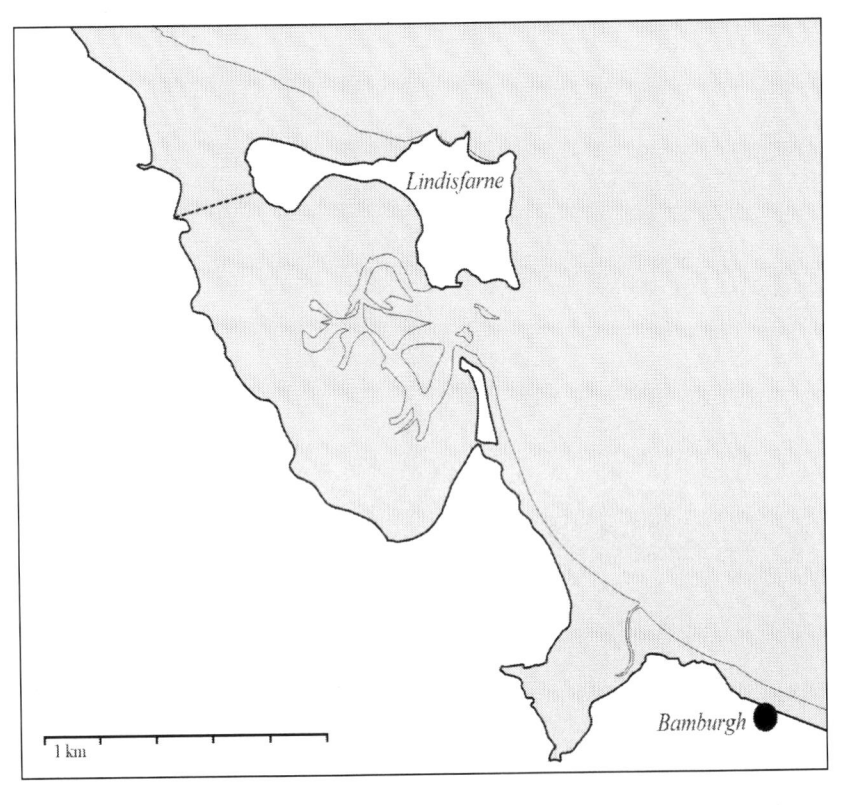

Fig. 47 Map of Lindisfarne, showing the island, sands and causeway, along with the position of the fort of Bamburgh

**Fig. 48 Bamburgh castle as seen from Lindisfarne, showing the
proximity of these two early Bernician sites**
Source: Akuppa

Lindisfarne region was not part of a natural and gradual northwards
expansion of Anglo-Saxon rule from a base around Hadrian's Wall,
but rather the result of a sixth-century marine migration to the
Lindisfarne region, just as the etymology of the name would require.[34]
The problem is that the written and archaeological evidence
additionally indicates that this same area was a crucial heartland of the
late sixth- and seventh-century Bernician kings. It is consequently
difficult to avoid associating the archaeologically observed mid- to
late sixth-century migration to the region around Lindisfarne with the
arrival of either the founders of the kingdom of Bernicia or the
ancestors of the same.[35] If this is correct, it is unlikely that another
group would be subsequently allowed to settle the island of
Lindisfarne, given the apparent status of the island as a royal territory
and the fact that the neighbouring fortress of Bamburgh was 'the
royal city' of the Bernicians.[36] Furthermore, neither the archaeological
nor the textual evidence supports the idea of a previous Anglo-Saxon
migration to the region that took place before the mid-sixth century.
The natural conclusion would, therefore, seem to be that the

migration of the *Lindisfaran* to Lindisfarne (recorded by the place-name 'the island of the *Lindisfaran*') was probably identical with the settlement of the ancestors of the historically recorded Bernician kings, as no other instance of migration to this area is recorded or plausible. That is to say, it seems quite possible that the Bernician royal *Idingas* were ultimately *Lindisfaran* who had migrated to this region from the Anglo-Saxon kingdom of *Lindissi*.[37]

This conclusion is, it has to be said, nowhere near as problematical as might be supposed. No explicit statement of the origins of the ancestors of the historical *Idingas* is found in the early medieval narrative sources which might contradict the idea that they were *Lindisfaran*. At the same time, it can scarcely be doubted that any mid-sixth-century group which migrated to the Lindisfarne–Bamburgh area must have come from the older Anglian settlements to the south (rather than directly from the continent), of which those in *Lindissi* were significant examples.[38] At present, therefore, we have no good reason to reject the suggestion that the founders of the kingdom of Bernicia were *Lindisfaran* who had moved up the coast to Lindisfarne–Bamburgh. Moreover, a further argument can be offered in support of both the credibility of the above derivation of Lindisfarne from 'the island of the *Lindisfaran*' and the suggestion that Anglo-Saxons from the Lincoln region were of central importance to the origins of Northumbria.

Although the Lindisfarne–Bamburgh region certainly seems to have been the early heartland of Bernician power, by the latter part of the seventh century a secondary royal heartland also existed (and had perhaps come to dominate) in the south of the kingdom around the River Tyne, with the famous monastery at Jarrow being a significant centre within this.[39] This monastery was royally endowed on a substantial scale in 681–2, possibly with the intention to create a royal family minster close by an important royal residence, and it has been argued by Ian Wood that Jarrow was in fact located next to the main base of the late seventh-century Northumbrian royal war fleet.[40] In the light of all of this, it is important to note that the name 'Jarrow' is actually an Old English population-group name, *Gyrwe*, with the early spellings all involving the dative plural ending, so that the name means 'at the settlement of the *Gyrwe*'.[41] The significance of this in the present context cannot be underestimated, as the existence of a significant Middle Anglian population group named the *Gyrwe* in southern Lincolnshire and northern Cambridgeshire has been discussed at length in the previous chapter.[42] Whilst it is not impossible that an identically formed population-group name – deriving from Old English *gyr* ('mud') – was coined in both the Fenland and the Jarrow region, the coincidence is arresting. Quite simply, it would seem that at the centre of both of the historically recorded Bernician 'heartlands' there was a place whose name appears to involve an Anglo-Saxon group-name which is well attested in the Lincoln region.

This pattern is replicated when we turn from historically defined major centres of early Northumbria to those observed archaeologically. In Bernicia most early Anglo-Saxon cemeteries seem to have been small. The three largest known cemeteries were all located at early royal sites in the Lindisfarne–Bamburgh region (Bamburgh, Yeavering, and Sprouston). Aside from these, by far the largest cemetery so far found is that at Norton in what was probably the far south of the Bernician kingdom, where 117 inhumations and three cremations have been excavated (compare, for example, the 15 inhumations from Howick Heugh).[43] Although the cemetery itself began in the early sixth century, the place-name Norton was probably coined in the ninth century or afterwards and therefore cannot reflect the name of the settlement or estate which this cemetery served.[44] However, only half a mile to the east of the cemetery is Billingham, a pre-Viking ecclesiastical estate-centre that bears a name which is 'one of the earliest Old English settlement forms to survive' in the region and which current place-name chronologies would place securely within the early Anglo-Saxon period.[45] Needless to say, this name – *Billingaham* in 1085, 'the estate/homestead of the *Billingas*'[46] – once again references a group-name which is also attested in Lincolnshire, where it seems to have belonged to a significant population group which inhabited a major *regio* of *Lindissi*.[47] This is, of course, intriguing, and in this context it may be worth noting that the excavators considered the cemetery at Norton to have been founded by settlers 'from a region further south in Anglian England, such as Yorkshire or Lincolnshire'.[48] Of course, an independent generation of this group-name in Northumbria is possible, but the coincidence is thought-provoking.

Turning to the southern part of Northumbria, we find a similar situation. Here, the probable original centre of the Anglo-Saxon kingdom of Deira was located in the vicinity of Sancton (East Yorkshire). This is not only the location of the largest and earliest Anglo-Saxon cemetery in Deira – which seems to have its origins in the fifth century and from which the remains of 454 cremated individuals have been excavated – but the site of the principal heathen shrine of Deira, according to Bede, was also to be found only a few miles to the north at Goodmanham.[49] Both Nick Higham and Christopher Loveluck have suggested that the position of Sancton on the Roman road running north from the Humber, combined with its characteristically Southumbrian burial rite, are suggestive of the foundation of Deira by immigrants who arrived via the Humber, probably from northern Lindsey. Moreover, there are close links between the cremation urns found at Sancton and those from the Lincolnshire cremation cemeteries of Cleatham, Elsham, South Elkington and Baston.[50] This, in itself, is highly noteworthy in the present context. The situation becomes even more interesting, however, when it is recognized that, just to the west of Sancton, there is an extensive district known as Spalding Moor (*Spaldinghemore* in 1172) that includes a hamlet called Spaldington on its south side, both of which names contain the population-group name *Spaldingas*.[51] Once again, the same group-name has been studied in the previous chapter as that of an important group within pre-Viking Lincolnshire (the *Spalde/Spaldingas*), and once again the coincidence is arresting, particularly as the Baston cremation cemetery has been tentatively associated with the Lincolnshire *Spalde/Spaldingas*.[52]

Whilst these instances of population-group names occurring both in Northumbria and in southern Lincolnshire might be individually dismissed as independently generated names, with their similarity to the Lincolnshire group-names being the result of coincidence, the combined weight of these coincidences is difficult to explain away. Furthermore, in each case the group-name is found at or next to some of the most important sites in Northumbria, as identifiable both from the archaeological and textual evidence (Fig. 46). Given this, the simplest and most credible solution may well be that Anglo-Saxon population groups from Lincolnshire did indeed play a major role in both the settlement of Northumbria and the foundation of the kingdoms of Bernicia and Deira, as the place-name Lindisfarne implies. Although this evidence is not sufficient to put the case beyond all doubt, unless all three of the above names are held to be mere coincidences then these place-names do suggest that a migration to Lindisfarne might be plausibly seen as part of a larger role played by the Anglo-Saxon population groups of the Lincoln region in Northumbrian prehistory, with this perhaps being a further indication of the importance of the Lincoln region in the early Anglo-Saxon period, as argued for earlier in this study.[53]

Summary: Lindisfarne and the *Lindisfaran*

The argument pursued in the present chapter has covered a number of areas and its findings can be summarized as follows. First and foremost, it has to be said that attempts to avoid deriving the place-name Lindisfarne from the group-name *Lindisfaran*, relying instead upon a British or Irish etymology, fail to carry conviction and are beset by problems. The only credible solution to the name Lindisfarne would appear to be that it does indeed involve the Old English population-group name *Lindisfaran*, and moreover that the *Lindisfaran* of Lindisfarne ('the island of the *Lindisfaran*') are identical with the *Lindisfaran* who lived in *Lindissi*. In other words, it would seem that at some point Lindisfarne was settled by migrants from *Lindissi*. Furthermore, this conclusion does not stand alone. For example, the archaeological evidence from the kingdom of Bernicia offers considerable support for this etymology, insofar as the area around and inland from Lindisfarne looks to have been settled by mid-sixth-century Anglo-Saxon immigrants, who – given the paucity of early Anglo-Saxon material to the immediate south of this region – probably had arrived there as the result of a marine migration from more southerly Anglo-Saxon centres. Equally, the idea that these migrants originated in the Lincoln region gains further credence from the fact that other major Lincolnshire population-group names are all similarly attested in place-names found at or close by key sites within Northumbria, whilst Sancton cremation cemetery – probably the original 'central place' of the kingdom of Deira – had strong links to the cemeteries of the Lincoln region.

The available evidence also raises the possibility that not only was Lindisfarne founded by *Lindisfaran* who had moved up the coast from Lincolnshire, but that these *Lindisfaran* went on to provide the Bernician ruling dynasty, the *Idingas*. Fundamentally, the archaeologically evidenced sixth-century migration to, and settlement of, the Lindisfarne–Bamburgh region is difficult to dissociate from the supposed foundation of the kingdom of Bernicia in the mid-sixth century, with both the literary and the archaeological evidence indicating that the core of the Bernician kingdom did indeed lie in the Lindisfarne–Bamburgh region. Given that Bamburgh, 'the royal city' of Bernicia, is only four miles from Lindisfarne, and Lindisfarne seems to have been a significant, early Bernician royal possession, it is hardly credible that any migration of *Lindisfaran* to Lindisfarne would have postdated the foundation of Bernicia. At the same time, however, there is no archaeological or early textual support for a migration of Anglo-Saxons from *Lindissi* to the Lindisfarne region that antedated the middle of the sixth century. The implication would therefore seem to be that the founders of the Bernician kingdom or their ancestors were themselves the *Lindisfaran* embodied in the etymology of Lindisfarne argued for here. Certainly, there is no early medieval evidence which might contradict this notion, and such an interpretation once again seems more than credible, given the Lincolnshire links of the probable original centre of the kingdom of Deira (Sancton) and the apparent presence of other major Lincolnshire group-names at or next to some of the most important sites in early Northumbria.[54]

This is just about as far as we can go with the available evidence. Such an arguably major role for the Anglo-Saxon population groups of the Lincoln region in the settlement and conquest of Northumbria is, needless to say, intriguing. Not only can it enable us to develop a more detailed understanding of the expansion of the area under Anglo-Saxon control in the fifth and sixth centuries, but it is also potentially useful in other ways. So, for example, a movement into the north by groups from the Lincoln region offers a very good context for recent suggestions that at least some members of the Northumbrian elite in the seventh century were somehow descended from the ruling house of *Lindissi*.[55] Similarly, an origin for the *Gyrwe* of Jarrow in the *Gyrwe* of southern Lincolnshire and Cambridgeshire can help to explain why Bede – who was based at Jarrow monastery –

seems to have been so interested in the Middle Anglian *Gyrwe* and accorded this *regio* a higher-than-normal status, referring to it a number of times, including once as a *prouincia*.[56] Finally, a Lincolnshire origin for the rulers of Northumbria would provide a credible context for the considerable Northumbrian interest in controlling *Lindissi* before 679, as was discussed in Chapter 4.[57]

As to why population groups from the Lincoln region were motivated to move into Northumbria and form settlements and communities there, this is very much open to debate. It is, of course, likely that simple proximity was a significant factor, at least with regard to Sancton and Deira, but other factors could well have played a role too. It might be worth considering, for example, whether the continued existence and regional dominance of the British 'country of **Lindēs*' into the sixth century might have acted to restrict the political and military freedom of action of the immigrant groups in the Lincoln region and so encouraged at least some of their members to seek more fruitful opportunities for military adventure and advancement in the British North.[58] Such a scenario is certainly not impossible, though its potential importance ought not to be overstated. There was, after all, a general expansion of Anglo-Saxon control and cultural influence in eastern Britain in this period, and the links between Lincolnshire and Northumbria may largely result from this process. Indeed, the archaeologically attested migration into the Lindisfarne–Bamburgh region actually broadly coincides with the suggested period in which British **Lindēs* came to an end.

Perhaps more significant is the possibility of some sort of 'pull' factor encouraging members of Anglo-Saxon population groups from the Lincoln region to move into the north, particularly with regard to the Lindisfarne region, which was so far beyond the pre-existing zones of major Anglo-Saxon activity. It has certainly been argued in the past that the evidence for a limited early Anglo-Saxon presence both around Hadrian's Wall and in southern Scotland best fits a model wherein the Anglo-Saxons were somehow employed by the Britons of these regions as a military force. Is it credible that such a situation might explain the presence of *Lindisfaran* in the Lindisfarne–Bamburgh region too?[59]

In considering this possibility, we do need to be wary of venturing too far into the realms of speculation. On the other hand, the notion that the *Lindisfaran* were allowed to settle in the far north in return for military service to the British rulers of the Gododdin, within whose territory Lindisfarne and Bamburgh probably originally lay, is not entirely without merit.[60] First, it is perhaps difficult to see the recorded 'dispersed and unfortified' sixth-century Anglo-Saxon settlements which existed inland of Lindisfarne as those of aggressive Anglian invaders who had seized control of the coast from a still-powerful British kingdom, as Ken Dark has recently pointed out.[61] Second, the early Welsh poem *Y Gododdin* would seem to imply that men from the Lincoln region fought in the mid- to late sixth-century Gododdin war-band at *Catraeth*, on the basis of the reading proposed earlier in this study. If this does reflect reality, rather than later poetic speculation as to the participants in this battle, then the coincidence is most intriguing and it would not seem unreasonable to associate the *lynwyssawr*, 'men of *Linnuis*/*Lindēs*', in the Gododdin war-band with the *Lindisfaran* from *Lindēs*/*Lindissi* who were settled in the south of the Gododdin's territory at this time. Indeed, such an association may gather some additional support from stanza A.47 of *Y Gododdin*, where the attacking army at *Catraeth* is referred to as 'the army of Gododdin and Bernicia'.[62] Of course, the matter is impossible to establish with certainty, given the nature of the materials available to us, but the above points are at least suggestive and it hardly needs mentioning that such an arrangement with the rulers of a British kingdom would probably have been more than familiar to members of the *Lindisfaran*.

Beyond Northumbria – Mercia and the *Hrepingas*

If there are indications that the Anglo-Saxon population groups of the Lincoln region played a central role in the process of conquering and Anglicizing Britain north of the Humber, founding settlements bearing their group-names at or close by some of the key sites in early Northumbria and even potentially providing the Bernician royal dynasty, what of other areas located away from the primary regions of immigration, such as Mercia and the West Midlands?

There is certainly some evidence suggestive of the origins of the 'Anglo-Saxons' involved in the conquest and Anglicization of the Midlands. For example, attention has been directed in the past to place-name evidence that would seem to indicate that the Mercian royal *Iclingas* were initially based in East/Middle Anglia before moving to their later middle Trent heartlands.[63] Similarly, the Worcestershire names Conderton (*Cantuaretun*), Whitsun Brook (*Wixenabroc*) and perhaps Phepson (*Fepsetnatune*) imply the presence of members of the *Cantware* of Kent and the Middle Anglian *Wixan* and *Feppingas* in this part of the West Midlands.[64] With regard to a possible role for population groups from the Lincoln region in Mercia and the West Midlands, the evidence we have is limited compared with Northumbria, but it is nonetheless important, being focused on Repton in Derbyshire, the site of a major seventh-century monastic estate-centre and the burial ground of the eighth- and ninth-century Mercian kings.[65]

The place-name Repton (*Hreopa dune/Hrypadun*) derives from a group-name *Hreope/Hrype* and means the 'Hill of the tribe called *Hreope/Hrype*', but what is particularly interesting is that this seems not to have been the only form of this group-name in existence in the pre-Viking period. It is now generally agreed that the group- and territory-name *Hrepingas*, which is recorded as the name of a large territory granted to Breedon monastery *c.* 675, was an alternative form of this group-name (compare *Spalde* and *Spaldingas*) and that the grant of the territory of the *Hrepingas* to Abbot Hædda probably records the foundation of Repton monastery.[66] This is significant for two reasons. The first is that the *Hreope/Hrepingas* have been consequently considered to be one of the major population groups of the original Mercian kingdom, alongside the *Tomsætan* and the *Pencersætan*.[67] The second is that the *-ingas* form of this group-name – *Hrepingas* – also occurs in Lincolnshire in the place-name Rippingale *(Repinghale, Repingehale)*, meaning 'the *halh* (valley) of the *Hrepingas*', where it seems to refer to a group that occupied a territory to the south of the *Billingas*.[68]

Ideally, of course, one would wish to have several more examples of such dual occurrences of a group-name in Mercia and the Lincoln region, as is found in Northumbria, in order to avoid the risks of being misled by coincidence or a relationship in the opposite direction.[69] On the other hand, the evidence of the *Hreope/Hrepingas* is at the very least intriguing in the context of the material discussed above, and the Rippingale area certainly seems to have seen notable and high-status activity in the early Anglo-Saxon period.[70]

Notes to Chapter 6

1   An early instance is found in Gervase of Tilbury's *Otia Imperialia*, ed. and
     trans. S. E. Banks and J. W. Binns (Oxford, 2002), II.25 at pp. 528–9,
     where he tries to solve the apparent similarity by claiming that Lincoln was
     once called Lindisfarne.

2   See above, p. 59, and C. Green, 'The British kingdom of Lindsey',
     Cambrian Medieval Celtic Studies, 56 (2008), 3–4 and fn. 15; T. Charles-
     Edwards and P. Wormald, 'Addenda' in J. M. Wallace-Hadrill, *Bede's
     Ecclesiastical History of the English People: A Historical Commentary* (Oxford,
     1988), pp. 234–5; E. Ekwall, *The Concise Oxford Dictionary of English Place-
     Names*, fourth edition (Oxford, 1960), p. 298; V. Watts, *The Cambridge
     Dictionary of English Place-Names* (Cambridge, 2004), p. 374; R. Coates and
     A. Breeze, *Celtic Voices, English Places. Studies of the Celtic Impact on Place-names
     in England* (Stamford, 2000), pp. 247–8.

3   See, for example, Watts, *Dictionary*, p. 374; J. T. Koch (ed.), *Celtic Culture, A
     Historical Encyclopedia* (Oxford, 2006), p. 1158; B. Cox, 'The place names of
     the earliest English records', *English Place-Name Society Journal*, 8 (1976), 24;
     Wallace-Hadrill, *Bede's Ecclesiastical History*, p. 234.

4   See Koch, *Celtic Culture*, p. 1158; *Historia Brittonum*, chapters 63 and 65, ed.
     and trans. J. Morris in *Nennius. British History and the Welsh Annals* (London,
     1980), pp. 79, 80; Coates & Breeze, *Celtic Voices*, pp. 241–2; and A. Breeze,
     '*Medcaut*, the Brittonic name of Lindisfarne', *Northern History*, 42 (2005),
     187–8.

5   Wallace-Hadrill, *Bede's Ecclesiastical History*, p. 234.

6   As in Watts, *Dictionary*, p. 374; Koch, *Celtic Culture*, p. 1158.

7   Watts, *Dictionary*, p. 374.

8   See below, p. 242; K. H. Jackson, *Language and History in Early Britain*
     (Edinburgh, 1953), p. 696.

9   The *-nd-* stage 'is only found in eastern names that may easily have been
     borrowed well before 500'; indeed, it had already become *-nn-* in the
     British-loan place-name (King's) Lynn (< *lindon*), which can scarcely have
     been first encountered by Anglian immigrants much after 500 – see P.
     Sims-Williams, 'Dating the transition to Neo-Brittonic: phonology and
     history, 400–600' in Alfred Bammesberger and A. Wollmann (eds), *Britain,
     400–600. Language and History* (Heidelberg, 1990), p. 247; P. Sims-Williams,
     The Celtic Inscriptions of Britain. Phonology and Chronology, c. 400–1200 (Oxford,
     2003), p. 283; Jackson, *Language and History*, p. 513. Compare, for example,
     the diphthongisation of Late British/Archaic Welsh *-ē-* to *-ui-*, which was
     only complete in Welsh writing by the second half of the eighth century,
     but must have occurred orally in the early sixth century (Sims-Williams,

'Dating the transition'; Sims-Williams, *Celtic Inscriptions*, especially pp. 281–90).

10 Coates & Breeze, *Celtic Voices*, pp. 243–59.

11 The group-name *Lindisware* occurs in 'Anglo-Saxon Chronicle' MS E, s.a. 678, ed. S. Irvine in *The Anglo-Saxon Chronicle. A Collaborative Edition. Volume 7: MS. E* (Cambridge, 2004), p. 33, and trans. D. Whitelock *et al* in *The Anglo-Saxon Chronicle: A Revised Translation* (London, 1961), p. 22.

12 Green, 'British kingdom', 3–4, fn. 15, and J. Insley and M. Eggers, 'Lindsey', *Reallexikon der Germanischen Altertumskunde*, 18 (Berlin, 2001), 475.

13 See, for example, N. P. Brooks, 'The creation and early structure of the kingdom of Kent' in S. Bassett (ed.), *The Origins of Anglo-Saxon Kingdoms* (London, 1989), pp. 68, 69, 72; D. N. Dumville, 'Essex, Middle Anglia and the expansion of Mercia' in Bassett, *Origins of Anglo-Saxon Kingdoms*, p. 127.

14 M. Gelling, 'The name Lindsey', *Anglo-Saxon England*, 18 (1989), 31–2, especially 32; Coates & Breeze, *Celtic Voices*, pp. 243–4.

15 As with Gelling, 'Lindsey', 32, whose etymology seems to have been the product of desperation rather than conviction, and is not credible for this and other reasons (above, pp. 79–80, endnote 15).

16 See especially the discussion by Charles-Edwards and Wormald in Wallace-Hadrill, *Bede's Ecclesiastical History*, p. 235; also Green, 'British kingdom', pp. 3–4, and above, p. 59. The key point is that *faran* can certainly refer to people who undertake or have undertaken temporary journeys, after which they return or returned to their homes, but it can also refer to people who have undertaken permanent journeys (migrations): Wallace-Hadrill, *Bede's Ecclesiastical History*, p. 235. See, for example, the 'Laws of Ine' (ed. and trans. F. L. Attenborough, *The Laws of the Earliest English Kings* (Cambridge, 1922), pp. 56, 57); the 'Vespasian Psalter', 10.2 (ed. H. Sweet, *The Oldest English Texts* (London, 1885), pp. 198, 461); and the 'Old English *Exodus*', line 555. In light of its meaning and the continental cognates cited below, the name is likely to have been a very early coinage, perhaps either as a general collective name for the immigrants engaged by the Britons of **Lindēs* to defend their territory (note, there is evidence for links between the Lincolnshire cremation cemeteries from the earliest phases of these sites: see K. Leahy, *The Anglo-Saxon Kingdom of Lindsey* (Stroud, 2007), pp. 50–1; K. Leahy, *'Interrupting the Pots': The Excavation of Cleatham Anglo-Saxon Cemetery* (York, 2007), pp. 127–8) or, alternatively, as that of a single immigrant group which later took control of **Lindēs* and so had their name more widely adopted (*i.e.* the group which provided the royal line of *Lindissi*, see above, pp. 101–03).

17 'Chronicle of Fredegar', IV.41, 44 and 55, ed. and trans. J. M. Wallace-Hadrill, *The Fourth Book of the Chronicle of Fredegar with its Continuations* (London, 1960); A. C. Murray, *Germanic Kinship Structure: Studies in Law and Society in Antiquity and the Early Middle Ages* (Toronto, 1983), pp. 89–97; M.

Innes, 'Land, freedom and the making of the medieval West', *Trans. Royal Hist.*, 16 (2006), 72; M. Lupoi, *The Origins of the European Legal Order* (Cambridge, 2000), p. 81; G. Halsall, 'Social identities and social relationships in early medieval Gaul' in I. Wood (ed.), *Franks and Alamanni in the Merovingian Period: An Ethnographic Perspective* (Woodbridge, 1998), p. 151; W. Goffart, *Rome's Fall and After* (London, 1989), p. 114.

18 See, for example, Wallace-Hadrill, *Bede's Ecclesiastical History*, p. 235; D. Herlihy, *Medieval Households* (Cambridge, Mass., 1985), pp. 45–6; W. Goffart, *Barbarians and Romans, A.D. 418–584: The Techniques of Accommodation* (Princeton, 1980), pp. 252–8; Murray, *Germanic Kinship Structure*, pp. 89–97; G. Althoff and C. Carroll, *Family, Friends and Followers: Political and Social Bonds in Medieval Europe* (Cambridge, 2004), p. 30; G. Tabacco, *The Struggle for Power in Medieval Italy: Structures of Political Rule* (Cambridge, 1989), pp. 93–4; T. S. Burns, *A History of the Ostrogoths* (Bloomington, 1984), pp. 167–8.

19 K. Malone, *Widsith*, 2nd edn (Copenhagen, 1962), p. 24. Note, however, that whilst this might offer further evidence in support of *faran* as a credible and legitimate group-name element, it probably has a different meaning from 'the people who migrated, moved permanently' in this instance.

20 Coates & Breeze, *Celtic Voices*, p. 242.

21 Perhaps, like New York, the site was 'so good they named it twice'? (Gerard Kenny, *New York, New York*, RCA 1978).

22 Coates & Breeze, *Celtic Voices*, pp. 249–55, partly inspired by the etymological speculations of Symeon of Durham in the twelfth century (*Libellus de Exordio*, ii.5).

23 See Coates & Breeze, *Celtic Voices*, pp. 250–5, for some acknowledgement of these and other issues. Here it is admitted that the name **Lindis-feranna* is – if it ever existed – likely to be 'unique, created in a special way', and the reader is invited to decide whether the supposed necessity for and plausibility of the etymology proposed can justify such 'specialness' (p. 252). If there ever was a stream called *Lindis*, then its name is surely more likely simply to derive from that of the island than *vice versa*, particularly given that *Lindis* as a standalone stream-name is etymologically dubious.

24 Coates & Breeze, *Celtic Voices*, p. 243. With regard to the plural 'domains, territories' (*feranna*), this is required in order to construct a hypothetical Archaic Irish form which would produce the recorded Old English forms with a final -*a* (Coates & Breeze, pp. 254–5), but one struggles to see why *ferann* ('domain, territory') would be plural in this hypothetical place-name other than for the convenience of the etymologist, despite Richard Coates' speculations (pp. 252, 254).

25 Needless to say, this rejection of an Irish etymology for Lindisfarne is a further argument against the idea that we can somehow have the group-

name *Lindisfaran* as derivative of the place-name Lindisfarne, as this theory depends upon there being a credible non-Old English etymology for the island-name. Note, Coates' proposed Irish etymology for the Farne Islands (Coates & Breeze, *Celtic Voices*, pp. 255–6) cannot be used in support of his Lindisfarne etymology, as it is derived from it, and if the latter is rejected then so must the former be too. However, his suggestion that their name means simply the islands 'of (Lindis)farne' may be worth consideration, whatever the origins of the name Lindisfarne.

26 This Old English etymology has been frequently suggested and discussed, although its implications have not usually been followed through (Ekwall, *Dictionary*, pp. 298–9; A. D. Mills, *A Dictionary of English Place-Names* (Oxford, 1991), p. 211; Watts, *Dictionary*, p. 374; Sawyer, *Anglo-Saxon Lincolnshire*, p. 47; S. Bassett, 'Lincoln and the Anglo-Saxon see of Lindsey', *Anglo-Saxon England*, 18 (1989), 8 and 30). The only real case to be offered against it has been that of Coates (Coates & Breeze, *Celtic Voices*, pp. 241–59), which depends fundamentally upon the group-name *Lindisfaran* having never really existed and instead being falsely derived from the place-name Lindisfarne, a position rejected above; otherwise, there are only some very minor possible issues with a few variants of the name Lindisfarne (discussed in Coates & Breeze, *Celtic Voices*, pp. 246, 253), and these are of debatable significance and meaning.

27 For example, Ekwall, *Oxford*, p. 299, and Bassett, 'Lincoln', 30, for this treatment of *Lindisfaran* within the name Lindisfarne. See also Watts, *Dictionary*, p. 374, who offered 'the island of the travellers to and from Lindsey' as an alternative to his British etymology of Lindisfarne.

28 Bassett, 'Lincoln', 30, speculates that frequent voyaging to and fro as a result of trading activity might explain this, but this does not seem particularly plausible given the early period with which we are here concerned (if the name Lindisfarne derives from an Old English population-group name *Lindisfaran*, it seems unlikely to have had its origins after 635, when the island was given to Bishop Aidán for a monastery: Bede, *Historia Ecclesiastica*, III.3).

29 Charles-Edwards and Wormald in Wallace-Hadrill, *Bede's Ecclesiastical History*, pp. 234–5; Ekwall, *Dictionary*, pp. 298–9.

30 On the Lindisfarne region, see, for example, C. Scull, 'Post-Roman phase I at Yeavering: a re-consideration', *Med. Arch.*, 36 (1992), especially pp. 60–1; R. Miket, 'A restatement of evidence from Bernician Anglo-Saxon burials' in P. A. Rahtz, T. M. Dickinson and L. Watts (eds), *Anglo-Saxon Cemeteries, 1979* (Oxford, 1980), pp. 289–306; S. J. Sherlock and M. G. Welch, *An Anglo-Saxon Cemetery at Norton, Cleveland* (London, 1992), pp. 1–9, 103–6; R. Cramp, 'Anglo-Saxon settlement' in J. C. Chapman and H. C. Mytum (eds), *Settlement in North Britain, 1000 BC – AD 1000* (Oxford, 1983), pp. 263–97; C. J. Scull and A. F. Harding, 'Two early medieval cemeteries at

Milfield, Northumberland', *Durham Archaeological Journal*, 6 (1990), 1–29; K. R. Dark and P. Dark, *Britain and the End of the Roman Empire* (Stroud, 2000), pp. 205–7; M. Ziegler, 'The Anglo-British cemetery at Bamburgh', *The Heroic Age*, 4 (2001). The evidence for sixth-century activity in this area derives from both mortuary and settlement archaeology. Whilst there is some debate over whether the earliest stages at Yeavering were British or Anglian (although Scull's argument for an Anglian origin appears persuasive), both models have the site as an Anglian settlement in the mid- to late sixth century (Scull, 'Post-Roman Phase I', 60; B. Hope-Taylor, *Yeavering. An Anglo-British Centre of Early Northumbria* (London, 1977), pp. 150–8, 310–13). Although such debates about origins are, owing to the nature of the evidence from these sites, possible for other early Bernician settlements too (for example, the sixth-century site at Thirlings), the presence of *Grubenhäuser* at these settlements is, as Scull has pointed out, indicative of Anglian occupation (Scull, 'Post-Roman Phase I', 61). On the nature of the Anglo-Saxon activity around Hadrian's Wall, see K. R. Dark, 'A sub-Roman re-defence of Hadrian's Wall?', *Britannia*, 22 (1992), 111–20; Dark, *Britain*, pp. 193–200; and C. A. Snyder, *An Age of Tyrants: Britain and the Britons A.D. 400–600* (Stroud, 1998), pp. 168–73. With regard to the early Anglo-Saxon material found in the area between the Lindisfarne region and the Wall, the fifteen inhumations at Howick Heugh (Northumberland) can be no more closely dated than the early Anglo-Saxon period generally and are unlikely to antedate the seventh century (Miket, 'Burials', pp. 293, 295, 298), and the same is probably true of the handful of burials from Great Tosson, Northumberland (Sherlock & Welch, *Norton*, p. 2; Cramp, 'Anglo-Saxon settlement', p. 269; Miket, 'Burials', pp. 294, 298; though see S. Lucy, 'Changing burial rites in Northumbria, A.D. 500–750' in J. Hawkes and S. Mills (eds), *Northumbria's Golden Age* (Stroud, 1999), pp. 34–5, 39).

31 This is suggested in N. J. Higham, *The Kingdom of Northumbria, AD 350–1100* (Stroud, 1993), p. 82; N. J. Higham, *The Northern Counties to AD 1000* (London, 1986), pp. 254, 256–60.

32 Bede, *Historia Ecclesiastica*, III.3, III.6, III.12, and III.16. Bede makes it clear that he considered Bamburgh (named, he says, after an early Bernician queen of *c.* 600) to have been 'the royal city' of seventh-century Bernicia – both an *urbs* and a *ciuitas* – and his notice of the granting of neighbouring Lindisfarne to the Ionan missionaries who were closely associated with the Bernician royal house implies that this island was also a significant royal possession in the early seventh century. I. N. Wood sees the Lindisfarne–Bamburgh area as the earliest Northumbrian centre, with the Wall/Tyne area becoming key in the latter part of the seventh century, taking over from Bamburgh (I. N. Wood, 'Bede's Jarrow' in C. A. Lees and G. R. Overing (eds), *A Place to Believe In: Locating Medieval Landscapes* (Philadelphia,

2006), pp. 76, 79–80, 83). Interestingly, Bede also names two important Bernician 'royal palaces', Yeavering and *Mælmin*, both of which seem to have been located just inland of Lindisfarne and Bamburgh (*Historia Ecclesiastica*, II.14). For the *Historia Brittonum* references, see chapters 61 and 63 (ed. and trans. Morris, *British History*, pp. 37, 38, 78 and 79).

33   On Yeavering, see Hope-Taylor, *Yeavering*, and Scull, 'Post-Roman Phase I'. See especially Ziegler, 'Bamburgh', on Bamburgh (with a potential total of around 1,000 burials), and I. M. Smith, 'Sprouston, Roxburghshire: an early Anglian centre on the eastern Tweed basin', *Proceedings of the Society of Antiquaries of Scotland*, 121 (1991), 261–94, on Sprouston as a late sixth-/early seventh-century Anglian royal centre with a cemetery containing at least 380 burials (pp. 280–1). Miket ('Burials') and Sherlock & Welch (*Norton*, p. 1) discuss the other known Bernician cemeteries, which are far smaller in scale. Norton was one of the largest, with 120 burials, but it was located well to the south of Hadrian's Wall.

34   It should be noted here that Higham (*Kingdom of Northumbria*, p. 82) has suggested that the statement in *Historia Brittonum* that a mid-sixth-century Bernician king named Ida *iunxit Dinguayrdi guurth Berneich*, 'joined Bamburgh to Bernicia' (§61: ed. and trans. Morris, *British History*, pp. 37, 78) means that the core of Bernicia lay elsewhere, and therefore that Ida was expanding into this region from southern Bernicia. However, even if this ninth-century legend could be relied on to recount events which occurred three hundred years earlier, this is by no means a necessary conclusion. For example, the statement could mean rather that Bamburgh was part of Ida's original territory and from it he conquered the British kingdom of *Berneich*, so that he thus could be said to have 'joined Bamburgh to *Berneich*'. Indeed, even if it does mean that Bamburgh was a secondary possession, then the 'original' core to which Ida – if he existed – was adding could simply be the island of Lindisfarne. In the light of all this, any attempt to overturn the above rejection of a land-based migration from the Wall on the basis of this statement in *Historia Brittonum* is unlikely to be credible.

35   This is particularly the case given that Bede places the origins of the Bernician kingdom in the mid-sixth century and associates it with Ida (Bede, *Historia Ecclesiastica*, V.24). See also the Northumbrian king-list found in the 'Moore Memoranda', which seems to confirm this dating (P. H. Blair, 'The *Moore Memoranda* on Northumbrian history' in C. Fox and B. Dickens (eds), *The Early Cultures of North-West Europe* (Cambridge, 1950), pp. 245–57). Whilst a mid-ninth-century chronicle fragment says that Ida's grandfather Oesa/Oessa was the first to come to Britain, too much has sometimes been made of this. Even if we had complete confidence in our accounts of Oessa and Ida and the historicity of these annals, this chronicle could not be used to argue that (contrary to the archaeological

evidence) Bernician settlement began two generations before Ida, only that Ida's ancestors arrived somewhere in Britain – not at all necessarily Northumbria – in the late fifth or early sixth century. However, it might well be suspected that this is not a 'genuine' Bernician legend at all, never mind an accurate historical record. The name Oesa/Oessa can hardly be separated from the name Oese/Ossa that occurs as a spelling of the name Oisc, the ancestor of the *Oiscingas* rulers of Kent, around whom 'first migrant' traditions certainly were gathered. In consequence, this supposed grandfather of Ida needs to be viewed with considerable suspicion, and such a borrowing would fit in with other apparent attempts to tie Bernician origins in with Kentish ones, as seen in the *Historia Brittonum*, chapters 38 and 56. See further, D. N. Dumville, 'A new chronicle-fragment of early British history', *EHR*, 88 (1973), 312–14; Higham, *Kingdom of Northumbria*, p. 77; N. P. Brooks, 'The creation and early structure of the kingdom of Kent' in Bassett, *Origins of Anglo-Saxon Kingdoms*, pp. 59–60, 63.

36 See Bede, *Historia Ecclesiastica*, III.6, III.12, and III.16, on Bamburgh and its status, and above, endnote 32.

37 J. N. L. Myres is one of the few who have explicitly recognized this implication of a derivation of *Lindisfarnae/Lindisfarena ea* from *Lindisfaran* + *ēg* (J. N. L. Myres, *The English Settlements* (Oxford, 1986), p. 199). Ida is first named as the ultimate ancestor of the Bernician royal dynasty in Bede's early eighth-century *Historia Ecclesiastica*, V.24.

38 It is occasionally suggested that the *Idingas* could have come to Lindisfarne–Bamburgh from the kingdom of Deira – as by Sherlock & Welch, *Norton*, p. 9 – but there is no early evidence in favour of this proposition, in contrast to the notion that the *Idingas* were *Lindisfaran*.

39 D. Rollason, *Northumbria, 500–1100. Creation and Destruction of a Kingdom* (Cambridge, 2003), pp. 50–1; Wood, 'Bede's Jarrow', especially pp. 79–80, 83–4.

40 Wood, 'Bede's Jarrow', especially pp. 71–3; J. Blair, *The Church in Anglo-Saxon Society* (Oxford, 2005), p. 88.

41 Bede, *Historia Ecclesiastica*, V.21; J. Insley, 'Jarrow (etymology of the name)', *Reallexikon der Germanischen Altertumskunde*, 16 (2000), 38.

42 Above, pp. 167–70.

43 Sherlock & Welch, *Norton*, pp. 1, 3; Smith, 'Sprouston', pp. 280–1; Ziegler, 'Bamburgh'; Miket, 'Burials', at p. 295 for Howick Heugh. On the boundary between Bernicia and Deira, see P. H. Blair, *Anglo-Saxon Northumbria* (London, 1984), essay V; Sherlock & Welch, p. 6; and Wood, 'Bede's Jarrow', pp. 77–9. The number of people buried in this cemetery may have been greater than reported, if antiquarian records of at least one body (with artefacts) being found in this area in the early nineteenth century relate to this cemetery (J. Brewster, *The Parochial History and*

Antiquities of Stockton-upon-Tees, 2nd edn (Stockton-upon-Tees, 1829), p. 10).

44   As noted by Sherlock & Welch, *Norton*, p. 9.

45   Sherlock & Welch, *Norton*, p. 9 and fig. 1, for the location of the cemetery
     relative to Billingham; Symeon of Durham, *Libellus de Exordio*, ii.5–6, iii.20,
     ed. and trans. D. Rollason, in *Symeon of Durham. Libellus de Exordio atque
     Procursu istius hoc est Dunhelmensis Ecclesie* (Oxford, 2000), pp. 92–4, 98–9,
     198–200. Rollason also notes (p. 94) an eighth- and a ninth-century grave
     marker from Billingham church. On place-name chronologies see, for
     example, B. Cox, 'The significance of the distribution of English place-
     names in *-hām* in the Midlands and East Anglia', *Journal of the English Place-
     Name Society*, 5 (1972–3), 15–73; J. Kuurman, 'An examination of the *-ingas*,
     -inga- place-names in the East Midlands', *Journal of the English Place-Name
     Society*, 7 (1974–5), 11–44; and M. Gelling, *Signposts to the Past. Place-names
     and the History of England*, 2nd edn (Chichester, 1988), pp. 111–12.

46   As Mills, *Dictionary*, p. 35, and Ekwall, *Dictionary*, p. 43, *pace* Watts,
     Dictionary, p. 56.

47   Above, pp. 185–200. See, for example, A. Woolf, 'Community, identity
     and kingship in early England' in W. O. Frazer and A. Tyrrell (eds), *Social
     Identity in Early Medieval Britain* (London, 2000), pp. 91–109, on subgroups
     within larger groups being able to have their own identities.

48   Sherlock & Welch, *Norton*, p. 105.

49   Higham, *Kingdom of Northumbria*, pp. 66–7; Bede, *Historia Ecclesiastica*, II.13;
     C. P. Loveluck, 'The development of the Anglo-Saxon landscape,
     economy and society "On Driffield", East Yorkshire, 400–750 AD', *Anglo-
     Saxon Studies in Archaeology and History*, 9 (1996), 29–30. See also H.
     Williams, 'Cemeteries as central places – place and identity in Migration
     Period eastern England' in B. Hårdh and L. Larsson (eds), *Central Places in
     the Migration and Merovingian Periods* (Stockholm, 2002), pp. 341–62.

50   Higham, *Kingdom of Northumbria*, p. 67; Loveluck, 'Anglo-Saxon landscape',
     p. 29. The links between the cemeteries have been recently discussed by
     Kevin Leahy in *Kingdom of Lindsey*, pp. 50–1, 101, and *'Interrupting the Pots'*,
     pp. 127–8. See also J. N. L. Myres, 'Some Anglo-Saxon potters', *Ant.*, 11
     (1937), 389–99, and C. J. Arnold, 'The Sancton-Baston potter', *Scottish
     Archaeological Review*, 2 (1983), 17–30.

51   Ekwall, *Dictionary*, pp. 432–3; Mills, *Dictionary*, pp. 175, 303–4. Spalding
     Moor was drained in the eighteenth century and it is now chiefly
     remembered by the place-name 'Holme on Spalding Moor' (H. E.
     Strickland, *A General View of the Agriculture of the East-Riding of Yorkshire*
     (York, 1812), pp. 29, 199; J. J. Sheahan and T. Whellan, *History and
     Topography of the City of York; the Ainsty Wapentake; and the East Riding of
     Yorkshire* (2 vols, Beverley, 1856), vol. 1, p. 576 and p. 584). It was partially
     mapped by John Cary on his map of the East Riding of Yorkshire,
     published in *Cary's New and Correct English Atlas* (London, 1787).

52 Above, pp. 183–5. It is certainly tempting to wonder whether the Sancton–Baston links might help to explain and/or reflect the presence of *Spaldingas* in the Sancton area.

53 We might also mention here the place-name Wintringham in North Yorkshire, found only around two miles to the south-west of the significant early Anglo-Saxon settlement and cemetery complex at West Heslerton, which seems to refer to a settlement of the *Wintringas* (Ekwall, *Dictionary*, p. 525; Mills, *Dictionary*, p. 364. Note, whilst the name Wintringham is likely to have been coined in the early Anglo-Saxon period, Heslerton probably belongs to a later period – see Cox, 'Earliest English records', and above). The personal name *Wintra* occurs more than once in an Anglo-Saxon context, and so an independent coinage of the group-name *Wintringas* in Deira is certainly not impossible. However, if the *Wintringas* mentioned in the Lincolnshire place-names Winteringham and Winterton were indeed a significant group within *Lindissi* (see above, p. 103), then this would constitute yet another intriguing coincidence to add to those discussed previously. See also below, endnote 70.

54 The suggestion, derived from the Bernician royal genealogy, that the Bernician kings considered the pagan god *Ing* to have been their divine patron – or considered themselves to be an *Inguionic* dynasty, deriving from continental *Inguiones* – may also be of relevance here (M. Miller, 'Royal pedigrees of the insular Dark Ages: a progress report', *History in Africa*, 7 (1980), 213; R. North, *Heathen Gods in Old English Literature* (Cambridge, 1997), especially pp. 42–3; K. I. Sandred, 'Ingham in East Anglia: a new interpretation', *Leeds Studies in English*, 18 (1987), 234–5). This is due to the fact that the most northerly of the four occurrences of the place-name Ingham is in *Lindissi*, three miles from the richest barrow burial in the kingdom (at Caenby), and this name means either 'the estate of the devotees of the deity *Ing*' or 'the estate of the *Inguione*', a tag to mark places as the royal property of a king who claimed to be of an *Inguionic* dynasty (Cameron, *Dictionary*, p. 69; K. Cameron, *The Place-Names of Lincolnshire, VI* (Nottingham, 2001), p. 184; Sandred, pp. 235–6).

55 J. Campbell, 'Bede (673/4–735)', in *The Oxford Dictionary of National Biography*, online edition (Oxford, 2004), *www.oxforddnb.com*; A. Thacker, 'Bede and the ordering of understanding' in S. DeGregorio (ed.), *Innovation and Tradition in the Writings of the Venerable Bede* (Morgantown, 2006), p. 40; above, p. 153.

56 See above, pp. 167–70, on the *Gyrwe*; Bede, *Historia Ecclesiastica*, III. 20, IV.6 and IV.19. The link between the two might also explain Bede's exceptional interest in St Æthelthryth, given that she was once married to a ruler of the South *Gyrwe* named *Tondberct* and later founded the monastery of Ely on what is often thought to have been South Gyrwean lands (above, pp. 169, 215).

57 Above, pp. 150–1. In light of the above, it may also be worth reconsidering J. N. L. Myres' suggestions with regard to the origins and significance of the name *Humbrenses*, which is used for the Northumbrians in the seventh century (Myres, *English Settlements*, pp. 174–6; J. N. L. Myres, 'The Teutonic Settlement of Northern England', *History*, 20 (1935), 250–62, though see Wallace-Hadrill, *Bede's Ecclesiastical History*, pp. 226–8).

58 This would, of course, require that the Britons of **Lindēs* not only exercised a degree of control and influence over the Anglo-Saxon groups within their borders, but also over those who lived beyond them, such as the *Spalde* and the *Gyrwe*. This is not necessarily implausible, however, particularly if Anglian settlement as a whole was initially controlled from Lincoln (see above, pp. 93–4). We might also note, tentatively, the claim of British military success on the river Glen *c.* 500 (discussed above, pp. 182–3).

59 Dark, 'Hadrian's Wall'; Dark, *Britain*, pp. 193–200; E. Proudfoot and C. Aliaga-Kelly, 'Towards an interpretation of anomalous finds and place-names of Anglo-Saxon origin in Scotland', *Anglo-Saxon Studies in Archaeology and History*, 9 (1996), 1–13.

60 On Lindisfarne and Bamburgh having originally lain within Gododdin territory, see, for example, Dumville, 'Northumbria', p. 217; Dark, *Britain*, p. 205; and D. P. Kirby, *The Earliest English Kings*, 2nd edn (London, 2000), p. 58.

61 Dark, *Britain*, pp. 206–7. For the interpretation of the Anglo-Saxons of the Lindisfarne–Bamburgh region as 'a band of pirates', see P. H. Blair, *An Introduction to Anglo-Saxon England*, 2nd edn (Cambridge, 1977), pp. 43–4, and compare D. N. Dumville, 'The origins of Northumbria' in Bassett, *Origins of Anglo-Saxon Kingdoms*, p. 218.

62 Above, pp. 95–9; J. T. Koch, *The Gododdin of Aneirin: Text and Context from Dark-Age North Britain* (Cardiff, 1997), pp. xviii–xxi, xxxviii–xxxix, xli.

63 For example, Myres, *English Settlements*, p. 185; E. Martin, 'The *Iclingas*', *East Anglian Archaeology*, 3 (1976), 132–4; and T. Williamson, *The Origins of Norfolk* (Manchester, 1993), pp. 71–2, though see N. P. Brooks, 'The formation of the Mercian kingdom' in Bassett, *Origins of Anglo-Saxon Kingdoms*, p. 164.

64 P. Sims-Williams, *Religion and Literature in Western England, 600–800* (Cambridge, 1990), p. 32; D. Hooke, *Worcestershire Anglo-Saxon Charter Bounds* (Woodbridge, 1990), pp. 125–9, 167–9, 190–3; Ekwall, *Dictionary*, pp. 120, 365, 514; Watts, *Dictionary*, p. 154.

65 M. Biddle and B. Kjølbye-Biddle, 'Repton' in M. Lapidge *et al* (eds), *The Blackwell Encyclopedia of Anglo-Saxon England* (Oxford, 1999), pp. 390–2.

66 Mills, *Dictionary*, p. 271; A. R. Rumble, '"Hrepingas" reconsidered' in A. Dornier (ed.), *Mercian Studies* (Leicester, 1977), pp. 169–72; A. Dornier, 'The Anglo-Saxon monastery at Breedon-on-the-Hill, Leicestershire' in A.

Dornier (ed.), *Mercian Studies* (Leicester, 1977), p. 158. On *Spalde/Spaldingas*, see above, p. 170.

67 Kirby, *Earliest English Kings*, p. 8; M. Welch, 'The archaeology of Mercia' in M. P. Brown and C. A. Farr (eds), *Mercia. An Anglo-Saxon Kingdom in Europe* (London, 2001), p. 147.

68 Watts, *Dictionary*, p. 501; Cameron, *Dictionary*, p. 102; A. Crowson *et al*, *Anglo-Saxon Settlement on the Siltland of Eastern England* (Heckington, 2005), p. 297.

69 A relationship in the opposite direction has been invoked to explain the presence of place-names involving the group-name *Hwicce* in Middle Anglia (Rutland and Northamptonshire), given that the *Hwicce* are far better known as a people and kingdom recorded in the West Midlands from the seventh century (Sims-Williams, *Religion and Literature*, p. 30; C. Hart, 'The Tribal Hidage', *Trans. Royal Hist.*, fifth series, 21 (1971), 138; F. M. Stenton, 'The historical bearing of place-name studies: the English occupation of southern England' in D. M. Stenton (ed.), *Preparatory to Anglo-Saxon England* (Oxford, 1971), pp. 269–70). However, it should be noted that recent work has considerably strengthened the place-name evidence for the *Hwicce* in Rutland, suggesting that A. H. Smith's interpretation of the *Hwicce* as a Middle Anglian group that moved westwards may be worthy of reconsideration (J. Insley and A. Scharer, 'Hwicce', *Reallexikon der Germanischen Altertumskunde*, 11 (2000), 288–9; B. Cox, *The Place-Names of Rutland* (Nottingham, 1994), pp. xxv–xxvi, 55–6, 61, 221–2; A. H. Smith, 'The Hwicce' in J. B. Bessinger and R. P. Creeds (eds), *Franciplegus: Medieval and Linguistic Studies in Honour of Francis Peabody Magoun Jr* (New York, 1965), pp. 60–2; A. H. Smith, *The Place-Names of Gloucestershire, IV* (Cambridge, 1965), p. 42).

70 See DCMS, *Treasure Annual Report 2003*, p. 83 (a high-status, gold sword pommel of the sixth century found in Rippingale parish in November 2002) and also Crowson *et al*, *Anglo-Saxon Settlement*, pp. 56–69, 297; Portable Antiquities Scheme NLM997, NLM4277. It should be noted that the group-name *Hreope/Hrype* is also present in the place-name Ripon (*Hrypum, Hreopum*) and related names in North Yorkshire (Watts, *Dictionary*, p. 501; Rumble, '"Hrepingas" reconsidered', pp. 170–1 – note especially Riponshire, *Ripeshire*). If the *Hrepingas* of Rippingale are indeed to be linked to the *Hreope/Hrype/Hrepingas* of Repton, with the Repton group being an offshoot of the Lincolnshire group, then the same interpretation should almost certainly be applied to the *Hreope/Hrype* of Ripon too. Certainly, a Lincolnshire origin for this Northumbrian population group would have a very good context in the evidence discussed above. In addition, this scenario for explaining the relationship between the Ripon and the Repton *Hreope* might well be thought to be more plausible than the notion that the group in the Mercian heartlands was an offshoot of the Deiran group, as

suggested by Watts (p. 501) and Stenton ('English Occupation', p. 270).

CONCLUSION

The significance of *Lindēs* and *Lindissi*

The period between the end of Roman imperial control in Britain and the conversion of the Anglo-Saxons to Christianity has been described in many different ways over the years, perhaps the most evocative of which is the 'Dark Ages'. Although this particular term is now less favoured in academic circles than it once was, it is still in common use. It also reflects some of the problems and assumptions that surround any study of the fifth and sixth centuries in Britain.[1] On the one hand, the period has often been considered 'dark' insofar as the sources for the fifth and sixth centuries are considered sufficiently unreliable and meagre for there to be some considerable difficulty in establishing even the general outline of events with confidence, never mind the specifics.[2] On the other hand, the period has also been so judged from a cultural perspective: the term 'Dark Ages' has always implied a strong pejorative judgement of these centuries, with their 'darkness' contrasting with the 'light' of Rome.[3] In this context, the name 'Dark Ages' for the fifth and sixth centuries refers to the supposed abandonment of Roman civilization and descent into barbarism that resulted from the Germanic conquests of the various provinces of the Western Roman Empire, with Britain seeing the Romano-British culture, institutions and even people swept from the land.

The present study does not completely remove the basis for either of the above judgements with regard to the Lincoln region. The available 'historical' sources remain meagre and difficult, and whilst one can quibble over 'decline' versus 'change',[4] there can be little doubt that urban life failed to survive the fifth century, or that the material culture of the post-Roman period was not in many ways much impoverished when compared with that of the fourth century. However, such judgements can be taken too far. There is now a sizeable corpus of both Anglo-Saxon and British archaeological material available for the fifth and sixth centuries from Lincolnshire, and if this is used in concert with the available historical, literary and linguistic evidence, then considerable progress can potentially be made in terms of understanding and explaining at least the general course of events which took place in the Lincoln region in this period. Similarly, the results of such an approach suggest that there are likely to be far stronger threads of what might be termed 'continuity' joining the seventh-century kingdom of *Lindissi* to the (Romano-)British past than has sometimes been assumed. As such, the fifth and sixth centuries in the Lincoln region might be said to look a little less 'dark' at the end of this study than they did at its start, and it is consequently worth asking whether the conclusions reached in the preceding chapters have any implications for some of the general questions that confront historians of this period.

Perhaps the most important of these questions is that of how the early Anglo-Saxon kingdoms came into being. On the one hand, it has been suggested that the Anglo-Saxon conquests resulted in an almost complete disintegration of the existing British political and administrative structures in the east, with kingdoms and kings only re-emerging from the mid–late sixth century as a result of the coalescence of many originally independent, local Anglo-Saxon territories.[5] On the other hand, there is little positive evidence in favour of such a scenario. Moreover, a credible alternative model has been suggested whereby the Anglo-Saxons simply took over the large British territories they encountered in order to form the recorded kingdoms. The local units (*regiones*) that have been identified as existing within the pre-Viking kingdoms would, on this model, merely represent administrative subdistricts rather than fossilized 'building blocks'.[6]

All told, the evidence from the Lincoln region would appear to support strongly the second of these competing hypotheses, especially with regard to the transition from *Lindēs* to *Lindissi*: the implication of the material analysed in the preceding chapters is that a Lincoln-based British polity (*Lindēs*) managed to survive and even prosper as late as the sixth century in an area of significant Anglo-

Saxon immigration, before being taken over almost intact by the Anglo-Saxons to form the kingdom of *Lindissi*. Even outside of *Lindēs-Lindissi* there is little real support for any hypothesis that involves the recorded Anglo-Saxon kingdoms having their origins in tiny 'proto-kingdoms' which gradually coalesced over time. Thus, for example, it seems likely that the *Gyrwe* were always a subordinate group inhabiting a subdistrict of the kingdom of Middle Anglia, rather than a truly independent 'kingdom'. This is a point of some importance, given that the *Gyrwe* have often been considered a prime example of the sort of independent small groups and 'kingdoms' that the first scenario suggests existed across all of eastern and southern Britain.

The evidence from Lincolnshire may also be of interest in other ways when it comes to questions of Anglo-Saxon kingdom-formation and the existence and annexation of British polities in post-Roman Britain. First, it can assist in explaining how the Anglo-Saxon takeover of British polities, as envisaged in the second scenario, might have progressed. In the case of *Lindēs*, it is suggested that this resulted from a British use of immigrant groups to help defend their territory, with control over these groups then weakening from the early sixth century until the Anglo-Saxons became the dominant political as well as military force within *Lindēs*.[7] Second, the evidence from *Lindēs-Lindissi* can provide a useful comparison for those areas of eastern and southern Britain where there are similar 'gaps' in the distribution of early Anglo-Saxon cemeteries. It has often been suspected that some of these gaps reflect post-Roman British polities, most especially that around London and the Chilterns. The conclusions reached in the present study can offer a model for such regions. In other words, it may well be that the situation in the Lincoln region both reflects and illuminates a broader pattern whereby at least some British polities in lowland Britain, based around major Late Roman centres (such as Lincoln, London, Verulamium and Silchester), survived the initial period of Anglo-Saxon immigration for some considerable period and were able to exert a degree of continuing control over Anglo-Saxon activity in their territories.[8]

Another key question is that of the extent of Anglian–British interaction and acculturation in the early Anglo-Saxon period. Most commentators now accept that there were large numbers of both Anglo-Saxons and Britons present in eastern Britain in the post-Roman centuries, with all that this implies with regard to interaction and acculturation.[9] The results of the present study corroberate this and, moreover, point to evidence for a British influence on aspects of pre-Viking culture which might have resulted from such interaction. In addition, they raise two further points that may be of a wider significance. One is that there seems to be at least some evidence that members of the British elite of *Lindēs joined with the new ascendancy and were eventually absorbed into Anglo-Saxon society. This may, of course, result from the unusual history of this region, and so not be applicable more widely – the archaeological evidence for post-Roman British elites in the Lincoln region is exceptionally rich in comparison with the rest of eastern Britain. Nonetheless, it is worthy of note. The other point is that we do need to be careful to take full account of the implications of such potentially widespread British survival and acculturation across much of eastern and southern Britain. Most especially, it seems likely that many Britons living within eastern Britain would not have acculturated before the end of the early Anglo-Saxon period (c. 650) and so would have remained effectively archaeologically 'invisible' throughout this period. This is potentially problematical when it comes to attempts to rely upon the distribution of early Anglo-Saxon artefacts (and their presence or absence on Late Roman settlement sites) to reach conclusions about early Anglo-Saxon population density and landscape abandonment. In this context, the discussion here of the *Spalde* and the district of Holland is of note.[10]

The last question to be highlighted here is that of the origins of the Anglo-Saxon groups and kingdoms that were located away from the primary regions of immigration. This question has often received only the briefest of treatments in academic studies of the kingdoms in question, largely due to the perceived difficulty in finding anything concrete to say on the matter. However, the discussion in Chapter 6 suggests that it is possible to make progress on this issue, with the available evidence indicating that the Anglo-Saxon population groups of the Lincoln region probably played a key role in the conquest and Anglicization of northern Britain, perhaps even providing the Bernician royal dynasty itself. This is, of course, of considerable significance for the history of regions other than that of Lincoln, and a case might additionally be made for a similar scenario with regard to the origins of the Midland kingdom of Mercia.

More could undoubtedly be said about the potential implications of the material discussed in the present study for our understanding of post-Roman Britain in general, but the above must suffice. Not only is there a case to be made for the Lincoln region having been an influential part of the fifth- and sixth-century political landscape in its own right, something which belies its relative lack of direct influence over events in the seventh century, but it seems likely that the evidence from Lincolnshire can also be used comparatively to help shed light on the history of other parts of early Anglo-Saxon England. In such circumstances, it can hardly be denied that both *Lindēs* and *Lindissi* possess a measure of wider historical significance.

Notes to Conclusion

1   D. B. Harden (ed.), *Dark Age Britain. Studies Presented to E. T. Leeds* (London, 1956) is an obvious example of the name 'Dark Age' being used for this period by twentieth-century academics, but there are many more recent academic books which feature the term too, including R. Hodges, *Dark Age Economics: The Origins of Towns and Trade AD 600–1000* (London, 1982); A. Williams *et al, A Biographical Dictionary of Dark Age Britain. England, Scotland and Wales, c. 500–c. 1050* (London, 1991); B. Crawford (ed.), *Scotland in Dark Age Europe* (St Andrews, 1994); and J. T. Koch, *The Gododdin of Aneirin: Text and Context from Dark-Age North Britain* (Cardiff, 1997).

2   As in S. Young, *The Celtic Revolution. In Search of 2000 Years that Changed the World* (London, 2009), p. 14.

3   See, for example, T. Mommsen, 'Petrarch's conception of the "Dark Ages"', *Speculum*, 17 (1942), 226–42.

4   See, for example, K. R. Dark, *Britain and the End of the Roman Empire* (Stroud, 2000), pp. 56–7; S. Esmonde-Cleary, 'Britain in the fourth century' in M. Todd (ed.), *A Companion to Roman Britain* (Oxford, 2004), pp. 418–9, 424–5.

5   H. Hamerow, 'The earliest Anglo-Saxon kingdoms' in P. Fouracre (ed.), *The New Cambridge Medieval History, I: c.500–c.700* (Cambridge, 2005), pp. 271–88; S. Bassett, 'In search of the origins of Anglo-Saxon kingdoms' in S. Bassett (ed.), *The Origins of Anglo-Saxon Kingdoms* (London, 1989), pp. 3–27; C. Scull, 'Archaeology, early Anglo-Saxon society and the Anglo-Saxon kingdoms', *Anglo-Saxon Studies in Archaeology and History*, 6 (1993), 72–9.

6 See B. Yorke, 'Anglo-Saxon *gentes* and *regna*' in H-W. Goetz *et al* (eds), *Regna and Gentes: The Relationship Between Late Antique and Early Medieval Peoples and Kingdoms in the Transformation of the Roman World* (Leiden, 2003), pp. 381–408, especially pp. 396–401; B. Yorke, 'Political and ethnic identity: a case study of Anglo-Saxon practice' in W. O. Frazer and A. Tyrrell (eds), *Social Identity in Early Medieval Britain* (London, 2000), pp. 82–6; and above, pp. 163–7.

7 See further above, pp. 87–9, 113–15. This does, of course, suggest that the traditional Gildasian model of the Anglo-Saxon arrival and conquest of eastern Britain may deserve more consideration than it is sometimes granted.

8 See, for example, K. R. Dark, *Britain and the End of the Roman Empire* (Stroud, 2000), pp. 97–103, on such British polities in southern and eastern Britain.

9 This is in contrast to earlier studies – such as R. Hodges, *The Anglo-Saxon Achievement. Archaeology and the Beginnings of English Society* (London, 1989), chapter two – which tended to treat a large-scale Anglo-Saxon migration and a large-scale British survival as mutually exclusive scenarios for post-Roman Britain.

10 Above, pp. 178–82. This applies equally to conclusions on supposedly 'British' burial rites in Anglo-Saxon cemeteries. Without making any judgements as to whether 'crouched burial' – which occurs chiefly in seventh-century graves – is a British rite or not, the specific argument that 'it seems nonsensical to suggest that such practices can … represent 'native survival', as crouched burial is not found to any great extent during the preceding two centuries', seems problematical in light of the above (S. Lucy, 'Early Medieval burials in East Yorkshire: reconsidering the evidence' in H. Geake and J. Kenny (eds), *Early Deira. Archaeological Studies of the East Riding in the Fourth to Ninth Centuries AD* (Oxford, 2000), p.14). Indeed, given that many Britons arguably did not acculturate until the seventh century or after, the above might actually be an argument in *favour* of this rite being British in origin.

APPENDIX
A GAZETTEER OF FIFTH- TO
SEVENTH-CENTURY CEMETERIES
IN LINCOLNSHIRE

The following gazetteer is based upon Kevin Leahy's 1993 survey of early Anglo-Saxon cemeteries known from Lindsey, which has been expanded and updated using the data collected by the local Historic Environment Records and the Portable Antiquities Scheme. As was the case with the earlier survey, single finds of metalwork have been omitted unless they are associated with human remains or likely to have come from a grave. With regard to the sites discussed in this gazetteer, cemeteries that were recorded in Leahy's list are associated with the number that they were allocated therein. Cemeteries not recorded by Leahy but present in the Historic Environment Records are cited by their respective record number(s) — the prefix HER indicates sites in the Lincolnshire Historic Environment Record, whilst NLSMR indicates sites in the North Lincolnshire Sites and Monuments Record. Finally, probable or possible cemeteries not listed by Leahy and known only from metal-detected finds are cited by their associated Portable Antiquities Scheme (PAS) record numbers.

It should be noted that the PAS keeps details of single finds, rather than 'sites'. As such, cemeteries cited here solely by PAS numbers derive from a complete survey of all early Anglo-Saxon material on the PAS that had been found in Lincolnshire through until late 2009. Following Leahy's lead from the earlier list, this dataset was examined for certain and potential concentrations of metal-detected material that might represent such cemeteries. Because the PAS assigns a separate record number to each find, some of these cemeteries have a considerable quantity of PAS numbers associated with them. Consequently, each of the cemeteries identified from this material is cited by only a handful of its associated PAS record numbers, which are intended as illustrative of the site as a whole. In most cases, full details of all of the relevant finds can be obtained from the latest (2010) PAS database — finds.org.uk/database — by using its 'Find objects within 2km radius of this artefact' option, which is available on Research accounts. Note, however, that finds with only a parish provenance also need to be taken account of, and these are usually assigned auto-generated find-spot grid references in the PAS database, something which has the potential to confuse the results of the above search option if allowance is not made for it.

Ancaster Small Anglo-Saxon cremation cemetery found 100 metres south of the Roman walls on the east side of Ermine Street; 40 urns found before 1870, with others since. (Leahy, 1993: no. 1)

Ancaster A fifth-century brooch and another small-long brooch are recorded as having been found at Ancaster. In addition, recent metal-detecting has recovered five pieces of the sixth to seventh centuries, including part of a hanging bowl and a sixth-century, gilded great square-headed brooch. (HER 30335; PAS NLM951)

Asgarby A sixth-century female grave was discovered in 1811 and an unusually rich male grave in 1915, along with pottery suggesting the presence of cremations. (Leahy, 1993: no. 2)

Aswarby and Swarby An early Anglo-Saxon sleeve clasp and two sixth-century brooches (one a great square-headed brooch) suggest a small burial ground belonging to the sixth century. Other finds from the parish include a buckle and a cremation-pot stamp from the east. (PAS NLM5662, LIN-E47E27, LIN-6C7948)

Aylesby Four sixth- and seventh-century brooches have been recovered via metal-detecting in the parish, probably from at least two separate sites. (PAS NLM201, NLM2879, NLM6071)

Barkston Six late fifth- or sixth-century items (including two cruciform brooches and a girdle hanger) have been metal-detected from this parish. (PAS LIN-8AB2D7, NLM-C70454)

Barnetby le Wold A sixth-century cruciform brooch and a fragment of a possible cremation urn, found close together, suggest the presence of a small, sixth-century cemetery. (PAS NLM-202521, NLM-E8A768)

Barton on Humber (Castledyke South) A very large sixth- to seventh-century cemetery, with finds including two hanging bowls. 196 burials excavated from a total of around 436. (Leahy, 1993: no. 3; Drinkall and Foreman, 1998)

Barton on Humber (West) An inhumation cemetery of the sixth century indicated by seven metal-detected finds, including small-long brooches, cruciform brooches and a girdle hanger. Further metal-detecting also indicates another small sixth-century inhumation cemetery to the south of Barton. (Leahy, 1993: no. 4; PAS NLM-2A14D4, NLM-AF5483)

Baston Anglo-Saxon cremation cemetery, dating from the late fifth to late sixth century. When excavated in 1966, 44 cremation urns were found along with two inhumations; an investigation and watching brief in 1989 and 1994 indicated that the full extent of the cemetery had been found in 1966. (HER 33387; Mayes and Dean, 1976)

Baston Large number of metal-detected finds testify to a separate and sizeable early Anglo-Saxon inhumation cemetery in the parish, to the south-east of the cremation centre. The finds are chiefly of the sixth century, but two Aberg Group I brooches (early to mid-fifth-century) suggest the possibility of a fifth-century start. In addition, there are indications of perhaps two further (and much smaller) burial sites in the metal-detected corpus from the parish, to the north and north-east of the cremation cemetery. (PAS LIN-9089F4, NLM960, NLM712, NLM4645)

Belton and Manthorpe Anglo-Saxon finds: at least five knives and part of a spearhead found in 1883. Probably part of an Anglo-Saxon inhumation cemetery. (HER 30433)

Binbrook Metal-detecting has recovered five brooches (including a fifth-century cruciform) from the parish, which are indicative of a small inhumation cemetery. (PAS NLM-0F8313, NLM-580982)

Blyborough Two brooches, two beads and a hanging bowl fragment have been found via metal-detecting in two separate locations in this parish. (PAS LIN-E2D1A5, LIN-B86833)

Bolingbroke Recent metal-detecting has recovered three finds, including a fifth-century cruciform brooch and a cremation urn fragment, from two sites located north-east of the West Keal cemetery. (PAS NLM-276356, NLM-616AB3)

Bonby Three metal-detected cruciform brooches from here suggest the presence of a sixth-century inhumation cemetery. (PAS NLM-14CBE4, NLM-EB2B44)

Bottesford Evidence of a mixed inhumation and cremation cemetery, of unknown size, including two brooches and a documented discovery of a cremation urn. (Leahy, 1993: no. 5)

Bourne Three fifth- to sixth-century brooches from a single site are suggestive of the presence of early Anglo-Saxon burials. A probable enamelled hanging-bowl escutcheon has also been recovered from the parish, as has a late sixth- or seventh-century sword pyramid. (PAS LIN-34C004, LIN-666425, NLM716)

Bracebridge Heath High-status 'warrior burial' of the seventh century, found with sword, shield and hanging bowl. (HER 60962)

Branston and Mere Four early Anglo-Saxon items metal-detected from the parish, suggestive of a small, sixth-century cemetery. (PAS LIN-8B0F05)

Brocklesby A sixth- to seventh-century inhumation cemetery, indicated by 13 pieces of early Anglo-Saxon metalwork, recovered via metal-detecting. (Leahy, 1993: no. 6)

Burgh-le-Marsh A late sixth- or early seventh-century male grave: possibly a barrow burial, although this has been disputed. (Leahy, 1993: no. 7; HER 43596)

Burton upon Stather (Bagmoor) A late fifth- to sixth-century cremation cemetery, containing 'many urns', destroyed by ironstone mining around 1928. (Leahy, 1993: no. 8)

Caenby The richest barrow burial in the region, with a mound which would seem to have been larger than that at Sutton Hoo; early seventh-century in date and excavated in 1850. (Leahy, 1993: no. 9)

Candlesby Armour, swords and shields found before 1882, which may be associated with a cruciform brooch. (Leahy, 1993: no. 10)

Careby, Aunby and Holywell Possible Anglo-Saxon cemetery, indicated by finds of ring-brooches, a bead and a steelyard. (HER 33604, 33605)

Carlton Scroop One or two (some confusion) fifth- to sixth-century Anglo-Saxon inhumation cemeteries, with reports of 30–40 bodies. Finds include a spearhead, and a brooch of *c.* 500. (Leahy, 1993: no. 11; HER 30380, 30381)

Castle Bytham Early Anglo-Saxon burial (female) found in 1850, well furnished with beaver tooth set in metal, silver-gilt ring-brooch inset with four gems, and other items. (HER 33614)

Caythorpe Mixed inhumation and cremation cemetery, probably discovered during ironstone mining. Ring-brooches, square-headed brooches, cruciform brooches, spearheads, shield boss etc. (Leahy, 1993: no. 12)

Claxby Four sixth-century brooches from Claxby indicate the presence of an inhumation cemetery of this date. (PAS NLM7022)

Cleatham Between 50 and 60 cremation urns discovered in 1856, with a very detailed excavation conducted in the 1980s by Kevin Leahy. 1,204 burials excavated out of a likely total of 1,528; probably mid-fifth- to seventh-century in date. (Leahy, 1993: no. 13; Leahy, 2007a)

Cleethorpes An excavated pot may indicate an early Anglo-Saxon inhumation inserted into a Bronze Age barrow. (Leahy, 1993: no. 14)

Coleby Around 80 inhumations, probably of early Anglo-Saxon date, excavated in the early nineteenth century. Accompanied by knives, spears, brooches, beads and pots. (Leahy, 1993: no. 15)

Denton Two bodies buried in a Roman villa, one associated with early sixth-century pottery. (HER 30019)

Donington-on-Bain A field a mile and a half north-east of the village apparently 'frequently turned up' cremation urns and partially burnt human and animal bone during ploughing in the nineteenth century; possible early Anglo-Saxon cremation cemetery? (HER 40725)

East Barkwith Two sixth-century cruciform brooches have been recorded from here via metal-detecting. (PAS LIN-290724, LIN-E85576)

Eagle and Swinethorpe Two sixth-century cruciform or small-long brooches from this parish, of sixth-century date. (PAS LIN-D196E5, LIN-D172B3)

Edenham Two cruciform brooches found; one of the fifth century and one of the sixth. The latter looks to have been cremated. (PAS NLM993)

Edlington with Wispington Fragments of two late fifth- to late sixth-century cruciform brooches have been recovered from a single site in this parish; a gilded sixth-century great square-headed brooch has also been found in the parish. (PAS LIN-415104, LIN-CA81C6)

Elsham Large cremation cemetery of the fifth to sixth centuries; 625 cremations excavated along with five inhumations. (Leahy, 1993: no. 16)

Elsham Recent metal-detected finds suggest an inhumation cemetery apparently located west of the cremation cemetery. Finds include three sixth-century cruciform brooches and a seventh-century Merovingian strap fitting. (PAS NLM2894, NLM24)

Farforth A small sixth-century inhumation cemetery indicated by a bronze-bound bucket and two brooch fragments. (Leahy, 1993: no. 17)

Fillingham Possible early Anglo-Saxon cemetery indicated by antiquarian references to spears and swords, along with finds of a cruciform and a small-long brooch. (Leahy, 1993: no. 18)

Flixborough Early Anglo-Saxon cremation urn and possible burial mound. (NLSMR 1982)

Folkingham A sixth-century inhumation cemetery discovered via metal-detecting. Finds include a Group V cruciform brooch, a great square-headed brooch, a spear and a rock-crystal bead. (PAS LIN-CF1D82)

Fonaby near Caistor A late fifth- to seventh-century mixed cemetery; 49 inhumations and 17 cremations recovered in 1956–7. (Leahy, 1993: no. 19)

Foston Five Anglo-Saxon, gilt square-headed brooches found by metal-detectorists, along with a stamped sherd of early Anglo-Saxon pottery and fragments of two brooches from nearby. Probable sixth-century inhumation cemetery site. (HER 34739, 30183)

Gayton le Wold A seventh-century buckle and a late fifth- to sixth-century sleeve clasp have been metal-detected from a site in this parish. (PAS NLM-0399A2)

Grantham Spitalgate early Anglo-Saxon inhumation cemetery. Said to be many spearheads, knives, shield bosses, and square-headed brooches found at this site. Recent metal-detecting has also recovered two early Anglo-Saxon small-long brooches from Grantham. (HER 30516)

Grantham A probable early Anglo-Saxon inhumation; part of a bronze buckle and a spearhead found. (HER 30529)

Grayingham Single early Anglo-Saxon female grave (with a necklace of amber beads) found around 1888. In recent years, two late fifth- to sixth-century items – a sleeve clasp and a girdle hanger – and a possible early Anglo-Saxon box-mount have been found by metal-detectorists in the parish. (Leahy, 1993: no. 20; PAS LIN-E22045, LIN-E3F5E6, LIN-E3C3A3)

Great Limber A probable Anglo-Saxon round barrow destroyed in 1787, which contained two cremation urns, one with a bone comb. (HER 50432)

Harlaxton Anglo-Saxon pots are recorded here, which may be indicative of an early Anglo-Saxon cemetery. Metal-detecting has recovered a late fifth- or early to mid-sixth-century circular brooch. (HER 30034; PAS NLM-861E47)

Harmston Four early Anglo-Saxon items metal-detected in this parish, including an annular and a small-long brooch. These suggest the presence of sixth-century grave(s), although only two items have rough locations and these are different. (PAS LIN-F71235, NLM6124)

Hatton A sixth-century pin fragment and a Group IV cruciform brooch have been discovered here via metal-detecting. (PAS LIN-FD3305)

Heckington Small number of probably early Anglo-Saxon graves reported, and 'Butts Hill' – now destroyed – may have been an Anglo-Saxon barrow. There are also an early Anglo-Saxon cruciform brooch, buckle and bracelet from the vicinity of the Cobham Roman villa. (Leahy, 1993: no. 21; HER 60866, 60325, 60870)

Heckington Modern metal-detecting has recovered numerous items which probably indicate a reasonably sizeable early Anglo-Saxon cemetery in the eastern part of the parish, associated with the trading site at Garwick. Finds include a high-status, seventh-century sword pommel, late fifth-/sixth-century small-long and cruciform brooches, and a mid-fifth-century brooch. (PAS LIN-7B7528, LIN-946BA2)

Heighington Up to six early Anglo-Saxon brooches found here via metal-detecting, which is suggestive of a small sixth-century cemetery, though not all items have locations recorded for them. (PAS LIN-0FD375, LIN-FA40C2)

Hemswell Four metal-detected brooches suggest the presence of a sixth-century cemetery somewhere in this parish. (PAS LIN-DE43D7)

Hibaldstow Metal-detecting has recovered five early Anglo-Saxon items from at least two sites within this parish, including a sixth-century great square-headed brooch. (PAS NLM-A81975, NLM6964, NLM-2C6AB6)

Holton le Moor Four metal-detected items are known from the parish, including part of a sixth- or seventh-century buckle and a strap fitting. (PAS NLM-0669D4, NLM-ED2FA1, NLM6574)

Honington Early Anglo-Saxon brooches, one cruciform and one small-long. (HER 30361)

Horncastle Sixth-century graves are known from the town, one with a sword and two spearheads; also remains of a small-long brooch found. More recently, metal-detecting has recovered other early Anglo-Saxon items from the parish. (Leahy, 1993: no. 22; PAS NLM6211)

Hougham Three early Anglo-Saxon items found by metal-detector: an early to mid-sixth-century cruciform brooch; a nice early to mid-sixth-century harness mount (a high-status piece); and a cremated sixth-century small-long brooch, probably indicative of a pyre site. (PAS NLM6090, NLM6073)

Ingham Metal-detected finds indicate the presence of an inhumation cemetery: a hanging bowl and fragments of a cruciform brooch and a sleeve clasp. (Leahy, 1993: no. 23)

Irby upon Humber (Welbeck Hill) A sizeable inhumation cemetery of the sixth century; 72 inhumations and five cremations. (Leahy, 1993: no. 24)

Keelby Kevin Leahy records a significant quantity of fifth- to sixth-century metal-detected material from Keelby in his gazetteer; subsequent finds have developed this picture further, revealing two significant cemeteries at separate locations in the parish. Finds include a sixth-century British Type G brooch and a very early fifth-century cruciform brooch, which was probably an heirloom piece. (Leahy, 1993: no. 25; PAS LIN-AC3AB3, NLM5759)

Kirkby la Thorpe Part of a probably seventh-century Anglo-Saxon cemetery recovered in 1999; nine inhumations excavated. A find of Anglo-Saxon shears in the nineteenth century may be associated with this site; in addition, metal-detecting has recovered a cruciform brooch and a fifth- or sixth-century small-long brooch from two separate sites in this parish. (HER 62057, 64333; PAS DENO-E0E7F5)

Kirton in Lindsey A seventh-century warrior burial, containing a sword, seax and bridle bit, was found *c.* 1920. Recent metal-detecting has also recovered two late fifth- to sixth-century cruciform brooches to the east of the village. (Leahy, 1993: no. 26; PAS NLM-554291)

Laceby A sixth- to seventh-century inhumation cemetery, with skeletons and early Anglo-Saxon grave-goods discovered between 1934 and 1939. Recent metal-detecting has recovered four sixth-century items from the parish. (Leahy, 1993: no. 27; PAS NLM-73C251)

Langtoft 'Post-Roman brooches', presumably early Anglo-Saxon, recorded here in the late 1980s. More recent metal-detecting has recovered a fifth- or sixth-century small-long brooch and a sixth- or seventh-century sleeve clasp. (HER 34752; PAS NLM992)

Leasingham Two fifth- or sixth-century small-long brooches discovered in this parish from metal-detecting. (PAS NLM752)

Legsby Metal-detecting has recovered ten items dating to the late fifth or sixth centuries, including three small-long brooches, a mid-fifth- to mid-sixth-century button brooch, and a fragment of a gilded great square-headed brooch. (PAS LIN-5D6605, LIN-A5AEE7)

Lenton, Keisby and Osgodby Large inhumation cemetery discovered via metal-detecting; mainly inhumations, but some cremation urns. Finds indicate that it dates chiefly to the sixth and seventh centuries, although there is one early (heirloom?) cruciform brooch; also part of a seventh-century drinking horn. (PAS LIN-273A14, LIN-43B873)

Little Ponton and Stroxton A fragment of a small-long brooch dating from *c.* 450–550 recorded via metal-detecting, along with a late fifth-century knob from a cruciform brooch and an early to mid-sixth-century small-long brooch, all from the same area. Also a scramasax, a shield boss and a gilt stud from the River Witham from this parish, at Saltersford. (HER 33970; PAS NLM5236)

Lissingleys Metal-detecting has revealed three Anglo-Saxon cemeteries around this site, located in the modern parishes of Lissington and Wickenby. Significant finds include a hanging-bowl mount, a silver sword ring and a silver sword mount. (PAS LIN-75B9C3, LIN-F2C275, LIN-3B4676)

Louth Metal-detected finds (including three small-long brooches) from just within the parish boundary suggest a sixth-century inhumation cemetery. (Leahy, 1993: no. 28)

Loveden Hill Second largest Anglo-Saxon cemetery in England with over 1,700 cremations excavated; also 44 inhumations. The cemetery appears to have been in use from the fifth to the seventh centuries. (Leahy, 1993: no. 29)

Lusby with Winceby A sixth-century inhumation cemetery is indicated by 16 metal-detected items, including a Frankish radiate-headed brooch and four cruciform brooches. (PAS LIN-9B0C06)

Maltby A fifth-century cruciform brooch, a mid-sixth- to mid-seventh-century sword pyramid, and an early Anglo-Saxon annular brooch have all been found at Maltby near Louth. (HER 40833, K. Leahy, personal communication)

Manthorpe Two spearheads, a buckle and a pot found during building work; possible early Anglo-Saxon cemetery site. (HER 30538)

Manton A hanging bowl discovered during sand-extraction probably comes from an inhumation grave. More recent metal-detecting has also recovered early Anglo-Saxon items from elsewhere in Manton parish, including a seventh-century disc brooch. (Leahy, 1993: no. 30; PAS NLM-013882)

Market Rasen Kevin Leahy records two mounts from a hanging bowl, along with finds of sleeve clasps and a fragment of cruciform brooch, which indicate the presence of an early Anglo-Saxon cemetery, though the hanging-bowl mounts and the other finds may not be from the same site. More recent metal-detecting has continued to add to this total from the parish, with the PAS recording four fifth- or sixth-century brooches. (Leahy, 1993: no. 31; PAS NLM-CDD252, NLM-CDB1D0)

Melton Ross A sixth-century inhumation cemetery, with some cremations indicated by burnt objects: between six and ten brooches, a sleeve clasp, a girdle hanger, an annular brooch and two knives were discovered whilst metal-detecting. (NLSMR 20333)

Middle Rasen A significant number of metal-detected finds indicate a sizeable early Anglo-Saxon inhumation cemetery; notable finds include a fifth-century cruciform brooch. A gold-sheet panel from a high-status seventh-century object has also been found in the parish. (PAS NLM-ED5CD1, NLM-A2D701, NLM-7CDDF5)

Navenby Five early Anglo-Saxon inhumations, probably seventh-century in date. (HER 61152)

Nettleton/Caistor Finds of skeletons and early Anglo-Saxon grave goods were made in 1855, with a possible outlier of this cemetery excavated in 1972 within Caistor parish. The hanging bowl from this cemetery is probably of the fifth century, and the cemetery as a whole is likely to date from the late fifth to perhaps the early seventh century (the latter date is suggested on the basis that use of hanging bowls in Anglo-Saxon graves seems to be a seventh-century rite). More recent metal-detecting has retrieved further sixth-century artefacts that probably belong to this site. (Leahy, 1993: no. 32; PAS NLM2815)

Newton and Haceby Six metal-detected items (including a fifth-century cruciform brooch) from this parish suggest an early Anglo-Saxon inhumation cemetery. (PAS LIN-61D118)

Normanton A sixth-century Anglo-Saxon inhumation cemetery: 30 burials have been excavated and there are indications that the cemetery extended beyond the area of excavation. (HER 35401)

North Hykeham Four or five brooches, a pin and part of a girdle hanger discovered via metal-detecting, which are probably indicative of two female burials interred by the middle of the sixth century; one of the brooches is mid-fifth-century in date, but the other items are later; as such, it ought to be considered an heirloom piece. (PAS LIN-DB6F46)

Northorpe Eight metal-detected finds (six of them fragments of cruciform brooches) indicate the presence of an inhumation cemetery. (Leahy, 1993: no. 34)

North Ormsby Three metal-detected finds, including a cruciform and a small-long brooch, suggest a sixth-century inhumation cemetery. (PAS NLM-50C8F2)

North Willingham Metal-detecting here has recovered a sixth-century small-long brooch and two different fifth- to seventh-century sleeve clasps. (PAS NLM-8439E4)

Osbournby Large Anglo-Saxon cemetery, with very many finds being discovered through metal-detecting, including part of a hanging bowl. The artefacts are generally indicative of a sixth- to seventh-century inhumation cemetery that included a small cremation element. (PAS LIN-EB33A6)

Osbournby Three cruciform brooches, a small-long brooch and two other pieces indicate a small sixth-century cemetery, which was separate from the main site noted above. Items from elsewhere in the parish suggest that there may have been other smaller burial sites here in the early Anglo-Saxon period too. (PAS LIN-18E954, LIN-F68575, NLM4229)

Osgodby Metal-detecting in the parish has recovered evidence of a sixth- to seventh-century cemetery, including two cruciform brooches and a sleeve clasp. (HER 54324)

Partney A barrow burial excavated in 1950, containing at least four burials (two adults and two children). Dated to *c.* 600, based on two cruciform brooches and other finds. (Leahy, 1993: no. 35)

Pointon and Sempringham Two cruciform brooches recovered through metal-detecting: one belongs to the sixth century and the other to the late fifth or sixth century. (PAS NLM997)

Quarrington Sizeable fifth- to seventh-century cremation cemetery (discovered in the early nineteenth century), with an inhumation element as found at other local cremation cemeteries. (Leahy, 1993: no. 36)

Quarrington A small inhumation cemetery of the fifth to sixth century has been recently excavated here, containing 15 inhumations. (HER 60375; Dickinson, 2004)

Revesby Three metal-detected finds, including a seventh-century sword pommel and a mid-sixth-century belt plate. (PAS NLM4176)

Riby Small seventh-century inhumation cemetery found during 1915 and 1916. (Leahy, 1993: no. 37)

Roxby (Sheffield's Hill) A sixth-century cemetery with a single cremation has been excavated here. A seventh-century cemetery was also found ten metres to the south of the sixth-century cemetery. 129 burials were found in total. (NLSMR 15987)

Roxby Metal-detecting has recovered early Anglo-Saxon items from several sites within the parish, suggesting that there is at least one small sixth-century burial site here in addition to the cemetery known from excavation. (PAS NLM-DE6635)

Ruskington 180 sixth- to seventh-century Anglo-Saxon inhumations, discovered at various times through the twentieth century, along with a small number of cremations. Metal-detecting continues to recover sixth- to seventh-century metalwork from the parish. (Leahy, 1993: no. 38; PAS LIN-D245D8)

Scotter Inhumations found before 1892, associated with an 'Anglian knife' and buried in the 'early Saxon manner'. Two sixth-century items – a bead and a small-long brooch – have also been found in the parish. (HER 50050; PAS NLM4499)

Searby A probably large, late fifth- to sixth-century inhumation cemetery discovered during chalk-digging between 1849 and 1864. Finds include a cruciform brooch and a garnet-set radiate-headed brooch. (Leahy, 1993: no. 39)

Silk Willoughby Anglo-Saxon pottery found in this parish, along with a sixth-century cruciform brooch, a small-long brooch and an early Anglo-Saxon spearhead. A Roman-coin pendant has also been found in the parish; these are usually early Anglo-Saxon in date. (HER 65167; PAS NLM4548)

Sixhills An inhumation cemetery indicated by significant quantities of metal-detected finds, which suggest a primarily sixth-century cemetery. (HER 54302)

Skendleby Two small-long brooches and a sixth- or seventh-century mount suggest the presence of a small inhumation cemetery. (PAS LIN-52AFE5)

Sleaford Very large inhumation cemetery of the late fifth to sixth/early seventh centuries: 242 out of *c.* 600 or more burials excavated. Some of the burials are extremely well furnished; six cremations were found at the site too. The next items may well be part of, or separate clusters of, this apparently very large cemetery, as may be the stray finds of a Roman-coin amulet and part of a sixth-century cruciform brooch from the parish. (Leahy, 1993: no. 40; HER 61960, 65290, 65288)

Sleaford A single female grave of the seventh century was found at Old Sleaford in 1916; other undated graves may also have been found in the area, according to the HER. (HER 60374, 60884)

Sleaford A small collection of early Anglo-Saxon grave goods, which are suggestive of a single female burial, were found during the construction of the Bass Maltings. (HER 65300)

South Carlton Small sixth- to early seventh-century cemetery; metal-detected finds led to the excavation of three inhumations and an urned cremation burial. Trenches dug in an attempt to establish whether there were any further burials failed to turn up evidence of such. (HER 54979)

South Elkington–Louth A very large mid-fifth- to sixth-century cremation cemetery; 290 urns excavated out of an estimated total of 1,200 original burials. (Leahy, 1993: no. 41)

South Ferriby A sixth-century inhumation cemetery, known from modern metal-detecting and finds recorded in 1907. (Leahy, 1993: no. 42)

South Rauceby Early Anglo-Saxon finds (a brooch of the fifth to sixth century, girdle hangers and a strap end) from a single site; probably indicative of a grave or small cemetery. (HER 60471)

South Willingham A cremation cemetery of unknown size; no finds survive. (Leahy, 1993: no. 43)

South Witham Probable early Anglo-Saxon mixed cremation and inhumation cemetery, destroyed in the mid-eighteenth century. Bodies, knife, urns and spears found. (HER 33616)

Spridlington A single sixth- or early seventh-century male burial with a shield boss was found at Spridlington House in 1974. (HER 51438)

Stamford Probable early Anglo-Saxon inhumation, found 1854. An urn, spear and bone found; the pottery is said to be sixth-century in date. (HER 30676)

Stenigot At least three individuals found in a seventh-century barrow. Finds include a bronze cauldron. (Leahy, 1993: no. 44)

Stickford Metal-detected finds, including three sixth-century cruciform brooches and a seventh-century girdle hanger. (PAS NLM2745)

Sudbrook Anglo-Saxon finds (tweezers, bracelet and beads) from Newton Sandpit suggest a probable early Anglo-Saxon female grave. (HER 30346)

Swaby Four Anglo-Saxon burials, unaccompanied so perhaps of seventh-century date. (HER 42837)

Swallow A very high-status, female grave assemblage, probably of the early seventh century, discovered and semi-excavated by metal-detectorists. (PAS LIN-E8F0C7)

Swaton A late fifth- or sixth-century buckle and a cremation urn have been found close to each other in this parish. (PAS LIN-74D863, LIN-7E3054)

Swinhope Three Roman coins re-used as pendants, a small-long brooch, some tweezers and a hanging-bowl mount indicate the presence of an early Anglo-Saxon inhumation cemetery. (PAS NLM6560, NLM-C8EF70)

Tallington Around 25 inhumations have been excavated here over several decades, representing a cemetery that apparently began in the sixth century and continued into the Middle Saxon period. (HER 33511)

Tathwell Nine metal-detected items, including a great square-headed brooch, have been found in Tathwell parish, indicating the presence of a sixth- to seventh-century cemetery; the earliest-reported finds seem to have been assigned the centre of the parish as a grid reference, but the later items have what appears to be a true NGR. (PAS NLM-85B475, NLM4737)

Tattershall Thorpe A smith's grave of the mid-seventh century. (HER 42790; Hinton, 2000)

Tetford Eleven graves discovered in 1958, via a partial excavation of what was probably a large seventh-century cemetery; finds include a seax and a bucket. Some distance to the south of this site, metal-detecting has recovered a seventh-century copper-alloy mount. (Leahy, 1993: no. 45; LIN-0825B6)

Thimbleby Two sixth-century cruciform brooches and other items recorded by Kevin Leahy have been supplemented by a number of more recent metal-detected finds discovered on at least two separate sites. These include a number of sixth-century brooches, sleeve clasps and some gold beaded wire, which is probably from a seventh-century triangular buckle. (Leahy, 1993: no. 46; PAS NLM-B895B4, LIN-F461F8, NLM4743)

Threekingham A fragment of a probably sixth-century small-long or cruciform brooch and a sixth-century sleeve clasp have been found very close to where two similar items were found previously; they may perhaps be associated with the 'many skeletons' found at Threekingham from 1780 to 1826. (HER 60899, 60041; PAS LIN-021528)

Torksey Three metal-detected items suggest the presence of a sixth- to seventh-century inhumation cemetery. (PAS NLM5772, NLM-B69663)

Waddington Eleven sixth-century graves found in 1947, with further graves excavated in recent years, including some of the seventh century. (Leahy, 1993: no. 47; HER 60377)

Walcot near Folkingham Four early Anglo-Saxon items (including part of a hanging bowl), metal-detected from two separate sites in this parish, are perhaps indicative of two sixth-century burials/small cemeteries. A sixth-century bucket mount has also been discovered in this parish. (PAS LIN-E64595, LIN-3394E7, LIN-679DD6)

Walesby A small sixth- to seventh-century inhumation cemetery, with 23 graves excavated and others probably yet to be uncovered. (Leahy, 1993: no. 48)

Welbourn Various early Anglo-Saxon artefacts found 1847; one or more female graves of *c.* 600. (Leahy, 1993: no. 49)

Wellingore A single female burial of the second half of the sixth century was excavated here in 2002. In addition, metal-detecting has recently found five early Anglo-Saxon items from a separate site nearby, indicative of a small cemetery of the sixth and seventh centuries. One of these was a seventh-century copper-and-gold sword pommel. (HER 62628; PAS LIN-87E077, LIN-871CD5)

Wellingore Fragments of three sixth-century brooches (two cruciform and one small-long) have been metal-detected in the far south of the parish. (PAS LIN-C66A27)

Welton-by-Lincoln Eleven graves found in 1971. Finds include a shield boss and annular brooches. (Leahy, 1993: no. 50)

Westborough and Dry Doddington Possible Anglo-Saxon cemetery. Anglo-Saxon pottery reported from the churchyard and near to a barrow. Metal-detecting has recovered seven sixth-century items: five cruciform brooches, one square-headed brooch, and a sleeve clasp. (HER 30205; PAS NLM-C2D9C4)

West Keal Very limited excavations and a pottery scatter covering around two acres suggest a large cremation cemetery of the fifth to sixth centuries. (Leahy, 1993: no. 51)

West Rasen Four metal-detected cruciform brooches, a disc brooch, a small-long brooch and a sleeve clasp indicate the presence of an inhumation cemetery. (PAS NLM-5E1AF5, NLM-1E18C6, NLM-242A81)

Winceby Finds of skeletons with what may have been Anglo-Saxon shield bosses suggest an early Anglo-Saxon cemetery, possibly associated with barrows in this area. (Leahy, 1993: no. 52)

Wold Newton Small cremation cemetery. Over 20 urns found in 1828 along the line of a 'tumulus'. (Leahy, 1993: no. 53)

Woolsthorpe Mixed cremation and inhumation cemetery, with 'numerous cinerary urns', discovered in 1885 during ironstone mining. (HER 30580)

Worlaby A sixth-century inhumation cemetery; twelve graves excavated and more ploughed out. Also, a single disturbed cremation. (Leahy, 1993: no. 54)

Wrawby A probable early Anglo-Saxon inhumation cemetery, containing nearly 100 burials, was recorded in antiquarian notes of the nineteenth century. Finds include spear heads, weapons, harness-buckles and coins. (NLSMR 20332)

BIBLIOGRAPHY

Abdy, R. and Williams, G. 'A catalogue of hoards and single finds from the British Isles, *c.* AD 410–675' in B. Cook and G. Williams (eds), *Coinage and History in the North Sea World, c. AD 500–1200* (Leiden, 2006), pp. 11–73

Alcock, L. *Arthur's Britain* (Harmondsworth, 1971)

Althoff, G. and Carroll, C. *Family, Friends and Followers: Political and Social Bonds in Medieval Europe* (Cambridge, 2004)

Arnold, C. J. 'The Sancton-Baston potter', *Scottish Archaeological Review*, 2 (1983), 17–30

Arnold, C. J. *Roman Britain to Saxon England* (Beckenham, 1984)

Arnold, C. J. *An Archaeology of the Early Anglo-Saxon Kingdoms*, 2nd edn (London, 1997)

Aston, M. 'Medieval settlement studies in Somerset' in M. Aston and C. Lewis (eds), *The Medieval Landscape of Wessex* (Oxford, 1994), pp. 219–37

Attenborough, F. L. (ed. and trans.) *The Laws of the Earliest English Kings* (Cambridge, 1922)

Bailey, K. 'The Middle Saxons' in S. Bassett (ed.), *The Origins of Anglo-Saxon Kingdoms* (London, 1989), pp. 108–22

Baker, J. T. *Cultural Transition in the Chilterns and Essex Region, 350 AD to 650 AD* (Hatfield, 2006)

Balkwill, C. J. 'Old English *wīc* and the origin of the hundred', *Landscape History*, 15 (1993), 5–12

Banks, S. E. and Binns, J. W. (eds and trans.) *Gervase of Tilbury: Otia Imperialia, Recreation for an Emperor* (Oxford, 2002)

Bassett, S. 'Beyond the edge of excavation: the topographical context of Goltho' in H. Mayr-Harting and R. I. Moore (eds), *Studies in Medieval History Presented to R. H. C. Davies* (London, 1985), pp. 21–39

Bassett, S. 'Lincoln and the Anglo-Saxon see of Lindsey', *Anglo-Saxon England*, 18 (1989), 1–31

Bassett, S. 'In search of the origins of Anglo-Saxon kingdoms' in S. Bassett (ed.), *The Origins of Anglo-Saxon Kingdoms* (London, 1989), pp. 3–27

Bassett, S. 'Church and diocese in the West Midlands' in J. Blair and R. Sharpe (eds), *Pastoral Care Before the Parish* (London, 1992), pp. 13–40

Bassett, S. 'Medieval ecclesiastical organisation in the vicinity of Wroxeter and its British antecedents', *Journal of the British Archaeological Association*, 145 (1992), 1–28

Behr, C. 'The origins of kingship in early medieval Kent', *Early Medieval Europe*, 9 (2000), 25–52 at pp. 39–45

Biddle, M. and Kjølbye-Biddle, B. 'Repton' in M. Lapidge, J. Blair, S. Keynes and D. Scragg (eds), *The Blackwell Encyclopedia of Anglo-Saxon England* (Oxford, 1999), pp. 390–2

Bishop, M. W. *An Archaeological Resource Assessment of Anglo-Saxon Nottinghamshire* (2000), www.le.ac.uk/ar/research/projects/eastmidsfw/pdfs/30nottas.pdf

Blackburn, M. 'Coin finds and coin circulation in Lindsey, *c.* 600–900' in A. Vince (ed.), *Pre-Viking Lindsey* (Lincoln, 1993), pp. 80–90

Blair, J. 'Frithuwold's kingdom and the origins of Surrey' in S. Bassett (ed.), *The Origins of Anglo-Saxon Kingdoms* (London, 1989), pp. 97–107

Blair, J. *Early Medieval Surrey: Landholding, Church and Settlement before 1300* (Stroud, 1991)

Blair, J. 'The Tribal Hidage' in M. Lapidge, J. Blair, S. Keynes and D. Scragg (eds), *The Blackwell Encyclopedia of Anglo-Saxon England* (Oxford, 1999), pp. 455–6

Blair, J. *The Church in Anglo-Saxon Society* (Oxford, 2005)

Blair, J. *Building Anglo-Saxon England* (Oxford, 2018)

Blair, J. 'Beyond the *Billingas*: from lay wealth to monastic wealth on the Lincolnshire fen-edge' (forthcoming)

Blair, P. H. 'The *Moore Memoranda* on Northumbrian history' in C. Fox and B. Dickens (eds), *The Early Cultures of North-West Europe* (Cambridge, 1950), pp. 245–57

Blair, P. H. *An Introduction to Anglo-Saxon England*, 2nd edn (Cambridge, 1977)

Blair, P. H. *Anglo-Saxon Northumbria* (London, 1984)

Booth, A. 'Reassessing the Long Chronology of the Penannular Brooch in Britain: Exploring Changing Styles, Use and Meaning Across a Millennium' (University of Leicester PhD Thesis, 2014)

Bradley, R., Jackson, R. and Willis, S. 'Ludford, Lincolnshire: small-scale investigations of a Roman roadside settlement', *Lincolnshire History & Archaeology*, 49 (2014), 23–36

Breeze, A. '*Medcaut*, the Brittonic name of Lindisfarne', *Northern History*, 42 (2005), 187–8

Brewster, J. *The Parochial History and Antiquities of Stockton-upon-Tees*, 2nd edn (Stockton-upon-Tees, 1829)

Brink, S. 'Political and social structures in early Scandinavia: a settlement-historical pre-study of the central place', *TOR*, 28 (1996), 235–82

Brink, S. 'Trading hubs or political centres of power? Maritime focal sites in early Sweden' in J. H. Barrett and S. J. Gibbon (eds), *Maritime Societies of the Viking and Medieval World* (Oxford, 2015), pp. 88–98

Briscoe, D. C. 'Two important stamp motifs in Roman Britain and thereafter', *Internet Archaeology*, 41 (2016), intarch.ac.uk/journal/issue41/2/

Bromwich, R. 'Concepts of Arthur', *Studia Celtica*, 10/11 (1975–6), 163–81

Brooks, N. P. *The Early History of the Church of Canterbury* (London, 1984)

Brooks, N. P. 'The creation and early structure of the kingdom of Kent' in S. Bassett (ed.), *The Origins of Anglo-Saxon Kingdoms* (London, 1989), pp. 55–74

Brooks, N. P. 'The formation of the Mercian kingdom' in S. Bassett (ed.), *The Origins of Anglo-Saxon Kingdoms* (London, 1989), pp. 159–70

Brooks, N. P. 'Historical introduction' in L. Webster and J. Backhouse (eds), *The Making of England. Anglo-Saxon Art and Culture, AD 600–900* (London, 1991), pp. 9–14

Bruce-Mitford, R. 'Late Celtic hanging bowls in Lincolnshire and South Humberside' in A. Vince (ed.), *Pre-Viking Lindsey* (Lincoln, 1993), pp. 45–70

Bruce-Mitford, R. *A Corpus of Late Celtic Hanging Bowls* (Oxford, 2005)

Burnham, B. C. and Wacher, J. *The Small Towns of Roman Britain* (Berkeley and Los Angeles, 1990)

Burns, T. S. *A History of the Ostrogoths* (Bloomington, 1984)

Caerwyn Williams, J. E. 'Review of John T. Koch, *The Gododdin of Aneirin*', *Studia Celtica*, 32 (1998), 282–91

Cameron, K. 'The meaning and significance of Old English *walh* in English place-names', *Journal of the English Place-Name Society*, 12 (1980), 1–53

Cameron, K. *The Place-Names of Lincolnshire, I* (Nottingham, 1985)

Cameron, K. *The Place-Names of Lincolnshire, II* (Nottingham, 1991)

Cameron, K. *The Place-Names of Lincolnshire, III* (Nottingham, 1992)

Cameron, K. *The Place-Names of Lincolnshire, IV* (Nottingham, 1996)

Cameron, K. *English Place Names*, 2nd edn (London, 1996)

Cameron, K. *Dictionary of Lincolnshire Place-Names* (Nottingham, 1998)

Cameron, K. *The Place-Names of Lincolnshire, VI* (Nottingham, 2001)

Campbell, J. 'Bede's *Reges* and *Principes*' in J. Campbell, *Essays in Anglo-Saxon History* (London, 1986), pp. 85–98

Campbell, J. 'Bede's words for places' in J. Campbell, *Essays in Anglo-Saxon History* (London, 1986), pp. 99–119

Campbell, J. 'Bede (673/4–735)', in *The Oxford Dictionary of National Biography*, (Oxford, 2004), online edition: www.oxforddnb.com

Campbell, J. 'Some considerations on religion in early England' in M. Henig and T. J. Smith (eds), *Collectanea Antiqua: Essays in memory of Sonia Chadwick Hawkes* (Oxford, 2007), pp. 67–73

Cary, J. *Cary's New and Correct English Atlas* (London, 1787)

Cessford, C. 'Where are the Anglo-Saxons in the Gododdin poem?', *Anglo-Saxon Studies in Archaeology and History*, 8 (1995), 95–8

Cessford, C. 'Northern England and the Gododdin poem', *Northern History*, 33 (1997), 218–22

Chadwick, H. M. *The Origin of the English Nation* (Cambridge, 1924)

Charles-Edwards, T. 'Language and society amongst the insular Celts, AD 400–1000' in M. Green (ed.), *The Celtic World* (London, 1995), pp. 703–36

Christie, N. 'Italy and the Roman to medieval transition' in J. Bintliff and H. Hamerow (eds), *Europe Between Late Antiquity and the Middle Ages* (Oxford, 1995), pp. 99–110

Clay, C. 'Roman forts in Lincolnshire' in S. Malone and M. Williams (eds), *Rumours of Roman Finds: Recent Work on Roman Lincolnshire*

(Heckington, 2010), pp. 30–42

Coates, R. *Toponymic Topics* (Brighton, 1988)

Coates, R. 'On some controversy surrounding *Gewissae/Gewissei, Cerdic* and *Ceawlin*', *Nomina*, 13 (1990), 1–11

Coates, R. 'Holland, the division of Lincolnshire' in R. Coates and A. Breeze, *Celtic Voices, English Places* (Stamford, 2000), pp. 162–4

Coates, R. 'Four pre-English river names in and around fenland: *Chater, Granta, Nene* and *Welland*', *Transactions of the Philological Society*, 103 (2005), 303–22

Coates, R. 'Two notes on names in *tūn* in relation to pre-English antiquities: Kirmington and Broughton, Lincolnshire', *Journal of the English Place-Name Society*, 37 (2005), 33–6

Coates, R. 'Invisible Britons: the view from linguistics' in N. J. Higham (ed.), *Britons in Anglo-Saxon England* (Woodbridge, 2007), pp. 172–91

Coates, R. 'Reflections on some major Lincolnshire place-names. Part one: Algarkirk to Melton Ross', *Journal of the English Place-Name Society*, 40 (2008), 35–95

Coates, R. 'Reflections on some major Lincolnshire place-names. Part two: Ness wapentake to Yarborough', *Journal of the English Place-Name Society*, 41 (2009), 57–102

Coates, R. and Breeze, A. *Celtic Voices, English Places. Studies of the Celtic Impact on Place-names in England* (Stamford, 2000)

Colgrave, B. (ed. and trans.) *Felix's Life of St Guthlac* (Cambridge, 1956)

Colgrave, B. (ed. and trans.) *The Earliest Life of St Gregory* (Cambridge, 1968)

Collingwood, R. G. and Myres, J. N. L. *Roman Britain and the English Settlements*, 2nd edn (Oxford, 1937)

Collins, R. 'Brooch use in the 4th- to 5th-century frontier' in R. Collins and L. Allason-Jones (ed.), *Finds From the Frontier: Material Culture in the 4th–5th Centuries* (London, 2010), pp. 64–77

Collins, R. 'Soldiers to warriors: renegotiating the Roman frontier in the fifth century' in F. Hunter and K. Painter, *Late Roman Silver: The Traprain Treasure in Context* (Edinburgh, 2013), pp. 29–43

Cool, H. 'The parts left over: material culture into the fifth century' in T. Wilmott and P. Wilson (eds), *The Late Roman Transition in the North* (Oxford, 2000), pp. 47–65

Cool, H. *Eating and Drinking in Roman Britain* (Cambridge, 2006)

Cool, H. 'A different life' in R. Collins and L. Allason-Jones (eds), *Finds from the Frontier: Material Culture in the 4th–5th Centuries* (London, 2010), pp. 1–9

Cool, H. 'Objects of glass, shale, bone and metal (except nails)', in P. Booth *et al* (eds), *The Late Roman Cemetery at Lankhills, Winchester: Excavations 2000–2005* (Oxford, 2010), pp. 266–309

Cool, H. 'Which "Romans"; what "home"? The myth of the "end" of Roman Britain' in F. K. Haarer *et al* (eds), *AD 410: The History and Archaeology of Late and Post-Roman Britain* (London, 2014), pp. 13–22

Cope-Faulkner, P. *Sempringham: Village to Priory to Mansion* (Heckington, 2011)

Cotterill, J. 'Saxon raiding and the role of the Late Roman coastal forts of Britain', *Britannia*, 24 (1993), 227–39

Coulston, J. C. N. 'Military equipment of the "long" 4th century on Hadrian's Wall', in R. Collins and L. Allason-Jones (eds), *Finds From the Frontier: Material Culture in the 4th–5th Centuries* (London, 2010), pp. 50–63

Courtney, P. 'The early Saxon Fenland: a reconsideration', *Anglo-Saxon Studies in Archaeology and History*, 2 (1981), 91–102

Cowie, R. 'Mercian London' in M. P. Brown and C. A. Farr (eds), *Mercia. An Anglo-Saxon Kingdom in Europe* (London, 2001), pp. 194–210

Cox, B. 'The significance of the distribution of English place-names in *-hām* in the Midlands and East Anglia', *Journal of the English Place-Name Society*, 5 (1972–3), 15–73

Cox, B. 'The place-names of the earliest English records', *English Place-Name Society Journal*, 8 (1976), 12–66

Cox, B. *The Place-Names of Rutland* (Nottingham, 1994)

Cox, B. 'The pattern of Old English *burh* in early Lindsey', *Anglo-Saxon England*, 23 (1994), 35–56

Cox, B. 'Yarboroughs in Lindsey', *English Place-Name Society Journal*, 28 (1994–5), 50–60

Cramp, R. 'Anglo-Saxon settlement' in J. C. Chapman and H. C. Mytum (eds), *Settlement in North Britain, 1000 BC – AD 1000* (Oxford, 1983), pp. 263–97

Crawford, B. (ed.) *Scotland in Dark Age Europe* (St Andrews, 1994)

Crerar, B. 'Contextualising Romano-British lead tanks: a study in design, destruction and deposition', *Britannia*, 43 (2012), 135–66

Crowson, A., Lane, T., Penn, K. and Trimble, D. *Anglo-Saxon Settlement on the Siltland of Eastern England* (Heckington, 2005)

Darby, H. C. 'The Fenland frontier in Anglo-Saxon England', *Antiquity*, 8 (1934), 185–201

Dark, K. R. 'A sub-Roman re-defence of Hadrian's Wall?', *Britannia*, 22 (1992), 111–20

Dark, K. R. 'St Patrick's *villula* and the fifth-century occupation of Romano-British villas' in D. N. Dumville (ed.), *Saint Patrick A.D. 493–1993* (Woodbridge, 1993), pp. 19–24

Dark, K. R. *Civitas to Kingdom: British Political Continuity 300–800* (London, 1994)

Dark, K. R. 'Proto-industrialisation and the end of the Roman economy' in K. R. Dark (ed.), *External Contacts and the Economy of Late Roman and Post-Roman Britain* (Woodbridge, 1996), pp. 1–21

Dark, K. R. 'Pottery and local production at the end of Roman Britain' in K. R. Dark (ed.), *External Contacts and the Economy of Late Roman and Post-Roman Britain* (Woodbridge, 1996), pp. 53–65

Dark, K. R. *Britain and the End of the Roman Empire* (Stroud, 2000)

Dark, K. R. 'Western Britain in Late Antiquity' in F. K. Haarer *et al* (eds), *AD 410: The History and Archaeology of Late and Post-Roman Britain* (London, 2014), pp. 23–35

Dark, K. R. and Dark, P. *The Landscape of Roman Britain* (Stroud, 1997)

Dark, P. 'Palaeoecological evidence for landscape continuity and change in Britain *ca* A.D. 400–800' in K. R. Dark (ed.), *External Contacts and the Economy of Late Roman and Post-Roman Britain* (Woodbridge, 1996), pp. 23–51

Darling, M. J. *A Group of Late Roman Pottery from Lincoln* (Lincoln, 1977)

Darling, M. and Precious, B. *A Corpus of Roman Pottery from Lincoln* (Oxford, 2014)

Daubney, A. 'Ancient British cult of Toutatis discovered in Lincolnshire', published on the Portable Antiquities Scheme website (12 July 2007), www.finds.org.uk/wordpress/?p=329

Daubney, A. 'The South Lincolnshire Productive Site', a lecture delivered at the Council for British Archaeology (East Midlands) AGM, 21 March 2009.

Daubney, A. 'The use of gold in late Iron Age and Roman Lincolnshire' in S. Malone and M. Williams (eds), *Rumours of Roman Finds: Recent Work on Roman Lincolnshire* (Heckington, 2010), pp. 64–74

Daubney, A. 'The use of precious metals in Late Roman Lincolnshire', a lecture delivered at the SLHA 'End of Roman Lincolnshire' conference, 20 March 2010

Daubney, A. 'The cult of Totatis' in S. Worrell, K. Leahy, M. Lewis and J. Naylor (eds), *A Decade of Discovery: Proceedings of the Portable Antiquities Scheme Conference 2007* (Oxford, 2010), pp. 109–20

Daubney, A. J. *Portable Antiquities, Palimpsests, and Persistent Places* (Leiden, 2016)

Davies, W. 'Annals and the origin of Mercia' in A. Dornier (ed.), *Mercian Studies* (London, 1977), pp. 17–29

Davies, W. and Vierck, H. 'The contexts of the Tribal Hidage: social aggregates and settlement patterns', *Frühmittelalterliche Studien*, 8 (1974), 223–93

DCMS, *Treasure Annual Report 2001*, Department for Culture, Media and Sport (London, 2003)

DCMS, *Treasure Annual Report 2002*, Department for Culture, Media and Sport (London, 2004)

DCMS, *Treasure Annual Report 2003*, Department for Culture, Media and Sport (London, 2004)

De la Bédoyère, G. *The Golden Age of Roman Britain* (Stroud, 1999)

Dickinson, T. M. 'Fowler's Type G Penannular brooches reconsidered', *Medieval Archaeology*, 26 (1982), 41–68

Dickinson, T. M. 'An early Anglo-Saxon Cemetery at Quarrington, near Sleaford, Lincolnshire: report on excavations, 2000–2001', *Lincolnshire History and Archaeology*, 39 (2004), 24–45

Dobney, K., Jaques, D. and Irving, B. *Of Butchers and Breeds: Report on Vertebrate Remains from Various Sites in the City of Lincoln* (Lincoln, 1996)

Dobney, K., Kenward, H., Ottaway, P. and Donel, L. 'Down, but not out: biological evidence for complex economic organization in Lincoln in the late 4th century', *Antiquity*, 72 (1998), 417–24

Dodgson, J. 'The significance of the distribution of the English place-name in *-ingas*, *-inga-* in south-east England', reprinted in K. Cameron (ed.), *Place-name Evidence for the Anglo-Saxon Invasion and*

Scandinavian Settlements (Nottingham, 1977), pp. 27–54

Dornier, A. 'The Anglo-Saxon monastery at Breedon-on-the-Hill, Leicestershire' in A. Dornier (ed.), *Mercian Studies* (Leicester, 1977), pp. 155–68

Drinkall, G. and Foreman, M. *The Anglo-Saxon Cemetery at Castledyke South, Barton-on-Humber* (Sheffield, 1998)

Dudley, H. *Early Days in North-West Lincolnshire* (Scunthorpe, 1949)

Duggan, M. 'Ceramic imports to Britain and the Atlantic seaboard in the fifth century and beyond', *Internet Archaeology*, 41 (2016), *intarch.ac.uk/journal/issue41/3/*

Dumville, D. N. 'A new chronicle-fragment of early British history', *English Historical Review*, 88 (1973), 312–14

Dumville, D. N. 'Some aspects of the chronology of the *Historia Brittonum*', *Bulletin of the Board of Celtic Studies*, 25 (1974), 439–45

Dumville, D. N. 'The Anglian Collection of royal genealogies and regnal lists', *Anglo-Saxon England*, 5 (1976), 23–50

Dumville, D. N. 'Kingship, genealogies and regnal lists' in P. H. Sawyer and I. N. Wood (eds), *Early Medieval Kingship* (Leeds, 1977), pp. 72–104

Dumville, D. N. 'Sub-Roman Britain: history and legend', *History*, 62 (1977), 173–92

Dumville, D. N. 'The historical value of the *Historia Brittonum*', *Arthurian Literature*, 6 (1986), 1–26

Dumville, D. N. 'Essex, Middle Anglia and the expansion of Mercia' in S. Bassett (ed.), *The Origins of Anglo-Saxon Kingdoms* (London, 1989), pp. 123–40

Dumville, D. N. 'The origins of Northumbria' in S. Bassett (ed.), *The Origins of Anglo-Saxon Kingdoms* (London, 1989), pp. 213–22

Dumville, D. N. 'The Tribal Hidage: an introduction to its texts and their history' in S. Bassett (ed.), *The Origins of Anglo-Saxon Kingdoms* (London, 1989), pp. 225–30

Dumville, D. N. 'The idea of government in sub-Roman Britain' in G. Ausenda (ed.), *After Empire: Towards an Ethnology of Europe's Barbarians* (Woodbridge, 1995), pp. 177–204

Dumville, D. N. and Lapidge, M. (eds) *Gildas: New Approaches* (Woodbridge, 1984)

Eagles, B. *The Anglo-Saxon Settlement of Humberside* (2 vols, Oxford, 1979)

Eagles, B. 'Lindsey' in S. Bassett (ed.), *The Origins of Anglo-Saxon Kingdoms* (London, 1989), pp. 202–12

Eagles, B. 'The archaeological evidence for settlement in the fifth to seventh centuries AD' in M. Aston and C. Lewis (eds), *The Medieval Landscape of Wessex* (Oxford, 1994), pp. 13–32

Ekwall, E. *English River-Names* (Oxford, 1928)

Ekwall, E. *The Concise Oxford Dictionary of English Place-Names*, 4th edn (Oxford, 1960)

Elsdon, S. M. *Old Sleaford Revealed. A Lincolnshire Settlement in Iron Age, Roman, Saxon and Medieval Times: Excavations 1882–1995* (Oxford, 1997)

Elton, G. *The English* (Oxford, 1992)

Esmonde-Cleary, S. *The Ending of Roman Britain* (London, 1989)

Esmonde-Cleary, S. 'Late Roman towns in Britain and their fate' in A. Vince (ed.), *Pre-Viking Lindsey* (Lincoln, 1993), pp. 6–13

Esmonde-Cleary, S. 'Changing constraints on the landscape' in D. Hooke and S. Burnell (eds), *Landscape and Settlement in Britain AD 400–1066* (Exeter, 1995), pp. 11–26

Esmonde-Cleary, S. 'Britain in the fourth century' in M. Todd (ed.), *A Companion to Roman Britain* (Oxford, 2004), pp. 409–27

Everson, P. 'Pre-Viking settlement in Lindsey' in A. Vince (ed.), *Pre-Viking Lindsey* (Lincoln, 1993), pp. 91–100

Everson, P. and Stocker, D. '"Coming from Bardney..." – the landscape context of the causeways and finds groups of the Witham valley' in S. Catney and D. Start (eds), *Time and Tide, The Archaeology of the Witham Valley* (Sleaford, 2003), pp. 6–15

Everson, P. and Stocker, D. *Custodians of Continuity? The Premonstratensian Abbey at Barlings and the Landscape of Ritual* (Heckington, 2011)

Everson, P. and Stocker, D. '"The Cros in the Markitte Stede": the Louth Cross, its monastery and its town', *Medieval Archaeology*, 61 (2017), 330–71

Everson, P. L., Taylor, C. C. and Dunn, C. J. *Change and Continuity: Rural Settlement in North-West Lincolnshire* (London, 1991)

Evison, V. I. 'The Dover ring-sword and other ring-swords and beads', *Archaeologia*, 101 (1967), 63–118

Faulkner, N. 'Later Roman Colchester', *Oxford Journal of Archaeology*, 13.1 (1994), 93–120

Faulkner, N. 'Verulamium: interpreting decline', *Archaeological Journal*, 153 (1996), 79–103

Faulkner, N. 'Urban stratigraphy and Roman history' in N. Holbrook (ed.), *Cirencester: The Roman Town Defences, Public Buildings and Shops* (Cirencester, 1998), pp. 371–85

Faulkner, N. *The Decline and Fall of Roman Britain* (Stroud, 2000)

Faull, M. 'British survival in Anglo-Saxon Northumbria' in L. Laing (ed.), *Studies in Celtic Survival* (Oxford, 1977), pp. 1–56

Featherstone, P. 'The Tribal Hidage and the ealdormen of Mercia' in M. P. Brown and C. A. Farr (eds), *Mercia. An Anglo-Saxon Kingdom in Europe* (London, 2001), pp. 23–34

Fellows-Jensen, G. 'The light thrown by the early place-names of Southern Scandinavia and England on population movement in the Migration Period' in E. Marold and C. Zimmermann (eds), *Nordwestgermanisch* (Berlin, 1995), pp.57–75

Fellows-Jensen, G. 'The Weevil's claw' in A. van Nahl, L. Elmevik and S. Brink (eds), *Namenwelten* (Berlin, 2004), pp. 76–89

Fenwick, H. 'The Lincolnshire Marsh: Landscape Evolution, Settlement Development and the Salt Industry' (University of Hull PhD Thesis, 2007)

Field, N. 'Romano-British pottery kilns in the Trent valley', *Lincolnshire History and Archaeology*, 19 (1984), 100–2

Field, N. 'Stow church', *Lincolnshire History and Archaeology*, 19 (1984), 105–06

Field, N. and Hurst, H. 'Roman Horncastle', *Lincolnshire History & Archaeology*, 18 (1983), 47–88

Filppula, M., Klemola, J. and Paulasto, H. *English and Celtic in Contact* (London, 2008)

Fitzpatrick-Matthews, K. J. 'Defining fifth-century ceramics in north Hertfordshire', *Internet Archaeology*, 41 (2016), intarch.ac.uk/journal/issue41/4/

Fitzpatrick-Matthews, K. J. and Fleming, R. 'The perils of periodization: Roman ceramics in Britain after 400 CE', *Fragments*, 5 (2016), 1–33

Fisher, G. 'Kingdom and community in early Anglo-Saxon eastern England' in L. Anderson Beck (ed.), *Regional Approaches to Mortuary Analysis* (New York, 1995), pp. 147–66

Foard, G. 'The administrative organisation of Northamptonshire in the Saxon period', *Anglo-Saxon Studies in Archaeology and History*, 4 (1985), 185–222

Foot, S. 'The kingdom of Lindsey' in A. Vince (ed.), *Pre-Viking Lindsey* (Lincoln, 1993), pp. 128–40

Forester, T. (trans.) *The Chronicle of Florence of Worcester* (London, 1854)

Foster, C. W. and Longley, T. (eds) *The Lincolnshire Domesday and the Lindsey Survey*, LRS, vol. 19 (Lincoln, 1924)

Freeman, E. A. *Old English History for Children*, 2nd edn (London, 1871)

Fulford, M. and Tyers, I. 'The date of Pevensey and the defense of an "*Imperium Britanniarum*"', *Antiquity*, 69 (1995), 1009–14

Gardiner, M. 'An early medieval tradition of building in Britain', *Arqueología de la Arquitectura*, 9 (2012), 231–46

Gavin, F. 'Insular Military Style silver pins in Late Iron Age Ireland' in F. Hunter and K. Painter (eds), *Late Roman Silver Within and Beyond the Frontier: The Traprain Treasure in Context* (Edinburgh, 2013), pp. 415–26

Gavin, F. 'Insular Ornamental Metalwork AD 300–500: 'Military Style' Inspired Art in Ireland and Britain' (2 vols, National University of Ireland, Galway, PhD Thesis, 2014)

Geake, H. 'When were hanging bowls deposited in Anglo-Saxon graves?', *Medieval Archaeology*, 43 (1999), 1–18

Gelling, M. 'English place-names derived from the compound *wīchām*' reprinted in K. Cameron (ed.), *Place-name Evidence for the Anglo-Saxon Invasion and Scandinavian Settlements* (Nottingham, 1977), pp. 8–26

Gelling, M. 'Latin loan-words in Old English place-names', *Anglo-Saxon England*, 6 (1977), 1–13

Gelling, M. 'Towards a chronology for English place-names' in D. Hooke (ed.), *Anglo-Saxon Settlements* (Oxford, 1988), pp. 59–76

Gelling, M. *Signposts to the Past. Place-names and the History of England*, 2nd edn (Chichester, 1988)

Gelling, M. 'The name Lindsey', *Anglo-Saxon England*, 18 (1989), 31–2

Gelling, M. 'Why aren't we speaking Welsh?', *Anglo-Saxon Studies in Archaeology and History*, 6 (1993), 51–6

Gelling, M. 'A brief history of English place-name studies', in M. Gelling, *Signposts to the Past*, 3rd edn (Chichester, 1997), pp. 9–20

Gelling, M. and Cole, A. *The Landscape of Place-Names*, 2nd edn

(Stamford, 2003)

Gerrard, J. 'How late is late? Pottery and the fifth century in southwest Britain' in R. Collins & J. Gerrard (eds), *Debating Late Antiquity in Britain AD 300–700* (Oxford, 2004), pp. 65–75

Gerrard, J. 'Finding the fifth century: a late fourth- and early fifth-century pottery fabric from south-east Dorset', *Britannia*, 41 (2010), 293–312

Gerrard, J. *The Ruin of Roman Britain: An Archaeological Perspective* (Cambridge, 2013)

Gerrard, J. 'Roman pottery in the fifth century: a review of the evidence and its significance' in F. K. Haarer *et al* (eds), *AD 410: The History and Archaeology of Late and Post-Roman Britain* (London, 2014), pp. 87–98

Gerrard, J. (ed.) *Romano-British Pottery in the Fifth Century*, *Internet Archaeology*, 41 (2016), intarch.ac.uk/journal/issue41/

Gerrard, J. 'The Black Burnished type 18 bowl and the fifth century', *Internet Archaeology*, 41 (2016), intarch.ac.uk/journal/issue41/5/

Gilmour, B. 'Sub-Roman or Saxon, pagan or Christian: who was buried in the early cemetery at St-Paul-in-the-Bail, Lincoln?' in L. Gilmour (ed.), *Pagans and Christians – from Antiquity to the Middle Ages* (Oxford, 2007), pp. 229–56

Gilmour, L. A. *Early Medieval Pottery from Flaxengate, Lincoln* (London, 1988)

Goffart, W. *Barbarians and Romans, A.D. 418–584: The Techniques of Accommodation* (Princeton, 1980)

Goffart, W. *Rome's Fall and After* (London, 1989)

Graham-Campbell, J. 'Dinas Powys metalwork and the dating of enamelled zoomorphic penannular brooches', *Bulletin of the Board of Celtic Studies*, 38 (1991), 220–32

Green, C. *Concepts of Arthur* (Stroud, 2007)

Green, C. 'The British kingdom of Lindsey', *Cambrian Medieval Celtic Studies*, 56 (2008), 1–43

Green, C. *The Origins of Louth: Archaeology and History in East Lincolnshire, 400,000 BC–AD 1086* (Louth, 2011)

Green, C. 'Tealby, the *Taifali*, and the end of Roman Lincolnshire', *Lincolnshire History & Archaeology*, 46 (2011), 5–10

Green, C. 'Stain Hill and the Lincolnshire Marshes in the Anglo-Saxon period', 2 November 2014, www.caitlingreen.org/2014/11/stainhill-anglo-saxon-marsh.html

Green, C. 'Ketsby DMV: a Roman–Early Modern settlement and pilgrimage site on the Lincolnshire Wolds', 4 February 2015, www.caitlingreen.org/2015/02/ketsby-dmv.html

Green, C. 'An early Anglo-Saxon pot from the Greetwell villa-palace', 8 April 2015, www.caitlingreen.org/2015/04/an-early-anglo-saxon-pot-from-greetwell.html

Gruffydd, R. G. 'In search of Elmet', *Studia Celtica*, 28 (1994), 63–79

Haddan, A. W. and Stubbs, W. (eds) *Councils and Ecclesiastical Documents Relating to Great Britain and Ireland* (3 vols, Oxford, 1869–79)

Hadley, D. M. *The Vikings in England: Settlement, Society and Culture* (Manchester, 2006)

Hadley, D. M. and Richards, J. D. 'The winter camp of the Viking Great Army, AD 872–3, Torksey, Lincolnshire', *Antiquaries Journal*, 96 (2016), 23–67

Hallam, S. J. *Settlement and Society. A Study of the Early Agrarian History of South Lincolnshire* (Cambridge, 1965)

Halsall, G. 'Social change around A.D. 600: an Austrasian perspective' in M. O. H. Carver (ed.), *The Age of Sutton Hoo* (Woodbridge, 1992), pp. 265–78

Halsall, G. 'Social identities and social relationships in early medieval Gaul' in I. Wood (ed.), *Franks and Alamanni in the Merovingian Period: An Ethnographic Perspective* (Woodbridge, 1998), pp. 141–75

Hamerow, H. 'Settlement mobility and the "Middle Saxon Shuffle": rural settlements and settlement patterns in Anglo-Saxon England', *Anglo-Saxon England*, 20 (1991), 1–18

Hamerow, H. *Early Medieval Settlements* (Oxford, 2002)

Hamerow, H. 'The earliest Anglo-Saxon kingdoms' in P. Fouracre (ed.), *The New Cambridge Medieval History, I: c.500–c.700* (Cambridge, 2005), pp. 263–88

Hamerow, H. *Rural Settlements and Society in Anglo-Saxon England* (Oxford, 2012)

Harden, D. B. (ed.) *Dark Age Britain. Studies Presented to E. T. Leeds* (London, 1956)

Härke, H. *Angelsächsische Waffengräber des 5. bis 7. Jahrhunderts* (Cologne, 1992)

Härke, H. 'Changing symbols in a changing society: the Anglo-Saxon weapon burial rite in the seventh century' in M. O. H. Carver (ed.), *The Age of Sutton Hoo* (Woodbridge, 1992), pp. 149–65

Härke, H. 'Early Anglo-Saxon social structure' in J. Hines (ed.), *The Anglo-Saxons from the Migration Period to the Eighth Century: An Ethnographic Perspective* (Woodbridge, 1997), pp. 125–60

Härke, H. 'Population replacement or acculturation? An archaeological perspective on population and migration in post-Roman Britain' in H. L. C. Tristram (ed.), *The Celtic Englishes III* (Hiedelberg, 2003), pp. 13–28

Härke, H. 'Anglo-Saxon immigration and ethnogenesis', *Medieval Archaeology*, 55 (2011), 1–28

Hart, C. 'The Tribal Hidage', *Transactions of the Royal Historical Society*, fifth series, 21 (1971), 133–57

Hase, P. H. 'The Church in the Wessex heartlands' in M. Aston and C. Lewis (eds), *The Medieval Landscape of Wessex* (Oxford, 1994), pp. 47–52

Hayes, P. P. 'Roman to Saxon in the south Lincolnshire Fens', *Antiquity*, 62 (1988), 321–6

Hayes, P. P. and Lane, T. W. *The Fenland Project, Number 5: Lincolnshire Survey, The South-West Fens* (Sleaford, 1992)

Haywood, J. *Dark Age Naval Power: A Reassessment of Frankish and Anglo-Saxon Seafaring Activity* (London, 1991)

Hearne, T. (ed.) *The Itinerary of John Leland the Antiquary* (9 vols, Oxford, 1770)

Hedeager, L. 'Kingdoms, ethnicity and material culture: Denmark in a European perspective' in M. O. H. Carver (ed.), *The Age of Sutton Hoo. The Seventh-Century in North-western Europe* (Woodbridge, 1992), pp. 279–300

Herlihy, D. *Medieval Households* (Cambridge, Mass., 1985)

Higginbottom, R. W. 'Roman coin hoards from Lincolnshire', *Lincolnshire History and Archaeology*, 15 (1980), 5–8

Higham, N. J. *The Northern Counties to AD 1000* (London, 1986)

Higham, N. J. *Rome, Britain and the Anglo-Saxons* (London, 1992)

Higham, N. J. *The Kingdom of Northumbria, AD 350–1100* (Stroud, 1993)

Higham, N. J. *The English Conquest: Gildas and Britain in the Fifth Century* (Manchester, 1994)

Higham, N. J. *An English Empire. Bede and the Early Anglo-Saxon Kings*

(Manchester, 1995)

Higham, N. J. *Arthur, Myth-Making and History* (London, 2002)

Higham, N. J. 'Northumbria's southern frontier: a review', *Early Medieval Europe*, 14.4 (2006), 391–418

Higham, N. J. (ed.), *Britons in Anglo-Saxon England* (Woodbridge, 2007)

Higham, N. J. and Ryan, M. J. *The Anglo-Saxon World* (London, 2013)

Hills, C. 'The Anglo-Saxon migration to Britain: an archaeological perspective' in H. Meller *et al* (eds), *Migration and Integration from Prehistory to the Middle Ages* (Saale, 2017), pp. 239–53

Hills, C. and Lucy, S. *Spong Hill IX: Chronology and Synthesis* (Cambridge, 2013)

Hines, J. *The Scandinavian Character of Anglian England in the pre-Viking Period* (Oxford, 1984)

Hines, J. 'Philology, archaeology and the *adventus Saxonum vel Anglorum*' in A. Bammesberger and A. Wollmann (eds), *Britain 400–600: Language and History* (Heidelberg, 1990), pp. 17–36

Hines, J. 'Britain after Rome' in P. Graves-Brown, S. Jones and C. Gamble (eds), *Cultural Identity and Archaeology: The Construction of European Communities* (London, 1996), pp. 256–70

Hines, J. *A New Corpus of Anglo-Saxon Great Square-Headed Brooches* (Woodbridge, 1997)

Hines, J. 'The Anglo-Saxon archaeology of the Cambridge region and the Middle Anglian kingdom', *Anglo-Saxon Studies in Archaeology and History*, 10 (1999), 135–49

Hines, J. 'The origins of East Anglia in a North Sea Zone' in D. Bates & R. Liddiard (eds), *East Anglia and its North Sea World in the Middle Ages* (Woodbridge, 2013), pp. 16–43

Hines, J. and Bayliss, A. (eds), *Anglo-Saxon Graves and Grave Goods of the 6th and 7th Centuries AD: A Chronological Framework*, Society for Medieval Archaeology Monograph, 33 (London, 2013)

Hinton, D. A. *A Smith in Lindsey: The Anglo-Saxon Grave at Tattershall Thorpe, Lincolnshire* (London, 2000)

Hodges, R. *Dark Age Economics: The Origins of Towns and Trade AD 600–1000* (London, 1982)

Hodges, R. *The Anglo-Saxon Achievement. Archaeology and the Beginnings of English Society* (London, 1989)

Hooke, D. *Worcestershire Anglo-Saxon Charter Bounds* (Woodbridge, 1990)

Hough, C. 'Some ghost entries in Smith's *English Place-Name Elements*', *Nomina*, 17 (1994), 19–30

Hough, C. 'Wilsill in Yorkshire and related placenames', *Notes and Queries*, 50.3 (2003), 253–7

Hope-Taylor, B. *Yeavering. An Anglo-British Centre of Early Northumbria* (London, 1977)

Huggett, J. 'Imported grave goods and the early Anglo-Saxon economy', *Medieval Archaeology*, 32 (1988), 63–96

Innes, M. 'Land, freedom and the making of the medieval West', *Transactions of the Royal Historical Society*, 16 (2006), 39–74

Insley, J. 'Gumeningas', *Reallexikon der Germanischen Altertumskunde*, 13 (1999), 191–3

Insley, J. 'Gyrwe', *Reallexikon der Germanischen Altertumskunde*, 13 (Berlin, 1999), 229–32

Insley, J. 'Jarrow (etymology of the name)', *Reallexikon der Germanischen Altertumskunde*, 16 (2000), 37–9

Insley, J. 'Kultische namen', *Reallexikon der Germanischen Altertumskunde*, 17 (Berlin, 2000), 425–37

Insley, J. 'The study of Old English personal names and anthroponymic lexika' in D. Geuenich, W. Haubrichs and J. Jarnut (eds), *Person und Name* (Berlin, 2002), pp. 148–76

Insley, J. 'Pre-conquest personal names', *Reallexikon der Germanischen Altertumskunde*, 23 (Berlin, 2003), 367–96

Insley, J. 'Siedlungsnamen §2. Englische', *Reallexikon der Germanischen Altertumskunde*, 28 (2005), 344–53

Insley, J. 'Wapentake', *Reallexikon der Germanischen Altertumskunde*, 33 (Berlin, 2006), 250–2

Insley, J. and Eggers, M. 'Lindsey', *Reallexikon der Germanischen Altertumskunde*, 18 (Berlin, 2001), 471–9

Insley, J. and Scharer, A. 'Hwicce', *Reallexikon der Geremanischen Altertumskunde*, 11 (2000), 287–96

Irvine, S. (ed.) *The Anglo-Saxon Chronicle. A Collaborative Edition. Volume 7: MS. E* (Cambridge, 2004)

Isaac, G. R. 'Readings in the history and transmission of the *Gododdin*', *Cambrian Medieval Celtic Studies*, 37 (1999), 55–78

Jackson, K. H. 'Once again Arthur's battles', *Modern Philology*, 43 (1945), 44–57

Jackson, K. H. 'On the name "Leeds"', *Antiquity*, 20 (1946), 209–10

Jackson, K. H. *Language and History in Early Britain* (Edinburgh, 1953)

Jackson, K. H. 'The site of Mount Badon', *The Journal of Celtic Studies*, 2 (1953–8), 152–5

Janes, D. 'The golden clasp of the Late Roman state', *Early Medieval Europe*, 5.2 (1991), 127–53

Jones, D. 'Aerial reconnaissance and prehistoric and Romano-British archaeology in northern Lincolnshire – a sample survey', *Lincolnshire History and Archaeology*, 23 (1988), 5–30

Jones, D. and Whitwell, B. 'Survey of the Roman fort and multi-period settlement complex at Kirmington on the Lincolnshire Wolds: a non-destructive approach', *Lincolnshire History and Archaeology*, 26 (1991), 57–62

Jones, D. 'Romano-British settlement in the Lincolnshire Wolds' in R. H. Bewley (ed.), *Lincolnshire's Archaeology from the Air* (Lincoln, 1998), pp. 69–80

Jones, G. 'Holy wells and the cult of St Helen', *Landscape History*, 8 (1986), 59–75

Jones, G. *Saints in the Landscape* (Stroud, 2007)

Jones, M. E. *The End of Roman Britain* (Ithaca, 1996)

Jones, M. J. 'The latter days of Roman Lincoln' in A. Vince (ed.), *Pre-Viking Lindsey* (Lincoln, 1993), pp. 14–28

Jones, M. J. 'St Paul in the Bail, Lincoln: Britain in Europe?' in K. Painter (ed.), *Churches Built in Ancient Times: Recent Studies in Early Christian Archaeology* (London, 1994), pp. 325–47

Jones, M. J. *Roman Lincoln: Conquest, Colony and Capital* (Stroud, 2002)

Jones, M. J. 'The Colonia era: archaeological account' in D. Stocker (ed.), *The City by the Pool: Assessing the Archaeology of the City of Lincoln* (Oxford, 2003), pp. 56–138

Jones, M. J. 'Recent research on the archaeology of the early Christian Church in Britain, c. 300–800' in S. Cresci *et al* (eds,) *Acta XV Congressus Internationalis Archaeologiae Christianae (Toledo 8–12.9 2008) — Episcopus, Civitas, Territorium, Studi Di Antichità Cristiana LXV* (Vatican City, 2013), pp. 1163–78

Phillips, G. and Keatman, M. *King Arthur: The True Story* (London, 1992)

Kelly, S. E. (ed.) *Charters of Selsey* (Oxford, 1998)

Keynes, S. *The Councils of Clofesho* (Leicester, 1994)

Keynes, S. 'England, 700–900' in R. McKitterick (ed.), *The New*

Cambridge Medieval History, II: c.700–c.900 (Cambridge, 1995), pp. 18–42

Keynes, S. 'Diocese and cathedral before 1056' in G. Aylmer and J. Tiller (eds), *Hereford Cathedral: A History* (London, 2000), pp. 3–20

Keynes, S. 'Between Bede and the *Chronicle*: London, BL, Cotton Vespasian B. vi, fols. 104–9' in K. O. O'Keeffe and A. Orchard (eds), *Latin Learning and English Lore: Studies in Anglo-Saxon Literature for Michael Lapidge* (Toronto, 2005), pp. 47–67

Kirby, D. P. *The Earliest English Kings*, 2nd edn (London, 2000)

Kitson, P. 'Quantifying qualifiers in Anglo-Saxon charter boundaries', *Folia Linguistica Historica*, 14 (1993), 29–82

Koch, J. T. 'When was Welsh literature first written down?', *Studia Celtica*, 20/21 (1985–6), 43–66

Koch, J. T. 'The cynfeirdd poetry and the language of the sixth century' in B. F. Roberts (ed.), *Early Welsh Poetry: Studies in the Book of Aneirin* (Aberystwyth, 1988), pp. 17–41

Koch, J. T. 'Gleanings from the *Gododdin* and other Early Welsh texts', *Bulletin of the Board of Celtic Studies*, 38 (1991), 111–18

Koch, J. T. *The Gododdin of Aneirin: Text and Context from Dark-Age North Britain* (Cardiff, 1997)

Koch, J. T. 'Marwnad Cunedda a diwedd y Brydain Rufeinig' in P. Russell (ed.), *Yr Hen Iaith: Studies in Early Welsh* (Aberystwyth, 2003), pp. 171–97

Koch, J. T. (ed.) *Celtic Culture, A Historical Encyclopedia* (Oxford, 2006)

Koch, J. T. and Carey, J. T. *The Celtic Heroic Age: Literary Sources for Ancient Celtic Europe and Early Medieval Ireland and Wales* (Aberystwyth, 2003)

Kuurman, J. 'An examination of the *-ingas, -inga-* place-names in the East Midlands', *Journal of the English Place-Name Society*, 7 (1974–5), 11–44

Laing, L. 'The Bradwell mount and the use of millefiori in post-Roman Britain', *Studia Celtica*, 33 (1999), 137–53

Laing, L. 'Romano-British metalworking and the Anglo-Saxons' in N. J. Higham (ed.), *Britons in Anglo-Saxon England* (Woodbridge, 2007), pp. 42–56

Lane, T. W. *The Fenland Project Number 8: Lincolnshire Survey, the Northern Fen-Edge* (Sleaford, 1992)

Lane, T. W. 'Invisible and irretrievable? Consideration of some non-ceramic aspects of Fenland salt production' in T. Lane and E. L. Morris (eds), *A Millennium of Saltmaking: Prehistoric and Romano-British Salt Production in the Fenland* (Heckington, 2001), pp. 459–65

Lane, T. W. and Hayes, P. 'Moving boundaries in the Fens of south Lincolnshire' in J. Gardiner (ed.), *Flatlands and Wetlands: Current Themes in East Anglian Archaeology* (Norwich, 1993), pp. 58–70

Laycock, S. 'Britannia: the threat within', *British Archaeology*, 87 (2006), 10–15

Laycock, S. *Britannia, The Failed State* (Stroud, 2008)

Leahy, K. 'The Anglo-Saxon settlement of Lindsey' in A. Vince (ed.), *Pre-Viking Lindsey* (Lincoln, 1993), pp. 29–44

Leahy, K. 'Three Roman rivet spurs from Lincolnshire', *Antiquaries Journal*, 76 (1996), 237–40

Leahy, K. 'The early Saxon context' in G. Drinkall and M. Foreman (eds), *The Anglo-Saxon Cemetery at Castledyke South, Barton-on-Humber* (Sheffield, 1998), pp. 6–17

Leahy, K. 'The formation of the Anglo-Saxon kingdom of Lindsey', *Anglo-Saxon Studies in Archaeology and History*, 10 (1999), 127–33

Leahy, K. *'Interrupting the Pots': The Excavation of Cleatham Anglo-Saxon Cemetery* (York, 2007)

Leahy, K. *The Anglo-Saxon Kingdom of Lindsey* (Stroud, 2007)

Leahy, K. 'Soldiers and settlers in Britain, fourth to fifth century – revisited' in M. Henig and T. J. Smith (eds), *Collectanea Antiqua: Essays in Memory of Sonia Chadwick Hawkes* (Oxford, 2007), pp. 133–43

Leland, J. *The Itinerary of John Leland the Antiquary*, ed. T. Hearne (Oxford, 1770)

Lingard, C. F. and Bonner, L. *Blyborough-Brigg 300mm Gas Pipeline, 1993, Archaeological Report* (1994)

Loveluck, C. P. 'The development of the Anglo-Saxon landscape, economy and society "On Driffield", East Yorkshire, 400–750 AD', *Anglo-Saxon Studies in Archaeology and History*, 9 (1996), 25–48

Lupoi, M. *The Origins of the European Legal Order* (Cambridge, 2000)

Lucy, S. 'Changing burial rites in Northumbria, A.D. 500–750' in J. Hawkes and S. Mills (eds), *Northumbria's Golden Age* (Stroud, 1999), pp. 12–43

Lucy, S. 'Early Medieval burials in East Yorkshire: reconsidering the evidence' in H. Geake and J. Kenny (eds), *Early Deira. Archaeological Studies of the East Riding in the Fourth to Ninth Centuries AD* (Oxford, 2000), pp. 11–18

Lucy, S. *The Anglo-Saxon Way of Death* (Stroud, 2000)

Maddicott, J. R. 'London and Droitwich, *c.* 650–750: trade, industry and the rise of Mercia', *Anglo-Saxon England*, 34 (2005), 7–58

Malone, K. *Widsith*, 2nd edn (Copenhagen, 1962)

Malone, S. '"Rumours of Roman finds": updating Roman Lincolnshire' in S. Malone and M. Williams (eds), *Rumours of Roman Finds: Recent Work on Roman Lincolnshire* (Heckington, 2010), pp. 1–14

Malone, S. 'A group of Romano-British lead tanks from Lincolnshire and Nottinghamshire' in S. Malone and M. Williams (eds), *Rumours of Roman Finds: Recent Work on Roman Lincolnshire* (Heckington, 2010), pp. 138–42

Malone, S. 'Lincolnshire Fenland Lidar', *HTL/APS Working Paper 1* (2014), www.academia.edu/5807526

Malone, S. *Viking Link: Boygrift to North Ing Drove, Lincolnshire Onshore Cable Route – Air-Photographic and Lidar Assessment* (Nottingham, 2017)

Mann, J. C. 'The creation of four provinces in Britain by Diocletian', *Britannia*, 29 (1998), 339–41

Mann, J. E. 'Roman coins' in M. Jones (ed.), *The Defences of the Lower City* (York, 1999), p. 51

Margary, I. D. *Roman Roads in Britain*, 3rd edn (1973)

Martin, E. 'The *Iclingas*', *East Anglian Archaeology*, 3 (1976), 132–4

Martin, T. F. 'Identity and the Cruciform Brooch in Early Anglo-Saxon England: An Investigation of Style, Mortuary Context, and Use' (4 vols, University of Sheffield PhD Thesis, 2011)

Martin, T. 'Women, knowledge and power: the iconography of early Anglo-Saxon cruciform brooches', *Anglo-Saxon Studies in Archaeology and History*, 18 (2013), 1–17

Martin, T. F. *The Cruciform Brooch and Anglo-Saxon England* (Woodbridge, 2015)

May, J. *Dragonby: Report on Excavation at an Iron Age and Romano-British Settlement in North Lincolnshire* (2 vols, Oxford, 1996)

May, J. 'The later Iron Age' in S. Bennett and N. Bennett (eds), *An*

Historical Atlas of Lincolnshire (Chichester, 2001), pp. 12–13

Mayes, P. and Dean, M. J. *An Anglo-Saxon Cemetery at Baston, Lincolnshire* (Lincoln, 1976)

McEvoy, B., Richards, M., Forster, M. and Bradley, D. G. 'The *Longue Durée* of genetic ancestry: multiple genetic marker systems and Celtic origins on the Atlantic facade of Europe', *American Journal of Human Genetics*, 75 (2004), 693–702

Miket, R. 'A restatement of evidence from Bernician Anglo-Saxon burials' in P. A. Rahtz, T. M. Dickinson and L. Watts (eds), *Anglo-Saxon Cemeteries, 1979* (Oxford, 1980), pp. 289–306

Miller, M. 'Royal pedigrees of the insular Dark Ages: a progress report', *History in Africa*, 7 (1980), 201–24

Miller, T. (ed. and trans.) *The Old English Version of Bede's Ecclesiastical History* (2 vols, London, 1890 and 1898)

Millett, M. *The Romanization of Britain* (Cambridge, 1990)

Millett, M. *Roman Britain* (London, 1995)

Mills, A. D. *A Dictionary of English Place-Names* (Oxford, 1991)

Mills, A. D. *A Dictionary of British Place-Names* (Oxford, 2011)

Mommsen, T. 'Petrarch's conception of the "Dark Ages"', *Speculum*, 17 (1942), 226–42

Moore, J. S. 'Quot homines? The population of Domesday England', *Anglo-Norman Studies*, 19 (1997), 307–34

Morris, J. *The Age of Arthur* (London, 1973)

Morris, J. (ed. and trans.) *Nennius. British History and the Welsh Annals* (London, 1980)

Murphy, P. 'The Anglo-Saxon landscape and rural economy: some results from sites in East Anglia and Essex' in J. Rackham (ed.), *Environment and Economy in Anglo-Saxon England* (York, 1994), pp. 23–39

Murray, A. C. *Germanic Kinship Structure: Studies in Law and Society in Antiquity and the Early Middle Ages* (Toronto, 1983)

Myres, J. N. L. 'The Teutonic Settlement of Northern England', *History*, 20 (1935), 250–62

Myres, J. N. L. 'Some Anglo-Saxon potters', *Antiquity*, 11 (1937), 389–99

Myres, J. N. L. 'Lincoln in the fifth century A.D.', *Archaeological Journal*, 103 (1946), 85–8

Myres, J. N. L. *The English Settlements* (Oxford, 1986)

Niecke, M. R. 'Penannular and related brooches: secular ornament or symbol in action?' in R. M. Spearman and J. Higgitt (eds), *The Age of Migrating Ideas: Early Medieval Art in Northern Britain and Ireland* (Edinburgh, 1993), pp. 128–34

North, R. *Heathen Gods in Old English Literature* (Cambridge, 1997)

O'Brien, E. *Post-Roman Britain to Anglo-Saxon England: Burial Practices Reviewed* (Oxford, 1999)

Oliver, R. 'Possible Roman roads from Caistor and a possible fort at Cleethorpes', *Lincolnshire History and Archaeology*, 41 (2006), 18–21

Oosthuizen, S. 'The origins of Cambridgeshire', *Antiquaries Journal*, 78 (1998), 85–109

Oosthuizen, S. 'Culture and identity in the early medieval Fenland landscape', *Landscape History*, 37 (2016), 5–24

Oosthuizen, S. *The Anglo-Saxon Fenland* (Oxford, 2017)

Oosthuizen, S. *The Emergence of the English* (Leeds, 2019)

Owen, A. E. B. 'Herefrith of Louth, saint and bishop: a problem of identities', *Lincolnshire History and Archaeology*, 15 (1980), 15–19

Owen, A. E. B. 'Salt, sea banks and medieval settlement on the Lindsey coast' in N. Field and A. White (eds), *A Prospect of Lincolnshire* (Lincoln, 1984), pp. 46–9

Owen, A. E. B. 'Louth before Domesday', *Lincolnshire History and Archaeology*, 32 (1997), 60–4

Owen, A. E. B. 'Roads and Romans in south-east Lindsey' in A. R. Rumble and A. D. Mills (eds), *Names, Places and People* (Stamford, 1997), pp. 254–68

Owen, A. E. B. and Coates, R. '*Traiectus/Tric*/Skegness: a Domesday name explained', *Lincolnshire History and Archaeology*, 38 (2003), 42–4

Padel, O. J. 'The nature of Arthur', *Cambrian Medieval Celtic Studies*, 27 (1994), 1–31

Padel, O. J. 'A new study of the *Gododdin*', *Cambrian Medieval Celtic Studies*, 35 (1998), 45–55

Page, T. 'Coptic bowl from Loveden Hill', *Lincolnshire History and Archaeology*, 21 (1986), 76–7

Parker, M. S. 'The province of Hatfield', *Northern History*, 28 (1992), 42–69

Parsons, D. 'British **Caraticos*, Old English *Cerdic*', *Cambrian Medieval Celtic Studies*, 33 (1997), 1–8

Pawley, S. 'Grist to the mill: a new approach to the early history of Sleaford', *Lincolnshire History and Archaeology*, 23 (1988), 37–41

Pawley, S. 'Medieval Old Sleaford' in S. M. Elsdon, *Old Sleaford Revealed. A Lincolnshire Settlement in Iron Age, Roman, Saxon and Medieval Times: Excavations 1882–1995* (Oxford, 1997), pp. 68–72

Perry, G. J. 'Beer, butter and burial: the pre-burial origins of cremation urns from the early Anglo-Saxon cemetery of Cleatham, North Lincolnshire', *Medieval Ceramics*, 32 (2011), 9–21

Perry, G. J. 'United in Death: The Pre-Burial Origins of Anglo-Saxon Cremation Urns' (University of Sheffield PhD Thesis, 2013)

Petts, D. *Pagan and Christian: Religious Change in Early Medieval Europe* (London, 2011)

Phillips, G. and Keatman, M. *King Arthur: The True Story* (London, 1992)

Phillips, C. W. (ed.) *The Fenland in Roman Times* (London, 1970)

Platt, G. *Land and People in Medieval Lincolnshire*, History of Lincolnshire, vol. IV (Lincoln, 1985)

Potter, T. W. *The Changing Landscape of South Etruria* (London, 1979)

Potter, T. W. 'The Roman Fenland: a review of recent work' in M. Todd (ed.), *Research on Roman Britain: 1960–89* (London, 1989), pp. 147–73

Potts, W. T. W. 'The pre-Danish estates of Peterborough Abbey', *Proceedings of the Cambridge Antiquarian Society*, 65 (1974), 13–27

Proudfoot, E. and Aliaga-Kelly, C. 'Towards an Interpretation of Anomalous Finds and Place-Names of Anglo-Saxon Origin in Scotland', *Anglo-Saxon Studies in Archaeology and History*, 9 (1996), 1–13

Rackham, O. J. *The History of the Countryside* (London, 1986)

Rahtz, P. 'Late Roman cemeteries and beyond' in R. Reece (ed.), *Burial in the Roman World* (London, 1977), pp. 53–64

Rahtz, P. 'Celtic society in Somerset, A.D. 400–700', *Bulletin of the Board of Celtic Studies*, 30 (1982), 176–200

Rahtz, P. 'Anglo-Saxon Yorkshire: current research problems' in H. Geake and J. Kenny (eds), *Early Deira: Archaeological Studies of the East Riding in the Fourth to Ninth Centuries AD* (Oxford, 2000), pp. 1–10

Reece, R. 'The end of the city in Roman Britain' in J. Rich (ed.), *The City in Late Antiquity* (London, 1992), pp. 136–45

Riley, D. N., Buckland, P. C. and Wade, J. S. 'Aerial reconnaissance and excavation at Littleborough-on-Trent, Notts.', *Britannia*, 26 (1995), 253–84

Rippon, S. 'Romano-British reclamation of coastal wetlands' in H. F. Cook and T. Williamson (eds), *Water Management in the English Landscape* (Edinburgh, 1999), pp. 101–22

Rippon, S. *Beyond the Medieval Village: The Diversification of Landscape Character in Southern Britain* (Oxford, 2009)

Rivet, A. L. F. and Smith, C. *The Place-Names of Roman Britain* (London, 1979)

Robertson, A. J. *Anglo-Saxon Charters* (Cambridge, 1939)

Roffe, D. 'The distribution of sokeland in south Kesteven', *South Lincolnshire Archaeology*, 1 (1977), 30–3

Roffe, D. 'Origins', *South Lincolnshire Archaeology*, 3 (1979), 11–16

Roffe, D. 'The seventh century monastery of Stow Green, Lincolnshire', *Lincolnshire History and Archaeology*, 21 (1986), 31–3

Roffe, D. '*On middan Gyrwan fenne*: intercommoning around the island of Crowland', *Fenland Research*, 8 (1993), 80–6

Roffe, D. 'Lissingleys and the meeting place of Lindsey' (2000), www.roffe.co.uk/lindsey.htm

Roffe, D. 'The lost settlement of *Burg* refound?' (2000), www.roffe.co.uk/burg.htm

Roffe, D. 'Osbournby' (2000), www.roffe.co.uk/osbournby.htm

Roffe, D. 'Medieval administration' in S. Bennett and N. Bennett (eds), *An Historical Atlas of Lincolnshire* (Chichester, 2001), pp. 38–9

Roffe, D. *Nottinghamshire and the North: A Domesday Study* (1987/2002), www.roffe.co.uk/phdframe.htm

Rollason, D. 'Lists of saints' resting places in Anglo-Saxon England', *Anglo-Saxon England*, 7 (1978), 61–93

Rollason, D. (ed. and trans.) *Symeon of Durham. Libellus de Exordio atque Procursu istius hoc est Dunhelmensis Ecclesie* (Oxford, 2000)

Rollason, D. *Northumbria, 500–1100. Creation and Destruction of a Kingdom* (Cambridge, 2003)

Rumble, A. R. '"Hrepingas" reconsidered' in A. Dornier (ed.), *Mercian Studies* (Leicester, 1977), pp. 169–72

Rumble, A. R. 'An edition and translation of the Burghal Hidage, together with Recension C of the Tribal Hidage' in D. Hill and

A. R. Rumble (eds), *The Defence of Wessex: The Burghal Hidage and Anglo-Saxon Fortifications* (Manchester, 1994), pp. 14–35

Salway, P. 'The Roman Fenland' in C. W. Phillips (ed.), *The Fenland in Roman Times* (London, 1970), pp. 1–21

Sandred, K. I. 'Ingham in East Anglia: a new interpretation', *Leeds Studies in English*, 18 (1987), 231–40

Sandred, K. I. 'East Anglian place-names: sources of lost dialect' in J. Fisiak and P. Trudgill (eds), *East Anglian English* (Cambridge, 2001), pp. 39–61

Sawyer, P. H. *Anglo-Saxon Charters: An Annotated List and Bibliography* (London, 1968)

Sawyer, P. H. *Anglo-Saxon Lincolnshire*, History of Lincolnshire, vol. III (Lincoln, 1998)

Schram, O. K. 'Fenland place-names' in B. Dickens (ed.), *The Early Cultures in North-West Europe* (Cambridge, 1950), pp. 427–41

Schrijver, P. *Studies in British Celtic Historical Phonology* (Amsterdam, 1995)

Scull, C. 'Further evidence from East Anglia for enamelling on early Anglo-Saxon metalwork', *Anglo-Saxon Studies in Archaeology and History*, 4 (1985), 117–24

Scull, C. 'Post-Roman phase I at Yeavering: a re-consideration', *Medieval Archaeology*, 36 (1992), 51–63

Scull, C. 'Archaeology, early Anglo-Saxon society and the Anglo-Saxon kingdoms', *Anglo-Saxon Studies in Archaeology and History*, 6 (1993), 65–82

Scull, C. 'Approaches to the material culture and social dynamics of the migration period in eastern England' in J. Bintliff and H. Hamerow (eds), *Europe Between Late Antiquity and the Middle Ages* (Oxford, 1995), pp. 71–83

Scull, C. 'Urban centres in pre-Viking England?' in J. Hines (ed.), *The Anglo-Saxons from the Migration Period to the Eighth Century: An Ethnographic Perspective* (Woodbridge, 1997), pp. 269–98

Scull, C. 'The *adventus saxonum* from an archaeological point of view: how many phases were there?' in G. Waxenberger and K. Kazzazi (eds), *Old English Runes: Interdisciplinary Perspectives on Approaches and Methodologies* (Berlin, forthcoming), pre-publication version at www.academia.edu/24427173/

Scull, C. J. and Harding, A. F. 'Two early medieval cemeteries at

Milfield, Northumberland', *Durham Archaeological Journal*, 6 (1990), 1–29

Sheahan, J. J. and Whellan, T. *History and Topography of the City of York; the Ainsty Wapentake; and the East Riding of Yorkshire* (2 vols, Beverley, 1856)

Sherlock, S. J. and Welch, M. J. *An Anglo-Saxon Cemetery at Norton, Cleveland* (London, 1992)

Simmons, B. 'Late Roman coastal defence around the Wash' in S. Malone and M. Williams (eds), *Rumours of Roman Finds: Recent Work on Roman Lincolnshire* (Heckington, 2010), pp. 47–52

Simmons, I. G. 'The emergence of the south Lindsey coast of the Wash before Domesday', *Midland History*, 42 (2017), 139–58

Sims-Williams, P. 'Gildas and the Anglo-Saxons', *Cambridge Medieval Celtic Studies*, 6 (1983), 1–30

Sims-Williams, P. *Religion and Literature in Western England, 600–800* (Cambridge, 1990)

Sims-Williams, P. 'Dating the transition to Neo-Brittonic: phonology and history, 400–600' in Alfred Bammesberger and A. Wollmann (eds), *Britain, 400–600. Language and History* (Heidelberg, 1990), pp. 217–61

Sims-Williams, P. 'The emergence of Old Welsh, Cornish and Breton orthography, 600–800: the evidence of Archaic Old Welsh', *Bulletin of the Board of Celtic Studies*, 38 (1991), 20–86

Sims-Williams, P. *The Celtic Inscriptions of Britain. Phonology and Chronology, c. 400–1200* (Oxford, 2003)

Smith, A. H. 'The Hwicce' in J. B. Bessinger and R. P. Creeds (eds), *Franciplegus: Medieval and Linguistic Studies in Honour of Francis Peabody Magoun Jr* (New York, 1965), pp. 56–64

Smith, A. H. *The Place-Names of Gloucestershire, IV* (Cambridge, 1965)

Smith, I. M. 'Sprouston, Roxburghshire: an early Anglian centre on the eastern Tweed basin', *Proceedings of the Society of Antiquaries of Scotland*, 121 (1991), 261–94

Smith, J. T. 'The Roman villa at Denton', *Lincolnshire Architectural and Archaeological Society Reports and Papers*, 10 (1964), 75–104

Snyder, C. A. *An Age of Tyrants: Britain and the Britons A.D. 400–600* (Stroud, 1998)

Southern, P. 'The army in late Roman Britain' in M. Todd (ed.), *A Companion to Roman Britain* (Oxford, 2004), pp. 393–408

Squires, K. E. 'Populating the pots: the demography of the early Anglo-Saxon cemeteries at Elsham and Cleatham, North Lincolnshire', *Archaeological Journal*, 169 (2012), 312–42

Squires, K. E. 'Piecing together identity: a social investigation of early Anglo-Saxon cremation practices', *Archaeological Journal*, 170 (2013), 154–200

Stancliffe, C. 'Oswald, "most holy and victorious king of the Northumbrians"' in C. Stancliffe and E. Cambridge (eds), *Oswald: Northumbrian King to European Saint* (Stamford, 1995), pp. 33–83

Stafford, P. *The East Midlands in the Early Middle Ages* (London, 1985)

Steane, K. 'St Paul-in-the-Bail – a dated sequence?', *Lincoln Archaeology*, 3 (1990–1), 28–31

Steane, K. *The Archaeology of the Upper City and Adjacent Suburbs* (Oxford, 2006)

Steane, K. and Vince, A. 'Post-Roman Lincoln: archaeological evidence for activity in Lincoln from the 5th to the 9th centuries' in A. Vince (ed.), *Pre-Viking Lindsey* (Lincoln, 1993), pp. 71–9

Stenton, F. M. 'Lindsey and its kings' in D. M. Stenton (ed.), *Preparatory to Anglo-Saxon England* (Oxford, 1971), pp. 127–35

Stenton, F. M. 'The historical bearing of place-name studies: the English occupation of Southern England' in D. M. Stenton (ed.), *Preparatory to Anglo-Saxon England* (Oxford, 1971), pp. 266–80

Stevenson, W. H. (ed.) *Asser's Life of King Alfred* (Oxford, 1904)

Stocker, D. 'The early Church in Lincolnshire: a study of the sites and their significance' in A. Vince (ed.), *Pre-Viking Lindsey* (Lincoln, 1993), pp. 101–22

Stocker, D. (ed.) *The City by the Pool: Assessing the Archaeology of the City of Lincoln* (Oxford, 2003)

Stocker, D. and Everson, P. 'The straight and narrow way: Fenland causeways and the conversion of the landscape in the Witham valley, Lincolnshire' in M. O. H. Carver (ed.), *The Cross Goes North: Processes of Conversion in Northern Europe, A.D. 300–1300* (Woodbridge, 2002), pp. 271–88

Stocker, D. *et al*, 'The Greetwell villa', LARA RAZ 7.23, Heritage Connect Lincoln (2003), www.heritageconnectlincoln.com/lara-raz/thegreetwell-villa/908

Strang, A. 'Explaining Ptolemy's Roman Britain', *Britannia*, 28 (1997),

1–30

Strickland, H. E. *A General View of the Agriculture of the East-Riding of Yorkshire* (York, 1812)

Stubbs, W. *Select Charters and Other Illustrations of English Constitutional History*, revised by H. W. C. Davis, 9th edn (Oxford, 1913)

Stuer, H. 'Helm und Ringschwert. Prunkbewaffnung und Rangabzeichen germanischer Krieger. Eine Übersicht', *Studien zur Sachsenforschung*, 6 (1987), 190–236

Sweet, H. (ed.) *The Oldest English Texts* (London, 1885)

Tabacco, G. *The Struggle for Power in Medieval Italy: Structures of Political Rule* (Cambridge, 1989)

Taylor, C. C. *Village and Farmstead* (London, 1983)

Taylor, G. 'An early to middle Saxon settlement at Quarrington, Lincolnshire', *Antiquaries Journal*, 83 (2003), 231–80

Taylor, J. 'Stonea in its Fenland context: moving beyond an Imperial Estate', *Journal of Roman Archaeology*, 13 (2000), 647–58

Thacker, A. '*Membra disjecta*: the division of the body and the diffusion of the cult' in C. Stancliffe and E. Cambridge (eds), *Oswald: Northumbrian King to European Saint* (Stamford, 1995), pp. 97–127

Thacker, A. 'Bede and the ordering of understanding' in S. DeGregorio (ed.), *Innovation and Tradition in the Writings of the Venerable Bede* (Morgantown, 2006), pp. 37–63

Thomas, A. C. 'Imported pottery in Dark-Age western Britain', *Medieval Archaeology*, 3 (1959), 89–111

Thomas, A. C. *Christianity in Roman Britain to AD 500* (London, 1981)

Thomas, A. 'Rivers of Gold? The coastal zone between the Humber and the Wash in the Mid Saxon period', *Anglo-Saxon Studies in Archaeology and History*, 18 (2013), 97–118

Thomas, G. W. 'On excavations in an Anglo-Saxon cemetery at Sleaford in Lincolnshire', *Archaeologia*, 50 (1887), 383–406

Thomas, M. G., Stumpf, M. P. H. and Härke, H. 'Evidence for an apartheid-like social structure in early Anglo-Saxon England', *Proceedings of the Royal Society*, 273 (2006), 2651–7

Thompson, E. A. 'Ammianus Marcellinus and Britain', *Nottingham Medieval Studies*, 34 (1990), 1–15

Thompson, F. H. 'Anglo-Saxon sites in Lincolnshire: unpublished material and recent discoveries', *Antiquaries Journal*, 36 (1956), 181–99

Todd, M. '*Famosa pestis* and Britain in the Fifth century', *Britannia*, 8 (1977), 319–25

Townend, P. *et al* 'The mystery in the marsh: exploring an Anglo-Saxon island at Little Carlton', *Current Archaeology*, 313 (2016), 28–34

Tristram, H. L. C. 'Why don't the English speak Welsh?' in N. J. Higham (ed.), *Britons in Anglo-Saxon England* (Woodbridge, 2007), pp. 192–214

Trollope, E. *Sleaford and the Wapentakes of Flaxwell and Aswardhurn* (London, 1887)

Turner, S. 'Aspects of the development of public assembly in the Danelaw', *Assemblage*, 5 (2000), www.assemblage.group.shef.ac.uk /5/turner.html

Tyler, D. 'An early Mercian hegemony: Penda and overkingship in the seventh century', *Midland History*, 30 (2005), 1–19

Ulmschneider, K. U. 'The archaeology of Middle Saxon England: the evidence of Lincolnshire and Hampshire compared' (2 vols, D.Phil Thesis, University of Oxford, 1998)

Ulmschneider, K. U. 'Settlement, economy, and the 'productive' site: Middle Anglo-Saxon Lincolnshire A. D. 650–780', *Medieval Archaeology*, 44 (2000), 53–79

Van de Noort, R. and Ellis, S. *Wetland Heritage of the Ancholme and Lower Trent Valleys: An Archaeological Survey* (Hull, 1998)

Van de Noort, R. *The Humber Wetlands: The Archaeology of a Dynamic Landscape* (Bollington, 2004)

Vikstrand, P. 'Pre-Christian sacral personal names in Scandinavia during the Proto-Scandinavian period' in W. Ahrens, S. Embleton and A. Lapierre (eds), *Names in Multi-Lingual, Multi-Cultural and Multi-Ethnic Contact: Proceedings of the 23rd International Congress of Onomastic Sciences* (Toronto, 2009), pp. 1012–18

Vince, A. G. 'Lincolnshire in the Anglo-Saxon Period, *c.* 450–1066' in S. Bennett and N. Bennett (eds), *An Historical Atlas of Lincolnshire* (Chichester, 2001), pp. 22–3

Vince, A. G. 'Lincoln in the early medieval era, between the 5th and 9th centuries: the archaeological account' in D. Stocker (ed.), *The City by the Pool. Assessing the Archaeology of the City of Lincoln* (Oxford, 2003), pp. 141–56

Vince, A. G. 'Coinage and urban development: integrating the archaeological and numismatic history of Lincoln' in B. Cook and G. Williams (eds), *Coinage and History in the North Sea World, c. AD 500–1200* (Leiden, 2006), pp. 525–43

Vince, A. and Jones, M. 'Discussion', in K. Steane *et al*, *The Archaeology of the Lower City and Adjacent Suburbs* (Oxford, 2016), pp. 470–516

Vince, A. G. and Williams, D. F. 'The characterization and interpretation of early to Middle Saxon granitic tempered pottery in England', *Medieval Archaeology*, 41 (1997), 214–20

Wacher, J. *The Towns of Roman Britain*, 2nd edn (London, 1995)

Walker, F. and Lane, T. *An Early to Middle Saxon Settlement at Quarrington, Lincolnshire*, Archaeological Project Services Report No. 49/96, (3 vols, Heckington, 1996)

Wallace-Hadrill, J. M. (ed. and trans.) *The Fourth Book of the Chronicle of Fredegar with its Continuations* (London, 1960)

Wallace-Hadrill, J. M. *Bede's Ecclesiastical History of the English People: A Historical Commentary* (Oxford, 1988)

Waller, M. *The Fenland Project, Number 9: Flandrian Environmental Change in Fenland* (Cambridge, 1994)

Ward, G. 'The parish boundary of Ingham-Coates', *The Lincolnshire Magazine*, 3.2 (1936), 42–5

Ward-Perkins, B. *From Classical Antiquity to the Middle Ages* (Oxford, 1984)

Ward-Perkins, B. 'Why did the Anglo-Saxons not become more British?', *English Historical Review*, 115 (2000), 513–33

Ward-Perkins, B. 'Specialised production and exchange' in A. Cameron, B. Ward-Perkins and M. Whitby (eds), *Cambridge Ancient History, XIV, Late Antiquity: Empire and Successors, AD 425–600* (Cambridge, 2000), pp. 346–91

Ward-Perkins, B. *The Fall of Rome and the End of Civilisation* (Oxford, 2005)

Warner, P. *The Origins of Suffolk* (Manchester, 1996)

Watts, V. *The Cambridge Dictionary of English Place-Names* (Cambridge, 2004)

Weale, M. E., Weiss, D. A., Jager, R. F., Bradman, M. and Thomas, M. G. 'Y chromosome evidence for Anglo-Saxon mass migration', *Molecular Biology and Evolution*, 19 (2002), 1008–21

Webster, G. 'A Romano-British pottery kiln at Rookery Lane, Lincoln', *The Antiquaries Journal*, 40 (1960), 214–20

Welch, M. 'The kingdom of the South Saxons: the origins' in S. Bassett (ed.), *The Origins of Anglo-Saxon Kingdoms* (London, 1989), pp. 75–83

Welch, M. *Anglo-Saxon England* (London, 1992)

Welch, M. 'The archaeological evidence for federate settlement in Britain within the fifth century' in F. Vallet and M. Kazanski (eds), *L'Armée Romaine et les Barbares du IIIe au VIIe Siècle* (Rouen, 1993), pp. 269–77

Welch, M. 'The archaeology of Mercia' in M. P. Brown and C. A. Farr (eds), *Mercia. An Anglo-Saxon Kingdom in Europe* (London, 2001), pp. 147–60

Wessex Archaeology, *Blackhills Farm and The Hollys, Wickenby, Lincolnshire. Archaeological Evaluation and Assessment of Results* (Salisbury, 2008)

Whitelock, D., Douglas, D.C. and Tucker, S. I. (trans.) *The Anglo-Saxon Chronicle: A Revised Translation* (London, 1961)

White, R. *Britannia Prima: Britain's Last Roman Province* (Stroud, 2007)

Whitwell, B. *The Coritani* (Oxford, 1982)

Whitwell, B. 'Late Roman settlement on the Humber and Anglian beginnings' in J. Price and P. R. Wilson (eds), *Recent Research in Roman Yorkshire* (Oxford, 1988), pp. 49–78

Whitwell, B. *Roman Lincolnshire*, History of Lincolnshire, vol. II, 2nd edn (Lincoln, 1992)

Whitwell, B. 'Some Roman small towns in north Lincolnshire and south Humberside' in A. E. Brown (ed.), *Roman Small Towns in Eastern England and Beyond* (Oxford, 1995), pp. 95–102

Whitwell, B. 'Roman Lincolnshire' in S. Bennett and N. Bennett (eds), *An Historical Atlas of Lincolnshire* (Chichester, 2001), pp. 14–15

Whyman, M. 'Invisible people? Material culture in 'Dark Age' Yorkshire' in M. O. H. Carver (ed.), *In Search of Cult* (Woodbridge, 1992), pp. 61–8

Whyman, M. 'Late Roman Britain in Transition, A.D. 300–500: A Ceramic Perspective from East Yorkshire' (University of York PhD Thesis, 2001)

Williams, A., Smyth, A. P. and Kirby, D. P. *A Biographical Dictionary of Dark Age Britain. England, Scotland and Wales, c. 500–c. 1050* (London, 1991)

Williams, H. 'Cemeteries as central places – place and identity in Migration Period eastern England' in B. Hårdh and L. Larsson (eds), *Central Places in the Migration and Merovingian Periods* (Stockholm, 2002), pp. 341–62

Williams, H. 'Assembling the dead' in A. Pantos and S. Semple (eds), *Assembly Places and Practices in Medieval Europe* (Dublin, 2004), pp. 109–34

Williams, I. (ed.) *Canu Aneirin* (Cardiff, 1938)

Williamson, T. *The Origins of Norfolk* (Manchester, 1993)

Williamson, T. 'Settlement chronology and regional landscapes: the evidence from the claylands of East Anglia and Essex' in D. Hooke (ed.), *Anglo-Saxon Settlements* (Oxford, 1988), pp. 153–75

Williamson, T. 'The environmental contexts of Anglo-Saxon settlement' in N. J. Higham and M. J. Ryan (eds), *The Landscape Archaeology of Anglo-Saxon England* (Manchester, 2010), pp. 133–56

Williamson, T. *The Origins of Hertfordshire* (Hatfield, 2010)

Willis, S. *The Roman Roadside Settlement and Multi-Period Ritual Complex at Nettleton and Rothwell, Lincolnshire* (London, 2013)

Willis, S. 'Report on the expenditure of the grant received from The Roman Society/Roman Research Trust for specialist consultancy reporting on the pottery finds from Hatcliffe Top, North-East Lincolnshire' (March 2018), www.romansociety.org/Portals/0/S_Willis_report.pdf

Willis, S. (ed.), *The Waithe Valley Through Time, I: The Archaeology of the Valley, and Excavation and Survey in the Hatcliffe Area* (London, 2019)

Willmott, H. and Daubney, A. 'Of saints, sows or smiths? Copper-brazed iron handbells in early medieval England', *Archaeological Journal*, 176 (2019), published online 31 January 2019, doi.org/10.1080/00665983.2019.1567970

Willmott, H. and Wright, D. W. 'Rethinking early medieval 'productive sites': trade, wealth and worship at Little Carlton, East Lindsey' (forthcoming)

Winterbottom, M. (ed. and trans.) *Gildas: De Excidio Britanniae* (London, 1978)

Wood, I. N. 'Internal crisis in fourth-century Britain', *Britannia*, 22 (1991) 313–15

Wood, I. N. '*Gentes*, kings and kingdoms – the emergence of states:

the kingdom of the Gibichungs' in H-W. Goetz, J. Jarnut and W. Pohl (eds), *Regna and Gentes: The Relationship Between Late Antique and Early Medieval Peoples and Kingdoms in the Transformation of the Roman World* (Leiden, 2003), pp. 243–69

Wood, I. N. 'The final phase' in M. Todd (ed.), *A Companion to Roman Britain* (Oxford, 2004), pp. 428–42

Wood, I. N. 'Bede's Jarrow' in C. A. Lees and G. R. Overing (eds), *A Place to Believe In: Locating Medieval Landscapes* (Philadelphia, 2006), pp. 67–84

Wood, M. *In Search of England: Journeys into the English Past* (London, 1999)

Woolf, A. 'Community, identity and kingship in early England' in W. O. Frazer and A. Tyrrell (eds), *Social Identity in Early Medieval Britain* (London, 2000), pp. 91–109

Woolf, A. 'The Britons: From Romans to Barbarians', in H-W. Goetz, J. Jarnut and W. Pohl (eds), *Regna and Gentes: The Relationship Between Late Antique and Early Medieval Peoples and Kingdoms in the Transformation of the Roman World* (Leiden, 2003), pp. 345–80

Woolf, A. 'Apartheid and economics in Anglo-Saxon England' in N. J. Higham (ed.), *Britons in Anglo-Saxon England* (Woodbridge, 2007), pp. 115–29

Yerburgh, R. *Sketches Illustrative of the Topography and History of New and Old Sleaford* (Creasey, Sleaford, 1825)

Yorke, B. 'Lindsey: the lost kingdom found?' in A. Vince (ed.), *Pre-Viking Lindsey* (Lincoln, 1993), pp. 141–50

Yorke, B. 'Fact or fiction? The written evidence for the fifth and sixth centuries AD', *Anglo-Saxon Studies in Archaeology and History*, 6 (1993), 45–50

Yorke, B. 'Political and ethnic identity: a case study of Anglo-Saxon practice' in W. O. Frazer and A. Tyrrell (eds), *Social Identity in Early Medieval Britain* (London, 2000), pp. 69–89

Yorke, B. 'Anglo-Saxon *gentes* and *regna*' in H-W. Goetz, J. Jarnut and W. Pohl (eds), *Regna and Gentes: The Relationship Between Late Antique and Early Medieval Peoples and Kingdoms in the Transformation of the Roman World* (Leiden, 2003), pp. 381–408

Yorke, B. *Nunneries and the Anglo-Saxon Royal Houses* (London, 2003)

Yorke, B. 'Pagan to Christian in Anglo-Saxon England' in R. Flechner and M. Ní Mhaonaigh (eds), *The Introduction of Christianity into the Early Medieval Insular World: Converting the Isles I* (Turnhout, 2016), pp. 237–57

Young, S. *The Celtic Revolution. In Search of 2000 Years that Changed the World* (London, 2009)

Youngs, S. 'Two medieval Celtic enamelled buckles from Leicestershire', *Transactions of the Leicestershire Archaeological and Historical Society*, 68 (1993), 15–22

Youngs, S. 'Recent finds of insular enamelled buckles' in C. E. Karkov, R. T. Farrell and M. Ryan (eds), *The Insular Tradition* (Albany, 1997), pp. 189–210

Youngs, S. 'Insular metalwork from Flixborough, Lincolnshire', *Medieval Archaeology*, 45 (2001), 210–20

Youngs, C. 'After Oldcroft: a British silver pin from Welton le Wold, Lincolnshire' in N. Crummy *et al* (eds), *Image, Craft and the Classical World* (Montagnac, 2005), pp. 249–54

Youngs, S. 'Britain, Wales and Ireland: holding things together' in K. Jankulak and J. M. Wooding (eds), *Ireland and Wales in the Middle Ages* (Dublin, 2007), pp. 80–101

Youngs, S. 'Missing material: early Anglo-Saxon enamelling' in C. E. Karkov and H. Damico (eds), *Aedificia Nova: Studies in Honor of Rosemary Cramp* (Kalamazoo, 2008), pp. 162–75

Ziegler, M. 'The Anglo-British cemetery at Bamburgh', *The Heroic Age*, 4 (2001), www.heroicage.org/issues/4/Bamburgh.html

INDEX

Printed in Great Britain
by Amazon

58866447R00228